Reader Series
in Library and Information Science

Published *Readers* in the series are:

Reader in Library Administration. 1969.
Paul Wasserman and Mary Lee Bundy.

Reader in Research Methods for Librarianship. 1970.
Mary Lee Bundy and Paul Wasserman.

Reader in the Academic Library. 1970.
Michael M. Reynolds.

Reader in Library Services and the Computer. 1971.
Louis Kaplan.

Reader in American Library History. 1971.
Michael H. Harris.

Reader in Classification and Descriptive Cataloging. 1972.
Ann F. Painter.

Reader in Technical Services. 1973.
Edward L. Applebaum.

Reader in Medical Librarianship. 1973.
Winifred Sewell.

Reader in
Government Documents

edited by

Frederic J. O'Hara

1973

 Microcard Editions

Published by NCR/Microcard Editions,
901 26th Street, N.W.
Washington, D.C. 20037

Printed in the United States of America

Foreword

Unlike many other academic disciplines, librarianship has not yet begun to exploit the contributions of the several disciplines toward the study of its own issues. Yet the literature abounds with material germane to its concerns. Too frequently the task of identifying, correlating, and bringing together material from innumerable sources is burdensome, time consuming or simply impossible. For a field whose stock in trade is organizing knowledge, it is clear that the job of synthesizing the most essential contributions from the elusive sources in which they are contained is overdue. This then is the rationale for the series, *Readers in Library and Information Science.*

The Readers in Library and Information Science will include books concerned with various broad aspects of the field's interests. Each volume will be prepared by a recognized student of the topic covered, and the content will embrace material from the many different sources from the traditional literature of librarianship as well as from outside the field in which the most salient contributions have appeared. The objectives of the series will be to bring together in convenient form the key elements required for a current and comprehensive view of the subject matter. In this way it is hoped that the core of knowledge, essential as the intellectual basis for study and understanding, will be drawn into focus and thereby contribute to the futherance of professional education and professional practice in the field.

Paul Wasserman
Series Editor

v

Contents

V

SOCIAL MEASUREMENT & STATISTICS

VI

INFORMATION HANDLING SYSTEMS

VII

COPYRIGHTS, PATENTS, AND TRADEMARKS

VIII

AMENDING THE LIBRARY SERVICES AND CONSTRUCTION ACT

IX

CAREERS IN FEDERAL LIBRARIES

Reader in
Government Documents

Introduction

This collection of articles and excerpts represents an attempt to pull together some of the available literature from our government that tells the reader how to use documents, what documents exist and are needed in certain fields, and what several Federal libraries and library related agencies have done, are doing, or plan to do in the future. In the process of selection many documents were searched, but surprisingly not too many were found in the fields indicated above. The titles quoted are not necessarily the "best." Suggestions for another collection would be most welcome.

In these pages I think you will find some indications of trends, some promising signs for the future, and some helpful aids to guide you through the maze of documents to the references or readings you need.

Brookville, L.I., N.Y.   Frederic J. O'Hara
Spring, 1972

I

DEPOSITORY LIBRARIES & THE SUPERINTENDENT OF DOCUMENTS CLASSIFICATION SCHEME

Because you need to know where to go to get the documents you want, if they're not in your own library, then you need to know about depository libraries. And, since many of these libraries arrange their documents by the SuDocs classification scheme, you'll need to know about it too. This will help you with "physical access." I personally feel that depository libraries are not known and not used enough by the general public. Perhaps you can promote their use in your state. An updated list of these libraries appears in the September issue each year of the *U.S. Government Monthly Catalog*, that most comprehensive listing of government documents issued by the Superintendent of Documents, Government Printing Office.

An Explanation of the Superintendent of Documents Classification System

Prepared by Norman Barbee, classification specialist under the supervision of Mrs. Mae S. Collins, Chief of Library, Division of Public Documents, United States Government Printing Office.

"This explanation of the classification system used by the Division of Public Documents was prepared to answer frequent inquiries received, and to provide an aid in the training of new personnel in this organization. The original edition was prepared by the late Mr. Joseph A. King. . . . It is hoped that this explanation will also provide a helpful guide for depository libraries which use the Superintendent of Documents classification system, as well as for other libraries and persons interested in, or concerned with the catalog numbers assigned to publications by this Division." From the Foreword.

INTRODUCTION

This system was formed in the Library of the Division of Public Documents sometime between 1895 and 1903. The first explanation of it was given in October 1903 by William Leander Post, then in charge of the Library, in the preface to List of Publications of the Agriculture Department 1862-1902, Department List No. 1, issued by the Superintendent of Documents in 1904.

Mr. Post gives credit for the basis of the system (classification by governmental author) to Miss Adelaide R. Hasse, who used this basis in assigning classification numbers to a List of Publications of the U.S. Department of Agriculture from 1841 to June 30, 1895, inclusive. Miss Hasse prepared the list while assistant librarian in the Los Angeles Public Library but it was published by the Department of Agriculture in 1896 as its Library Bulletin No. 9.

Like other classification systems in use for many years, this one has expanded as the Federal Government has grown, and has changed in some details and methods of use, though still retaining the principles upon which it is based.

It has one fundamental weakness—the position in the scheme, of the publications of any Government author (i.e. department, bureau, office, etc.), is determined by the current organizational status of the author. Thus it is at the mercy of any Government reorganization which may be directed by the President, by Congress, or by the head of a department or agency, with the result that the publications of some authors may be located in as many as three different places in the scheme.

Despite this fundamental weakness, it has stood the test of time as a workable arrangement for publications of the United States Government, having been used for over 50 years by the Library of the Division of Public Documents (the Office of the Superintendent of Documents in earlier years) for the collection of public documents which has accumulated as a by-product of the Division's cataloging and publishing functions, and as a catalog system for the stocks of Government publications sold by the Superintendent of Documents.

SOURCE: Reprinted from United States Government Printing Office. Division of Public Documents. Library. *An Explanation of the Superintendent of Documents Classification System as currently used in the Library of the Division of Public Documents, U.S. Government Printing Office, and as catalog numbers for the stocks of Government publications sold by the Superintendent of Documents.* Prepared by Norman Barbee. (Washington: 1970). Introduction and pp. 1-17.

PRINCIPLES OF THE SYSTEM

The basis of the classification is the grouping together of the publications of any Government author—the various departments, bureaus, and agencies being considered the authors. In the grouping, the organizational structure of the United States Government is followed, that is, subordinate bureaus and divisions are grouped with the parent organization.

Author Symbols

Each executive department and agency, the Judiciary, Congress, and other major independent establishments are assigned a place in the scheme. The place is determined by the alphabetical designation assigned to each, as "A" for Agriculture Department, "Ju" for Judiciary, and "NS" for National Science Foundation, the designation usually being based on the name of the organization. (See attached Table I for symbols currently in use.)

Subordinate Offices

To set off the subordinate bureaus and offices, numbers are added to the symbols with figure "1" being used for the parent organization and the secretary's or administrator's office. Beginning with the figure "2" the numbers are applied in numerical order to the subordinate bureaus and offices, these having been arranged alphabetically when the system was established, and new subordinate bureaus or offices having been given the next highest number. A period follows the combination of letters and numbers representing the bureau or office. For example:

Agriculture Department (including Secretary's Office)	A 1.
Forest Service	A 13.
Information Office	A 21.
Rural Electrification Administration	A 68.

Series Designations

The second breakdown in the scheme is for the various series of publications issued by a particular

TABLE I

DEPARTMENT AND AGENCY SYMBOLS CURRENTLY IN USE

A	Agriculture Department
AC	Arms Control and Disarmament Agency
C	Commerce Department
CC	Federal Communications Commission
CR	Civil Rights Commission
CS	Civil Service Commission
CZ	Panama Canal Company and Canal Zone Government
D	Defense Department
DC	District of Columbia
FA	Fine Arts Commission
FCA	Farm Credit Administration
FHL	Federal Home Loan Bank Board
FM	Federal Mediation and Conciliation Service
FMC	Federal Maritime Commission
FP	Federal Power Commission
FR	Federal Reserve System Board of Governors
FT	Federal Trade Commission
FTZ	Foreign Trade Zones Board
GA	General Accounting Office
GP	Government Printing Office
GS	General Services Administration
HE	Health, Education, and Welfare Department
HH	Housing and Urban Development Department (Formerly Housing and Home Finance Agency)
I	Interior Department
IA	United States Information Agency
IC	Interstate Commerce Commission
J	Justice Department
Ju	Judiciary (Courts of the United States)
L	Labor Department
LC	Library of Congress
LR	National Labor Relations Board
NA	National Academy of Sciences
NAS	National Aeronautics and Space Administration
NC	National Capital Planning Commission
NCU	National Credit Union Administration
NF	National Foundation on the Arts and the Humanities
NMB	National Mediation Board
NS	National Science Foundation
P	Post Office Department
Pr	President of United States
PrEx	Executive Office of the President
RA	National Railroad Adjustment Board
RnB	Renegotiation Board
RR	Railroad Retirement Board
S	State Department
SBA	Small Business Administration
SE	Securities and Exchange Commission
SI	Smithsonian Institution
T	Treasury Department
TC	Tariff Commission
TD	Transportation Department
VA	Veterans Administration
X and Y	Congress

bureau or office. A number is assigned to each series and this number is followed by a colon.

In the beginning the following numbers were assigned for the types of publications common to most Government offices:

1: Annual reports
2: General publications (unnumbered publications of a miscellaneous nature)
3: Bulletins
4: Circulars

In setting up classes for new agencies or bureaus, these numbers were reserved for those types of publications. Later, new types common to most offices evolved and the following additional numbers were set aside in the classes of new agencies for particular types of series:

5: Laws (administered by the agency and published by it)
6: Regulations, rules, and instructions
7: Releases
8: Handbooks, manuals, guides

Any additional series issued by an office are given the next highest numbers in order of issuance—that is, as an office begins publication of a series the next highest number not already assigned to a series is assigned to the new series of the particular office.

Related Series

New series which are closely related to already existing series are now tied-in to the existing series so as to file side by side on the shelf. Originally no provision was made for this except in the case of separates from publications in a series. Tie-in is provided by use of the shilling mark after the number assigned to the existing series, followed by a digit for each related series starting with "2." (The "1" is not generally used in this connection since the existing series is the first.) Separates are distinguished by use of a lower case letter beginning with "a" rather than by numbers.

A theoretical example of these "tie-in" classes is as follows:

4: Circulars
4/a: Separates from Circulars (numbered)
4/b: Separates from Circulars (unnumbered)
4/2: Administrative Circulars
4/3: Technical Circulars

Class Stem

Thus by combining the designations for authors and those for the series published by the authors, we obtain the class stems for the various series of publications issued by the United States Government. For example:

A 1.10: Agriculture Yearbook
A 13.1: Annual Report of Chief of Forest Service
A 57.38: Soil Survey Reports

Book Numbers

The individual book number follows the colon. For numbered series the original edition of a publication gets simply the number of the book. For example, Department of Agriculture Leaflet 381 would be A 1.35:381. For revisions of numbered publications, the shilling mark and additional figures beginning with 2 are added, as: A 1.35:381/2, A 1.35:381/3, etc.

In the case of annuals, the last three digits of the year are used for the book number, e.g., Annual Report of Secretary of Agriculture, A 1.1:954. For reports or publications covering more than one year, a combination of the dates is used, e.g., Annual Register of the U.S. Naval Academy, 1954–1955 is D 208.107:954–55.

Unnumbered publications (other than continuations) are given a book number based on the principal subject word of the title, using a 2-figure Cutter table. An example is Radioactive Heating of Vehicles Entering the Earth's Atmosphere, NAS 1.2:R 11, "Radioactive" being the key subject word and the Cutter designation being R 11. Another publication, Measurements of Radiation from Flow Fields of Bodies Flying Speeds up to 13.4 Kilometers per Second, issued by the same agency, falling in the same series class (NAS 1.2:), and having the same Cutter number for the principal subject word, is individualized by adding the shilling mark and the figure 2, as NAS 1.2:R 11/2. Subsequent different publications in the same subject group which take the same Cutter designation would be identified as R 11/3, R 11/4, etc.

In assigning book numbers to unnumbered separates or reprints from whole publications, the 3-figure Cutter table is used. This is done for the purpose of providing for finer distinctions in class between publications whose principal subject words begin with the same syllable. The 3-figure table is also sometimes used in regular unnumbered series for the same purpose.

Another use of the 3-figure Cutter table is for non-Government publications which although not officially authored by a particular Government bureau or agency, may have been written by some of its personnel, or may be about it and its work, and it is desirable to have them filed on the shelf with the organization's own publications. The book numbers assigned to the non-Government publications are treated as decimals so as to file with the same subject groups but yet not disturb the sequence of book numbers of publications actually authored by the organization.

Revisions of unnumbered publications are identified by addition of the shilling mark and the last three digits of the year of revision. For example, if the first publication mentioned in the preceding paragraph was revised in 1964, the complete classification would read NAS 1.2:R 11/964. Subsequent revisions in the same year would be identified as 964-2, 964-3, etc.

Periodicals and other continuations are identified by number, or volume and number as the case may be. Volume and number are separated by use of the shilling mark. Some examples are:

Current Export Bulletin, No. 732,
   C 42.11/2:732
Marketing Information Guide, Vol. 17, No. 1,
   C 41.11:17/1

Unnumbered periodicals and continuations are identified by the year of issuance and order of issuance throughout the year. The last three digits of the year are used, and a number corresponding to the order of issuance within the year is added, the two being separated by the shilling mark. An example is:

United States Savings Bonds Issued and Redeemed, January 31, 1954, T 63.7:954/1

SPECIAL TREATMENT OF PUBLICATIONS OF CERTAIN AUTHORS

While the foregoing principles and rules govern the classification of the publications and documents of most Government authors, special treatments are employed for those of certain Government agencies. These consist of classes assigned to:

(1) Some series issued by the Interstate Commerce Commission
(2) Boards, Commissions, and Committees established by act of Congress or under authority of act of Congress, not specifically designated in the Executive Branch of the Government nor as completely independent agencies
(3) Congress and its working committees
(4) Multilateral international organizations in which the United States participates
(5) Publications of the President and the Executive Office of the President including Committees and Commissions established by executive order and reporting directly to the President

Interstate Commerce Commission

The classes assigned to publications of this agency were revised in December 1914 to provide better groupings of material than could formerly be given due to the lack of bureau breakdowns within the Commission at that time. Accordingly, those publications of the Commission as a whole, such as annual reports, general publications, bulletins, circulars, etc., continued to follow the regular form of classification, while all others were grouped by subject. This subject grouping took the place of bureau breakdowns and was designated by adding the first three or four letters of the subject word to the main agency designation of IC 1. Thus those publications relating to "accidents" were grouped under IC 1 acci., those relating to "express companies" were under IC 1 exp., and similarly for other subjects. The series designations and individual book numbers were then assigned under each subject grouping as though it were a regular bureau. For example, Accident Bulletin Number 3 is classed as IC 1 acci.3:3. A list of current subject breakdowns is contained in Table II attached.

Boards, Commissions, and Committees

Those agencies established by act of Congress or under authority of act of Congress, not specifically designated in the Executive Branch of the Government nor as completely independent agencies, are grouped under one of the agency symbols assigned to Congressional publications—namely,

TABLE II

CURRENT SUBJECT BREAKDOWNS OF THE INTERSTATE COMMERCE COMMISSION

Symbol	Publications Relating to:
IC 1 acci.	Accidents
IC 1 act.	Acts to regulate commerce
IC 1 blo.	Block signals
IC 1 def.	Defense Transport Administration
IC 1 elec.	Electric Railways
IC 1 exp.	Express companies
IC 1 hou.	Hours of service
IC 1 loc.	Locomotive inspection
IC 1 mot.	Motor carriers
IC 1 pip.	Pipe line companies
IC 1 rat.	Rates
IC 1 saf.	Safety
IC 1 sle.	Sleeping car companies
IC 1 ste.	Steam roads
IC 1 val.	Valuation of property
IC 1 wat.	Water carriers

Y 3. This place in the scheme is reserved for all such agencies. The classification numbers of the publications of these agencies are then literally pushed over to the right so that instead of the series designation following the period, the individual agency designation follows it. This agency designation is the Cutter author number from the 2-figure table for the first main word of the agency name, followed by the colon. Thus the agency designation for Atomic Energy Commission is Y 3.At 7: and that of Selective Service System is Y 3.Se 4:. The shilling mark and numbers are used to distinguish between author designations of agencies having the same or similar first principal word in their names as Y 3.F 31/8: for Federal Deposit Insurance Corp. and Y 3.F 31/13: for Federal Inter-Agency River Basin Committee.

Series designations for publications of these agencies then follow the colon instead of preceding it. These series designations are assigned in the regular way.

Individual book numbers are then added to the series designations with no separation if the individual book numbers begin with letters, and are separated by the shilling mark if they begin with numbers. Thus the Annual Report of the Atomic Energy Commission for the year 1961 is Y 3.At 7: 1/961 while the unnumbered AEC Report on Status Centrifuge Technology is classed as Y 3.At 7:2G 21.

Table III attached gives a list of current Boards, Commissions, and Committees with their class symbols.

TABLE III

AGENCY SYMBOLS OF BOARDS, COMMISSIONS, AND COMMITTEES ESTABLISHED BY ACT OF CONGRESS OR UNDER AUTHORITY OF ACT OF CONGRESS

(Not specifically designated in the Executive Branch of the Government nor as completely independent agencies.)

Y 3.Ad9/7:	Advisory Commission on Information
Y 3.Ad9/8:	Advisory Commission on Intergovernmental Relations
Y 3.Am3:	American Battle Monuments Commission
Y 3.At7:	Atomic Energy Commission
Y 3.B61:	Committee on Purchase of Blind-Made Products
Y 3.C49/2:	Civil War Centennial Commission
Y 3.C63/2:	Coastal Plains Regional Commission
Y 3.C66:	Coinage Joint Commission
Y 3.D37/2:	Delaware River Basin Commission
Y 3.Ed8/2:	National Advisory Council on Education of Disadvantaged Children
Y 3.Eq2:	Equal Employment Opportunity Commission
Y 3.Ex7/3:	Export-Import Bank of United States
Y 3.F31/8:	Federal Deposit Insurance Corporation
Y 3.F31/13:	Federal Inter-Agency River Basin Committee
Y 3.F31/14:	Federal Inter-Agency Committee on Recreation
Y 3.F31/17:	Federal Radiation Council
Y 3.F76/3:	Foreign Claims Settlement Commission
Y 3.F82:	Four Corners Regional Commission
Y 3.G79/3:	Great Lakes Basin Commission
Y 3.H73:	Permanent Committee for the Oliver Wendall Holmes Devise
Y 3.In2/6:	Indian Claims Commission
Y 3.In8/6:	Interdepartmental Committee on Children and Youth
Y 3.In8/8:	Inter-Agency Committee on Water Resources
Y 3.In8/13:	Interdepartmental Committee on Nutrition for National Defense
Y 3.In8/15:	Commission on International Rules of Judicial Procedure
Y 3.In8/16:	Interagency Committee on Automatic Data Processing
Y 3.In8/17:	Interdepartmental Committee to Coordinate Federal Urban Area Assistance Programs
Y 3.In8/21:	Interdepartmental Committee on Status of Women
Y 3.J66:	Joint Publications Research Service
Y 3.L58:	Lewis and Clark Trail Commission
Y 3.M33:	Maritime Advisory Committee
Y 3.M69:	Missouri Basin Inter-Agency Committee
Y 3.M84:	Mortgage Interest Rates Commission
Y 3.N21/16:	National Advisory Council on International Monetary and Financial Problems
Y 3.N21/21:	National Capital Transportation Agency
Y 3.N21/23:	National Visitors Center Study Commission
Y 3.N21/24:	National Water Commission
Y 3.N21/25:	National Commission on Product Safety

Table III (continued)

Y 3.N42/2:	New England Regional Commission
Y 3.N42/3:	New England River Basins Commission
Y 3.Oz1:	Ozarks Regional Commission
Y 3.P11/2:	Pacific Southwest Inter-agency Committee
Y 3.P96/7:	Public Land Law Review Commission
Y 3.Se4:	Selective Service System
Y 3.Sh6:	Ship Structure Committee
Y 3.Sp2/7:	Cabinet Committee on Opportunity for Spanish Speaking
Y 3.Su1:	Subversive Activities Control Board
Y 3.T22:	National Commission on Technology, Automation, and Economic Progress
Y 3.T25:	Tennessee Valley Authority
Y 3.Up6:	Upper Great Lakes Regional Commission
Y 3.W29:	Water Resources Council

Congress and its Working Committees

The working committees of Congress such as Appropriations, Judiciary, etc., are grouped under one of the agency symbols assigned to Congress—namely, Y 4. As in the case of the Y 3. classifications outlined above, an author designation based on the name of the Committee follows the period and is followed by the colon. Thus the House Committee on Judiciary is Y 4.J 89/1: and the Senate Committee on Judiciary is Y 4.J 89/2:, the shilling mark and the figures 1 and 2 being used to distinguish between the two committees. If other committees were to be appointed having the word "judiciary" as the principal subject word of their name, J 89/3:, J 89/4:, etc., would be used as the author designations. (See Table IV attached for symbols of current committees.)

No regular *numbered* series designations are normally used after the colon for the publications of Congressional Committees since they are for the most part simply unnumbered hearings or committee prints. These are given book numbers by use of the two-figure Cutter tables based on the principal subject word of the title of each as for unnumbered publications in the regular classification treatment.

Where series do occur within the publications of a Committee they have been treated in various ways. Some examples follow.

Congressional Directory. This has been given a series designation of "1" following the colon, as Y 4.P93/1:1. Individual book numbers are then marked off by use of the shilling mark following the series designation, as Y 4.P93/1:1/ with the particular issue being designated by Congress and session, as Y 4.P93/1:1/84-1.

Economic Indicators. This monthly periodical issued by the Joint Economic Committee has been

TABLE IV

AGENCY SYMBOLS OF CURRENT CONGRESSIONAL COMMITTEES

(Temporary select and special committees not included)

Y 4.Ae8:	Aeronautical and Space Sciences (Senate)
Y 4.Ag4:	Special Committee on Aging (Senate)
Y 4.Ag8/1:	Agriculture (House)
Y 4.Ag8/2:	Agriculture and Forestry (Senate)
Y 4.Ap6/1:	Appropriations (House)
Y 4.Ap6/2:	Appropriations (Senate)
Y 4.Ar5/2:	Armed Services (House)
Y 4.Ar5/3:	Armed Services (Senate)
Y 4.At7/2:	Joint Committee on Atomic Energy
Y 4.B22/1:	Banking and Currency (House)
Y 4.B22/3:	Banking and Currency (Senate)
Y 4.C73/2:	Commerce (Senate)
Y 4.D36:	Joint Committee on Defense Production
Y 4.D63/1:	District of Columbia (House)
Y 4.D63/2:	District of Columbia (Senate)
Y 4.Ec7:	Joint Economic Committee
Y 4.Ed8/1:	Education and Labor (House)
Y 4.F49:	Finance (Senate)
Y 4.F76/1:	Foreign Affairs (House)
Y 4.F76/2:	Foreign Relations (Senate)
Y 4.G74/6:	Government Operations (Senate)
Y 4.G74/7:	Government Operations (House)
Y 4.H81/3:	House Administration (House)
Y 4.In8/4:	Interstate and Foreign Commerce (House)
Y 4.In8/11:	Joint Committee on Internal Revenue Taxation
Y 4.In8/13:	Interior and Insular Affairs (Senate)
Y 4.In8/14:	Interior and Insular Affairs (House)
Y 4.In8/15:	Internal Security Committee (House)
Y 4.J89/1:	Judiciary (House)
Y 4.J89/2:	Judiciary (Senate)
Y 4.L11/2:	Labor and Public Welfare (Senate)
Y 4.L61/2:	Joint Committee on the Library
Y 4.M53:	Merchant Marine and Fisheries (House)
Y 4.N22/4:	Joint Committee on Navajo-Hopi Indian Administration
Y 4.P84/10:	Post Office and Civil Service (House)
Y 4.P84/11:	Post Office and Civil Service (Senate)
Y 4.P93/1:	Joint Committee on Printing
Y 4.P96/10:	Public Works (Senate)
Y 4.P96/11:	Public Works (House)
Y 4.R24/4:	Joint Committee on Reduction of Federal Expenditures
Y 4.R86/1:	Rules (House)
Y 4.R86/2:	Rules and Administration (Senate)
Y 4.Sci2:	Science and Astronautics (House)
Y 4.Sm1:	Small Business Select Committee (House)
Y 4.Sm1/2:	Small Business Select Committee (Senate)
Y 4.V64/3:	Veterans' Affairs (House)
Y 4.W36:	Ways and Means (House)

assigned a place in the group of publications issued by this Committee by use of the Cutter designation following the colon (instead of the regular numerical series designation), based on the subject word "Economic" as Y 4.Ec7:Ec7. The book numbers for individual issues are then designated by year of issue and number corresponding to the month of issue as 954-1 for January 1954, 954-2 for February 1954, etc. These are added to the series designation of "Ec7" following the colon and separated by the shilling mark, as: June 1954 issue, Y 4.Ec7/954-6.

Serially Numbered Hearings and Committee Prints. Hearings and the committee prints of some Congressional Committees are numbered as serials within each Congress. These are designated by Congress and number (separated by the shilling mark) immediately following the colon, as: House Judiciary Committee Serial 13, 83d Congress would be Y 4.J89/1:83/13, the number of the Congress taking the place of the usual numerical series designation. These are filed behind the hearings and committee prints bearing letter and number Cutter designation—that is, to the right on the shelf.

Congressional Bills, Documents, and Reports. These numbered series of publications issued by Congress are not given a place in the scheme by use of lettered symbols but are simply filed at the end of all other classifications by Congress, session, and individual number with abbreviations being used for the series titles. The order of filing and the manner of designation is as follows:

Series	Individual examples
Senate Bills	91-2:S.528
House Bills	91-2:H.R.15961
Senate Joint Resolutions	91-2:S.J.Res.172
House Joint Resolutions	91-2:H.J.Res.1098
Senate Concurrent Resolutions	91-2:S.Con.Res.70
House Concurrent Resolutions	91-2:H.Con.Res.578
Senate Resolutions	91-2:S.Res.304
House Resolutions	91-2:H.Res.108
Senate Reports	91-2:S.rp.885
House Reports	91-2:H.rp.983
Senate Documents	91-2:S.doc.82
House Documents	91-2:H.doc.342

Other Congressional Publications. Attached as Table V is a list of currently published Congressional series not explained above with notes as to methods of assigning book numbers.

Multilateral International Organizations in which the United States Participates

Many of the publications of these organizations are published simultaneously by the United States

TABLE V

CLASSIFICATION OF CONGRESSIONAL PUBLICATIONS
(Other than bills, documents, and reports)

X.	Congressional Record (bound). Congress and session form the series designation with individual book numbers made up of volume and part. For example: 83d Congress, 2d session, volume 100, part 2, classified X.83/2:100/pt.2.
X/a.	Congressional Record (daily). These are numbered throughout each session with no volume numbers. For example: 83d Congress, 2d session, number 32 is classified X/a.83/2:32.
XJH:	Journal of the House of Representatives. These are simply designated by Congress and session as XJH:83-2.
XJS:	Journal of the Senate. Designated by Congress and session as XJS:83-2.
Y 1.1:	Here are classified joint miscellaneous publications pertaining to both House and Senate, individual book numbers being formed by 2-figure Cutter designations based on the principal subject word of the title. This class may also be used by libraries desiring to file them serially for reports of organizations chartered by Congress such as the Boy Scouts of America, Disabled American Veterans, etc., with dates of the reports being added to the 3-figure Cutter designations for the titles of the organizations. For example, the 1954 report of the Boy Scouts of America would be classified Y 1.1:B691/954.
Y 1.2:	House of Representatives miscellaneous publications. Individual book numbers are assigned in the usual manner for unnumbered publications.
Y 1.2/2:	Calendars of the United States House of Representatives and history of legislation. Book numbers are assigned by Congress, session, and individual number as Y 1.2/2:84-1-13.
Y 1.3:	Senate miscellaneous publications. Individual book numbers are assigned in the usual manner for unnumbered publications. The volumes of the Journal of executive proceedings are given the Cutter designation Ex3 with the volume numbers added as: Y 1.3:Ex3/v.91,pt.2.
Y 1.3/2:	Executive calendar [relating to nominations and treaties]. Book numbers are assigned by date and number as: Y 1.3/2:955/1.
Y 1.3/3:	Calendar of business. Book numbers are assigned by Congress and individual number as Y 1.3/3:84-16.
Y 1.Cong.sess:	Senate Executive documents and reports. Congress and session numbers form the series designations for these two series with the individual document letters or report numbers (preceded by the letters "rp") forming the individual book num-

Table V (continued)

	bers as: Y 1.83/2:A (Senate Executive Document A) and Y 1.83/2:rp.5 (Senate Executive Report 5).
Y 2.	This class was originally assigned for Congressional bills and resolutions and may be so used in libraries desiring to keep such material in one group. Classification is completed by use of Congress and session, and individual bill or resolution numbers preceded by the abbreviations S. for Senate bills, H.R. for House bills, S. con. res. for Senate concurrent resolutions, H. res. for House resolutions, etc.
Y 3.	Boards, Commissions, and Committees. (See main text.)
Y 4.	Congressional Committees. (See main text.)
Y 5.	Contested elections. Not used in recent years.
Y 6.	Impeachments. Not used in recent years.
Y 7.1:	Memorial Addresses on life and character of deceased members of Congress. Individual book numbers are assigned by use of the 3-figure Cutter table based on the name of the deceased member.

and other countries. The United States portions of these organizations may also publish separately, for example, the United States National Commission for UNESCO. Since participation by the United States is in the realm of foreign relations, such publications are classed under the State Department with two main class designations assigned as follows:

S 3. Arbitrations and Mixed Commissions to Settle International Disputes
S 5. International Congresses, Conferences, and Commissions

The individual organizations are then treated as subordinate bureaus or offices, a number being assigned to each as it begins to publish, but following the period rather than preceding it as in regular class construction. Individual book numbers are assigned after the colon, using the 2-figure Cutter table and based on the principal subject word of the title.

If the organization proves to be a prolific publisher, however, issuing several definite series of publications, each is distinguished by adding the shilling mark and digits beginning with 2 to the number assigned to the organization as a bureau designation, as in the case of related series in regular class construction. For example some of the

series issued by the U.S. National Commission for UNESCO are classed as follows:

S 5.48/9: Addresses
S 5.48/10: Maps and posters
S 5.48/11: Executive committee, summary of notice of meetings

Individual book numbers are then assigned in the regular way.

Publications of the President and the Executive Office of the President including Committees and Commissions Established by Executive Order and reporting directly to the President

The agency symbol assigned to the President of the United States is Pr followed by the number corresponding to the ordinal number of succession to the presidency as Pr 37, Richard M. Nixon, 37th president of the United States. Breakdowns under the agency symbol follow normal methods of classification expansion. However, in recent years, presidents have appointed many special committees and commissions to study particular problems and to report their findings directly to the Chief executives. These organizations usually cease to exist after making their report. Since their publications are usually few in number, normal bureau treatment is not practical and special treatment is therefore indicated to prevent establishment of classes which will not be used, and in addition to keep together the publications of all such organizations appointed by one president.

Therefore, beginning with those appointed by President Eisenhower, one series class (Pr --.8:) has been assigned for all such committees and commissions. A Cutter designation using the 2-figure table is then assigned to each based on the principal subject word of its name as Pr 34.8:H81, President's Advisory Committee on Government Housing Policies and Programs. Publications of the committee are distinguished by addition of the shilling mark and Cutter numbers based on the principal subject word of the title as in normal classification.

Beginning with the administration of President Kennedy, the continuing offices assigned to the President, which make up the Executive Office of the President, have been given permanent classes under the symbol PrEx. Thus with a change in administration it will no longer be necessary to change the classes for such offices as Bureau of the Budget, National Security Council, Office of Emergency Planning, etc. These have been given breakdowns as subordinate offices of the Executive Office of the President, the Bureau of the Budget for example, being assigned PrEx2. Series and book numbers are then assigned in the usual manner.

Government Depository Libraries: The Present Law Governing Designated Depository Libraries

Prepared by the Joint Committee on Printing,
Senator B. Everett Jordan, Chairman.

This law should not only be known and understood by all librarians but it should be made known to any and all citizens (and others) who may have need for the vast amount of information that is freely available to them through their over 1000 "Designated Depository Libraries." "The law requires that the Government publications, when forwarded to a depository shall be made available for the free use of the general public, and must be retained permanently by all depository libraries not served by a regional depository, and by regional depositories themselves in either printed or microform copy."

DESIGNATED DEPOSITORY LIBRARIES

AUTHORIZATION

The law now in force provides for a class of libraries in the United States in which certain Government publications are deposited for the use of the public. These libraries are known in the office of the Superintendent of Documents, Government Printing Office, where the distribution is made, as designated depository libraries. Title 44 of the United States Code which is the authority for the operation of the depository program was codified and enacted during the 90th Congress. Sections of title 44 and excerpts from the Statutes at Large affecting the program will be found in the appendix at the end of this pamphlet. In the revised title 44, simplified language has been substituted for awkward and obsolete terms, and superseded and obsolete statutes were eliminated. The statutes are intended to remain substantively unchanged even though changes in terminology and style have been made by the codification of title 44.

NUMBER

Under the present provisions of title 44 of the United States Code, the depository list comprises the following described libraries:

State libraries	50
2 libraries for each congressional district to be designated by the Representative from that district (or at large in the case of undistricted States)	870
2 libraries to be designated in any part of the State by each Senator	200
2 libraries to be designated by the Resident Commissioner from Puerto Rico	2

SOURCE: Reprinted from U.S. Congress. Joint Committee on Printing. *Government Depository Libraries: The Present Law Governing Designated Depository Libraries.* Joint Committee Print, 92d Congress, 1st Session, Revised April 1971. (Washington: 1971). pp. 1–5, 35–39.

2 libraries to be designated by the Commissioner of the District of Co-
  lumbia_____ 2
1 library to be designated by the Governor of Guam_____ 1
1 library to be designated by the Governor of American Samoa_____ 1
2 libraries to be designated by the Governor of the Virgin Islands (1 on
  the island of St. Thomas and 1 on the island of St. Croix)_____ 2
The libraries of the land-grant colleges_____ 69
The libraries of the executive departments in Washington_____ 12
Libraries of independent agencies and of major bureaus and divisions of
  departments and agencies_____ [1] 125
The libraries of the U.S. Air Force, Coast Guard, Merchant Marine, Military, and Naval Academies_____ 5

In addition, the following libraries were designated by special
legislation:

American Antiquarian Society Library, Worcester, Mass_____ 1
The Public Library of the District of Columbia_____ 1

The estimated theoretical total number of authorized depository
libraries is, therefore, 1,341. However, of the 1,045 currently on the
list, some are not included in this total since in several instances there
are three or more depository libraries in the same congressional
district, all designated by Representatives, due to redistricting after
each decennial census.

If a depository designated by a Representative already exists
within a congressional district or one in Puerto Rico designated by
the Resident Commissioner, before an additional one may be designated by such a designator, a certified statement of justification of
the need for an additional depository must be furnished by the head
of the library to be designated. This justification must also be signed
by the head of every existing depository library within the congressional district or the Commonwealth of Puerto Rico, or by the head
of the library authority of the State or Commonwealth. A similar
justification is required in the case of a senatorial designation when
the Senator or his predecessor has already designated an existing
depository.

DISCONTINUANCE

Once a library has been designated a depository it cannot be
removed from the list and another library designated in its place
upon the election of a new Member of Congress. It remains a depository until it ceases to exist or vacates the privilege at its own request
(sec. 5, Sundry Civil Act, approved June 23, 1913, 38 Stat. 75, as
amended). It can, however, be removed by the Superintendent of
Documents for failure to abide by the laws governing the depository
program (44 U.S.C. 1910, Oct. 22, 1968, 82 Stat. 1286).

REGIONAL DEPOSITORIES

The 1962 amendments to the law provided for the designation of
not more than two libraries in each State and the Commonwealth of
Puerto Rico to be regional depositories. Such designations may be
made by the Senators from the States and the Resident Commissioner
in the case of Puerto Rico.

Libraries designated to be regional depositories must already be
designated depositories.

Designation as a regional depository requires prior approval of the
head of the library authority of the State or the Commonwealth of
Puerto Rico.

In addition to fulfilling the requirements for regular depositories,

---

[1] An estimated number.

they must receive and retain at least one copy of all Government publications made available to depositories, either in printed or microform copy (except those authorized to be discarded by the Superintendent of Documents).

Within the region they serve, the regional depositories must provide interlibrary loan, reference service, and assistance for regular depository libraries in the disposal of unwanted Government publications as provided by law. They have the authority to permit regular depository libraries within the areas served by them to dispose of Government publications which they have retained for at least 5 years after first offering them to other depository libraries within their area, then to other libraries, and then if not wanted to discard.

BOOKS FURNISHED

Depository libraries are permitted to receive one copy of all publications of the U.S. Government, except those determined by their issuing components to be required for official use only or those required for strictly administrative or operational purposes which have no public interest or educational value, and publications classified for reasons of national security. In addition to the exceptions noted, the so-called cooperative publications, which must necessarily be sold in order to be self-sustaining, are also excluded. These are primarily certain publications of the Library of Congress and those of the National Technical Information Service.

SELECTIVE PLAN

In view of the repeated requests from librarians of the designated depository libraries to be granted the privilege of selecting those public documents of the United States most suitable for their libraries, and which they would prefer to receive, instead of being compelled as formerly to receive the whole output of the Government Printing Office, all libraries are now on a selective basis. A classified list of the series and groups of Government publications available for selection has been furnished to all depositories for their use in making selections. This list which is revised from time to time is furnished in card form with one card for each series or group of publications giving the distribution item number, the issuing agency, the series or group title, and brief descriptions where needed.

As new series are begun by existing Government agencies, or new agencies are established, additional cards for the list are furnished to depositories for them to select the new material if desired. Cards are furnished in duplicate and selections are made by return to the Superintendent of Documents of one card for each series or group selected, properly marked with the depository's assigned library number. (This library number is assigned by the Superintendent of Documents for administrative purposes in control of selections and distribution of publications.)

The annual appropriation act for the Government Printing Office, beginning with July 1, 1922, provides that no part of the sum appropriated shall be used to supply the depository libraries with any publications not requested by such libraries, and that request must be made in advance of printing. There is therefore no retroactive distribution of depository publications as only sufficient copies are printed to provide distribution to those libraries which have selected the series or group in which a particular publication falls, prior to time of printing.

DISPOSAL OF BOOKS

The law requires that the Government publications, when forwarded to a depository, shall be made available for the free use of the general public, and must be retained permanently by all depository libraries not served by a regional depository, and by regional depositories themselves in either printed or microform copy. The exceptions allowed by the present law are superseded publications and those issued later in bound form, which may be discarded as authorized by the Superintendent of Documents.

Depository libraries which are served by regional depositories may dispose of publications which they have retained for at least 5 years with the permission of and in accordance with instructions from the regional depository which serves their area.

Depository libraries within executive departments and independent agencies of the Federal Government are authorized to dispose of unwanted Government publications after first offering them to the Library of Congress and the National Archives.

HISTORY OF EARLY LEGISLATION

Before the establishment of designated depositories, or any systematic methods for the distribution of public documents, special acts were passed at various times providing for the printing of a sufficient number of copies of the public journals of the Senate and House of Representatives for distribution to the executives of the several States and each branch of the State and territorial legislatures. Provision was also made at times for supplying these journals, the acts, and sometimes the documents and reports, to each, university and college incorporated in each State, as well as to the incorporated historical societies throughout the country.

During the 13th Congress, second session, December 27, 1813, a resolution was adopted embodying these provisions which had heretofore been covered by special legislation, and not only directing distribution for a Congress, but "for every future Congress." Two hundred copies in addition to the usual number was the limit named for documents, and this, of course, was more than sufficient for the needs at that early day.

By joint resolutions approved July 20, 1840, and April 30, 1844, the number of copies of journals and documents printed was increased to 300.

A resolution of January 28, 1857, as amended by resolution of March 20, 1858, was the real basis of the institution of depositories. By these provisions the journals and documents which up to that time, were deposited in the Library of Congress for distribution by the Librarian, and 250 copies of those delivered to the Department of State for distribution by that Department to colleges and other literary institutions, were transferred to the jurisdiction of the Secretary of the Interior "for distribution to such colleges, public libraries, atheneums, literary and scientific institutions, and boards of trade or public associations as may be designated to him by the Representative in Congress from each congressional district and by the Delegate from each Territory in the United States."

The following February, at the second session, 35th Congress (Feb. 5, 1859), an act was passed providing for "keeping and distributing all public documents" (11 Stat. 379). This act charged the Secretary of the Interior with "receiving, arranging, safekeeping, and distribution" of public documents "of every nature," already or hereafter directed by law to be printed or purchased for the use of the Government, "except such as are for the special use of Congress or the executive departments." It also empowered him to remove from the Congressional Library and other places all accumulations of books, journals, etc., and appropriated $22,000 for the purpose. He was directed by the act to keep accurate statistics of the receipt and distribution of all books.

Section 5 of this act further amended the resolution of January 28, 1857, by providing for the designation of a library by each of the Senators, and directing that the distribution should be made first to such States as had not yet been covered by distribution, and that in the future the distribution should be kept equal in each congressional district and territory.

All books, maps, charts, etc., heretofore deposited in the Department of State were also turned over to the Secretary of the Interior.

The act of February 5, 1859, was in force without amendment until March 2, 1861, at the 36th Congress, second session, when a long act to amend was passed (12 Stat. 244), the most important feature of which as affecting general distribution was contained in the first section, which gave the Secretary of the Interior the right to designate libraries to receive publications of which the edition was not sufficient to supply the regular depositories to be named by the Senators and Representatives. His power of selection was limited, however, by a proviso in section 2, which stated that in the future the public documents to be distributed by the Secretary of the Interior should be sent to the institutions already designated, unless he should be satisfied that any such institution was no longer a suitable depository for the same. This act also contained a clause repealing all acts or parts of acts inconsistent with its provisions.

Upon the basis of these acts the Revised Statutes were compiled, and chapter 7, sections 497 to 511, pages 82 to 85, contain all operative provisions reenacted at that time and superseding all former enactments.

No legislation can be found prior to that contained in the General Printing Act of January 12, 1895, affecting the State and territorial libraries, and it is thought that it became customary to send documents regularly to these libraries, under the discretionary powers vested in the Secretary of the Interior, which would account for their appearance on the depository list many years prior to 1895.

APPENDIX

LAWS IN FORCE RELATING TO GOVERNMENT DEPOSITORY LIBRARIES

(EXTRACT FROM PUBLIC LAW 90-620)

90TH CONGRESS, H.R. 18612

October 22, 1968

To enact title 44, United States Code, "Public Printing and Documents", codifying the general and permanent laws relating to public printing and documents.

*   *   *   *   *   *   *

Chapter 19—DEPOSITORY LIBRARY PROGRAM

*   *   *   *   *   *   *

§ 1901. Definition of Government publication

"Government publication" as used in this chapter, means informational matter which is published as an individual document at Government expense, or as required by law.

§ 1902. Availability of Government publications through Superintendent of Documents; lists of publications not ordered from Government Printing Office

Government publications, except those determined by their issuing components to be required for official use only or for strictly administrative or operational purposes which have no public interest or educational value and publications classified for reasons of national security, shall be made available to depository libraries through the facilities of the Superintendent of Documents for public information. Each component of the Government shall furnish the Superintendent of Documents a list of such publications it issued during the previous month, that were obtained from sources other than the Government Printing Office.

§ 1903. Distribution of publications to depositories; notice to Government components; cost of printing and binding

Upon request of the Superintendent of Documents, components of the Government ordering the printing of publications shall either increase or decrease the number of copies of publications furnished for distribution to designated depository libraries and State libraries so that the number of copies delivered to the Superintendent of Documents is equal to the number of libraries on the list. The number thus delivered may not be restricted by any statutory limitation in force on August 9, 1962. Copies of publications furnished the Superintendent of Documents for distribution to designated depository libraries shall include—

the journal of the Senate and House of Representatives;

all publications, not confidential in character, printed upon the requisition of a congressional committee;

Senate and House public bills and resolutions; and

reports on private bills, concurrent or simple resolutions;

but not so-called cooperative publications which must necessarily be sold in order to be self-sustaining.

The Superintendent of Documents shall currently inform the components of the Government ordering printing of publications as to the number of copies of their publications required for distribution to depository libraries. The cost of printing and binding those publications distributed to depository libraries obtained elsewhere than from the Government Printing Office, shall be borne by components of the Government responsible for their issuance; those requisitioned from the Government Printing Office shall be charged to appropriations provided the Superintendent of Documents for that purpose.

§ 1904. Classified list of Government publications for selection by depositories

The Superintendent of Documents shall currently issue a classified list of Government publications in suitable form, containing annotations of contents and listed by item identification numbers to facilitate the selection of only those publications needed by depository libraries. The selected publications shall be distributed to depository libraries in accordance with regulations of the Superintendent of Documents, as long as they fulfill the conditions provided by law.

§ 1905. Distribution to depositories; designation of additional libraries; justification; authorization for certain designations

The Government publications selected from lists prepared by the Superintendent of Documents, and when requested from him, shall be distributed to depository libraries specifically designated by law and to libraries designated by Senators, Representatives, and the Resident Commissioner from Puerto Rico, by the Commissioner of the District of Columbia, and by the Governors of Guam, American Samoa, and the Virgin Islands, respectively. Additional libraries within areas served by Representatives or the Resident Commissioner from Puerto Rico may be designated by them to receive Government publications to the extent that the total number of libraries designated by them does not exceed two within each area. Not more than two additional libraries within a State may be designated by each Senator from the State. Before an additional library within a State, congressional district or the Commonwealth of Puerto Rico is designated as a depository for Government publications, the head of that library shall furnish his Senator, Representative, or the Resident Commissioner from Puerto Rico, as the case may be, with justification of the necessity for the additional designation. The justification, which shall also include a certification as to the need for the additional depository library designation, shall be signed by the head of every existing depository library within the congressional district or the Commonwealth of Puerto Rico or by the head of the library authority of the State or the Commonwealth of Puerto Rico, within which the additional depository library is to be located. The justification for additional depository library designations shall be transmitted to the Superintendent of Documents by the Senator, Representative, or the Resident Commissioner from Puerto Rico, as the case may be. The Commissioner of the District of Columbia may designate two depository libraries in the District of Columbia, the Governor of Guam and the Governor of American Samoa may each designate one depository library in Guam and American Samoa, respectively, and the Governor of the Virgin Islands may designate one depository library on the island of Saint Thomas and one on the island of Saint Croix.

§ 1906. Land-grant colleges constituted depositories

Land-grant colleges are constituted depositories to receive Government publications subject to the depository laws.

§ 1907. Libraries of executive departments, service academies, and independent agencies constituted depositories; certifications of need; disposal of unwanted publications

The libraries of the executive departments, of the United States Military Academy, of the United States Naval Academy, of the United States Air Force Academy, of the United States Coast Guard Academy, and of the United States Merchant Marine Academy are designated depositories of Government publications. A depository library within each independent agency may be designated upon certification of need by the head of the independent agency to the Superintendent of Documents. Additional depository libraries within executive departments and independent agencies may be designated to receive Government publications to the extent that the number so designated does not exceed the number of major bureaus or divisions of the departments and independent agencies. These designations may be made only after certification by the head of each executive department or independent agency to the Superintendent of Documents as to the justifiable need for additional depository libraries. Depository libraries within executive departments and independent agencies may dispose of unwanted Government publications after first offering them to the Library of Congress and the Archivist of the United States.

§1908. American Antiquarian Society to receive certain publications

One copy of the public journals of the Senate and of the House of Representatives, and of the documents published under the orders of the Senate and House of Representatives, respectively, shall be transmitted to the Executive of the Commonwealth of Massachusetts for the use and benefit of the American Antiquarian Society of the Commonwealth.

§1909. Requirements of depository libraries; reports on conditions; investigations; termination; replacement

Only a library able to provide custody and service for depository materials and located in an area where it can best serve the public need, and within an area not already adequately served by existing depository libraries may be designated by Senators, Representatives, the Resident Commissioner from Puerto Rico, the Commissioner of the District of Columbia, or the Governors of Guam, American Samoa, or the Virgin Islands as a depository of Government publications. The designated depository libraries shall report to the Superintendent of Documents at least every two years concerning their condition.

The Superintendent of Documents shall make firsthand investigation of conditions for which need is indicated and include the results of investigations in his annual report. When he ascertains that the number of books in a depository library is below ten thousand, other than Government publications, or it has ceased to be maintained so as to be accessible to the public, or that the Government publications which have been furnished the library have not been properly maintained, he shall delete the library from the list of depository libraries if the library fails to correct the unsatisfactory conditions within six months. The Representative or the Resident Commissioner from Puerto Rico in whose area the library is located or the Senator who made the designation, or a successor of the Senator, and, in the case of a library in the District of Columbia, the Commissioner of the District of Columbia, and, in the case of a library in Guam, American Samoa, or the Virgin Islands, the Governor, shall be notified and shall then be authorized to designate another library within the area served by him, which shall meet the conditions herein required, but which may not be in excess of the number of depository libraries authorized by law within the State, district, territory, or the Commonwealth of Puerto Rico, as the case may be.

§1910. Designations of replacement depositories; limitations on numbers; conditions

The designation of a library to replace a depository library, other than a depository library specifically designated by law, may be made only within the limitations on total numbers specified by section 1905 of this title, and only when the library to be replaced ceases to exist, or when the library voluntarily relinquishes its depository status, or when the Superintendent of Documents determines that it no longer fulfills the conditions provided by law for depository libraries.

§1911. Free use of Government publications in depositories; disposal of unwanted publications

Depository libraries shall make Government publications available for the free use of the general public, and may dispose of them after retention for five years under section 1912 of this title, if the depository library is served by a regional depository library. Depository libraries not served by a regional depository library, or that are regional depository libraries themselves, shall retain Government publications permanently in either printed form or in microfacsimile form, except superseded publications or those issued later in bound form which may be discarded as authorized by the Superintendent of Documents.

§ 1912. Regional depositories; designation; functions; disposal of publications

Not more than two depository libraries in each State and the Commonwealth of Puerto Rico may be designated as regional depositories, and shall receive from the Superintendent of Documents copies of all new and revised Government publications authorized for distribution to depository libraries. Designation of regional depository libraries may be made by a Senator or the Resident Commissioner from Puerto Rico within the areas served by them, after approval by the head of the library authority of the State or the Commonwealth of Puerto Rico, as the case may be, who shall first ascertain from the head of the library to be so designated that the library will, in addition to fulfilling the requirements for depository libraries, retain at least one copy of all Government publications either in printed or microfacsimile form (except those authorized to be discarded by the Superintendent of Documents); and within the region served will provide interlibrary loan, reference service, and assistance for depository libraries in the disposal of unwanted Government publications. The agreement to function as a regional depository library shall be transmitted to the Superintendent of Documents by the Senator or the Resident Commissioner from Puerto Rico when the designation is made.

The libraries designated as regional depositories may permit depository libraries, within the areas served by them, to dispose of Government publications which they have retained for five years after first offering them to other depository libraries within their area, then to other libraries.

§ 1913. Appropriations for supplying depository libraries; restriction

Appropriations available for the Office of Superintendent of Documents may not be used to supply depository libraries documents, books, or other printed matter not requested by them, and their requests shall be subject to approval by the Superintendent of Documents.

§ 1914. Implementation of depository library program by Public Printer

The Public Printer, with the approval of the Joint Committee on Printing, as provided by section 103 of this title, may use any measures he considers necessary for the economical and practical implementation of this chapter.

The following sections are also taken from title 44 of the United States Code:

§ 701. "Usual number" of documents and reports; distribution of House and Senate documents and reports; binding; reports on private bills; number of copies printed; distribution

*   *   *   *   *   *   *

(c) Of the number printed, the Public Printer shall bind a sufficient number of copies for distribution as follows:

Of the House documents and reports, bound—to the Senate library, fifteen copies: to the Library of Congress, not to exceed one hundred and fifty copies, as provided by section 1718 of this title; to the House of Representatives library, fifteen copies; to the Superintendent of Documents, as many copies as are required for distribution to the State libraries and designated depositories.

Of the Senate documents and reports, bound—to the Senate library, fifteen copies; to the Library of Congress, copies as provided by sections 1718 and 1719 of this title; to the House of Representatives library, fifteen copies; to the Superintendent of Documents, as many copies as may be required for distribution to State libraries and designated depositories. In binding documents the Public Printer shall give precedence to those that are to be distributed to libraries and to designated depositories. But a State library or designated depository entitled to documents that may prefer to have its documents in unbound form, may do so by notifying the Superintendent of Documents to that effect prior to the convening of each Congress.

§ 719. Classification and numbering of publications ordered printed by Congress; designation of publications of departments; printing of committee hearings

Publications ordered printed by Congress, or either House, shall be in four series, namely:

one series of reports made by the committees of the Senate, to be known as Senate reports;

one series of reports made by the committees of the House of Representatives, to be known as House reports;

one series of documents other than reports of committees, the orders for printing which originate in the Senate, to be known as Senate documents, and

one series of documents other than committee reports, the orders for printing which originate in the House of Representatives, to be known as House documents.

The publications in each series shall be consecutively numbered, the numbers in each series continuing in unbroken sequence throughout the entire term of a Congress, but these provisions do not apply to the documents printed for the use of the Senate in executive session. Of the "usual number", the copies which are intended for distribution to State libraries and other designated depositories of annual or serial publications originating in or prepared by an executive department, bureau, office, commission, or board may not be numbered in the document or report series of either House of Congress, but shall be designated by title and bound as provided by section 738 of this title; and the departmental edition, if any, shall be printed concurrently with the "usual number". Hearings of committees may be printed as congressional documents only when specifically ordered by Congress or either House.

§ 738. Binding of publications for distribution to libraries

The Public Printer shall supply the Superintendent of Documents with sufficient copies of publications distributed in unbound form to be bound and distributed to the State libraries and other designated depositories for their permanent files. Every publication of sufficient size on any one subject shall be bound separately and receive the title suggested by the subject of the volume and the others shall be distributed in unbound form as soon as printed. The library edition as well as all other bound sets of congressional numbered documents and reports shall be arranged in volumes and bound in the manner directed by the Joint Committee on Printing.

§ 906. Congressional Record: gratuitous copies; delivery; subscriptions

The Public Printer shall furnish the Congressional Record only as follows:

*   *   *   *   *   *   *

to the Superintendent of Documents as many daily and bound copies as may be required for distribution to depository libraries;

*   *   *   *   *   *   *

The following chapter is taken from Statutes at Large Volume 57 part 1:

243. An Act to designate the Public Library of the District of Columbia a public depository for governmental publications.—*Be it enacted by the Senate and House of*

Representatives of the United States of America in Congress assembled, That the Public Library of the District of Columbia is hereby constituted a designated depository of governmental publications and the Superintendent of Documents shall supply to such library one copy of each such publication in the same form as supplied to other designated depositories.

Approved September 28, 1943.

○

Instructions to Depository Libraries

Prepared by the Superintendent of Documents

"The depository instructions have been revised to reflect changes as a result of the Depository Library Act of 1962. This booklet is to provide guidance regarding the rights and duties of libraries officially designated as depositories for United States Government publications. They supersede the 1955 edition of Cumulative Instructions to Depository Libraries." From an introductory letter by the then Superintendent of Documents, Carper W. Buckley.

SECTION 1. GENERAL INFORMATION CONCERNING YOUR DEPOSITORY STATUS

Your library is an official depository for United States Government Publications.

It has been designated as such in one of the following ways:

1. By the United States Representative of your Congressional district or his predecessor.
2. By one of your State's United States Senators or his predecessor.
3. By virtue of being a land-grant college.
4. By special act of Congress.

In accepting the privilege of being a depository library you have agreed to abide by the law and regulations governing officially designated depositories.

You are not required to receive all United States Government publications which are made available to depositories. You may select those series best suited to the needs of your patrons. You are urged to use caution in selecting publications so that there will be no waste of Government funds and so that you can properly handle those you do select and make them readily available. Keep in mind that the depository collection is a *permanent* one and that publications cannot be disposed of except as outlined in the later paragraphs on Disposition of Depository Publications.

Government publications supplied to depository libraries should receive the same care and treatment as privately published material, such as books and periodicals. They need not be held together as a special depository collection. If they can circulate as do other books in your collection, so much the better. (Those libraries wishing to keep their depository collection intact may find it convenient to purchase extra copies of many Government publications for use in circulation.)

Many Federal Government publications are valuable as reference and bibliographical sources, and this type of material in many instances can profitably be made a part of a reference-room collection.

There are also important periodicals published by the Federal Government. They can form a valuable part of the periodical collection of the library and need not be segregated merely because they are received through depository designation.

If the practice of the depository library is to keep pamphlet material in vertical files, then similar Government publications may be kept in the same way.

It is necessary to issue many Government publications unbound or in paper covers. Libraries are expected to include these publications in their binding program along with books, periodicals, and other privately published materials. Binders are not usually furnished for looseleaf material.

Depository-collection items which are lost or worn out, etc., should be subject to the same replacement policy as the library maintains for non-Government materials.

Use of the Superintendent of Documents classification scheme is not mandatory for depository libraries. Any library should carefully weigh it

SOURCE: U.S. Government Printing Office. Division of Public Documents. Superintendent of Documents. *Instructions to Depository Libraries.* (Washington: 1962), pp. 1-13.

against other classification schemes before adopting it.

Every effort should be made to insure that the depository collection is used and that publications are not merely stored or placed in inaccessible locations.

SECTION 2. REGIONAL DEPOSITORIES

Libraries designated to be regional depositories must already be designated depositories.

Designation as a regional depository requires prior approval of the head of the library authority of the State or the Commonwealth of Puerto Rico. A United States Senator or the Resident Commissioner in the case of Puerto Rico, may make the designation.

In addition to fulfilling the requirements for refular depositories, they must receive and retain at least one copy of all Government publications made available to depositories, either in printed or microfacsimile form (except those authorized to be discarded by the Superintendent of Documents).

Within the region they serve, the regional depositories must provide interlibrary loan, reference service, and assistance for regular depository libraries in the disposal of unwanted Government publications as provided by law. They have the authority to permit regular depository libraries within the areas served by them, to dispose of Government publications which they have retained for at least five years after first offering them to other depository libraries within their area, then to other libraries, and then if not wanted to discard.

SECTION 3. CORRESPONDENCE WITH THE SUPERINTENDENT OF DOCUMENTS

In writing, always mention that you are a depository library and cite your assigned library number.

To avoid misrouting and insure prompt response, address all letters, claims, amendment of selections, replies to surveys for new items, etc. to:

Library
Division of Public Documents
U. S. Government Printing Office
Washington 25, D. C.

unless self-addressed envelopes or labels are furnished to you.

Use the claim forms only for requests for publications selected but not received. All other matters should be handled in separate correspondence.

Always give the item number from the Classified List, the series title or publication title, and the Superintendent of Documents classification number when writing concerning depository publications.

SECTION 4. PERIODIC REPORTS

At least every two years the Superintendent of Documents sends to all depository libraries questionnaires concerning the use made of the publications furnished as well as conditions under which they are kept. All libraries are required to answer these questionnaires fully and promptly, as they serve as part of the inspection of depositories provided by law. It is impossible for the Superintendent to make periodic visits to each library personally, though he visits as many as time and funds permit.

SECTION 5. TERMINATION AS A DEPOSITORY LIBRARY

Any depository library has the right to relinquish its privilege at any time by addressing a letter to the Superintendent of Documents stating that the library no longer wishes to be a depository for United States Government publications.

The privilege may also be taken away by the Superintendent of Documents for failure of the library to meet the standards required by law or for consistent disregard of notices and instructions, resulting in unnecessary expense to the Government in administering the program for that particular library.

Upon termination of the depository privilege, either by request or for cause, the library shall request of the Superintendent instructions concerning disposition to be made of the depository publications on hand. The library must also submit a list of those holdings that it wishes to keep permanently, as all depository publications remain the property of the United States Government.

SECTION 6. SELECTION OF PUBLICATIONS BY DEPOSITORY LIBRARIES

The basis of selection is the Classified List of United States Government Publications, which was last revised in 1950.

The Classified List comprises those series or groups of publications which are prepared by the various departments and agencies of the Government having public interest or educational value. Excluded are publications required for strictly administrative or operational purposes, those classified for reasons of national security, and so-called cooperative publications.

Selections from the 1950 Revision of the Classified List which went into effect on November 27, 1950, now supersede all previous selections. The 1950 list consists of one 3" X 5" card for each series or group of publications available for selection by libraries. Each card gives the Item Number, issuing agency, series title, Superintendent of Documents classification number, information on the series when necessary, and a space for the depository's assigned number. An annotated list by class, revised or supplemented each year, is also furnished beginning in 1963.

The Item Number assigned to a series in the Classified List remains the governing item number for that series regardless of change of title or transfer of the issuing agency or change of name of the issuing agency. An item number assigned to a series may also govern the distribution of a closely related series of similar nature, if one would give incomplete information without the other (for example, a series of numbered manuals and a series of unnumbered manuals with similar content issued by the same agency).

Two sets of item cards have been furnished to designated depositories, one set to be kept intact for the library's records, and the other to be used in making selections by return to the Library, Division of Public Documents of one item card, properly marked with the depository's assigned number, for each series selected.

It is important that selections by a library be centrally controlled within the library and that records be accurately kept, in order that misunderstandings will not occur and that the library's records of items selected will agree with those kept in the Division of Public Documents. In making your selections, keep in mind the amount of space available to you, as well as the adequacy of your staff for classifying, cataloging, and shelving the publications listed. You will receive notification as new series of publications are announced, in order that you may select them, if your desire.

SECTION 7. SURVEYS FOR NEW ITEMS

As new series of publications are printed by the United States Government, new item numbers are added to the 1950 Revision of the Classified List of publications available for selection by depositories.

Two 3" X 5" item cards are sent to each library for the new item, together with a sample copy of the first printed issue, whenever possible. If the library desires to receive future issues in the series, it should return one item card, properly marked with the assigned Depository Library Number. A self-addressed envelope, directed to the Library of the Division of Public Documents, is provided for returning the card, which must be received within the time prescribed. Returns received after the date indicated in the survey notice cannot be used as the basis of claims for missed publications (libraries outside the contiguous United States excepted).

If the library selects the new item, the sample copy furnished should be kept as the regular depository distribution for the item. If not selected, the sample copy may be discarded.

SECTION 8. AMENDMENT OF SELECTIONS

Selections can be amended at any time, but, in the case of Congressional material, distribution cannot be provided for added libraries until the start of a new session of Congress, unless copies happen to be available through discontinuance by some other depository. This is particularly true of the Congressional Serial Set, which may not be bound and distributed until long after being printed and then only in sufficient numbers to supply libraries which had selected the bound volumes prior to the beginning of the session which they cover.

Publications cannot be furnished retroactively. New selections will take effect only when new issues in the series selected are ordered printed.

Only series for which item cards have been furnished and made part of the Classified List can be added to a depository's selections.

Additions to selections are made by sending, to

the Library, Division of Public Documents, one item card or a typewritten facsimile, with the depository library number correctly marked on it.

Selections are discontinued by written request giving the item number and series title of the item to be dropped.

SECTION 9. DAILY DEPOSITORY SHIPPING LIST

Since August 1, 1951, the Documents Division has prepared a daily shipping list of all depository publications distributed on that day, with the exception of the Federal Register and the daily Congressional Record. The list, showing the item numbers under which the publications were distributed, the titles and series numbers of the publications, and the Superintendent of Documents classification numbers, is issued daily Monday through Friday, except on holidays. *Each library receives a copy of each day's list*, even though none of the item numbers listed were selected by the library.

The shipping list serves as an invoice for the day's shipment. Immediately upon receipt of a package the indicated item numbers on the list should be checked against the library's selections to determine whether any items previously selected have been omitted from the shipment.

The attention of all concerned with the depository collection should be brought to the fact that the shipping list is also used by the Division of Public Documents as a quick means of informing depositories of corrections of previous lists, of issuance of special publications which are available only upon individual request, *and of new item numbers being added to the Classified List.*

SECTION 10. CLAIMS FOR COPIES OF PUBLICATIONS SELECTED BUT NOT RECEIVED

All claims for nonreceipt of depository publications *must be postmarked within 10 days from the date of receipt of the Daily Depository Shipping List on which the publications were listed.*

Except for issues of the Federal Register and the daily Congressional Record, claims can be made only for publications actually listed on the Depository Shipping List. The Monthly Catalog cannot be used as a basis for claims.

Special claim forms are provided to all depository libraries and must be used in preference to regular letters.

The Division of Public Documents can provide only one copy of each publication to depository libraries. Duplicate copies of publications can be supplied by this Office only from the sales stock which is purchased with an entirely separate appropriation and which is accounted for in a completely different manner. The depository distribution and the sales distribution are two entirely separate functions and are in no way interchangeable.

When depository publications are ordered, the number of requests on hand when the publication is printed is used as the basis for determining the number of copies to be supplied to depositories. For this reason, requests which come in after the publication has gone to press cannot be honored. Claims for Congressional serial volumes cannot be honored unless the library had selected the particular item number prior to the time the individual reports or documents were ordered printed; that is, prior to the beginning of the session of Congress and not at the time the volumes are bound.

The Division of Public Documents makes every effort to provide a fast and accurate distribution service of depository publications. In distributing several million publications each year to depositories, it is inevitable that a few mistakes will be made. In all cases where depositories have selected publications in advance but have failed to receive them, this Office will endeavor to obtain a copy for the depository. In some instances, it will be impossible to honor claims because the supply of the publication has been exhausted. Before the depository is informed that no copy can be made available, the Documents Division will make every effort to obtain one.

SECTION 11. DISPOSITION OF DEPOSITORY PUBLICATIONS

All depositories libraries *not* served by a designated regional depository *must retain permanently* one copy of all Government publications received under depository distribution, except superseded publications or those issued later in bound form, in either printed form or in microfacsimile form.

Superseded publications may simply be discarded.

Those received later in bound form and those

for which microfacsimile copies are substituted should be offered to some other public library or educational institution in your vicinity which might find use for them. Failing to find such a taker after reasonable effort you may dispose of them in any appropriate manner but should such disposition take the form of sale, either as second-hand books or as waste paper, the proceeds with a letter of explanation should be sent to this Office as all depository publications remain the property of the United States Government.

Depository libraries which *are* served by regional depositories (at present this applies only to libraries in the State of Wisconsin and in New York State outside of the city of New York) may dispose of publications which they have retained for at least five years with the permission of and in accordance with instructions from the regional depository which serves their area.

The following are some of the types of material which may be disposed of by all depositories:

1. Daily Congressional Record, after bound volumes are received. However, depositories wishing to keep the Appendix pages should remove them from the daily issues as they are no longer carried into the bound volumes.
2. Slip laws, after bound Statutes at Large are received.
3. House and Senate Bills and Resolutions, 1 year after the close of the Congress.
4. Any materials which are cumulated in later issues, such as Supplement to the United States Code, the Code of Laws of the District of Columbia, pocket supplements to the Code of Federal Regulations (with the exception of Title 3), Internal Revenue Bulletin (if the Cumulative Bulletins are received), etc., after the later cumulation is received.
5. Any publication which is revised after the revised edition is received, regardless of whether it carries a new number in the series.
6. Pages from loose-leaf publications that are supplanted by new pages.
7. Separates, upon receipt of final bound volumes.
8. Senate and House reports and documents, upon receipt of the serial set volumes.
9. Compilations of laws and regulations issued by various agencies, upon receipt of new editions.

10. Lists and indexes of publications of various agencies, upon receipt of *complete* new editions (e.g. list of publications of the Bureau of Mines, Index of Congressional committee hearings issued by the Senate Library, etc.). Small spot lists, such as publication announcements, may be discarded at the end of 6 months or when they have lost their timeliness.
11. Annual or biennial publications of a statistical nature which merely revise figures or information and bring them up-to-date, such as Postal Guide, Light Lists, etc., upon receipt of a new issue. This permission does *not* apply to annual publications such as annual reports of departments and agencies, each of which covers the activities of the organization for a specific period of time.
12. Material which has an expiring-effect date, such as Civil Service examination announcements, Agricultural Conservation Program Handbooks, etc. On such material only the latest issues need be kept.
13. Any publication which is superseded by another which is stated to contain similar information.

SECTION 12. SUBSTITUTION OF MICROFACSIMILE COPIES FOR DEPOSITORY PUBLICATIONS

Permission is granted to all designated United States Government depositories to substitute microfacsimile copies for any holdings of United States Government publications provided the microfacsimile copies are properly referenced and located so as to be readily accessible to users and the necessary reading equipment is available for whichever type of microfacsimile is substituted for the original.

Libraries availing themselves of permission for substitution should send the Library, Division of Public Documents, United States Government Printing Office, Washington 25, D. C. a list of the material for which microfacsimile copies have been substituted.

Microfacsimiles are not furnished to depositories by the Superintendent of Documents and must be obtained from commercial producers of the same.

II

LAWS, REGULATIONS, THE CONGRESS & THE COURTS

You don't have to be a lawyer to understand the legislative and judicial processes and products . . . but it might help. However, since you probably don't have time for a law degree you might find some assistance from the following readings. Most of these "how to do it" pieces have just recently been revised. You should also know that there is no substitute for getting right in there and wallowing in the Federal Register, the Statutes, and the like. This doesn't diminish the value of the instructions provided here, but it's just to remind you that you can't learn to play tennis by just reading a book on it.

And don't forget that there are other helps too: the *U.S. Code* itself describes Congress and the Courts, and the *House* and *Senate Manuals* go into the nature of the various kinds of Congressional legislation.

Guide to Federal Register Finding Aids

Prepared by the Office of the Federal Register, National Archives and Records Service, General Services Administration.

The purpose of this guide is to give users of the Federal Register publications a better understanding of the indexes and other finding aids to Federal statutes, Proclamations, Executive orders, and other Presidential materials, and agency rules and other legal instruments published by the Office of the Federal Register pursuant to law and the Code of Federal Regulations.

These materials are published in the daily Federal Register, *the* Code of Federal Regulations, *the* slip laws, *and the* United States Statutes at Large *from the original acts of Congress and the Executive rules and notices filed with the Office. From related source material, the Office publishes the U.S.* Government Organization Manual, *the* Public Papers of the Presidents of the United States, *and the* Weekly Compilation of Presidential Documents.

Each of the publications named above includes appropriate subject indexes and numerical finding aids designed to facilitate its use and reduce research time. This guide describes the indexes and finding aids and indicates where they may be found. It also includes a table of special information lists that are useful to researchers generally.

This guide is arranged as follows:

Alphabetical List of Finding Aids.
Table 1–Researching Agency Materials.
Table 2–Researching Presidential Materials.
Table 3–Researching Statutory Materials.
Table 4–Special Information Lists.

ALPHABETICAL LIST OF FINDING AIDS

	Finding aid item
Acts Approved by the President, weekly list .	49
Acts Requiring Publication in the Federal Register, list.	57
Agency abolitions and transfers:	
Executive agencies abolished, transferred, or terminated	50
National defense, abolished agencies or transfers of functions relating to	16
Bills enacted into law:	
Legislative history.	43

	Finding aid item
Private	39
Public.	38
CFR:	
Checklist.	50
Current and superseded volumes, list	53
Subtitles and chapters, alphabetical list. . .	10
Titles and chapters, table	9
Codification guides:	
CFR Parts Affected:	
Cumulative	3B, 21B
Daily	3A, 21A

SOURCE: Reprinted from U.S. National Archives and Records Service. Office of the Federal Register. *Federal Register,* vol. 34, no. 225, part II, Saturday Nov. 22, 1969. (Washington: 1969). pp. 18785–18794.

Finding aid item

Finding aid item

Table 1—Researching Agency Materials

This table describes the principal finding aids used to locate agency materials published in the daily *Federal Register,* the *Code of Federal Regulations* (CFR), and the *United States Government Organization Manual.* The finding aids are listed under the name of the publication containing the source materials to which they lead.

FEDERAL REGISTER

1. Contents table.
2. Subject index.
3. Codification guide (lists of CFR parts or sections affected).
4. Parallel Table of Statutory Authorities and Rules.
5. Table of Presidential documents affected by Federal Register documents.
6. Land Management Bureau (Interior Department), Table of Public Land Orders.
7. Securities and Exchange Commission, Tables of Interpretative Releases.
8. General Index.
9. Table of CFR Titles and Chapters.
10. Alphabetical List of CFR Subtitles and Chapters.

CODE OF FEDERAL REGULATIONS

11. List of Sections Affected.
12. Redesignation tables.
13. Parallel Tables of Presidential Documents and Agency Rules.
14. Parallel Table of Statutory Authorities and Rules.
15. Guide to Record Retention Requirements.
16. Tabulation of Abolished Agencies or Transfers of Functions Relating to National Defense.

U. S. GOVERNMENT ORGANIZATION MANUAL

17. Subject index.
18. List of Names.

FEDERAL REGISTER

The following finding aids lead to agency source materials published in the daily *Federal Register.*

Finding Aid	Location
1. Contents table. Identifies by subject, agency documents published in the Federal Register.	Federal Register, each issue, third page.
2. Subject index. Analyzes contents of the Federal Register for the period covered.	Federal Register, separately issued as follows: *Monthly* for Jan., Feb., Apr., May, July, Aug., Oct., Nov., and Dec.; *Quarterly* for Jan.-Mar., Apr.-June, July-Sept.; *Annually.*

Finding Aid	*Location*
3. Codification guide.	
Identifies by CFR number, agency regulations and rule-making proposals (and Presidential documents) currently published in the Federal Register.	
A. *List of CFR Parts Affected (Daily).*	
Lists CFR parts affected by documents appearing in each day's issue.	Federal Register, each issue, following table of Contents.
B. *Cumulative List of CFR Parts Affected.*	
Lists CFR parts affected by documents published during a particular month.	Federal Register, end of each issue, beginning with the second issue of each month.
C. *List of CFR Sections Affected.*	
i. *Current.* Lists CFR sections amended or otherwise affected by documents published in the Federal Register beginning January 1 of a particular year. Entries indicate nature of changes effected.	Federal Register, separately published each month until entire year has been cumulated. (Portions of the list are also published in pertinent units of the CFR.)
ii. *Prior years.* Lists CFR sections affected by Federal Register documents published from 1949 through 1963. Enables users to determine text in effect on any given date during the period covered.	Issued as separate CFR units.
4. Parallel Table of Statutory Authorities and Rules.	
Leads from sections of the United States Code to agency rules published in the Federal Register which contain new citations implementing statutory authority.	Included with List of CFR Sections Affected, at end (see Finding aid 3 C i).
5. Table of Presidential Documents Affected by Federal Register Documents.	3 CFR: 5-year compilations, Table 4 (before 1948), Table 7) and Annual Supplements, Table 4.
Leads to documents published in the Federal Register each year since 1945, which have amended or otherwise affected Presidential documents.	
6. Land Management Bureau (Interior Department), Table of Public Land Orders.	
A. *1948–present.*	43 CFR Ch. II, Appendix
Lists orders and includes dates, subjects, and citations to publication in the Federal Register.	
B. *1943–1947.*	3 CFR, 1943–1948 Comp., Table 5.
Separate table for each year.	
7. Securities and Exchange Commission, Tables of Interpretative Releases.	
List by number, interpretative releases directed to individuals, partnerships, and corporations with respect to laws and regulations affecting their business conduct, including citations to publication in the Federal Register.	
A. Accounting matters.	17 CFR Part 211.
B. Securities Act of 1933.	17 CFR Part 231.
C. Securities and Exchange Act of 1934.	17 CFR Part 241.
D. Public Utility Holding Act of 1935.	17 CFR Part 251.
E. Trust Indenture Act of 1939.	17 CFR Part 261.
F. Investment Advisors Act of 1940.	17 CFR Part 276.
G. Corporate Reorganizations.	17 CFR Part 281.

CODE OF FEDERAL REGULATIONS

The following finding aids lead to agency source materials published in the *Code of Federal Regulations* (CFR).

Finding Aid	*Location*
8. General Index. Leads to regulatory areas of the CFR.	Issued as a separate unit of the CFR; revised annually.
9. Table of CFR Titles and Chapters. Lists titles of the CFR (broad subject areas) and chapters within each title (generally the name of the issuing agency).	Each CFR unit, at end; CFR General Index, at beginning.
10. Alphabetical List of CFR Subtitles and Chapters. Lists agencies prescribing regulations published in the CFR, showing location.	Each CFR unit, at end; CFR General Index, at beginning; and Government Organization Manual, Appendix C.
11. List of Sections Affected. Lists CFR sections affected by Federal Register documents.	See Finding aid 3 C.
12. Redesignation tables. Key new CFR section numbers to former section numbers for major recodifications of regulations.	CFR units, at end, as appropriate.

13. Parallel Tables of Presidential Documents and Agency Rules.
Lead to currently effective rules in the CFR which include or cite Presidential documents, specifying whether the Presidential document is codified, cited as authority, quoted, or cited in the text.
  A. Proclamations.
  B. Executive orders.
  C. Other Presidential documents.
	3 CFR Ch. I.
	3 CFR Ch. II.
	3 CFR Ch. III.

14. Parallel Table of Statutory Authorities and Rules. Leads from sections of the United States Code to CFR provisions which cite the statutory provisions as rule-making authority or as being interpreted or applied by the administering agency.	2 CFR Ch. I, revised annually as of Jan. 1. (Current additions to this table are carried cumulatively with the monthly List of CFR Sections Affected (Finding aid 3 C i).)
15. Guide to Record Retention Requirements. Digests provisions of the United States Code and the CFR with respect to the keeping of records; includes an index to categories of persons, groups, and products covered.	1 CFR, Appendix A. Also published in Federal Register annually, and available in pamphlet form on separate order.
16. Tabulation of Abolished Agencies or Transfers of Functions Relating to National Defense. Lists agencies within 32A CFR (National Defense, Appendix) which have been abolished or whose emergency planning functions have been transferred since October 10, 1953, citing the order effecting the change.	32A CFR Ch. I.

U.S. GOVERNMENT ORGANIZATION MANUAL

The following finding aids lead to agency source materials published in the *United States Government Organization Manual.*

Finding Aid	*Location*
17. Subject Index. Analyzes contents of the official organization handbook of the Federal Government.	Government Organization Manual, at end.
18. List of Names. Lists key officials with page references to titles of their positions.	Government Organization Manual, at end.

TABLE 2–RESEARCHING PRESIDENTIAL MATERIALS

This table describes the principal finding aids used to locate Presidential materials published in the daily *Federal Register,* the *Code of Federal Regulations* (CFR), the *Public Papers of the Presidents of the United States,* the *Weekly Compilation of Presidential Documents,* and the *United States Statutes at Large.* The finding aids are listed under the name of the publication containing the materials to which they lead.

FEDERAL REGISTER

19. Contents table.
20. Subject index
21. Codification guide.
22. Presidential Documents Published in the Federal Register.
23. Table of Presidential documents affected by Federal Register documents.
24. Tabulation of Executive orders related to 32A CFR.
25. Alphabetical list of customs collection districts.

CODE OF FEDERAL REGULATIONS

26. Index.
27. Tables of Presidential documents.
28. Parallel Tables of Presidential Documents and Agency Rules.

29. Statutes Cited As Authority for Presidential Documents.
30. Tabulation of Executive orders related to 32A CFR.

PUBLIC PAPERS OF THE PRESIDENTS

31. List of items.
32. Index.

WEEKLY COMPILATION OF PRESIDENTIAL DOCUMENTS

33. Indexes.

U.S. STATUTES AT LARGE

34. List of Proclamations.
35. Tables of Laws Affected (Presidential documents).

FEDERAL REGISTER

The following finding aids lead to Presidential source materials published in the daily *Federal Register.*

Finding Aid	*Location*
19. Contents table. Identifies by subject, Proclamations, Executive orders, and other Presidential documents published in the Federal Register.	Federal Register, beginning on third page.
20. Subject index. Analyzes contents of the Federal Register, including the documents issued by or relating to the President.	Federal Register, separately issued as follows: *Monthly* for Jan., Feb., Apr., May, July, Aug., Oct., Nov., and Dec.; *Quarterly* for Jan.-Mar., Apr.-June, and July-Sept.; *Annually.*
21. Codification guide. Lists by number, Proclamations, Executive orders, and other Presidential documents published in the Federal Register; includes earlier Presidential documents affected during the period covered.	
A. *List of CFR Parts Affected (Daily).* Lists documents published and affected in each day's issue.	Federal Register, following contents table, under "3 CFR."
B. *Cumulative List of CFR Parts Affected.* Lists documents published and affected during the month.	Federal Register, at end, beginning with second issue of each month; under "3 CFR."
C. *List of CFR Sections Affected.* Lists of documents published and affected beginning Jan. 1 of each year.	Federal Register, published separately as monthly supplements; under "3 CFR."

Finding Aid	*Location*
22. Presidential Documents Published in the Federal Register. Lists Proclamations, Executive orders, and other Presidential documents published in the Federal Register during the period covered.	Public Papers of the Presidents, each volume, Appendix B.
23. Table of Presidential documents affected by Federal Register documents. Lists Proclamations, Executive orders, and other Presidential documents affected by documents published in the Federal Register each year since 1945.	3 CFR, annual supplements, Table 4 (before 1948, Table 7), and 5-year compilations, Table 4.
24. Tabulation of Executive orders related to 32A CFR. Lists Executive orders directly related to regulations in 32A CFR (National Defense, Appendix), including Federal Register citations.	32A CFR, at beginning.
25. Alphabetical list of customs collection districts. Leads to Executive orders issued since March 3, 1913, which make organization changes in customs collection districts; includes Federal Register citations for orders issued after March 1936.	19 CFR 1.2.

CODE OF FEDERAL REGULATIONS

The following finding aids lead to Presidential source materials published in the *Code of Federal Regulations* (CFR).

Finding Aid	*Location*
26. Index. Leads to Proclamations, Executive orders, and other Presidential documents published in the CFR.	
A. Annual.	3 CFR, annual supplements, at end.
B. Five-year compilations.	3 CFR, 5-year compilations, at end.
27. Tables of Presidential documents. List by number, Presidential documents published in the CFR.	
A. Proclamations.	3 CFR, annual supplements and 5-year compilations, Table 1.
B. Executive orders.	3 CFR, annual supplements and 5-year compilations, Table 2.
C. Other Presidential documents.	3 CFR, annual supplements and 5-year compilations, Table 3.
28. Parallel Tables of Presidential Documents and Agency Rules. List by number, Presidential documents included or cited in currently effective rules in the CFR, specifying whether the Presidential document is codified, cited as authority, quoted, or cited in the text.	
A. Proclamations.	3 CFR Ch. I.
B. Executive orders.	3 CFR Ch. II.
C. Other Presidential documents.	3 CFR Ch. III.
29. Statutes Cited as Authority For Presidential Documents. Leads to Presidential documents which cite statutes as issuing authority; lists revised statutes and U.S.C. citations numerically, and lists Statutes at Large provisions chronologically.	3 CFR, annual supplements, Table 5, and 5-year compilations, Table 5.

Finding Aid	*Location*
30. Tabulation of Executive orders related to 32A CFR. Lists Executive orders directly related to regulations in Title 32A (National Defense, Appendix), including CFR position.	32A CFR, at beginning.

PUBLIC PAPERS OF THE PRESIDENTS

The following finding aids lead to Presidential source materials published in the *Public Papers of the Presidents of the United States.*

Finding Aid	*Location*
31. List of items. Lists by number and subject, items included in volumes of the Public Papers of the Presidents.	Public Papers of the Presidents, each volume, at beginning.
32. Index. Leads to items included in volumes of the Public Papers of the Presidents.	Public Papers of the Presidents, each volume, at end.

WEEKLY COMPILATION OF PRESIDENTIAL DOCUMENTS

The following finding aids lead to Presidential source materials published in the *Weekly Compilation of Presidential Documents.*

Finding Aid	*Location*
33. Indexes:	
A. Index of contents of current issues.	Weekly Compilation, each issue, at beginning.
B. Index to prior issues cumulated for a 3-month period.	Weekly Compilation, each issue, at end.
C. Seminannual: Subject index to documents published during a 6-month period.	Weekly Compilation, separately published.
D. Annual: Subject index to documents published during the year.	Weekly Compilation, separately published.

U.S. STATUTES AT LARGE

The following finding aids lead to Presidential materials published in the *United States Statutes at Large.*

Finding Aid	*Location*
34. List of Proclamations. Lists by number, Proclamations issued during each session of Congress, including title, date of issuance, and page number of the Statutes volume where text is published.	Statutes at Large, each volume, at beginning.
35. Tables of Laws Affected (Presidential documents). List by Number, Presidential documents (since 1956) which are amended, repealed, or otherwise expressly affected, or referred to or otherwise cited by provisions of public laws: Expressly affected: Table 6—Reorganization Plans. Table 8—Executive Orders and Proclamations. Referred to or cited: Table 16—Reorganization Plans. Table 18—Executive Orders and Proclamations.	Statutes at Large: Separate pamphlet for Vol. 70; at end of each volume beginning with Vol. 71; 10-year cumulation in separate volume for 1956-1965.

TABLE 3–RESEARCHING STATUTORY MATERIALS

This table describes the principal finding aids published by the Office of the Federal Register which pertain to statutory materials published in the *United States Statutes at Large,* the *Revised Statutes,* the *United States Code,* and related legislative source materials.

36. Subject Index (Statutes at Large).
37. Individual Index (Statutes at Large).
38. List of Bills Enacted into Public Law.
39. List of Bills Enacted into Private Law.
40. List of Public Laws.
41. List of Private Laws.
42. List of Concurrent Resolutions.
43. Guide to Legislative History of Bills Enacted into Public Law.

44. Tables of Laws Affected.
45. Parallel Tables of Statutory Authorites and Rules.
46. Statutes Cited as Authority for Presidential documents.
47. Guide to Record Retention Requirements.
48. "How to Find U.S. Statutes and U.S. Code Citations."

Finding Aid	*Location*
36. Subject Index (Statutes at Large). Leads to laws and concurrent resolutions enacted during each session of Congress, reorganization plans, proposed and ratified amendments to the Constitution, and Presidential Proclamations published with the Statutes.	Statutes at Large, each volume, at end.
37. Individual Index (Statutes at Large). Lists persons and private entities mentioned in the text of public and private laws enacted during a given session of Congress.	Statutes at Large, each volume, at end.
38. List of Bills Enacted into Public Law. Lists by number, Senate bills, House bills, and joint resolutions enacted into law during a given session of Congress (since 1963), including corresponding public law number.	Statutes at Large, each volume, at beginning.
39. List of Bills Enacted into Private Law. Lists by number, Senate bills, House bills, and joint resolutions enacted into law during a given session of Congress (since 1963), including corresponding private law number.	Statutes at Large, each volume, at beginning.
40. List of Public Laws. Lists by number, public laws enacted during a given session of Congress, including subject, date of enactment, and Statutes page numbers.	Statutes at Large, each volume, at beginning.
41. List of Private Laws. Lists by number, private laws enacted during a given session of Congress, including subject, date of enactment, and Statutes page numbers.	Statutes at Large, each volume, at beginning.
42. List of Concurrent Resolutions. Lists in chronological order, concurrent resolutions passed during a given session of Congress, including subject, date of passage, and the Statutes page numbers.	Statutes at Large, each volume, at beginning.
43. Guide to Legislative History of Bills Enacted Into Public Law. Lists by number, public laws enacted during a given session of Congress giving background sources, including approval dates, Statutes volume and page numbers, bill numbers, committee names and report numbers, dates of consideration and passage, and pertinent Congressional Record references.	Statutes at Large, each volume (since 1963), at end. *Note:* Separate history for each public law is carried on each slip law print.

Finding Aid	*Location*

44. Tables of Laws Affected.

Lists (since 1956) laws and other Federal instruments amended, repealed, or otherwise expressly affected, or referred to or otherwise cited by provisions of public laws:

Expressly affected:

Table 1—General Legislation.
Table 2—Revised Statutes.
Table 3—Internal Revenue Code of 1939.
Table 4—Internal Revenue Code of 1954.
Table 5—Positive Law Titles.
  (a) United States Code.
  (b) District of Columbia Code.
  (c) Panama Canal Code.
Table 6—Reorganization Plans.
Table 7—Veterans' Regulations.
Table 8—Executive Orders and Proclamations.
Table 9—Treaties and International Agreements.

Public laws expressing relationships in general terms (such as, "notwithstanding any other provision of law," "all laws in conflict with this law are hereby repealed," etc.):

Table 10—Provisions Respecting General Repeals, Conflicts, Etc.

Referred to or cited:

Table 11—General Legislation.
Table 12—Revised Statutes.
Table 13—Internal Revenue Code of 1939.
Table 14—Internal Revenue Code of 1954.
Table 15—Positive Law Titles.
  (a) United States Code.
  (b) District of Columbia Code.
  (c) Panama Canal Code.
Table 16—Reorganization Plans.
Table 17—Veterans' Regulations.
Table 18—Executive Orders and Proclamations.
Table 19—Treaties and International Agreements.

Location: Statutes at Large: Separate pamphlet for Vol. 70; at end of each volume beginning with Vol. 71; 10-year cumulation in separate volume for 1956–1965.

45. Parallel Tables of Statutory Authorites and Rules.

A. *Table of United States Code Citations.* Lists sections of the United States Code which are (a) cited as rulemaking authority or (b) noted as being interpreted or applied by currently effective rules codified in the CFR.

Location: 2 CFR Ch. I, revised annually.

B. *Additions to 2 CFR.* Lists sections of the United States Code added to 2 CFR because of new or amended citations of authority in documents currently published in the Federal Register.

Location: Included with List of CFR Sections Affected, at end (see Finding aid 3 C i).

46. Statutes Cited as Authority for Presidential Documents.

Lists statutes cited as issuance authority by Presidential documents published during a given year.

Location: 3 CFR: 5-year compilations, Table 5, and in annual supplements, Table 5.

47. Guide to Record Retention Requirements.

Digests provisions of the United States Code and the CFR with respect to the keeping of records; includes an index to categories of persons, groups, and products covered.

Location: 1 CFR, Appendix A. Also published in Federal Register annually and available in pamphlet form on separate order.

Finding Aid	*Location*
48. "How To Find U.S. Statutes and U.S. Code Citations." Presents typical reference situations and illustrated procedures for finding accurate up-to-date citations to U.S. Statutes at Large and the U.S. Code.	Separate pamphlet published by the House Committee on the Judiciary, sold by Superintendent of Documents, Government Printing Office.

TABLE 4—SPECIAL INFORMATION LISTS

The following special lists, published by the Office of the Federal Register, are not direct finding aids to agency, Presidential, or legislative materials, but contain information useful to legal researchers and others interested in such materials.

49. Acts Approved by the President.
50. CFR Checklist.
51. Executive agencies abolished, transferred, or terminated.
52. FAA Advisory Circulars Checklist.
53. Lists of current and superseded CFR volumes.
54. Nominations Submitted to the Senate.

55. Presidential Reports to Congress.
56. White House Releases.
57. List of Acts Requiring Publication in the Federal Register.
58. Checklist of White House Press Releases.
59. Digests of other White House announcements.

List	*Location*
49. Acts Approved by the President. Lists Acts approved by the President during a given week, including legislative and law numbers, and titles.	Weekly Compilation of Presidential Documents, at end.
50. CFR Checklist. Shows the issuance date and price of current bound volumes and supplements of the Code of Federal Regulations.	Federal Register, first issue of each month, under 1 CFR.
51. Executive agencies abolished, transferred, or terminated. Lists Federal departments, commissions, boards, that have been abolished, transferred, or terminated since March 4, 1933.	Government Organization Manual, Appendix A.
52. FAA Advisory Circulars Checklist.	Federal Register, published triennially.
53. Lists of current and superseded CFR volumes. List by title, volumes of the CFR which are currently effective and those which have been superseded since January 1, 1945.	CFR, most volumes and supplements, at end.
54. Nominations Submitted to the Senate. Lists Presidential nominations to various positions, indicating the individual, legal residence, and position for which nominated.	Weekly Compilation of Presidential Documents each issue, at end.
55. Presidential Reports to Congress. Lists the reports, including subject, House document number if so published, date sent to Congress, and White House release date, if so issued.	Public Papers, each volume, Appendix C.
56. White House Releases. Lists press releases and other White House announcements of concern to the President.	Public Papers, each volume, Appendix A.
57. List of Acts Requiring Publication in the Federal Register. Cites in chronological order, provisions of U.S. Statutes at Large and U.S. Code requiring or authorizing publication of documents in the Federal Register.	1 CFR, Appendix B.

List	*Location*
58. Checklist of White House Press Releases. Lists releases of the Office of the White House Press Secretary which have not been included in the issue.	Weekly Compilation, each issue, at end.
59. Digests of other White House announcements. Digests of other announcements not included in the issue.	Weekly Compilation, each issue, at end.

Enactment of a Law: Procedural Steps in the Legislative Process

Prepared by Floyd M. Riddick

There are very few government documents on this subject. This one, by the Senate's own Parliamentarian, covers the passage of a bill, from its introduction through the various parliamentary stages until its enactment into law. It is a revision of an earlier document on the same subject.

CONGRESS

"All legislative powers" of the Federal Government are vested by the Constitution in the Congress of the United States, which consists of two branches—the Senate and the House of Representatives.

The Senate is composed of 100 Members. Each State, regardless of area or population, is entitled, under the Constitution, to two Senators. It is presided over by the Vice President of the United States, who is the President of the Senate. Senators are elected for terms of 6 years, and are divided into three classes, so that the terms of one-third thereof expire every 2 years.

Membership of the House is apportioned on the basis of the population of the several States, the number now being fixed at 435, but each State shall have at least one Representative. The House is presided over by the Speaker, who is chosen by its Members at the beginning of a Congress or when a vacancy occurs in that office. Members of the House are elected for 2-year terms, being the same as the duration of a Congress.

Vacancies in the representation of any State in the Senate may be filled at a special election called for such purpose or by a temporary appointment by the Governor. In the latter case the appointee serves until the vacancy is filled by election in the manner provided by law. Vacancies in the House of Representatives can only be filled by an election for that purpose.

In addition to the 435 Members of the House, there is in that body a Resident Commissioner from Puerto Rico. He has the same rights and privileges as a Representative with respect to attending sessions of the House, engaging in debate, and serving on committees, but he does not have the right to vote.

SOURCE: U.S. Congress. Senate. *Enactment of a Law: Procedural Steps in the Legislative Process.* Prepared under the direction of Francis R. Valeo, Secretary of the Senate by Floyd M. Reddick, Parliamentarian of the Senate. Senate Document No. 35, 90th Congress, 1st Session. (Washington: 1967), pp. 1–29.

SESSIONS OF A CONGRESS

The life of a Congress is 2 years, and it shall assemble at least once every year, to begin at noon on the 3d day of January, unless by law it fixes a different day.   Thus, each Congress has at least two sessions. The President, under the Constitution, may call a special session of Congress or either body thereof, whenever in his judgment it is necessary.   He may even adjourn them to such time as he shall think proper in case of "disagreement between them, with respect to the time of adjournment."

Bills and resolutions started on their way to enactment but left unfinished at the end of any session of a Congress, except the last, are proceeded with at the next session as if no adjournment had taken place; however, at the end of a Congress all measures die on which final action has not been taken.   Treaties and protocols, which are considered by the Senate only, remain from session to session until they are disposed of; the consideration of these, however, must be resumed anew at the beginning of a new Congress.   Nominations must be submitted or resubmitted to the Senate each session.

Both Houses ordinarily meet at noon each day, but either may change its hour of meeting.   The daily sessions are terminated at their own pleasure, usually between 4 and 6 p.m.; but they may be continued into the evening if necessary or essential.   Neither House can recess or adjourn for more than 3 days without the consent of the other.

PROCEDURAL STEPS IN THE LEGISLATIVE PROCESS
FORMS AND DESIGNATION OF LEGISLATIVE BUSINESS

All proposed legislation, and nearly all formal actions by either of the two Houses, take the form of a bill or resolution.   When bills and resolutions are introduced or submitted they take one of the following forms: In the Senate, they are designated with the prefix "S. ———," for Senate bills; "S.J. Res. ———," for Senate joint resolutions; "S. Con. Res. ———," for Senate concurrent resolutions; and "S. Res. ———," for Senate resolutions.   In the House of Representatives, they take the following designations: "H.R. ———," for House bills; "H.J. Res. ———," for House joint resolutions; "H. Con. Res. ———," for House concurrent resolutions; and "H. Res. ———," for House resolutions.   The bills and resolutions are numbered ad seriatim, in the chronological order in which they are introduced.

Senate and House bills and Senate and House joint resolutions, when passed by both Houses in identical form and approved by the President, become public or private law—public laws affect the Nation as a whole; private laws relate only to an individual, private matters, or claims against the Government. The procedure to the enactment on both are identical, with the exception of joint resolutions proposing amendments to the Constitution of the United States, which under the Constitution must be passed in each House by a two-thirds vote of the Members present and voting, a quorum being present. They are not sent to the President for his approval but to the Administrator of the General Services Administration, who transmits them to the various States for ratification by at least three-fourths of the legislatures thereof.

Concurrent resolutions by either House do not become law; they are not signed by the President, nor by the Speaker and the Vice President. They are attested by the Secretary of the Senate and Clerk of the House and transmitted after approval to the Administrator of the General Services Administration for publication in the Statutes at Large. Concurrent resolutions have the force of both Houses, and must be approved by them in identical form to be effective— they are used for matters such as the creation of joint investigating committees or printing matters in which both Houses have a concern.

A House or Senate resolution (H. Res. ———— and S. Res. ————) only has the force of the House passing it, and the action by one House on such instrumentality is final—resolutions of one House are used to fill some of the legislative needs of that House such as creating investigating committees or to express its sentiments.

ORIGIN OF LEGISLATION

Legislation originates in several ways. The Constitution provides that the President "shall from time to time give to the Congress information of the state of the Union, and recommend to their consideration such measures as he shall judge necessary and expedient."

The President fulfills this duty either by personally addressing a joint session of the two Houses or by sending messages in writing to the Congress or to either body thereof, which are received and referred to the appropriate committees. The President usually presents or submits his annual message on the state of the Union shortly after the beginning of a session.

The right of petition is guaranteed the citizens of the United States by the Constitution, and numerous petitions and memorials on all types of subjects are sent to Congress. These are laid before the two Houses by their respective presiding officers or submitted by individual Members of the House and Senate in their respective bodies, and are usually referred to the appropriate committees of the House in which they were submitted.

Bills to carry out the recommendations of the President are usually introduced by the chairmen of the various committees or subcommittees thereof which have jurisdiction of the subject matter recommended by the President   Sometimes the committees themselves may submit and report to the Senate "original bills" to carry out such recommendations.

The ideas for legislative proposals may come from the individual Representative or Senator, from any of the executive departments of the Government, from private organized groups or associations, or from any individual citizen.

The bills or resolutions (legislative proposals), however, can be introduced in their respective Houses only by Senators and Representatives. When introduced they are referred to the standing committees which have jurisdiction of the subject matter.

Members frequently introduce bills that are similar in purpose, in which case the committee considering them may take one of the bills, and add the best features of the others for reporting to the parent body, or draft an entirely new bill and report it (known as an original bill) in lieu of the others.

Under article 1, section 7 of the Constitution of the United States, all bills for raising revenue shall originate in the House of Representatives; but the Senate may propose or concur in amendments as on other bills.

ANNUAL APPROPRIATIONS

Legislative proposals when enacted and become law are referred to generally as "legislative authority."

Funds for carrying on the work of the Government pursuant to "legislative authority" are provided in general and special appropriation bills, which usually originate in the House. The procedure is, briefly, as follows: The heads of the various departments and agencies of the Government prepare estimates on the cost of doing their work for the year and submit these estimates to the Director of the Bureau of the Budget. He gives them careful consideration from which he prepares a budget for expenditures for each of the Government establishments based on their own official estimates. This budget is submitted to the President and, after his approval, is transmitted to the Congress.

The Committee on Appropriations of the House drafts these various appropriations bills, based on the budget submitted by the President. After passage of these bills by that body they are transmitted to the Senate, where they are referred to its Committee on Appropriations. After due consideration by the latter committee they are reported back to the Senate, usually with amendments, for passage by the Senate.

The budget is for the guidance of Congress; it is not obligatory upon either House to follow its recommendations. The budget estimates are regularly increased or decreased by Congress.

The Government operates its business on a fiscal rather than a calendar year basis, beginning on July 1 of each year and ending on the following June 30.

INTRODUCTION AND REFERENCE OF PROPOSED LEGISLATION IN SENATE

During the morning hour of each legislative day, Rule VII of the Senate provides that, after the Journal is read and the Presiding Officer lays before the Senate messages, reports, and communications of various types, he shall call for, in the following order:

"The presentation of petitions and memorials.

"Reports of standing and select committees.

"The introduction of bills and joint resolutions.

"Concurrent and other resolutions."

Under recent practices, however, nearly all of the bills and resolutions are presented to the clerks at the Presiding Officer's desk for processing throughout the day, and without any comment from the floor. A few of them are still introduced from the floor, and any Senator, when making such introductions, usually discusses his proposal when he presents it. Only one Senator may introduce a bill or resolution, but commonly he does it for himself and other Senators as cosponsors.

The rules require that every bill and joint resolution have three readings, each on a different legislative day, before passage—two of these to occur before reference to a committee. This is seldom done any more, however, since all bills and resolutions are available in printed form. The reading requirement on different days is no longer called into play except in the case of procedural conflicts but this requirement can be forced on the Senate on demand of a single Senator.

A legislative day comprises the period between the meeting of the Senate following adjournment and its next adjournment, which period by recessing from day to day may include several calendar days.

After the second reading of each, or after such assumption, and usually on the same day, bills are referred (under authority of the Presiding Officer) to the standing committee having jurisdiction over the subject matter. The Senate itself, by a majority vote, may determine to which committee a bill will go by appealing the proposed reference thereof. Sometimes bills are submitted and by unanimous consent immediately passed without reference; or they are ordered to lie on the table, or placed directly on the calendar, later to be taken up and passed without reference, or to be referred to a particular committee on motion.

Endorsements showing the author and reference are made at the Presiding Officer's desk on each bill. These various proceedings are shown in the Congressional Record of that day and are noted in the Minute Book kept by the Journal clerk. After being referred the bill is sent by a page to the Office of the Secretary of the Senate and numbered by the Congressional Record clerk. He delivers it to the bill clerk, who makes an entry in the Bill Book, showing the number, author, title, date, and reference. It is then turned over to the assistant Journal clerk for proper notation in the Senate Journal of the proceedings of that day, and is subsequently sent to the Government Printing Office to be printed.

On the following morning, printed copies of the bill are delivered to the Secretary's Office, and to the Senate and House document rooms and are thus made available to the public.

The original bill is then returned from the Printing Office and placed in the file of the Senate.

SENATE COMMITTEE CONSIDERATION

A clerk in the Secretary's office delivers a printed copy of each bill to the committee to which it was referred, taking a receipt therefor. The clerk of each committee enters bills upon his Calendar of Business of the said committee.

Committees as a rule have regular meeting days, but they may meet at the call of their chairman at other times.

At sittings of a committee, matters on its calendar are usually the order of business, but any issue within its jurisdiction may be the order of the day, for example: an investigation of an agency of the Government over which it has jurisdiction or to hear an official discuss policies and operations of his agency.

Any committee may refer its pending bills to its subcommittees for study and reports thereon. Most of the committees have standing subcommittees, and frequently ad hoc subcommittees are appointed to study and report on particular pieces of legislation or to make a study of a certain subject.

Committees or subcommittees generally hold hearings on all major controversial legislation before drafting the proposal into a final form for reporting to the Senate. The length of hearings and the number of witnesses testifying vary, depending upon the time element, the number of witnesses wanting to be heard, the desires of the committee to hear witnesses, et cetera. Recommendations of the administration in conjunction with the Bureau of the Budget are sought by the committees on nearly all major legislation, but they are in no way obligated to accept such recommendations.

A subcommittee makes reports to its full committee, and the latter may adopt such reports without change, amend them in any way it desires, reject them, or adopt an entirely different report.

After consideration of any bill, the full committee may report it to the Senate favorably with or without amendments, submit an adverse report thereon, or vote not to report anything.

Committees necessarily do not act on all bills referred to them. And any Senator has the right, under the rules, to enter a motion to discharge a committee from its further consideration of any bill. Rarely are measures discharged from a committee on motion. By unanimous consent, some bills are discharged from one committee and sent to another. If a motion to discharge is agreed to, the bill is thereby taken out of the jurisdiction of that committee, and placed on the Senate Calendar of Business or referred to another committee.

COMMITTEE REPORTS

The chairman, or some other member of the committee designated for that purpose, reports bills to the Senate, and when reported they are placed on the Senate Calendar of Business, unless unanimous consent is given for immediate consideration.

The action taken by the committee appears on the copy of the bill reported, and a written report nearly always accompanies the bill, which is numbered ad seriatim.   The reports, like the bills, are printed by the Government Printing Office for distribution.

A reported bill passes through the same channels in the Secretary's Office as an introduced bill, for notation of the proper entries on the records.   It is reprinted, showing the calendar and report numbers, the name of the Senator reporting it, the date, and whether with or without amendment.   Matters proposed to be stricken out of a bill by the committee are shown in line type, while matters proposed to be inserted are shown in italic.

The minority members of a committee, on leave of the Senate, may submit their views in opposition to those of the committee, and any member of the committee may likewise submit his individual views on the bill in question.

SENATE CONSIDERATION

Bills or resolutions of importance are usually brought before the Senate for consideration by motion of the majority leader, agreed to by a majority vote.   Most bills and resolutions, however, are taken up by unanimous consent or on call of the Calendar.   The majority and minority leaders are the spokesmen for their respective parties and in consultation with their respective policy committees implement and direct the legislative schedule and program.

Rule VIII governs the consideration of bills on call of the Senate Calendar, and is as follows:

At the conclusion of the morning business for each day, unless upon motion the Senate shall at any time otherwise order, the Senate will proceed to the consideration of the Calendar of Bills and Resolutions, and continue such consideration until 2 o'clock; and bills and resolutions that are not objected to shall be taken up in their order, and each Senator shall be entitled to speak once and for 5 minutes only upon any question; and the objection may be interposed at any stage of the proceedings, but upon motion the Senate may continue such consideration * * *.

On Mondays, when there is a morning hour, the call of the Calendar may be dispensed with only by unanimous consent; but on any other legislative day following the close of morning business, a Senator obtaining recognition may move to take up any bill on the Calendar.

Under recent practices, the call of the Calendar is usually pursuant to a unanimous consent order, but in accordance with the above rule, except that it continues until concluded instead of 2 o'clock.

After the amendment stage, the bill is ordered engrossed and read a third time.   This reading is usually by title only, but, upon demand, the engrossed bill must be read in full.   The question is then put upon its passage, which is carried by a majority vote.

The preamble of a bill, if any, and the title are acted upon after passage of the bill.

At any time before its passage, a bill may be laid on the table; postponed indefinitely, either of which motions has the effect of killing the bill; made a special order for a day certain, which requires a two-thirds vote; laid aside temporarily; recommitted to the committee which reported the bill; referred to a different committee; or displaced by taking up another bill by a majority vote.

Most bills are passed by a voice vote only, but before the result is announced, a division of the Senate may be demanded. Before the result of a voice or division vote has been announced, a rollcall vote may be had upon the demand of one-fifth of the Senators present.

Only one motion to reconsider the passage of a bill is in order, and that must be made by a Senator voting with the prevailing side. A bill cannot be transmitted to the House of Representatives while a motion to reconsider its passage remains unacted upon.

Debate in the Senate is unlimited unless by unanimous consent an agreement is reached to limit and control time on a pending bill or question, or unless by a two-thirds vote, a quorum being present, cloture is invoked.

ENGROSSED BILLS

The printed bill used at the desk by the Senate during its consideration as the official desk copy, showing the amendments adopted, if any, and endorsed as having passed, is sent to the Secretary's Office and delivered to the bill clerk. Again, he makes the proper entries on his records. He then turns it over to the enrolling clerk who makes an appropriate entry on his records and sends it to the Government Printing Office to be printed in the form in which it passed the Senate, on special white paper. This printed Act is attested by the Secretary as having passed the Senate as of the proper date, and is termed as the official engrossed bill.

After the passage of a bill by one body, it technically becomes an Act (not yet effective as a law) but it nevertheless continues to be generally referred to as a bill.

BILLS SENT TO HOUSE

Engrossed bills are messaged to the House of Representatives by one of the clerks in the Secretary's Office, who is announced by the Doorkeeper of the House.[1] Upon being recognized by the Speaker, the clerk announces that the Senate has passed a bill (giving its number and title) in which the concurrence of the House is requested.

Upon receipt of the message from the Senate, the Speaker refers the measures contained therein to appropriate committees. If, however, a substantially similar House bill has been favorably reported by a committee, the Senate bill, unless it creates a charge upon the Treasury, may not be referred but remain on the Speaker's table. It may subsequently be taken up or substituted for such House bill when consideration of the latter is had.

---

[1] (Senate Journal, Apr. 23, 1789.) The original rule provided: When a bill or other message shall be sent from the Senate to the House of Representatives, it shall be carried by the Secretary, who shall make one obeisance to the Chair on entering the door of the House of Representatives, and another on delivering it at the table into the hands of the Speaker. After he shall have delivered it, he shall make an obeisance to the Speaker, and repeat it as he retires from the House.

HOUSE COMMITTEE CONSIDERATION

Senate bills and resolutions when messaged to the House are referred by the Speaker to the appropriate House committees, just as he refers all bills and resolutions introduced in the House, and they are all processed in much the same fashion as in the Senate—that is, endorsed for reference, recorded in Journal, information on each printed in Congressional Record, and printed by Government Printing Office for distribution.   The House committees, like the Senate, have committee calendars of business and usually have regular meeting days [but may also meet on the call of their chairman] for the consideration of business pending before them.

The procedure of House committees in considering and reporting bills is much the same as those of the Senate; they also have standing subcommittees and ad hoc subcommittees.

After a House committee has concluded consideration of a proposed bill, it votes to report it to the House, with or without amendments. If the committee acts in the affirmative, the bill is reported and a written report usually accompanies each reported measure.   When reported it is placed on at least one of the four House calendars, namely: Union Calendar, House Calendar, Consent Calendar, and Private Calendar.   If it is a noncontroversial public bill it may at the same time be placed on either the Union or House and the Consent Calendars.

There is one other House calendar called the Discharge Calendar. Only bills discharged from committees are ever placed on this calendar.

HOUSE CONSIDERATION

The House calendars have little relationship to the order in which the House transacts its business.

In addition to the calendars, the House has special legislative days which have been established to expedite certain types of unprivileged business.   The special legislative days are: Calendar Wednesday (every Wednesday), District of Columbia (considered on second and fourth Mondays), and Suspension of the Rules (considered first and third Mondays).   The Consent Calendar business is transacted on the first and third Mondays, and Private Calendar business on the first and third Tuesdays.   Discharge Calendar business, if any, comes up on the second and fourth Mondays.

The business privileged for consideration in the House on special legislative days is defined in each instance.   Generally speaking, after the regular routine business each morning, including the reading of the Journal, the House proceeds to the consideration of bills or resolutions if any are to be acted on that day.   The order varies somewhat, as follows: (1) On special calendar and special legislative days, bills and resolutions are called up in pursuance of the procedure defined by the rules in each instance as mentioned above; (2) under unanimous consent bills are called up in pursuance of such requests made and granted by the House regardless of the regular rules of procedure; (3) privileged bills including general appropriation bills, general revenue bills, conference reports, special reports, and the like may be called up by the Members in charge of them at almost any time, interrupting other less privileged business, providing the Representative in charge is recognized by the Speaker; and (4) bills are regularly voted the next business in order, usually by adopting a special rule [simple House resolution], reported by the Rules Committee.   The procedure for consideration of such measures is defined in each instance in the special rule.   A special rule to call up a bill may be debated an hour before it is voted on.

Bills called up under the latter category are usually major or controversial pieces of legislation.

Bills which are first considered in the Committee of the Whole of the House are read for amendment under the 5-minute rule, after which the Committee of the Whole reports them back to the House for action on any amendments that may have been adopted, and final passage.

In the House as in the Senate, under the rules, bills are read three times before they are passed.   After a Senate bill is passed by the House, with or without amendment, it is returned to the Senate; if there are amendments, the amendments are engrossed before being messaged to the Senate.   All House bills passed are engrossed and messaged to the Senate.   All House engrossments are printed on blue paper.

For more details on procedure in the House in its passage of bills, see House Document No. 103 of the 88th Congress, first session, prepared by Charles J. Zinn.

SENATE ACTION ON HOUSE AMENDMENTS

Senate bills returned with House amendments in due course are laid before the Senate by the Presiding Officer upon the request or motion of a Senator, usually the author of the bill or the Senator who reported it from the committee   All amendments are read and may be considered en bloc   Various motions for the disposition of House amendments to a Senate bill, when they are laid before the Senate for action, are available to Senators, including the motions "to amend" or "to agree," and they take precedence over a motion to disagree and ask for a conference with the House on the amendments.   Usually this latter motion may include authority for the Presiding Officer to appoint the conferees on the part of the Senate; otherwise, the Senate may appoint them directly.   The number is usually three or five, and occasionally a larger number, especially in the case of the general appropriation bills.   Sometimes the House amendments are agreed to by the Senate, agreed to with amendments, or sent to conference.

In the case a motion to amend is made and agreed to, such amendments made by the Senate to the House amendments are transmitted to the House with a request for its concurrence therein.   If the House concurs or agrees in all of the Senate amendments, the legislative action in the passage of the bill is completed.   The House, however, may amend the Senate amendments to the House amendments, this being the second, and therefore the last, degree in which amendments may be made.   The House amendments to the Senate amendments to the House amendments are transmitted to the Senate, usually with a request for concurrence therein.   As in the case of the original amendments, the Senate may agree to some, and disagree to others and asks a further conference with the House thereon.   A conference may be asked at any stage of consideration of amendments in disagreement.   If the Senate agrees to all of the House amendments to the Senate amendments to the House amendments, such action brings the two Houses into complete agreement, and likewise completes the legislative steps.

If the Senate concurs in all of the original House amendments to a Senate bill that also completes the legislative action on the measure.

BILLS ORIGINATING IN THE HOUSE

If a bill or resolution originates in the House, it takes the same steps as set forth above, except in reverse, i.e.: A House committee considers it first; it is passed by the House; it is messaged to the Senate and referred to a Senate committee; the committee reports it to the Senate and it is then acted on by that body.   Lastly, it is returned to the House for concurrence in Senate amendments, if any.

CONFERENCES

If the Senate agrees to send a bill to conference, and the conferees are named, the Senate informs the House, by message, of its action. All papers accompany the various messages between the Houses, and neither body can act unless the papers are in its possession.   It is the usual practice of the House to insist upon its amendments en bloc, agree to the request for a conference, and appoint its conferees. They do not have to be the same in number as the Senate conferees. If the Senate's request is granted, the House so notifies the Senate. The papers, comprising the Senate engrossed bill, the House engrossed amendments, the Senate engrossed amendments to the latter, if any, and the various messages of transmittal, are delivered to the Senate conferees by a clerk in the Secretary's Office who takes a receipt therefor.   At the meetings of the conferees, the amendments only are before the conferees for compromise.   A majority of each group controls its action, so that if one group has a larger number of conferees it has no voting advantage over the other.

After deliberations, the conferees may make one or more of various recommendations: For example, (1) that the House recede from all or certain of its amendments; (2) that the Senate recede from its disagreement to all or certain of the House amendments, and agree to the same; or (3) they may even report an inability to agree in all or in part.   Usually, however, there is compromise.

Conferees have limited powers.   They can deal only with the actual matters in disagreement.   They cannot insert new matter, or leave out matter agreed to by both Houses, and if they exceed their authority a point of order will lie against the report. Each House, at a certain stage, may instruct its conferees, but such action is not often taken, as conferences are presumed to be full and free.

Where one House passes a bill of the other House with an amendment in the nature of a substitute, the conferees usually report a substitute (a third version) on the same subject matter, but all of the provisions of each such substitute by the conferees must be a germane modification of the House- or Senate-passed versions or it will be subject to a point of order.

CONFERENCE REPORTS

The recommendations of the conferees are incorporated in written reports made in duplicate, which must be signed by a majority of each group of conferees. If there are amendments upon which they were unable to agree, a statement to this effect is included in the reports.

Where one House passes a bill by striking out all after the enacting clause and substituting a complete new bill therefor, the conferees may not report amendments in disagreement. In such case, the conferees could take the version of the House or of the Senate or write a third bill (a substitute for the Senate- and House-passed versions). One report, together with the papers, is taken by the House conferees, or managers, as they are termed in that body, and subsequently presented by them to the House, with an accompanying explanatory statement as to its effect upon the matters involved. The report must lie over a day in the House for printing, except during the last 6 days of a session. The Senate conferees also may present their report for printing, but that is seldom the case.

The House agreeing to a conference on a bill acts first on the conference report, but neither House can act on such a report unless it has the papers. Conference reports are privileged in both the Senate and House. They cannot be amended, but must be voted upon as an entirety. If the conferees reported any amendments in disagreement, they are acted on after the conference report is adopted. The report, if adopted by one house, is transmitted, with the papers, to the other, with a message announcing its action.

The Senate conferees may present their report and ask for its immediate consideration, since it does not have to lie over a day, as in the House; but on motion, which is not debatable, the Senate may act immediately. A conference report agreed to by one House may not be recommitted by the other.

If conferees reach a complete agreement on all of the House amendments to a Senate bill, and the House adopts that report, the adoption of the report by the Senate completes the legislative action on the bill. If, however, there were amendments upon which an agreement had not been reached by the conferees, the adoption of the report by both Houses leaves the parliamentary status of these particular amendments in disagreement the same as if no conference had been held.

If the amendments on which an agreement could not be reached were House amendments, and the House acted on the report first, it could then recede from its amendments, eliminating the amendments in disagreement; and then, when the Senate should adopt the report, the bill would have been cleared for the President's signature. If they were Senate amendments and the House acted first, the House could concur in the Senate amendments or concur in them with amendments. If the Senate amendments were concurred in by the House that would clear the amendments in disagreement, and when the Senate agreed to the conference report the bill would be cleared for the President's signature. If the House should concur in the Senate amendments reported in disagreement with amendments, when the Senate agreed to the report it could concur in the House amendments to the Senate amendments which would clear the bill for the President's signature. If the amendments reported in disagreement are not disposed of pursuant to one of the above suggestions, a further conference on these amendments could be requested by one House and agreed to by the other. But until they are compromised or cleared by one or the other Houses in accordance with proper procedure, the bill cannot become law, but will die.

When conferees report amendments in disagreement in both Houses the conference report is the first order of business, after which in each house, the amendments in disagreement are taken up and disposed of.

If the bill is sent back to conference, usually the same conferees are appointed by each House. If a conference report is rejected by one of the Houses, it so notifies the other body and usually requests another conference; but sometimes it merely notifies it of its action, leaving further steps to be taken by the latter.

Endorsements showing the various legislative steps, and when taken, are made on the House or Senate engrossed bill involved, as the case might be. If and when the two Houses reach a complete agreement on all of the amendments, the papers are delivered to the enrolling clerk of the House or Senate, as the case may be. He prepares a copy of the bill in the form as finally agreed upon by the two Houses, and sends it to the Government Printing Office for "enrollment," which means in reference to written documents, going back as far as the 15th Century, "written on parchment." The original papers are retained in the files of the Senate, if a Senate bill, until the end of the Congress, when they are sent to the Archives. Likewise, they are retained in the files of the House, if a House bill.

SIGNATURES OF SPEAKER AND VICE PRESIDENT

Upon receipt of an enrolled bill from the Government Printing Office, if a Senate bill, the Secretary of the Senate makes an endorsement thereon certifying that the bill originated in the Senate; if a House bill it is received and so certified by the Clerk of the House. If, after examination, the bill is found to be in the form agreed upon by both Houses, a slip is attached thereto stating that the bill (giving its number and title) has been examined and found truly enrolled. It is then delivered to the enrolling clerk of the House or Senate, depending upon whether it is a House or Senate bill,[2] and presented to the Speaker of the House for his signature, announced in open session.

Under the law, every enrolled bill, whether it originates in the Senate or in the House is signed first by the Speaker. The bill is then transmitted by messenger to the Senate, where it is likewise signed by the Vice President, or in his absence, the President pro tempore, or if both are absent, by the Acting President pro tempore.

Under the rules of the House, the Committee on House Administration is charged, when an enrolled bill has been duly signed by the Speaker and the Vice President (or by the duly authorized presiding officers of the two bodies), to present the same, when the bill originates in the House, to the President of the United States for his signature "and report the fact and date of such presentation to the House." If it is a Senate bill this responsibility of presenting the bill to the President falls on the Secretary of the Senate.

PRESIDENTIAL ACTION—APPROVAL OR VETO

The President, under the Constitution, has 10 days (Sundays excepted), after the bill has been presented to him, in which to act upon it. If the subject matter of the bill is within the jurisdiction of a department of the Government, or affects its interests in any way, he may, in the meantime, in his discretion, refer the bill to the head of such department for investigation and a report thereon. The report of such official may serve as an aid to the President in reaching a decision on the question of approval. If the President approves the bill, he signs it, giving the date, and transmits this information, by messenger, to the Senate or the House, as the case might be. In the case of revenue and tariff bills, which, under the Constitution, originate in the House of Representatives, the hour of approval is usually indicated. The enrolled bill is delivered to the Administrator of the General Services Administration, who designates it as a public or private law, depending upon its purpose, and gives it a number. Public and private laws are numbered separately and serially. An official copy is sent to the Government Printing Office, to be used in making the so-called slip law print. The enrolled bill itself is deposited in the files of the General Services Administration.

In the event the President does not desire to approve a bill, but is unwilling to veto it, he may, by not returning it to the Senate within the 10-day period after it is presented to him, permit it to become a law without his approval. The Administrator of the General Services Administration makes an endorsement on the bill that having been presented to the President of the United States for his approval and not having been returned to the House of Congress in which it originated within the time prescribed by the Constitution, it has become a law without his approval.

The Supreme Court of the United States in the case of *Edwards* v. *U.S.* (286 U.S. 482), decided that where the 10-day period extends

---

[2] The enrollment of bills in the House is under the jurisdiction and control of its Committee on House Administration; in the Senate, under the Secretary of the Senate.

beyond the date of the final adjournment of a session of the Congress, the President may, within such time, approve and sign the bill, which thereby becomes a law. If, however, in such a case, the President does not approve and sign the bill prior to the expiration of that period, it fails to become a law. This is what is known as a pocket veto.

If the President does not favor the bill, he may veto it; that is to say, he may return it to the Senate or House (Senate bills to Senate and House bills to House) without his approval, together with his objections thereto, unless Congress, by final adjournment, prevents its return by the end of the 10-day period.

The procedure in respect to a vetoed bill is prescribed by Article I, section 7, of the Constitution of the United States, which reads, in part, as follows:

If he approve he shall sign it, but if not he shall return it, with his objections to that House in which it shall have originated, who shall enter the objections at large on their Journal, and proceed to reconsider it. ˙ If after such reconsideration two-thirds of that House shall agree to pass the bill, it shall be sent, together with the objections, to the other House, by which it shall likewise be reconsidered, and if approved by two-thirds of that House, it shall become a law. But in all such cases the votes of both Houses shall be determined by yeas and nays, and the names of the persons voting for and against the bill shall be entered on the Journal of each House respectively.

The constitutional provision for reconsideration by the Senate is met, under the precedents, by the reading of the veto message and the adoption of a motion (1) to act on it immediately; (2) referring it, with the accompanying papers, to a standing committee; (3) ordering that it lie on the table, to be subsequently considered; or (4) ordering its consideration postponed to a definite day. The House procedure is much the same.

If, upon reconsideration by either House, it does not receive a two-thirds vote, the President's veto is sustained and the bill fails to become a law.

If a Senate bill which has been vetoed is passed by the Senate by the required two-thirds vote, an endorsement to this effect is made on the back of the bill by the Secretary of the Senate, who then transmits it, together with the accompanying message, to the House of Representatives for its action thereon. If likewise reconsidered and passed by that body, a similar endorsement is made thereon by the Clerk of the House. The bill, which has thereby been enacted into law, is not again presented to the President of the United States, but is delivered by the Clerk of the House to the Administrator of the General Services Administration for deposit in the Archives, and is printed, together with the attestations of the Secretary of the Senate and the Clerk of the House of its passage over the President's veto; if a House bill, the House would have to act first.

FIGURE I

(Senate bill as introduced in Senate and referred to committee)

90TH CONGRESS
1ST SESSION

S. 1432

IN THE SENATE OF THE UNITED STATES

APRIL 5, 1967

Mr. RUSSELL (for himself and Mrs. SMITH) introduced the following bill;
which was read twice and referred to the Committee on Armed Services

---

A BILL

To amend the Universal Military Training and Service Act,
and for other purposes.

1   *Be it enacted by the Senate and House of Representa-*

2 *tives of the United States of America in Congress assembled,*

3 That the Universal Military Training and Service Act is

4 amended as follows:

5   (1) Section 1 (a) (50 App. U.S.C. 451 (a)) is

6 amended to read as follows:

7   "(a) This Act may be cited as the 'Selective Service

8 Act of 1967'."

    *   *   *   *   *   *   *

**(Sample copy of part of first page and end of last page of this 7-page
introduced bill)**

3   "(1) family responsibilities; and

4   "(2) employment necessary to maintain the na-

5 tional health, safety, or interest."; and

6   (2) by inserting the following item in the analysis:

"673a. Ready Reserve: members not assigned to, or participating satisfactorily in, units."

FIGURE II

(Senate bill as reported in the Senate with amendments for Senate consideration)

Calendar No. 204

90TH CONGRESS
1ST SESSION

S. 1432

'[Report No. 209]

IN THE SENATE OF THE UNITED STATES

APRIL 5, 1967

Mr. RUSSELL (for himself and Mrs. SMITH) introduced the following bill; which was read twice and referred to the Committee on Armed Services

MAY 4, 1967

Reported by Mr. RUSSELL, with amendments

[Omit the part struck through and insert the part printed in italic]

A BILL

To amend the Universal Military Training and Service Act, and for other purposes.

1   *Be it enacted by the Senate and House of Representa-*
2   *tives of the United States of America in Congress assembled,*
3   That the Universal Military Training and Service Act is
4   amended as follows:
5   (1) Section 1(a) (50 App. U.S.C. 451(a)) is
6   amended to read as follows:
7   "(a) This Act may be cited as the 'Selective Service
8   Act of 1967'."

(Sample copy of first page and end of last page of this 7-page reported bill)

*   *   *   *   *   *   *

14   "(2) employment necessary to maintain the na-
15   tional health, safety, or interest."; and
16   (2) by inserting the following item in the analysis:

"673a. Ready Reserve: members not assigned to, or participating satisfactorily in, units."

FIGURE III

(Senate report to accompany S. 1432, as reported)

Calendar No. 204

90TH CONGRESS	SENATE	REPORT
1st Session		No. 209

AMENDING AND EXTENDING THE DRAFT LAW

MAY 4, 1967.—Ordered to be printed

Mr. RUSSELL, from the Committee on Armed Services, submitted the following

REPORT

[To accompany S. 1432]

The Committee on Armed Services, to which was referred the bill (S. 1432) to amend the Universal Military Training and Service Act, and for other purposes, having considered the same, reports favorably thereon with amendments and recommends that the bill as amended do pass.

PURPOSE

This bill would—

(1) Extend for a period of 4 years, from July 1, 1967, through July 1, 1971, the following provisions of law:

(*a*) The authority to induct persons into the Armed Forces;

(*b*) The authority to issue selective service calls for physicians, dentists, and allied specialists;

(*c*) The suspension of permanent limitations on the active duty strength of the Armed Forces;

(*d*) The authority to pay a quarters allowance to all enlisted members of the Armed Forces who have dependents, irrespective of the rank of these members, if the dependents are not furnished Government quarters; and

(*e*) The authority for special pay to physicians, dentists, and veterinarians.

*   *   *   *   *   *   *

(Sample copy of part of first page and end of last page of this 26-page Senate report)

*   *   *   *   *   *   *

§ 673a. Ready Reserve: members not assigned to, or participating satisfactorily in, units

(*a*) *Notwithstanding any other provision of law, the President may order to active duty any member of the Ready Reserve of an armed force who—*

(*1*) *is not assigned to, or participating satisfactorily in, a unit of the Ready Reserve;*

(*2*) *has not fulfilled his statutory reserve obligations; and*

(*3*) *has not served on active duty for a total of 24 months.*

(*b*) *A member who is ordered to active duty under this section may be required to serve on active duty until his total service on active duty equals 24 months. If his enlistment or other period of military service would expire before he has served the required period under this section, it may be extended until he has served the required period.*

(*c*) *To achieve fair treatment among members of the Ready Reserve who are being considered for active duty under this section, appropriate consideration shall be given to—*

(*1*) *family responsibilities; and*

(*2*) *employment necessary to maintain the national health, safety, or interest.*

FIGURE IV

(Engrossed Senate bill—Passed by Senate and ready for messaging to House of Representatives)

90TH CONGRESS
1ST SESSION

S. 1432

AN ACT

To amend the Universal Military Training and Service Act, and for other purposes.

1   *Be it enacted by the Senate and House of Representa-*

2   *tives of the United States of America in Congress assembled,*

3   That the Universal Military Training and Service Act is

4   amended as follows:

5   (1) Section 1 (a)   (50 App. U.S.C. 451 (a)) is

6   amended to read as follows:

7   "(a) This Act may be cited as the 'Selective Service

8   Act of 1967'."

*   *   *   *   *   *   *

(Sample copy of part of first page and end of last page of this 6-page engrossed bill)

*   *   *   *   *   *   *

8   "(1) family responsibilities; and

9   "(2) employment necessary to maintain the na-

10   tional health, safety, or interest."; and

11   (2) by inserting the following item in the analysis:

"673a. Ready Reserve: members not assigned to, or participating satisfactorily in, units."

Passed the Senate May 11 (legislative day, May 10), 1967.

Attest:

Francis R. Valeo

Secretary.

FIGURE V

(Senate-passed bill as received by the House of Representatives and referred to its committee)

90TH CONGRESS
1ST SESSION

S. 1432

IN THE HOUSE OF REPRESENTATIVES

MAY 15, 1967

Referred to the Committee on Armed Services

AN ACT

To amend the Universal Military Training and Service Act, and for other purposes.

1   *Be it enacted by the Senate and House of Representa-*
2   *tives of the United States of America in Congress assembled,*
3   That the Universal Military Training and Service Act is
4   amended as follows:
5   (1) Section 1(a) (50 App. U.S.C. 451(a)) is
6   amended to read as follows:
7   "(a) This Act may be cited as the 'Selective Service
8   Act of 1967'."
9   (2) Section 6(c) (2) (A) (50 App. U.S.C. 456(c)
10   (2) (A)), is amended to read as follows:

(Sample copy of first page and end of last page of this 6-page bill as passed by Senate and referred to committee in House)

*   *   *   *   *   *   *

10   tional health, safety, or interest."; and
11   (2) by inserting the following item in the analysis:

"673a. Ready Reserve: members not assigned to, or participating satisfactorily in, units."

Passed the Senate May 11 (legislative day, May 10),
1967.

Attest:

FRANCIS R. VALEO,
Secretary.

FIGURE VI

(Senate-passed bill as reported for consideration by House)

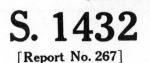

Union Calendar No. 116

90TH CONGRESS
1ST SESSION

S. 1432

[Report No. 267]

IN THE HOUSE OF REPRESENTATIVES

MAY 15, 1967

Referred to the Committee on Armed Services

MAY 18, 1967

Reported with an amendment, committed to the Committee of the Whole House
on the State of the Union, and ordered to be printed

[Strike out all after the enacting clause and insert the part printed in italic]

AN ACT

To amend the Universal Military Training and Service Act,
and for other purposes.

1   *Be it enacted by the Senate and House of Representa-*
2   *tives of the United States of America in Congress assembled,*
3   ~~That the Universal Military Training and Service Act is~~
4   ~~amended as follows:~~
5   ~~(1) Section 1(a) (50 App. U.S.C. 451(a)) is amended~~
6   ~~to read as follows:~~

**(Sample copy of part of first page and end of last page of this 21-page
bill as reported to House for its consideration)**

*   *   *   *   *   *   *

11   *SEC. 5. Sections 302 and 303 of title 37, United States*
12   *Code, are each amended by striking out "July 1, 1967"*
13   *whenever that date appears and inserting in place thereof*
14   *"July 1, 1971".*

Passed the Senate May 11 (legislative day, May 10),
1967.

Attest: FRANCIS R. VALEO,
                                        Secretary.

FIGURE VII

(House of Representatives Report Numbered 267 to accompany S. 1432, as reported to House)

90TH CONGRESS *1st Session*	HOUSE OF REPRESENTATIVES	REPORT No. 267

MILITARY SELECTIVE SERVICE ACT OF 1967

MAY 18, 1967.—Committed to the Committee of the Whole House on the State of the Union and ordered to be printed

Mr. RIVERS, from the Committee on Armed Services, submitted the following

REPORT

[To accompany S. 1432]

The Committee on Armed Services, to whom was referred the bill (S. 1432) to amend the Universal Military Training and Service Act, and for other purposes, having considered the same, report favorably thereon with an amendment and recommend that the bill as amended do pass.

The amendment is as follows:

Strike all after the enacting clause and insert in lieu thereof the following:

That the Universal Military Training and Service Act is amended as follows:
(1) Section 1(a) (50 App. U.S.C. 451(a)) is amended to read as follows:
"(a) This Act may be cited as the 'Military Selective Service Act of 1967'."
(2) Section 4 (50 App. U.S.C. 454) is amended by:
(a) Inserting after the first proviso of subsection (a) the following:
"*Provided further*, That, notwithstanding any other provision of law, any registrant who has failed or refused to report for induction shall continue to remain liable for induction and when available shall be immediately inducted." , and
(b) Adding the following new subsection (g) to read as follows:

*　　　*　　　*　　　*　　　*　　　*　　　*

(Sample copy of part of first page and end of last page of this 47-page House report)

Section 3

This section would continue for four years the authority to pay allowances for quarters to enlisted members in pay grades E–1, E–2, E–3, and E–4 (with 4 or less years of service) if these members have dependents.

If the authority to pay these allowances under the Dependents Assistance Act is not continued, these enlisted members would be entitled to a quarters allowance of only $45 a month, regardless of the number of their dependents, and even this lower allowance would be payable only if quarters were not furnished to the enlisted member.

Section 4

This section would continue for four years the so-called Doctors Draft Act.

Section 5

This section would continue for those officers who enter on active duty after June 30, 1967, authority for the payment of special pays to physicians, dentists, and veterinarians.

FIGURE VIII

(Engrossed House amendments to S. 1432—Passed by House of Representatives and ready for messaging to Senate*)

In the House of Representatives, U. S.,

May 25, 1967.

Resolved, That the bill from the Senate (S. 1432) entitled "An Act to amend the Universal Military Training and Service Act, and for other purposes", do pass with the following

AMENDMENT:

Strike out all after the enacting clause and insert: *That the Universal Military Training and Service Act is amended as follows:*

(1) Section 1(a)(50 App. U.S.C. 451(a)) is amended to read as follows:

"(a) This Act may be cited as the 'Military Selective Service Act of 1967'."

(2) Section 1(c)(50 App. U.S.C. 451(c)) is amended to read as follows:

"(c) The Congress further declares that in a free society the obligations of serving in the armed forces should be enforced through the provisions of this Act only when necessary to insure the security of this Nation, and the opportu-

(Sample copy of first page and end of last page of this 17-page print of House engrossed amendments)

*   *   *   *   *   *   *

Sec. 5. Sections 302 and 303 of title 37, United States Code, are each amended by striking out "July 1, 1967" whenever that date appears and inserting in place thereof "July 1, 1971".

Attest:

Jennings

* Printed on blue paper.

Clerk.

FIGURE IX

(Conference report on S. 1432—to be approved by both Houses before becoming law)

90TH CONGRESS *1st Session*	HOUSE OF REPRESENTATIVES	REPORT No. 346

AMENDING AND EXTENDING THE DRAFT ACT AND RELATED LAWS

JUNE 8, 1967.—Ordered to be printed

Mr. RIVERS, from the committee of conference, submitted the following

CONFERENCE REPORT

[To accompany S. 1432]

The committee of conference on the disagreeing votes of the two Houses on the amendment of the House to the bill (S. 1432) to amend the Universal Military Training and Service Act, and for other purposes, having met, after full and free conference, have agreed to recommend and do recommend to their respective Houses as follows:

That the Senate recede from its disagreement to the amendment of the House and agree to the same with an amendment as follows:

In lieu of the matter proposed to be inserted by the House amendment insert the following: *That the Universal Military Training and Service Act is amended as follows:*

(1) Section 1(a) (50 App. U.S.C. 451(a)) is amended to read as follows:
"(a) This Act may be cited as the 'Military Selective Service Act of 1967'."
(2) Section 4 (50 App. U.S.C. 454) is amended by:

*   *   *   *   *   *   *

(Sample copy of part of first page and end of last page of this 7-page conference report)

*   *   *   *   *   *

"(c) To achieve fair treatment among members of the Ready Reserve who are being considered for active duty under this section, appropriate consideration shall be given to—
"(1) family responsibilities; and
"(2) employment necessary to maintain the national health, safety, or interest."; and
(2) by inserting the following item in the analysis:
"673a. Ready Reserve: members not assigned to, or participating satisfactorily in, units."
And the House agree to the same.

L. MENDEL RIVERS,
PHILIP J. PHILBIN,
F. EDW. HÉBERT,
MELVIN PRICE,
WILLIAM H. BATES,
L. C. ARENDS,
Managers on the Part of the House.

RICHARD B. RUSSELL,
JOHN STENNIS,
STUART SYMINGTON,
HENRY M. JACKSON,
MARGARET CHASE SMITH,
STROM THURMOND,
Managers on the Part of the Senate.

FIGURE X

(Enrolled bill signed by President)

PUBLIC LAW 90-40

S. 1432

Ninetieth Congress of the United States of America

AT THE FIRST SESSION

Begun and held at the City of Washington on Tuesday, the tenth day of January,
one thousand nine hundred and sixty-seven

An Act

To amend the Universal Military Training and Service Act, and for other
purposes.

Be it enacted by the Senate and House of Representatives of the
United States of America in Congress assembled, That the Universal
Military Training and Service Act is amended as follows:

(1) Section 1(a) (50 App. U.S.C. 451(a)) is amended to read as
follows:

"(a) This Act may be cited as the 'Military Selective Service Act of
1967'."

(2) Section 4 (50 App. U.S.C. 454) is amended by:

(a) Inserting after the first proviso of subsection (a) the following:
"*Provided further,* That, notwithstanding any other provision of law,
any registrant who has failed or refused to report for induction shall
continue to remain liable for induction and when available shall be
immediately inducted.", and

(b) Adding the following new subsection (g) to read as follows:

"(g) The National Security Council shall periodically advise the
Director of the Selective Service System and coordinate with him the
work of such State and local volunteer advisory committees which
the Director of Selective Service may establish, with respect to the
identification, selection, and deferment of needed professional and
scientific personnel and those engaged in, and preparing for, critical
skills and other essential occupations. In the performance of its duties
under this subsection the National Security Council shall consider the
needs of both the Armed Forces and the civilian segment of the
population."

(3) Section 5(a) (50 App. U.S.C. 455(a)) is amended by inserting
"(1)" immediately after "SEC. 5. (a)"; and by adding at the end thereof
a new paragraph as follows:

"(2) Notwithstanding the provisions of paragraph (1) of this subsection, the President in establishing the order of induction for registrants within the various age groups found qualified for induction
shall not effect any change in the method of determining the relative
order of induction for such registrants within such age groups as has
been heretofore established and in effect on the date of enactment of
this paragraph, unless authorized by law enacted after the date of
enactment of the Military Selective Service Act of 1967."

(4) Section 6(c)(2)(A) (50 App. U.S.C. 456(c)(2)(A)), is
amended to read as follows:

"(2)(A) Any person, other than a person referred to in subsection
(d) of this section, who—

"(i) prior to the issuance of orders for him to report for induction; or

"(ii) prior to the date scheduled for his induction and pursuant
to a proclamation by the Governor of a State to the effect that the
authorized strength of any organized unit of the National Guard
of that State cannot be maintained by the enlistment or appointment of persons who have not been issued orders to report for
induction under this title; or

"(iii) prior to the date scheduled for his induction and pursuant
to a determination by the President that the strength of the Ready
Reserve of the Army Reserve, Naval Reserve, Marine Corps Reserve, Air Force Reserve, or Coast Guard Reserve cannot be main-

S. 1432—7

"(c) To achieve fair treatment among members of the Ready Reserve who are being considered for active duty under this section, appropriate consideration shall be given to—

"(1) family responsibilities; and

"(2) employment necessary to maintain the national health, safety, or interest."; and

(2) by inserting the following item in the analysis:

"673a. Ready Reserve: members not assigned to, or participating satisfactorily in, units."

Speaker of the House of Representatives.

Vice President of the United States and
President of the Senate.

APPROVED

JUN 3 0 1967

How Our Laws Are Made

By Joseph Fischer, Esq.

"During recent years a wholesome interest in the Federal legislative process has developed on the part of students and the general public in the United States. This interest, no doubt, will increase because of the lowering of the voting age, from 21 to 18. Because of this desire for information about the legislative process there is a great need for a concise factual explanation of how the Congress goes about making our laws. The explanation has to be brief but adequately detailed to provide a reasonably complete picture of the entire process—simple but sufficiently authoritative to reflect the technical aspects of the procedure. HOW OUR LAWS ARE MADE is just such an explanation. The young student may read it with understanding and the more sophisticated reader may be satisfied with the details.

The late Dr. Charles J. Zinn, who served as law revision counsel of this committee for many years, had a deep interest in the legislative process and was regarded as a leading authority on the subject. He authored HOW OUR LAWS ARE MADE in 1952. It was printed as a House document in 1953 and has been reprinted since then eleven times. The document was so well received that more than 1,800,000 copies have been distributed throughout the United States and in other parts of the world.

Prior editions of this brochure have been translated and published in the Korean, German, Portuguese, French, Spanish, Arabic, and Italian languages.

A Peace Corps volunteer in Nepal several years ago reported that the native school teachers in a small village there were so interested in the United States Federal legislative process that they borrowed his copy of HOW OUR LAWS ARE MADE and several of them carefully transcribed it in longhand for their own use.

This edition has been revised and updated by Joseph Fischer, Esquire, law revision counsel for the committee, to reflect changes in legislative procedure brought about by the enactment of the "Legislative Reorganization Act of 1970."

I hope that this edition will be widely disseminated and read throughout the United States and abroad."

> From the Foreword by Hon. Emanuel Celler,
> Member of Congress, and Chairman, Committee
> on the Judiciary.

I. INTRODUCTION

This handbook is intended to provide a readable and nontechnical outline of the background and the numerous steps of our Federal lawmaking process from the origin of an idea for a legislative proposal through its publication as a statute. This is a matter about which the average citizen should be well informed so that he may be able to understand the everyday news reports and discussions concerning the work of the Congress.

The Federal legislative process is ordinarily a lengthy and somewhat

SOURCE: Reprinted from U. S. House of Representatives. HOW OUR LAWS ARE MADE. Revised and Updated by Joseph Fischer, Esq. 1971. pp. vii-viii, 1-63. 92nd Congress, 1st Session. House Document Number 144.

complex one that is often the butt of scorn and jibes by the uninformed and by those who seek to undermine our Constitutional way of life. On the one hand, complaints are heard about "the law's delays" both with regard to the administration of justice by our courts and the enactment of laws by the Congress. On the other hand, with an inconsistency that is significant, it is not uncommon for the same individuals to charge that a particular bill has been "steamrollered" through the Congress. Manifestly, no system of enacting laws to govern more than 200 million persons can be perfect in all its details with respect to every single piece of legislation. However, by and large, neither of these complaints is justified and, discounting the sly but vicious attacks by hostile persons or groups that often make dupes of otherwise well-intentioned persons, the invective against our deliberative lawmaking procedure is quite likely to stem from a fundamental lack of information and understanding regarding that procedure.

Rather than being an object of petty criticism, the Federal legislative process should be recognized as one of the bulwarks of our representative system and should receive the fullest support and understanding.

One of the most practical safeguards of the American democratic way of life is that process which, with its jealous care for the protection of minorities, gives ample opportunity to all sides to be heard and make their views known. The fact that a proposal cannot become a law without consideration and approval by both Houses of the Congress is an outstanding virtue rather than a defect of the Congressional system. The result of the open and full discussions provided for under our Constitution is frequently the notable improving of a bill by amendment before it becomes law, or the complete defeat of a bad proposal.

Inasmuch as the large majority of laws originate in the House of Representatives this discussion will be directed principally to the procedure in that body.

II. THE CONGRESS

Article I, section 1, of the United States Constitution, provides that—

All legislative Powers herein granted shall be vested in a Congress of the United States, which shall consist of a Senate and House of Representatives.

The Senate is composed of 100 Members—two from each State, irrespective of population or area—elected by the people in conformity with the provisions of the 17th amendment to the Constitution. That amendment changed the former Constitutional method under which Senators were chosen by the respective State legislatures. A Senator must be at least 30 years of age, and have been a citizen of the United States for nine years and, when elected, a resident of the State for which he is chosen. The term of office is six years and so arranged that the terms of both Senators from a particular State do not terminate at the same time—one-third of the total membership being elected every second year. Of the two Senators from a State serving at the same time the one who was elected first—or if both were elected at the same time, the one elected for a full term—is referred to as the "senior" Senator from that State. The other is referred to as the "junior" Senator. The Constitution further provides that, in case of the death or resignation of a Senator during his term, the governor of the State must call a special election unless the State legislature has authorized him to appoint a successor until the next general election, at which time a successor is elected for the balance of the term. Most of the State legislatures have granted their governors the power of appointment.

Each Senator has one vote.

As constituted in 1971—the 92d Congress—the House of Representatives is composed of 435 Members elected every two years from among the 50 States, apportioned to their total populations, exclusive of untaxed Indians. The permanent number of 435 was established following the Thirteenth Decennial Census in 1910, as directed in article I, section 2, of the Constitution, and was increased temporarily to 437 for the 87th Congress, to provide for one Member each for Alaska and Hawaii. It seems undesirable to make a considerable increase in the number of Members, because a larger body, similar to the British House of Commons, consisting of 630 members, would be too unwieldy. The Constitution limits the number of Representatives to not more than one for every 30,000 of population, and, under a former apportionment in one State a particular Member represented more than 900,000 constituents, while another in the same State was elected from a district having a population of only 175,000. The Supreme Court[1] has since held unconstitutional a Missouri statute permitting a maximum population variance of 3.1 percent from mathematical equality. The Court said that the variances among the districts were not unavoidable and, therefore, were invalid. This is an interpretation of the Court's earlier decision that "as nearly as is practicable one man's vote in a Congressional election is to be worth as much as another's".

A law enacted in 1967 has abolished all "at-large" elections (i.e., Members elected by the voters of the entire State rather than in a Congressional district within the State) except, of course, in States entitled to only one Representative. (2 U.S.C., §2c)

A Representative must be at least 25 years of age and have been a citizen of the United States for seven years and, when elected, a resident of the State in which he is chosen. In case of the death or resignation of a Member during his term, the governor of his State may call a special election for the choosing of a successor to serve for the unexpired portion of the term.

Each Representative has one vote.

In addition to the Representatives from 50 States, there is a Resident Commissioner from the Commonwealth of Puerto Rico, as authorized by an act of 1917 (48 U.S.C., § 891) and in 1970 the Congress by Pub. L. 91–405, created the office of Delegate to the House of Representatives from the District of Columbia. The Resident Commissioner and the Delegate have most of the prerogatives of Representatives, with the important exception of the right to vote on matters before the House.

Representatives and Senators are both technically "Members of Congress," since the Congress consists of the two bodies, but the term "Member" is popularly used to refer to a Member of the House of Representatives only.

Under the provisions of section 2 of the 20th amendment to the Constitution, Congress must assemble at least once every year, at noon on the 3d day of January, unless by law they appoint a different day.

A Congress lasts for two years, commencing in January of the year following the biennial election of Members.

Unlike some other parliamentary bodies, both the Senate and the

---

[1] Kirkpatrick v. Preisler, 394 U.S. 526.

House of Representatives have equal legislative functions and powers (except that only the House of Representatives may initiate revenue bills), and the designation of one as the "upper" House and the other as the "lower" House is not appropriate.

The Constitution authorizes each House to determine the rules of its proceedings. Pursuant to that authority the House of Representatives adopts its rules on the opening day of each Congress. The Senate operates under its rules adopted in 1884 and amended from time to time since then.

The chief function of the Congress is the making of laws. In addition, the Senate has the function of advising and consenting to treaties and to certain nominations by the President. In the matter of impeachments, the House of Representatives presents the charges—a function similar to that of grand juries—and the Senate sits as a court to try the impeachment. Both Houses meet in joint session on January 6th, following a presidential election, to count the electoral votes. If no candidate receives a majority of the total electoral votes, the House of Representatives chooses the President from among the three candidates having the largest number of votes, and the Senate chooses the Vice President from the two candidates having the largest number of votes for that office.

III. SOURCES OF LEGISLATION

Sources of ideas for legislation are unlimited, and proposed drafts of bills originate in many diverse quarters. First of these is, of course the idea and draft conceived by a Member himself. This may emanate from his election campaign during which he had promised to introduce legislation on a particular subject, if elected. His entire campaign may have been based upon one or more such proposals. Or, through his experience after taking office he may have become aware of the need for amendment or repeal of existing laws or the enactment of a statute in an entirely new field.

In addition, his constituents—either as individuals or by corporate activity such as bar associations, labor unions, manufacturers' associations, and chambers of commerce—may avail themselves of the right to petition, which is guaranteed by the First Amendment to the Constitution, and transmit their proposals to him. Many excellent laws have originated in this way since some of those organizations, because of their vital concern with various areas of legislation, have considerable knowledge regarding the laws affecting their interests and have the services of expert legislative draftsmen at their disposal for this purpose. If the Member is favorably impressed by the idea he may introduce the proposal in the form in which it has been submitted to him or he may first redraft it. In all events he may consult with the official legislative counsel to frame the ideas in suitable legislative language and form for introduction.

In modern times the "executive communication" has become a prolific source of legislative proposals. This is usually in the form of a letter from a member of the President's Cabinet or the head of an independent agency—or even from the President himself—transmitting a draft of a proposed bill to the Speaker of the House of Representatives and the President of the Senate. Despite the system of separation of powers, section 3 of article II of the Constitution imposes an obligation on the President to report to the Congress from time to time on the state of the Union and to recommend for consideration such measures as he deems necessary and expedient. Many of these executive communications follow upon the President's message on the state of the Union delivered to the Congress in accordance with the mandate set out in section 3 of article II of the Constitution. The communication is then referred to the standing committee having jurisdiction of the subject matter embraced in the proposal since a bill may be introduced only by a Member of Congress. The chairman of that committee usually introduces the bill promptly either in the form in which it was received or with such changes as he deems necessary or desirable. This practice prevails even when the majority of the House and the President are not of the same political party, although there is no constitutional or statutory requirement that a bill be introduced to effectuate the recommendations. Otherwise, the message may be considered by the committee or one of its subcommittees to determine whether a bill should be introduced. The most important of the regular executive communications is the annual message from the President transmitting the proposed budget to the Congress. This, together with testimony by officials of the various branches of the Government before the Appropriations Committees of the House and Senate, is the basis of the several appropriation bills that are drafted by the House Committee on Appropriations.

Several of the executive departments and independent agencies have staffs of trained legislative counsel whose functions include the drafting of bills to be forwarded to the Congress with a request for their enactment.

The drafting of statutes is an art that requires great skill, knowledge, and experience. In some instances a draft is the result of a study covering a period of a year or more by a commission or committee designated by the President or one of his Cabinet officers. The Administrative Procedure Act and the Uniform Code of Military Justice are only two of many examples of enactments resulting from such studies. In addition, Congressional committees sometimes draft bills after studies and hearings covering periods of a year or more. Bills to codify the laws relating to crimes and criminal procedure, the judiciary and judicial procedure, the Armed Forces, and other subjects, have each required several years of preparation.

IV. FORMS OF CONGRESSIONAL ACTION

The work of the Congress is initiated by the introduction of a proposal in one of four principal forms. These are: the bill, the joint resolution, the concurrent resolution, and the simple resolution. By far the most customary form used in both Houses is the bill. During the 91st Congress (1969–1970), there were introduced in both Houses, nearly 25,000 bills and less than 1,700 joint resolutions. Of this number, 20,015 bills and 1,421 joint resolutions originated in the House of Representatives.

For the sake of simplicity this discussion will be confined generally to the procedure on a House of Representatives bill, but a brief comment will be made about each of the forms.

BILLS

A bill is the form used for most legislation, whether permanent or temporary, general or special, public or private.

The House of Representatives Manual prescribes the form of a House bill, as follows:

A BILL

For the establishment, etc. [as the title may be].

*Be it enacted by the Senate and House of Representatives of the
United States of America in Congress assembled, That, etc.*

The enacting clause was prescribed by law in 1871 and is identical
in all bills, whether they originate in the House of Representatives
or in the Senate.

Bills may originate in either the House of Representatives or the
Senate, with one notable exception provided for by the Constitution.
Article I, section 7, of the Constitution, provides that all bills for
raising revenue shall originate in the House of Representatives but
the Senate may propose or concur with amendments, as on other bills.
Customarily, the general appropriation bills also originate in the
House of Representatives although there is no Constitutional require-
ment to that effect.

Article I, section 8, prescribes the matters concerning which the
Congress may legislate, while section 9 of the same article places certain limitations upon Congressional action.

A bill originating in the House of Representatives is designated by
the letters "H.R." followed by a number which it retains throughout
all its parliamentary stages. The letters, of course, signify "House
of Representatives" and not, as is sometimes supposed, "House resolution." A Senate bill is designated by the letter "S." followed by
its number.

A bill becomes the law of the land only after—

(1) Presidential approval; or

(2) failure by the President to return it with his objections to
the House in which it originated within 10 days while the Congress is in session; (See Fig. 11, p. 62) or

(3) the overriding of a Presidential veto by a two-thirds vote
in each House. (See Fig. 12, p. 63.)

It does not become law without the President's signature if the
Congress by their adjournment prevent its return with his objections.
This is known as a "pocket veto."

JOINT RESOLUTIONS

Joint resolutions may originate either in the House of Representatives or in the Senate—not, as may be supposed, jointly in both
Houses. There is little practical difference between a bill and a joint
resolution and, although the latter are not as numerous as bills, the
two forms are often used indiscriminately. Statutes that have been
initiated as bills have later been amended by a joint resolution, and
vice versa. Both are subject to the same procedure—with the exception of joint resolutions proposing an amendment to the Constitution which must be approved by two-thirds of both Houses and are
thereupon sent directly to the Administrator of General Services for
submission to the several States for ratification, and which are not
presented to the President for his approval.

The form of a House joint resolution is prescribed by the House of
Representatives Manual, as follows:

JOINT RESOLUTION

Authorizing, etc. [as the title may be].

*Resolved by the Senate and House of Representatives of the United
States of America in Congress assembled, That all, etc.*

The resolving clause is identical in both House and Senate joint resolutions, having been prescribed by statute in 1871. It is frequently preceded by one or more "whereas" clauses indicating the necessity for or the desirability of the joint resolution.

The term "joint" does not signify simultaneous introduction and consideration in both Houses.

A joint resolution originating in the House of Representatives is designated "H.J. Res." followed by its individual number which it retains throughout all its parliamentary stages. One originating in the Senate is designated "S.J. Res." followed by its number.

Joint resolutions become law in the same manner as bills.

CONCURRENT RESOLUTIONS

A matter affecting the operations of both Houses are usually initiated in the form of a concurrent resolution. These are not normally legislative in character but are used merely for expressing facts, principles, opinions, and purposes of the two Houses. They are not equivalent to a bill and their use is narrowly limited within these bounds.

The term "concurrent" does not signify simultaneous introduction and consideration in both Houses.

A concurrent resolution originating in the House of Representatives is designated "H. Con. Res." followed by its individual number, while a Senate concurrent resolution is designated "S. Con. Res." together with its number. Upon approval by both Houses they are signed by the Clerk of the House and the Secretary of the Senate and transmitted to the Administrator of General Services for publication in a special part of the Statutes at Large. They are not presented to the President for action as in the cases of bills and joint resolutions unless they contain a proposition of legislation, which, of course, is not within their scope in their modern form.

SIMPLE RESOLUTIONS

A matter concerning the operation of either House alone is initiated by a simple resolution. A resolution affecting the House of Representatives is designated "H. Res." followed by its number, while a Senate resolution is designated "S. Res." together with its number. They are considered only by the body in which they were introduced and upon adoption are attested to by the Clerk of the House of Representatives or the Secretary of the Senate, as the case may be, and are published in the Congressional Record.

V. INTRODUCTION AND REFERENCE TO COMMITTEE

Any Member, the Resident Commissioner and the Delegate from the District of Columbia in the House of Representatives may introduce a bill at any time while the House is actually sitting by simply placing it in the "hopper" provided for the purpose at the side of the Clerk's desk in the House Chamber. He is not required to ask permission to introduce the measure or to make any statement at the time of introduction. Printed blank forms for use in typing the original bill are supplied through the stationery room. The name of the sponsor is endorsed upon it, and since April 1967, a bill may be sponsored by up to 25 Members. This constitutes a change in the former practice and conforms more closely to the Senate practice where unlimited multiple sponsorship is permitted. Occasionally a Member may insert the words "by request" after his name to indicate that the introduction of the measure is in compliance with the suggestion of some other person.

The procedure is somewhat more formal in the Senate as governed by the standing rules of that body. At the time reserved for the purpose, a Senator who wishes to introduce a measure rises and states that he offers a bill for introduction, and sends it by page to the Secretary's desk. If objection is offered by any Senator the introduction is postponed until the next day. If there is no objection the bill is read by title for the first and second reading. Frequently, Senators obtain consent to have the bill printed at that point in the body of the Congressional Record, following their formal statement. Moreover, several Senators may, and frequently do, join together in the introduction of a single bill and the names of all are endorsed upon it.

In the House of Representatives it is no longer the custom to read bills—even by title—at the time of introduction. The title is entered in the Journal and printed in the Congressional Record, thus preserving the purpose of the old rule. The bill is assigned its legislative number by the Clerk and referred to the appropriate committee by the Speaker with the assistance of the Parliamentarian. These details appear in the daily issue of the Congressional Record. It is then sent to the Government Printing Office where it is printed that same night in its introduced form, and printed copies are available the next morning in the document rooms of both Houses. (See Fig. 1, p. 47.)

One copy is sent to the office of the chairman of the committee to which it has been referred, for action by that committee.

Perhaps the most important phase of the Congressional process is the action by committees. That is where the most intensive consideration is given to the proposed measures and where the people are given their opportunity to be heard. Nevertheless, this phase where such a tremendous volume of hard work is done by the Members is sometimes overlooked by the public, particularly when complaining about delays in enacting laws.

The Legislative Reorganization Acts of 1946, and 1970, the result of widespread proposals for "streamlining" the Congress, establish the existing committee structure of the House and Senate. Prior to the Reorganization Act of 1946 the House had 48 standing committees and there were 33 in the Senate which corresponded generally to those of the House. In addition there were a number of select or special committees, usually of an investigative character, that did not normally consider pending legislation. There are, at present, twenty-one standing committees in the House of Representatives and seventeen in the Senate, as well as several select committees. In addition, there are several standing joint committees of the two Houses.

An important one created by the Legislative Reorganization Act of 1970, is the Joint Committee on Congressional Operations. This committee has the duty to:

>   (1) make a continuing study of the organization and operation of the Congress of the United States; recommend improvements in such organization and operation with a view toward strengthening Congress, simplifying its operations, improving its relationships with other branches of the United States Government, and enabling it better to meet its responsibilities under the Constitution of the United States; and

>   (2) identify any court proceeding or action which, in the opinion of the Joint Committee, is of vital interest to the Congress, or to either House of the Congress, as a constitutionally established institution of the Federal Government and call such proceeding or action to the attention of that House of the Congress

which is specifically concerned or to both Houses of the Congress if both Houses are concerned.

The committee also has supervision and control over the operations of the Office of Placement and Office of Management, established for the Congress by the same Act. The committee is required to report, from time to time, to the Congress its recommendation with respect to matters within the jurisdiction of the committee.

The only joint committee that may report legislation is the Joint Committee on Atomic Energy, which reports identical bills to each House simultaneously.

Each committee has jurisdiction over certain subject matters of legislation and all measures affecting a particular area of the law are referred to that committee which has jurisdiction over it. For example, the Committee on the Judiciary has jurisdiction over measures relating to judicial proceedings, civil and criminal, generally, and 18 other categories, of which Constitutional amendments, revision and codification of statutes, civil liberties, antitrust, patents, copyrights and trademarks, are but a few. In all, the rules provide for more than 190 different classifications of measures which are to be referred to the respective committees in the House and more than 170 in the Senate. Membership on the various committees is divided between the two major political parties in proportion to their total membership in the House. Until 1953, with the exception of the Members serving on the Committee on the District of Columbia, the former Committees on Un-American Activities and on Expenditures in the Executive Departments, or the Committee on House Administration, a Member could not serve on more than one standing committee of the House. This limitation was removed in January 1953, and now all members may serve on more than one committee. In January 1971, the majority party of the House determined in caucus that (1) the chairman of a full committee may not be the chairman of more than one subcommittee of that committee, (2) a Member may not be chairman of more than one legislative subcommittee, and (3) a Member may not serve on more than two committees having legislative jurisdiction. These limitations do not apply to committees performing housekeeping functions and joint committees.

A Member usually seeks election to that committee which has jurisdiction of a field in which he is most qualified and interested. For example, the Committee on the Judiciary is composed entirely of lawyers. Not a few Members are nationally recognized experts in the specialty of their particular committee or subcommittee.

Members rank in seniority in accordance with the order of their appointment to the committee, with the ranking majority Member being elected chairman. This aspect of the committee system has been the object of criticism but it insures the selection of a chairman with experience, for which there is no substitute, and a more practical and foolproof method has never been suggested. However, in January 1971, the majority party of the House, in caucus, adopted a resolution which was designed to afford those Members, who opposed the seniority system, an opportunity to challenge the selection of a chairman on that basis alone.

Most of the committees have two or more subcommittees that in addition to having general jurisdiction, specialize in the consideration of particular classifications of bills.

Each committee is provided with a professional and clerical staff to assist it in the innumerable administrative details and other problems involved in the consideration of bills. The professional staff is appointed on a permanent basis without regard to political affiliations. The clerical staff is appointed by a majority vote of the committee and handles correspondence and stenographic work for the committee staff and the chairman and ranking minority Member on matters related to committee work. In recent years there has been a move to provide a minority staff for committees and a number of committees have obtained authority to engage one or more experts to be assigned to the minority Members.

The Legislative Reorganization Act of 1970 and the Rules of the House authorize two additional professional staff members for each standing committee and the minority may request as a matter of right the appointment of two professional and one clerical staff member, subject to final approval by the committee. These minority staff provisions do not apply to the Committee on Appropriations, because the minority Members of that committee have in the past been entitled to more than two employees, subject to committee decision, and to the Committee on Standards of Official Conduct because of its bipartisan nature.

Under certain conditions a standing committee may appoint consultants on a temporary or intermittent basis and may also provide financial assistance to members of its professional staff for the purpose of acquiring specialized training, whenever the committee determines that such training will aid the committee in the discharge of its responsibilities.

VI. CONSIDERATION BY COMMITTEE

The chairman of the committee to which a bill has been referred may, on his own initiative, or at the request of the sponsor, refer the bill to a subcommittee for consideration. One of the first actions taken is the transmittal of copies of the bill to the departments or agencies concerned with the subject matter and frequently to the General Accounting Office with a request for an official report of views on the necessity or desirability of enacting the bill into law. Ample time is given for the submission of the reports and when received they are accorded serious consideration but are not binding upon the committee in determining whether or not to act favorably on the bill. The reports are submitted first to the Office of Management and Budget to determine whether the bill is consistent with the program of the President.

With the exception of the Committees on Government Operations, on Rules, on Internal Security, on Standards of Official Conduct, and on Appropriations, committees may not, without special permission, meet while the House is reading a measure for amendment under the five-minute rule, but they may also be permitted to meet during a recess up to the expiration of the Constitutional term.

PUBLIC HEARINGS

If the bill is of sufficient importance, and particularly if it is controversial, the committee will usually set a date for public hearings. Each committee (except the Committee on Rules) is required to make public announcement of the date, place, and subject matter of any hearing to be conducted by the committee on any measure or matter at least one week before the commencement of that hearing, unless the committee determines that there is good cause to begin the hearing at an earlier date. If the committee makes that determination, it must make such public announcement at the earliest possible date. Public announcement is also published in the Daily Digest portion of the Congressional Record as soon as possible after such public announcement is made by the committee and often noted in newspapers and periodicals, and personal notice, usually in the form of a letter, but possibly in the form of a subpena, is frequently sent to individuals, organizations, and Government departments and agencies that are known to be interested.

All hearings and business meetings are required to be public, except when the committee by majority vote determines otherwise. Hearings on the budget are to be held within 30 days after its transmittal to Congress. They are to be open except when they relate to national security.

On the day set for the public hearing an official reporter is present to record the testimony in favor of and against the bill. Suitable accommodations are provided for the public and witnesses.

The bill may be read in full at the opening of the hearings and a copy is inserted in the record. After a brief introductory statement by the chairman and often by the ranking minority Member or other committee member, the first witness is called. Members or Senators who wish to be heard are given preference out of courtesy and because of the limitations on their time. Cabinet officers and high-ranking civil and military officials of the Government, as well as any private individual who is interested, may appear and testify either voluntarily or at the request or summons of the committee.

Committees require, so far as practicable, that witnesses who appear before it file with the committee, in advance of their appearance, a written statement of their proposed testimony and limit their oral presentations to a brief summary of their arguments.

Minority party members of the committee are entitled to call witnesses of their own to testify on a measure during at least one day of the hearing.

All committee rules in the House must provide for the application of the five-minute rule in the interrogation of witnesses until such time as each Member of the committee who so desires has had an opportunity to question a witness.

A typewritten transcript of the testimony taken at a public hearing is made available for inspection in the office of the clerk of the committee and frequently the complete transcript is printed and distributed widely by the committee.

EXECUTIVE SESSION

After hearings are completed the subcommittee usually will consider the bill in an executive session that is popularly known as "the marking-up" session. The views of both sides are studied in detail and at the conclusion of deliberation a vote is taken to determine the action of the subcommittee. It may decide to report the bill favorably to the full committee, with or without amendment, or unfavorably, or suggest that it be "tabled." Each member of the subcommittee, regardless of party affiliation, has one vote.

The proceedings in executive session are generally confidential but the subject matter considered and the actions taken are open to the public.

COMMITTEE MEETINGS

Standing committees are required to have regular meeting days not less frequently than once a month, but the Chairman may call and convene additional meetings. A majority of the committee may call a special meeting within seven calendar days after filing a written notice with the committee, specifying the matter to be considered. At these meetings reports may be made by subcommittees. Full discussions are had on the reports, and amendments may be offered. Committee amendments are only proposals to change the bill as introduced and are subject to acceptance or rejection by the House itself. The absence of a quorum is the subject of a point of order—that is, an objection that the proceedings are out of order because the required number of Members is not present—thus insuring adequate participation by both sides in the action taken. A vote is taken to determine the action of the full committee, which is usually either to report the bill favorably, with or without amendments, or to table it. Since tabling a bill is normally effective in preventing action on it, adverse reports to the House by the full committee are not ordinarily made. On rare occasions, a committee may report a bill without recommendation.

PUBLIC INSPECTION OF RESULTS OF ROLLCALL VOTE IN COMMITTEE

The result of each rollcall vote in any meeting of a committee must be made available by that committee for inspection by the public at reasonable times in the offices of that committee. Information so available for public inspection includes a description of each amendment, motion, order, or other proposition and the name of each Member voting for and each Member voting against such amendment, motion, order, or proposition, and whether by proxy or in person, and the names of those Members present but not voting.

With respect to each record vote by a committee on a motion to report a bill or resolution of a public character, the total number of votes cast for, and the total number of votes cast against, the reporting of such bill or resolution is required to be included in the committee report.

PROXY VOTING

A vote by a member of a committee with respect to a measure or other matter may not be cast by proxy unless that committee, by written rule adopted by the committee, permits voting by proxy and requires that the proxy authorization shall be in writing, shall designate the person who is to execute the proxy authorization, and shall be limited to a specific measure or matter and any amendments or motions pertaining thereto.

POINTS OF ORDER WITH RESPECT TO COMMITTEE PROCEDURE

A point of order does not lie with respect to a measure reported by a committee on the ground that hearings upon such measure were not conducted in accordance with required committee procedure; except that a point of order on that ground may be made by a Member of the committee which reported the measure if, in the committee, that point of order was (A) timely made and (B) improperly overruled or not properly considered.

BROADCASTING COMMITTEE HEARINGS

For the first time beginning with the 1st Session of the 92d Congress it is permissible to cover open committee hearings in the House by television, radio, still photography or by any of those methods of coverage. This permission is granted under well defined conditions as outlined in clause 33 of Rule XI of the Rules of the House of Representatives. As stated in the rule:

> The coverage of committee hearings by television broadcast, radio broadcast, or still photography is a privilege made available by the House and shall be permitted and conducted only in strict conformity with the purposes, provisions, and requirements of this clause.

VII. REPORTED BILLS

If the committee votes to report the bill favorably to the House one of the members is designated to write the committee report. The report usually describes the purpose and scope of the bill and the reasons for its recommended approval. Frequently, a section-by-section analysis is set forth in detail explaining precisely what each section is intended to accomplish. Under the rules of the House all changes in existing law must be indicated and the text of laws being repealed must be set out. This is known as the "Ramseyer" rule; a similar rule in the Senate is known as the "Cordon" rule. Committee amendments must also be set out at the beginning of the report and explanations of them are included. Executive communications requesting the introduction and consideration of the bill are usually quoted in full.

If at the time of approval of a measure or matter by a committee (except the Committee on Rules) a member of the committee gives notice of intention to file supplemental, minority, or additional views, that member is entitled to not less than three calendar days (Saturdays, Sundays and legal holidays excluded) in which to file with the clerk of the committee those views and they must be included in the report on the measure. Committee reports, with certain exceptions, must be filed while the House is actually sitting unless unanimous consent is obtained from the House to file at a later time.

The report is assigned a report number when it is filed, and it is delivered to the Government Printing Office for printing during that night. Beginning with the 91st Congress, in 1969, the report number contains a prefix-designator which indicates the number of the Congress. For example, the first House report in 1969 was numbered 91–1.

The bill also is printed when reported (see Fig. 2, p. 49) and committee amendments are indicated by showing new matter in italics and deleted matter in stricken-through type. The report number is also printed on the bill and the calendar number is shown on both the first and back page of the bill and on the report. (See Fig. 3, p. 51.)

Committee reports are perhaps the most valuable single element of the legislative history of a law. They are used by the courts, executive departments and agencies, and the public generally, as a source of information regarding the purpose and meaning of the law.

FILING OF REPORTS

Reports of committees are required to be filed promptly but in any event, the report on a measure which has been approved by the committee must be filed within seven calendar days (exclusive of days on which the House is not in session) after the day on which there has been filed with the clerk of the committee a written request signed by a majority of the members of the committee, for the reporting of that measure. Upon the filing of the request, the clerk of the committee must transmit immediately to the chairman of the committee notice of the filing of that request. This does not apply to a report of the Committee on Rules with respect to the rules, joint rules, or order of business of the House or to the reporting of a resolution of inquiry addressed to the head of an executive department.

AVAILABILITY OF REPORTS AND HEARINGS

With certain exceptions (relating to emergency situations, such as a measure declaring war or other national emergency) a measure reported by a committee (except the Committees on Appropriations, on House Administration, on Rules, and on Standards of Official Conduct) may not be considered in the House unless the report of that committee has been available to the Members of the House for at least three calendar days (excluding Saturdays, Sundays, and legal holidays) prior to the consideration of that measure in the House. If hearings were held on a measure so reported, the committee is required to make every reasonable effort to have those hearings printed and available for distribution to the Members of the House prior to the consideration of the measure in the House. With respect to general appropriation bills they may not be considered until printed committee hearings and a committee report thereon have been available for the Members of the House for at least three calendar days (excluding Saturdays, Sundays, and legal holidays).

COST ESTIMATES IN REPORTS

The Legislative Reorganization Act of 1970 and the Rules of the House for the 92d Congress require that each report in connection with a bill or joint resolution of a public character shall contain, by the committee making the report, an estimate of the costs which would be incurred in carrying out that bill or joint resolution in the fiscal year reported and in each of the five fiscal years thereafter or for the duration of the program authorized by the bill or resolution if less than five years. In the case of a measure involving revenues the report shall contain only an estimate of the gain or loss in revenues for a one-year period. The report is also required to contain a comparison of the estimates of those costs with the estimate made by a Government agency and submitted to that committee.

These provisions, however, do not apply to the Committees on Appropriations, on House Administration, on Rules and on Standards of Official Conduct.

VIII. LEGISLATIVE REVIEW BY STANDING COMMITTEES

In order to assist the House in—(1) its analysis, appraisal, and evaluation of the application, administration, and execution of the laws enacted by the Congress, and (2) its formulation, consideration, and enactment of any modifications of or changes in those laws, and of additional legislation, as may be necessary or appropriate, each standing committee is required to review and study, on a continuing basis, the application, administration, and execution of those laws, or parts thereof, which is within the jurisdiction of that committee.

Each standing committee is required to submit to the House, not later than January 2 of each odd-numbered year beginning on or after January 1, 1973, a report on the activities of that committee during the Congress ending at noon on January 3 of such year.

These provisions do not apply to the Committees on Appropriations, on House Administration, on Rules, and on Standards of Official Conduct.

IX. CALENDARS

A calendar of the House of Representatives, together with a history of all measures reported by a standing committee of either House, is printed each day the House is sitting for the information of those interested.

As soon as a bill is favorably reported it is assigned a calendar number on one of the two principal calendars of business; namely, the so-called Union Calendar and the House Calendar.

UNION CALENDAR

The rules of the House provide that there shall be:

First. A calendar of the Committee of the Whole House on the State of the Union, to which shall be referred bills raising revenues, general appropriation bills, and bills of a public character directly or indirectly appropriating money or property.

This is commonly known as the Union Calendar and the large majority of public bills and resolutions are placed on it upon being reported to the House.

HOUSE CALENDAR

The rules further provide that there shall be:

Second. A House Calendar, to which shall be referred all bills of a public character not raising revenue nor directly or indirectly appropriating money or property.

The public bills and resolutions that are not placed on the Union Calendar are referred to the House Calendar.

CONSENT CALENDAR

If a measure pending on either of these calendars is of a noncontroversial nature it may be placed on the so-called Consent Calendar. The House rules provide that after a bill has been favorably reported and is on either the House or Union Calendar any Member may file with the Clerk a notice that he desires the bill placed upon the Consent Calendar. On the first and third Mondays of each month immediately after the reading of the Journal the Speaker directs the Clerk to call the bills that have been for three days on the Consent Calendar in the order of appearance on that calendar. If objection is made to the consideration of any bill so called it is carried over on the calendar without prejudice to the next day when the Consent Calendar is again called, and if then objected to by three or more Members it is immediately stricken from the calendar and may not thereafter during the same session of that Congress be placed on the Consent Calendar again. If objection is not made and if the bill is not "passed over" by request, it is passed by unanimous consent without debate. Ordinarily the only amendments considered are those sponsored by the committee that reported the bill.

To avoid the passage without debate of measures that may be controversial or are sufficiently important or complex to require full discussion there are six official objectors—three on the majority side and three on the minority side—who make a careful study of bills on the Consent Calendar. If a bill involves the expenditure of more than a fixed maximum amount of money or if it changes national policy or has other aspects that any of the objectors believes demand explanation and extended debate, it will be objected to and will not be passed by consent. That action does not necessarily mean the final defeat of the bill since it may then be brought up for consideration in the same way as any other bill on the House or Union Calendars.

PRIVATE CALENDAR

All bills of a private character, namely bills for relief in the nature of claims against the United States or private immigration bills, are referred to the Private Calendar which is called on the first and third Tuesdays of each month. If objection is made by two or more Members to the consideration of any measure so called it is recommitted to the committee which reported it. As in the case of the Consent Calendar there are six official objectors, three on the majority side and three on the minority side, who make a careful study of each bill or resolution on the Private Calendar and who will object to a measure that does not conform to the requirements for that calendar, thereby preventing the passage without debate of nonmeritorious bills and resolutions.

DISTRICT OF COLUMBIA BUSINESS

The second and fourth Mondays in each month, after the disposition of motions to discharge committees and after the disposal of such business on the Speaker's table as requires reference only, are set apart, when claimed by the Committee on the District of Columbia, for the consideration of any business that is presented by that committee.

X. OBTAINING CONSIDERATION OF MEASURES

Obviously certain measures pending on the House and Union Calendars are more important and urgent than others and it is necessary to have a system permitting their consideration ahead of those that do not require immediate action. Since all measures are placed on those calendars in the order in which they are reported to the House, the latest bill reported would be the last to be taken up if the calendar number alone were the determining factor.

SPECIAL RESOLUTIONS

To avoid such delays and to provide some degree of selectivity in the consideration of measures it is possible to have them taken up out of order by procuring from the Committee on Rules a special resolution or "rule" for their consideration. That committee, which is composed of majority and minority members but with a larger proportion of majority members than other committees, is specifically granted jurisdiction over resolutions relating to the order of business of the House. Usually the chairman of the committee that has favorably reported the bill appears before the Committee on Rules accompanied by the sponsor of the measure and one or more members of his committee in support of his request for a resolution providing for its immediate consideration. If the Rules Committee is satisfied that the measure should be taken up it will report a resolution reading substantially as follows with respect to a bill on the Union Calendar:

> *Resolved*, That immediately upon the adoption of this resolution it shall be in order for the House to resolve itself into the Committee of the Whole House on the State of the Union and proceed to consider the bill (H.R. ——) entitled, etc., debate to be limited to — hours, one-half to be controlled by the chairman of the Committee on ——, and one-half by the ranking minority member of such committee.

If the measure is on the House Calendar the resolution reads substantially as follows:

> *Resolved*, That immediately upon the adoption of this resolution the House shall proceed to consider the bill (H.R. ——) entitled,

etc., and at the end of — hours a vote shall be taken on all pending
amendments and on the bill to final passage.

The resolution may waive points of order against the bill and limit
floor amendments. This is known as a "closed rule."

There are several other methods of obtaining consideration of bills
that either have not been reported by a committee or, if reported,
for which a special order or "rule" has not been obtained.

MOTIONS FOR CONSIDERATION OF MEASURES MADE IN ORDER BY PREVIOUS RESOLUTION

If, within seven calendar days after a measure has, by resolution,
been made in order for consideration by the House, a motion has not
been offered for its consideration, the Speaker may, in his discretion,
recognize a Member of the committee which reported the measure to
offer a motion that the House shall consider it, if the Member has been
duly authorized by that committee to offer the motion.

MOTION TO DISCHARGE COMMITTEE

A Member may present to the Clerk a motion in writing to discharge
a committee from the consideration of a public bill or resolution which
has been referred to it 30 days prior thereto. Under this rule a Member
may also file a motion to discharge the Committee on Rules from
further consideration of a resolution providing either a special order
of business, or a special rule for the consideration of a public bill or
resolution favorably reported by a standing committee, or a special
rule for the consideration of a public bill or resolution which has
remained in a standing committee 30 days or more without action.
This motion may be made only when the resolution, from which it is
moved to discharge the Committee on Rules, has been referred to
that committee at least seven days prior to the filing of the motion
to discharge. The motion is placed in the custody of the Clerk, who
arranges some convenient place for the signature of Members. When
a majority of the total membership of the House have signed the
motion it is entered on the Journal, printed with the signatures
thereto in the Congressional Record, and referred to the Calendar of
Motions to Discharge Committees.

On the second and fourth Mondays of each month, a Member who
has signed a motion to discharge, which has been on the calendar at
least seven days, may seek recognition to call up the motion. The bill
or resolution is then read by title only. After 20 minutes' debate,
one-half in favor of the proposition and one-half in opposition thereto,
the House proceeds to vote on the motion to discharge.

If the motion prevails to discharge the Committee on Rules from
a resolution pending before the committee, the House immediately
votes on the adoption of that resolution.

If the motion prevails to discharge one of the standing committees
of the House from a public bill or resolution pending before the
committee, a Member who signed the motion may move that the
House proceed to the immediate consideration of the bill or resolution
under the general rules of the House. If the House by vote decides
against the motion for immediate consideration, the bill or resolution
is referred to its proper calendar with the same rights and privileges
it would have had if reported favorably by the standing committee.

MOTION TO SUSPEND THE RULES

On the first and third Mondays of each month and during the last
6 days of a session the Speaker may entertain a motion to suspend

the operation of the regular rules and pass a bill or resolution. Arrangement must be made in advance with the Speaker to recognize the Member who wishes to offer the motion. Before being considered by the House the motion must be seconded by a majority of the Members present, and by teller vote, if demanded. Then the proposition is debated for 40 minutes, one-half by those in favor of the proposition and one-half by those in opposition thereto. The motion may not be amended and if amendments to the bill are proposed they must be included in the motion when it is made. The rules may be suspended only by affirmative vote of two-thirds of the Members voting, a quorum being present.

CALENDAR WEDNESDAY

On Wednesday of each week, unless dispensed with by unanimous consent or by affirmative vote of two-thirds of the Members voting (a quorum being present), the standing committees are called in alphabetical order. A committee when named may call up for consideration any bill reported by it on a previous day and pending on either the House or Union Calendar. Not more than two hours of general debate is permitted on any measure called up on Calendar Wednesday and all debate must be confined to the subject matter of the measure, the time being equally divided between those for and those against it. The affirmative vote of a simple majority of the Members present is sufficient to pass the measure.

PRIVILEGED MATTERS

Under the rules of the House certain matters are regarded as privileged matters and may interrupt the order of business, as for example, reports from the Committee on Rules, from the Committee on Appropriations on the general appropriation bills, and from the Committee on Ways and Means on bills raising revenues.

At any time after the reading of the journal, a member, by direction of the appropriate committee, may move that the House resolve itself into the Committee of the Whole House on the State of the Union for the purpose of considering bills raising revenues, or general appropriation bills. General appropriation bills may not be considered in the House until three days after printed committee reports and hearings on them have been available to the members. The limit on general debate is generally fixed by unanimous consent.

Other examples of privileged matters are conference reports, amendments to measures by the other body, and veto messages from the President of the United States. The Member in charge of such a matter may call it up at practically any time for immediate consideration. Usually, this is done after consultation with both the majority and minority floor leaders so that the Members of both parties will have advance notice and will not be taken by surprise.

XI. CONSIDERATION

Our democratic tradition demands that bills be given consideration by the entire membership with adequate opportunity for debate and the proposing of amendments.

COMMITTEE OF THE WHOLE HOUSE

In order to expedite the consideration of bills and resolutions the House resorts to a parliamentary usage which enables it to act with a quorum of only 100 Members instead of the normally requisite 218. This consists of resolving itself into the Committee of the Whole House on the State of the Union to consider a measure. All measures on the Union Calendar—involving a tax, making appropriations, or authorizing payments out of appropriations already made—must be first considered in a Committee of the Whole House.

Upon the adoption of a resolution that the House resolve itself into the Committee of the Whole House, the Speaker leaves his chair after appointing a Chairman to preside. Debate on the adoption of the resolution in the House is limited to one hour.

The special resolution or "rule" reported by the Committee on Rules fixes the length of the debate in the Committee of the Whole. This may vary according to the importance and controversial nature of the measure. As provided in the resolution the control of the time is divided equally—usually between the chairman and the ranking minority member of the committee that reported the measure. Members seeking to speak for or against the measure usually arrange in advance with the Member in control of the time on their respective side to be allowed a certain amount of time in the debate. Others may ask the Member speaking at the time to yield to them for a question or a brief statement. Frequently permission is granted a Member by unanimous consent to extend his remarks in the Congressional Record if sufficient time to make a lengthy oral statement is not available during actual debate.

The conduct of the debate is governed principally by the standing rules of the House which are adopted at the opening of each Congress. Another recognized authority is Jefferson's Manual which was prepared by Thomas Jefferson for his own guidance as President of the Senate from 1797 to 1801. The House, in 1837, adopted a rule which still stands, providing that the provisions of Jefferson's Manual should govern the House in all cases to which they are applicable and in which they are not inconsistent with the standing rules and orders of the House. In addition there is a most valuable compilation of precedents up to the year 1935 set out in Hinds' Precedents and Cannon's Precedents, consisting of 11 volumes, to guide the action of the House. An extremely useful and concise synopsis of up-to-date precedents is contained in a single volume entitled Cannon's Procedure in the House of Representatives. Recent rulings of the Speaker are set out as notes to the current House Manual, so that most parliamentary questions arising during the course of debate are susceptible of ruling backed up by a precedent of action in a similar situation. The Parliamentarian of the House is present in the House Chamber in order to assist the Chairman or the Speaker in making a correct ruling on such questions.

SECOND READING

During the general debate an accurate account is kept of the time used on both sides and when all the time allowed under the rule has been consumed the Chairman terminates the debate. Then begins the "second reading of the bill," section by section, at which time amendments may be offered to a section when it is read. The rules permit a Member five minutes to explain his proposed amendment, after which the Member who is first recognized by the Chair is allowed to speak for five minutes in opposition to it, and there is no further debate on that amendment, thereby effectively preventing any attempt at filibuster tactics. There is, however, a device whereby a Member may offer a pro forma amendment—"to strike out the last word"—without intending any change in the language, and be allowed five minutes for debate, thus permitting a somewhat more comprehensive debate. Each amendment is put to the Committee of the Whole for adoption.

At any time after a debate is begun, under the five minute rule, upon proposed amendments to a section or paragraph of a bill the committee may by majority vote of the Members present, close debate on the section or paragraph. However, if debate is closed on any section or paragraph before there has been debate on any amendment which a Member has caused to be printed in the Congressional Record after the reporting of the bill by the committee but at least one day prior to floor consideration of such amendment, the Member who caused the amendment to be printed in the Record is given five minutes in which to explain such amendment, after which the first person to obtain the floor has five minutes to speak in opposition to it, and there is no further debate on that proposed amendment; but such time for debate is not allowed when the offering of the amendment is dilatory.

When an amendment is offered, while the House is meeting in the Committee of the Whole, the Clerk is required to transmit to the majority committee table five copies of the amendment and five copies to the minority committee table, and at least one copy of the amendment to the majority cloak room and at least one copy to the minority cloak room.

VOTING

There are three methods of voting in the Committee of the Whole, which are also employed, together with an additional method, in the House. These are the voice vote (viva voce), the division, the teller vote, and finally the yea-and-nay vote which is used only in the House and not in the Committee of the Whole. If a Member objects to the vote on the ground that a quorum is not present there may be an automatic rollcall vote.

To obtain a voice vote the Chair simply states, "As many as are in favor (as the question may be) say 'Aye'." "As many as are opposed, say 'No'." The Chair determines the result on the basis of the volume of ayes and noes. This is the form in which the vote is ordinarily taken in the first instance. If it is difficult to determine the result by this method, a division may be demanded and the Chair then states that a division has been demanded and "as many as are in favor will rise and stand until counted." After counting those in favor he calls upon those opposed to stand and be counted, thereby determing the number in favor of and those opposed to the question.

If a demand for a teller vote is supported by one-fifth of a quorum (20 in the Committee of the Whole, and 44 in the House) the Chair appoints one teller from each side and directs the Members in favor of the proposition to pass between the tellers and be counted. After counting, a teller announces the number in the affirmative and the Chair directs the Members opposed to pass between the tellers and be counted. When the count is stated by a teller the Chair announces the result. If before tellers are named a Member requests tellers with clerks and that request is supported by at least one-fifth of a quorum, the names of those voting on each side of the question and the names of those not voting are recorded by clerks or by electronic device, and are entered in the Journal and published in the Congressional Record. Members have not less than twelve minutes from the naming of tellers with clerks to be counted.

Pending the installation of appropriate electronic equipment, a procedure has been devised whereby Members cast their votes on paper ballots. Green ballots are used by Members voting "aye" after filling in their names on the ballot. Those Members voting "no" cast their ballots by using red cards provided for that purpose. The ballots are deposited in two boxes, one marked "yea" with green trimming, the other "no" with red trimming.

When the ballots are tallied the Chair announces the result, and thereupon Members wishing to be recorded as "present" may do so by announcing their presence to the Chair.

If the yeas and nays are demanded, the Speaker directs those in favor of taking the vote by that method to stand and be counted. The assent of one-fifth of the Members present (as distinguished from one-fifth of a quorum in the case of a demand for tellers) is necessary for ordering the yeas and nays. When the yeas and nays are ordered (or a point of order is made that a quorum is not present) the Speaker directs that as many as are in favor of the proposition will, as their names are called, answer "Aye"; as many as are opposed will answer "No." The Clerk calls the roll and reports the result to the Speaker who announces it to the House. The Speaker is not required to vote but may do so when his vote would be decisive.

THE COMMITTEE "RISES"

At the conclusion of the consideration of the bill for amendment, the Committee of the Whole "rises" and reports the bill to the House with such amendments as have been adopted.

ACTION BY THE HOUSE

If the previous question (passage of the bill) has been deemed ordered by the terms of the special resolution, the House immediately votes on whatever amendments have been reported by the Committee of the Whole in the sequence in which they were reported. Upon completion of voting upon the amendments the House immediately votes upon the passage of the bill with such amendments as it has adopted.

In those cases where the previous question has not been deemed ordered the House may engage in debate lasting 1 hour, at the conclusion of which the previous question is ordered and the House votes on the passage of the bill. During the debate it is in order to offer amendments to the bill or to the committee amendments.

Measures which do not have to be considered in the Committee of the Whole are, of course, considered in the House in the first instance in accordance with the terms of the special resolution limiting debate thereon.

The Speaker puts the question: Shall the bill be engrossed and read a third time? and, if decided in the affirmative, it is read a third time by title only. In 1965 the House rules were amended to abolish the third reading of the bill in full on the demand of a Member—a practice that was sometimes used as a dilatory tactic. Upon passage of the bill by the House a *pro forma* motion to reconsider it is automatically made and laid upon the table—i.e., action is postponed indefinitely—to forestall such a motion at a later date, since the vote of the House upon a proposition is not final and conclusive upon the House until there has been an opportunity to reconsider it.

MOTIONS TO RECOMMIT

After the previous question has been ordered on the passage of a bill or joint resolution, it is in order to make one motion to recommit and the Speaker is required to give preference in recognition for that purpose to a Member who is opposed to the bill or joint resolution. However, with respect to a motion to recommit with instructions after the previous question has been ordered, it is always in order to debate the motion for ten minutes before the vote is taken, the time to be equally divided between the proponents and opponents of the motion.

SYSTEM OF LIGHTS AND BELLS

Because of the large number and the diversity of daily tasks that they have to perform it is not practicable for Members to be present in the House (or Senate) Chamber at every minute that the body is actually sitting. Furthermore, many of the routine matters do not require the personal attendance of all the Members. In order to procure their presence when needed for a vote or to constitute a quorum, systems of electric lights and bells or buzzers are provided in various parts of the Capitol Building and of the House and Senate Office Buildings.

In the House the Speaker has ordered that the bells and lights comprising the system be utilized as follows:

Tellers—one ring and one light on left side of the light panel;

Tellers with Clerks—one ring and one light on left when tellers are ordered; two rings and two lights on left when recorded tellers are ordered and tellers are named;

"Yeas and Nays"—two rings and two lights on left;

Call of the House—three rings and three lights on left;

Adjournment—four rings and four lights on left;

Recess—five rings and five lights on left;

Civil Defense Warning—six rings and six lights on left.

The light on the far right—seven—indicates that the House is in Session.

In the Senate the following system of lights and bells are used:

One long ring at hour of convening; one ring—"Yeas" and "Nays"; two rings—Quorum Call; three rings—Call of absentees; four rings—Adjournment or Recess; five rings—Five minutes remaining on "Yea" and "Nay" vote; six rings—Morning business concluded.

One red light remains lighted at all times while Senate is in actual session.

ROLLCALLS AND QUORUM CALLS

In order to speed up and expedite rollcalls and quorum calls, the Legislative Reorganization Act of 1970, provides alternative methods for pursuing these procedures.

When a call of the House in the absence of quorums is ordered, the Speaker of the House or the Chairman of the Committee of the Whole House may order the Clerk of the House to lay out tally sheets on which the presence of the Members is recorded by the Clerk or the Member may record his own name. When a quorum is recorded the Clerk is required to notify the presiding officer of this fact, and thereupon it is in order to entertain a privileged motion, without debate, to dispense with further proceedings under the call, and if carried the business of the House or of the Committee of the Whole resumes without further call of the House. For a period of 30 minutes after the start of the call, Members who are present may have their presence recorded on the tally sheets. Absent Members are recorded in the Journal of the House, and the former requirement that in all calls of the House the doors shall be closed has been dispensed with, except when so ordered by the Speaker.

In lieu of the calling of the names of Members in the manner pro-

vided for under other provisions of the Rules of the House upon any
rollcall or quorum call, the names of the Members voting or present
may be recorded through the use of appropriate electronic equipment
when they become available. In that case, the Clerk is required to
enter in the Journal and publish in the Congressional Record, in
alphabetical order in each category, a list of the names of those
Members recorded as voting in the affirmative, of those Members
recorded as voting in the negative, and of those Members voting
present, as the case may be, as if their names had been called in the
manner provided for under other provisions of Rules. [See Rule XV of
the Rules of the House.]

However, unless the Chairman invokes the procedure for the call of
the roll under the Rule providing for tally sheets as described under
this sub-heading, whenever a Committee of the Whole House or of the
Whole House on the State of the Union is without a quorum, which
consists of one hundred Members, the Chairman is required to cause
the roll to be called, and thereupon the committee rises, and the
Chairman reports the names of the absentees to the House, which
are entered on the Journal; but if on such call a quorum appears, the
committee resumes its sitting without further order of the House.

PAIRING OF MEMBERS

When a Member anticipates that he will be unavoidably absent at
the time a vote is to be taken he may arrange in advance to be recorded as being either in favor of, or opposed to, the question by being
"paired" with a Member who is also to be absent and who holds contrary views on the question. A specific pair of this kind shows how he
would have voted if he had been present. Occasionally, a Member
who has arranged in advance to be paired, actually is present at the
time of voting. He then votes as he would have voted if he had not
been paired, and subsequently withdraws his vote and asks to be
marked "present" to protect his colleague. This is known as a "live
pair". If his absence is to continue for several days during which a
number of different questions are to be voted upon he may arrange a
"general pair". A general pair does not indicate how he would have
voted on the question, but merely that he and the Member paired
with him would not have been on the same side of the question.

XII. ENGROSSMENT AND MESSAGE TO SENATE

The preparation of a copy of the bill in the form in which it has
passed the House is sometimes a detailed and complicated process
because of the large number and complexity of amendments to some
bills adopted by the House. Frequently these amendments are offered
during a spirited debate with little or no prior formal preparation.
The amendment may be for the purpose of inserting new language,
substituting different words for those set out in the bill, or deleting
portions of the bill. It is not unusual to have more than 100 such
amendments, including those proposed by the committee at the
time the bill is reported and those offered from the floor during the
consideration of the bill in the chamber. Some of the amendments
offered from the floor are written in longhand and others are typewritten. However, when an amendment is offered in the Committee of
the Whole, the Clerk is required to furnish the majority and minority,
tables, five copies each of the amendment and one copy each to the

majority and minority cloakrooms. Each must be inserted in precisely the proper place in the engrossed bill, with the spelling and punctuation exactly the same as it was adopted by the House. Obviously, it is extremely important that the Senate receive a copy of the bill in the precise form in which it has passed the House. The preparation of such a copy is the function of the enrolling clerk.

There is an enrolling clerk in each House, constituting a division of the office of the Clerk of the House of Representatives and of the Secretary of the Senate. He receives all the papers relating to the bill, including the official Clerk's copy of the bill as reported by the standing committee and each amendment adopted by the House. From this material he prepares the engrossed copy of the bill as passed, containing all the amendments agreed to by the House. (See Fig. 4, p. 52.) At this point the measure ceases technically to be called a bill and is termed "an act" signifying that it is the act of one body of the Congress, although it is still popularly referred to as a bill. The engrossed bill is printed on blue paper and a certificate that it passed the House of Representatives is signed by the Clerk of the House. The engrossed bill is delivered by a reading clerk to the Senate, while that body is actually sitting, in a rather formal ceremonious manner befitting the dignity of both Houses. The reading clerk is escorted into the chamber by the Secretary or another officer of the Senate and upon being recognized by the President of the Senate states that the House has passed the bill, giving its number and title, and requests the concurrence of the Senate.

XIII. SENATE ACTION

The President of the Senate refers the engrossed bill to the appropriate standing committee of the Senate in conformity with the rules. The bill is immediately reprinted and copies are made available in the document rooms of both Houses. (See Fig. 5, p. 53.) This printing is known as the "Act print" or the "Senate referred print."

COMMITTEE CONSIDERATION

The standing committee gives the bill the same kind of detailed consideration as it received in the House, and may report it with or without amendment, or "table" it. A committee member who wishes to express his individual views, or a group of Members who wish to file a minority report, may do so, if he or they give notice, at the time of the approval of the measure, by a standing committee, of intention to file supplemental, minority or additional views, in which event those views may be filed within three days with the clerk of the committee and they become a part of the report.

Any Senator may enter a motion to discharge a committee from further consideration of a bill which it has failed to report after what is deemed to be a reasonable time. If the motion is agreed to by a majority vote, the committee is discharged and the bill is placed on the Calendar of Bills under the standing rules. Upon being reported by the committee the bill is reprinted with committee amendments indicated by line-through type and italics. The calendar number and report number are indicated on the first and back page, together with the name of the Senator making the report. (See Fig. 6, p. 55.) The committee report and any minority or individual views accompanying the bill are also printed at the same time. (See Fig. 7, p. 57.)

CHAMBER PROCEDURE

The rules of procedure in the Senate differ to a large extent from those in the House. At the time that a bill is reported (and in the Senate this is a more formal matter than in the House of Representatives inasmuch as the Senator usually announces orally that he is submitting the report) the Senator who is making the report may ask unanimous consent for the immediate consideration of the bill. If the bill is of a noncontroversial nature and there is no objection the Senate may pass the bill with little or no debate and with only a brief explanation of its purpose and effect. Even in this instance the bill is subject to amendment by any Senator. A simple majority vote is necessary to carry an amendment as well as to pass the bill. If there is any objection the report must lie over one day and the bill is placed upon the calendar.

The Legislative Reorganization Act of 1970, requires that a measure reported by a standing committee of the Senate shall not be considered unless the report of that committee has been available to Senate Members for at least three days (excluding Saturdays, Sundays, and legal holidays) prior to consideration of the measure in the Senate. This requirement, however, may be waived by agreement of the majority and minority leaders and does not apply in certain emergency situations.

There is only one Calendar of Bills in the Senate, there being no differentiation, as there is in the House, between (1) bills raising revenue, general appropriation bills, and bills of a public character appropriating money or property, and (2) other bills of a public character not appropriating money or property.

At the conclusion of the morning business for each legislative day the Senate proceeds to the consideration of the Calendar of Bills. Bills that are not objected to are taken up in their order, and each Senator is entitled to speak once and for five minutes only upon any question. Objection may be interposed at any stage of the proceedings, but upon motion the Senate may continue consideration after the call of the calendar is completed, and the limitations on debate then do not apply.

On any day but Monday, following the announcement of the close of morning business, any Senator obtaining recognition may move to take up any bill out of its regular order on the calendar. Frequently, this is the majority leader. The five-minute limitation on debate does not apply to the consideration of a bill so taken up and debate may continue until the hour when the President of the Senate lays down the unfinished business of the day. At that point consideration of the bill is discontinued and the measure reverts back to the Calendar of Bills and may again be called up at another time under the same conditions.

When a bill has been objected to and passed over on the call of the calendar it is not necessarily lost. The majority leader, after consulting the majority policy committee of the Senate, and the minority leadership determines the time at which it will be called up for debate. At that time a motion is made to consider the bill. The motion, which is debatable, if made after the morning hour, is sometimes the occasion for lengthy speeches, on the part of Senators opposed to the measure, intended to prevent or defeat action. This is the tactic known as "filibustering." Upon obtaining the floor Senators may speak as long as they please but may not speak more than twice upon any one question in debate on the same day without leave of the Senate. Debate, however, may be closed if 16 Senators sign a motion to that effect and the motion is carried, without debate, by two-thirds of the Members of the Senate present and voting.[1]

---

[1] Until 1959, the rules required the assent of two-thirds of the total membership of the Senate to close debate.

While a measure is being considered it is subject to amendment and each amendment, including those proposed by the committee that reported the bill, is considered separately. Generally there is no requirement that proposed amendments be germane to the subject matter of the bill except in the case of general appropriation bills. Under the rules of the Senate a "rider," that is, an amendment proposing substantive legislation to an appropriation bill is prohibited, but this prohibition may be suspended by two-thirds vote on a motion to permit consideration of such an amendment upon one day's notice in writing. After final action upon the amendments the bill is ready for engrossment and the third reading, which is usually by title only, although if demanded, it must be read in full. The Presiding Officer then puts the question upon the passage and the vote is usually taken viva voce although a yea-and-nay vote is in order if demanded by one-fifth of the Senators present. A simple majority is necessary for passage. Before an amended measure is cleared for its return to the House of Representatives (or an unamended measure is cleared for enrollment) a Senator who voted with the prevailing side, or who abstained from voting, may make a motion within the next two days to reconsider the action. If the measure was passed without a record vote any Senator may make the motion to reconsider. That motion is usually "tabled", that is, action on it is postponed indefinitely, and its tabling constitutes a final determination. If, however, the motion is granted, the Senate, by majority vote, may either affirm its action, which then becomes final, or reverse it.

The original engrossed House bill, together with the engrossed Senate amendments, if any, is thereupon returned to the House with a message stating the action taken by the Senate. Where amendments have been made by the Senate the message requests that the House concur in them.

XIV. FINAL ACTION UPON AMENDED BILL

Upon their return to the House the official papers relating to the amended measure are placed upon the Speaker's table to await House action on the Senate amendments. If the amendments are of a minor or noncontroversial nature the chairman of the committee that originally reported the bill—or any Member—may, at the direction of the committee, ask unanimous consent to take the bill with the amendments from the Speaker's table and agree to the Senate amendments. At this point the Clerk reads the title of the bill and the Senate amendments. If there is no objection the amendments are then declared to be agreed to, and the bill is ready to be enrolled for presentation to the President. Lacking such unanimous consent, bills that do not require consideration in the Committee of the Whole are privileged and may be called up from the Speaker's table by motion for immediate consideration of the amendments, a simple majority being necessary to carry the motion and thereby complete floor action on the measure. However, nongermane amendments added by the Senate, to a House passed bill require for adoption, on demand of a Member, a separate vote on each amendment if, originating in the House, such amendment would be subject to a point of order on a question of germaneness. Before a separate vote is taken, it is in order to debate the amendment for forty minutes, one-half of the time to be given to debate in favor of, and one-half to debate in opposition to, the amendment. An amendment of the Senate to a House bill is subject to a point of order that it shall first be considered in the Committee of the Whole House on the State of the Union, if, originating in the House, it would be subject to that point.

If, however, the amendments are substantial or controversial the Member may request unanimous consent to take the bill with the Senate amendments thereto from the Speaker's table, disagree to the amendments and request a conference with the Senate on the disagreeing votes of the two Houses. If there is objection it becomes necessary to obtain a special resolution from the Committee on Rules unless the Speaker, in his discretion, recognizes a Member for a motion, authorized by the committee having jurisdiction of the subject matter of the bill, to disagree to the amendments and ask for a conference. If there is no objection to the request, or if the motion is carried, the Speaker thereupon appoints the managers (as the conferees are called) on the part of the House and a message is sent to the Senate advising it of the House action. The Speaker customarily, but not necessarily, follows the suggestions of the chairman of the committee in charge of the bill in designating the managers on the part of the House from among the Members of the committee. The number, as fixed by the Speaker, is frequently three, consisting of two Members of the majority party and one of the minority, but may be greater on important bills. Representation of both major parties is an important attribute of all our parliamentary procedure but, in the case of conference committees, it is rather more important that the conferees represent the views of the House on the House measure and all the conferees may be of the same political party.

If the Senate agrees to the request for a conference a similar committee is appointed by unanimous consent by the Presiding Officer of the Senate. Both political parties may be represented on the Senate conference committee also, but the Senate committee need not be the same size as the House committee.

The conference committee is sometimes popularly referred to as the "Third House of Congress."

The request for a conference can be made only by the body in possession of the papers. Occasionally the Senate, anticipating that the House will not concur in its amendments, votes to insist on its amendments and requests a conference upon passage of the bill without returning the bill to the House. This practice serves to expedite the matter because several days' time may be saved by the designation of the Senate conferees before returning the bill to the House. The matter of which body requests the conference is not without significance inasmuch as the one asking for the conference acts last upon the report to be submitted by the conferees.

Although the managers on the part of each House meet together as one committee they are in effect two separate committees, each of which votes separately and acts by a majority vote. For this reason the number of the respective managers is largely immaterial.

The conferees are strictly limited in their consideration to matters in disagreement between the two Houses. Consequently they may not strike out or amend any portion of the bill that was not amended by the Senate. Furthermore, they may not insert new matter that is not germane to the differences between the two Houses. Where the Senate amendment revises a figure or an amount contained in the bill, the conferees are limited to the difference between the two numbers and may not increase the greater nor decrease the smaller figure. Neither House may alone, by instructions, empower its managers to make a change in the text to which both Houses have agreed, but the managers for both bodies may be given that authority by a concurrent resolution adopted by a majority of each House.

However, where the Senate amendment to the bill strikes out all after the enacting clause and inserts a substitute bill for the House provisions the conferees have the entire subject before them. This is so even though particular sections of the substitute may be identical to sections in the version of the bill as it passed the House. When a disagreement to an amendment in the nature of a substitute is committed to a conference committee it is in order for the managers on the part of the House to propose a substitute which is a germane modification of the matter in disagreement, but the introduction of language in that substitute presenting a specific additional topic, question, issue, or proposition not committed to the conference committee by either House does not constitute a germane modification of the matter in disagreement. Moreover, their report may not include matter not committed to the conference committee by either House, nor may their report include a modification of any specific topic, question, issue, or proposition committed to the conference committee by either or both Houses if that modification is beyond the scope of that specific topic, question, issue, or proposition as so committed to the conference committee.

An amendment by the Senate to a general appropriation bill or to any other bill which would be in violation of the rules of the House, if the amendment had originated in the House, or an amendment by the Senate providing for an appropriation upon a bill other than a general appropriation bill, may not be agreed to by the managers on the part of the House, unless a specific authority to agree to such an amendment is first given by the House by a separate vote on each specific amendment.

MEETINGS AND ACTION OF CONFEREES

The meetings of the conferees are customarily held in executive session on the Senate side of the Capitol, with only the conferees and staff members or other expert assistants in attendance, although in rare instances Members or other persons have been admitted to make arguments.

There are generally three forms of recommendations available to the conferees when reporting back to their bodies, *viz.*, that:

    1. the Senate recede from all (or certain of) its amendments;

    2. the House recede from its disagreement to all (or certain of) the Senate amendments and agree thereto; and

    3. the House recede from its disagreement to all (or certain of) the Senate amendments and agree thereto with amendments.

In many instances the result of the conference is a compromise growing out of the third type of recommendation available to the conferees. The complete report may, of course, be comprised of one, two, or all three of these recommendations with respect to the various amendments. Occassionally the conferees find themselves unable to reach an agreement with respect to one or more amendments and so report back a statement of their inability to agree on those particular amendments. These may then be acted upon separately. This partial disagreement is, of course, not practicable where the Senate strikes out all after the enacting clause and substitutes its own bill which must be considered as a single amendment.

If they are unable to reach any agreement whatsoever the conferees report that fact to their respective bodies and the amendments are in the position they were before the conference was requested. New conferees may be appointed in either or both Houses. In addition, the Houses may instruct the conferees as to the position they are to take. The practice of instructing the original conferees at the time of their appointment is rarely used today.

After House conferees on any bill or resolution in conference between the two bodies have been appointed for twenty calendar days and have failed to make a report, the House rules provide for a motion of the highest privilege to discharge the House conferees and to appoint new conferees, or to instruct them. Further, during the last six days of any session it is a privileged motion to move to discharge, appoint, or instruct House conferees after House conferees shall have been appointed 36 hours without having made a report.

CONFERENCE REPORTS

When the conferees, by majority vote of each group, have reached complete agreement (or find that they are able to agree with respect to some but not all amendments) they embody their recommendations in a report made in duplicate which must be signed by a majority of the conferees appointed by each body. The minority portion of the managers have no authority to file a statement of minority views in connection with the report. Starting with the 92d Congress, in 1971, the report is required to be printed in both Houses and must be accompanied by an explanatory statement prepared jointly by the conferees on the part of the House and the conferees on the part of the Senate. (See Fig. 8, p. 58.) The statement must be sufficiently detailed and explicit to inform the Congress as to the effect which the amendments or propositions contained in the report will have upon the measure to which those amendments or propositions relate. The engrossed bill and amendments and one copy of the report are delivered to the body which is to act first upon the report; namely, the body that had agreed to the conference requested by the other.

In the Senate the presentation of the report is always in order except when the Journal is being read or a question of order or motion to adjourn is pending, or while the Senate is dividing; and when received, the question of proceeding to the consideration of the report, if raised, is immediately put and is determined without debate. The report is not subject to amendment in either body and must be accepted or rejected as an entirety. If the time for debate is limited, the time allotted must be equally divided between the majority and minority party. If the Senate, acting first, does not agree to the report it may by majority vote order it recommitted to the conferees. When the Senate agrees to the report its managers are thereby discharged and it then sends the original papers to the House of Representatives with a message advising that body of its action.

A report that contains any recommendations which go beyond the differences between the two Houses is subject to a point of order in its entirety. Any change in the text as agreed to by both Houses renders the report subject to the point of order and the matter is before the House *de novo*.

The presentation of the report in the House of Representatives is always in order, except when the Journal is being read, while the roll is being called, or the House is dividing on any proposition. The report is considered in the House and may not be sent to the Committee of the Whole on the suggestion that it contains matters ordinarily requiring consideration in that Committee. The report may not be received by the House if the required statement does not accompany it.

It is, however, not in order to consider the report of a committee of conference unless the report and the accompanying statement have been printed in the Record, at least three calendar days (excluding Saturdays, Sundays, and legal holidays) prior to the consideration of the report by the House; but this provision does not apply during the last six days of the session. Nor is it in order to consider the report unless copies of the report and accompanying statement are then available on the floor. The time allotted for debate in the consideration of any report is equally divided between the majority party and the minority party. If the House does not agree to the report, the report may not be recommitted to the conferees since the Senate has already agreed to it and discharged its managers.

Where the report discloses an inability of the conferees to reach complete agreement the amendments of the Senate in disagreement may be voted upon separately and may be adopted by a majority vote after the adoption of the report itself as though no conference had been had with respect to those amendments. The Senate may recede from all amendments, or from certain of its amendments, insisting upon the others with or without a request for a conference with respect to them. If the House does not accept the amendments insisted upon by the Senate the entire conference process begins again with respect to them.

CUSTODY OF PAPERS

The custody of the original official papers is important in conference procedure inasmuch as either body may act only when in possession of the papers. As indicated above the request for a conference may be made only by the body in possession. The papers are then transmitted to the body agreeing to the conference and by it to the managers of the House which asked. The latter in turn carry the papers with them to the conference and at its conclusion turn them over to the managers of the House that agreed to the conference. The latter deliver them to their own House, which acts first on the report and then messages the papers to the other House for final action on the report.

Each group of conferees, at the conclusion of the conference, retains one copy of the report which has been made in duplicate, and signed by a majority of the managers of each body—the House copy signed first by the House managers and the Senate copy signed first by its managers.

Obviously a bill cannot become a law of the land until it has been approved in identical terms by both Houses of the Congress. When the bill has finally been approved by both Houses all the original papers are transmitted to the enrolling clerk of the body in which the bill originated.

XV. ENROLLMENT

When the bill has been agreed to in identical form by both bodies—either without amendment by the Senate, or by House concurrence in the Senate amendments, or by agreement in both bodies to the conference report—a copy of the bill is enrolled for presentation to the President.

The preparation of the enrolled bill is a painstaking and important task since it must reflect precisely the effect of all amendments, either by way of deletion, substitution, or addition, agreed to by both bodies. The enrolling clerk of the House in which the bill originated receives the original engrossed bill, the engrossed Senate amendments, the signed conference report, the several messages from the Senate, and a notation of the final action by the House, for the purpose of preparing the enrolled copy. From these he must prepare meticulously the final form of the bill, as it was agreed to by both Houses, for presentation to the President. (See Fig. 9, p. 60.) On occasion there have been upward of 500 amendments, particularly after a conference, each of which must be set out in the enrollment exactly as agreed to, and all punctuation must be in accord with the action taken.

The enrolled bill is printed on parchment paper, with a certificate on the reverse side of the last page, to be signed by the Clerk of the House stating that the bill originated in the House of Representatives (or by the Secretary of the Senate when the bill has originated in that body). It is examined by the Committee on House Administration for accuracy. When the committee is satisfied with the accuracy of the bill it attaches a slip stating that it finds the bill truly enrolled and sends it to the Speaker of the House for his signature. All bills, regardless of the body in which they originated, are signed first by the Speaker and then by the President of the Senate. The Speaker and the President of the Senate may sign bills only while their respective House is actually sitting unless advance permission is granted to them to sign during a recess or after adjournment. After both signatures are affixed the bill is returned to the committee for the purpose of being presented to the President for his action under the Constitution.

XVI. PRESIDENTIAL ACTION

The Constitution provides that—

Every Bill which shall have passed the House of Representatives and the Senate, shall, before it becomes a Law, be presented to the President of the United States.

In actual practice the clerk of the Subcommittee on Enrolled Bills delivers the original enrolled bill to an employee at the White House and obtains a receipt therefor, and the fact of the delivery is then reported to the House by the chairman of the subcommittee. Such delivery to a White House employee has customarily been regarded as presentation to the President and as commencing the 10-day Constitutional period for Presidential action.

Copies of the enrolled bill are usually transmitted by the White House to the various departments interested in the subject matter so that they may advise the President who, of course, cannot be personally familiar with every item in every bill.

If the President approves the bill he signs it and usually writes the word "approved" and the date, the only Constitutional requirement being that he sign it. (See Fig. 9, p. 60.)

The Supreme Court has stated that undoubtedly the President when approving bills may be said to participate in the enactment of laws, which the Constitution requires him to execute.

The bill may become law without the President's signature by virtue of the Constitutional provision that if he does not return a bill with his objections within 10 days (Sundays excepted) after it has been presented to him, it shall be a law in like manner as if he had signed it. (See Fig. 11, p. 62.) However, if the Congress by their adjournment prevent its return, it does not become law. The latter event is what is known as a "pocket veto," that is, the bill does not become law even though the President has not sent his objections to the Congress.

Notice of the signing of a bill by the President is usually sent by message to the House in which it originated and that House informs the other, although such action is not necessary to the validity of the act. The action is also noted in the Congressional Record.

A bill becomes law on the date of approval (or passage over the President's veto), unless it expressly provides a different effective date.

VETO MESSAGE

By the terms of the Constitutional provision, if the President does not approve the bill "he shall return it, with his objections to that House in which it shall have originated, who shall enter the objections at large on their Journal, and proceed to reconsider it." It is the usual but not invariable rule that a bill returned with the President's objections shall be voted on at once and when laid before the House the question on the passage is considered as pending. A vetoed bill is always privileged, and a motion to take it from the table is in order at any time.

The Member in charge moves the previous question which is put by the Speaker, as follows: "The question is, Will the House on reconsideration agree to pass the bill, the objections of the President to the contrary notwithstanding?" The Clerk calls the roll and those in favor of passing the bill answer "Aye," and those opposed "No." If fewer than two-thirds of the Members present (constituting a quorum) vote in the affirmative the bill is killed, and a message is usually sent to the Senate advising that body of the decision that the bill shall not pass. If, however, two-thirds vote in the affirmative the bill is sent with the President's objections to the Senate together with a message advising it of the action in the House.

A similar procedure is had in the Senate where again a two-thirds affirmative vote is necessary to pass the bill over the President's objections. If then passed by the Senate the measure becomes the law of the land notwithstanding the objections of the President, and it is ready for publication as a binding statute. (See Fig. 12, p. 63.)

XVII. PUBLICATION

One of the important steps in the enactment of a valid law is the requirement that it shall be made known to the people who are to be bound by it. Obviously, there would be no justice if the state were to hold its people responsible for their conduct before it made known to them the unlawfulness of such behavior. That idea is implicit in the Constitutional prohibition against enacting *ex post facto* laws. In practice, our laws are published immediately upon their enactment so that they may be known to the people.

If the President approves a bill, or allows it to become law without his signature, the original enrolled bill is sent from the White House to the Administrator of General Services for publication. If a bill is passed by both Houses over the objections of the President the body which last overrides the veto likewise transmits it. There it is assigned a public law number. The public law numbers run in sequence starting anew at the beginning of each Congress, and since 1957 are prefixed for ready identification by the number of the Congress—e.g., the first public law of the 92d Congress is designated Public Law 92–1 and subsequent laws of this Congress will also contain the same prefix designator.

"SLIP LAWS"

The first official publication of the statute is in the form generally known as the "slip law." (See Fig. 10, p. 61.) It is an unbound pamphlet and each law is published separately. Since the beginning of the 82d Congress, in 1951, the slip laws have been printed by photoelectric offset process from the original enrolled bill. This process insures accuracy and saves both time and expense in preparing the copy. A heading indicates the public law number and bill number, and the date of approval. If the statute has been passed over the veto of the President, or has become law without his signature because he did not return it with his objections, an appropriate statement is inserted in lieu of the usual notation of approval. ∕

The Office of the Federal Register, General Services Administration, which prepares the slip laws, provides marginal editorial notes giving the citations to laws mentioned in the text and other explanatory details. It also includes an informative guide to the legislative history of the law consisting of the committee report number, the name of the committee in each House, as well as the date of consideration in each House, with a reference to the Congressional Record pages.

Copies of the slip laws are delivered to the document rooms of both Houses where they become available to officials and the public immediately. They may also be obtained by annual subscription or individual purchase from the Superintendent of Documents at the Government Printing Office.

STATUTES AT LARGE

For the purpose of providing a permanent collection of the laws of each session of the Congress the bound volumes, which are called the Statutes at Large, are prepared by the General Services Administration. When the latest volume containing the laws of the second session of the 91st Congress becomes available it will be No. 84 in the series. Each volume contains a complete index and a table of contents and, since 1956, a table of earlier laws affected, as well as a most useful table showing the legislative history of each law in the volume. There are also extensive marginal notes referring to laws in earlier volumes and earlier and later matters in the same volume.

Under the provisions of a statute originally enacted in 1895 these volumes are legal evidence of the laws contained in them and will be accepted as proof of those laws in any court in the United States.

The Statutes at Large are simply a chronological arrangement of the laws exactly as they have been enacted. There is no attempt to arrange the laws according to their subject matter or to show the present status of an earlier law that has been amended on one or more occasions. That is the function of a code of laws.

UNITED STATES CODE

The United States Code contains a consolidation and codification of the general and permanent laws of the United States arranged according to subject matter under fifty title headings, in alphabetical order to a large degree. It sets out the current status of the laws, as amended, without repeating all the language of the amendatory acts except where necessary for that purpose and is declared to be prima facie evidence of those laws. Its purpose is to present the laws in a concise and usable form without requiring recourse to the many volumes of the Statutes at Large containing the individual amendments.

The code is prepared by the House of Representatives Committee on the Judiciary under the supervision of its law revision counsel. New editions are published every six years and cumulative supplements are published after the conclusion of each regular session of the Congress.

Nineteen of the fifty titles have been revised and enacted as law, and one has been eliminated by consolidation with another. Those titles are now legal evidence of the law and the courts will receive them as proof of those laws. It is hoped that eventually all the titles will be revised and enacted into law and that thereafter they will be kept up to date by direct amendment.

DISTRICT OF COLUMBIA CODE

The laws for the seat of the government—the District of Columbia—are also enacted by the Congress and are similarly set out in the Statutes at Large and consolidated in the District of Columbia Code in 49 titles. Thirteen of the titles—relating to the judiciary and judicial procedure, criminal procedure, decedents' estates and fiduciary relations, and commercial instruments and transactions—have been revised and enacted as law. This code is also prepared by the House Committee on the Judiciary in much the same fashion as the United States Code.

APPENDIX

SELECT LIST OF GOVERNMENT PUBLICATIONS

*Constitution of the United States of America, Analysis and Interpretation, with
annotations of cases decided by the Supreme Court of the United States to
June 22, 1964; prepared by the Legislative Reference Service, Library of
Congress, Norman J. Small, editor, and Lester S. Jayson, supervising editor.
[A new edition is now in the process of preparation.]

*House Rules and Manual:
Constitution, Jefferson's Manual and Rules of the House of Representatives
of the United States, prepared by Lewis. Deschler, Parliamentarian. New
editions are published each Congress.

*Senate Manual:
Containing the standing rules, orders, laws, and resolutions affecting the busi-
ness of the United States Senate; Jefferson's Manual, Declaration of Inde-
pendence, Articles of Confederation, Constitution of the United States, etc.
Prepared under the direction of the Senate Committee on Rules and
Administration. New editions are published each Congress.

*Hinds' Precedents of the House of Representatives:
Including references to provisions of the Constitution, laws, and decisions
of the Senate, by Asher C. Hinds.
Vols. 1–5 (1907).
Vols. 6–8 (1935), as compiled by Clarence Cannon, are supplementary
to vols. 1–5 and cover the 28-year period from 1907 to 1935, revised
up to and including the 73d Congress.
Vols. 9–11 (1941) are index-digest to vols. 1–5.

*Cannon's Procedure in the House of Representatives:
By Clarence Cannon, A.M., LL.B., LL.D., Member of Congress, sometime
Parliamentarian of the House, Speaker pro tempore, Chairman of the
Committee of the Whole, Chairman of Committee on Appropriations, etc.
New editions are published from time to time.

*Senate Procedure:
By Charles L. Watkins, Parliamentarian, and Floyd M. Riddick, Assistant
Parliamentarian, of the Senate (1964).

Calendars of the House of Representatives and History of Legislation:
Published each day the House is in session; prepared under the direction of
the Clerk of the House of Representatives.

Committee Calendars:
Published periodically by most of the standing committees of the House of
Representatives and Senate, containing the history of bills and resolutions
referred to the particular committee.

*Digest of Public General Bills and Selected Resolutions:
A brief synopsis of public bills and resolutions, and changes made therein
during the legislative process; prepared by American Law Division, Legislative Reference Service, Library of Congress, and published during each
session in 5 cumulative issues with biweekly supplementation as needed.

*Congressional Record:
Proceedings and debates of the House and Senate, published daily, and bound
with an index and history of bills and resolutions at the conclusion of each
session of the Congress.†

Journal of the House of Representatives:
Official record of the proceedings of the House, published at the conclusion
of each session under the direction of the Clerk of the House.

Journal of the United States Senate:
Official record of the proceedings of the Senate, published at the conclusion
of each session under the direction of the Secretary of the Senate.

*United States Statutes at Large:
Containing the laws and concurrent resolutions enacted, and reorganization
plans and proclamations promulgated during each session of the Congress,
published annually under the direction of the Administrator of General
Services by the Office of the Federal Register, National Archives and
Records Service, General Services Administration, Washington, D.C.
20408.
Supplemental volume: Tables of Laws Affected, Volumes 70–83 (1956–69),
containing tables of prior laws amended, repealed, or patently affected by
provisions of public laws enacted during that period.
Additional parts, containing treaties and international agreements other than

---

treaties, published annually under the direction of the Secretary of State until 1950.

*United States Treaties and Other International Agreements:
Compiled and published annually since 1950 under the direction of the Secretary of State.

*Treaties and Other International Agreements of the United States of America, 1776–1949:
A consolidation of the text of treaties and other international agreements prior to 1950, compiled under the direction of Charles I. Bevans, Assistant Legal Adviser, Department of State (in preparation).

*United States Code:
The general and permanent laws of the United States in force on the day preceding the commencement of the session following the last session the legislation of which is included; arranged in 50 titles; prepared under the direction and supervision of the House of Representatives, Committee on the Judiciary. New editions are published every 6 years and cumulative supplements are published annually.

*District of Columbia Code:
The general and permanent laws relating to and in force in the District of Columbia (except such laws as are of application to the District of Columbia by reason of being general and permanent laws of the United States) in force on the day preceding the commencement of the session following the last session the legislation of which is included; arranged in 49 titles; prepared under the direction and supervision of the House of Representatives, Committee on the Judiciary. New editions are published every 6 years and cumulative supplements are published annually.

*Federal Register:
Presidential Proclamations, Executive Orders, and Federal agency orders, regulations, and notices, and general documents of public applicability and legal effect, published daily. The regulations therein amend the Code of Federal Regulations. Published by the Office of the Federal Register, National Archives and Records Service, General Services Administration, Washington, D.C. 20408.

*Code of Federal Regulations:
Cumulates in bound volumes the general and permanent rules and regulations of Federal agencies published in the Federal Register, including Presidential documents. Revised as of January 1 of each year. Published by the Office of the Federal Register, National Archives and Records Service, General Services Administration, Washington, D.C. 20408.

*Weekly Compilation of Presidential Documents:
Containing statements, messages, and other Presidential materials released by the White House up to 5:00 p.m. Friday of each week, published every Monday by the Office of the Federal Register, National Archives and Records Service, General Services Administration, Washington, D.C. 20408.

*Public papers of the Presidents of the United States:
Containing public messages and statements, verbatim transcript of the President's News Conference and other selected papers released by the White House each year, since 1945, compiled by the Office of the Federal Register, National Archives and Records Service, General Services Administration, Washington, D.C. 20408.

*Enactment of a Law, by Floyd M. Riddick, Parliamentarian of the Senate, under the direction of Francis R. Valeo, Secretary of the Senate: Senate Document No. 35, 90th Congress, 1st session, 1967.

History of the United States House of Representatives, by Dr. George B. Calloway, Senior Specialist in American Government, Legislative Reference Service, Library of Congress: House Document No. 250, 89th Congress, 1st Session, 1965. [New edition in preparation.]

Veto Power of the President, by Charles J. Zinn: Committee Print of the House Committee on the Judiciary, 82d Congress, 1st Session, 1951.

Extent of the Control of the Executive by the Congress of the United States, by Dr. Charles J. Zinn: Committee Print of the House Committee on Government Operations, 87th Congress, 2d Session, 1962.

[Figure 1—Introduced Print*]

90TH CONGRESS
1ST SESSION

H. R. 8629

IN THE HOUSE OF REPRESENTATIVES

APRIL 17, 1967

Mr. CELLER introduced the following bill; which was referred to the Committee on the Judiciary

A BILL

To amend the Act of July 4, 1966 (Public Law 89–491).

1   *Be it enacted by the Senate and House of Representa-*

2 *tives of the United States of America in Congress assembled,*

3 That the Act of July 4, 1966 (80 Stat. 259), is hereby

4 amended as follows:

5   1. By adding in section 2 (b) (3) the words "the

6 Secretary of Commerce," after the words, "the Secretary

7 of Defense,".

8   2. By deleting in section 3 (d) the words "two years

9 after the date of the enactment of this Act," and inserting

10 in lieu thereof "July 4, 1969.".

I

1   3. By deleting section 7 (a) and inserting in lieu thereof

2 the following:

3   "SEC. 7. (a) There are authorized to be appropriated

4 without fiscal year limitation such sums as may be necessary

5 for the expenses of the Commission."

---

*All illustrations in this document are reduced in size.

[Figure 2—Reported Print]

Union Calendar No. 182

90TH CONGRESS
1ST SESSION

H. R. 8629

[Report No. 509]

IN THE HOUSE OF REPRESENTATIVES

APRIL 17, 1967

Mr. CELLER introduced the following bill; which was referred to the Committee on the Judiciary

JULY 25, 1967

Reported with an amendment, committed to the Committee of the Whole House on the State of the Union, and ordered to be printed

[Omit the part struck through and insert the part printed in italic]

A BILL

To amend the Act of July 4, 1966 (Public Law 89–491).

1   *Be it enacted by the Senate and House of Representa-*

2 *tives of the United States of America in Congress assembled,*

3 *That the Act of July 4, 1966 (80 Stat. 259), is hereby*

4 *amended as follows:*

5   1. By adding in section 2 (b) (3) the words "the

6 Secretary of Commerce," after the words, "the Secretary

7 of Defense,".

8   2. By deleting in section 3 (d) the words "two years

9 after the date of the enactment of this Act," and inserting

10 in lieu thereof "July 4, 1969.".

1   3. By deleting section 7 (a) and inserting in lieu thereof

2 the following:

3   ~~"SEC. 7. (a) There are authorized to be appropriated~~

4 ~~without fiscal year limitation such sums as may be necessary~~

5 ~~for the expenses of the Commission."~~

6   *"SEC. 7. (a) There is authorized to be appropriated not*

7 *to exceed $450,000 for the period through fiscal year 1969."*

[Figure 3—House Committee Report*]

| 90TH CONGRESS
1st Session | HOUSE OF REPRESENTATIVES | REPORT
No. 509 |

AMERICAN REVOLUTION BICENTENNIAL COMMISSION

JULY 25, 1967.—Committed to the Committee of the Whole House on the State of the Union and ordered to be printed

Mr. ROGERS of Colorado, from the Committee on the Judiciary, submitted the following

REPORT

[To accompany H.R. 8629]

The Committee on the Judiciary, to whom was referred the bill (H.R. 8629) to amend the act of July 4, 1966 (Public Law 89–491), having considered the same, report favorably thereon with an amendment and recommend that the bill do pass.

The amendment is as follows:

On page 2, strike lines 3 through 5 and insert in lieu thereof the following:

"SEC. 7. (a) There is authorized to be appropriated not to exceed $450,000 for the period through fiscal year 1969."

EXPLANATION OF AMENDMENT

The purpose of the amendment is to limit the authorization for appropriations to $450,000 during the period through fiscal year 1969.

PURPOSE OF THE BILL

The purpose of H.R. 8629 is threefold: First, it would add the Secretary of Commerce as an ex officio member of the Commission; second, it would extend the date on which the Commission shall report to the President by 1 year—from July 4, 1968, to July 4, 1969; third, it would authorize the appropriation of public funds to finance the work of the Commission.

STATEMENT

Public Law 89–491, approved July 4, 1966, established the American Revolution Bicentennial Commission to commemorate the American

[Rule XIII of the Rules of the House now require the report to contain an estimate of the costs involved in the reported bill except as to certain committees]

*First page only.

[Figure 4—Engrossed Bill*]

90TH CONGRESS
1ST SESSION

H. R. 8629

AN ACT

To amend the Act of July 4, 1966 (Public Law 89–491).

1   *Be it enacted by the Senate and House of Representa-*
2   *tives of the United States of America in Congress assembled,*
3   That the Act of July 4, 1966 (80 Stat. 259), is hereby
4   amended as follows:

5   1. By adding in section 2 (b) (3) the words "the
6   Secretary of Commerce," after the words, "the Secretary
7   of Defense,".

8   2. By deleting in section 3 (d) the words "two years
9   after the date of the enactment of this Act," and inserting
10   in lieu thereof "July 4, 1969.".

11   3. By deleting section 7 (a) and inserting in lieu thereof
12   the following:

13   "SEC. 7. (a) There is authorized to be appropriated not
14   to exceed $450,000 for the period through fiscal year 1969."

Passed the House of Representatives August 7, 1967.

Attest: **W. PAT JENNINGS,**

Clerk.

---

*Printed on blue paper.

[Figure 5—Senate Referred ("Act") Print]

90TH CONGRESS
1ST SESSION

H. R. 8629

IN THE SENATE OF THE UNITED STATES

AUGUST 8, 1967

Read twice and referred to the Committee on the Judiciary

AN ACT

To amend the Act of July 4, 1966 (Public Law 89–491).

1   *Be it enacted by the Senate and House of Representa-*

2   *tives of the United States of America in Congress assembled,*

3   That the Act of July 4, 1966 (80 Stat. 259), is hereby

4   amended as follows:

5   1. By adding in section 2 (b) (3) the words "the

6   Secretary of Commerce," after the words, "the Secretary

7   of Defense,".

8   2. By deleting in section 3 (d) the words "two years

9   after the date of the enactment of this Act," and inserting

10   in lieu thereof "July 4, 1969.".

II

1   3. By deleting section 7 (a) and inserting in lieu thereof

2   the following:

3   "SEC. 7. (a) There is authorized to be appropriated not

4   to exceed $450,000 for the period through fiscal year 1969."

Passed the House of Representatives August 7, 1967.

Attest: W. PAT JENNINGS,

Clerk.

[Figure 6—Senate Reported Print]

Calendar No. 592

90TH CONGRESS
1ST SESSION

H. R. 8629

[Report No. 609]

IN THE SENATE OF THE UNITED STATES

AUGUST 8, 1967
Read twice and referred to the Committee on the Judiciary

OCTOBER 11 (legislative day, OCTOBER 10), 1967
Reported by Mr. DIRKSEN, with an amendment

[Insert the part printed in italic]

AN ACT

To amend the Act of July 4, 1966 (Public Law 89–491).

1   *Be it enacted by the Senate and House of Representa-*

2 *tives of the United States of America in Congress assembled,*

3 That the Act of July 4, 1966 (80 Stat. 259), is hereby

4 amended as follows:

5   1. By adding in section 2(b)(3) the words "the

6 Secretary of Commerce," after the words, "the Secretary

7 of Defense,".

8   2. By deleting in section 3(d) the words "two years

9 after the date of the enactment of this Act," and inserting

10 in lieu thereof "July 4, 1969.".

II

1   3. By deleting section 7(a) and inserting in lieu thereof

2 the following:

3   "Sec. 7. (a) There is authorized to be appropriated not

4   to exceed $450,000 for the period through fiscal year 1969."

5   *4. By deleting in section 2(b)(1) the word "Four"*

6   *and inserting in lieu thereof the word "Six"; and by deleting*

7   *in section 2(b)(2) the word "Four" and inserting in lieu*

8   *thereof the word "Six".*

Passed the House of Representatives August 7, 1967.

Attest: W. PAT JENNINGS,

Clerk.

[Figure 7—Senate Committee Report*]

Calendar No. 592

90TH CONGRESS ⎱   SENATE   ⎰ REPORT
1st Session ⎰   ⎱ No. 609

EXTENDING THE AMERICAN REVOLUTION BICENTEN-NIAL COMMISSION

OCTOBER 11 (legislative day, OCTOBER 10), 1967.—Ordered to be printed

Mr. DIRKSEN, from the Committee on the Judiciary, submitted the following

REPORT

[To accompany H.R. 8629]

The Committee on the Judiciary, to which was referred the bill (H.R. 8629) to amend the act of July 4, 1966 (Public Law 89–491), having considered the same, reports favorably thereon with an amendment and recommends that the bill as amended do pass.

AMENDMENT

On page 2, after line 4, insert the following:

4. By deleting in section 2(b)(1) the word "Four" and inserting in lieu thereof the word "Six"; and by deleting in section 2(b)(2) the word "Four" and inserting in lieu thereof the word "Six".

PURPOSE OF AMENDMENT

The purpose of the amendment is to increase the Senate membership on the Commission from four members to six members, and to increase the House of Representatives membership on the Commission from four members to six members.

PURPOSE

The purpose of the proposed legislation, as amended, is fourfold: First, it would add the Secretary of Commerce as an exofficio member of the Commission; second, it would extend the date on which the

[With certain exceptions, the Legislative Reorganization Act of 1970, requires the report to contain an estimate of the costs involved in the bill]

*First page only.

[Figure 8—Conference Committee Report]

90TH CONGRESS } HOUSE OF REPRESENTATIVES { REPORT
1st Session   No. 987

AMERICAN REVOLUTION BICENTENNIAL COMMISSION

NOVEMBER 28, 1967.—Ordered to be printed

Mr. ROGERS of Colorado, from the committee of conference, submitted the following

CONFERENCE REPORT

[To accompany H.R. 8629]

The committee of conference on the disagreeing votes of the two Houses on the amendment of the Senate to the bill (H.R. 8629) to amend the act of July 4, 1966 (Public Law 89–491), having met, after full and free conference, have agreed to recommend and do recommend to their respective Houses as follows:

That the Senate recede from its amendment.

BYRON G. ROGERS,
BASIL WHITENER,
ANDREW JACOBS, Jr.,
RICHARD H. POFF,
CHARLES E. WIGGINS,
Managers on the Part of the House.

EVERETT M. DIRKSEN,
JOHN L. McCLELLAN,
Managers on the Part of the Senate.

STATEMENT OF THE MANAGERS ON THE PART OF THE HOUSE

The managers on the part of the House at the conference on the disagreeing votes of the two Houses on the amendment of the Senate to the bill (H.R. 8629) to amend the act of July 4, 1966 (Public Law 89-491), submit the following statement in explanation of the effect of the action agreed upon by the conferees and recommended in the accompanying conference report:

The Senate passed H.R. 8629 with an amendment. The House disagreed to the amendment and requested a conference; the Senate then agreed to the conference.

H.R. 8629 as it passed the House added the Secretary of Commerce as an ex officio member of the American Revolution Bicentennial Commission, extended the time within which the Commission shall report to the President to July 4, 1969, and authorized the appropriation of funds to finance the work of the Commission.

These provisions are not in disagreement.

The Senate amendment added a provision which increased from four members to six members each the House and Senate membership on the Commission.

The conference report recommends that the Senate recede from its amendment.

BYRON G. ROGERS,
BASIL WHITENER,
ANDREW JACOBS, Jr.,
RICHARD H. POFF,
CHARLES E. WIGGINS,

Managers on the Part of the House.

[Legislative Reorganization Act of 1970, and the Rules of the House now require the statement to be prepared jointly by conferees on the part of the House and conferees on the part of the Senate]

FORMAT OF JOINT EXPLANATORY STATEMENT OF THE COMMITTEE OF CONFERENCE

The managers on the part of the House and the Senate at the conference on the disagreeing votes of the two Houses on the amendment(s) of the House (Senate) to the bill (joint resolution) [number] ...... (title) ...... submit the following joint statement to the House and the Senate in explanation of the effect of the action agreed upon by the managers and recommended in the accompanying conference report:

――― ―――,		――― ―――,
――― ―――,		――― ―――,
――― ―――,		――― ―――,
Managers on the part of the House.		*Managers on the part of the Senate.*

[Figure 9—Enrolled Bill Signed by President]

H. R. 8629   PUBLIC LAW 90-187

Ninetieth Congress of the United States of America

AT THE FIRST SESSION

Begun and held at the City of Washington on Tuesday, the tenth day of January, one thousand nine hundred and sixty-seven

An Act

To amend the Act of July 4, 1966 (Public Law 89-491).

Be it enacted by the Senate and House of Representatives of the United States of America in Congress assembled, That the Act of July 4, 1966 (80 Stat. 259), is hereby amended as follows:

1. By adding in section 2(b)(3) the words "the Secretary of Commerce," after the words, "the Secretary of Defense,"..

2. By deleting in section 3(d) the words "two years after the date of the enactment of this Act," and inserting in lieu thereof "July 4, 1969.".

3. By deleting section 7(a) and inserting in lieu thereof the following:

"SEC. 7. (a) There is authorized to be appropriated not to exceed $450,000 for the period through fiscal year 1969."

Speaker of the House of Representatives.

Vice President of the United States and President of the Senate.

APPROVED

DEC 12 1967

DEC 13 1967
RECEIVED

THE WHITE HOUSE
NOV 1967
RECEIVED

[Figure 10—Slip law]

Public Law 90-187
90th Congress, H. R. 8629
December 12, 1967

An Act

81 STAT. 567

To amend the Act of July 4, 1966 (Public Law 89-491).

Be it enacted by the Senate and House of Representatives of the United States of America in Congress assembled, That the Act of July 4, 1966 (80 Stat. 259), is hereby amended as follows: **American Revolution Bicentennial Commission.**

1. By adding in section 2(b)(3) the words "the Secretary of Commerce," after the words, "the Secretary of Defense,".

2. By deleting in section 3(d) the words "two years after the date of the enactment of this Act," and inserting in lieu thereof "July 4, 1969.".

3. By deleting section 7(a) and inserting in lieu thereof the following:

"SEC. 7. (a) There is authorized to be appropriated not to exceed **Appropriation.** $450,000 for the period through fiscal year 1969."

Approved December 12, 1967.

LEGISLATIVE HISTORY:

HOUSE REPORTS: No. 509 (Comm. on the Judiciary) and No. 987 (Comm. of
            Conference).
SENATE REPORT No. 609 (Comm. on the Judiciary).
CONGRESSIONAL RECORD, Vol. 113 (1967):
    Aug. 7: Considered and passed House.
    Oct. 12: Considered and passed Senate, amended.
    Nov. 28: Senate agreed to conference report.
    Nov. 29: House agreed to conference report.

[Figure 11—Copy of Act which became a law without approval of the President]

Public Law 91-295
91st Congress, H. R. 5554
June 30, 1970

An Act

To provide a special milk program for children.

84 STAT. 336

Be it enacted by the Senate and House of Representatives of the United States of America in Congress assembled, That section 3 of the Child Nutrition Act of 1966 is amended to read as follows:

"SEC. 3. There is hereby authorized to be appropriated for the fiscal year ending June 30, 1970, and for each succeeding fiscal year, not to exceed $120,000,000, to enable the Secretary of Agriculture, under such rules and regulations as he may deem in the public interest, to encourage consumption of fluid milk by children in the United States in (1) nonprofit schools of high school grade and under, and (2) nonprofit nursery schools, child-care centers, settlement houses, summer camps, and similar nonprofit institutions devoted to the care and training of children. For the purposes of this section 'United States' means the fifty States, Guam, and the District of Columbia. The Secretary shall administer the special milk program provided for by this section to the maximum extent practicable in the same manner as he administered the special milk program provided for by Public Law 89-642, as amended, during the fiscal year ending June 30, 1969."

Child Nutrition
Act of 1966,
amendment.
80 Stat. 885.
42 USC 1772.

"United States."

[Note by the Office of the Federal Register.—The foregoing Act, having been presented to the President of the United States on Wednesday, June 17, 1970, for his approval and not having been returned by him to the House of Congress in which it originated within the time prescribed by the Constitution of the United States, has become a law without his approval on June 30, 1970.]

LEGISLATIVE HISTORY:

HOUSE REPORT No. 91-110 (Comm. on Agriculture).
SENATE REPORT No. 91-842 (Comm. on Agriculture and Forestry).
CONGRESSIONAL RECORD:
    Vol. 115 (1969): May 6, considered and passed House.
    Vol. 116 (1970): May 11, considered and passed Senate, amended.
                     June 16, House concurred in Senate amendment.

[Figure 12—Endorsements on Act which became a law after Presidential veto]

Public Law 91–296
91st Congress, H.R. 11102
June 30, 1970

JOHN W. MCCORMACK

Speaker of the House of Representatives.

JAMES B. ALLEN
Acting President of the Senate pro tempore.

IN THE HOUSE OF REPRESENTATIVES, U.S.,
June 25, 1970.

The House of Representatives having proceeded to reconsider the bill (H. R. 11102) entitled "An Act to amend the Public Health Service Act to revise, extend, and improve the program established by title VI of such Act, and for other purposes", returned by the President of the United States with his objections, to the House of Representatives, in which it originated, it was

Resolved, That the said bill pass, two-thirds of the House of Representatives agreeing to pass the same.

Attest:

W. PAT JENNINGS
Clerk.

I certify that this Act originated in the House of Representatives.

W. PAT JENNINGS
Clerk.

IN THE SENATE OF THE UNITED STATES,
June 30, 1970.

The Senate having proceeded to reconsider the bill (H. R. 11102) entitled "An Act to amend the Public Health Service Act to revise, extend, and improve the program established by title VI of such Act, and for other purposes", returned by the President of the United States with his objections, to the House of Representatives, in which it originated, it was

Resolved, That the said bill pass, two-thirds of the Senators present having voted in the affirmative.

Attest:

FRANCIS R. VALEO
Secretary.

○

How To Find U.S. Statutes and U.S. Code Citations

Prepared by Mrs. Dorothy Muse

"One of the important functions of the Committee on the Judiciary of the House of Representatives is to prepare the United States Code, setting forth the present status of the general and permanent laws of the United States arranged in fifty titles according to subject matter. The code is an essential tool of anyone who is interested in knowing the status of the laws enacted by the Congress. It is based upon the acts of Congress that are set forth in the Revised Statutes of 1873 and the annual volumes of the Statutes at Large, which are published by the U. S. Statutes Branch, Office of the Federal Register, National Archives and Records Service, General Services Administration. That Office has made the slip laws and the Statutes at Large increasingly useful by a number of helpful innovations during the past few years.

This pamphlet ... was originated and prepared by Mrs. Dorothy Muse, under the direction of Mr. Ernest Galdi, of the U. S. Statutes Branch, as a guide to enable interested persons in locating the laws in the United States Statutes at Large and in the United States Code. A brief description on how to use this pamphlet is set out in the introduction.

The Committee on the Judiciary is publishing this pamphlet as an additional service to the Congress, and the bench and bar of the United States as part of its program of assistance in statutory research." From the Forward by Hon. Emanuel Celler, Chairman, Committee on the Judiciary, House of Representatives.

INTRODUCTION

This "How To Find" guide is designed to enable the user to obtain—quickly and easily—an up-to-date and accurate citation to the United States Statutes at Large and the United States Code.

In using the chart, the reader should read the items from left to right across the two pages.

The *first* column contains the typical references which require further citing, which are (1) Revised Statutes section, (2) date of law, (3) name of law, (4) number of law, (5) Statutes citation, and (6) Code citation; the *second, third,* and *fourth* columns point to the official published volumes in which the citations may be found and suggest logical sequences to follow in making the search; *column five* suggests additional finding aids, some of which especially are useful for citing current legislation; and the *last* column shows some examples of the citations resulting from following the steps in the chart.

The careful following of the steps set forth carries the assurance that each search will be complete and that all appropriate points will be covered.

Publications referred to in abbreviated form are identified and described in a convenient list on the last page.

SOURCE: Reprinted from U. S. House of Representatives. Committee on the Judiciary. *How To Find U. S. Statutes And U. S. Code Citations.* Committee Print 71–1. (Washington: 1971), pp. iv and 1–8.

HOW TO FIND CITATIONS TO THE UNITED
THE UNITED

IF YOU HAVE this reference—	AND YOU USE THESE basic finding aids—	
	U.S. STATUTES AT LARGE (new volume added each year)	U.S. CODE [1] (new edition each 6 years)
1. Revised Statutes Section.................. [e.g., Rev. Stat. 56]	[Revised Statutes, 1873, were published as pt. 1, vol. 18, U.S. Statutes at Large; 2d edition published in 1878.]	Use U.S.C. tables volume to find U.S.C. section; verify text; then—
2. Date of Law: [2] (a) For any year *up to* and *through* year of last edition of U.S.C. [e.g., June 22, 1942];	Use Stat. volume for that year to check the List of Public Laws; get law number and verify page number from List; then—	Use U.S.C. tables volume to find U.S.C. section; verify text; then—
(b) For any year *after* year of last edition of U.S.C. and *through* year of latest Supplement;	Use Stat. volume for that year to check the List of Public Laws; get law number and verify page number from List; then—	----------------------------
(c) For current year..................	----------------------------	----------------------------
3. Name of Law: (a) For any year *up to* and *through* year of last edition of U.S.C. [e.g., Consumer Credit Protection Act];	----------------------------	Use U.S.C. popular names index (preceding general index) to obtain Stat. and U.S.C. citations; verify both; then—
(b) For any year *after* year of last edition of U.S.C. and *through year* of latest Supplement;	----------------------------	----------------------------
(c) For current year..................	----------------------------	----------------------------

See footnotes at end of table, p. 128.

STATES STATUTES AT LARGE AND TO STATES CODE

PLUS latest published— U.S. CODE SUPPLEMENT (*all* changes since last edition)	AND/OR THESE additional finding aids— (See "REFERENCES" at end of pamphlet)	YOU SHOULD GET this citation—
Check latest U.S.C. Supplement for recent changes; verify text.	Check Table 3 in latest U.S.C. Cong. & Adm. News for changes during current period; if Code section is included, verify text in same publication or in slip law.	Rev. Stat. 56. 2 U.S.C. 64.
Check latest U.S.C. Supplement for recent changes; verify text.	Check Table 3 in latest U.S.C. Cong. & Adm. News for changes during current period; if Code section is included, verify text in same publication or in slip law.	56 Stat. 377. 36 U.S.C. 171-178.
Use tables volume in latest U.S.C. Supplement to find U.S.C. section; verify text.	Check Table 3 in latest U.S.C. Cong. & Adm. News for changes during current period; if Code section is included, verify text in same publication or in slip law.	
	Use slip law or U.S.C. Cong. & Adm. News *text* to get law number and Stat. citation and to verify subject matter; then use Table 2, U.S.C. Cong. & Adm. News to find U.S.C. classification.	
Check latest U.S.C. Supplement for recent changes; verify text.		
Use U.S.C. popular names index (preceding general index) to obtain Stat. and U.S.C. citation; verify both; then—	Check Table 3 in latest U.S.C. Cong. & Adm. News for changes during current period; verify any changes in same publication or in slip law. Other sources: Index of Popular Names in U.S. Statutes at Large *Laws Affected Tables, 1956-70;* Digest of U.S. Supreme Court Reports; Shepard's Federal Acts by Popular Names or Short Titles; U.S.C.A. Popular Name Table; FCA tables volume.	82 Stat. 146. 15 U.S.C. 1601 note.
	Use House Calendar *index* and *numerical list* to get bill number, then law number (if assigned); or U.S.C. Cong. & Adm. News *index* or Table 10; use slip law or U.S.C. Cong. & Adm. News *text* to get Stat. citation and to verify date and subject matter; then, with law number, use Table 2, U.S.C. Cong. & Adm. News to find U.S.C. classification.	

HOW TO FIND CITATIONS TO THE UNITED
THE UNITED

IF YOU HAVE this reference—	AND YOU USE THESE basic finding aids—	
	U.S. STATUTES AT LARGE (new volume added each year)	U.S. CODE (new edition each 6 years)
4. Number of Law:		
(a) For any year *up to* and *through* year of last edition of U.S.C. and the law—		
(1) *does not* have a numerical prefix [e.g,. Public Law 706];	[You will need additional in-information, such as the Congress, the year, or the Stat. volume—year 1946 used here; then] use the Stat. volume to check the List of Public Laws; get and verify page number from List; then—	Use U.S.C. tables volume to find U.S.C. section; verify text; then—
(2) *does* have a numerical prefix [e.g., Public Law 85–227];	Use Stat. volume for the Congress indicated by the numerical prefix; check the List of Public Laws; get and verify page number from List; then—	Use U.S.C. tables volume to find U.S.C. section; verify text; then—
(b) For any year *after* last edition of of U.S.C. and *through* year of latest Supplement [e.g., Public Law 92–75];	Use Stat. volume for the Congress indicated by the numerical prefix; check the List of Public Laws; get and verify page number from List; then—	------------------
(c) For current year----------	------------------	------------------
5. Stat. Citation: [3]		
(a) For any year *up to* and *through* year of last edition of U.S.C. [e.g., 72 Stat. 997];	Use Stat. volume to get date and law number; verify subject matter, then—	Use U.S.C. tables volume to find U.S.C. section; verify text; then—
(b) For any year *after* year of last edition of U.S.C. and *through* year of latest Supplement;	Use Stat. volume to get date and law number; verify subject matter; then—	------------------
(c) For current year----------	------------------	------------------

See footnotes at end of table, p. 124.

STATES STATUTES AT LARGE AND TO
STATES CODE—Continued

PLUS latest published— U.S. CODE SUPPLEMENT (*all* changes since last edition)	AND/OR THESE additional finding aids— (See "REFERENCES" at end of pamphlet)	YOU SHOULD GET this citation—
Check latest U.S.C. Supplement for recent changes; verify text.	Check Table 3 in latest U.S.C. Cong. & Adm. News for changes during current period; if Code section is included, verify text in same publication or in slip law.	60 Stat. 968. 25 U.S.C. 601–607.
Check latest U.S.C. Supplement for recent changes; verify text.	Check Table 3 in latest U.S.C. Cong. & Adm. News for changes during current period; if Code section is included, verify text in same publication or in slip law.	71 Stat. 512. 42 U.S.C. 418 and note.
Use tables volume in latest U.S.C. Supplement to find U.S.C. section; verify text.	Check Table 3 in latest U.S.C. Cong. & Adm. News for changes during current period, if Code section is included, verify text in same publication or in slip law.	85 Stat. 213. 46 U.S.C. 1451 *et seq.*
------------------------------	Use slip law or U.S.C. Cong. & Adm. News *text* to get Stat. citation and to verify date and subject matter; then, with law number, use Table 2, U.S.C. Cong. & Adm. News to find U.S.C. classification.	
Check latest U.S.C. Supplement for recent changes; verify text; then—	Check Table 3 in latest U.S.C. Cong. & Adm. News for changes during current period; if Code section is included, verify text in same publication or in slip law.	72 Stat. 997. 29 U.S.C. 301–309.
Use tables volume in latest U.S.C. Supplement to find U.S.C. section; verify text; then—	Check Table 3 in latest U.S.C. Cong. & Adm. News for changes during current period; if Code section is included, verify text in same publication or in slip law.	
------------------------------	Use slip law or U.S.C. Cong. & Adm. News *text* to verify subject matter, date, and law number. Table 2, U.S.C. Cong. & Adm. News may be used to find U.S.C. classification.	

HOW TO FIND CITATIONS TO THE UNITED STATES STATUTES AT LARGE AND TO THE UNITED STATES CODE—Continued

IF YOU HAVE this reference—	AND YOU USE THESE basic finding aids—		PLUS latest published— U.S. CODE SUPPLEMENT (all changes since last edition)	AND/OR THESE additional finding aids— (See "REFERENCES" at end of pamphlet)	YOU SHOULD GET this citation—
	U.S. STATUTES AT LARGE (new volume added each year)	U.S. CODE¹ (new edition each 6 years)			
6. U.S.C. Citation:					
(a) For any year *up to* and *through* year of last edition of U.S.C. [e.g., 7 U.S.C. 182];		Check section in U.S.C. to verify subject matter and determine appropriate Stat. citation; verify text against Stat. volume; then—	Check latest U.S.C. Supplement for recent changes; verify text; then—	Check Table 3 in latest U.S.C. Cong. & Adm. News for changes during current period; If Code section is included, verify text in same publication or in slip law.	42 Stat. 159. 7 U.S.C. 182.
(b) For any year *after* year of last edition of U.S.C. and *through* year of latest supplement;			Check section in latest U.S.C. Supplement to verify subject matter and determine appropriate Stat. citation; verify text against Stat. volume; then—	Check Table 3 in latest U.S.C. Cong. & Adm. News for changes during current period; If Code section is included, verify text in same publication or in slip law.	
(c) For current year				Check Table 3 in latest U.S.C. Cong. & Adm. News; If Code section is included, get page number on which text of law appears, get law number from that page (footnote should show Code citation there), then get specific Stat. citation from slip law and verify subject matter.	

¹ If U.S. Code is not available, use U.S.C.A. or F.C.A. and their supplements.

² You will need some knowledge of the subject matter If more than one law was signed on the same day:

³ You will need some knowledge of the subject matter If more than one law appears on the same page.

PRINCIPAL FINDING AIDS*

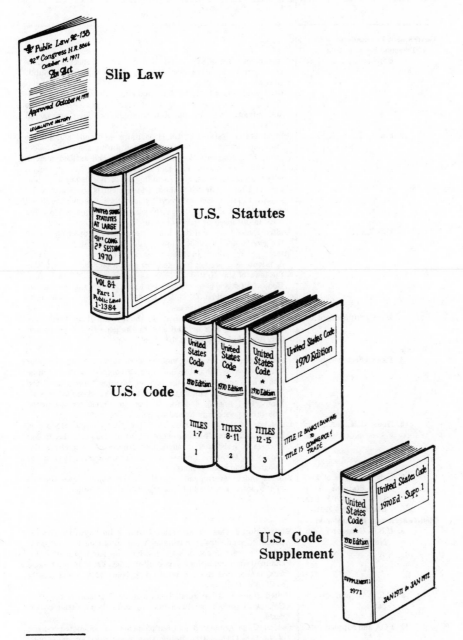

Slip Law

U.S. Statutes

U.S. Code

U.S. Code
Supplement

*For description see "REFERENCES" at end of pamphlet.

REFERENCES

Title	Description
Government Publications:	
A. Principal Finding Aids	
1. Slip law	A pamphlet print of each public and private law enacted by Congress, issued a few days after being signed by the President; public (but not private) slip laws carry Statutes page numbers, annotations, guide to legislative history, and citation to any related Presidential statement accompanying the signing; text of both public and private laws with annotations cumulated later and bound as Statutes volume.
2. Stat	United States Statutes at Large; contains all public and private laws and concurrent resolutions enacted during a session of Congress, plus reorganization plans, proposed and ratified amendments to the Constitution, and proclamations by the President, with finding aids at the end, including legislative history in tabular form and Laws Affected Tables; arrangement is chronological by approval date in each category; by law, these volumes are "legal evidence" (1 U.S.C. 112); only the general and permanent laws are codified (arranged by subject in titles) in the U.S.C.
3. U.S.C.	United States Code and its annual, cumulative Supplements; only the general and permanent laws of the United States are codified (arranged by subject in titles) in the U.S. Code; temporary, local, or private laws are not included; the code establishes "prima facie the laws of the United States" except "whenever titles of such Code shall have been enacted into positive law the text thereof shall be legal evidence" (1 U.S.C. 204(a)); to date, 19 titles have been enacted into positive law.
4. U.S.C. Supplement	Annual, cumulative supplements to the United States Code; contains all changes in or additions to the general and permanent laws since the last edition of the Code.
B. Others	
5. Laws Affected Tables	Published in each Statutes volume since 1956, showing the prior laws affected by the public laws in each volume; the first cumulation was a separate 223-page booklet covering the 5-year period 1956-60, the second cumulation was 463 pages and covered the 10-year period 1956-65, and the 15-year cumulation for the period 1956-70 has been computerized, available in early 1972.
6. House Calendar	Calendars of the U.S. House of Representatives and History of Legislation (1 publication)—very useful for following day-to-day progress of legislation through both Houses of Congress; index, usually on Mondays; final edition covers the session (1st) or the Congress (end of 2d session).
7. Index Analysis of Federal Statutes, 1789-1873; Index to Federal Statutes, 1874-1931.	Subject index covering all general and permanent laws through 46 Stat. (Mar. 4, 1931); useful for tracing early legislation.
Non-Government Publications:	
8. U.S.C. Cong. and Adm. News.	United States Code Congressional and Administrative News—published semimonthly during each session of Congress; monthly when Congress is not in session. Gives slip law information, including legislative history; has subject index, list of popular name acts, tables; material is currently supplemental to and annually codified in U.S.C.A.
9. U.S.C.A. and pocket parts.	United States Code Annotated—an annotated version of the U.S. Code with periodic supplements and annual, cumulative pocket parts.
10. FCA and supplements.	Federal Code Annotated and supplements—an annotated version of the U.S. Code with monthly, then cumulative, annual supplements.
11. Shepard's popular names.	Shepard's Federal Acts by Popular Names or Short Title—a pamphlet, supplemented in Shepard's Citations; reissued intermittently.

The United States Courts

By Joseph F. Spaniol, Jr., Esq., Administrative Office of the United States Courts

"The system of courts, comprising the judicial branch of the United States Government under the Constitution, is a logical arrangement designed to provide equal protection under the laws to individuals in all walks of life. Following the guidelines established by the Constitution and with careful regard and respect for the prerogatives of the States, the Congress has set up a number of district courts and courts of appeals in addition to the Supreme Court provided for by article III of the Constitution. The jurisdiction of the courts of original jurisdiction and the method of appeal from their decisions has been carefully devised and enacted into law by the Congress, and other so-called "legislative courts" with limited jurisdiction have also been established to round out the system.

Information regarding this judicial system has not been readily available to the interested layman in a form that is brief and understandable. This excellent handbook, by Joseph F. Spaniol, Jr., Esq., of the Administrative Office of the United States Courts, explains in layman's language and in a concise form, just what the judicial branch is, and describes the system of courts clearly and briefly. It was first published as House Document 180 of the 88th Congress and has been brought up to date by the author. I know of no other publication of its kind and I hope that it will receive widespread circulation among students and other persons who are interested in understanding this extremely important coordinate part of our scheme of Government." From the Foreward by Hon. Emanual Celler, Member of Congress and Chairman, Committee on the Judiciary.

THE UNITED STATES COURTS

The position of the United States courts in our governmental organization is not difficult to understand when that organization is seen as a whole. Our government is a dual one—Federal and State—and the Federal Government in turn has three separate branches—the Legislative, the Executive, and the Judicial. The United States courts constitute the Judicial Branch of the Federal Government. Thus, the powers of the United States courts are first of all limited as Federal powers—they can exercise only those powers granted by the United States Constitution to the Federal Government—and secondly are limited as judicial—they cannot exercise powers belonging to the Legislative or Executive Branches of the Government.

SOURCE: Reprinted from U.S. Congress. House of Representatives. *The United States Courts Their Jurisdiction and Work.* House Committee Print, 92d Congress, 1st Session. (Washington: 1971). pp. 1–15.

The Judicial Branch

The Constitution assures the equality and independence of the Judicial Branch from the Legislative and Executive Branches. Although Federal judges are appointed by the President of the United States with the advice and consent of the Senate, and although funds for the operation of the courts are appropriated by the Congress, the independence of the United States courts is provided for in three respects:

First, under the Constitution these courts can be called upon to exercise only judicial powers and to perform only judicial work. Judicial power and judicial work involve essentially the application and interpretation of the law in the decision of real differences, that is, in the language of the Constitution, the decision of "Cases" and "Controversies." The courts cannot be called upon to make laws— the function of the Legislative Department—nor to enforce and execute laws—the function of the Executive Department.

Secondly, Federal judges "hold their Offices during good Behavior", that is, as long as they desire to be judges and perform their work. They can be removed from office against their will only by impeachment.

Third, the Constitution provides that the "Compensation" of Federal judges "shall not be diminished during their continuance in office." Neither the President nor the Congress can reduce the salary of a Federal judge.

These three provisions—for judicial work only, for holding office during good behavior, and for undiminished compensation—are designed to assure judges of independence from outside influence so that their decisions may be completely impartial.

State and United States Court Systems

Throughout the United States there are two sets of judicial systems. One set is that of the State and local courts established in each State under the authority of the State government. The other is that of the United States courts set up under the authority of the Constitution by the Congress of the United States.

The State courts have general, unlimited power to decide almost every type of case, subject only to the limitations of State law. They are located in every town and county and are the tribunals with which citizens most often have contact. The great bulk of legal business concerning divorce and the probate of estates and all other matters except those assigned to the United States courts, is handled by these State courts.

The United States courts, on the other hand, have power to decide only those cases in which the Constitution gives them authority. They are located principally in the larger cities. The controversies in only a few carefully selected types of cases set forth in the Constitution can be heard in the United States courts.

Cases Which the United States Courts Can Decide

The controversies which can be decided in the United States courts are set forth in section 2 of Article III of the United States Constitution. These are first of all "Controversies to which the United States shall be a party," that is, cases in which the United States Government itself or one of its officers is either suing someone else or is being sued by another party. Obviously it would be inappropriate that the United States Government depend upon the State governments for the courts in which to decide controversies to which it is a party.

Secondly, the United States courts have power to decide cases where State courts are inappropriate or might be suspected of partiality. Thus, Federal judicial power extends "to Controversies between two or more States; between a State and Citizens of another State; between Citizens of different States; between Citizens of the same State claiming Lands under Grants of different States, * * *." If the State of Missouri sues the State of Illinois for pollution of the Mississippi River, the courts of either Missouri or Illinois would be inappropriate and perhaps not impartial forums. These suits may be decided in the United States courts. At various times State feeling in our country has run high, and it has seemed better to avoid any suspicion of favoritism by vesting power to decide these controversies in the United States courts.

State courts are also inappropriate in "Cases affecting Ambassadors, other public Ministers and Consuls" and in cases "between a State, or the Citizens thereof, and foreign States, Citizens, or Subjects." The United States Government has responsibility for our relations with other nations, and cases involving their representatives or their citizens may affect our foreign relations so that such cases should be decided in the United States courts.

And, thirdly the Constitution provides that the judicial power extends "to all Cases, in Law and Equity, arising under this Constitution, the Laws of the United States, and Treaties made, or which shall be made, under their Authority" and "to all Cases of admiralty and maritime jurisdiction." Under these provisions the United States courts decide cases involving the Constitution, laws enacted by Congress, treaties, or laws relating to navigable waters.

The Constitution declares what cases may be decided in the United States courts. The Congress can and has determined that some of these cases may also be tried in State courts and that others may be tried only in the United States courts. Thus Congress has provided that, with some exceptions, cases arising under the Constitution or laws of the United States or between citizens of different States may be tried in the United States courts only if the amount involved exceeds $10,000 and even then may be tried in either the State or the United States courts. The Congress has also provided that maritime cases and suits against consuls can be tried only in the United States courts. When a State court decides a case involving Federal law, it in a sense acts as a United States court, and its decision on Federal law may be reviewed by the United States Supreme Court.

In any event this discussion should make it clear that the United States courts cannot decide every case which arises, but only those which the Constitution and the laws enacted by the Congress allot to them. And as you may suspect from the length of this discussion, whether a case is one which may be decided by the United States courts is an extremely technical and complicated matter which lawyers and judges frequently spend a great deal of time resolving.

THE UNITED STATES COURT SYSTEM

The United States court system to which decision of the types of cases just discussed has been entrusted has varied a great deal throughout the history of our country. The Constitution merely provides: "The judicial Power of the United States, shall be vested in one Supreme Court, and in such inferior Courts as the Congress may from time to time ordain and establish." Thus, the only indispensable court is the Supreme Court, and the Congress has from time to time established and abolished various other United States courts.

At the present time the United States court system may be likened to a pyramid. At the apex of the pyramid stands the Supreme Court

of the United States, the highest court in the land. On the next level
stand the United States courts of appeals, 11 in all. On the next level
stand the United States district courts, 89 in all, the United States
District Court for the District of Columbia and the district courts in
the Canal Zone, Guam, and the Virgin Islands. In a sense certain
administrative agencies may be included here because the review of
their decisions may be directly in the courts of appeals. Some agency
reviews, however, are handled by the district courts.

A person involved in a suit in a United States court may thus
proceed through three levels of decision. His case will be heard and
decided by one of the courts or agencies on the lower level. If either
party is dissatisfied with the decision rendered, he may usually have
review of right in one of the courts of appeals. Then, if he is still
dissatisfied, but usually only if his case involves a matter of great
national importance, he may obtain review in the Supreme Court of
the United States.

This pyramidal organization of the courts serves two purposes. First,
the Supreme Court and the courts of appeals can correct errors which
have been made in the decisions below. Secondly, these higher courts
can assure uniformity of decision by reviewing cases where two or
more lower courts have reached different results. The chart on page 3
shows the organization of the United States courts.

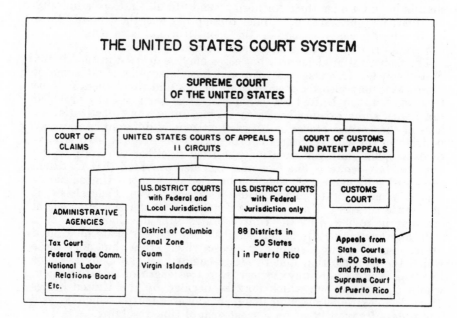

THE SUPREME COURT

The highest court is the Supreme Court of the United States. It
consists of nine Justices, appointed for life by the President with the
advice and consent of the United States Senate. One Justice is designated the Chief Justice and he receives a salary of $62,500 a year. The
other justices receive $60,000 a year. The officers appointed by the
Court include a Clerk to keep its records, a Marshal to maintain order
and supervise the administrative affairs of the court, a Reporter to
publish its opinions, and a Librarian to serve the justices and the
lawyers of the Supreme Court bar.

The Court meets on the first Monday of October each year. It continues in session usually until June and receives and disposes of about 3,400 cases each year. Most of these cases are disposed of by the brief decision that the subject matter is either not proper or not of sufficient importance to warrant full Court review. But each year between 200 and 250 cases of great importance and interest are decided on the merits. About half of these decisions are announced in full published opinions.

The official address of the Supreme Court is: The Supreme Court of the United States, Washington, D.C. 20543. Currently the following justices are serving on the Supreme Court:

	Appointed	Assignment as circuit justice
Chief Justice of the United States: Warren E. Burger	June 23, 1969	District of Columbia and 4th circuits.
Associate Justices:		
Hugo L. Black	Aug. 18, 1937	5th circuit.
William O. Douglas	Apr. 15, 1939	9th circuit.
John M. Harlan	Mar. 17, 1955	2d circuit.
William J. Brennan, Jr	Oct. 15, 1956	1st and 3d circuits.
Potter Stewart	Oct. 14, 1958	6th circuit.
Byron R. White	Apr. 12, 1962	10th circuit.
Thurgood Marshall	Aug. 30, 1967	7th circuit.
Harry A. Blackmun	June 9, 1970	8th circuit.

The United States Courts of Appeals and
The United States District Courts

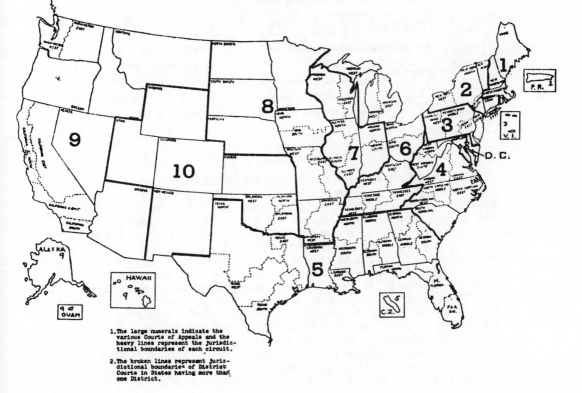

1. The large numerals indicate the various Courts of Appeals and the heavy lines represent the jurisdictional boundaries of each circuit.

2. The broken lines represent jurisdictional boundaries of District Courts in States having more than one District.

COURTS OF APPEALS

The intermediate appellate courts in the United States judicial system are the courts of appeals in 11 circuits. Each circuit includes three or more States, except the District of Columbia Circuit. The map on page 5 of this pamphlet shows how the United States is divided among the circuits. The States of Alaska and Hawaii and the territory of Guam are included in the ninth circuit, Puerto Rico is included in the first circuit, the Virgin Islands in the third circuit, and the Canal Zone in the fifth circuit. Each court consists of between 3 and 15 judges depending upon the amount of work in the circuit, and the judge with the longest service, who has not reached his 70th birthday, is the chief judge. Each judge receives a salary of $42,500 a year. There are now 97 circuit judges.

The 11 United States courts of appeals currently are receiving about 11,700 cases every year. A disappointed suitor in a district court usually has a right to have the decision of his case reviewed by the court of appeals of his circuit. In addition to appeals from the district courts, the courts of appeals receive many cases to review actions of various Federal administrative agencies for errors of law.

The judicial business of the courts of appeals is conducted through the office of the clerk of the court located in one of the principal cities in each circuit. The following chart shows the location, number of authorized judges, and postal address of the clerk's office in each circuit.

Court of Appeals	Number of authorized judgeships	Location and postal address
District of Columbia Circuit (District of Columbia)	9	Washington, D.C. 20001.
1st Circuit (Maine, Massachusetts, New Hampshire, Rhode Island, and Puerto Rico).	3	Boston, Mass. 02109.
2d Circuit (Connecticut, New York, and Vermont)	9	New York, N.Y. 10007.
3d Circuit (Delaware, New Jersey, Pennsylvania, and the Virgin Islands).	9	Philadelphia, Pa. 19107.
4th Circuit (Maryland, North Carolina, South Carolina, Virginia, and West Virginia).	7	Richmond, Va. 23219.
5th Circuit (Alabama, Florida, Georgia, Louisiana, Mississippi, Texas, and the Canal Zone).	15	New Orleans, La. 70130.
6th Circuit (Kentucky, Michigan, Ohio, and Tennessee)	9	Cincinnati, Ohio 45202.
7th Circuit (Illinois, Indiana, and Wisconsin)	8	Chicago, Ill. 60604.
8th Circuit (Arkansas, Iowa, Minnesota, Missouri, Nebraska, North Dakota, and South Dakota).	8	St. Louis, Mo. 63101.
9th Circuit (Alaska, Arizona, California, Hawaii, Idaho, Montana, Nevada, Oregon, Washington, and Guam).	13	San Francisco, Calif. 94101.
10th Circuit (Colorado, Kansas, New Mexico, Oklahoma, Utah, and Wyoming).	7	Denver, Colo. 80202.

DISTRICT COURTS

The United States courts where cases are initially tried and decided are the district courts. There are 93 of these courts, 88 in the 50 States, and one each in the District of Columbia, the Canal Zone, Guam, Puerto Rico, and the Virgin Islands. Each State has at least one court; but many States have two or three districts, and Califironia, Texas, and New York have four districts each. A district itself may be divided into divisions and may have several places where the court hears cases. Each district has from 1 to 27 judges depending upon the volume of cases which must be decided. For each district there is a clerk's office, a United States marshal's office, and one or more referees in bankruptcy, United States magistrates, probation officers and court reporters. In addition, there is a United States attorney's office in each district. Four hundred and one district judgeships are authorized by law, and the salary of each judge is $40,000 a year. In districts having two or more judges, the judge senior in service who has not reached 70 years of age is the chief judge. The district courts are currently receiving about 87,300 civil cases, 38,100 criminal cases, and 194,400 bankruptcy cases every year.

Some district courts, namely those in the District of Columbia, the Canal Zone, Guam, and the Virgin Islands, have jurisdiction over local cases as well as those arising under Federal law. These courts thus differ in several respects from the other 89 United States district courts. In these places the Federal Government does not share the judicial power as it does with the State governments in the several States and with the Commonwealth Government in Puerto Rico. Thus, these courts are not limited to the types of cases defined in the Constitution as part of the Federal judicial power, but decide all types of cases as do State courts. Then, too, the judges in the Canal Zone, Guam and the Virgin Islands are not appointed for life, but for terms of 8 years, and are not protected against diminution of their salaries during their terms of office. These courts may also be given duties which are not strictly judicial in nature.

Because of these differences, territorial courts have been called "legislative courts" to distinguish them from the "constitutional courts." The name indicates that these courts have been created, not in the exercise of Congress' power to establish courts under the judiciary article of the Constitution, but under its powers in the legislative article over the Territories and other fields of Federal authority. The United States Court of Appeals for the District of Columbia Circuit and the United States District Court for the District of Columbia, although they may be given work outside the judiciary article, are constitutional courts.

The chart appearing in the appendix gives the location of the principal office of the clerk of each district court, the number of authorized district judgeship positions for the district, and the postal address.

THE UNITED STATES COURT OF CLAIMS

The official seal of the United States Court of Claims describes it as "For the Republic and For its Citizens." The court was established in 1855 and has since been known as the "keeper of the nation's conscience," for it is here that the individual citizen or corporation may sue the Federal Government for money damages in a wide variety of claims wherein the Congress has waived the sovereign immunity of the United States. Aliens and their governments may also bring suits provided their courts give us the same privilege.

The Court of Claims is a constitutional court and has nationwide jurisdiction. Its seven judges sit in Washington, D.C., but there are 15 commissioners who serve as the trial judges of the court and sit in any section of the country most convenient to the parties. An individual commissioner hears evidence in a case in the same manner as a Federal district judge does in conducting a trial without a jury. In each case the commissioner thereafter prepares findings of fact, an opinion, and recommendations for conclusions of law which are, on exceptions by a party, reviewed by a panel of three judges, as authorized by law, or by the Court sitting *en banc*. The court's final judgments are subject to review by the Supreme Court on writ of *certiorari*. In complex cases, where there is no legal right to recover, either House of Congress may refer such a claim to the chief commissioner of the Court for findings and a recommendation as to whether there is an equitable basis upon which Congress itself should compensate the claimant.

This is a busy court with a heavy docket of cases, and a large volume of decisions is handed down annually. The usual case is a technical one involving complicated issues and large amounts, for there is no monetary ceiling on the court's jurisdiction. Suits against the Government for money damages must be tried in the Court of Claims if the amount exceeds $10,000 except in tax refund claims where the district courts have concurrent jurisdiction, and in tort claims where district courts have exclusive jurisdiction. The court has appellate jurisdiction over the district courts in tort cases by agreement of the parties. It also has appellate jurisdiction over the Indian Claims Commission.

The Federal Government is the nation's largest contractor, purchaser and employer. The complexity of its operations and their impact on individual citizens is nowhere better illustrated than in the litigation in this court.

Citizens who pay Federal taxes under formal protest may sue in the Court of Claims for refunds with interest. Citizens may bring suits for damages for the taking of private property for public use without just compensation in violation of the Fifth Amendment to the Constitution. Constitutional and statutory rights are constantly in issue. Often they involve personnel of the military services, active and retired, and their dependents. Civil service employes seek back pay for alleged illegal dismissal from office. Contractors sue for breach of contract. Oyster growers have sought compensation for damages to their beds by dredging operations for harbor or channel improvements. Farmers blame the Army Engineers for building structures in rivers that allegedly cause floods upon their lands. Inventors find this court the only one where they can claim patent infringements by the Government. They appear in a wide variety of matters, many reflecting the nation's involvement in procurement of sophisticated weapons' system for national defense.

This special court hears the largest claims in the world. But, the court prides itself on giving the same careful consideration to small claims. In most cases it is the court of first and last resort for the citizen who challenges the might of the State. In the Court of Claims the Federal Government is just another litigant with no more nor fewer rights than those of the humblest citizen.

THE UNITED STATES COURT OF CUSTOMS AND PATENT APPEALS AND THE UNITED STATES CUSTOMS COURT

Two other special courts have been created by the Congress to deal with particular types of cases. The United States Court of Customs and Patent Appeals consists of five judges appointed for life and hears appeals from the Customs Court, the Tariff Commission and the Patent Office. Appeals from the decisions of this court may be heard by the United States Supreme Court on writ of *certiorari*.

The Customs Court consists of nine judges appointed for life and determines controversies concerning the classification and valuation of imported merchandise. The court sits at New York City and from time to time at other major port cities.

The following chart shows the location, number of authorized judgeships and postal addresses of the three special courts:

Court	Number of authorized judgeships	Location and postal address
Court of Claims	7	717 Madison Place NW., Washington, D.C. 20005.
Court of Customs and Patent Appeals	5	717 Madison Place NW., Washington, D.C. 20005.
Customs Court	9	1 Federal Plaza, New York, N.Y. 10007.

In addition to maintaining courts, the Judicial Branch of the United States Government includes several organs for its own administration and self-government, and for the study and formulation of new procedures to reduce problems of the law's delay. The courts govern themselves through Judicial Councils and Judicial Conferences in each of the 11 circuits and through the Judicial Conference of the United States for all the circuits. Each circuit has a Judicial Council consisting of the judges of its Court of Appeals, which has the power to take such steps, including particularly the assignment of judges, as may be required to dispose efficiently of the volume of cases in each district. The Judicial Conference of the circuit consists of all the district and circuit judges in that circuit and invited members of the bar who meet together annually to discuss common problems and to make recommendations for the improvement of the administration of justice.

On the national level, the Judicial Conference of the United States consists of the Chief Justice of the United States, the chief judges of the 11 circuits, the Chief Judge of the Court of Claims, the Chief Judge of the Court of Customs and Patent Appeals, and a district judge from each circuit chosen for a term of 3 years by the judges of the circuit at an annual Judicial Conference of the Circuit. The Judicial Conference of the United States meets at least once every year to resolve administrative problems affecting all the circuits and to make recommendations to Congress concerning legislation affecting the Federal judicial system.

The administrative duties of the Federal court system are performed by the Administrative Office of the United States Courts which prepares and submits to Congress the budget for the courts; receives reports from and exercises some degree of supervision over the clerical staffs of the courts, the probation officers, referees in bankruptcy, United States magistrates, reporters, and other court personnel; audits and disburses money for the operation of the courts through the United States marshals; compiles and publishes statistics on the volume and distribution of business in the courts; supplies a professional secretariat and legal and statistical services to committees of the Judicial Conference of the United States; and conducts studies of court procedures under the direction of and for the Judicial Conference, and for other interested groups including committees of the Congress.

THE FEDERAL JUDICIAL CENTER

In 1968 the Congress passed Public Law 90–219 authorizing the establishment of a Federal Judicial Center to carry on research activities and to conduct training programs for judges and other court personnel. The Judicial Center is the research and development arm for the Federal judiciary. An independent Board made up of the Chief Justice of the United States, Chairman, two circuit judges, three district judges, and the Director of the Administrative Office of the United States Courts, guides the work of the Center and appoints its Director. The circuit and district judges who are members of the Board are elected by the Judicial Conference of the United States and they serve for staggered terms. This new establishment is a sister agency to the Administrative Office of the United States Courts.

The Judicial Center is concerned with solving problems of court congestion by developing new methods and procedures for improving efficiency in the management of court affairs. Its education and training activities include orientation programs or seminars for newly appointed judges, United States magistrates, referees in bankruptcy and other court officials, as well as training sessions for clerks and deputy clerks.

The Director is Honorable Alfred P. Murrah, a Senior Judge who has retired from active judicial service on the United States Court of Appeals for the Tenth Circuit. At the present time the headquarters of the Center are in historic Dolley Madison House located on the east side of Lafayette Square, 1520 H Street, NW., in Washington, D.C.

LAW AND PROCEDURE IN THE UNITED STATES COURTS

The organization of the United States courts set up to handle the types of cases designated in the Constitution for decision by the Judicial Branch of the Federal Government has been described. For many years there was much confusion as to whether these types of cases were merely to be decided by a different court system or whether in addition they were to be decided according to different rules of law and a different procedure.

The question of the rule of law to apply in these types of cases was largely determined by the supremacy clause making the Constitution, statutes, and treaties of the United States Government the supreme law of the land. However, until 1938 the United States courts in suits between citizens of different States also purported to apply a general law, not the law of any State; but now it is settled that the law applied in the United States courts is the same as the law which would be applied in a State court in similar cases

The question of procedure, conversely, was long governed by the rule that the United States courts, except where Federal statutes otherwise provided, followed the procedure of the courts in the State where they were sitting. However, again in 1938, Rules of Civil Procedure prepared by an advisory committee and approved by the Supreme Court became effective to give the United States courts their own rules of practice. And in 1946 Federal Rules of Criminal Procedure prepared in a similar fashion became effective. Both rules of practice have adopted the simplest, most modern, and best procedure and have been models for procedural reform in the States. In 1966 these Rules of Civil and Criminal Procedure were extensively revised and up-dated. Then in 1968 the Supreme Court adopted uniform rules of Federal Appellate Procedure for the United States Courts of Appeals. Thus, today the United States courts decide cases involving citizens of different States according to the same rules of law as would govern the case in a State court, but decide them by Federal procedure.

ILLUSTRATION: AN AUTOMOBILE ACCIDENT

This whole rather complex problem of the various cases that may be tried in the United States courts may be illustrated for you by the story of an automobile collision. Bill Smith from Chicago, driving his car on an Illinois road, has a collision with another vehicle. Ordinarily no suit arising out of that accident could be tried in a United States court; it would be heard and decided in a State court. But if the other vehicle were an army truck driven by a soldier, Bill Smith may want to sue the United States, or the United States may decide to sue Bill Smith. In either event Bill Smith or the United States may commence a suit in the United States district court in Illinois.

If the other vehicle belonged to a private person who lived in Illinois, Bill Smith or the other owner may sue only in the State court, unless under certain circumstances the suit involved some provision of the Federal statutes or the Federal Constitution. If, on the other hand, the other vehicle belonged to John Jones who lived in St. Louis, Mo., then either John Jones or Bill Smith may sue in a United States district court because they were from different States.

These possible suits have been civil cases brought to compensate the parties for damage done, and it is unlikely that a criminal case brought by the Government would arise. Yet, if either Bill Smith or the other driver had been handling his car so recklessly as to warrant a criminal prosecution for reckless driving, manslaughter, etc., the suit would be brought by the State of Illinois in the State court. Let us suppose, however, that the other driver was in a car which he had stolen in Indiana and had driven into Illinois. Then that driver might be prosecuted by the United States Government in the United States district court under Federal law for transporting a stolen automobile from one State into another.

If either Bill Smith or his adversary is dissatisfied with the decision of the United States district court, he may appeal to a United States court of appeals, and is still dissatisfied after a decision by that court, he may seek review in the United States Supreme Court on questions of Federal law which arose in the proceedings. So you can see how an accident usually gives rise to suits which can be tried in State courts only, but which under special circumstances may be tried or reviewed in the United States courts.

The Work of the United States District Courts

The work of the United States district courts is partly reflected in the statistics on the types of cases which are filed every year. In the fiscal year ended June 30, 1970, exactly 87,321 civil cases were filed in these courts. Of these 24,965 involved the United States either as a party plaintiff or party defendant. The United States as plantiff commenced about 550 cases under the food and drug laws, 2,430 cases to collect money due on promissory notes, 3,250 civil commitment proceedings under the Narcotic Addict Rehabilitation Act, and about 6,750 other cases. The United States was a defendant in about 1,600 habeas corpus cases and 1,730 cases involving motions to vacate criminal sentences, 1,980 Tort Claims Act cases, 1,285 tax cases and many others. These figures show the important role the district courts play in enforcing Federal statutes and in achieving justice even when the United States Government is involved in a law suit.

Private parties brought into the district courts during 1970 fiscal year 62,356 cases of which 34,846 involved questions arising under Federal laws. The largest category of these cases (about 11,600) was that involving petitions for writs of habeas corpus by persons held in custody who have alleged violations of Federal constitutional rights. About 23,000 cases came into the district courts in suits between private persons from different States. Of this number about 7,600 were concerned with personal injuries arising out of motor vehicle accidents. An additional 4,656 civil cases of a local nature were filed in the District Court for the District of Columbia and in the territorial courts.

Of the 38,102 criminal cases brought into the district courts during the year ended June 30, 1970, 3,700 involved embezzlement or fraud, 3,860 forgery and counterfeiting, 4,090 the interstate transportation of a stolen automobile, 1,360 failure to pay the tax on alcoholic beverages and 3,700 the violation of the Selective Service laws. The remainder involved the violation of a host of other laws. In these criminal cases the United States courts share with the officers of the law and the United States attorneys the enforcement of criminal laws for the protection of all citizens.

An important work performed by the United States district courts is the supervision by probation officers of persons convicted of crimes, but placed on probation rather than sent to prison. During the fiscal year 1970 over 13,500 persons were placed on probation by the district courts. Thus, the Federal prisons were relieved of an expensive burden and these persons were afforded a greater chance of "going straight" away from contaminating prison influences. In addition, during the year the probation officers received for supervision from prison authorities 7,100 persons released on parole, or other release procedure. On June 30, 1970, the probation officers had under supervision over 38,400 persons. The work of the probation officers also includes an investigation of almost every person convicted of crime in a district court and the submission to the court of a report to be used by the judge in determining the sentence to be imposed.

During the fiscal year 1970 the referees in bankruptcy attached to the district courts undertook the administration of the property of approximately 194,400 persons unable to pay their debts, for the purpose of enabling creditors to receive a proper share of the money due to them.

In its work of enforcing the Federal laws, deciding controversies between citizens, sentencing convicted criminal defendants, distributing the estates of debtors and rehabilitating violators of the law, the United States courts perform an essential and vital function in the American pattern of democratic government.

JOSEPH F. SPANIOL, Jr.,
Assistant Director for Legal Affairs,
Administrative Office of
The United States Courts.

WASHINGTON, D.C., *February 1, 1971.*

APPENDIX

U.S. DISTRICT COURT DIRECTORY AS OF FEB. 1, 1971

District court	Number of authorized judgeships [1]	Location and postal address
Alabama:		
Northern district	4	Birmingham, Ala. 35202.
Middle district	2	Montgomery, Ala. 36101.
Southern district	2	Mobile, Ala. 36602.
Alaska	2	Anchorage, Alaska 99501.
Arizona	5	Phoenix, Ariz. 85025.
Arkansas:		
Eastern district	2	Little Rock, Ark. 72203.
Western district	2	Fort Smith, Ark. 72902.
California:		
Northern district	11	San Francisco, Calif. 94102.
Eastern district	3	Sacramento, Calif. 95841.
Central district	16	Los Angeles, Calif. 90012.
Southern district	5	San Diego, Calif. 92101.
Canal Zone	1	Ancon, C.Z.
Colorado	4	Denver, Colo. 80201.
Connecticut	4	New Haven, Conn. 06505.
Delaware	3	Wilmington, Del. 19899.
District of Columbia	15	Washington, D.C. 20001.
Florida:		
Northern district	2	Tallahassee, Fla. 32302.
Middle district	6	Jacksonville, Fla. 32201.
Southern district	7	Miami, Fla. 33101.
Georgia:		
Northern district	6	Atlanta, Ga. 30301.
Middle district	2	Macon, Ga. 31202.
Southern district	2	Savannah, Ga. 31402.
Guam	1	Agana, Guam 96910.
Hawaii	2	Honolulu, Hawaii 96803.
Idaho	2	Boise, Idaho 83702.
Illinois:		
Northern district	13	Chicago, Ill. 60604.

[1] Footnote at end.

U.S. DISTRICT COURT DIRECTORY AS OF FEB. 1, 1971—Continued

District court	Number of authorized judgeships [1]	Location and postal address
Eastern district	2	East St. Louis, Ill. 62202.
Southern district	2	Springfield, Ill. 62705.
Indiana:		
Northern district	3	Hammond, Ind. 46325.
Southern district	4	Indianapolis, Ind. 46204.
Iowa:		
Northern district	1½	Cedar Rapids, Iowa 52401.
Southern district	1½	Des Moines, Iowa 50309.
Kansas	4	Wichita, Kans. 67201.
Kentucky:		
Eastern district	2½	Lexington, Ky. 40501.
Western district	3½	Louisville, Ky. 40202.
Louisiana:		
Eastern district	10	New Orleans, La. 70130.
Western district	4	Shreveport, La. 71102.
Maine	1	Portland, Maine 04112.
Maryland	7	Baltimore, Md. 21202.
Massachusetts	6	Boston, Mass. 02109.
Michigan:		
Eastern district	10	Detroit, Mich. 48226.
Western district	2	Grand Rapids, Mich. 49502.
Minnesota	4	St. Paul, Minn. 55101.
Mississippi:		
Northern district	2	Oxford, Miss. 38655.
Southern district	3	Jackson, Miss. 39205.
Missouri:		
Eastern district	4	St. Louis, Mo. 63101.
Western district	4	Kansas City, Mo. 64106.
Montana	2	Butte, Mont. 59701.
Nebraska	3	Omaha, Nebr. 68101.
Nevada	2	Reno, Nev. 89502.
New Hampshire	1	Concord, N.H. 03302.
New Jersey	[1] 10	Trenton, N.J. 08605.
New Mexico	3	Albuquerque, N. Mex., 87103.
New York:		
Northern district	2	Utica, N.Y. 13503.
Eastern district	9	Brooklyn, N.Y. 11201.
Southern district	27	New York, N.Y. 10007.
Western district	3	Buffalo, N.Y. 14202.
North Carolina:		
Eastern district	[1] 3	Raleigh, N.C. 27602.
Middle district	2	Greensboro, N.C. 27402.
Western district	2	Asheville, N.C. 28802.
North Dakota	2	Fargo, N. Dak. 58103.
Ohio:		
Northern district	8	Cleveland, Ohio 44114.
Southern district	5	Columbus, Ohio 43215.
Oklahoma:		
Northern district	1⅔	Tulsa, Okla. 74103.
Eastern district	1⅔	Muskogee, Okla. 74402.
Western district	2⅔	Oklahoma City, Okla. 73102.
Oregon	3	Portland, Oreg. 97205.
Pennsylvania:		
Eastern district	19	Philadelphia, Pa. 19107.
Middle district	[1] 4	Scranton, Pa. 18501.
Western district	10	Pittsburgh, Pa. 15219.
Puerto Rico	3	San Juan, P.R. 00905.
Rhode Island	2	Providence, R.I. 02903.
South Carolina	5	Columbia, S.C. 29201.
South Dakota	2	Sioux Falls, S. Dak. 57101.
Tennessee:		
Eastern district	3	Knoxville, Tenn. 37901.
Middle district	2	Nashville, Tenn. 37203.
Western district	3	Memphis, Tenn. 38103.
Texas:		
Northern district	6	Dallas, Tex. 75221.
Eastern district	3	Beaumont, Tex. 77704.
Southern district	8	Houston, Tex. 77601.
Western district	5	San Antonio, Tex. 78206.
Utah	2	Salt Lake City, Utah 84101.
Vermont	2	Burlington, Vt. 05402.
Virginia:		
Eastern district	6	Norfolk, Va. 23510.
Western district	2	Roanoke, Va. 24006.
Virgin Islands	1	St. Thomas, V.I. 00801.
Washington:		
Eastern district	1½	Spokane, Wash. 99210.
Western district	3½	Seattle, Wash. 98104.
West Virginia:		
Northern district	1½	Elkins, W. Va. 26241.
Southern district	2½	Charleston, W. Va. 25301.
Wisconsin:		
Eastern district	3	Milwaukee, Wis. 53202.
Western district	1	Madison, Wis. 53701.
Wyoming	1	Cheyenne, Wyo. 82001.

[1] The use of fractions indicates that a judge is authorized to serve in more than 1 district. Included in these figures are 3 temporary judgeship positions which will expire as vacancies occur. Under the law creating these positions it was provided that the 1st vacancies occurring thereafter may not be filled. These temporary positions are located in the district of New Jersey, the eastern district of North Carolina and the middle district of Pennsylvania.

BIBLIOGRAPHY

The United States Government Organization Manual, 1969–70, Superintendent of Documents, Government Printing Office, Washington, D.C., $3.00.

Bunn, Jurisdiction and Practice of the Courts of the United States (5th ed. 1949).

The Constitution of the United States of America. Revised and Annotated. U.S. Library of Congress, Legislative Reference Service. Washington, D.C., Government Printing Office, 1964.

Dimock, American Government in Action (1946), particularly pp. 479–483.

"Supreme Court, United States", by Felix Frankfurter in Vol. 14 of the Encyclopedia of the Social Sciences 474 (1934).

Frankfurter and Landis. The Business of the Supreme Court (1927).

Hart and Wechsler, The Federal Courts and the Federal System. Brooklyn, New York. The Fountain Press (1953).

Hurst, Willard. The Growth of American Law (1950).

Warren, Supreme Court in United States History, Boston. Little, Brown and Company, 1926 (Revised Edition, 2 volumes).

Wolfson and Kurland, Jurisdiction of the Supreme Court of the United States (By Reynolds Robertson and Francis R. Kirkham, 1936. Revised Edition by Wolfson and Kurland, 1951). New York, Matthew Bender & Company, Inc.

Wright, Federal Courts, West Publishing Co., St. Paul, Minn., 1963.

"The Federal Courts," 13 Law & Contemporary Problems 1–273 (Winter 1948).

Annual Reports of the Director of the Administrative Office of the United States Courts.

Title 28, United States Code, contains the law governing the organization of the United States courts and court officers.

○

III

OUR NATIONAL LIBRARY, NATIONAL ARCHIVAL REPOSITORY, AND THE U.N.

To paraphrase a well-known phrase: "No library is an island." If you understand this then you'll know that it's important for you to be aware of the resources, collections, and services of other libraries and repositories of the materials of communication. Two of the most important of these in the U.S. are described ever so briefly on the following pages: the Library of Congress, our National library, and the National Archives. Both deserve your close attention.

One should also know about United Nations documents if he is to keep in touch with and relate to the rest of the world. Hence this third article, an excellent piece for your information.

[Information Resources in the] Library of Congress

Prepared by the National Referral Center for Science and Technology

In addition to being the "research arm" of Congress, LC is truly the national library of the United States. As far as I know a complete description of its services and collections has not been brought together in any single volume, although there are many separate publications and articles on various aspects of the library. On the following pages you'll find a very concise summary of its resources, services, and publications. This is the minimum amount of information that every librarian should have on this "probably the world's largest library." For more, I refer you to LC's latest Catalog of Publications in Print. It's revised annually in March.

LIBRARY OF CONGRESS

1st St. and Independence Ave. SE.
Washington, D.C. 20540
Tel: (202) 783-0400

The Library of Congress is a general reference and research library for public use, as well as a library for the use of Congress. Its general book collection (approximately 13.5 million volumes) is in the custody of the Stack and Reader Division, which makes books available to readers in the Main Reading Room or in the Thomas Jefferson Reading Room in the Annex adjoining the Main Library Building. All persons over high school age are permitted to use the reading rooms. Study desks are available for full-time scholars and researchers doing advanced work that requires relative quiet and reservation of books. Typing and recording devices are permitted in specified areas.

The information resources of organizational units of the Library that maintain special collections or offer specialized services are described below, together with representative publications relating to their collections or services. Information regarding the ordering of both free and priced publications will be found in *Library of Congress Publications in Print,* revised annually and obtainable without charge from the Office of the Secretary of the Library at the address given above.

Information Office

Tel: (202) 783-0400 *Ext.* 605

Areas of Interest: Events, services, and programs of the Library of Congress.

Publications: *Calendar of Events in the Library of Congress* (monthly public announcements of concerts, literary or other events, exhibits, and new publications of general interest); fact sheets about the Library; news announcements for public information media; *Library of Congress Information Bulletin* (a weekly staff news publication).

Information Services: Answers inquiries from the public (and from the press and other media serving the public) about the organization, functions, history, activities, programs, and services of the Library; operates an information counter to direct visitors to exhibitions, reading rooms, or other units as appropriate and to provide information to visitors through various priced or free Library publications; sells facsimiles, greeting cards, and notepapers both by mail and over the counter, but provides free informational materials and sells other Library publications (postcards, literary recordings, brochures, exhibit catalogs, and bibliographies) *only* over the counter.

SOURCE: Reprinted from U.S. Library of Congress. National Referral Center for Science and Technology. *A Directory of Information Resources in the United States: Federal Government.* (Washington: 1967). pp. 182–194.

Card Division

Tel: (202) 967-8205

Areas of Interest: Sale and distribution of Library of Congress catalog cards and technical publications.

Information Services: The Division sells catalog cards for all types of library materials (books, serials, music, films, phonorecords, maps, etc.). Cards may be ordered by author, title, serial number, subject, or series. Standing orders are accepted for any well-defined subject. Proofsheets, less expensive than cards and containing five cards to a sheet, are available in any of 25 broad categories, including Maps, Medicine, Plant and Animal Industry, Science, Social and Political Science, Technology, Geography and Anthropology, titles from the U.S. Department of Health, Education, and Welfare, and titles from the U.S. Geological Survey. Information on prices and availability may be obtained from the Division. The Division also sells bound volumes of catalog cards and other guides to the collections, such as *Subject Headings Used in the Dictionary Catalogs of the Library of Congress, Library of Congress Classification Schedules,* and the monthly, quarterly, and annual cumulations of the various catalogs of the Library of Congress.

Copyright Office

Tel: (202) 967-8262

Areas of Interest: Registration of claims to copyright in 13 classes of literary and artistic works; recordation of documents pertaining to copyrights.

Holdings: Records for all works registered in the United States since 1870—approximately 11 million claims. (Copyright records for the period 1790–1870 are in the Rare Book Division.)

Publications: Information circulars, catalogs of copyright entries, bulletins of reported decisions of the Federal courts on copyright cases, and articles on copyright for publication in encyclopedias and similar works.

Information Services: Answers inquiries by telephone, personal visit, or correspondence; serves as host to foreign copyright experts or persons acquiring expertise in United States copyright; holds seminars for publishing houses on registration procedures; maintains liaison with the various bar committees interested in copyright, furnishing speakers on occasion.

Decimal Classification Office

Tel: (202) 967-8361

Areas of Interest: Library subject classification; classified bibliography.

Publications: *Dewey Decimal Classification and Relative Index* (17th ed., 1965, and 9th abridged ed., 1965); *Decimal Classification Additions, Notes, and Decisions* (irregular).

Information Services: Answers inquiries; makes referrals; provides advisory services on structure, use, and interpretation of Dewey Decimal Classification.

Division for the Blind and Physically Handicapped

Tel: (202) 967-7303

Areas of Interest: Literature in braille, talking-book records and tape, and other materials, devices, and systems to provide reading services to the blind and physically handicapped; sound reproduction systems for the blind, including modified phonographs (talking-book machines); indexing of recordings; speech compression; braille musical scores.

Holdings: Braille and recorded books and magazines available for loan to the blind and physically handicapped through the regional libraries listed below; specialized reading materials in braille and on tape to supplement the services of the regional libraries; catalogs of braille material and talking books in media for the blind and physically handicapped; library of braille musical scores and music instruction texts.

Publications: *Talking Book Topics* and *Braille Book Review* (bimonthly); catalogs and indexes of books, magazines, and articles available in braille or as talking books; information brochures and circulars concerning services and resources of the Division and other organizations.

Information Services: Makes its holdings available for direct loan to the legally blind and physically handicapped through 34 cooperating regional libraries without charge (reading materials for the blind and physically handicapped are carried free by the U.S. mails); provides general reference services on matters pertaining to the interests and welfare of the blind and physically handicapped; answers technical inquiries on the braille system; provides bibliographic services for blind and physically handicapped readers throughout the U.S.; serves as a national resource in providing specialized reading materials through the regional libraries. Information regarding the direct loan of talking books to the blind and physically handicapped may be obtained from the 34 cooperating libraries, located as follows:

Alabama
  Library for the Blind
  Alabama Institute for the Deaf and Blind
  P.O. Box 455
  Talladega, Ala. 35160
    Tel: (205) 362-7934

Alaska *see* Washington

Arizona *see* California

Arkansas *see* Oklahoma

California (southern), Arizona
  Braille Institute of America
  741 North Vermont Ave.
  Los Angeles, Calif. 90029
    Tel: (213) 663-1111 *Ext.* 32

California (northern), Nevada
  Blind Section
  California State Library
  P.O. Box 2037
  Sacramento, Calif. 95809
    Tel: (916) 445-4552

Canal Zone *see* District of Columbia

Colorado
  Division of Work with the Blind
  Denver Public Library
  90 Lowell Blvd.
  Denver, Colo. 80219
    Tel: (303) 934-0930

Connecticut *see* New York State

Delaware *see* Pennsylvania (east)

District of Columbia, Canal Zone, Puerto Rico, Virgin Islands
    Regional Librarian for the Blind
    Division for the Blind and Physically Handicapped
    Library of Congress
    Washington, D.C. 20540
      Tel: (202) 967-7406

Florida
  Talking Book Library
  Florida Council for the Blind
  P.O. Box 2299
  Daytona Beach, Fla. 32015
    Tel: (305) 252-0070

Georgia
  Library for the Blind
  State Department of Education
  1050 Murphy Ave. SW.
  Atlanta, Ga. 30310
    Tel: (404) 753-5607

Guam *see* Hawaii

Hawaii, Guam
  Library for the Blind
  402 Kapahulu Ave.
  Honolulu, Hawaii 96815
    Tel: (808) 79-888

Idaho *see* Oregon

Illinois
  Services to the Blind
  Chicago Public Library
  4544 North Lincoln Ave.
  Chicago, Ill. 60625
    Tel: (312) 561-7210

Indiana
  Services for the Blind
  Indiana State Library
  140 North Senate Ave.
  Indianapolis, Ind. 46204
    Tel: (317) 633-5404

Iowa
  Library
  Iowa Commission for the Blind
  4th and Keosauqua Sts.
  Des Moines, Iowa 50309
    Tel: (515) 283-0153

Kansas *see* Missouri

Kentucky *see* Ohio

Louisiana, Mississippi
  Department for the Blind
  Louisiana State Library
  P.O. Box 131
  Baton Rouge, La. 70821
    Tel: (504) 342-5681 *Ext.* 363

Maine *see* Massachusetts

Maryland *see* Virginia

Massachusetts, Maine, New Hampshire, Rhode Island
  The Library
  Perkins School for the Blind
  Watertown, Mass. 02172
    Tel: (617) 924-3434 *Ext.* 31

Michigan (outside Wayne County)
  Michigan State Library for the Blind
  735 East Michigan Ave.
  Lansing, Mich. 48913
    Tel: (517) 373-1591

Michigan (Wayne County)
  Wayne County Library
  33030 Van Born Rd.
  Wayne, Mich. 48184
    Tel: (313) 722-8000

Minnesota, North and South Dakota
  Library for the Blind
  Minnesota Braille and Sight Saving School
  Faribault, Minn. 55021
    Tel: (507) 334-6411 *Ext.* 279

Mississippi *see* Louisiana

Missouri, Kansas
  Wolfner Library for the Blind
  3844 Olive St.
  St. Louis, Mo. 63108
    Tel: (314) 533-0352

Montana *see* Washington

Nebraska
  Library for the Blind
  Nebraska Public Library Commission
  State Capitol
  Lincoln, Nebr. 68509
    Tel: (402) 477-5211

Nevada *see* California (northern)

New Hampshire *see* Massachusetts

New Jersey
  Library for the Blind and Handicapped
  1700 Calhoun St.
  Trenton, N.J. 08638
    Tel: (609) 292-6450

New Mexico
  Services to the Blind
  New Mexico State Library
  300 Don Gasper
  Santa Fe, N. Mex. 87501
    Tel: (505) 827-2103

New York State, Connecticut, Vermont
  New York State Library
  226 Elm St.
  Albany, N.Y. 12202
    Tel: (518) 474-5935

New York City, Long Island
  Library for the Blind
  New York Public Library
  166 Ave. of the Americas
  New York, N.Y. 10013
    Tel: (212) 925-1011

North and South Carolina
  Regional Library for the Blind
  North Carolina State Library
  1124 Hillsboro St.
  Raleigh, N.C. 27603
    Tel: (919) 829-7228

North Dakota *see* Minnesota

Ohio (south of Columbus), Kentucky, Tennessee
  Public Library of Cincinnati
  617 College St.
  Cincinnati, Ohio 45202
    Tel: (513) 241-2636 *Ext.* 40

Ohio (north, including Columbus)
  Cleveland Public Library
  325 Superior Ave.
  Cleveland, Ohio 44114
    Tel: (216) 241-6647

Oklahoma, Arkansas
  Oklahoma State Library
  1108 Northeast 36th St.
  Oklahoma City, Okla. 73111
    Tel: (405) 521-3671

Oregon, Idaho
  Books for the Blind
  Library Association of Portland
  205 Northeast Russell St.
  Portland, Oreg. 97212
    Tel: (503) 223-7201

Pennsylvania (east of Harrisburg), Delaware
  Library for the Blind
  Free Library of Philadelphia
  1700 Spring Garden St.
  Philadelphia, Pa. 19130
    Tel: (215) 563-5433

Pennsylvania (west of Harrisburg), West Virginia
  Library for the Blind
  Carnegie Library of Pittsburgh
  Federal and East Ohio Sts.
  Pittsburgh, Pa. 15212
    Tel: (412) 321-0111

Puerto Rico *see* District of Columbia

Rhode Island *see* Massachusetts

South Carolina *see* North Carolina

South Dakota *see* Minnesota

Tennessee *see* Ohio

Texas
  Blind Services Division
  Texas State Library
  1201 Brazos
  Austin, Tex. 78711
    Tel: (512) 475-2619

Utah, Wyoming
  Division for the Blind
  Utah State Library
  1488 South State St.
  Salt Lake City, Utah 84115
    Tel: (801) 328-5855

Vermont *see* New York State

Virgin Islands *see* District of Columbia

Virginia, Maryland
  Virginia State Library for the Blind
  3003 Parkwood Ave.
  Richmond, Va. 23221
    Tel: (703) 644-4111 *Ext.* 6356

Washington, Montana, Alaska
  Library for the Blind

Seattle Public Library
425 Harvard Ave. East
Seattle, Wash. 98102
   Tel: (206) 324-0201

West Virginia *see* Pennsylvania (west)

Wisconsin
   Milwaukee Public Library
   814 West Wisconsin Ave.
   Milwaukee, Wis. 53233
   Tel: (414) 276-7578 *Ext.* 246

Wyoming *see* Utah

General Reference and Bibliography Division

   Tel: (202) 967-8064

   Areas of Interest: Subjects not within the scope
.of the subject-oriented divisions of the Library of
Congress.

   Publications: *A Guide to the Study of the
United States of America: Representative Books
Reflecting the Development of American Life and
Thought; John Fitzgerald Kennedy, 1917–1963: A
Chronological List of References; The Presidents
of the United States, 1789–1962; A Selected List
of References; Union Lists of Serials; A Bibliog-
raphy; Literary Recordings: A Checklist of the
Archive of Recorded Poetry and Literature in the
Library of Congress.*

   Information Services: This Division provides
reference services in subjects not within the scope
of the subject-oriented divisions of the Library.
Services are provided by the Public Reference
Section to readers in the Main Reading Room of
the Main Building and in the Thomas Jefferson
Reading Room in the Annex. Special services in
the field of local history and genealogy are available in the Local History and Genealogy Reading
Room adjacent to the Thomas Jefferson Room.
The Division maintains extensive reference collections in all reading rooms for immediate use by
readers and reference personnel. The Bibliography
and Reference Correspondence Section offers
advisory service on bibliographical operations
(to facilitate this activity it has issued *Bibliographical Procedures & Style; A Manual for Bibliograph-
ers in the Library of Congress*). The four sections
of the Division, whose information resources are
described below, render special services and prepare bibliographies and other publications in their
fields of specialization.

African Section

   Tel: (202) 967-7318

   Areas of Interest: Sub-Saharan Africa, including
adjacent Indian Ocean Islands; Africa-oriented research and publication centers; Africa-oriented
publications, with particular emphasis on serials
and offical publications of African governments.

   Holdings: A collection of pamphlets, political
ephemera, and special reference materials, supplementing the Library's holdings on Africa.

   Publications: *Africa South of the Sahara: A
Selected, Annotated List of Writings* (1963);
Serials for African Studies (1961); *Agricultural
Development Schemes in Sub-Saharan Africa: A
Bibliography* (1963); *A List of American Doctoral
Dissertations on Africa* (1962); bibliographies of
publications of African governments.

   Information Services: Answers inquiries; makes
referrals; provides reference and bibliographic services. Special reference materials are available for
on-site use only.

Arms Control and Disarmament Section

   Tel: (202) 967-8248

   Areas of Interest: All aspects of arms control
and disarmament.

   Publications: *Disarmament Digest* (weekly), abstracts for the use of the U.S. Arms Control and
Disarmament Agency; *Arms Control and Disarmament* (quarterly), bibliography with abstracts
and annotations of current literature in the English, French, German, and Russian languages.

   Information Services: Answers inquiries; makes
referrals; provides advisory and reference services.
Services are primarily for the U.S. Arms Control
and Disarmament Agency, members of Congress,
and executive agencies. Services to institutions
and scholars are provided when staff time is
available.

Children's Book Section

   Tel: (202) 967-8289

   Areas of Interest: Books for children, preschool
age to high school.

   Holdings: A reference collection relating to English and foreign language children's books (his-

tory, criticism, basic catalogs, bibliographies, and indexes, subject lists, review media, professional journals, pamphlets, and books on folklore, storytelling, and the writing and illustrating of children's books); a dictionary catalog (author, title, and subject) and a separate file of illustrator entries, both begun early in 1966, which contain annotated cards for new children's books (and will eventually include all children's books in print); a Library of Congress classified shelflist of all juvenile fiction and nonfiction books added to the collections since 1957 and of earlier nonfiction.

Publications: *Children's Literature: A Guide to Reference Sources* (1966); *Children's Books* (annual), an annotated list of new juvenile books; *Fables* (catalog of an exhibit); "Serving Those Who Serve Children,"a reprint from *The Quarterly Journal of the Library of Congress.*

Information Services: Answers reference and research inquiries; provides bibliographic information about children's books, *but does not serve children.*

International Organizations Section

Tel: (202) 967-7797

Areas of Interest: Governmental and nongovernmental groups that are internationally organized, financed, and sponsored (history, structure, operation, activities, and publications); proceedings of international meetings; future international meetings.

Holdings: Programs and preconference documents; pamphlets and data on international organizations.

Publications: *World List of Future International Meetings* (bimonthly). Entries are arranged in two parts: Part I covers meetings in the fields of science, technology, agriculture, and medicine; Part II covers meetings in the social, cultural, commercial, and humanistic fields. The index covers both parts and contains subjects, sponsors, and geographical locations.

Information Services: Answers inquiries; makes referrals; provides consulting and reference services as staff time permits.

Geography and Map Division

Tel: (202) 967-7473

Areas of Interest: Maps, charts, atlases, globes, models, and other cartographic forms; literature

and bibliographical records about maps, mapmakers, and sources; history of cartography and cartographic techniques; geographical publications (books, pamphlets, reports, etc.); developments in geography as a modern discipline.

Holdings: Nearly 3,000,000 maps and charts, 30,000 atlases, several hundred globes and models, and a 50,000-card bibliography of cartographical literature. The materials are current and historical, foreign and domestic, commercial and official. Current issues of some 200 geographical and cartographical periodicals are available for reference use. The cartographic collections contain both air and water navigation charts, topographic map sets, and thematic maps of several hundred special subjects, including manuscript and rare items, historical maps, and maps dealing with geology, climate, vegetation, population, transportation and communication, resources, industries, and wars.

Publications: Bibliographies; locator aids describing specialized cartographic groups. A list of publications and a pamphlet describing the Division's services and collections are available without charge.

Information Services: Within limitations of staff time, the staff answers inquiries by telephone or correspondence, and provides reference service to the public in the Map Reading Room. Materials are available for loan to members of Congress, Federal agencies, and authorized libraries. Reproductions of maps not protected by copyright may be ordered through the Library's Photoduplication Service.

Hispanic Foundation

Tel: (202) 967-8302

Areas of Interest: Spanish, Portuguese, Brazilian, and Spanish-American culture (humanities, literature, social sciences, and current events).

Holdings: The Archives of Hispanic Literature on Tape (original voice recordings of writers and poets of Latin America, Spain, and Portugal). The Foundation maintains a collection of reference materials in the Hispanic Society Reading Room.

Publications: *Handbook of Latin American Studies* (annual), a selective, annotated bibliography of world-wide literature in 18 subject fields; since 1964 even-numbered volumes cover the humanities and odd-numbered volumes the social sciences. *National Directory of Latin Americanists* (1966), biobibliographies of specialists in the social sciences and the humanities. Other bibliographies, guides, and indexes relating to Latin America, Spain, and Portugal in the social sciences and the humanities.

Information Services: Answers inquiries by telephone or correspondence; prepares bibliographies; provides reference services in the Hispanic Society Room.

Information Systems Office

Library of Congress Automation Techniques Exchange (LOCATE)

Tel: (202) 967-8193

Areas of Interest: Automation of libraries.
Holdings: Reports on library automation projects.

Information Services: Answers inquiries; provides reference services. File materials are accessible for on-site use. Services are primarily for libraries, commercial firms, and individuals involved in library research.

Law Library

Tel: (202) 967-7403

Areas of Interest: Federal and State laws of the United States; secular systems of law (common law and Roman law); the religious legal systems, such as Canon, Islamic, Hindu, and Buddhist law; international law; legal history and biography; philosophy of law and jurisprudence.

Holdings: Almost $1\frac{1}{2}$ million volumes located principally in the Library of Congress (a working collection is maintained in the Capitol for the use of Congress). The collections include: Federal and State session laws, statutes, and reports; original records and briefs of the U.S. Supreme Court and the U.S. Courts of Appeals; bar association reports; opinions of the U.S. Attorney General; legal directories; Anglo-American treatises; reports of American and foreign trials; legal periodicals; extensive collections in various special branches of the law; English yearbooks, statutes, and treatises printed prior to the year 1600; 290 volumes of legal incunabula; extensive collections of legislation, court decisions, legal treatises, and periodicals of foreign countries.

Information Services: Answers inquiries; provides reference services; permits on-site use of the

collections. Requests from Congress, the courts, and Government agenices are given priority; inquiries from the public are answered within limitations of staff time. (The Law Library does not provide legal advice.)

Loan Division

Tel: (202) 967-7449
        967-7493 (*Government Order Desk*)

Publications: *Library and Reference Facilities in the Area of the District of Columbia* (7th ed., 1966).

Information Services: The Division loans books and certain other Library of Congress materials to members of Congress, other Government officials, Government agency libraries, the diplomatic corps, and the judiciary. Interlibrary loans are made to public, university, and special libraries throughout the world.

Manuscript Division

Tel: (202) 967-7287

Areas of Interest: Correspondence and other manuscript materials relating to eminent Americans, American history and culture, and Latin America.

Holdings: About 28 million manuscripts and documents, including personal papers of 23 Presidents of the United States and other eminent Americans, records of nationally important organizations, manuscripts concerning the history of Latin America, and more than 3 million pages of reproductions of materials relating to America in foreign archives and libraries. (Most manuscript maps and music, medieval manuscripts, manuscripts in oriental languages, and microfilms of manuscripts unrelated to United States history are in the custody of other divisions of the Library.)

Publications: Registers of papers in the Manuscript Division and indexes to Presidents' papers.

Information Services: Reference services are provided in the Division's reading room, where properly identified scholars engaged in serious research may examine manuscripts under the supervision of attendants. Manuscripts may be copied (but not always by photocopying, because of restrictions of donors).

Microfilm Reading Room

Tel: (202) 967-7421

Areas of Interest: Microreproductions of printed materials, including rare books, periodicals, maps, and manuscripts.

Holdings: Over 400,000 items on microfilm and other forms of transparent and opaque microreproductions. Among the many special collections on microfilm are early American and Latin American imprints, doctoral dissertations, books printed in English before 1640, books from the Library's general collection copied for preservation purposes, early archives of Genoa and Venice, manuscript and early printed books on the history of science, and manuscripts from the monasteries at Mount Sinai and Mount Athos.

Information Services: Reference service is provided in the Microfilm Reading Room, and reading machines are available for all types of microforms in the collection.

Music Division

Tel: (202) 967-7351

Areas of Interest: Music of western civilization and its history; American music and its documentation; opera; chamber music; manuscripts of master composers; correspondence of composers and musicians; early music literature; rare flutes and flute-type instruments; phonorecords.

Holdings: Over 3,000,000 items. Copyright deposits of music and books form the bulk of the collection. In addition, there are extensive collections of rare and early music, rare books, original manuscripts, autograph correspondence, music literature in all western languages, operatic material, Stradivari instruments (for use in endowed concerts), more than 1,500 flutes and flute-type instruments, a comprehensive body of flute music and literature, and sound recordings (including nonmusical recordings).

Information Services: Answers inquiries; makes referrals; provides consulting and reference services; makes interlibrary loans. The collections are accessible for on-site use with the exception of certain restricted categories and rare materials which are accorded special care and supervision. Arrangements may be made for the use of sound recordings in serious research. The Division will supply information on special services made possible through gifts of money administered by the Library Trust Fund Board; these include the compostion, dissemination, and performance of chamber music, the commission of new works by prominent composers, the loan to radio stations of broadcast tapes of concerts held in the Library of Congress under foundation auspices, lectures on music, and financial aid in the publication of historical studies in the field of American music.

Archive of Folk Song

Tel: (202) 967-7513

Areas of Interest: Folk and primitive music (its musical, literary, historical, international, and intercultural phenomena), with special emphasis on American folk expressions; preservation of important musical events; folklore related to music.

Holdings: Sound recordings of over 90,000 musical specimens (songs, chants, dances, etc.), including 4,000 cylinders of rare American Indian music, some 1,600 cylinders of Anglo-American traditional songs, and recordings of Negro music, Latin American and Caribbean music, and music from African and Asian countries; folklorist manuscripts gathered by the Federal Writers' Project; plaints, worksongs, and ballads collected in rural areas, remote mountain communities, and prisons.

Information Services: Answers inquiries; makes referrals; provides reference services. A reading room and limited listening facilities are available. Recordings of many items in the collections may be purchased from the Music Division's Recorded Sound Section.

Recorded Sound Section

Tel: (202) 967-7320

Areas of Interest: Recordings of music, literature, history, drama, etc.

Publications: Catalogs of poetry and folk music recordings offered for sale.

Information Services: Answers inquiries; makes referrals; provides advisory services on equipment and costs for recording expenditions in the field. Unrestricted, noncommercial recordings in the Music Division collections are duplicated for a fee.

National Referral Center for Science and Technology

Tel: (202) 967-8265

Areas of Interest: Governmental, industrial, academic, public, and private organizations and institutions, and individuals, who have specialized knowledge in any area of the physical, biological, engineering, or social sciences.

Holdings: An inventory of information resources in the United States. The inventory includes broad and specific areas of interest for each organization or individual, holdings (literature and report collections, unpublished data, specimen collections, etc.), titles of representative publications, and the types of information services available.

Publications: *A Directory of Information Resources in the United States: Physical Sciences, Biological Sciences, Engineering* (1965); *Social Sciences* (1965); *Water* (1966); *Federal Government with a Supplement of Government-Sponsored Information Resources* (1967).

Information Services: Provides names, addresses, telephone numbers, and brief descriptions of appropriate information resources. The Center does not provide technical details in answer to inquiries nor furnish bibliographic assistance. It functions as an intermediary, directing those who have questions concerning specific subjects to organizations or individuals with specialized knowledge of those subjects. Services are available without charge, by telephone, correspondence, or through personal visits.

Office of the Secretary of the Library

Tel: (202) 967-7707

Areas of Interest: Mail distribution of free publications of the Library of Congress.

Information Services: Distributes (by mail) without charge *Information for Readers in the Library of Congress, Library of Congress Publications in Print* (annual), and other free publications of the Library; answers inquiries regarding the availability of Library publications offered for sale by the Card Division or the U.S. Government Printing Office.

Orientalia Division

Tel: (202) 967-7521

Areas of Interest: Literature of all disciplines (except law, technical agriculture, and clinical medicine) produced in and relating to East, Southeast, South, Central, and West Asia and the Middle East.

Holdings: Over one million volumes, administered by five Sections: the Chinese and Korean, Hebraic, Japanese, Near East, and South Asia. (The Division has custody of books and periodicals in all oriental languages.)

Information Services: Each of the five Sections of the Orientalia Division answers inquiries, makes referrals, and provides reference services. Reference services are also provided in respect to the Library's extensive holdings of Western-language works relating to the areas of the Division's concern; these, however, are not in the custody of the Orientalia Division, but are available in the general classified collections.

Chinese and Korean Section

Tel: (202) 967-7477 (*Chinese collection*)
            967-7777 (*Korean collection*)

Areas of Interest: Chinese local histories; Ch'ing dynasty history; Chinese agriculture, botany, and materia medica; Chinese authors; Korean history, literature, and social organization.

Holdings: Approximately 355,000 volumes in the Chinese language; over 6,000 serial titles (about 360 currently received); 1,074 reels of microfilm of rarities in the National Library of Peiping; union catalogs of Chinese and Korean books and union card files of Chinese and Korean serials in the U.S.; books in the Manchu, Mongol, and Nashi languages. The Korean collection consists of more than 30,000 volumes and over 1,300 serial titles (about 530 currently received).

Publications: *A Catalog of Chinese Local Histories in the Library of Congress* (1942); *Eminent Chinese of the Ch'ing Period* (2 vols., 1943–44); *Korea, An Annotated Bibliography of Publications in Far Eastern Languages* (1950); *A Descriptive Catalog of Rare Chinese Books in the Library of Congress* (2 vols., 1957).

Hebraic Section

Tel: (202) 967-7358

Areas of Interest: Culture and languages of the Ancient Near East; Ethiopia; Israel; Jews and Judaism from Biblical times to the present (history, bibliography, biography, religion, cultural, and social conditions); Jewish settlements in various lands; the Bible; Zionism; anti-Semitism; political and economic conditions of the Jews.

Holdings: Over 80,000 volumes of Hebrew, Yiddish, Aramaic, Syriac, Ethiopic, and related languages and literatures, including 15,000 in Yiddish. The Section maintains the National Union Catalog of Hebraica and the National Union Catalog of Yiddish Books.

Japanese Section

Tel: (202) 967-7500

Areas of Interest: Japanese history, literature, and institutions; humanistic and social sciences in Japan, Formosa, Korea, and Manchuria; science and technology of Japan.

Holdings: Nearly 500,000 volumes and about 8,000 periodical titles in the Japanese language. Special collections include prewar publications of the South Manchuria Railway Company and of the Government-Generals of Formosa and Korea and pre-1945 publications banned by the Japanese Ministry of Home Affairs. There are union catalogs of Japanese books and serials, and 2,900 reels of microfilm, including selected archives of Japanese Government agencies from 1868 to 1945.

Near East Section

Tel: (202) 967-7252

Areas of Interest: Literature produced by and concerning the Near and Middle East and North Africa; languages and linguistic sciences of the area extending from Afghanistan in the East to Morocco in the West, and from Turkey and Central Asia in the North to the Sudan in the South, excluding only Israel; ancient, medieval, modern, and political history of the areas; Islam and Islamic culture.

Holdings: Over 55,000 volumes in the languages of the area, the largest segments of the vernacular collection being in Arabic, Turkish, Persian, and Armenian, with smaller groups of material in Mongolian, Azerbaijani, Pushtu, Uzbek, Kazakh, and other Central Asian languages; over 5,000 volumes on all phases of Islam; reference works and union catalogs of materials in Near Eastern languages.

South Asia Section

Tel: (202) 967-7600

Areas of Interest: India, Pakistan, Bhutan, Ceylon, Tibet, Sikkim, Burma, Thailand, Cambodia, Laos, Vietnam, Malaysia, Brunei, Singapore, Indonesia, and the Philippines (anthropology, art, archeology, current political developments, his-

tory, law, philosophy, religion, sciences, social institutions, contemporary conditions, and linguistic disciplines).

Holdings: About 44,000 books in the vernacular languages of the area; union catalogs of vernacular books for South and Southeast Asia; a subject catalog on Southeast Asia. Over 1,000 manuscripts from the subject countries are in the custody of the Library's Manuscript Division.

Publications: *Southeast Asia: An Annotated Bibliography of Selected Reference Sources in Western Languages* (1964); *Southeast Asia Publication Sources* (1960).

Photoduplication Service

Tel: (202) 967-8282

Areas of Interest: Photoreproduction standards and techniques; archival preservation and storage of library materials; bibliographic control of microforms.

Holdings: Library of Congress master negative microfilm collection, totaling more than 80,000 reels, including microfilms of the Presidential Papers, the manuscript collections in the library at Mt. Sinai and the library of the Greek and Armenian Patriarchiates in Jerusalem, early State records of the U.S., official papers in the Japanese Ministry of Foreign Affairs, current and retrospective files of more than 1,000 domestic and foreign newspapers and other serials, and more than 10,-000 monographs. The Photoduplication Service is custodian of over 100,000 scientific and technical reports released through the Publication Board of the Department of Commerce prior to June 1, 1961.

Information Services: The Service supplies photoreproductions of materials in the Library of Congress collections to Government agencies, to institutions, and to individuals for a fee, subject to copyright and other restrictions. Types of reproductions include microfilms, microfilm enlargement prints, photostats, electrostatic prints, blueprints, ozalid prints, photographs, slides, and color transparencies. The Photoduplication Service will answer inquiries concerning availability of items in the Library of Congress collections and prepare cost estimates. Price lists and order forms are available. Catalogs, lists, and circulars describing the more significant collections and cooperative microfilming projects are available upon request.

Preservation Office

Tel: (202) 967-7445

Areas of Interest: Preservation of books, maps, films, charts, manuscripts, and other library materials; lamination of documents; bookbinding; lighting of exhibit cases housing books and papers; physical security of library collections.

Information Services: Answers inquiries; makes referrals; provides consulting services; provides short lists of literature citations.

Prints and Photographs Division

Tel: (202) 967-7217

Areas of Interest: Prints, photographs, drawings, posters, and related categories of applied graphic arts; documentation of American history of civilization.

Holdings: Almost three million items, including: artists' prints from the 15th through the 20th century; historical prints (largely of the 19th and 20th centuries), including engravings and lithographs of views, portraits, battles, and advertisements; Archives of American Graphic Humor (political cartoons, etc.); extensive photographic portrait and geographical files; events and human interest photos; master photographs; Historic American Buildings Survey (measured drawings, photographs, and pertinent data); Archive of Hispanic Culture (Latin American art and architecture); American and foreign theatrical posters and contemporary poster art.

Publications: *A Guide to the Special Collection of Prints and Photographs in the Library of Congress* (1955); *Pictorial Americana: A Select List of Photographic Negatives* (1955); *Civil War Photographs, 1861-1865* (1961); other catalogs.

Information Services: Answers inquiries; provides reference services but cannot make lengthy searches or extensive editorial selections. Copies of pictures may be ordered from the Library's Photoduplication Service, subject to copyright and other restrictions. Price lists are available. Prints and photographs may be borrowed for exhibits by institutions, subject to interlibrary loan and Library of Congress regulations.

Motion Picture Section

Tel: (202) 967-7721

Areas of Interest: Early American and contemporary motion pictures.

Holdings: About 86,000 reels, including the archival collection of representative motion pictures (1942 to present), early American films (1900-1925), German, Italian, and Japanese features, newsreels, and documentary films (1930-45), and paper print collection of early films deposited for copyright (1897-1915) and now copied onto 16mm film.

Publications: Bibliographies and film lists on particular subjects.

Information Services: Scholarly and research activities are served through personal visits and by correspondence. No films are loaned but copies may be ordered if copyright and donor restrictions are observed.

Process Information Unit

Tel: (202) 967-7567

Areas of Interest: Location of books and other materials in the Library of Congress; status of Library of Congress materials being processed.

Holdings: Process File, a constantly changing card catalog of temporary entries, recording the status and location of materials until printed cards are filed into the principal catalogs of the Library.

Information Services: Provides reference service concerning location and status of material on order or in process of being cataloged; provides information concerning the number and location of copies of materials already in the Library of Congress.

Publications Office

Tel: (202) 967-8381

Areas of Interest: Publications of the Library of Congress.

Publications: *The Quarterly Journal of the Library of Congress* (supplement to the *Annual Report of the Librarian of Congress*).

Information Services: Answers inquiries about current, forthcoming, and out of print publications of the Library of Congress.

Rare Book Division

Tel: (202) 967-7478

Areas of Interest: Rare books, pamphlets, serials, and broadsides, including incunabula; Americana; rare Bibles; personal libraries of famous people; special collections about famous political or literary figures; gastronomy; magica; cryptography; dime novels.

Holdings: Approximately 300,000 volumes, pamphlets, magazines, and newspapers. Half of these holdings are maintained as separate collections. There are more than 40 such collections, all but two of which are represented by individual card catalogs or published catalogs. They include libraries of famous persons (Thomas Jefferson, Woodrow Wilson, Abraham Lincoln, Theodore Roosevelt), comprehensive collections of books about famous persons (Walt Whitman, Rudyard Kipling, Benjamin Franklin, Abraham Lincoln), the collection of illustrated books assembled by Lessing J. Rosenwald, and several generic collections, such as miniature books, Bibles, English imprints (1501–1640), pre-1801 American imprints, American juvenilia, examples of early printing (1501–20), and over 5,600 incunabula.

Information Services: The collections are accessible for on-site use by the public in the Division's reading room, in accordance with Library of Congress regulations for the use of rare material. Inquiries are answered by telephone and correspondence.

Science and Technology Division

Tel: (202) 967-8043

Areas of Interest: All aspects of science and technology (except technical agriculture and clinical medicine, which are subject specialities of the National Agricultural Library and the National Library of Medicine).

Holdings: The subject fields of science and technology are represented in the Library of Congress by more than 2 million books, nearly 20,000 current journal titles, and some 800,000 technical reports. The Division's Science Reading Room maintains a reference collection of books in the basic sciences, including technical dictionaries, encyclopedias, and handbooks; all major abstracting and indexing journals in the physical, earth, biomedical, and social sciences are represented for purposes of current and retrospective searching. The Division also has custody of an extensive collection of technical reports (now numbering 800,000), including those issued by the Atomic Energy Commission, the National Aeronautics and Space Administration, the Department of Defense, and other Government agencies.

Publications: *Aerospace Medicine and Biology: A Continuing Bibliography with Indexes* (monthly); *Antarctic Bibliography* (irregular); *Bibliography on Snow, Ice, and Permafrost; with Abstracts* (irregular); other bibliographies and

guides to the collections. A publications list is available.

Information Services: The Science Reading Room and its staff of subject and language specialists provide a broad range of reference services, including guidance in the use of abstracting and indexing publications. A literature-searching service is available on a fee basis, and bibliographies are prepared for other Government agencies on a transfer-of-funds basis.

Serial Division

Tel: (202) 967-8051

Areas of Interest: Serial publications of all types, including newspapers, magazines, journals, and serials issued irregularly; official publications at the Federal, State, and municipal levels, domestic and foreign; pamphlets, including leaflets, reprints, and circulars.

Holdings: More than 35,000 periodical titles and 18,000 Government serials, all current and unbound; the Library's pamphlet collection of approximately 124,000 items; 5,000 volumes of catalogs and other guides to serial publications; selected U.S. newspapers from all States and a comprehensive selection from foreign countries. About 1,500 current domestic and foreign newspapers are retained, almost all in the form of microfilm. (Newspaper files for 1800 and earlier are in the custody of the Rare Book Division.) The entire newspaper collection comprises some 15,000 domestic and foreign titles (128,000 bound volumes and 122,000 reels of microfilm).

Publications: *African Newspapers in Selected American Libraries; Popular Names of U.S. Government Reports;* surveys of official government publications of the German Federal Republic, the German Democratic Republic, etc.; other specialized reference tools and guides to the serial collections.

Information Services: Answers inquiries and provides reference services to readers through the Newspaper Reading Room and the Periodical and Government Publication Reading Room. The latter reading room also services the pamphlet collection. Requests requiring extensive searching are referred to private researchers who provide services on a fee basis.

Serial Record Division

Searching and Reference Section

Tel: (202) 967-7531

Areas of Interest: Serial publications (in the Roman, Cyrillic, Greek, and Hebraic alphabets) received by the Library of Congress, excluding newspapers, but including bound and unbound periodicals, directories, Government documents and other publications issued in successive parts (usually at regular intervals) and intended to be continued indefinitely.

Holdings: A serial record card catalog of all Library of Congress serial holdings in the alphabets noted above, with the exception of newspapers.

Publications: *New Serial Titles,* a continuing union list covering serials issued since Jan. 1, 1950 (monthly since 1953, with annual and quinquennial cumulations).

Information Services: Answers inquiries concerning titles, starting and ceasing dates, volume and issue numbers, frequency, and location of all non-newspaper series in the Library of Congress. Questions regarding policies or procedures of the Serial Record Division should be directed to the Division office, *tel:* (202) 967-8083.

Slavic and Central European Division

Tel: (202) 967-7739

Areas of Interest: Cultural, political, social, and economic aspects of Albania, Austria, Bulgaria, Czechoslovakia, Estonia, Finland, Germany, Greece, Hungary, Latvia, Lithuania, Poland, Rumania, the Soviet Union, Switzerland, and Yugoslavia.

Holdings: The Division's Slavic Room maintains a reference collection of about 7,500 volumes on the Slavic countries and the Soviet Union. It has custody of and services current unbound Slavic and Baltic newspapers and periodicals (approximately 3,000 titles are received regularly). The Division also maintains the Cyrillic Union Catalog, which consists of several hundred thousand cards recording materials in Cyrillic types held by the Library of Congress and other major research libraries in the United States and Canada, and a card file listing recent articles on Eastern and Southeastern Europe in Western European languages.

Publications: *Newspapers of the Soviet Union in the Library of Congress, Newspapers of East Central and Southeastern Europe in the Library*

of Congress, and other lists for facilitating bibliographic access to the collections; *The USSR and Eastern Europe: Periodicals in Western Languages* and other comprehensive bibliographies; a series of bibliographic area guides, of which those on Rumania and Bulgaria have been published so far. A list of publications is available without charge.

Information Services: Provides specialized reference and consulting services in person, by telephone, or by correspondence. General reference service to readers is provided through the facilities of the Slavic Room.

Union Catalog Division

Tel: (202) 967-8125

Areas of Interest: Physical location of books in U.S. and Canadian libraries; American imprints from 1801 to 1876.

Holdings: National Union Catalog of pre-1956 imprints, consisting of about 15 million cards, representing about 8 million titles or editions to be found in the Library of Congress and more than 700 other libraries in the U.S. and Canada. (Imprints after 1955 are recorded in the printed *National Union Catalog;* Chinese, Japanese, Korean, Hebrew, and Yiddish Union Catalogs are maintained in the Orientalia Division; the pre-1956 Slavic Union Catalog is maintained by the Library's Cyrillic Bibliographic Project; 1956 and later Slavic imprints are recorded in the printed *National Union Catalog.*) The National Union Catalog Division also maintains the Card Index to Special Collections in North American Libraries; the American Imprints Inventory, a comprehensive record of materials printed in the U.S. from 1801 to 1876; the National Register of Microform Masters; and the Microfilming Clearing House, a record of extensive microfilming projects.

Publications: *National Union Catalog, A Cumulative Author List* (monthly, with quarterly, annual, and quinquennial cumulations).

Information Services: Provides book-locating services for libraries and scholars for purposes of interlibrary loan, but extensive searching is referred to searchers on a fee basis. Local resources and the printed catalogs should be consulted before a search is requested.

The National Archives and Its Records—Readings

From several pamphlets prepared by the National Archives and Records Service

This agency is the final repository for the permanently valuable non-current records of our Federal Government. The only records kept here are those that have "enduring value." Those of temporary worth are destroyed after stated periods of time. These records come from Congress, the White House, every executive department, most of the independent agencies, and several of the Federal courts, and they range in date from the Revolutionary War period (circa 1774) through World War II to the present. Such materials are, of course, of use to the several government agencies themselves, e.g. for the legal purpose of determining precedent. But they can also be of use to the librarian, the researcher, and the general public. The following readings describe some of NA's record collections and the services offered in connection with their use.

AGE AND CITIZENSHIP RECORDS IN THE NATIONAL ARCHIVES

The National Archives has very few original records of birth, marriage, and death, but it has other records that are useful in establishing a person's age and citizenship. The principal records in its care that can be so used and the kinds of data that an inquirer should furnish in requesting a search of them are set forth briefly below. The National Archives will supply either information from these records or photocopies of all except records of naturalization. Anyone who wishes may examine the records in the National Archives research rooms or may hire an agent to examine them.

Adoption and Guardianship Records

The National Archives has records of adoptions only for the District of Columbia, 1907–37. These records, which are indexed, give the age and occasionally the date and place of birth of each person adopted. The National Archives will search for adoptions recorded in 1907 or later if the full name of the person adopted and the names of the foster parents are given.

The National Archives has guardianship papers only for the District of Columbia, 1802–78. These papers sometimes show, besides the name of the ward of the court, his age or the date of his birth. The National Archives will search the guardianship papers if given the ward's full name and the approximate dates of the wardship.

Birth Records

The National Archives has records of births at Army camps, posts, and stations, 1884–1912, with some records as late as 1920. It will search these records if provided with the name of the child, the names of his parents, the place of his birth, and the month and year of his birth.

The National Archives also has records through 1935 of many births, registered at American foreign-service offices, of children of American

SOURCE: General Services Administration. National Archives and Records Service. (Washington: 1965–70).

Age and Citizenship Records in the National Archives. Leaflet 7.
Compiled Military Service Records in the National Archives. Leaflet 9.
Genealogical Records in the National Archives. Leaflet 5.
Genealogical Sources Outside the National Archives. Leaflet 6.
Pension and Bounty-Land Warrant Application Files in the National Archives. Leaflet 8.
Records in the National Archives Relating to Confederate Soldiers. Leaflet 10.

citizens residing abroad. Requests for information about such births registered less than 75 years ago should be addressed to the Department of State, Washington, D.C. 20520. For information about earlier registrations, requests should be addressed to the National Archives.

For information about other original records of birth, marriage, and death an inquirer should address the bureau of vital statistics, the church, or other appropriate local depository in the appropriate State, county, or city. To obtain a birth certificate, he should address the bureau of vital statistics in the capital city of the State in which the birth occurred, giving the date and place of birth. If there is no record of birth on file, the bureau will explain the procedure for filing a delayed birth certificate. The Superintendent of Documents, U. S. Government Printing Office, Washington, D.C. 20402, can supply the leaflets *Where To Write for Birth and Death Records* (15c) and *Where To Write for Marriage Records* (10c).

Census Schedules

The National Archives has both original and microfilmed population census schedules for 1850, 1860, and 1870 and microfilm copies only for 1880. These schedules usually show the name and age and the State, Territory, or country of birth of every free inhabitant of the United States. The National Archives has also a microfilm copy of the card index to entries of the 1880 schedules that relate to households including a child aged 10 or under. The cards give the names, ages, and birthplaces of all members of such households. There is a separate cross-reference card for each child, aged 10 or under, whose surname is different from that of the head of the household in which he is listed. Prices and contents for rolls containing positive microfilm copies of the schedules and the index are listed in *Federal Population Censuses, 1790–1890,* which may be obtained on request from the Publications Sales Branch, The National Archives, Washington, D.C. 20408. Microfilm readers are usually available in the larger public and research libraries.

Prices of paper photocopies of pages will be furnished by the National Archives if an inquirer can identify the schedules he wants by census year, name of State, volume numbers, and page numbers. Stamped page numbers, when shown, should be cited.

The Bureau of the Census at Pittsburg, Kans.,

has the population census schedules for 1880 and later (except those for 1890, which were almost totally destroyed by fire in 1921) and will search them for a fee. Requests for searches by the Bureau should be made on its form entitled "Application for Search of Census Records." The form, which shows the fees for searches, can be obtained from the Personal Census Service Branch of the Bureau of the Census, Pittsburg, Kans. 66762.

Homestead Applications

Applications in the National Archives for homestead lands, 1862–1950, show for each applicant his age and whether he was native-born or naturalized. If an applicant was not native-born, his application file contains evidence of his naturalization or of his intention to become a citizen.

The National Archives will search, for the period 1862–1908, the homestead applications for Alabama, Alaska, Arizona, Florida, Louisiana, Nevada, or Utah if given the full name of the applicant and the State or Territory in which the land was located. It will search these records for all other public land States or Territories if given, besides the applicant's name, (1) the number of the land entry file or a description of the land by township, range, section, and fraction of section or (2) the name of the land office and either the date when the original application was filed or the date of the final certificate. If such exact information cannot be furnished, the National Archives can sometimes make a successful search if given the name of the nearest town and the direction and approximate distance of the land from that town. An inquirer may be able to obtain the legal description of a piece of land by writing to the recorder of deeds in the county seat of the county in which the land is located.

If given the full name of the applicant and the State or Territory in which the land was located, the National Archives will search, for the period July 1, 1908–December 31, 1950, the homestead applications for all public land States and Territories.

Naturalization Records

The National Archives has naturalization proceedings of the District of Columbia courts, 1802–

1926. These records show for each person who petitioned for naturalization his age or date of birth, his nationality, and whether citizenship was granted. The National Archives has photocopies and indexes (made by the Work Projects Administration) of naturalization documents, 1787–1906, filed by courts in Maine, Massachusetts, New Hampshire, and Rhode Island. The National Archives will search for information about naturalizations that occurred before September 27, 1906, if given the full name of the petitioner and the approximate date of naturalization. Persons who wish information about citizenship granted elsewhere before September 27, 1906, should send their inquiries to the clerk of the Federal, State, or other court that issued the naturalization certificate.

The Immigration and Naturalization Service, Washington, D.C. 20536, has duplicate records of all naturalizations that occurred after September 26, 1906. Inquiries about citizenship granted after that date should be sent to the Service on a form that can be obtained from any of the Service's district offices. Local postmasters will give the address of the nearest district office.

Passenger Lists

The National Archives has incomplete series of custom passenger lists and immigration passenger lists, mostly on microfilm, for ships arriving from abroad at various Atlantic and Gulf of Mexico ports. These lists give the names of passengers and usually their ages and countries of origin. The National Archives will search all lists shown below that are more than 50 years old—those less than 50 years old are not available at this time for reference purposes—if, in addition to the name of the passenger and the name of the port of entry, the following information is given: the name of the vessel and the approximate date of its arrival or the name of the port of embarkation and the exact date of arrival.

Port	Customs Passenger lists	Immigration Passenger lists	Indexes
Baltimore	1820–91	1891–1909	1820–1952
Boston	1820–74 *and* 1883–91	1891–1943	1848–91 *and* 1902–20
New Orleans	1820–1902	1903–45	1853–1952
New York	1820–97	1897–1942	1820–46 *and* 1897–1943
Philadelphia	1800–82	1883–1945	1800–1948
Certain minor ports	1820–73	1893–1945	1890–1924

The National Archives has also several incomplete indexes to names on these lists, which it will consult if the port of entry and supposed year of arrival are given.

Persons needing information from lists less than 50 years old to establish their citizenship or to support claims for social security benefits should write to the Immigration and Naturalization Service. Forms to be used can be obtained from the nearest district office of the Service, the location of which is available from any postmaster.

Information about the arrival of vessels at the port of New York, 1890–1930, and at the ports of Baltimore, Boston, and Philadelphia, 1904–26 is included in the *Morton Allan Directory of European Passenger Steamship Arrivals* (New York, Immigration Information Bureau, Inc., 1931). This directory is available in most large public and research libraries.

The passenger lists or microfilm copies of the lists for the ports and periods indicated above may be consulted at the National Archives unless they are being repaired or photocopied.

Passport Applications

The National Archives has passport applications and related papers, 1791–1905, of United States citizens who intended to travel abroad and will make limited searches for age and citizenship information in such of these records as are at least 75 years old. The name of the person who applied for a passport and the place and approximate date of application should be supplied. Requests for information from passport records less than 75 years old should be addressed to the Passport Office, Department of State, Washington, D.C. 20520.

Pension Application Files

The pension application files in the National Archives relate to claims based on service in the Armed Forces as late as 1934, except for service in World War I or with the Confederate forces in the Civil War. These files often give the ages or dates of birth, and sometimes the places of birth, of servicemen and their dependents or widows.

The National Archives will search for a particular file if the inquirer furnishes the following information: full name of the serviceman and name of the war in which he served or the inclusive dates of his service. The search is more likely to be fruitful if additional information is given, such as the name of the organization with which the man served or the State from or in which he entered the service, his residence before and after service, and the name of his widow, if any. If a pension application file for the serviceman is found, the National Archives will examine it to see if it contains any information about the birth or citizenship of the inquirer. If the file contains such information a photocopy of the relevant page will be furnished gratis provided that it is required as proof to obtain some Federal benefit to which the inquirer is entitled by law; otherwise, the established fee for a photocopy will be charged.

Inquiries about pension files for military service in World War I or after 1933 should be sent to the Veterans Administration, Washington, D.C. 20420. Inquiries about civilian employees of the U.S. Government separated from service after 1909 should be sent to the National Personnel Records Center, GSA (Civilian Personnel Records), 111 Winnebago Street, St. Louis, Mo. 63118.

Personnel Records

Most of the extant personnel records for civilian employees of the Federal Government whose service terminated before 1910 are in the National Archives. These records may contain information about the date and place of birth of an employee. The National Archives will search personnel records if given the full name of the employee at the time of service, the name and address of the employing agency, and the approximate dates of employment. The personnel records for most civilian employees whose service terminated after 1909 are in the National Personnel Records Center, GSA (Civilian Personnel Records), 111 Winnebago Street, St. Louis, Mo. 63118.

Seamen's Protection-Certificate Applications

The National Archives has applications of seamen on American vessels for "protection certificates," or certificates of American citizenship, 1916-40. Such applications are usually supported by evidence of the date and place of birth and of the citizenship of the seaman. The National Archives will search the application files if given the

following information: the full name of the seaman and the port from which the certificate was issued and, if available, the number or date of the certificate.

COMPILED MILITARY SERVICE RECORDS IN THE NATIONAL ARCHIVES

Compiled service records for volunteer soldiers who fought in various wars from the Revolution through the Philippine Insurrection are on file in the National Archives. Those less than 75 years old, however, are subject to a restriction imposed by the Department of Defense that prohibits disclosure of personal information. The compiled service records contain virtually no genealogical information, but they are of value for proving the military service of a forebear. The National Archives cannot abstract or summarize these records for inquirers but can furnish photocopies of them for a fee sufficient to cover the cost of reproduction.

Detailed information on the compiled service records for Confederate soldiers is in a separate pamphlet entitled *Records in the National Archives Relating to Confederate Soldiers.*

History of the Records

The compilation of the service records was originally undertaken by the War Department to permit more efficient and expeditious checking of medical and military records in connection with claims for pensions and other benefits. All entries specifically referring to each soldier in the muster rolls, returns, hospital registers, and related records that were available were recorded as "abstracts" on separate cards. The abstracts were verified in a separate operation of comparison, and great care was taken to ensure their accuracy. The cards for each war were then arranged by State, thereunder by military organization, and thereunder alphabetically by name.

The compiled service records for the Revolutionary War are fragmentary because many of the original service records were burned in a fire that occurred on November 8, 1800, in the offices occupied by the Secretary of War. Other records were lost in 1814 when Government buildings in Washington were burned by the British army.

Description of the Records

The compiled military service record of each volunteer soldier is kept in a jacket-envelope filed with those for other soldiers who fought in the same war and regiment or other unit. The record consists of (1) one or more card abstracts of entries relating to the soldier as found in the original rolls, returns, registers, or other records, and (2) sometimes, particularly for the later wars, one or more original documents relating solely to that soldier. The abstracts in the jacket for any soldier, if the original record of his service was complete, may serve to trace that service from beginning to end, but they normally do little more than account for where he was at a given time. They normally show the soldier's rank, military organization, and term of service. Sometimes they also show his age, the place of his enlistment, and the place of his birth.

Most of the original records from which the card abstracts were made are among the holdings of the National Archives, but there is rarely any need to consult them about the service of a soldier because of the care and thoroughness with which the service data they contain were abstracted. The original records are much used, however, for general historical purposes, for example, the history of military campaigns. The National Archives cannot do genealogical or historical research in these records in response to inquiries but will be glad to furnish simple factual information for general historical purposes if it is readily accessible in the records and does not have to be compiled.

How to Order Copies

To find the record of a particular volunteer soldier for whom there is a compiled military service record, the National Archives needs:

(1) the exact name under which he was carried on the Army rolls,
(2) the war in which he served,
(3) the State from which he entered service, and
(4) the designation of the regiment or other unit in which he served.

If this information is supplied, it is usually a simple matter to locate the record.

To simplify the searching process inquirers are asked to fill out Form NAR–288, Order for Photocopies Concerning Veteran. The completed form should be sent to the National Archives and Records Service with a check or money order for $1, payable to the General Services Administration. The $1 fee should be paid for each order form sent. If no record is found for the soldier inquired about, the fee will be returned.

Upon receipt of an order, since the compiled service records seldom contain genealogical information, the National Archives will first search the pension and bounty-land warrant application files. It will search for a compiled service record only if no pension or bounty-land warrant application is found or if the inquirer specifically states that he wants the compiled record. The National Archives has no pension or bounty-land warrant applications for Confederate soldiers or compiled service records for soldiers who served in the Regular Army.

What You Will Receive

If a compiled service record for the soldier in question is found, the National Archives will send photocopies of the card abstracts in his jacket-envelope or, if the abstracts are numerous, photocopies of those that are not merely repetitions. The original papers that may be in the jacket-envelope are not usually copied because most of them are mere financial vouchers containing information of no lasting interest. Occasionally other papers, mainly pertaining to routine matters such as details to duty or furloughs, are to be found in the jacket-envelope. Upon request the National Archives will report the cost of reproducing all papers in a jacket-envelope in addition to the card abstracts.

Identifying a Soldier

If the soldier's name supplied by an inquirer is not exactly the same as that under which the soldier was carried on the Army rolls, or if the unit in which he served is not known or is given incorrectly, the staff of the National Archives may find it difficult to identify the soldier correctly. There are usually many more soldiers of the same or nearly the same name than the average inquirer would imagine, and the name under which a soldier was carried on the Army rolls may differ in various ways from the name by which he was known to members of his family.

In attempting to identify a soldier, where the information supplied is not sufficient, the National Archives will try to match initials and variant spellings of the surname given in a standard list of variant spellings. If it is able to reduce the possibilities to a very few individual records, it will attempt identification by comparing the contents of these records with any information supplied by the inquirer that is likely to be useful for the purpose. If the soldier's identity seems obvious or very probable, the National Archives will furnish a photocopy of the record for the soldier it thinks is the correct one.

The National Archives cannot go beyond making identifications that are relatively easy to make. It cannot undertake to do extensive research or to evaluate conflicting or uncertain evidence in the records. If such research or evaluation is necessary, it will offer to furnish reproductions of all the records involved.

State Records

It should be remembered that, even though the War Department made every effort to assemble all available official information, many of the series of the compiled service records are not complete. In some cases a soldier may have served in a State militia unit never mustered into the service of the Continental, Federal, or Confederate States Governments. Records of service in such units, if extant, are most likely to be in the State archives or in the custody of the State Adjutant General.

GENEALOGICAL RECORDS IN THE NATIONAL ARCHIVES

The National Archives has custody of millions of records relating to persons who have had dealings with the Federal Government. These records may contain full information about the person or give little information beyond a name. Searches in the records may be very time consuming as many records lack name indexes. The National Archives is not staffed to make extensive searches but, given enough identifying information, will try to find a record about a specific person.

Most of the records, subject to the restrictions and limitations described below, may be freely consulted in the National Archives or in the Washington National Records Center, Washington, D.C.

20409. Photocopies of most of the records can be supplied for a moderate fee per page by the National Archives or the Center. A list is available, on request, of organizations and institutions in the Washington area that will provide the names of private persons who do research for a fee. A more detailed description of records of genealogical interest is contained in *Guide to Genealogical Records in the National Archives* (GS 4.6/2: G28), which may be purchased for 65 cents from the Superintendent of Documents, U.S. Government Printing Office, Washington, D.C. 20402.

Census Schedules

Population Censuses

A census of the population has been taken every 10 years since 1790. The National Archives has the 1790–1870 schedules, a microfilm copy of the 1880 schedules, and the surviving fragments of the 1890 schedules. (Practically all of the 1890 census schedules were destroyed by fire in 1921. The remaining entries are for small segments of the population in Perry County, Ala., the District of Columbia, Columbus, Ga., Mound Township, Ill., Rockford, Minn., Jersey City, N.J., Eastchester and Brookhaven Township, N.Y., Cleveland and Gaston Counties, N.C., Cincinnati and Wayne Township, Ohio, Jefferson Township, S. Dak., and Ellis, Hood, Kaufman, Rusk, and Trinity Counties, Tex.)

The 1790–1840 schedules show the names of the heads of households only; other family members are tallied unnamed in age and sex groups. For the 1850 and 1860 censuses, separate schedules list slaveowners and the age, sex, and color (but not the name) of each slave. The 1850–90 schedules include the name, age, and State, Territory, or country of birth of each free person in a household. Additional information is included with each succeeding census.

The available schedules for the 1790 census were published by the Federal Government in the early 1900's and have since been privately reprinted. The published census schedules for 1790 are for Connecticut, Maine, Maryland, Massachusetts, New Hampshire, New York, North Carolina, Pennsylvania, Rhode Island, South Carolina, and Vermont. Schedules for each State are listed in a separate, indexed volume. The schedules for the remaining States—Delaware, Georgia, Kentucky,

New Jersey, Tennessee, and Virginia—were burned during the War of 1812. As a substitute for the Virginia schedules, the Federal Government published names obtained from State censuses and tax lists, thereby listing about half of the known population of the State in 1790. Over the years additional lists of names have been published privately, and they provide more of the missing information for Virginia and other States whose 1790 schedules were destroyed. The Government has not published other census listings, but many privately published lists are available from libraries and other sources. Although the lists vary considerably in format and geographic scope, they frequently save researchers from fruitless searches and help locate a specific entry in the actual records.

Also helpful in locating specific census entries are the following unpublished indexes in the National Archives:

- 1810 Census—a card index for Virginia only.
- 1880 Census—a microfilm copy of a card index to entries for each household that included a child aged 10 or under. On the cards are the name, age, and birthplace of each member of such households, and there is a separate cross-reference card for each child aged 10 or under whose surname is different from that of the head of the household in which he is listed. The cards are arranged by State and thereunder by the Soundex system; that is, alphabetically by the first letter of the surname, thereunder by the sound of the surname, and thereunder alphabetically by given name of the head of the household.
- 1890 Census—a card index to the 6,160 names on the surviving 1890 schedules.

Other Censuses

The National Archives has the 1890 special schedules of Union veterans and widows of veterans for Washington, D.C., about half of Kentucky, and for States in alphabetical order from Louisiana through Wyoming. Schedules for the other States no longer exist. The schedules give the name and post office address of each living veteran and of each veteran's widow (along with the name of her veteran husband) and information about the service of each veteran named.

Whenever possible, the National Archives is acquiring microfilm copies of the mortality schedules of the 1850–80 censuses from the various depositories where they are held. The schedules show the name; the month and cause of death; and the State, Territory, or country of birth of each person who died during the year that preceded the taking of each of the censuses.

The National Archives staff will, free of charge, search the census schedules and indexes for a specific name in response to an inquiry received on GSA Form 7029, Request for Census Search. For schedules not indexed, the staff can make a very limited search for a particular name in a given year's schedules if provided the State and county in which the person lived. If the county had a large population, particularly after 1850, the specific town or township is needed. If the residence was in one of the larger cities, the street address or ward is also needed. This information can be found in city directories and ward maps that are normally available in city and State libraries, historical societies, and archives. When a requested entry is found, the fee for a photocopy of the census page on which it appears will be given. If the search is too extensive for the National Archives staff to undertake, the cost of the microfilm roll on which the desired schedules are included will be given.

Microfilm

The National Archives has microfilmed all of the available census schedules and the indexes to them, and positive microfilm copies are available at a moderate cost per roll. These microfilm rolls are arranged alphabetically by State and thereunder alphabetically by country. Each roll usually contains all of the schedules for one or several counties. The National Archives publication *Federal Population Census, 1790–1890,* which contains a roll listing and indicates the price for each roll, will be mailed upon request.

Claims for Pensions and Bounty Land

Under numerous laws passed since the Revolutionary War period, money and land have been awarded to Army, Navy, and Marine veterans and to their widows and other dependents. Each claim —whether for bounty land or pensions, whether or not submitted by the veteran, whether or not approved—is filed under the name of the veteran on whose service the applicant based his claim. The National Archives has bounty-land-warrant application files based on service in wartime between 1775 and 1855 and pension application files based on military service for the Confederate States of America were authorized by some Southern States but not by the Federal Government until 1959. Inquiries about State pensions should be addressed to the State Archives or equivalent agency at the capital of the veteran's State of residence after the war.

Since the form and contents of papers submitted in support of claims have varied over the years, the information in the files is not uniform. A veteran's claim will probably show his place and date of birth, place of residence after service, and a summary of military service. A dependent's claim normally includes the dependent's age and residence, relationship to the veteran, and information about the veteran's death. A widow's application usually includes her maiden name, the date of her marriage to the veteran, and the names of their children.

Inquiries about pension and bounty-land claims should be submitted on GSA Form 6751, Order for Photocopies Concerning Veteran, and accompanied by the required remittance in the form of a check or money order. Printed on the form are instructions about its use and an explanation of how orders are processed. When a claim file is found, documents that normally contain information of a personal nature about the veteran and his family will be selected and photocopies. The selected documents furnished generally contain the basic information in the pension file, as the remaining documents rarely contain any additional genealogical data. If an inquirer wishes to have photocopies of all the reproducible papers in the claim file, they can be furnished for a moderate cost per page. *The National Archives staff cannot undertake to read all the documents in the claim file or to answer questions about them.* If no claim file is found, the remittance will be refunded.

Some of the information requested on the form will be found in *Index of Revolutionary War Pension Applications,* revised and published in 1966 by the National Genealogical Society; in *Report From the Secretary of War . . . in Relation to the Pension Establishment of the United States,* published in three volumes in 1835 as Senate Document 514, 23d Congress, 1st session; and in *List of Pensioners on the Roll January 1, 1883,* published in five volumes in 1883 as Senate Executive Docu-

ment 84, 47th Congress, 2d session. These publications are available in some of the larger public and research libraries.

Army Service Records

Records relating to service in the U.S. Regular Army by officers (1789–1916) and by enlisted men (1789–1912) during both peacetime and wartime, as well as those of persons serving during wartime in volunteer units raised by States and mustered into Federal Service (1775–1903), are in the National Archives. There also are compiled military service records for soldiers in the Army of the Confederate States of America. Records of officers serving in the Regular Army vary in content so much that it is not feasible to describe here their form or content. Records of enlisted men serving in the Regular Army are contained in registers of enlistments which show for each recruit his name, age, place of birth, date and place of enlistment, regiment or company, and date and cause of discharge, or, where applicable, date of death or date of desertion and sometimes of apprehension or return after desertion. The compiled military service records both of volunteer officers and enlisted men serving in wartime and of Confederate soldiers normally show the soldier's rank, military organization, and term of service and occasionally his age, place of enlistment, and place of birth. These records do not contain information about the soldier's family.

The National Archives will search the registers of enlistments or the compiled military service records in response to an inquiry on GSA Form 6751, Order for Photocopies Concerning Veteran, when accompanied by the required remittance. For an effective search it is necessary that the form be as complete as possible. Whenever information is desired about military service in the Union Army in the Civil War, the name of the State from which the soldier served must be given. If a compiled military service record or an entry in an enlistment register is found, photocopies of the records will be supplied if the service was rendered more than 75 years ago (records of more recent service are subject to restrictions imposed by the Department of Defense). If the records in the National Archives relate to service within the past 75 years, a written statement of the service of the soldier will be sent free of charge. In that case and in any case where no record is found, the remittance will be returned.

Requests for information about Army officers separated after 1916 and Army enlisted personnel separated after 1912 should be made on Standard Form 180, Request Pertaining to Military Records, and sent to the National Personnel Records Center (Military Personnel Records), 9700 Page Boulevard, St. Louis, Mo. 63132.

Naval and Marine Service Records

The National Archives has records relating to American naval and marine service in the Revolutionary War (1775–83), in the U.S. Navy (for officers, 1798–1902, and for enlisted men, 1798–1885), and in the U.S. Marine Corps (1798–1895). There are also records for some persons who served in the Confederate Navy and Marine Corps (1861–65).

Naval and marine service records of the Revolutionary War period are fragmentary, including only such information as a serviceman's name and rank, the name of the vessel on which he served, and the dates of his service or the dates when he was paid. Confederate naval and marine service records give the serviceman's name and rank and sometimes his station. If he was imprisoned, a record may give such information as the date of his capture, the place of his imprisonment, and the date of his parole. Only those requests for information about naval and marine service during the Revolutionary War and about service in the Confederate Navy and Marine Corps should be sent on GSA Form 6751, Order for Photocopies Concerning Veteran, and accompanied by the required remittance. All other requests regarding naval and marine service records in the National Archives should be by letter as the National Archives does not have compiled service records for naval and marine personnel.

Records relating to the service of commissioned officers in the U.S. Navy after the Revolution and before 1846 give for each officer such information as his name, rank, State of birth, State of residence, dates of service, and, sometimes, age or date of birth. Records for 1846 and later occasionally give the date and place of the officer's death in service or the date of his retirement. Records relating to a Navy enlisted man's service before 1846 usually give only his name and rating, the name of the vessels on which he served, and the dates of his service. Later records give also the enlisted man's age and place of birth and occasionally his place of enlistment.

Records of commissioned officers in the U.S. Marine Corps usually show each officer's name and rank and the date of his appointment or of his acceptance of a commission. They may also give his age and information about his residence. Service records for enlisted marines usually show the man's name, age, and the date, place, and term of his enlistment.

The National Archives will make a limited search in its naval and marine service records in response to letters of inquiry. If a request concerns a Navy or Marine officer or enlisted man, his name and the name of the war in which he served or the dates of his service should be given. If the request concerns a Navy enlisted man, the name of at least one vessel on which he served (with approximate dates) must also be given and, if possible, his place of enlistment.

Requests for information about Navy officers separated since 1902, Navy enlisted men separated since 1885, and Marine Corps officers and enlisted men separated after 1895 should be made on Standard Form 180, Request Pertaining to Military Records. Send these requests to the National Personnel Records Center (Military Personnel Records), 9700 Page Boulevard, St. Louis, Mo. 63132.

Passenger Lists

The National Archives has incomplete series of customs passenger lists and immigration passenger lists of ships arriving from abroad at Atlantic and Gulf of Mexico ports. The following table shows the dates of passenger lists and related indexes in the National Archives:

Port	Customs passenger lists	Immigration passenger lists	Indexes
Baltimore	1820–91	1891–1909	1820–1952
Boston	1820–74 and 1883–91	1891–1943	1848–91 and 1902–20
New Orleans	1820–1902	1903–45	1853–1952
New York	1820–97	1897–1942	1820–46 and 1897–1943
Philadelphia	1800–82	1883–1945	1800–1948
Certain minor ports	1820–73	1893–1945	1890–1924

Supplementing the indexes listed above is a general index to quarterly reports of arrivals at most ports except New York, 1820–74.

A customs passenger list normally contains the

following information for each passenger: his name, age, sex, and occupation; the country from which he came; and the country to which he was going; and, if he died in passage, the date and circumstances of his death. The immigration passenger lists that are more than 50 years old (those less than 50 years old are not available for reference purposes) vary in informational content but usually show the place of birth and last place of residence in addition to the information found in the customs passenger lists. Some of the immigration passenger lists include the name and address of a relative in the country from which the passenger came.

The National Archives will search the customs passenger lists if in addition to the name of the passenger and the name of the port of entry an inquirer can supply the following information: the name of the vessel and the approximate date of its arrival or the name of the port of embarkation and the exact date of arrival. It will also search the immigration passenger lists over 50 years old if an inquirer can give the full name and age of the passenger and names and ages of accompanying passengers, the name of the port of entry, the name of the vessel, and the exact date of arrival. The National Archives will also consult such indexes as it has to the names on the customs and immigration passenger lists provided an inquirer can supply the name of the port of entry and the supposed year of arrival.

Microfilm copies of passenger lists more than 50 years old are available for use in the National Archives.

The Morton Allan Directory of European Passenger Steamship Arrivals (New York, Immigration Information Bureau, Inc., 1931) lists by year, steamship company, and exact date the names of vessels arriving at the ports of New York, 1890–1930, and of Baltimore, Boston, and Philadelphia, 1904–26. This publication is available in some of the larger public and research libraries.

Records About Indians

There are in the National Archives many records relating to Indians who kept their tribal status. The records, arranged by tribes, are dated chiefly 1830–1940. They include lists of Indians (chiefly Cherokee, Chickasaw, Choctaw, and Creek) who moved west during the period 1830–46; annuity pay rolls, 1841–1949; annual census rolls, 1885–1940; and Eastern Cherokee claim files, 1902–10.

The lists normally contain the name of the head of the family, the number of persons in the family by age and sex groups, the description of property owned before removal (including the location of real property), and the dates of departure from the East and arrival in the West.

Annuity pay rolls (except those early ones that give little but the names of heads of families) show the name, age, and sex of each person who received payment.

The annual census rolls normally show for each person listed his Indian or English name or both (names are grouped by family), age, sex, and relationship to the head of the family and sometimes to another enrolled Indian. Occasionally on the rolls may be found supplementary information, such as the names of persons who died or were born during the year. The National Archives will search the records if it is given the Indian's name (preferably both his English and his Indian name), the name of his tribe, and the approximate date of his association with the tribe.

The Eastern Cherokee claim files usually contain the name of the applicant, his residence, the date and place of his birth, the name and age of his spouse, the names of his father and mother and of his children, and other genealogical information. For a search of the claim files, the name of the claimant (or his claim number) and his age when the claim was filed or the date of his birth are necessary. Such additional information about the claimant as his place of residence when the claim was filed, the name of his spouse, and the names of his parents or children will facilitate the search.

Records About District of Columbia Residents

Records relating to District of Columbia residents in the Washington National Records Center, Washington, D.C. 20409, include, in addition to naturalization records (see below), copies of wills, 1801–88; records relating to the administration of estates, 1801–78; and guardianship papers, 1802–78. Although the records relating to the administration of estates are concerned mostly with financial transactions involving the property and debts of a decedent, they show his name and sometimes the names of members of his family. Copies of wills contain, besides the name of the decedent, the names of legatees and their relationships to him. Guardianship papers give the name of each ward of the court and at times his age and the names of his parents.

A search of these records requires the name of the person in question, the type of record involved, and the approximate date of the transaction.

Naturalization Records

The Washington National Records Center, Washington, D.C. 20409, has naturalization proceedings of the District of Columbia courts, 1802–1926. These records show, for each person who petitioned for naturalization, his age or date of birth, his nationality, and whether citizenship was granted. The National Archives has photocopies and indexes of naturalization documents, 1787–1906, filed by courts in Maine, Massachusetts, New Hampshire, and Rhode Island. These records were copied and indexed by the Work Projects Administration in the late 1930's. The Washington National Records Center and the National Archives will search these records for information about naturalizations that occurred before September 27, 1906, if given the full name of the petitioner and the approximate date of naturalization. Persons who wish information about citizenship granted elsewhere before September 27, 1906, should send their inquiries to the clerk of the Federal, State, or other court that issued the naturalization certificate.

The Immigration and Naturalization Service, Washington, D.C. 20536, has duplicate records of all naturalizations that occurred after September 26, 1906. Inquiries about citizenship granted after that date should be sent to the Service on a form that can be obtained from any of the Service's district offices. Local postmasters will give the address of the nearest district office.

Land Records

The land records (dated chiefly 1800–1950) in the Washington National Records Center include bounty-land warrant files, donation land entry files, homestead application files, and private land claim files relating to the entry of individual settlers on land in the public land States. There are no land records for the Thirteen Original States and Maine, Vermont, West Virginia, Kentucky, Tennessee, Texas, and Hawaii. Records for these States are maintained by State officials, usually in the State capital. The donation land entry files and homestead application files show, in addition to the name of the applicant, the location of the land and the date he acquired it, his residence or post office address, his age or date and place of birth, his marital status, and, if applicable, the given name of his wife or the size of his family. If an applicant for homestead land was of foreign birth, his application file contains evidence of his naturalization or of his intention to become a citizen. Supporting documents show the immigrant's country of birth and sometimes the date and port of arrival. Genealogical information in records relating to private land claims varies from the mention of the claimant's name and location of the land to such additional information as the claimant's place of residence when he made the claim and the names of his relatives, both living and dead.

The Washington National Records Center, Washington, D.C. 20409, will search these land records for Alabama, Alaska, Arizona, Florida, Louisiana, Nevada, or Utah for the period 1800–July 1, 1908, if the full name of the applicant and the name of the State or Territory in which the land was located are given. A search of the records for all other public land States or Territories, 1800–1950, requires, in addition to the applicant's name, (1) the number of the land entry file or a description of the land by township, range, section, and fraction of section or (2) the name of the land office and either the date when the original application was filed or the date of the final certificate. An inquirer may be able to obtain the legal description of land by writing to the county recorder of deeds in the county seat of the county in which the land was located.

GENEALOGICAL SOURCES OUTSIDE THE NATIONAL ARCHIVES

A genealogist tracing the history of a family needs to examine all the pertinent records he can find, and he will find many such records outside the National Archives. He will begin, as a rule, by referring to such records as the family Bible, diaries, and letters and by contacting older family members who can often provide leads to informative documentary sources. He also will learn how to find and use some of these sources by referring to books such as the following:

- Gilbert Harry Doane, *Searching for Your*

Ancestors (Minneapolis: University of Minnesota Press, rev. 1960).
- American Society of Genealogists, *Genealogical Research: Methods and Sources* (Washington, 1960).

These books, as well as others cited in this leaflet, may be found in many of the larger public and research libraries.

Documentary sources in the National Archives are described briefly in a leaflet entitled *Genealogical Records in the National Archives.* Some records, such as census schedules, naturalization proceedings, and military service records, which can be used as sources of genealogical information in the 19th century, are subject to restrictions in later periods. They may be used chiefly by the individuals mentioned in them for legal and other purposes, such as proving age and citizenship. Records of this type are discussed in the leaflet *Age and Citizenship Records in the National Archives.* Both of these leaflets are available free of charge in limited quantities from the Publications Sales Branch, National Archives Building, General Services Administration, Washington, D.C. 20408. Some of the more generally useful genealogical sources elsewhere in the United States are described below.

Federal Census Schedules

The original general schedules of the decennial population census of 1880 and the original special schedules of the decennial nonpopulation censuses of 1850–80 are in various depositories in the States and the District of Columbia. Some depositories also have the copies of the Federal population census schedules from 1830 to 1870 that were given to the States at the time of the original enumerations. Many State archival agencies and large public libraries have photocopies (usually microfilm) of some of the general schedules of the decennial population censuses, 1790–1880, as well as of the remnant special schedules of a census in 1890 of surviving Union veterans or the widows of deceased Union veterans of the Civil War. Many States and the National Archives have original or microfilm copies of Federal mortality schedules of the population censuses, 1850–80, which contain information about deaths of persons often not available elsewhere. The names and addresses of more than 200 depositories, with information on their census holdings, appear in

an article by W. Neil Franklin, "Availability of Federal Population Census Schedules in the States," in the *National Genealogical Society Quarterly* (Vol. 50, Nos. 1 and 2, March and June 1962).

The 1790 population census schedules have been published by the U.S. Government Printing Office in 12 indexed volumes. Although the original edition is out of print, the volumes have been reprinted by non-Government agencies.

Naturalization Records

Before 1906, naturalization proceedings could be held in a Federal, State, or local court. Records of such proceedings in Federal courts outside of the District of Columbia are commonly to be found in records of the district court for the district in which the proceedings took place. If the proceedings were held in a State or local court, the clerk of the court will, as a rule, have the records. The *Check List of Historical Records Survey Publications,* cited below under State and Local Records, may give a citation to a records inventory that will tell where the naturalization records were in the late 1930's. Published guides to manuscript holdings in various depositories in the States may also help locate naturalization records.

Holdings of the Library of Congress

The Local History and Genealogy Room of the Library of Congress has an extensive collection of useful materials relating to local history and genealogy. The collection includes American and foreign-compiled genealogies; periodicals published by State historical societies and genealogical organizations; publications of patriotic and hereditary societies, such as lineage books and lists of members of families; published works on immigrations to the United States, for example, the Scotch-Irish, German, and Huguenot; published rosters of American soldiers and sailors who participated in wars in which the Thirteen Colonies and the United States were involved; histories of localities in the United States and in foreign countries; guides to records in State archival agencies and historical societies; biographical works; and lists of passengers arriving in the United States that have been printed in various publications.

The Library does not prepare family trees or

undertake genealogical research. The small staff assigned to administer the local history and genealogy collection is able to do a limited amount of searching in the catalogs and indexes to the collection for specific titles of books and to see if a particular reference can be found in a given volume. The staff assists readers in the use of catalogs and indexes to the collection. The following leaflets are available free of charge from the General Reference and Bibliography Division, The Library of Congress, Washington, D.C. 20540: *Reference Services and Facilities of the Local History and Genealogy Room, Guides to Genealogical Research: A Selected List,* and *Surnames: A Selected List of Books.*

The Library has a limited amount of material of genealogical interest in its Manuscript and Rare Book Divisions. It also has on microfilm and microcards a collection of material on local history and genealogy, which is not available in any other form in the Library. Other collections in the Library, such as newspapers, city directories, and maps, are also of value in genealogical research.

The National Union Catalog in the Library gives the location of important books in the major libraries in the United States and Canada. The Library's Photoduplication Service will supply, for a fee, photocopies of materials in its collections if there are no copyright or other restrictions on them. Information for persons who plan to do research at the Library of Congress is in the booklet *Information for Readers in the Library of Congress,* available free of charge from the Central Services Division, and on the sheet *Hours of Public Service in the Library of Congress,* available free of charge from the Stack and Reader Division.

Holdings of Other Libraries

Some other libraries have large genealogical collections. For example, the library of the National Society, Daughters of the American Revolution, 1776 D Street NW., Washington, D.C. 20006, has a large collection of genealogical materials in printed, processed, and typewritten form. They include copies of entries in family Bibles and of inscriptions on tombstones, abstracts of court records, lineage books, abstracts of Revolutionary War pension and bounty land warrant application files in the National Archives, and copies of church records. The library of the society is open not only to members but also (for a small fee) to non-

members. It is closed to nonmembers during the month of April. The society does not do original research but will furnish the names of genealogists who will do research in its holdings for a fee. For the names and addresses of other libraries having large genealogical collections, see *Subject Collections,* compiled by Lee Ash and Denis Lorenz (New York: R. R. Bowker Co., 1967).

Most large public and research libraries, whether they have genealogical collections or not, have materials that can be used for genealogical research. Among them are files of newspapers, which are invaluable in tracing lineages. They contain notices of births, marriages, and deaths and of the changes of family residence from one community to another. See Clarence S. Brigham, *History and Bibliography of American Newspapers, 1690–1820* (2 vols.; Worcester, Mass.: American Antiquarian Society, 1947); and Winifred Gregory, *American Newspapers, 1821–1936, a Union List of Files Available in the United States and Canada* (New York: H. W. Wilson Co., 1937).

A useful tool for finding printed sources that contain information on persons who came to America before 1826 is the publication *A Bibliography of Ship Passenger Lists, 1538–1825,* compiled by Harold Lancour, revised and enlarged by Richard J. Wolfe (New York: New York Public Library, 1963).

Sources in Genealogical Societies

Genealogical societies can be helpful to persons tracing their ancestry. One of the many such societies in the United States is the National Genealogical Society, 1921 Sunderland Place NW., Washington, D.C. 20036. Its periodical, the *National Genealogical Society Quarterly,* has published thousands of records and many articles on families and the locations of source materials in all parts of the United States and some foreign countries, especially England and Germany. The society has issued special publications dealing with such varied topics as migration trails east of the Mississippi River, Lancaster County (Pennsylvania) tax lists, Chatham County (Georgia) wills, medieval English records, heraldry, and genealogical research in German-speaking lands. The publications of genealogical societies are available in most of the larger libraries having genealogical collections. The advertising columns of most genealogical publications are open to persons who wish to obtain or exchange information about particular families. One of the available lists of genealogical societies is published annually in the June issue of *The Genealogical Helper* by the Everton Publishers, P.O. Box 368, Logan, Utah 84321.

State and Local Records

Some State, county, and municipal records have great value for genealogists. Records of births and deaths may be on file in State bureaus of vital statistics, or they may be kept by a county or municipal offical—usually the county, city, or town clerk. Many State governments made no attempt before the 20th century to centralize vital records. Marriage and divorce records are usually filed with either an official of the county in which the marriage or divorce occurred or the State official having custody of vital records. In some instances, however, marriage records are kept in the office of a town or city official. The Superintendent of Documents, U.S. Government Printing Office, Washington, D.C. 20402, sells three helpful leaflets: *Where to Write for Birth and Death Records* (15 cents), *Where to Write for Marriage Records* (15 cents), and *Where to Write for Divorce Records* (10 cents).

There are records for the ports of Baltimore and Boston that were created as a result of State legislation relating to immigrants. Lists of aliens who arrived at Baltimore during the years 1833–66 and an alphabetical index to them are maintained by the city of Baltimore. For information about these lists, write to the Department of Legislative Reference, City Hall, Baltimore, Md. 21202. Massachusetts has lists of aliens who arrived at Boston during the years 1848–91. For information about these lists, write to the Archives Division, Office of the Secretary of the Commonwealth, State House, Boston, Mass. 02133. An index to the Boston lists is in the Boston Public Library, Copley Square, Boston, Mass. 02117; the Genealogical Society of the Church of Jesus Christ of Latter Day Saints, 107 South Main Street, Salt Lake City, Utah 84111; and the National Archives.

Some States have records of military service performed in State or colonial units, State or colonial land transactions affecting individuals, censuses authorized by Federal, State, or territorial legislation, and claims for pension and other benefits based on military service. Such records are often deposited in the State archives. If they are not, the State archivist or a compara-

ble official can usually direct an inquirer to them. For information about Confederate pension application files, write to the appropriate official in the capital of the State from which the service was rendered or where the pensioner resided at the time of his death.

In addition to vital records, county records of genealogical interest include wills, records of the administration and distribution of estates, deeds, leases, court records relating to orphans and guardianship, and lists of voters and taxpayers. Municipal records of similar interest include tax lists, registers of voters, and court records. For information about such records, write to the appropriate county, town, or city official.

Some books that may be of assistance in the use of State and local records are listed below:

- Sargent B. Child and Dorothy P. Holmes, *Check List of Historical Records Survey Publications* (Washington: Work Projects Administration, rev. 1943), which lists published inventories of State, county, and municipal records; transcriptions of public records in the States; and guides to vital records.
- Henry J. Dubester, *State Censuses, an Annotated Bibliography of Censuses of Population Taken After the Year 1790 by States and Territories of the United States* (Washington: U.S. Government Printing Office, 1948). Out of print.
- Noel C. Stevenson, *Search and Research* (Salt Lake City: Deseret Book Co., rev. 1959).
- Society of American Archivists, State and Local Records Committee, *Directory of State and Provincial Archivists, 1968.*
- American Association for State and Local History, *Directory: Historical Societies and Agencies in the United States and Canada, 1969–70.*

Church Records

Church records contain information about births, baptisms, marriages, deaths, and burials and give the names of members of families. Church records may also help trace movements of individuals from one community to another.

Information about the record holdings of many of the leading denominations can be found in the October 1961 and other issues of *The American Archivist,* published quarterly by the Society of American Archivists.

The following books may also help locate church records:

- *Check List of Historical Records Survey Publications,* cited under State and Local Records, which lists inventories of church records in the States.
- E. Kay Kirkham. *A Survey of American Church Records* (2 vols.; Salt Lake City: Deseret Book Co., 1959–60).

PENSION AND BOUNTY LAND WARRANT APPLICATION FILES IN THE NATIONAL ARCHIVES

From the earliest days of English settlement in America, the Colonies gave financial aid to persons disabled in military or naval service and to the dependents of those who were killed. After the Colonies declared their independence, the Continental Congress passed resolutions promising compensation to all who were disabled in the Revolutionary War, all who continued in service to the end of the war, and the widows or orphans of officers who were killed in the war. But since the Congress lacked funds, it relied on the States to provide for compensation in the form of money or land. And some States provided benefits independently of the Congress.

Pension Files

During the first session of the First Congress under the Constitution, an act was approved making the United States responsible for the payment of disability pensions that had been granted by the States for service in the Revolutionary War. Acts passed by Congress during the next three decades limited benefits to those who were disabled in service and to dependents of those who were killed or died as a result of service. In 1818, however, Congress provided that every person who had served in the Revolutionary War for 9 months or until the end of the war and was "in need of assistance from his country for support" should be pensioned. Later legislation removed the requirement of need.

Following the precedent set for Revolutionary War veterans, Congress has authorized pensions for those who served in succeeding wars, including the Indian wars, and in the peacetime Military Establishment. Pensions for peacetime service, however, have been limited to veterans who suf-

fered service-connected disabilities or to dependents of those who died as a result of their service.

The records of pensions granted or applied for under most of these laws are in the National Archives. The pension files relate to claims based on service rendered between 1775 and 1916. Pension claims based on naval service are interfiled with those for military service.

The National Archives does not have applications received by the Secretary of War through November 8, 1800, as those applications together with their supporting papers were apparently destroyed in the War Department fire of that date. A few records, however, relating to those early claims still exist, and certain information from them has been abstracted on cards, which are interfiled in the series of Revolutionary War pension and bounty land warrant application files.

A typical pension file contains the application of the claimant, documents submitted as evidence of identity and service, and records of action taken on the claim. The claimant may have been a veteran, a veteran's widow, his minor children, or other dependents. Since a claimant might apply for a pension under several acts of Congress, a pension file may contain more than one application for a single claimant. Or it may contain applications for several claimants, since all applications for pensions that were based on the service of the same serviceman for the same period of time were usually filed together. The documents submitted in support of a pension claim may include discharge papers or affidavits attesting to the service rendered, leaves from family Bibles, and copies of records of birth, marriage, and death. For service in the Civil War and later a pension file may also include Bureau of Pensions questionnaires containing genealogical information. Many such questionnaires were sent to pensioners by the Bureau in 1898 and 1915.

Pensions based on military service for the Confederate States of America were authorized by some Southern States but not by the Federal Government until 1959. Inquiries about State pensions should be addressed to the State Archives or equivalent agency at the capital of the veteran's State.

Bounty Land Warrant Application Files

In 1776 and later the Continental Congress provided for granting land in the public domain to those who would agree to remain in the armed forces until the end of the war or until discharged by the Congress and to dependents of those who were killed. Laws passed by Congress between 1796 and 1855 also authorized the granting of warrants for land to those who had served in the Revolutionary War, the War of 1812, Indian wars, and the war with Mexico and also for services of militia volunteers and State troops between June 18, 1812, and March 22, 1852. The bounty land warrant application files relate to claims based on service rendered in wartime between 1775 and 1855.

The documents in a bounty land warrant application file are similar to those in a pension file. They include the application of the claimant, who may have been the veteran, his widow, or his heirs; a discharge certificate or affidavits attesting to the service rendered; and the jacket on which actions taken on the claim are noted. Since Congress enacted many laws relating to bounty land, more than one application may be found in a bounty land warrant application file. Many of these application files have been combined with pension files. All the claims in such a consolidated file, however, are based on the service of the same serviceman in the same war.

Information in the Records

A pension or bounty land warrant application file normally shows the name, rank, and military or naval unit of the serviceman and the period of his service. If the serviceman made the application, the file usually shows his age or date of birth and his place of residence, and sometimes his place of birth. If his widow made the application, the file normally shows her age and place of residence, her maiden name, the date and place of her marriage to the serviceman, and the date and place of his death. When an application was made in behalf of minor children or by heirs of the serviceman, their names and sometimes their ages or dates of birth are in the file. Questionnaires returned by Civil War and later pensioners normally show the names of children.

How To Get Copies of the Records

For the convenience of those who wish to obtain information from pension and bounty land war-

rant application records without coming to Washington, the National Archives furnishes photocopies of documents in the files for a fee. It will search for a pension or bounty land warrant application file if, in addition to the full name of the veteran and the war in which he served or the dates of his service, an inquirer can supply certain identifying information. This information should be sent in on GSA Form 6751, Order for Photocopies Concerning Veteran, which will be furnished free on request. The form should be filled out, according to the printed instructions on it, with as much of the information called for as possible and returned to the National Archives and Records Service with a $1 check or money order for each record requested. The form also contains an explanation of our procedures in handling requests.

Some of the information requested on the form will be found in *Index of Revolutionary War Pension Applications,* revised and published in 1966 by the National Genealogical Society; in *Report From the Secretary of War . . . in Relation to the Pension Establishment of the United States,* published in three volumes in 1835 as Senate Document 514, 23d Congress, 1st session; and in *List of Pensioners on the Roll January 1, 1883,* published in five volumes in 1883 as Senate Executive Document 84, 47th Congress, 2d session. These publications are available in most of the larger public and research libraries.

What You Will Receive

In the National Archives finds a pension or bounty land warrant application file for the veteran in question, it will supply photocopies of selected documents that normally contain information of a personal nature about the veteran and his family. *The National Archives is unable to read all the documents in the file or to answer specific questions about them.* But if the inquirer wishes to have photocopies of all the other papers in the file, they will be furnished for a moderate additional cost.

If no pension or bounty land warrant application file is found for the veteran in question, the remittance of $1 will be returned to the inquirer.

Inquirers who are unable to supply the information necessary for the National Archives to make an effective search in the pension and bounty land warrant application files may examine or hire someone to examine specified files in the National Archives research rooms.

RECORDS IN THE NATIONAL ARCHIVES RELATING TO CONFEDERATE SOLDIERS

Compiled service records for most men, but not all men, who served in the Confederate States Army are on file in the National Archives. They contain virtually no genealogical information, but they are of value for proving the Confederate military service of a forebear. The National Archives is unable to abstract or summarize these records for inquirers but can furnish photocopies of them for a fee sufficient to cover the cost of reproduction.

Their History

When Richmond was evacuated by the Confederate Government in April 1865, the centralized military personnel records of the Confederate Army were taken to Charlotte, N.C., by the Confederate Adjutant and Inspector General, Gen. Samuel Cooper. When the Confederate civil authorities left Charlotte after agreeing to an armistice between the armies in North Carolina, President Jefferson Davis instructed Cooper to turn the records over, if necessary, to "the enemy, as essential to the history of the struggle." When Gen. Joseph E. Johnston learned, after the armistice, that the records were at Charlotte, he turned them over to the Union commander in North Carolina, saying: "As they will furnish valuable materials for history, I am anxious for their preservation, and doubt not that you are too."

The records in question were taken to Washington, where along with other Confederate records captured by the Union Army, they were preserved in the War Department. In the years 1878–1901 a former Confederate general, Marcus J. Wright, was employed by the War Department to locate missing Confederate records and borrow them for copying if the possessors were not disposed to give them to the War Department. In 1903 Secretary of War Elihu Root persuaded the Governors of most Southern States to lend to the War Department for copying such Confederate military personnel records as were then in the possession of their respective States.

Their Value

Supplementing the Confederate records surrendered or captured at the end of the war with other records collected or copied has resulted in a unique body of official information about the service of Confederate soldiers. The Confederate Army, unlike the Union Army, did not provide the States with copies of muster rolls for military units it had taken over from them. Copies kept by unit commanders were in many cases turned over, in the years after the war, to the States involved; but the States had no files, created during the war, of muster rolls for the units they had furnished. They or their citizens have therefore long had to rely on the information contained in the War Department Collection of Confederate Records, now in the National Archives. The need for access to this information first became acute when Southern States began providing benefits for Confederate veterans. It has continued to be important to patriotic organizations composed of proven descendants of Confederate veterans.

In order to make information about the service of Confederate soldiers more readily and completely available, the War Department began in 1903 to compile a service record for each soldier by copying off the entries pertaining to him in muster rolls and other original records. This project was interrupted by World War I but was completed in 1927 with the aid of a special appropriation. The result is an immense file of "compiled military service records," from which inquiries about Confederate soldiers are answered.

Because of the efforts made over many years to incorporate all available information into this file, it is by far the most complete and accurate source of information about Confederate soldiers. Thus, a special study has shown that the chances of finding in this file the record of a Confederate soldier from North Carolina are about 50 percent greater than the chances of finding the soldier's record in John W. Moore's *Roster of North Carolina Troops in the War Between the States* (4 vols., Raleigh, 1882), although the latter work was compiled from the Confederate muster rolls in the custody of the Federal War Department.

Description of the Records

The compiled military service record of a Confederate soldier is kept in a jacket-envelope filed with jacket-envelopes for other soldiers in the same regiment or similar unit. The record consists of one or more card abstracts and usually, also, one or more original documents. Each card abstract is a copy, made in the 20th century by the Federal War Department, of an entry in original records such as Confederate muster rolls, returns, and descriptive rolls and Union prison and parole records. The card abstracts in the jacket for any soldier, if the original record of his service was complete, may serve to trace that service from beginning to end, but they normally do little more than account for where he was at a given time. The only information of genealogical interest they are likely to give is his age and place of enlistment.

The original Confederate and Union records, from which the card abstracts just discussed were made, are among the holdings of the National Archives; but there is rarely any need to consult them about the service of a soldier because of the care and thoroughness with which the service data they contain were abstracted. The original records are much used, however, for general historical purposes, for example, the history of military campaigns and of home-front activities of the Confederate Government. The National Archives is unable to do genealogical or historical research in these records in response to letter inquiries but will be glad to furnish simple factual information for general historical purposes if it is readily accessible in the records and does not have to be compiled.

How To Order Copies

To find the record of a particular Confederate soldier for whom a compiled military service record exists, the National Archives needs:

(1) the exact name under which he was carried on the rolls of the Confederate Army,

(2) the State from which he entered the Confederate service, and

(3) the designation of the regiment or other unit in which he served, for example, the "23rd Alabama Infantry."

If this information can be supplied, it is usually a simple matter to locate the man's compiled military service record. And to simplify further the searching process inquirers are asked to fill out Form NAR 288, Order for Photocopies Concerning Veteran. Since this form is also used for in-

quiries about Union veterans, it calls for some information that is not pertinent to inquiries for Confederate soldiers.

The completed form should be sent to the National Archives and Records Service with a check or money order for $1, payable to the General Services Administration. The $1 fee should be paid for each order form sent. If the National Archives cannot find a record for the soldier inquired about, it will return the fee.

What You Will Receive

The National Archives, if it finds a compiled service record for the soldier about whom you have inquired, will send you photocopies of the card abstracts in his jacket-envelope, or, if such abstracts are numerous, photocopies of such of them as are not merely repetitions. The original papers that may be in the jacket-envelope are not normally copied because most such papers are financial vouchers containing information of no more than casual interest. Occasionally other papers are to be found in the jacket-envelope, but these usually pertain to routine matters such as details to duty or furloughs. Upon request the National Archives will report to you the cost of reproducing all papers in a jacket-envelope in addition to the card abstracts.

Identifying a Soldier

If the soldier's name as supplied by an inquirer is not exactly the same as that under which the soldier was carried on the rolls of the Confederate Army, or if the unit in which the soldier served is not known to the inquirer or is given incorrectly by him, the staff of the National Archives may find it difficult to identify the soldier correctly. There are usually far more soldiers of the same or nearly the same name than the average inquirer would imagine, and the name under which a soldier was carried on the rolls of the Confederate Army may differ in various ways from the name by which he was known to members of his family.

In attempting to identify a soldier, where the information supplied does not suffice for the purpose, the National Archives will try to match initials and variant spellings of the surname given in a standard list of variant spellings. If it is able to reduce the possibilities to a very few individual records, it will attempt identification by comparing the contents of these records with any information supplied by the inquirer that is likely to be useful for the purpose. If the soldier's identity seems obvious or very probable, the National Archives will furnish a photocopy of the record for the soldier it thinks is the correct one. If the attempted identification proves to be incorrect, it should be remembered that it was made in an effort to be helpful.

The National Archives cannot go beyond making identifications that are relatively easy to make. It cannot undertake to do extensive research or to evaluate conflicting or dubious evidence in the records. If such research or evaluation is necessary, it will offer to furnish reproductions of all the records involved.

State Records

It should be remembered that, owing to the hazards to which records of the Confederate Army were subjected during the war and particularly at the end of the war, the War Department Collection of Confederate Records is not complete, even though every effort was made to assemble all available official information. In some cases a soldier may have served in a State militia unit never mustered into the service of the Confederate States Government. Records of service in such units, if extant, are most likely to be in the State archives or in the custody of the State Adjutant General. Southern States are also likely to have records relating to the payment of State benefits to Confederate veterans.

United Nations Documents

By Harry N. M. Winton

Although a little dated (as to the number of Member States and the like), this authoritative article is one of the best short pieces that I've been able to find on the subject. Harry Winton, recently retired, was Chief of the Documents Reference Section of the Dag Hammarskjold Library of the United Nations for many years. I think every school, college, and public librarian should have at least the basic information on this important international agency and its publications. This article provides that.

On the 26th of June the United Nations will celebrate the twentieth anniversary of the signing of its Charter at the United Nations Conference in San Francisco in 1945.[1] The purposes of the Organization are declared by Article 1 of that Charter to be:

To maintain international peace and security;
To develop friendly relations among nations, based on respect for the principle of equal rights and self-determination of peoples, and to take other appropriate measures to strengthen universal peace;
To achieve international co-operation in solving international problems of economic, social, cultural, or humanitarian character, and in promoting and encouraging respect for human rights and for fundamental freedoms for all without distinction as to race, sex, language, or religion; and
To be a centre for harmonizing the actions of nations in the attainment of these common ends.

Membership has grown from the fifty-one original signatories in 1945 to 114 Member States today.[2] The six principal organs named in the Charter are the General Assembly, the Security Council, the Economic and Social Council, the Trusteeship Council, the International Court of Justice, and the Secretariat. In the course of its work the General Assembly and the three Councils have established many subsidiary bodies, both permanent and *ad hoc*; and the staff of the Secretariat, although chiefly at work at Headquarters in New York and at the European Office in Geneva, is to be found in branch offices and information centers and on mission throughout the world.

The functions of the principal and subsidiary organs of the United Nations and the nature of their publications are well described in *Everyman's United Nations*.[3] For a more detailed examination of the documents and publications of the United Nations, *A Guide to the Use of United Nations Documents* contains suggestions for research purposes, as well as information regarding the management of collections of this material.[4] Prepared at New York University, the *Guide* is the result of extensive experience with this excellent and well-managed depository collection.

Of the intergovernmental agencies related to the United Nations, some of the more specialized agencies are older than the United Nations itself. The International Telecommunication Union (ITU), for instance, originated in 1865, and the International Labor Organization (ILO) was created in 1919 at the same time as The League of Nations. Other specialized agencies, among these the United Nations Educational, Scientific and Cultural Organization (UNESCO), were founded, like the United Nations itself, during the Second World War. Still other agencies, such as the World Health Organization (WHO), were later created by the United Nations. Each of these organizations is autonomous, with its own headquarters, and is responsible for distribution of its publications by sale, exchange or deposit. These agencies are discussed in *Everyman's United Nations;* the publications and documents examined in *A Guide to the Use of United Nations Documents.*

The International Court of Justice, seated at The Hague, publishes through A. W. Sijthoff's Pub-

SOURCE: Reprinted from Harry N. M. Winton, "United Nations Documents," *Drexel Library Quarterly*, I (October, 1965), pp. 32–41, by permission of the publisher and the author.

lishing Company, Leyden. Other than press releases, the Court distributes no mimeographed material. Its publications appear, except for the *Yearbook*, in bilingual (French and English) printed series. The sales numbers appearing on individual publications form a continuous series, indicating the order of publication. The series of Court publications include: *Reports of Judgments, Advisory Opinions and Orders*, each available in separate paper cover editions, as well as in annual cumulative clothbound volumes; *Pleadings, Oral Arguments, Documents*, issued in cloth-bound volumes for each case; *Acts and Documents Concerning the Organization of the Court*, in a single clothbound volume; and the *Yearbook*, in separate French and English editions, clothbound.[5] Court publications are available from the Sales Section, and are listed, as published, in the *United Nations Documents Index.*[6]

In considering the published materials of other principal organs (the General Assembly, the three Councils, the Secretariat and subsidiaries of these organs) the term "documents" includes mimeographed material distributed during the sessions of these organs: reports, memoranda, and notes from the Secretary-General; Secretariat studies; draft resolutions; communications from governments, other inter-governmental agencies and non-governmental organizations; petitions; and meeting records. All of these are in regular document symbol series. The term "publications" includes sales publications, priced items offered for sale or subscription: monographs, yearbooks, bulletins, periodicals, the *Official Records* and the *Treaty Series*. Nearly all publications are printed or photo-offset, only a few are mimeographed. The term "public information material" includes leaflets and pamphlets issued free of charge by the Office of Public Information, as distinct from publications prepared for sale by that Office.

It should be recognized that the United Nations is not primarily a publisher but a political organization, with vital functions in economic, social and humanitarian areas, in addition to its efforts to maintain peace and security and to further the development of international law. Despite the value of its sales publications in various subject fields and of its *Official Records* and the *Yearbook of the United Nations* (as official records of its work) the bulk of United Nations mimeographed documentation never reaches formal publication. Although much of this material (meeting records, draft resolutions, committee reports) is of interest primarily to students of international organization,

it includes also many reports and studies of value to other subject and area specialists. All of this material, fortunately, is listed and indexed in the *United Nations Documents Index*, since much of it receives little attention elsewhere.

A United Nations document is distinguished by a symbol which identifies the organ or office of issue. The basic series symbol (A/-) identifies the documents of the General Assembly and forms the first element in the series symbol of every subsidiary organ of the General Assembly: committees, commissions, conferences, etc. Other major series include the Security Council (S/-), the Economic and Social Council (E/-), the Trusteeship Council (T/-), and the Secretariat (ST/-).[7] Documents are stocked *by symbol number* in the warehouse for a period of two years, at which time most are discarded to make room for stocks of current documents. The mimeographed editions of documents republished in the printed Official Records, where they retain their symbols, are destroyed as the *Official Records* are issued; such documents constitute a minority of the total documentation. All documents, however, are retained on microfilm for permanent preservation in the archives, in document symbol order, series by series.[8] It is therefore important to cite the symbol in any request for current documents and in any reference or citation. A sales publication number or the symbol of a current document is of more consequence than full title information to a stock clerk, to whom pagination and date of issue are equally irrelevant.

The problems of documentation are today more complicated for the United Nations than in the past for the League of Nations. The United Nations has a greater number of principal and subsidiary organs; membership is far more extensive; operations are geographically more widespread; the volume of documentation is greater and the demand for rapid reproduction and distribution more exigent. Most United Nations publications and documents appear in at least three languages as contrasted with two (English and French) for the League. The active cooperation of intergovernmental and international non-governmental organizations is now in far greater evidence. Public interest in the activities of the United Nations is greater than in the League of Nations. This increase in interest is actively served by press, radio, and television, as well as professional study of international relations. It may be noted also that printing operations today are far more widespread than were those of the League. Allocation of printing contracts is not only anticipated by member nations, the practice also makes possible good printing at lower costs than those available in New York and Geneva. The logistics of distribution is further complicated by the distant locations of regional offices and major conferences, which require printing and reproduction of materials in the local areas. Also, a situation such as a dock strike in New York Harbor further complicates and delays the receipt of bulk shipments of printed materials from abroad and seriously affects the delivery of books, periodicals and government publications to the United Nations Library.

In addition, facilities available to the Economic Commission for Africa (in Addis Ababa), the Economic Commission for Asia and the Far East (in Bangkok), and the Economic Commission for Latin America (in Santiago de Chile) are so far adequate only for distribution of commission documents within the respective areas. Consequently, the Publishing Service at Headquarters has the responsibility for producing general documents in the main series of these commissions for distribution outside these areas. This does not, however, include reproducing documents of subsidiary organs of the commissions or commission libraries. The latter, obviously, was an unavoidable decision in view of the workload at Headquarters, regrettable because of the pertinence and value of these documents to the study of the regions in question.

English, French, Spanish, Russian, and Chinese are the official languages of the United Nations, and simultaneous interpretation services are available in major meetings for all five. However, publication in all five languages is limited to the *Official Records* of the General Assembly and the Security Council, to conventions concluded under the auspices of the United Nations, and to public information material. Usually documents are distributed simultaneously in three working languages, usually English, French, and Spanish; but in English, French and Russian for the Security Council and the Economic Commission for Europe. Material also appears in Arabic and many another non-official language, and this is usually limited to public information material and the press releases of Information Centers. The *Treaty Series* publishes texts of treaties and other international agreements in the original languages of each instrument, with translations in English and French as required.[9]

The United Nations is generous in supplying requests for free copies of a current document issued at Headquarters. Requests should be directed to the Public Inquiries Unit of the Office of Public Information. Since documents are not sales items, such requests should not be included in acquisition orders to the Sales Section. The Public Inquiries Unit will also handle requests for free public information material, much of which is also identified by symbol. *The United Nations Documents Index* indicates documents issued other than in New York or Geneva, but these are not available from United Nations Headquarters. No document more than two years old is any longer in stock.

Sales publications include the *Official Records*, the *Treaty Series* periodicals (which do not bear sales numbers) and monographs, yearbooks and bulletins, which have sales numbers indicating subject categories.

Adopting the practice of the League of Nations, the Sales Section has assigned sales numbers to monographic publications in seventeen subject categories. This permits the placement of standing orders for monographs in specific subject categories. The sales number consists of the year of issue, the subject category in Roman numerals, and the number assigned to the individual title. For example, the report of a study group convened at United Nations Headquarters by the Resources and Transport Division of the Department of Economic and Social Affairs has been published under the title, *Water Desalination: Proposals for a Costing Procedure and Related Technical and Economic Considerations.* This bears the same sales number (65.II.B.5) for the English, the French, and the Spanish editions. The sales number indicates that this is the fifth sales publication issued in 1965 in subject category II.B. (economic development).

Currently available publications are listed by subject categories in *United Nations Publications . . . a Reference Catalogue*,[10] supplemented by the *Monthly Sales Bulletin* and by leaflets which group publications by subject matter or regional interest. These may be obtained from the Sales Section of the United Nations.

Sales numbers are not applied to periodicals and *Official Records*, nor to the *United Nations Treaty Series*, successor to the League of Nations *Treaty Series* (published from 1920 to 1946 in 205 volumes, containing a total of 4,823 treaties). The United Nations *Treaty Series*, which has reached its 478th volume, has published 7,547 treaties and international agreements.[11] The most complete cumulation of documents appears in the *Official Records of the General Assembly*,[12] where the records of all plenary and committee meetings of each session of the General Assembly are republished. Most sessional plenary and committee documents are available in the *Annexes*. Individual supplements contain the major annual and special reports to the General Assembly from the Secretary-General and other organs, the budget and the resolutions of the session. Meeting records and documents, other than reports to the General Assembly of the numerous extra-sessional committees appear only in mimeographed form, not in the *Official Records*.

The *Official Records* of the three councils, the former Atomic Energy Commission, and the Disarmanent Commission re-publish only the sessional plenary meetings, documents and resolutions, but do not include committee documents (other than reports to the councils) nor meeting records of either sessional or non-sessional committees. Only reports of the numerous commissions and other subsidiary organs of the Economic and Social Council appear in its *Official Records*. The documents and meeting records of these bodies remain in mimeographed form, except for economic surveys and occasional special studies re-issued as separate sales publications. Reports of Administering Authorities to the Trusteeship Council are regularly published by the governments involved and transmitted in either English or French to the Council. These have never been included in *Official Records*, which since 1952 have also excluded petitions and communications concerning Trust Territories and related observations of the Administering Authorities.

As an indication of the volume of distribution of United Nations materials from Headquarters alone, let me cite a few figures for 1964.[13] In that year the Publishing Service distributed a total of 25,415,856 copies of documents and publications (19,298,803 documents and 6,117,053 publications). Of this total, 17,731,562 copies were sent out on "initial distribution," in accordance with pre-arranged quotas, and 7,684,294 were distributed in response to "secondary requests," including sales orders, sales in the bookshop at Headquarters, and requests from Information Centers. In addition to this formidable mass of material, the Publishing Service also dispatched 823,983 other items for the Office of Public Information—sales promotion leaflets, free public information material, filmstrips and press-releases, and *received* by pouch for local distribution 313,595 mimeographed documents. During the year the Index Section of the Dag Hammarskjold Library indexed 8,724 United Nations documents.

To assure that documents and publications are readily available throughout the world there is a system of depository libraries to which documents and publications are sent by specific arrangement.[14] Depository libraries are designated by the Publications Board with the advice and cooperation of the Dag Hammarskjold Library. Each member-nation is entitled to one depository library, and in addition the national parliamentary library may be designated a depository upon request of the government concerned. Additional depositories may be designated when size of area and population so dictate. The United Nations cannot, obviously, afford to supply free to every library and learned institution its documents and publications, and the depositories must accept the obligation to keep the material in good order and available for use. Depositories are asked to select one language of publication and, on the basis of the capacity to handle the material, are designated as either complete depositories to receive all printed publications and generally-distributed mimeographed documents or as limited depositories receiving printed publications only. The depository arrangement does not include the publications of the International Court of Justice. The Registrar of the Court designates depositories for Court publications, many of which are otherwise United Nations depositories. There are now 256 depository libraries throughout the world, including 34 in the United States.

NOTE ON THE DAG HAMMARSKJOLD LIBRARY

The Dag Hammarskjold Library, at the headquarters of the United Nations, occupies a building constructed and furnished by a generous gift of funds from the Ford Foundation. The building was dedicated in 1961 and named in memory of the late Secretary-General. The Dag Hammarskjold Library is a private library, serving the staff of the Secretariat and the Permanent Missions, members of the press accredited to the United Nations and representatives of non-governmental organizations in consultative status with the United Nations. The library staff comprises 92 persons, of whom 39 are professional librarians and 53 are in the general service category. The staff is truly international, representing 36 countries and 30 languages.

The Dag Hammarskjold Library is also a special library, with holdings designed to serve official users in the subject areas in which the United Nations functions. There is no intention to create a large general library in competition with other great libraries in New York and on the eastern seaboard. The aim, rather, is to maintain a working collection of basic and current materials in international law and relations and in economic and social fields, assembled with attention to national and linguistic balance and representative of different points of view.

The most used reference materials comprise dictionaries, encyclopaedias, world-wide directories, bibliographies, biographical dictionaries, indexes, legal codes, treaty collections, constitutions and similar basic works, Official publications of governments, especially gazettes and statistical publications, and current newspapers are received regularly. The map collection embraces about 60,000 maps and many atlases, gazetteers, guides and other geographical reference works.[15]

Since this material forms a working collection, the need for weeding is constant.[16] The Library does not acquire historical material relating to the distant past, nor material in subject areas in which the United Nations is not concerned, such as belles-lettres, natural sciences, medicine and technology. When necessary to consult materials in these areas, the Library uses the resources of other great libraries, which generously cooperate with interlibrary loans and permission to consult holdings.

The publications and documents of the United Nations and its specialized agencies, in all languages, form a major part of the holdings,[17] supplemented by a steadily growing collection of books, pamphlets and periodicals dealing with the work of these organizations. In 1950, the collection of League of Nations publications and documents was augmented, and an excellent collection of books, pamphlets and periodicals concerning international relations in the period 1919-1945 acquired, by gift of the Woodrow Wilson Foundation to the Dag Hammarskjold Library

The Library publishes the monthly *United Nations Documents Index* and sessional indexes to proceedings for the General Assembly, the Economic and Social Council, on annual index to proceedings of the Security Council, the *Check List* of United Nations Documents, indexes to the *Treaty Series,* and provides occasional indexes for inclusion in other publications. Bibliographical work of the Library is reflected in bibliographies compiled as documents for various conferences and bibliographies prepared as documents in its own series, including a *Bibliographical Style Manual.*[18]

The Library acts as purchaser for a great many publications required by technical assistance projects or field offices, and has also assisted libraries of the regional economic commissions to acquire needed publications until these libraries developed to the point where the staffs could perform this work.

Finally, the collections of the Dag Hammarskjold Library have been made available to many non-official users for information not elsewhere available, although access to the Library is necessarily limited to qualified scholars and publicists.

NOTES

[1] Fifty of the fifty-one original Members signed at San Francisco; Poland signed on October 15, 1945; and the Charter came into effect on October 24, 1945.

[2] Indonesia withdrew from the Organization on March 1, 1965.

[3] *Everyman's United Nations: the Structure, Functions and Work of the Organization and its Related Agencies during the Years 1945-1962, and a United Nations Chronology for 1963,* 7th ed., New York: United Nations, 1964. (Sales no. 64.I.9, $5.00 cloth; $1.95 paperbound.)

[4] Brenda Brimmer (and others), *A Guide to the Use of United Nations Documents,* New York: Oceana Publications, Inc., 1962.

[5] For further information on the publications of the Court, see International Court of Justice, Yearbook, 1963-1964 (The Hague, 1964), chapter VII. (Court Sales no. 288)

[6] *United Nations Documents Index,* vol. 1, no. 1, January 1950–date. New York, United Nations, 1950–date. Monthly; with two annual cumulations, $10.00.

[7] See List of United Nations Documents Series Symbols, New York: United Nations, 1965. (Documents ST/LIB/ SER.B/Rev. 1; sales no. 65.I.6, $2.00).

[8] The English texts are also reproduced in symbol series order by Readex Microprint Corporation, 5 Union Square, New York, N. Y. 10003.

[9] Brimmer (and others), *Guide to the Use of United Nations Documents,* p. ix, notes the usefulness of United Nations publications to language students in contemporary subject fields.

[10] Documents ST/CS/SER.J/3, covering 1945-1963, and ST/CS/SER.J/3/ Add.1 are available free on request from the Sales Section.

[11] This covers the period from December 14, 1946 to September 30, 1963, when 6,943 treaties had been registered with the Secretariat; and 604 treaties had been filed and recorded (the latter group includes treaties entered into by the United Nations and one or more specialized agencies; treaties entered into prior to the Charter but which were not included in the *Treaty Series* of the League of Nations; and treaties transmitted by parties not members of the United Nations). The issues of the *Statement of Treaties and International Agreements* for November and December 1964 (documents ST/LEG/SER.A/213,214) indicate that at the close of 1964 a total of 8,141 treaties had been registered or filed and recorded (7,531 in the first group, 610 in the second).

[12] Consult *United Nations Official Records 1948-1962; a Reference Catalogue* (doc. ST/CS/SER/J/2; sales no. 64.I.3. $0.50).

[13] In 1964 there were 1,375 meetings at Headquarters. This figure had usually been above 2,000 during 1961-1963, but during its 19th session, 1964, the General Assembly did not organize its General Committee and its seven Main Committees; it took action which could be achieved without voting only on certain items of the provisional agenda. There were therefore no committee meeting records and almost no committee documents.

[14] *Principles Governing United Nations Depository Libraries,* New York, United Nations July 17, 1963. (ST/PB/4/Rev.1.)

[15] During 1964 the Library acquired 9,927 books, 72,135 government documents, 114,890 issues of newspapers and periodicals, and 1,899 maps.

[16] In 1964, 3,590 volumes were withdrawn. Most newspapers and periodicals are discarded at the end of six months or a year. Major newspapers are retained on microfilm, other periodicals either permanently or for a specified number of years.

[17] During 1964 the Library checked in 100,399 copies of United Nations material and 20,900 copies of specialized agency material.

[18] *Bibliographical Style Manual.* New York: United Nations, 1963. (Document ST/LIB/SER.B/8; sales number 63.I.5; $0.75.)

IV

COMMISSIONS AND COMMITTEES

Here we have one of the most important (to librarians) advisory commission reports in many a year. And the legislation establishing the resultant *National Commission*, I would rank with the initial Library Services Act of the 84th Congress, not for what it is but for what it promises for the future of librarianship in this country. Watch for their activities and reports!

And, the Federal Library Committee has already proven its worth in its few short years of existence. You can keep uptodate with FLC by reading their *Newsletter* which is distributed by the Library of Congress.

Report of the National Advisory Commission on Libraries

Douglas M. Knight, Chairman

"The [President's] Committee found it a highly stimulating report, containing numerous ideas which would strengthen the role of libraries in our society. It reflected the painstaking and energetic efforts of the Commission to look at the varied problems confronting libraries and librarians as they seek to supply a variety of services in the midst of growing demands . . . The Committee urges a wide distribution of the Report. Its recommendations should be considered and discussed by individuals and groups at Federal, State, and local levels, both in and out of the library community. It should encourage all of these groups as they make plans for even more effective services." From the letter of transmittal accompanying the Report and sent to the President by Wilbur J. Cohen, Chairman, President's Committee on Libraries, and Secretary of Health, Education, and Welfare.

REPORT OF THE NATIONAL ADVISORY COMMISSION ON LIBRARIES

HON. CARL D. PERKINS
OF KENTUCKY
IN THE HOUSE OF REPRESENTATIVES
Monday, October 14, 1968

Mr. PERKINS. Mr. Speaker, in the closing hours of a congressional year, it is traditional that we review our accomplishments and set forth some goals for future action. Accordingly, as chairman of the House Education and Labor Committee, I point with pride to the progress we have made in advancing and strengthening the Nation's library resources. Title II of the Higher Education Act, which we have recently extended in the Higher Education Amendments of 1968, will continue for another 3 years Federal assistance to help provide college library resources, training and research in librarianship, and cooperative cataloging by the Library of Congress.

In connection with this important program, I wish to call my colleagues' attention to the recent report of the National Advisory Commission on Libraries. As you know, when this Commission was established in September of 1966, it was directed "to appraise the role and adequacy of our libraries, now and in the future, as sources for scholarly research, as centers for the distribution of knowledge, and as links in our Nation's rapidly evolving communications networks."

During the 90th Congress, we have considered and approved various programs, in addition to HEA, title II, such as the Public Broadcasting Act, Interlibrary Cooperation, and the new Networks for Knowledge, which, to me, all appear related to the work of the Library Commission, soon to be disbanded now that its report has been transmitted to the President.

In reading the Commission's report, I find that this initial study makes it clearly evident that the job has just begun if we really mean to serve the educational needs of all our people. The first recommendation of the advisory panel is the establishment of a National Commission on Libraries and Information Science as a continuing Federal planning agency. It is my hope that early in the 91st Congress we will consider this recommendation and take positive action.

At this time, I insert the report of the National Advisory Commission on Libraries in the RECORD so that all the Members may have the benefit of its findings and recommendations:

THE SECRETARY OF HEALTH,
EDUCATION, AND WELFARE,
Washington, D.C., October 3, 1968.

The PRESIDENT,
The White House,
Washington, D.C.

DEAR MR. PRESIDENT: The Report of the National Advisory Commission on Libraries, established in September 1966, by your Executive Order Number 11301, is attached. The Report has been reviewed by the members of the President's Committee on Libraries.

The Committee found it a highly stimulating report, containing numerous ideas

SOURCE: *Congressional Record, Extension of Remarks*, Report of the National Advisory Commission on Libraries. vol. 114, no. 173, October 21, 1968. (Washington: 1968). pp. E-9355-E-9368.

which would strengthen the role of libraries in our society. It reflected the painstaking and energetic efforts of the Commission to look at the varied problems confronting libraries and librarians as they seek to supply a variety of services in the midst of growing demands.

Libraries are the keepers of our history and our culture. But they are not merely storehouses for the relics of the past, but meeting places for people and ideas, vital partners in our system of education.

The Committee urges a wide distribution of the Report. Its recommendations should be considered and discussed by individuals and groups at Federal, State and local levels, both in and out of the library community. It should encourage all of these groups as they make plans for even more effective services.

Respectfully yours,

WILBUR J. COHEN,
Chairman, President's Committee on Libraries.

LIBRARY SERVICES FOR THE NATION'S NEEDS: TOWARD FULFILLMENT OF A NATIONAL POLICY—REPORT OF THE NATIONAL ADVISORY COMMISSION ON LIBRARIES, JULY 1968

ACKNOWLEDGMENTS

The appendixes of this Report of the National Advisory Commission on Libraries contain lists of the witnesses who offered testimony and organizations which submitted useful special studies. Many other individuals in one way or another contributed to the efforts of the Commission. It is appropriate here to mention our particular thanks to Dr. Frederick H. Wagman, Director, University Library, The University of Michigan, whose preliminary compilation of written materal at the request of the Commission served as indispensable resource for discussions at its final meetings and enabled the distillation of content for the December 1967 preliminary Report and the present Report to be completed within the limited time available. Finally, the Commission wishes to thank the officials and agencies of the Federal Government, whose cooperation has been most helpful from the beginning.

LETTER OF TRANSMITTAL

NATIONAL ADVISORY COMMISSION ON LIBRARIES,
Washington, D.C., July 1, 1968.

Hon. WILBUR J. COHEN,
Secretary, Department of Health, Education, and Welfare; Chairman, President's Committee on Libraries, Washington, D.C.

DEAR MR. SECRETARY: In accordance with the Executive Order of the President of the United States, we are pleased to transmit to the President's Committee on Libraries the recommendations of the National Advisory Commission on Libraries. The Commission believes that its six broad objectives for the transitional and future development of library and information services can be achieved responsibly and realistically through the structural and organizational recommendations set forth in these pages.

The Commission has tried diligently to meet its charge as set forth in Chapter 1 of this Report. We have met eleven times as a full Commission to discuss library problems and potentials as perceived by a most interesting diversity of viewpoints represented by our membership. We have heard formal testimony and had informal discussions with technological experts, librarians, people from government and private agencies, and a variety of users and producers of both conventional literary material and newer forms of informational transfer. Regional hearings were held in communities throughout the country by members of the Commission to ascertain the people's library needs at the grass roots of our nation. Special studies on a number of relevant topics, in most cases specially commissioned by us, were submitted to the Commission and contributed to our deliberations on problems and issues. Already, areas for vital new research are evident.

On the basis of deliberations through early December 1967, the Commission had agreed on its recommendations and reached some basic conclusions on fulfilling the national policy we recommend for library services appropriate to the needs of the people. We presented these conclusions and our specific recommendations in a preliminary Report dated December 1967. Since then, the Commission has prepared a chapter analyzing its response to the President's charge, completed a statement on library manpower for Chapter 3, and made certain other refinements and modifications in the five basic recommendations now set forth in Chapter 4.

The work we have started can continue most meaningfully through the combined efforts of many existing and evolving entities, coordinated by the overall planning efforts of our recommended National Commission on Libraries and Information Science. There must be continuing, coordinated study and action in the years ahead—it is an ongoing, never-ending venture. Because the results of all the activities of the present Commission can continue to provide resource on library and information science and service in the future, we are supplementing our Report with a forthcoming volume which will be based on a variety of materials and data, including the special studies, in an attempt to synthesize and document a complex set of problems and issues.

At this time, it is our hope that the President's Committee on Libraries will study our Report and commend our proposals for action to the early attention of the President and the Congress. The problems are urgent. A sound beginning can be made.

Sincerely yours,

DOUGLAS M. KNIGHT,
Chairman, National Advisory Commission on Libraries, President, Duke University.

MEMBERSHIP OF THE NATIONAL ADVISORY COMMISSION ON LIBRARIES

Chairman: Douglas M. Knight, President, Duke University, Durham, North Carolina.

Vice Chairman: Frederick H. Burkhardt, President, American Council of Learned Societies, New York, New York.

Estelle Brodman, Librarian and Professor of Medical History, Washington University School of Medicine, St. Louis, Missouri.

Launor F. Carter, Vice President and Manager, Public Systems Division, System Development Corporation, Santa Monica, California.

Verner W. Clapp, Consultant, Council on Library Resources, Washington, D.C.

Carl Elliott, Attorney at Law, Jasper, Alabama.

Alvin C. Eurich, President, Academy for Educational Development, New York, New York.

Mildred P. Frary, Director of Library Services, City Schools Libraries, Los Angeles, California.

Herman H. Fussler, Director of the University Library and Professor in the Graduate Library School, The University of Chicago, Chicago, Illinois.

Marian G. Gallagher, Professor of Law and Law Librarian, University of Washington, Seattle, Washington.

Emerson Greenaway, Director, Free Library of Philadelphia, Philadelphia, Pennsylvania.

Caryl P. Haskins, President, Carnegie Institution of Washington, Washington, D.C.

William N. Hubbard, Jr., Dean, University of Michigan Medical School, Ann Arbor, Michigan.

Dan Lacy, Senior Vice President, McGraw-Hill Book Company, New York, New York.

Mrs. Merlin M. Moore, Supervisor of Economic Education, State Department of Education, State Capitol, Little Rock, Arkansas.

Carl F. J. Overhage, Professor of Engineering, Massachusetts Institute of Technology, Cambridge, Massachusetts.

Harry H. Ransom, Chancellor, University of Texas, Austin, Texas.

Wilbur L. Schramm, Director, Institute for Communication Research, Stanford University, Stanford, California.

Mrs. George Rodney Wallace, Trustee, Fitchburg Public Library, Fitchburg, Massachusetts.

Stephen J. Wright, President, United Negro College Fund, Inc., New York, New York.

Staff of the commission

Melville J. Ruggles, Executive Director (November 1, 1966–December 31, 1967).

Daniel J. Reed, Deputy Director (January 1, 1967–December 31, 1967).

E. Shepley Nourse, Editor (August 15, 1967–).

Mary Alice Hedge, Administrative Officer (August 1, 1967–).

Richard K. Burns, Research Associate (September 11, 1967–December 31, 1967).

FOREWORD

When the President appointed the National Advisory Commission on Libraries more than a year ago, he gave it a demanding task, and one with urgent as well as enduring aspects. He asked the Commission to consider the nation's library structure, the nature of the present and wisest possible future involvement of Federal support in the development of national library and informational resources, and the most effective shaping of those resources to our common need as we can picture it over the next decade. This third concern of the Commission has been for resources of every kind, and needs at every level. We know very well how difficult it is to relate Federal and local, public and private sources of support and definitions of purpose, but we have tried to suggest some of the ways in which that crucial job can be done.

Our recommendations will be understood best, I think, by seeing them as they result from our basic concern for adequate library resources. This concern may in its turn seem simple or self-evident until we look at the history of libraries and the needs of this country in the late 20th century—needs which grow equally from the individual citizen and the large corporation, the pioneering university and the complex Federal agency. The historical growth of libraries is a vivid commentary on our problems today, in fact, for we see at major periods in the

past the development of one or two particular kinds of library. Today we have the whole array of libraries alive at once; our world demands this variety, while our achievements and our great need grow from it. We are Alexandrian or Renaissance citizens in our development of great book and manuscript collections which range across the past of Western culture; we are Roman or Baroque in many of our superb private and personally shaped libraries; we are medievalists in our development of libraries for specialized fields of learning; and we continue the public or national traditions of the 18th and 19th centuries in our great Federal, municipal, and university libraries. Just as we have an astonishing range of demands on our libraries, so we have range in the kinds of library we create and support.

But what in fact do we mean by a library? We must ask this elementary question, because we are surrounded, almost overwhelmed, by the tangible fact of libraries. We take their meaning, like their existence, too much for granted. That existence, and meaning are best understood, perhaps, by realizing what libraries are *not*—not warehouses of books and manuscripts, not collections of reading rooms, and not sets of reading devices. Any library is instead a particular kind of meeting-place, and it grows from certain major attributes of the human mind and spirit. It is not a neutral spot, not passive, and yet it does not have restrictive purpose or direction as a thoughtful radio or television show does. A library differs from other systems of communication, indeed, precisely because its value and power emerge from the use which we as individuals choose to make of it.

A library—great or small, privately or publicly supported—has two major and unique functions. First, it makes possible meetings of mind and idea which are not limited by our normal boundaries of time, space, and social or economic level. An effective library gives us the option of moving to the far side of the world, to the fifth century B.C., or to the company of prophets and princes. And we do all this, not by the transient means of fantasy, but by the enduring power of our own human awareness. We can become more than we were; we can, if we wish it, increase our individual stature as well as our public effectiveness.

To say this is to suggest the second great function of a library. It is the institution in our society which allows and encourages the development, the extension of ideas—not their passive absorption, but their active generation. Here our image of the conventional reading room many interfere. We picture a hundred silent, inert figures, and forget that each is making some active reckoning with all that he thought to be true before he confronted a new range of ideas or conditions. He may be more active at that quiet moment, in fact, than at any other time in his life. The technical means of his encounter may be a record, a tape, a film, a print-out or—most radical of all—a book. Libraries are not bounded by means; they will and should employ any means to achieve their ends.

At a time of great technical virtuosity it is important to realize that in the predictable future new means of information storage and retrieval will not displace the book. Nor will they lessen the need for materials, buildings, or skilled staff. Instead they will extend and supplement what we now have, and our investments during the next decade must take equal account of the enduring purposes of libraries and the diverse emergent means of strengthening them.

Clearly, of course, libraries cannot achieve their ends for the illiterate or the indifferent. They are dependent on teachers, writers, parents to set interest alight, but they are the means of meeting the interest, and giving it range beyond those who first stirred it. This creative center which is a library should not be defined by the adequacy of its space, equipment, and collections alone, but by the adequacy of its people—those who first teach the mind to inquire, and those in the libraries who can show it *how* to inquire. The librarian of today and tomorrow must have many technical and professional skills, but above all he must have skill with people. He is a teacher whose subject is learning itself, and his class has no limits on age, field of study, or degree of competence. The national policy which we propose is as a result based equally on the need for skilled and sensitive people, bold and yet imaginative technical means, and support from every sector of the economy as well as every major level of government.

Douglas M. Knight,
Chairman, National Advisory Commission on Libraries, President, Duke University.

CHAPTER 1.—THE COMMISSION'S CHARGE

In the Executive Order of September 2, 1966 (see Appendix A), the National Advisory Commission on Libraries was charged to:

(1) Make a comprehensive study and appraisal of the role of libraries as resources for scholarly pursuits, as centers for the dissemination of knowledge, and as components of the evolving national information systems;

(2) Appraise the policies, programs, and practices of public agencies and private institutions and organizations, together with other factors, which have a bearing on the role and effective utilization of libraries;

(3) Appraise library funding, including Federal support of libraries, to determine how funds available for the construction and support of libraries and library services can be more effectively and efficiently utilized; and

(4) Develop recommendations for action by Government or private institutions and organizations designed to ensure an effective and efficient library system for the Nation.

The Commission tried conscientiously to meet these charges. In particular, it attempted a broad look at the complex roles of libraries in relation to user needs in a changing society, and it developed some recommendations for structural adaptations that can foster evolutionary development and enable continuing, coordinated study and action in the years ahead. The Commission's conclusions with respect to major objectives and its five specific recommendations for realizing these objectives are the basic subject matter of this Report. Chapters 2 through 4 present the rationale for the Commission's response to point 4 in the Executive Order.

Here in Chapter 1, however, it seems appropriate to comment on the response of the National Advisory Commission on Libraries to the first three points set forth in the Executive Order.

In some areas the Commission feels it would be presumptuous to make premature judgments on the basis of current evidence,

but even in these cases some tentative judgments can be made. The discussion that follows touches on many areas, including some still confused by question affecting the philosophy, administration, and financing of library and information services for the nation's needs. Tackling the imponderables is part of the job ahead.

Evolving responsiveness to user needs

With respect to point 1 in the original charge, the National Advisory Commission on Libraries approached its appraisal of the role of libraries in several ways. It arranged to hear a variety of testimony (see Appendixes C and D); it sponsored several major studies on basic aspects of the roles of libraries—notably the System Development Corporation report on *Technology and Libraries* and the American Council of Learned Societies' study *On Research Libraries* (see Appendix B); and its members have discussed the issues at some length and familiarized themselves with many of the other major studies that fall into this general area. As a result of this effort, the Commission has reached a number of conclusions that have led to its specific recommendations.

The Commission believes that libraries are both essential and major elements in providing resources for scholarship in almost all fields of knowledge, in serving as centers for the dissemination of knowledge, and in serving as components in the evolving national information systems. The library role in these matters is in fact so critical that the Commission believes that libraries serving these purposes must be significantly strengthened. This increased strength will require a variety of different approaches and techniques; Federal support, long-range planning, and better coordination are all urgent requirements.

In the Statement by the President accompanying the Executive Order, three serious questions were asked about the future of our libraries. One of these was quite similar to the item in point 1 of the Commission's charge about the role of libraries as components of evolving national information systems. It asked:

What part can libraries play in the development of our communications and information-exchange networks?

In considering the role of libraries in national information systems and in communications and information-exchange networks, the Commission found many uncertainties, often further complicated by semantic confusion and a tendency to polarize conventional written information and scientific and technical data. The National Advisory Commission on Libraries favors resolving the uncertainties through multiple but coordinated planning and experimentation. It urges an evolutionary development responsive to user needs, whether it is simple interlibrary cooperation or a highly technical communications system. Some points supporting this conclusion appear to be already evident.

Libraries are reservoirs of information whose means and ends of distribution are determined by the function the information is to serve in the hands of the user rather than by some abstract set of values inherent in the term "library" itself. Similarly, one cannot evaluate electronic and computer-processed information stores except in terms of improving the function of the ultimate user of this information.

The requirements for effective library and information access for students, scholars, and practitioners in various disciplinary areas and at various levels display sharp and complex variations. Consequently, sweeping generalizations with respect to user needs are likely to be misleading through incompleteness and inaccuracy. For example, some misunderstandings exist because the need for books has now been joined by needs for information in other formats. In some technical fields traditional books may be playing a decreasing role as reservoirs of information. In other fields the need for traditional literary information may actually be increasing. But in all fields the needs are multiple and are likely to become more so as new multidisciplinary relationships emerge and develop simultaneously with further highly specialized needs.

At the beginning levels of formal education, we find that the close adaptation of elementary school libraries to the functional needs of changing teaching patterns has made the book only one of many information resources handled by the information center of the elementary school. It is at other levels within the formal educational system—the secondary school, college, and university levels—that library needs are most evident and least satisfied. Here the more traditional understanding of the library asserts itself and a wide variety of measures will be needed, including more collaborative efforts among these libraries, to insure their long-range effectiveness. As for academic research, the library responses to these needs display, even where there appears to be great strength, severe stresses and great unevenness in access.

The roles of the public library are changing. The relative inefficiency of completely self-planned instruction and the increasing availability of organized instruction within the community have decreased the function of the public library as the university of the poor. Nevertheless, as educational demands upon the public library by the educational system itself increase, and as the sophistication of the community increases, the public library becomes an essential element within the community as an information reservoir for multiple user groups.

It follows from the foregoing paragraphs that naturally evolving systems that clearly serve the needs of users should be given support in their own right at this time. No one can perceive the final nature of communications and information-exchange networks, nor the quality of a national information system—with a single exception. The exception is that such a system will finally be made up of a large number of highly specialized individual components, each one of which should be designed to serve the needs of a defined user group.

The specialized libraries, such as the National Library of Medicine, one of our three existing national libraries, can therefore be looked upon as important models of how a library alters or develops its role and activity to serve a defined group—in this case the medical scientists and practitioners. The National Library of Medicine also engages in cooperative activities. Likewise the largest of our national libraries, the Library of Congress, has demonstrated many kinds of cooperation with other units, thus exemplifying how the understanding of the need of response to a user group (e.g., the Congress) does not exclude sensitivity to cooperation with the larger whole.

Libraries badly need support in establishing new means of intercommunication and cooperation. Only after this kind of support of the existing order has been established can it be reliably estimated what the role of these units is in the evolving national information system.

To summarize, then, and to place the Commission's response to the very broad point 1 of its charge in somewhat clearer focus, the following observations are relevant here. These are shared by members of the Commission and recur many times throughout this Report in various contexts.

First, in order to improve the access of our society to information, the Commission believes the basic necessity is to foster development by an evolutionary process. An example is the application of technology, which can play an extremely important role in improving library and informational operations; the Commission does not presently see a technological solution that will make either the printed book or the library itself quickly obsolete—nor does it see any near-term system that will inexpensively provide instant access to all knowledge at any location.

Second, if the present unsatisfactory situation, described particularly in Chapter 3 of this Report, is to be improved, the Commission believes there should be augmented Federal support for: (a) national or regional resource collections and services for infrequently used research materials in a carefully planned pattern; (b) nationally oriented indexing, cataloging, abstracting, and other bibliographical services; (c) basic and applied research in library operations and in the intellectual problems, technology, and economics of information transfer and dissemination.

Third, it is apparent that public, school, and academic libraries will all be obligated to change many of their methods of work, their interrelationships, and some of their roles and objectives in the years ahead. If these libraries are to be responsive to contemporary and future requirements, the Commission believes that changes will have to take place at a much faster rate than has heretofore been the case. To effect more rapid rates of change and response, funds, among other things, will be required that are not now available.

Fourth, there are, and there will continue to be, many information dissemination and data-handling functions that may be handled in part or entirely outside the walls of traditional libraries—e.g., indexing, abstracting, literature evaluation, synthesis, and computer or other means of access to extensive economic, sociological, scientific, and other data banks. These services are of great importance in insuring effective access to the resources collected, organized, preserved, and made available primarily through libraries—especially those of a scholarly research nature.

Fifth, the Commission believes that the nation's library and other information systems will continue to be a shared responsibility of Federal agencies, the States, municipalities, educational institutions, and many other public and private organizations. No monolithic Federal or other centralized administrative control seems either feasible or desirable. There will have to be many different kinds of informations systems and working relationships among a variety of institutions if we are to provide effective access to relevant information for our society. New systems, roles, and relationships are likely to emerge at very different rates of speed in response to widely varying user needs.

Finally, it should be stated here that the tasks of analyzing the needs, planning, setting standards, allocating resources, measuring performance, and coordinating efforts will be difficult and complex in the years ahead. Effective progress will require the sustained effort of the persent Commission's recommended ongoing National Commission on Libraries and Information Science working with Federal agencies, the national libraries, and many other institutions, groups, and individuals.

The fragmentation of efforts

The second of the President's charges required the National Advisory Commission on Libraries to "Appraise the policies, programs, and practices of public agencies and private institutions and organizations, together with other factors, which have a bearing on the role and effective utilization of libraries."

In an effort to accomplish this appraisal, a number of the special studies referred to earlier were planned by the Commission to concentrate on the various kinds of libraries and the different public agencies involved. These studies by competent authorities included one on the Federal Government and libraries by Duke University, one on State libraries and library agencies by Nelson Associates, Inc.; one on research libraries by the American Council of Learned Societies; three on undergraduate and junior college libraries, public libraries, and school libraries, respectively, all by Nelson Associates, Inc.; and one on special libraries by the American Documentation Institute. The Commission also heard testimony from representatives of all types of libraries, from Federal and State agencies concerned, and from library associations.

It is impossible to present any reliable appraisal of the policies, programs, and practices of even a single type among the multitudinous agencies and institutions that are involved in giving library and information services to the American people. An overriding conclusion, however, evident from all the studies and hearings, is that there is an extremely wide range in both the character and the adequacy of library services and library resources. The incomparable holdings of the great university libraries contrast starkly with the nearly empty shelves of new community colleges and similar institutions. Residents of some large cities and affluent suburbs enjoy a wealth of library services denied to residents of most rural areas. The schools of suburbia are likely to have superb libraries, the schools of urban and rural slums none at all—at least until the Elementary and Secondary Education Act of 1965 (P.L. 89–10, P.L. 89–750) began to offer assistance. What kind of library service an American has available to him may have the widest possible variation, depending on his means and where he lives. In general, the areas of greatest poverty and social need and the institutions confronting the most critical social and educational problems are those with the least adequate library services. Where such great efforts are required to induce nonusers of library services to become users, we face a great lack.

More detailed appraisals of particular strengths and weaknesses are reflected in the definitions of objectives and the recommendations for action that make up the ensuing chapters of this Report. A forthcoming book planned by the Commission and based on Commission materials, including a number of the special studies, will attempt a further analysis of the multiplicity of users and uses of library and information services. Surely one of the primary tasks of the present Commission's recommended ongoing National Commission on Libraries and Information Science will be broad planning toward understanding and coordinating the present fragmented situation.

In the Statement by the President accompanying the Executive Order establishing the National Advisory Commission on Libraries, there was a question, somewhat related to point 2 in the charge but directed toward the fragmentation of Federal efforts:

Are our Federal efforts to assist libraries intelligently administered, or are they too fragmented among separate programs and agencies?

As mentioned above, there are many current complexities in evaluating and even identifying some of the programs and the relationships between them. The Commission clearly believes that coordination of and cooperation between the organic units of the whole body of library efforts, both within the Federal Government and supported by it, are inadequate. Such a body needs a central nervous system. In pursuing this analogy, it is important to emphasize that a central nervous system is the servant of the organs— that each has its own independent and discrete function on behalf of the whole. The central nervous system cannot substitute for the function of the organ, but the function of the organ serves the whole body only when it is coordinated.

For this reason the National Advisory Commission on Libraries does not recommend that one of the organic units—for instance the largest of the national libraries, the Library of Congress—should dominate all of the other organic units in this coordination. Rather, the Commission recommends that a body roughly analogous to that serving the national Library of Medicine as its Regents should be established as a Board of Advisers to the Library of Congress, and that an Institute should be established within the Office of the Secretary of Health, Education, and Welfare to coordinate developmental efforts. The brain of this system is that overall planning and advisory agency, the National Commission on Libraries and Information Science, already referred to several times here in Chapter 1.

The present Commission believes that, within this system it has recommended, the haphazard fragmentation of efforts can be circumvented and the strength of diversity maximized.

Sources and uses of funds

The third point in the charge to the National Advisory Commission on Libraries was to "Appraise library funding, including Federal support of libraries, to determine how funds available for the construction and support of libraries and library services can be more effectively and efficiently utilized." Attention was further directed to the following question from the President's Statement:

Are we getting the most benefit for the taxpayer's dollar spent?

The pitiful incompleteness and tardiness of library statistics, and their lack of comparability, make it impossible to give specific quantitative responses to this series of questions. No one knows precisely, or even with close approximation, what the total present library expenditures of the nation are, or even what the Federal contributions to those expenditures are—nor can even approximately reliable specific estimates be made of the costs of remedying the serious deficiencies in library service that we all know exist.

Estimated needs suggest extensive expenditures in order to approach the various sets of standards adopted by the American Library Association (ALA). According to figures supplied to the Commission by the United States Office of Education in June 1968, it would require a lump sum expenditure in 1968 of $1.6 billion to stock school libraries optimally. Just to make up the backlog of space required to construct centralized public school libraries where they did not exist in 1961 would require $2.145 billion. Space requirements for replacement and new growth for public libraries have been estimated at $1.132 billion for the period 1962–75. As for academic libraries, available figures compare present trend with optimum trend over the total period 1962–75: $1.945 billion compared with $9.891 billion for books and materials, $120 million compared with $360 million for new construction.

Obviously such large amounts are beyond immediate achievement, but the estimates afford some general measure of the magnitude of the financial problem that lies ahead in the development of library services. The present Commission has not attempted to make its own specific estimate of the dollar needs of libraries—in part because the members have not found it possible to evaluate existing standards and do not believe an adequate factual basis for a reliable estimate exists, and in part because any estimate would quickly be made obsolete by changing needs and costs—but primarily because the principal need is to create machinery for continuing examination of changing library needs, for devising means of meeting them, and for determining priorities and costs. This would be the task of the permanent National Commission on Libraries and Information Science proposed in this Report.

It already seems perfectly clear, however, that the need for additional financial support for our libraries is great at present and will grow rapidly in the future. Population growth, our more extensive educational commitments, the rapidly increasing role of research, the greater complexity of our society, and our determination to achieve a massive improvement in the educational and vocational status of the poorer and less-educated among our citizens will join to require very substantial increases in the quantity and quality of library services.

The present Commission has explored possible means of reducing the unit cost of library service to offset in some degree the total financial impact of the need for greatly increased services. Interlibrary cooperation, the establishment of interlibrary networks, and the more extensive employment by libraries of new information technology have all been considered in this connection. As other sections of this Report indicate, the Commission believes that all of these developments have great potentialities for library service and should be vigorously pursued. Their value, however, will almost certainly rest in making it possible for us to have library services of a form and scope now unattainable—for example in making the holdings of the great research libraries more realistically available to users in smaller communities and institutions— rather than in reducing the cost of services. In reality, the effective employment of these new devices and methods will itself require a large additional investment of funds.

The unit cost of library services is, in fact, almost certain to rise substantially over the foreseeable future. Three fourths or more of the cost of library service consists of salaries. These will undoubtedly rise steadily as the general wage and salary level of society rises with higher productivity. Indeed, the acute shortage of professional personnel is likely to drive library salaries up even faster than the general salary level. The absence of opportunities to increase man-hour productivity comparable to those available in industry, coupled with increases in salary rates, will produce substantial and inescapable increases in unit costs. This is the same problem the nation faces in connection with increasing costs of education and medical services.

Since the principal reason for the steady increase in the cost of library services, as of other social services, is the rising affluence of the country, the means exist to meet these costs. It is inescapable, however, that these should be met from sources of public income that rise hand-in-hand with increases in the gross national product. Public libraries and school libraries are now financed primarily from local real estate taxes, which are inelastic and respond very slowly to increases in national income; many college and university libraries are heavily dependent on endowment income and student fees, which are also capable of only limited increase. The role of State support for many of these types of libraries has been substantially enlarged and should be further increased as a partial response to the inflexibility of other sources of support. Even State income, however, based as it is largely on low income taxes and sales taxes, responds relatively slowly to rises in the general level of productivity and is critically low in just those states especially in need of large-scale expansion of library services.

For all these reasons, the Commission believes that over the coming decade very large increases in Federal support of libraries will be necessary and, indeed, inescapable. Even if this necessity did not exist, however, there would be ample justification for an increase in the Federal component of library support. The problem of research libraries is peculiarly a national one: we need to develop national centers of research collections, national backstopping facilities to improve access to research materials, national plans for coordination, national catalogs and bibliographies, and other apparatus that will improve the accessibility of relevant information. The employment of the newer information technology in libraries—including research to develop its applications, the formulation of uniform or compatible information storage and retrieval systems, and the creation of library networks—are also inescapably national problems whose solutions require national participation and support.

Even on the level of local school and public libraries, there is a great and distinct national interest. Especially with a population so mobile as that of the United States, the whole nation must have a concern for the level of educational and informational services throughout the country. Illiteracy, ignorance, limited education, and lack of vocational skills, and other poverty-engendering deprivations, wherever orginating, spread their impact by migration and otherwise throughout the country. Library development is an essential element in such national objectives as the elimination of poverty and the achievement of rapid social and economic development, and it requires and deserves national support.

As for the effective utilization of funds already available for the construction and support of libraries and library services, it should be pointed out that, during the life of the Commission, the Federal contribution to libraries had just been greatly expanded under the Elementary and Secondary Education Act of 1965 and the Higher Education Act of 1965 (P.L. 89–329, P.L. 90–35, P.L. 90–82), and appropriate procedures and staffing were still being worked out. There was some inevitable confusion and it is too early to reach dependable judgments about the efficiency of the Federal program. In general, however, the Commission hopes that the administration of these acts may be moving toward the quite high level of efficiency already achieved in the administration of the Library Services and Construction Act (P.L. 88–269, P.L. 89–511, P.L. 90–154) and the library components (Titles III and XI) of the National Defense Education Act (P.L. 88–665).

There are, however, some fundamental weaknesses in the present pattern of Federal library support:

a. It is given under a large number of different acts in addition to the four mentioned above. Some such diffusion is inevitable, and even to some degree desirable since it would be unwise to pull library components out of many different Federal programs and put them into one act, thus separating libarary support from the objectives it is intended to serve. But there is substantial overlapping and lack of coordination among these different acts at present, and they have not been planned as part of a comprehensive whole.

b. There is no program of Federal support for research libraries as such.

c. There is no central program for the development of the newer information technology and its application to libraries.

d. Although manpower is a most critical library problem, Federal support has been almost wholly given to buildings and materials, with limited support for training and almost none for salaries.

e. Effective employment of Federal funds within the States, especially for school and public libraries, and effective State support both depend on strong State library planning and administrative services, which do not always exist.

The National Advisory Commission on Libraries has stated in this Report a number of conclusions and recommendations to strengthen these aspects of Federal support.

Particularly relevant in this respect are the permanent National Commission on Libraries and Information Science to undertake broad central planning toward coordination; a central Federal Institute of Library and Information Science for research and development; aid to research libraries as well as other libraries; improved manpower recruitment, training, and utilization; and strengthening of State libraries. The Commission believes the adoption of these approaches would substantially improve both the efficiency and the effectiveness of library funding and the use of Federal funds.

The criterion of social value

In retrospect, examining the objectives and recommendations presented in this Report in relation to the original charge, the National Advisory Commission on Libraries believes that questions now unanswered will yield to the diverse approaches and interlinked continuing bodies recommended. There clearly already are, and will continue to be, many challenging problems for the scrutiny of the continuing National Commission on Libraries and Information Science—the very fact that the present Commission, in only the few months since completion of its preliminary Report, has developed additional conclusions and recommendations for the present Report is encouraging evidence of the validity of the commission function in overall planning and advising.

One theme emerges throughout all the activities of the National Advisory Commission on Libraries since its first meeting in November 1966. This is a strong social-benefit awareness, a service orientation that pervades every existing and conceivable library and information function. Perhaps it is not too soon to propose the criterion of social value as the most important in decision-making—whether for broad central planning, more specific planning, or immediate problem-solving. We should look at the value to our people and our culture that accrues from the activities of the user whose functions are to be enhanced by improved availability of library and information services. A library can be understood only as it enhances a socially valuable function, one of which—and one that all libraries can enhance—is the personal intellectual and ethical development of every individual in our society. The variety of the other socially valuable functions determines the need for variety in kinds of libraries.

In this spirit of social awareness, the National Advisory Commission on Libraries developed its recommendations for a National Library Policy, presented in the following chapter.

CHAPTER 2. A NATIONAL LIBRARY POLICY

Recommendation: That it be declared National Policy, enunciated by the President and enacted into law by the Congress, that the American people should be provided with labrary and informational services adequate to their needs, and that the Federal Government, in collaboration with State and local governments and private agencies, should exercise leadership in assuring the provision of such services.

Increasingly over the years the need for a national library policy has become apparent—a policy which could permit plans that take into consideration the needs for library service of the American people as a whole. Recent developments which have profoundly affected not only the supply and the use of informational materials, but also the way in which information is used, have made the recognition of this need inescapable.

As long ago as circa 1730, when Benjamin Franklin and his youthful colleagues were establishing what was perhaps the first communal library in the American colonies, he gave expression to the basic principle of modern library service. By "clubbing our books to a common library," he wrote, each member had "the advantage of using the books of all the other members, which would be nearly as beneficial as if each owned the whole." Today, some Americans share the use of collections of millions of volumes, while others still lack access even to meager and deficient library facilities.

By the end of the 19th century the country possessed many thousands of academic, public, and other libraries, all based on Benjamin Franklin's principle of clubbing. These libraries were all more or less self-sufficient institutions, necessarily limited by their local resources, but providing important services to local communities of users. But the need for more broadly based services was already recognized and growing, and interlibrary lending, union catalogs, and other products of interlibrary cooperation were responding to this need.

During the next 50 years, however, it became clear that the library needs of the country could not be met merely by cooperation between independent units having local responsibilities. Several of the State governments led the way in developing regional library services organized around their State libraries, while increasingly through the period the libraries of the country were taking advantage of central services—of which the Library of Congress catalog-card system is the archetype—for reducing their costs and increasing their effectiveness. Finally, in 1956, in the Library Services Act (P.L. 597), Congress took a major step to enable the Federal Government, in collaboration with the States, to extend public library services to that third of the nation's population, mainly in rural areas, that still lacked them.

That Act was just in time. Since 1956 the accelerated momentum of events has made cumulative demands upon the libraries of the country which they were quite unprepared to meet, but the experience gained under the Library Services Act has proved invaluable for suggesting methods for meeting library problems.

It is now clear that library services are needed, to greater or less extent, directly or indirectly, by the entire citizenry of the country. Such services are increasingly essential for education, scholarship, and private inquiry; for research, development, commerce, industry, national defense, and the arts; for individual and community enrichment; for knowledge alike of the natural world and of man—in short, for the continuity of civilization on the one hand and increasingly for the preservation of man's place in nature on the other.

It is also now clear that these needs can no longer be met by spontaneous independent institutions having merely local responsibilities and claiming merely local support, no matter how willing they may be to assist. Indeed, these institutions through the years are persistently further and further from self-sufficiency and increasingly dependent

upon the services of external bodies—public and private, State and Federal, domestic and foreign—without which their costs would skyrocket and their services diminish.

A principal reason for this exists in the sheer mass of new information continuously being added to the existing stock as a result of the ceaseless probings of scholarship and research—information which is requisite for the increasingly complex activities of civilization and of modern communities, yet which is beyond the capacity of individual libraries to acquire, organize, store, search, and make available for service. For the efficient handling of this information, a system of specialized agencies is needed. Elements of such an arrangement actually do exist, but on an unplanned and spontaneous basis. The situation requires rationalization through the execution of careful plans in the national interest.

There are other reasons why libraries can less and less attempt to serve as self-sufficient entities but must more and more derive strength from membership in regional or national systems or networks. One of these is the increasing mobility both of people and of industry—a mobility that tends not only to diversify, but also to intensify the demands upon local libraries for specialized materials. Another is the enormous increase in personnel costs that all service organizations, including libraries, are forced to sustain, costs that compel them wherever possible to substitute mechanisms and automatons for manual operations. A special aspect of this process is the inevitable impact of electronic technology on information transfer—a process already under way in the development of methods for storage of information in electronic memories, processing by computer, distribution by wire or microwave, and service to the consumer by telefacsimile or cathode-ray-tube display.

To avoid haphazard and fragmented response to the inevitable forces of a changing society, a national plan is required that can be used to guide the next steps of all participants toward a recognized and achievable goal of adequate library service to all Americans. Because of the deep involvement of the Federal Government as producer, processor, and user of information, and because this is a matter closely touching the national welfare, the leadership of the Federal Government is essential to the success of any plan.

A prerequisite to the development of such a plan is a clear enunciation of the policy on which the plan is to be based. In consequence, the first recommendation of the National Advisory Commission on Libraries, on which all its further recommendations rest, is that it be declared National Policy, enunciated by the President and enacted into law by the Congress, that the American people should be provided with library and informational services adequate to their needs, and that the Federal Government, in collaboration with State and local governments and private agencies, should exercise leadership in assuring the provision of such services.

The international dimension

A National Library Policy for meeting the needs of our own citizens does not preclude an international awareness and responsibility. In fact a national policy statement on international book and library activities already exists—it was approved by the President on January 4, 1967. Subsequent directives to government agencies have further elucidated this policy for the encouragement of education through exchanges of books and of teachers and students, fostering indigenous book publishing and distribution facilities, support for programs of library development, training programs for library personnel, liaison between American and foreign libraries, increased exchange of reference and bibliographic information, and joint undertakings in the development of library technology.

The National Advisory Commission on Libraries shares the enthusiasm of the library profession toward achieving these goals and urges the appropriation of funds to implement the International Education Act (P.L. 89–698). The Commission also commends the idea of a clearinghouse at the Library of Congress to which foreign scholars and libraries might apply for needed publications.

The contribution of our library profession and our libraries to the improvement of international relations over the years has been noteworthy. Their acquisitions programs have attempted to develop rich resources of information from all parts of the world to meet the ever increasing needs of our citizens. They have aided in the work of creating understanding of our society and our policies by making publications of the United States available to libraries abroad. They have participated on a continuing basis in the work of international library associations and of the United Nations Educational, Scientific, and Cultural Organization (UNESCO) in its program of fostering education and librarianship abroad, and they have helped restore libraries ravaged by war and natural disasters.

Today, when it is clearly in our national interest to help the emerging countries develop progressive educational systems and provide a basis, through education and knowledge, for peaceful coexistence in the community of nations, the American library profession can—through participation in both publicly and privately supported efforts—make a greater contribution than ever before.

The United States can demonstrate to the world that we support our convictions regarding intellectual freedom by providing free access to all types of information and all shades of opinion for all citizens. Our libraries can strive to become a vital positive force in the social and intellectual reconstruction of a broadening and changing society. The National Advisory Commission on Libraries believes that the basic first step for the Federal Government is to state a National Library Policy toward the provision of services truly adequate to the nation's needs.

CHAPTER 3. OBJECTIVES FOR OVERCOMING
CURRENT INADEQUACIES

In order to fulfill the National Policy and provide library and informational services adequate to the nation's needs, current inadequacies must be faced. The purpose of this chapter is to discuss some areas where objectives are needed: where existing deficiencies threaten to undermine the success of any coherent development into the future. These deficiencies already severely limit or deny effective access to libraries and relevant knowledge for many individuals, but the situation can and must be remedied. A variety of complex responses and changes are required, and these responses and changes need to be developed in a sustained, consistent, and evolutionary manner over a period of time—and with a substantial degree of Federal leadership and participation. The National Advisory Commission on Libraries recommends that immediate national attention be given to six broad and fundamental objectives. The long-range development of an adequate library and information system will be dependent to a large degree on the achievement of these objectives.

Formal education at all levels

Objective: Provide adequate library and informational services for formal education at all levels.

First of all, we must reduce some serious current deficiencies in those libraries serving not only every level of formal education, but also the increasingly blurred boundary lines between these levels.[1] School library deficiencies, labeled "a national disgrace" by former Commissioner of Education, Francis Keppel, have truly serious consequences for our entire system of education. The habit of reading, skill in reading, and skill in identifying and using pertinent information are vital in the learning process, in dealing with concepts, in making wise judgments, in pursuing a vocation or profession, in extending the frontiers of knowledge, and in the liberation and extension of the mind of man.

Recent Federal legislation has already had visible impact on elementary and secondary school library development, in part by encouraging much greater local effort in library improvement. Nevertheless, and in spite of differences from one system to another, the needs of our schools in general for books and other library materials, for adequate physical facilities in which to house libraries, and for staff are so enormous that continued Federal assistance is necessary. The Commission believes that appropriations for school library resources should be increased as soon as possible to at least the full amount authorized by the Elementary and Secondary Education Act of 1965 (P.L. 89–10, P.L. 89–750). At this time some school buildings have no libraries in any sense of the word; too often meager materials are housed with notable inadequacy. Provision for libraries should be made mandatory in any Federal legislation supporting the construction of new school buildings or the expansion of existing buildings that do not already have adequate library facilities. It should be noted that libraries in schools serving educationally deprived children appear to be extremely deficient, and it would be advisable to bolster the library assistance provided by the Elementary and Secondary Education Act with supplementary legislation to help solve this problem in our large cities where so many disadvantaged children reside. To provide for a more efficient use of materials, equipment, and personnel, local and State school library agencies should be further encouraged to form community and regional systems to provide centralized consultation and acquisitions and processing services for school library materials.

The implementation of a national plan to raise elementary and secondary school libraries to full and continuing adequacy will require far better data on school libraries than are now available. Investigations should also be undertaken on the relative cost and utility of the various types of library materials, which are often indistinguishable from instructional materials; on differing patterns of service, supervision, and library organization; on appropriate standards; on the various means of coordinating school library districts to provide centralized consultant, processing, and materials-evaluation services; and on the means of stimulating the production of special library materials for students and preschool children in disadvantaged or bilingual communities, where children lack the preschool preparation and relative linguistic and cultural sophistication of children from middle-class American families.

One of the most complex problems that will have to be resolved in any national planning for genuine adequacy of library service to the total span of education relates to the difficulty of coordinating the various library agencies that serve high school and college students in urban areas. Because high schools, urban colleges, and junior colleges are often remote from areas where many of their students reside, and because it is frequently difficult and costly to provide the maintenance services necessary to keep the school library open evenings and weekends, and because the school collections are often inadequate to the needs, students have been resorting to their local public libraries in such large numbers as seriously to overload the public library. Coordination of public library directors, teachers, school principals, and various librarians within different geographic jurisdictions is not an easy administrative matter, but evidence suggests that there is a serious lack of such coordination even within areas where the jurisdictional boundaries of the public library and school library systems coincide. New thinking and planning are critically needed regarding the distribution of responsibility and financial support to the various types of libraries within each region if we are to serve the increasing demands of formal education.

As college enrollments have increased since World War II, we have witnessed an almost phenomenal increase in the number of junior and community colleges. In no other type of institution serving higher education are library shortcomings so glaring. The great majority of library collections of junior colleges are considered substandard, and a high percentage of the libraries of four-year colleges are also weak. Of all the difficulties that beset the college library, the most visible is that of inadequacy of library buildings. The Higher Education Facilities Act of 1963 (P.L. 88-204, as amended) has been a tremendous stimulus and support for college library construction. Substantial amounts have been granted under this Act for undergraduate college library buildings, but in many instances the combination of Federal aid and local resources has led only to an alleviation of the pressing immediate need for more library space, and not to solutions viable for long periods.

The National Advisory Commission on Libraries believes it to be of great national importance that the libraries serving the undergraduate students and facilities of our two-year and four-year colleges, and also the undergraduate colleges in our universities, be equipped and staffed to do their jobs with full adequacy. To help achieve this goal, the Commission believes that sums appropriated under the authority of the Higher Education Act of 1965 to strengthen the collections of college libraries should be increased substantially, and in the administration of grants for this purpose, special attention should be given to improvement of the collections of the two-year and four-year colleges that are most seriously in need. Additionally, the limitation on grants for the construction of academic library buildings under the Higher Education Facilities Act of 1963 (P.L. 88-204 as amended) should be raised to permit a Federal contribution of three fourths of the construction cost, as provided, for example, in the Medical Library Assistance Act (P.L. 89-291).

For long-range college library development, plans should be developed for centralized services to college libraries in acquisitions, processing, and storage of little-used material; in effecting cooperative arrangements that will give college students and faculty members efficient bibliographic and physical access to the resources of research libraries; in arranging for advisory services to college librarians, especially with respect to the utilization of technological aids to library work; and in persuading the States and other responsible agencies that adequate libraries are essential rather than marginal or optional facilities.

As formal education progresses into graduate and professional schools of the university and the continuing education of practitioners, the informational needs become more complex and the boundary lines between education and research become blurred. Inadequacies in serving the nation's research needs are discussed later in this chapter under other objectives, but it is appropriate to point out here that a dynamic relationship exists between all the areas for which the National Advisory Commission on Libraries has identified inadequacies and suggested objectives.

The public at large

Objective: Provide adequate library and informational services for the public at large.

Serving the informal educational needs at all levels might well be the stated function of the only libraries to which the undifferentiated general public has access today—the public libraries. There are inadequacies here too, and there are strong arguments for overcoming these in order to strengthen the health of our democracy.

The public library reaches the entire population as does no other aspect of library service. Parents of preschool children rely on it for the picture and storybooks that are the child's first introduction to the mystery of reading. Elementary school children go to the public library for books when school is out and during vacation, as do high school students, who also use it for assistance in homework and term papers. Urban college students living at home find the public library more convenient than their college libraries. Adults rely on it for recreation and continuing education. Businessmen may turn to it for practical information, as do housewives, craftsmen, and hobbyists. The larger public libraries are major research resources. More recently we have turned to the library as one of the social agencies needed to assist in liberating the prisoners of urban ghettos from ignorance and poverty. For all men and women, it is the one place through which they may reach the world's collected informational and intellectual resources.

Yet, important as the public library is,

there are few social services so unequally provided to the American people. Residents of some cities can command the resources of enormous institutions holding many hundreds of thousands, or even millions, of volumes. At the other extreme, some 20 million Americans, largely in rural areas, have no public library service at all, and some 10 million more have access only to very small libraries with very inadequate collections and little or no service from professional librarians. Indeed, only residents of cities of substantial size or of areas served by well-sustained county or regional library systems are likely to have access to reasonably adequate library service. It is essential that measures be taken to extend at least basic local public library service to every American. The encouragement of library systems, interlibrary loans, and other similar approaches can give everyone ultimate access to all the library resources he needs.

The unequal distribution of service is not the only inadequacy. Even where public library service is available, indeed even in some of the better served cities, it is usually far below any reasonable standard of adequacy. More than two thirds of all public libraries fail to meet American Library Association (ALA) standards as to the minimum adequate size of collections, and not one in 30 meets ALA standards for per-capita financial support.

There are a number of other quite critical problems in current public library services. One is the heavy burden of high school and college student use of the public library. This pressure will in part be relieved as the educational libraries are strengthened. But students turn to the public library not only because of its relative strength, but because of its convenience. This motive will not be lessened by the improvement of a high school library, for it may still be closed on evenings and weekends, or by the improvement of a college library that may be distant from a student's home. Diverting students away from the public library would deprive them of definite conveniences. The desirable objective would be to assist the public library in developing the means to meet the pressure and serve the student better. Public libraries need to be included in programs of assistance to educational libraries.

Another special problem, shared by many urban services, arises from the fact that patterns of public library service in metropolitan areas by no means correspond to the pattern of local governmental jurisdiction. In particular, the public library of the central city may be called on to render service to residents of the entire metropolitan area, without any financial support from suburban jurisdictions. The situation is doubly complicated when the metropolitan area, as in several of our large cities, extends across state lines. Further means of support and coordination must be found.

Still other problems stem from the fact that the nature of the informational and reading needs of the residents of core cities has radically changed in the last decade, so radically as to require substantial changes in the outlook, collections, and services of the core-city branches of urban public libraries if they are to become effective instruments in the attack on poverty, ignorance, and semiliteracy. The public libraries require assistance, financial and professional, in equipping themselves to meet these new needs.

One of the principal tasks of the National Commission on Libraries and Information Science, proposed in Chapter 4, should be to develop a national plan, calling on Federal, State, and local sources of support for making adequate public libraries service available to all Americans. Such a plan should give special attention to the problems of large cities with difficult educational problems, of metropolitan areas with multiple jurisdictions, and of rural areas entirely or almost entirely lacking public library services. The planning give attention to the coordination of school, college, and public library services. It should consider arrangements for the maximum use of cooperative library systems, and assure compensation to larger or more specialized libraries—public or private—when they give service to such systems that extends beyond the demands of their normal clientele. The National Advisory Commission on Libraries believes the plan should provide for substantially increased levels of support on a matching-fund basis.

The term "public library" includes county libraries serving townships without libraries, or with very inadequate ones, and State libraries. State libraries support the public library system in their respective States and provide assistance to school libraries. They are entrusted, usually, with planning State library systems and with the administration of State aid to public libraries. In some instances they are required to provide legal collections and other resources necessary for the work of State government. The deficiencies some State library agencies face are so severe that one recommendation of the National Advisory Commission on Libraries is specifically directed to this problem area.

Research in all fields at all levels

Objective: Provide materials to support research in all fields at all levels.

A third broad national goal must be the development and implementation of a plan that will insure that the nation has the research resources required for its increasingly complex informational and research needs. The publication of new books and new editions of older titles (exclusive of government publications, dissertations, pamphlets, and most subscription books) doubled between 1950 and 1966. The growth of knowledge and the phenomenal increase in its use is reflected not only in the increased production of books, but in the proliferation of such information-bearing records as journals, research reports, dissertations, microfilms, audiorecordings, and other materials. Increases in the use of all publications are difficult to assess, but a recent report states that the use of scientific literature has been increasing by 12 to 17 percent per year. In addition, there are major new areas of research concern (such as Asia, Africa, the Middle East, and Eastern Europe) requiring acquisitions programs for large quantities of material that are very costly, very difficult to acquire, and very expensive to catalog and organize for effective use.

The increase in research conducted by universities and sponsored by Federal and State agencies, corporations, and foundations, has made demands upon university libraries that have not been satisfied by either the growth of library collections or staffs. All agencies of government, foundations, industries, and other organizations that subsidize research by contracts, grants-in-aid, fellowships, and other means should be made aware of the greatly augmented burden on the library that their grants and subventions commonly entail. This should be taken into account in the planning of grants and programs. Continuity of such funding is critically important.

Although many libraries share in carrying the burden of acquiring, organizing, and servicing this vast body of material for the nation, the principal burden at the present time falls upon a relatively small number of university libraries, the three great national libraries (the Library of Congress, the National Library of Medicine, and the National Agricultural Library), and a number of very large public libraries and privately supported research libraries. Rapid increases in the costs and scope of required publications and of the staffs for handling them, as well as the added needs for sufficient space, are severely straining the very limited resources of all these institutions. Existing programs of Federal assistance are not in general addressed to the development or the accessibility of research materials. It is essential to develop and fund a more systematic and comprehensive national program to assist these libraries in the acquisition, organization, housing, and servicing of materials likely to be of research value to the nation.

Research, basic or applied, requires source materials and itself produces new informational output—this is true of the arts and humanities as well as the natural and physical sciences, the social and behavioral sciences, and many technical areas. As society continues to demand both new knowledge and more rapid application of knowledge for its own betterment, the proliferation of information may defeat its own purpose unless it is adequately recorded, acquired, and available for use.

Bibliographic access

Objective: Provide adequate bibliographic access to the nation's research and informational resources.

It is not enough simply to acquire research and informational resources. To insure that their existence and relevance will be known to those who need them, an adequate apparatus for indexing, cataloging, abstracting, and evaluating their content must be developed.

The work of bibliographic organization of vast collections of books and other materials, and of providing the tools that permit any user to determine their location quickly, grows in complexity with every volume added to the collections and with the proliferation in the sources, the subjects, the languages, and the forms in which pertinent materials appear. Under the Higher Education Act of 1965 (P.L. 89–329, P.L. 90–35, P.L. 90–82), funds totaling $3 million were provided in 1967 to enable the Library of Congress to expand its acquisitions and cataloging program in an effort to provide cataloging data for any foreign book that an American library might purchase. This appropriation has now been increased substantially and the program, if sustained, may prove to be the most far-reaching service to scholarly and many other national bibliographic needs of all Federal library undertakings.

At present the technology of electronically storing, updating, querying, and transmitting bibliographic data is emerging. In Chapter 4, the National Advisory Commission on Libraries sets forth its recommendation for a vigorous program of research and development leading toward national networks that will provide better access to improved bibliographic and related services.

Bibliographic access to the content of the many thousands of journals and research reports in our libraries is inadequate and uneven. There is no agency: (1) to initiate and develop national technical standards that could help to insure coverage of all journals contributing to the total research effort, (2) to coordinate the work of various association-supported, governmental, and commercial enterprises, and (3) to assist in determining priorities in funding.

Despite the seeming wealth of service of all kinds to assist in providing bibliographic access to information in the sciences and technology, several deficiencies in the present pattern are obvious. Except for medicine, agriculture, and the Library of Congress, the responsibility of the Government agencies for coverage is naturally based primarily on the particular objectives and literature requirements of the agency. The commercial services respond only to demonstrably large-scale need in special fields, and the work of the various scientific associations is not well coordinated. As a consequence, there are both extensive overlapping of effort and tremendous gaps in coverage. Moreover, a proprietary attitude in both the Government agencies and the scientific societies as regards their bibliographic products is a natural consequence of their desire to satisfy the special requirements of their users.

There is no direction by any national agency concerned with the total information problem. As separate services proliferate, grow, and succeed, the prospect for standardization and compatibility diminishes. There is clearly a need for national planning and coordination to insure, for all subject fields, including the humanities and social and behavioral sciences, adequate systems of bibliographical control.

Physical access

Objective: Provide adequate physical access to required materials or their texts throughout the nation.

Plans to strengthen national holdings of research resources and their effective subject or bibliographical control must also provide for effective physical access to the texts themselves. Even the largest research, university, corporate, or Federal library cannot hope to achieve self-sufficiency, despite the fact that it must possess library resources adequate for all but the most unusual needs of its staff or constituency. As the college library looks to the university library in its locality, so must the university library depend on the holdings of other institutions and the national libraries to satisfy requests for publications that it has not acquired. The public library, in turn, may look to State library agencies, other public libraries, or to academic libraries for materials needed by readers.

The demands for research information extend far beyond the requirements of scholars employed at universities. Industry must be able to draw upon the resources that our university libraries offer, since the duplication of their holdings in the depth and extent necessary for many industrial research purposes is almost inconceivable. Moreover, the needs of governmental agencies at all levels, of the professions, of the private scholar, all require access to research and other information not necessarily available in the immediate vicinity. Means must be found to make the full text of documents available in some suitable form and at locations convenient to all users, with minimum delay and at manageable and equitably distributed costs. The problems of physical access are likely to be further complicated in future unless efforts are made to discourage the continued use of book paper with a rapid rate of deterioration.

The present cooperative arrangements between libraries to make materials available are slow and inefficient and are costly to the relatively small number of libraries that are called upon to provide a major part of this service without recompense. Furthermore, the present difficulties in the way of interinstitutional physical access to publications forces research and other libraries, at high cost, to acquire, catalog, and house large amounts of little-used materials. These costs might be significantly reduced if new and effective patterns of joint physical access to materials can be developed. It is apparent that national, regional, and State planning is needed to facilitate physical access to publications generally, utilizing any technological aids that it is feasible to employ.

Such planning will obviously entail: (1) support from Federal, State, and other sources for improvement of interlibrary loan and copying services, which the research and certain other libraries can no longer provide gratuitously at high cost to themselves; (2) the establishment of regional library networks and of resource libraries to serve them; and (3) support for agencies, such as the Center for Research Libraries, which should have Federal assistance in their efforts to serve research and informational needs in all parts of the country. Finally, it will be important in the public interest, whether under the present copyright law or any revision that may be adopted, that arrangements for the protection of copyright proprietors do not unreasonably hinder access to and use of information.

Library manpower

Objective: Provide adequate trained personnel for the varied and changing demands of librarianship.

Recent analyses undertaken by the library profession, as well as the testimony of almost all witnesses before the National Advisory Commission on Libraries, indicate that the problem of manpower shortage in our libraries is of such critical severity as to merit its being singled out for special mention. All estimates of the number of professional personnel needed to fill existing vacancies and for normal attrition of staff in public, academic, and special libraries exceed the number of librarians graduated each year by the 42 accredited schools of librarianship in the United States and Canada. With respect to the provision of librarians qualified for positions in elementary and secondary school libraries, the situation is even more unsatisfactory.

Before the library profession can hope to enroll the requisite number of persons for training in the schools of librarianship, a variety of obstacles must be overcome. First, librarianship should be made more attractive as a career for men as well as for women. As is true of most professions in which women predominate at the lower and middle levels of responsibility, the prestige of librarianship as a whole is lower in the public view than it deserves to be, and the financial rewards are less tempting than in many other professions that require professional education. General public ignorance of the variety of interesting specialized career opportunities within the broad field of librarianship also make recruitment difficult. A further handicap is the discrepancy between the status, salaries, and fringe benefits accorded the librarians of many academic institutions and those available to their colleagues employed in teaching and research. Finally, there is a long tradition of recruitment for librarianship among only the humanistically oriented college students. Too few scientifically oriented young people understand that the profession of librarianship embraces all categories of specialists who mediate between the sources of recorded information and the people who need access to information in all subject fields and at all levels of sophistication.

A second major obstacle is the inadequacy of the 42 accredited graduate schools of librarianship in the United States and Canada with respect to financial support for staff and physical facilities. It is not known how many qualified applicants for library training may be lost for this reason. To complicate matters still further, all schools of librarianship contend with a shortage of qualified teachers, with a scarcity of fellowships to encourage the advanced study requisite for the preparation of future faculty, and with inadequate support for workshops, institutes, and other programs to enhance the competence of librarians already employed and help them adjust to changing demands. Equally important is the inadequacy of support for working librarians who wish to take advantage of opportunities for specialized training or advanced training when these do exist.

Paralleling these dilemmas is the slowness of the library profession itself in achieving agreement regarding the nature and extent of education or training needed for employment in the various specializations of librarianship, and in enlisting more fully the aid of the various disciplines of the social, behavioral, and applied sciences in preparing library science students for the changing requirements of library management and for the evolving role of the library in our society.

The resolution of library and information science manpower problems will be difficult, but they can yield to a number of specific measures. First, the library profession should undertake a program of ongoing research in librarianship in order to improve functional efficiency and facilitate the establishment of the variety of training programs needed now and in the future. Research in library education itself should be encouraged, as well as curricular experimentation.

Second, library administrators should employ every effort to make all professional library work intellectually and socially challenging to retain the best minds that enter the profession.

Third, the Federal Government, which has already acknowledged its responsibility for the improvement of library service under its constitutional mandate on the general welfare, should assist the profession through a number of undertakings. The United States Office of Education should analyze the library personnel situation on a regular basis, compare it with standards established by itself or the library associations, and publish its findings. It should, further, maintain a clearinghouse of information on all innovations in library education and training and on all efforts of libraries to make more efficient use of personnel. Further, the Office of Education should provide advisory aid to library schools, library associations, and others interested in recruiting people to library work in adequate numbers to carry out the various existing and emerging specialized tasks required.

To assist the library profession, the proposed National Commission on Libraries and Information Science should give high priority to an exploration of professional education and training, including experimentation with alternate modes of library training. The Commission should assist also with achieving improved salary scales and providing better promotional possibilities to make librarianship more attractive as a career.

Finally, Federal assistance in developing library personnel should be provided: (1) by direct aid to schools offering graduate and undergraduate training, postgraduate inservice training, and refresher courses; (2) by aid in the publication of suitable texts for such training; (3) by support of special programs to train potential teachers of librarianship; and (4) by greatly increased provision of funds for fellowships for undergraduate, graduate, and special library training.

Conclusion

These, then, are six areas where current inadequacies exist, and future inadequacies are foreseen unless all participants in the management and use of information can look to coherent national planning and coordinated research and development. The nation's needs for library and information service can be expressed in terms of the need to serve formal education, the public at large, and research of all kinds. The need to provide appropriate ways of locating information (bibliographic access) and acquiring it for use (physical access) is basic. Manpower is a pervasive and very urgent problem area. The six interrelated objectives discussed above form the context for the recommendations of the National Advisory Commission on Libraries set forth in Chapter 4.

CHAPTER 4. RECOMMENDATIONS FOR ACHIEVING
THE OBJECTIVES

In order to serve the needs of education at all levels, the general public in all its diversity, and research in all fields of knowledge, the problems of access to continually burgeoning information and efficient utilization of manpower must be resolved. Some dilemmas are immediately pressing and can be handled by immediate action. Other dilemmas are foreseen as still emerging over the transition period to the long future, and thus provision must be made for constant adaptation to inevitably changing needs and improved understanding of these needs. The National Advisory Commission on Libraries believes the five recommendations discussed below provide both a sound base for the future and a realistic means of coping with current inadequacies.

National Commission on Libraries and Information Science

Recommendation: Establishment of a National Commission on Libraries and Information Science as a continuing Federal planning agency.

In order to implement and further develop the national policy of library services for the nation's needs, the most important single measure that can be undertaken is the establishment of a continuing Federal planning agency. It is noteworthy that almost all representatives of library, scholarly, scientific, and other professional associations who testified before the National Advisory Commission on Libraries gave high priority in their recommendations to the creation of such a Federal planning agency. The present Commission's efforts to analyze current and future national library needs, assess the strengths and weaknesses of existing library resources and services, and evaluate the effects of library legislation, leave the members with the absolute conviction that the goal of library adequacy will be achieved only as a consequence of long-range planning and fostering of the evolutionary process of library development. This will require taking advantage of present and emerging knowledge in information science; it will require encouraging and exploiting future research.

The proposed National Commission should be charged with the responsibility of preparing full-scale plans to deal with the nation's library and information needs, and for advising the Federal Government and other agencies, institutions, and groups—both public and private, with respect to those needs. It should be empowered to conduct, or have conducted, such studies and analyses as are necessary for the fulfillment of its responsibilities; it should have ready access to information relevant to its purposes from other Government agencies concerned with library and information services; and it should be empowered to recommend legislation which is needed to enhance and strengthen the nation's library and information services.

The National Commission should be established by the Congress. Its members should be appointed by the President with the advice and consent of the Senate. The National Commission should report at least once a year to the President and to the Congress on its activities, recommendations, and plans in the areas of its responsibility and concern. This report should be published.

The present National Advisory Commission on Libraries recommends that this proposed National Commission on Libraries and Information Science be constituted of not more than 15 private citizens of distinction. This group shall include, but not necessarily be restricted to, persons competent in the library and information science professions. The Chairman should be appointed by the President from among its members. A rotating, staggered membership is suggested so that individuals serve for a term of five or six years.

To accomplish its complex and broad mission the National Commission should be provided with a staff adequate in number and strong in expertise, and with funds sufficient to enable it to exercise the extensive research and planning functions which will be necessary if it is to provide sound advice to the President and the Congress. A suggested location appropriate for the National Commission on Libraries and Information Science is in the Office of the Secretary of Health, Education, and Welfare.

The Library of Congress: The National Library of the United States

Recommedation: Recognition and strengthening of the role of the Library of Congress as the National Library of the United States and establishment of a Board of Advisers.

The National Advisory Commission on Libraries believes that the role of the Library of Congress as the National Library of the United States should be recognized and strengthened, and it specifically recommends:

1. That the Congress define the responsibilities of the Library of Congress as follows: (a) to serve as the principal reference and research arm of the Congress, thus serving the nation through this body; (b) to assemble, maintain, and provide national availability for comprehensive national research collections of materials from all countries and in all fields of knowledge, except those for which the National Library of Medicine and the National Agricultural Library have accepted responsibility; (c) to catalog these materials promptly and offer its catalog cards for sale to other libraries; and (d) to provide basic national bibliographical, reference, and copyright services. The Commission suggests that these functions of the Library of Congress, already largely exercised in fact, should be further recognized by adding an appropriate phrase to its title, so that its formal designation would be: "The Library of Congress: The National Library of the United States."

2. That a Board of Advisers to the Library of Congress be created. Its chairman and members should be drawn from the public, including scholarly and research organizations, the scientific community, universities and colleges, and research librarianship, and they should be appointed by the President of the Senate and the Speaker of the House of Representatives. The recommended functions of this proposed Board of Advisers are to review the Library's operations and services and to advise the Librarian of Congress—and, as desired, the appropriate Committees of Congress—on matters that would assist the Library in the development of its collections and the performance of its national services. The Board should be required to prepare and submit an annual report to the Congress and to the Librarian of Congress. This report should be published.

The rationale for the Commission's conclusions lies chiefly in the fact that, by far-reaching legislation and generous appropriations over the last 70 years, the Congress has created in the Library of Congress perhaps the greatest of the world's national libraries. It has the principal national research collections in most fields of knowledge, except of course those served by its two companion national institutions, the National Library of Medicine and the National Agricultural Library. It is a source of last resort to which other libraries can turn for inter-library loans and for microfilms of materials. It provides a means of acquisitions, for other libraries' collections as well as for its own, of public documents and other research materials not available through the book trade, especially from Asia, Africa, Latin and South America, and Eastern Europe.

The catalog cards of the Library of Congress provide a basis for the catalogs of most American libraries. The Library houses and maintains the *National Union Catalog,* one of the greatest and most nearly indispensable of our bibliographical tools. The publication of its own catalogs in book form has provided a major reference resource for libraries here and abroad. Many of its other bibliographic services have become essential to research libraries and to scholars. Since 1948 the Library of Congress has published the best continuing bibliography of Russian books compiled outside the Soviet Union. It edits the indispensable *National Union List of Serials* and publishes regularly a list of new serial titles received by principal American and Canadian libraries. It provides the subject apparatus for the national listing of doctoral dissertations, maintains a *National Register of Microcopy Masters,* and publishes a *National Union Catalog of Manuscript Collections.*

The Library of Congress performs many other national services as well. It is the chief agency in providing Braille and "talking" books for the blind. It has undertaken major responsibility for a national program to preserve the physically deteriorating book stocks of libraries. On a contractual basis it has provided a major bibliographical and documentation service to a number of Federal agencies concerned with scientific and technological research.

The Library of Congress in general—and, in their respective fields, the National Library of Medicine and the National Agricultural Library—have the ultimate in comprehensive national research collections and provide national bibliographical services that are absolutely indispensable to research and scholarship in many fields and to the whole system of American research libraries. Comprehensive as the collections and bibliographic services of the Library of Congress now are, however, they need further strengthening in a number of areas.[2] This strengthening of the Library of Congress through provision of a Board of Advisers, definition of the Library's responsibilities, and recognition of the role it already plays as a great national library, is the main thrust of the Commission's recommendations here.

It is a great credit to the wisdom and vision of the Congress that the Library of Congress has been so responsive to many needs. Today all the nation's requirements for library services are becoming so complex that the Library, which has never had a charter or basic constituent act defining its responsibilities, must be formally recognized for its national role and provided with advisers that can help to steer its future responsiveness.

The National Advisory Commission on Libraries does not recommend that the Library of Congress have responsibility for the development, administration, or coordination of a national library system or for the administration of programs of library assistance or grants such as those carried on by the United States Office of Education, the National Science Foundation, and other agencies. That would be a deterrent to its main function as a national library. The Commission believes that the indispensable role of the Library of Congress is in the development and availability of its unmatched collections and in its unique cataloging and bibliographic services. These should be strengthened in every possible way.

Federal Institute of Library and Information Science

Recommendation: Establishment of a Federal Institute of Library and Information

Science as a principal center for basic and applied research in all relevant areas.

The National Advisory Commission on Libraries recommends that a Federal Institute of Library and Information Science be established to become a principal national center of research on library and information science in all its aspects. The Institute should have as one of its major responsibilities the system engineering and technical direction involved in the design and implementation of an integrated national library and information system, but the mission of this proposed Institute must range beyond matters of technological development and application to research into the changing needs of information users and the effectiveness of libraries and information systems in meeting these needs.

This recommendation is based on the striking contrast between the serious inadequacies of the nation's libraries and the rapid progress in the tec'nology of information transfer. One of the great challenges of our day is to apply new technology to the operations of our libraries and thereby give each individual in our society easy and comprehensive access to the information resources he needs to make his work competent and his life meaningful.

The Commission recognizes that this goal will not be achieved by a single sweeping innovation, but rather by a succession of technical advances, some already within reach, others attainable by short-term efforts, and some approachable only through prolonged research activities. The times at which elements of new technology are introduced into specific libraries will also vary with the type of library service. Books and card files will be the mainstays of most small libraries for many years to come, but the large research libraries and a few special libraries will press for the earliest possible exploitation of new developments. Ultimately, the new technology will provide effective links from all information resources to all information users.

The uses of microfilm and document copiers are already familiar to every serious library user, even to some elementary school pupils. In the near future, gradual reduction in the costs of microfilm duplicates and full-size paper copiers will make on-demand duplication compete even more with traditional circulation of books and other materials in responding to many kinds of readers' needs. At a later time, as communication costs come down, we shall also see a more extensive adoption by libraries of telefacsimile transmission to distant users.

Of greater potential importance for future libraries than any past technical innovation will be the utilization of high-speed digital computers and their associated information-handling equipment, for the employment of computers in libraries has already led to high hopes for improved access to informational resources, in spite of the exponential growth of knowledge. Computers will most likely be applied to library operations in three successive stages. The computer has already demonstrated its usefulness as a rapid and efficient accounting device for the control of such library functions as acquisitions, circulation, serial records, and binding, as well as for general business operations; this is the first stage. Second, we are witnessing the initial successful attempts to apply the computer to bibliographic operations. The third and most exciting stage of computer involvement, which we are only beginning to approach, is the interaction between the library and the on-line computer community, in which a time-shared central computer is used as a general intellectual tool by many users working simultaneously at different terminals in a network. Development work is now in progress on the transmission of bibliographic data in such networks and on the more formidable problem of storing and transmitting the full text of documents.

In the course of time, different local networks will be interconnected and we shall see the emergence of regional, national, and international information-transfer networks. What we know today by the term "interlibrary cooperation" will be superseded by a much more fluid pattern of providing access to distant users without preventing concurrent access by local users. The evolution of these networks is the brightest promise of the new technology for libraries, but there are many technical, economic, and other problems that must be resolved before such networks can be operational.

The realization of all that is implied in this array of new technology can be achieved only by a substantial program of research and development. This Commission urges that the Federal Government should actively promote research and development in all aspects of technology as it relates to libraries and information transfer. To this end, the proposed National Commission on Libraries and Information Science should develop an integrated plan of support and cooperation involving the various Federal agencies now sponsoring such research and development work. Such a plan would greatly aid the continuation and strengthening of the current grant and contract program, which involves research and development projects at universities, private and public libraries, nonprofit research and development organizations, professional societies, and private companies.

The major Federal Institute recommended by the National Advisory Commission on Libraries can play an important role in the over-all plan. This Institute should itself undertake multidisciplinary research, development, and prototype application of all types of new technology as they relate to library and information science activities. Its program should be built on a foundation of basic research efforts directed toward better tools for the analysis of library and information requirements, quantitative measures for judging the value of existing systems and services, and an understanding of the relative value of various information-transfer media and of the role of interactive systems.

Supported by such basic investigations, the major research and development activities of the program should aim for further multidisciplinary efforts to improve library work—for example: (1) through applications of new technology for purposes of saving labor, improving speed and accuracy, maximizing convenience and dependability, reducing costs, and performing tasks previously impossible; (2) through more effective devices for organizing, storing, transmitting, displaying, and copying information; (3) through more effective organization of manpower and service units; (4) through superior understanding of the theoretical foundations of library work and of the storage, organization, and communication of knowledge; (5) through understanding, based on comprehensive studies of both users and nonusers of libraries, both as to their library requirements and also the reasons for nonuse; and (6) through the resolution of legal problems, such as those relating to the photocopying of copyrighted material.

The apex of the overall plan for research and development should be a system of interconnected libraries, established as a prototype network, a model for information transfer by advanced techniques. Such a network, after attaining full operational success, would become the first step in the evolution of an integrated national library system. The National Advisory Commission on Libraries recommends that the proposed Institute should be given the system engineering and technical direction responsibilities for the design and implementation of such a system.

In all planning of technological applications in library work, in all library network or systems planning, a crucial element is the development and application of national standards for the compatibility and convertibility of data systems and techniques among libraries. The proposed Institute should take a leading part in bringing about such standardization.

Administratively and organizationally, the Government can choose among many different patterns in establishing a research and development Institute of the type here contemplated. It is recommended that this Institute be esablished wihin the Office of the Secretary of Health, Education, and Welfare. If may be helpful to point out that the models that were prominent in the Commission's thinking were the National Institutes of Health and the National Laboratories of the Atomic Energy Commission.

U.S. Office of Education

Recommendation: Recognition and full acceptance of the critically important role the United States Office of Education currently plays in meeting needs for library services.

Recent legislation and Federal appropriations providing for: (1) major research programs that greatly accelerate the growth of new knowledge and (2) additional massive support for education at all levels place new and large responsibilities on the Office of Education. Its task would become even greater with the adoption of the National Advisory Commission on Libraries' proposals for a National Policy on library services for the nation's needs, the creation of a nationwide library network, and the widespread use of technological aids to improve library services.

The Commission recognizes the steps which the Office of Education has taken during this past year to strengthen and to increase the efficiency of its operations. The proposed organization of the Office's activities that affect libraries must focus on the most critical library problems: programs, professional education, facilities, research, planning, and development. In addition, the National Center for Educational Statistics must be in a position to collect on a continuing basis the pertinent and adequate library data—urgently required and not now available—for an appraisal of present programs and formulating plans for the future. But to carry out these key functions, the Office's staff must immediately be strengthened. The Commission urges the approval without delay of support for professionally trained, experienced

people, with supporting staff, to serve in the library programs of the Office, particularly within its Division of Library Services and Educational Facilities. To provide the essential overall leadership, the National Advisory Commission on Libraries specifically recommends the appointment of an Associate United States Commissioner for Libraries, responsible directly to the Commissioner of Education.

With its library and information services programs properly organized and staffed, the Office of Education would be in a far better position to administer present and impending Federal legislation and to conduct efficiently more extensive activities on behalf of the libraries. It could then plan, extend, and coordinate, at the national level, all types of library services for schools, colleges, continuing and adult education, public libraries, research, industry, government, and other agencies. In doing so, it would assist greatly in providing the service to libraries so vital in our time.

The critically important role of the Office of Education in meeting the nation's need for services in support of libraries must be clearly recognized and fully accepted by the Federal Government.

State library agencies

Recommendation: Strengthening State library agencies to overcome deficiencies in fulfilling their current functions.

Because State library agencies are unable to fulfill their current role adequately, far less their participative role in new joint ventures toward the objectives discussed in Chapter 3, State library agencies must be strengthened. This can best be done at this time by amendment of the Library Services and Construction Act (P.L. 88–269, P.L. 89–511, P.L. 90–154) authorizing aid specifically for such agencies to enable them: (1) to overcome staff shortages, (2) to provide better consultative services to public libraries, (3) to offer special information and library services to State Government, (4) to insure that a full range of library services is offered to the handicapped and disadvantaged, (5) to initiate and encourage research into library problems, and (6) to coordinate library planning for total library service. These are the areas where serious deficiencies currently exist.

In the long-range development of State-related library services, the principle of State matching should be retained. The National Advisory Commission on Libraries believes that Federal programs should give increasing attention to the building and strengthening of regional and interstate library programs where these appear to respond more effectively and efficiently to library needs.

Conclusion

The five recommendations discussed above are the result of the deliberations of the National Advisory Commission on Libraries from its establishment by Executive Order September 2, 1966, through June 1968. They are intended to provide structural innovations and realignments for a planned and coordinated approach to society's changing needs in the years ahead, as well as immediate actions to solve immediate problems. The order of presentation and relative length of descriptive text do not imply order of importance. All are major recommendations. Some relate to all the objectives discussed in Chapter 3; others relate more to one objective than another. All are aimed toward fulfillment of the National Policy presented in Chapter 2:

Recommendation: That it be declared National Policy, enunciated by the President and enacted into law by the Congress, that the American people should be provided with library and informational services adequate to their needs, and that the Federl Government, in collaboration with State and local governments and private agencies, should exercise leadership in assuring the provision of such services.

SUMMARY OF OBJECTIVES AND RECOMMENDATIONS

The fundamental recommendation of the National Advisory Commission on Libraries, on which further recommendations are based, is that it be declared National Policy, enunciated by the President and enacted into law by the Congress, that the American people should be provided with library and informational services adequate to their needs, and that the Federal Government, in collaboration with State and local governments and private agencies, should exercise leadership assuring the provision of such services.

Objectives for overcoming current inadequacies

Provide adequate library and informational services for formal education at all levels.

Provide adequate library and informational services for the public at large.

Provide materials to support research in all fields at all levels.

Provide adequate bibliographic access to the nation's research and informational resources.

Provide adequate physical access to required materials or their texts throughout the nation.

Provide adequate trained personnel for the varied and changing demands of librarianship.

Recommendations for achieving the objectives

1. Establishment of a National Commission on Libraries and Information Science as a continuing Federal planning agency.

2. Recognition and strengthening of the role of The Library of Congress as the National Library of the United States and establishment of a Board of Advisers.

3. Establishment of a Federal Institute of Library and Information Science as a principal center for basic and applied research in all relevant areas.

4. Recognition and full acceptance of the critically important role the United States Office of Education currently plays in meeting needs for library services.

5. Strengthening State library agencies to overcome deficiencies in fulfilling their current functions.

APPENDIX A

TEXT OF THE PRESIDENT'S STATEMENT AND THE EXECUTIVE ORDER ESTABLISHING THE PRESIDENT'S COMMITTEE ON LIBRARIES AND THE NATIONAL ADVISORY COMMISSION ON LIBRARIES

1. STATEMENT BY THE PRESIDENT

Our nation is providing better education to more citizens today than ever before. The result of this expanding effort in education is a rising demand for information—and a tidal wave of new information touching every aspect of our lives: health, education, jobs, national defense, goods and services, transportation, communications and environmental use.

But merely piling up valuable new knowledge is not enough; we must apply that knowledge to bettering our lives.

In our effort to do this, we depend heavily upon the nation's libraries. For this reason, the Federal government will spend, next year, more than $600 million in the library field.

But money alone cannot do the job. We need intelligent planning and advice to see that our millions are spent well. We need to ask serious questions about the future of our libraries:

What part can libraries play in the development of our communications and information-exchange networks?

Are our Federal efforts to assist libraries intelligently administered, or are they too fragmented among separate programs and agencies?

Are we getting the most benefit for the taxpayer's dollar spent?

To help answer these questions, I have signed today an Executive Order creating the National Advisory Commission on Libraries, composed of distinguished citizens and experts.

I have asked the Commission to appraise the role and adequacy of our libraries, now and in the future, as sources for scholarly research, as centers for the distribution of knowledge, and as links in our nation's rapidly evolving communications networks.

I have also asked the Commission to evaluate policies, programs, and practices of public agencies and private organizations—and to recommend actions which might be taken by public and private groups to ensure an effective, efficient library system for the nation.

I believe that this new Commission, aided by public and private efforts, will bring real advances in our progress toward adequate library service for every citizen.

Dr. Douglas Knight, president of Duke Univeristy in Durham, North Carolina, will serve as the Commission chairman.

The other members are: [3]

Proposed Membership for the National Library Commission:

Douglas M. Knight, President of Duke University, Chairman.

Verner Clapp, President, Council on Library Resources.

Herman Fussler, Library, University of Chicago.

Carl Overhage, M.I.T., Cambridge, Massachusetts.

Theodore Waller, President, Teaching Materials Corporation, New York (resigned December 28, 1966).

Wilbur Schramm, Director, Institute for Communication Research, Stanford University.

Launor Carter, Senior Vice President, System Development Corporation, Santa Monica.

Caryl Haskins, Carnegie Institution, Washington, D.C.

William N. Hubbard, Jr., Dean, University of Michigan Medical School, and Chairman, Educom.

Alvin Eurich, President, Aspen Institute for Humanistic Studies, Colorado.

Stephen Wright, former President of Fisk University, Nashville, Tennessee.

Harry Ransom, Chancellor, University of Texas, Austin.

Carl Elliott, former Congressman from Alabama.

Estelle Brodman, Medical Library, Washington University, St. Louis, Missouri.

2. EXECUTIVE ORDER NO. 11301

By virtue of the authority vested in me as President of the United States, it is ordered as follows:

Section 1. *Establishment of Committee.* (a) There is hereby established the President's Committee on Libraries (hereinafter referred to as the "Committee").

(b) The membership of the Committee shall consist of the Secretary of Health, Education, and Welfare, who shall be the Chairman of the Committee, the Secretary of Agriculture, the Director of the Office of Science and Technology, and the Director of the National Science Foundation, and may include, in addition, the Librarian of Congress who is hereby invited to be a member of the Committee. Each member of the Committee may designate an alternate, who shall serve as a member of the Committee whenever the regular member is unable to attend any meeting of the Committee.

Section 2. *Duties of the Committee.* (a) The Committee shall:

(1) Appraise the role of libraries as resources for scholarly pursuits, as centers for the dissemination of knowledge, and as components of the Nation's rapidly evolving communications and information-exchange network;

(2) Evaluate policies, programs, and practices of public agencies and private institutions and organizations with reference to maximum effective and efficient use of the Nation's library resources; and

(3) Develop recommendations for action by Government or by private institutions and organizations designed to ensure an effective and efficient library system for the Nation.

(b) Such recommendations shall take into account the final report of the National Advisory Commission on Libraries established by Section 3 of this order, which report shall be transmitted to the President with the recommendations of the Committee.

Section 3. *Establishment of Commission.* (a) To assist the Committee in carrying out its functions under Section 2 of this order, there is hereby established the National Advisory Commission on Libraries (hereinafter referred to as the "Commission").

(b) The Commission shall be composed of not more than twenty members appointed by the President, none of whom shall be officers or full-time employees of the Federal Government. The President shall designate the Chairman of the Commission from among its members.

(c) The Commission shall meet on call of the Chairman.

(d) Each member of the Commission may be compensated for each day such member is engaged upon work of the Commission, and shall be reimbursed for travel expenses, including per diem in lieu of subsistence, as authorized by law (5 U.S.C. 55a; 5 U.S.C. 73b-2) for persons in the Government service employed intermittently.

Section 4. *Duties of the Commission.* (a) The Commission shall transmit to the Committee its independent analysis, evaluation, and recommendations with respect to all matters assigned to the Committee for study and recommendations.

(b) In carrying out its duties under subsection (a), above, the Commission shall:

(1) Make a comprehensive study and appraisal of the role of libraries as resources for scholarly pursuits, as centers for the dissemination of knowledge, and as components of the evolving national information systems;

(2) Appraise the policies, programs, and practices of public agencies and private institutions and organizations, together with other factors, which have a bearing on the role and effective utilization of libraries;

(3) Appraise library funding, including Federal support of libraries, to determine how funds available for the construction and support of libraries and library services can be more effectively and efficiently utilized; and

(4) Develop recommendations for action by Government or private institutions and organizations designed to ensure an effective and efficient library system for the Nation.

(c) The Commission shall submit its final report and recommendations to the Committee no later than one year after the date of its first meeting, and shall make such interim reports as it deems appropriate for improving the utilization of library resources.

Section 5. *Federal departments and agencies.* (a) The Committee or the Commission is authorized to request from any Federal department or agency any information deemed necessary to carry out its functions under this order; and each department or agency is authorized, consistent with law and within the limits of available funds, to furnish such information to the Committee or the Commission.

(b) Each department or other executive agency the head of which is named in Section 1(b) of this order shall, as may be necessary, furnish assistance to the Committee or the Commission in accordance with the provisions of Section 214 of the Act of May 3, 1945 (59 Stat. 134; 31 U.S.C. 691), or as otherwise permitted by law.

(c) The Department of Health, Education, and Welfare is hereby designated as the agency which shall provide administrative services for the Commission.

Section 6. *Termination of the Committee and the Commission.* The Committee and the Commission shall terminate ninety days after the final report of the Commission is submitted to the Committee.

LYNDON B. JOHNSON.

THE WHITE HOUSE, *September 2, 1966.*

APPENDIX B
SELECT LIST OF SPECIAL STUDIES

One of the most ambitious endeavors undertaken by the National Advisory Commission on Libraries was to call for more than a dozen special studies on a wide range of subjects. Social science, history, political science, economics, information science, education, and library science were only some of the disciplines contributing to the studies—all of which were performed within the limited space of a few months.

Most of these special studies, commissioned by or made available to the Commission, contributed at least partially to Commission decision-making, although there was by no means a total endorsement of every position or recommended action in even the most highly acclaimed studies. All will be made available to the United States Office of Education for consideration for the Educational Research Information Center (ERIC), and several will appear elsewhere—notably in a forthcoming book based on Commission activity.

The list on the following page includes those special studies the Commission judged to be relevant to the problems with which it was concerned and worthy of serious consideration, although a few are of mostly descriptive value. Studies, or parts of studies, that were not completed in time for careful study by the membership are not included on the list, nor are those deemed to be of little or no immediate relevance to Commission decision-making in the form in which they were submitted.

TITLE OF STUDY AND AGENCY CONDUCTING STUDY

1. Technology and Libraries, System Development Corporation.

2. On Research Libraries,[4] American Council of Learned Societies.

3. The Impact of Technology, on the Library Building,[3] Educational Facilities Laboratories.

4. The Federal Government and Libraries, Duke University.

5. American State Libraries and State Library Agencies, Nelson Associates, Inc.

6. Impact of Social Change on Libraries, National Book Committee.

7. On the Economics of Library Operation, Mathematica.

8. The Use of Libraries and the Conditions That Promote Their Use, The Academy for Educational Development, Inc.

9. Special Libraries: Problems and Cooperative Potentials, American Documentation Institute.

10. School Libraries in the United States, Nelson Associates, Inc.

11. Undergraduate and Junior College Libraries in the United States, Nelson Associates, Inc.

12. Public Libraries in the United States, Nelson Associates, Inc.

13. Libraries and Industry, Programming Services, Inc.

APPENDIX C
LIST OF REGIONAL HEARINGS

Another project of the National Advisory Commission on Libraries was designed to acquire information on the people's needs for library and informational services. This was the series of regional hearings, held during the summer and early fall of 1967, at which subcommittees of Commission membership heard testimony from variety of citizens, businessmen, professional people, farmers, white-collar and blue-collar workers, students, teachers, parents, and local, state, and national officials in communities of varying size throughout the nation. There was testimony representing the blind, the aged, and virtually all religious and ethnic groups in America.

The results contributed particularly to the Commission's consensus on the objective to "provide adequate library and informational services for the public at large" and on the recommendation for strengthening State library agencies. The need to solve library problems by effective manpower utilization was pervasive throughout all the hearings. The forthcoming book based on Commission materials will include highlights from the regional hearings and a complete list of all who testified. A summary table appears below:

REGIONAL HEARINGS

Locale	Date, 1967	Number of witnesses
St. Louis, Mo. [1]	Apr. 12	7
Tampa, Fla.	Sept. 8	25
Great Falls, Mont.	Sept. 11	30
Portland, Oreg.	Sept. 13	34
Anchorage, Alaska	Sept. 15	22
Nome, Alaska [2]	Sept. 16	
Bismarck, N. Dak.	Sept. 18	42
Wilkes-Barre, Pa.	Sept. 22	23
Baton Rouge, La.	Oct. 4	48
Lubbock, Tex.	Oct. 6	47
Pikeville, Ky.	Oct. 20	64
Tucson, Ariz.	Oct. 27	24

[1] This earlier meeting was actually held before the series of regional hearings was established.
[2] No transcript has been received in the Commission office, hence there is no record of the number of witnesses giving testimony.

APPENDIX D
LIST OF COMMISSION MEETINGS AND WITNESSES AND GUESTS AT EACH

The Members of the National Advisory Commission on Libraries convened formally on eleven occasions to hear testimony, to converse with both witnesses and guests, and to deliberate among themselves on a broad range of topics relevant to the study of library and informational services for the nation's needs. A list of these meetings of the full Commission appears below. The titles of the witnesses who gave formal testimony and of the guests who visited are shown as they were at the time of each meeting.

I. NOVEMBER 30, 1966, WASHINGTON, D.C.

Guests: S. Douglass Cater, Jr., Special Assistant to the President; Harold Howe II, Commissioner of Education; Louis Hausman, Assistant to the Commissioner of Education; Jerome N. Bluestein, Administrative Officer, Office of the Commissioner of Education.

II. JANUARY 7 AND 8, 1967, NEW ORLEANS, LA.

Witnesses: An informal meeting was held on January 8 with representatives of the Association of Research Libraries Liaison Committee and the Committee on National Library-Information Systems. There is no transcript of this meeting.

III. FEBRUARY 13, 1967, WASHINGTON, D.C.
Witnesses

Burton W. Adkinson, Head, Office of Science Information Service, National Science Foundation.

Scott Adams, Deputy Director, National Library of Medicine.

Andrew A. Aines, Technical Assistant, Office of Science and Technology, and Acting Chairman of the Committee on Scientific and Technical Information (COSATI) of the Federal Council for Science and Technology (FCST).

Foster E. Mohrhardt, Director, National Agricultural Library.

IV. MARCH 5 AND 6, 1967 NEW YORK, N.Y.
Witnesses

Kathleen Molz, Editor, *Wilson Library Bulletin.*

Jean Connor, Director, Division of Library Development, New York State Library.

Edward G. Freehafer, Director, New York Public Library.

Frank L. Schick, Director, School of Library and Information Science, University of Wisconsin (Milwaukee).

Bill M. Woods, Executive Director, Special Libraries Association.

Frank E. McKenna, President, Special Libraries Association.

Lester E. Asheim, Director, Office for Library Education, American Library Association.

John M. Cory, Executive Director, New York Metropolitan Reference and Research Library Agency.

John A. Humphry, Director, Brooklyn Public Library.

Paul Wasserman, Dean, School of Library and Information Services, University of Maryland.

Eric Moon, Editor, *Library Journal*, R. R. Bowker Publishing Company.

V. APRIL 18 AND 19, 1967, CHICAGO, ILL.

Witnesses

American Library Association Representatives: Mary V. Gaver, President; David H. Clift, Executive Director.

American Library Association Panel Members: Ralph U. Blasingame, Associate Professor, Graduate School of Library Science, Rutgers University; Keith Doms, Director, Carnegie Library of Pittsburgh; Frances B. Jenkins, Professor, Graduate School of Library Science, University of Illinois; Marion A. Milczewski, Director, University of Washington Libraries; Frederick H. Wagman, Director, University of Michigan Library; Eileen Thornton, Librarian, Oberlin College, Harold G. Johnston, Director, Detroit Metropolitan Library Project; Genevieve M. Casey, State Librarian, Michigan State Library; Gertrude E. Gscheidle, Chief Librarian, Chicago Public Library; Jesse H. Shera, Dean, School of Library Science, Western Reserve University; Don R. Swanson, Dean, Graduate Library School, University of Chicago; Ralph H. Parker, Dean, Library School, University of Missouri; James L. Lundy, President, University Microfilms; James G. Miller, Principal Scientist, Educom.

VI. MAY 22 AND 23, 1967, WASHINGTON, D.C.

Witnesses

Present from the Library of Congress: L. Quincy Mumford, Librarian of Congress; John G. Lorenz, Deputy Librarian of Congress; Elizabeth E. Hamer, Assistant Librarian; Marlene D. Morrisey, Executive Assistant to the Librarian of Congress; Paul L. Berry, Director, Administrative Department; Lewis C. Coffin, Law Librarian; Roy P. Basler, Director, Reference Department; William J. Welsh, Acting Director, Processing Department; Marvin W. McFarland, Chief, Science and Technology Division; Abraham L. Kaminstein, Register of Copyrights; Lester S. Jayson, Director, Legislative Reference Service; Paul R. Reimers, Coordinator of Information Systems.

Alice Ball, Executive Director, United States Book Exchange.

Germaine Krettek, Associate Executive Director, American Library Association, and Director, ALA Washington Office.

Edwin Castagna, Chairman, Legislation Committee, American Library Association.

Paul Howard, Executive Secretary, Federal Library Committee.

Henry J. Gartland, Director of Libraries, Veterans Administration.

Burton E. Lamkin, Chief, Library and Information Retrieval Branch, Federal Aviation Administration.

Hubert E. Sauter, Deputy Director, Clearinghouse of Federal Scientific and Technical Information.

Melvin S. Day, Deputy Assistant Administrator, Office of Technical Utilization, National Aeronautics and Space Administration.

Edward J. Bruenenkant, Director, Division of Technical Information, U.S. Atomic Energy Commission.

Walter C. Christensen, Staff Assistant for Scientific Information, Department of Defense.

Representatives from the Office of Education: Harold Howe II, Commissioner of Education; Grant Venn, Associate Commissioner, Bureau of Adult and Vocational Education; Lee Burchinal, Director, Division of Research Training and Dissemination; Ray Fry, Director, Division of Library Services and Educational Facilities; Eugene Kennedy, Chief, Library and Information Science Research Branch; Alexander Mood, Assistant Commissioner, National Center for Educational Statistics; Morris Ullman, Chief, Adult, Vocational, and Library Studies Branch.

VII. JUNE 25 AND 26, 1967, SAN FRANCISCO, CALIF.

Guests: Maryann Reynolds, Librarian, Washington State Library; Lucile Nix, Library Consultant, Georgia State Department of Education, Public Library Unit (Library Extension Service); Carma Leigh, Librarian, California State Library.

VIII. SEPTEMBER 6 AND 7, 1967, WASHINGTON, D.C.

Guests: Carolyn I. Whitenack, Associate Professor, Library and Audiovisual Education, Purdue University; Mary Helen Mahar, Chief of School Library Section and Acting Chief, Instruction Research Branch, U.S. Office of Education; William Knox, Vice-President, McGraw-Hill, Inc.; J. Lee Westrate, Senior Management Analyst, Bureau of the Budget; Louis B. Wright, Director, Folger Shakespeare Library.

IX. OCTOBER 9, 10, AND 11, 1967, WASHINGTON, D.C.

Guest: Barnaby C. Keeney, Chairman, National Endowment for the Humanities.

ADDITIONAL HEARING

November 27 and 28, 1967 (Washington, D.C.).

May 1, 1968 (New York, New York).

---

[1] As evidenced, for example, by such phenomena as advanced-placement credit for college-level courses taken in high school and early-entrance programs to professional education.

[2] This is true, for example, in connection with the previously mentioned acquisition and prompt central cataloging of foreign research materials not available through normal trade channels. To a considerable extent, this must now be accomplished through the transfer of funds appropriated to the United States Office of Education under Title II–C of the Higher Education Act of 1965 (P.L. 89–329) and the transfer of foreign currencies accumulated under Public Law 480.

[3] See beginning of report for the final official list of Commission membership.

[4] Not financed or only partially financed by the Commission but offered to ERIC.

An Act To Establish a National Commission on Libraries & Information Science and for Other Purposes

Public Law 91–345, 91st Congress.

This is a piece of legislation that will prove to be of interest and importance to all librarians and information scientists in the country. It came into being as a result of recommendations made in a report by the National Advisory Commission on Libraries. The report itself was published in the Congressional Record for October 21, 1968, on pages E-9355 through E-9368. I am reminded of the one theme that runs through that report. As the Report on page E-9359, phrases it: "This [theme] is a strong social-benefit awareness, a service orientation that pervades every existing and conceivable library function ... A library can be understood only as it enhances a socially valuable function, one of which—and one that all librarians can enhance—is the personal intellectual and ethical development of every individual in our society."

Public Law 91-345
91st Congress, S. 1519
July 20, 1970

An Act

To establish a National Commission on Libraries and Information Science, and for other purposes.

Be it enacted by the Senate and House of Representatives of the United States of America in Congress assembled, That this Act may be cited as the "National Commission on Libraries and Information Science Act".

National Commission on Libraries and Information Science Act.

STATEMENT OF POLICY

SEC. 2. The Congress hereby affirms that library and information services adequate to meet the needs of the people of the United States are essential to achieve national goals and to utilize most effectively the Nation's educational resources and that the Federal Government will cooperate with State and local governments and public and private agencies in assuring optimum provision of such services.

COMMISSION ESTABLISHED

SEC. 3. (a) There is hereby established as an independent agency within the executive branch, a National Commission on Libraries and Information Science (hereinafter referred to as the "Commission").

(b) The Department of Health, Education, and Welfare shall provide the Commission with necessary administrative services (includ-

SOURCE: U.S. Laws, Statutes, etc. *An Act To Establish a National Commission on Libraries and Information Science, and for other purposes.* Public Law 91-345. 91st Congress, S.1519. Approved July 20, 1970. (Washington: 1970). pp. 1–3.

ing those related to budgeting, accounting, financial reporting, personnel, and procurement) for which payment shall be made in advance, or by reimbursement, from funds of the Commission and such amounts as may be agreed upon by the Commission and the Secretary of Health, Education, and Welfare.

84 STAT. 440
84 STAT. 441

CONTRIBUTIONS

Sec. 4. The Commission shall have authority to accept in the name of the United States grants, gifts, or bequests of money for immediate disbursement in furtherance of the functions of the Commission. Such grants, gifts, or bequests, after acceptance by the Commission, shall be paid by the donor or his representative to the Treasurer of the United States whose receipts shall be their acquittance. The Treasurer of the United States shall enter them in a special account to the credit of the Commission for the purposes in each case specified.

FUNCTIONS

Sec. 5. (a) The Commission shall have the primary responsibility for developing or recommending overall plans for, and advising the appropriate governments and agencies on, the policy set forth in section 2. In carrying out that responsibility, the Commission shall—

(1) advise the President and the Congress on the implementation of national policy by such statements, presentations, and reports as it deems appropriate;

Advice to President and Congress.

(2) conduct studies, surveys, and analyses of the library and informational needs of the Nation, including the special library and informational needs of rural areas and of economically, socially, or culturally deprived persons, and the means by which these needs may be met through information centers, through the libraries of elementary and secondary schools and institutions of higher education, and through public, research, special, and other types of libraries;

Studies, surveys, etc.

(3) appraise the adequacies and deficiencies of current library and information resources and services and evaluate the effectiveness of current library and information science programs;

(4) develop overall plans for meeting national library and informational needs and for the coordination of activities at the Federal, State, and local levels, taking into consideration all of the library and informational resources of the Nation to meet those needs;

(5) be authorized to advise Federal, State, local, and private agencies regarding library and information sciences;

(6) promote research and development activities which will extend and improve the Nation's library and information-handling capability as essential links in the national communications networks;

(7) submit to the President and the Congress (not later than January 31 of each year) a report on its activities during the preceding fiscal year; and

Report to President and Congress.

(8) make and publish such additional reports as it deems to be necessary, including, but not limited to, reports of consultants, transcripts of testimony, summary reports, and reports of other Commission findings, studies, and recommendations.

(b) The Commission is authorized to contract with Federal agencies and other public and private agencies to carry out any of its functions under subsection (a) and to publish and disseminate such reports, findings, studies, and records as it deems appropriate.

Contract authority.

(c) The Commission is further authorized to conduct such hearings at such times and places as it deems appropriate for carrying out the purposes of this Act.

Hearings.

(d) The heads of all Federal agencies are, to the extent not prohibited by law, directed to cooperate with the Commission in carrying out the purposes of this Act.

84 STAT. 441

84 STAT. 442

MEMBERSHIP

Appointments
by President.

Terms of
office.

Compensation,
travel ex-
penses.

SEC. 6. (a) The Commission shall be composed of the Librarian of Congress and fourteen members appointed by the President, by and with the advice and consent of the Senate. Five members of the Commission shall be professional librarians or information specialists, and the remainder shall be persons having special competence or interest in the needs of our society for library and information services, at least one of whom shall be knowledgeable with respect to the technological aspects of library and information services and sciences. One of the members of the Commission shall be designated by the President as Chairman of the Commission. The terms of office of the appointive members of the Commission shall be five years, except that (1) the terms of office of the members first appointed shall commence on the date of enactment of this Act and shall expire two at the end of one year, three at the end of two years, three at the end of three years, three at the end of four years, and three at the end of five years, as designated by the President at the time of appointment, and (2) a member appointed to fill a vacancy occurring prior to the expiration of the term for which his predecessor was appointed shall be appointed only for the remainder of such term.

(b) Members of the Commission who are not in the regular full-time employ of the United States shall, while attending meetings or conferences of the Commission or otherwise engaged in the business of the Commission, be entitled to receive compensation at a rate fixed by the Chairman, but not exceeding the rate specified at the time of such

84 STAT. 442

35 F.R. 6247.

service for grade GS–18 in section 5332 of title 5, United States Code, including traveltime, and while so serving on the business of the Commission away from their homes or regular places of business, they may be allowed travel expenses, including per diem in lieu of subsistence, as authorized by section 5703 of title 5, United States Code, for persons employed intermittently in the Government service.

83 Stat. 190.

(c) (1) The Commission is authorized to appoint, without regard to the provisions of title 5, United States Code, covering appointments in the competitive service, such professional and technical personnel as may be necessary to enable it to carry out its function under this Act.

Professional and technical personnel, appointment.

80 Stat. 378.

(2) The Commission may procure, without regard to the civil service or classification laws, temporary and intermittent services of such personnel as is necessary to the extent authorized by section 3109 of title 5, United States Code, but at rates not to exceed the rate specified at the time of such service for grade GS–18 in section 5332 of title 5, United States Code, including traveltime, and while so serving on the business of the Commission away from their homes or regular places of business they may be allowed travel expenses, including per diem in lieu of subsistence, as authorized by section 5703 of title 5, United States Code, for persons employed intermittently in the Government service.

AUTHORIZATION OF APPROPRIATIONS

SEC. 7. There are hereby authorized to be appropriated $500,000 for the fiscal year ending June 30, 1970, and $750,000 for the fiscal year ending June 30, 1971, and for each succeeding year, for the purpose of carrying out the provisions of this Act.

Approved July 20, 1970.

LEGISLATIVE HISTORY:

HOUSE REPORTS: No. 91-240 accompanying H.R. 10666 (Comm. on Education and Labor) and No. 91-1226 (Comm. of Conference).
SENATE REPORT No. 91-196 (Comm. on Labor and Public Welfare).

CONGRESSIONAL RECORD:
    Vol. 115 (1969): May 23, considered and passed Senate.
    Vol. 116 (1970): April 20, considered and passed House, amended,
                     in lieu of H.R. 10666.
                     June 29, House agreed to conference report.
                     July 6, Senate agreed to conference report.

National Commission Membership Announced

Members of the National Commission on Libraries and Information Science:

For a term expiring July 19, 1971: Andrew A. Aines, Technical Assistant for Scientific and Technological Information, Communication and Computers to the Director of the Office of Science and Technology, Washington, D.C.; and Catherine D. Scott, Head Librarian of Bellcomm, Inc., Washington, D.C. For a term expiring July 19, 1972: Martin Goland, President, Southwest Research Institute, San Antonio, Tex.; Louis A. Lerner, publisher, Lerner Home Newspapers, Chicago, Ill.; and Charles A. Perlik, Jr., President, American Newspaper Guild, Washington, D.C. For a term expiring July 19, 1973: John G. Kenemy, President, Dartmouth College, Hanover, N.H.; Mrs. Bessie B. Moore, Director of Economic and Environmental Education, State Department of Education, Little Rock, Ark.; and Alfred R. Zipf, Executive Vice President, Bank of America, San Francisco, Calif.

For a term expiring July 19, 1974: Joseph Becker, President, Becker and Hayes, Inc., Bethesda, Md.; Carlos A. Cuadra, Manager of Library and Education Systems Department, System Development Corp., Santa Monica, Calif.; and John E. Velde, Jr., Vice President, Velde, Roelfs and Company, Pekin, Ill. For a term expiring July 19, 1975: W. O. Baker, Vice President of Research, Bell Telephone Laboratories, Morristown, N.J.; Frederick Burkhardt, President, American Council of Learned Societies, New York, N.Y.; and Leslie W. Dunlap, Dean of Library Administration, University of Iowa, Iowa City, Iowa.

Charles H. Stevens, Associate Director for Library Development, Project INTREX at the Massachusetts Institute of Technology, has been appointed the first Executive Director of the National Commission on Libraries and Information Science, Washington, D.C.

Frederick Burkhardt, President of the American Council of Learned Societies, who was named head of the Commission by President Nixon earlier this year, expressed satisfaction with the Commission's choice. "The library field and the information community as a whole have awaited this appointment with some anticipation, and we are fortunate indeed to find a man who is at once a librarian of acknowledged national stature and

an expert on the technical aspects of information retrieval systems," he said. "We have every expectation that Mr. Stevens will bring to his new duties a balanced consideration for the mounting problems of traditional libraries as well as for innovations in the field."

Mr. Stevens, who will take a leave of absence from M.I.T. to accept the new post, has been on the staff of Project INTREX since its inception at M.I.T. six years ago. INTREX (for *IN*formation *TR*ansfer *EX*periments) is a computer-based prototype technical library system, combining recent advancements in digital data processing and video technology to give the library user remote access to computer catalog data and microfiche texts.

SOURCE: The above news item is from the *FLC* (Federal Library Committee) *Newsletter*, No. 60, December 1971, p. 2.

The Federal Library Mission: A Statement of Principles and Guidelines, and The Federal Library Committee: Three Years of Progress, 1965–1968

Prepared by The Federal Library Committee

The collections and services of Federal libraries constitute an important resource for providing information needed in daily operation of the Government, in the conduct of agency research programs, and in connection with the needs of non-governmental groups such as libraries, research institutions, and the general public. Therefore, both the statement and the progress report that follow are important in that they tell of FLC's recent and continuing efforts in "establishing a common understanding of Federal libraries among the Government's information services so as to insure full utilization of library resources."

PREFACE

The Federal Library Committee is an inter-agency committee established under the auspices of the Bureau of the Budget and the Library of Congress.[1] Its membership consists of representatives of the cabinet departments and six independent agencies, the latter selected for two year terms on a rotating basis. The Committee was organized to:

(1) consider policies and problems relating to Federal libraries;

(2) evaluate existing Federal library programs and resources;

(3) determine the priorities among library issues requiring attention;

(4) examine the organization and policies for acquiring, preserving, and making information available;

(5) study the need for and potential of technological innovation in library practices;

(6) study library budgeting and staffing problems including the recruiting, education, training, and remuneration of librarians.

In considering its responsibilities the Committee has concluded that immediate priority must be given to establishing a common understanding of the role of Federal libraries among the Government's information services so as to insure full utilization of library resources. Therefore, the Committee has formulated this statement of mission and guidelines for its implementation.

The Committee plans subsequent statements on specific library operations and services with a view to raising the general level of Federal library performance.

INTRODUCTION

All Federal agencies require information to operate effectively. Managerial decisions and professional expertise necessary to successful accomplishment of agency missions depend on an informed staff. The increased complexity of Government, the accelerated growth of knowledge, and the explosion of documentation have focused attention on the need to increase effectiveness of all mechanisms providing information services to Federal agencies among which Federal libraries are of special importance.

The most urgent library problem confronting Federal agencies is identical with that confronting non-Federal institutions, i.e., the problem of providing library service adequate to meet urgent growing demands. The gravity of this problem was recognized by the President when on Septem-

SOURCE: Library of Congress. Federal Library Committee. *The Federal Library Mission: A Statement of Principles and Guidelines.* (Washington: 1966). pp. 1–9, and *The Federal Library Committee: Three Years of Progress, 1965–1968.* (Washington: 1969). pp. 1–13.

,ber 2, 1966 he issued Executive Order No. 11301, creating a National Advisory Commission on Libraries to "evaluate policies, programs, and practices," affecting the nation's libraries.

The key elements of the problem include:

1. A staggering increase in production of information accompanied by an overwhelming demand for access to all types of information;
2. The growing complexity of our civilization, the increasing educational level of our population, and its changing cultural characteristics which have created and will continue to create new and heavier demands upon Government and upon educational and research institutions such as libraries;
3. Cumulative deficiencies in library resources, staff, and services which are not equal to present and anticipated demands;
4. The development of new data processing techniques which are revolutionizing information handling and are placing new pressures on libraries.

Essential to the solution of this urgent problem is a clear understanding within Federal agencies of (1) the services Federal libraries can provide to support missions of their agencies, and (2) the resources the libraries must have to develop those services. The statement of library mission that follows and the appended guidelines are a basis for attacking the problem.

THE FEDERAL LIBRARY MISSION

1. Definition and Scope

Federal libraries support the missions and programs of their agencies principally by providing bibliographically related information services. To achieve this objective they have at least four basic responsibilities.

a. To collect and organize pertinent recorded information, in whatever form required, to meet managerial, research, educational, informational, and other program responsibilities;
b. To provide ready access to their materials and to assist users in locating required information;
c. To disseminate pertinent information from their collections on a selective basis;
d. To make their collections and services known to present and potential users.

2. Library Functions

To discharge these basic responsibilities, Federal libraries perform a range of tasks including assistance to users through literature searching, reference service, bibliographic work, professional guidance to readers, lending and borrowing materials, and by supporting these services through selecting, acquiring, cataloging, indexing, and abstracting pertinent materials. The effective performance of these functions requires continuing appraisal of the information needs of the agency.

3. Relation to Federal Community

The collections of Federal libraries constitute an important resource for providing information needed in daily operation of the Government, and in the conduct of agency research programs. Interlibrary lending, inter-agency reference assistance, cooperative cataloging, literature searching, and other forms of cooperation are essential to full and efficient use of this resource.

4. Relation to Research Community and the General Public

Increasingly, a community of interest has developed among Federal and non-Federal library users. Federal libraries support those missions of their agencies that relate to non-Governmental groups by extending their library services to other libraries, research institutions, and the general public.

GUIDELINES
For Adequate Federal Library Service

Government agencies[2] require library services fully responsive to their research and other information needs. This can only be achieved through increased administrative attention, guidance, and support. Agency management should see that its library managerial policies are consistent with the foregoing statement of the Federal Library Mission. The Guidelines which follow provide Government agencies a means for strengthening their library management, resources, and services. Implementation of these guidelines demands intensive program planning and development.

The Guidelines are arranged in three closely related categories: Organization and Management; Library Resources; and Library Services.

A. Organization and Management

Sound organizational and management practices are necessary to insure that agency libraries provide adequate service, responsive to agency needs. Basic to the effectiveness of these practices, however, are full communication and understanding of program goals, a competent library staff, and adequate administrative support for library improvement.

The following practices are recommended:

1. Each agency should formulate a written policy stating its library's mission and its place in the organizational structure. This should be reviewed at regular intervals or at least not less than every five years.
   a. Each Federal library should maintain current operation manuals that explain the agency's mission to the library staff and that establish procedures to serve that mission.
   b. To insure responsiveness to user needs, each agency should locate its library or libraries organizationally where they can maintain most effective communication with agency program and planning officials.
2. Each agency should see that its library program is professionally administered and that the library staff is sufficient in number and adequately trained to fulfill library responsibilities.
3. Agencies should budget for library needs in the same manner as for the needs of other professional services which support agency missions. In doing so, the following factors should be considered:
   a. The full range of services the library must provide in support of the agency mission;
   b. Increased effectiveness of agency management and professional activity to be

achieved by using the specialized services provided by the library;
   c. The extent and nature of specialized agency research activities requiring library services;
   d. The range of subject areas the library must cover to fulfill its mission;
   e. The availability of other pertinent information resources and the expenditures required to exploit them in support of the agency mission.
4. The agency should require pertinent reports from its libraries including up-to-date statistical records of library operations, services, and resources upon which sound management and policy decisions can be made. The libraries should make such reports compatible with other library reporting practices currently being developed by the Office of Education.

B. Library Resources

Basic physical resources of a library consist of recorded information such as, but not limited to: books, documents, periodicals, serials, technical reports, dissertations, pamphlets, manuscripts, films, micro texts, slides, audio discs or tapes, computer tapes, maps and photos, and the necessary related equipment.

The following guidelines are designed to assure that Government libraries have adequate resources organized for optimum accessibility.

1. The agency should require its library to provide, in sufficient quantity, those resources necessary to carry out the agency's mission. In addition to reference materials, these resources should include the indexes and bibliographic tools required to identify pertinent literature available in other libraries.
2. The agency should require from its libraries a carefully developed, written acquisition policy based upon the agency's mission and related library responsibility. The policy should include scope, coverage, and retention guidelines.
3. Each library should develop a policy statement governing the organization of its resources by means of cataloging, indexing, abstracting, and other bibliographic procedures which may include use of machine techniques. The statement should define the scope, coverage, and form of the catalog and

its relation to other pertinent bibliographic tools. The agency should require its library to cooperate in, and make the fullest practical use of, centralized cataloging and indexing services.

C. Library Services

Library services comprise those which involve knowledge of, and interpretation and exploitation of, the collections and their bibliographic apparatus and those which involve lending materials, directional assistance, and record keeping. Where the services enumerated below are not provided, the agency, with assistance from its library, should re-examine the library program in relation to current information needs, and develop a modern program of library services including:

1. Providing factual information responsive to specific inquiries, including when appropriate, the selection and synthesis of information from various sources and directing the inquirers' attention to related information beyond the immediate scope of the query;
2. Providing an organized program for selective dissemination of information based on systematic analysis of agency and staff information needs through interest profiles and program analysis;
3. Compiling comprehensive or selective bibliographies selected for specific purposes and produced either on the initiative of the library or upon request. Such bibliographies may be current or retrospective and should, when appropriate, include annotations or abstracts;
4. Performing literature searches for the purpose of documenting and producing state-of-the-art reviews;
5. Providing professional guidance to readers in the use of library collections and bibliographic resources, and acquainting them with other information sources such as individual subject specialists, information centers, and research organizations;
6. Lending library materials or photo-copying when appropriate;
7. Borrowing, for official use, materials from other Federal or private libraries;
8. Systematically providing information about agency library resources, services, and programs to encourage maximum use of these facilities.

In addition to these services, each agency should define the extent of library service it is willing to provide to other agencies as part of a cooperative network of Federal library resources.

Membership in FLC is as follows:

PERMANENT MEMBERSHIP—Library of Congress (Librarian of Congress, Chairman), National Agricultural Library, National Library of Medicine, Department of State, Department of the Treasury, Department of Defense, Department of Justice, Department of the Interior, Department of Commerce, Department of Labor, Department of Health, Education, and Welfare, Department of Housing and Urban Development, Department of Transportation.

ROTATING MEMBERSHIP, 1971-73—Federal Communications Commission, General Services Administration, National Aeronautics and Space Administration, National Science Foundation, Supreme Court of the United States, Veterans Administration.

OBSERVERS—Office of Management and Budget and Office of Science and Technology of the Executive Office of the President, Library of Congress, Bureau of Libraries and Educational Technology of the Office of Education of the Department of Health, Education, and Welfare.

THE FEDERAL LIBRARY COMMITTEE
Three Years of Progress
1965-1968

At the expiration of its three-year grant from the Council of Library Resources, the Federal Library Committee wishes to express its deep appreciation for the support it has received and to report upon its accomplishments.

The Committee is now firmly established. The Library of Congress in its requests for appropriations for Fiscal 1969, asked for funds to support the FLC secretariat (one Executive Secretary and one secretarial assistant). These positions were neither specifically granted nor denied by the Appropriations Committees. In recognition of the value of the Committee, as a service to Federal libraries, and as a national-library activity, the Librarian decided to establish these positions, however, from the funds allowed LC under its main appropriations heading, "Library of Congress Salaries and Expenses."

A research program, resulting directly from project proposals made by the Committee and amounting to approximately $300,000 is being funded by the U. S. Office of Education. Additional research funds amounting to more than $20,000 have also been made available to the Committee by other agencies and organizations. The compilation of a *Guide to Laws and Regulations on Federal Libraries* has been completed and is being published by the R. R. Bowker Company in August. The U. S. Office of Education has published the Committee's *Survey of Special Libraries Serving the Federal Government,* and *Procurement of Library Materials in the Federal Government* is in press. In addition, 22 issues of the Federal Library Committee *Newsletter* have been published and widely distributed. Most of them have had a *Roster of Vacancies* as an appendix.

The work of the Committee is done through a group of nine task forces involving more than one hundred Federal librarians.

The remainder of this report will be concerned with the substance of the Committee's program—past, present, and future. We are attempting to establish a broad base for developing library service to the Federal Government through fundamental research on the nature of library and information services in Government programs and the application of these findings to the improvement of services.

Federal Library Mission

As one phase of this work, the Committee developed *The Federal Library Mission, A Statement of Principles and Guidelines,* which enunciated an essential Federal library policy by applying basic principles of management to library problems. This statement was widely circulated throughout the Federal library service. It was sent to the heads of 44 Federal Agencies. Forty-one of these responded, indicating positive concurrence. Further follow-up on implementation is being planned. A copy of the statement is attached and a sample response follows:

The extensive study of SEC library policies and operations which we undertook as a result of your letter of November 14, 1967, has resulted in a number of improvements in the organization, orientation, and operations of the SEC Library, with consequent benefits to the staff of the Commission in their work. These improvements were developed and installed by a Library Committee working along the lines suggested in "The

Federal Library Mission: A Statement of Principles and Guidelines."

The Library Committee, chaired by our Solicitor and composed of our Director of Records and Service, our Librarian, and representatives of the various divisions and offices of the Commission, developed a written policy and a Library Handbook, copies of which I enclose. The Committee also has given the Librarian valuable guidance in planning the scope and content of the collections and services to meet the evolving information needs of the Commission.

This guidance from senior management and operating officials has proved so beneficial, not only in tangible ways, but also in terms of added appreciation and understanding of Library resources, services, and needs by the officials concerned, that we will continue the Committee indefinitely.

Interlibrary Loan

The Committee has approved a *Federal Interlibrary Loan Code.* This was tested for one year on an experimental basis and then formally adopted. The Code enunciates basic policies and responsibilities of Federal libraries in relation to each other and to the Nation's libraries generally. It is an important step in opening up Federal library resources to qualified researchers. Other steps will be described later in this report.

Procurement of Library Materials

One of the most difficult and annoying problems which face Federal librarians is the procurement of library materials from vendors. This problem has several facets:

1. The procurement laws and regulations are designed to meet general needs of the Government, but library procurement is so small in comparison to general procurement that library needs have had little impact upon their formulation.
2. In library procurement, the element of service is a much more important and more complex factor than in procurement in general.
3. Interpretation of laws and regulations has varied so greatly within the Government, and even within individual agencies, that many regulations have become more restrictive than helpful. In addition, the values of standardized procedures have been lost to a large extent.

In its *Procurement of Library Materials in the Federal Government*, the Committee's Task Force has defined the problems, clarified the regulations, and described successful procurement programs for various kinds of library materials. Initial reaction by Federal librarians who have seen the preliminary draft indicate that the document will be extremely valuable in facilitating library procurement. After a reasonable period for use and evaluation, the Committee will review the procurement problem and consider whether revision and codification of laws and regulations affecting procurement of library materials is needed, either in whole or in part. It will inform Federal librarians of current changes and developments through the medium of the *FLC Newsletter*.

Laws and Regulations

The *Guide to Laws and Regulations on Federal Libraries* consists of an analysis and interpretation of those laws and regulations which particularly affect operation of Federal libraries. In addition, there is an appendix giving the text of the laws, as well as of regulations, at the Department level. For the first time, Federal librarians will have access to the basic documents which authorize their programs and operations. They will benefit greatly by a comparative study of these varying provisions. It is likely that as a result of comments and criticisms, a second edition will be needed in a few years and this second edition will be a real improvement over the first. During the interval, the Committee will consider the advisability of revising and codifying those laws and regulations directly related to Federal library operation.

Statistics

In its program to develop the basic information and data necessary for realistic analysis and planning for a viable and useful Federal library program, the Committee secured the cooperation of the National Center for Educational Statistics in the Office of Education in a pilot statistical survey of special libraries serving the Federal Government. The resulting publication is perhaps the most comprehensive collection of Federal library management data ever made. The fact that this collection covers less than one-fourth of Federal

libraries emphasizes the paucity of information available to library planners and the need for a comprehensive program to obtain library management and research data which is essential in developing a dynamic library and information service responsive to the needs of Government.

The Committee plans to convene a meeting of representatives of Federal agencies, the National Center for Education Statistics, the Bureau of the Budget, and other interested organizations, such as associations, consulting firms, etc., to consider the kinds of statistics which should be provided by Federal libraries, the frequency of their collection that would be desirable, their usefulness in planning and administering Federal library programs, and their compatability with national standards for library statistics. Out of this it is planned to develop an ongoing statistical program which will furnish the data mentioned above.

Recruiting

One of the most critical problems facing Federal libraries is the manpower shortage and this has occupied the attention of an FLC Task Force from the beginning of its organization.

A network of recruiters has been established in every Civil Service region. These recruiters have been furnished with recruiting literature and other helpful information.

A monthly roster of vacancies has been published as an appendix to the *FLC Newsletter* and approximately 120 vacancies are listed in each issue. A study of factors that deter the recruitment of librarians for the Federal service has been made. The data is now being analyzed and a report will be compiled for presentation to the Civil Service Commission. Present indications are that many Federal libraries are not competitive in the matter of salaries, ability to expedite employment, or flexible in meeting competition. Further contact will be made with the Civil Service Commission in an attempt to have librarians designated in a "shortage category," which gives certain advantages, and to overcome other deterrents to recruiting.

Federal libraries do have some concessions: Recent graduates in the upper $\frac{1}{4}$ of their class can be recruited at the Grade 9 level, travel and moving costs can be paid to the first post of duty, experienced librarians recruited from non-Government positions for the upper grades may be paid at a level within the grade which will compete with the salary received outside Government. Other inducements available for occupations not in a shortage category are not available to librarians. In the lower grades where most recruiting occurs, recruits from outside may not be paid above the base of the grade.

Education

The Committee has, since its inception, been concerned with the educational needs of Federal librarians and other library workers. Since this concern was closely associated with manpower and recruiting problems, the Task Force on Recruitment accepted some responsibility until an Education Task Force was organized in February 1968. In 1967, the Civil Service Commission, with cooperation of the Committee, conducted a study on *The Needs for Continuing Education of Librarians*. The Task Force on Education negotiated with Catholic University and with the Office of Education, about a project to study the kinds of education needed for work in Federal libraries and information centers. The result is a grant of $86,000 by the Office of Education to Catholic University for the purpose of determining the skill and educational needs for work in Federal libraries and information centers. The information thus obtained is to be used as a base for curriculum development in library and information science for a program reaching beyond a Master's degree to the doctorate and post doctorate levels. Because of the advanced development of some Federal libraries and information centers in the application of new technologies and concepts of information services, it is thought that this study will have great significance, not only to Federal libraries but to the entire library community.

In cooperation with the Committee, the Library of Congress has initiated a series of orientation programs for Federal librarians which explains the nature of the Library's services and resources which are available to other libraries. These courses which consume approximately 20 hours, are now being given (in five consecutive mornings) twice each year. Every session has been filled to capacity and there is a waiting list of potential participants. The course is flexible enough to meet varying conditions. In May 1967, it was given in 2½ full days as part of two FLC workshops on automation and procurement for Federal librarians from outside the Washington area. In

June 1968, it was reduced to two days and given to library school faculties who were attending a two week institute on "Federal Library Resources, Services, and Programs" given by the Catholic University of America.

The last named institute was also developed with the help and cooperation of the Federal Library Committee. The Committee has been concerned about the negative attitude toward Federal library service which seems too prevalent in many library schools, and which the Committee feels has an inhibitory effect on recruiting. It is hoped that the success of this institute will help overcome this difficulty. Since only 20 schools were represented in the 1968 institute, others may be necessary in following years.

Resources of Federal Libraries

The Office of Education has provided a grant of $140,000 to the Biological Sciences Communication Project of George Washington University for the purpose of providing an analysis in depth of the scope and coverage of a selected list of Government research libraries. A Task Force has worked for more than two years developing a methodology for such a study and has made two pilot studies with the assistance of the Biological Sciences Communication Project. CLR funds were used for this purpose. It is expected that the current study will furnish basic data upon which decisions regarding delegation of responsibility for information services in specific subject areas could be made and that, in addition, it will assist in the development of Federal library networks and in unlocking resources of great value to research. A printout of the listing will become an essential reference tool for interlibrary loans. The methodology developed should become a useful technique in other resource studies. The identification of gaps in holdings should prove as valuable in library program planning as the identification of strong collections.

Automation

On behalf of the Federal Library Committee, the Office of Education has contracted with the Information Dynamics Corporation for a study of *Development Trends in Library and Information Center Automation*. This study represents the second phase of the Committee's effort to establish a reasonable basis for predicting and guiding the development of automated operations in Federal libraries. The first phase of the Task Force's work produced a summary of library automation developments as revealed in the literature. A third phase will be concerned with an analysis of trends, and prediction of possible future developments. A fourth phase will attempt to develop a group of systems and sub-systems of automated procedures which will be flexible enough to be used in Federal library situations and which will facilitate development of automated networks. The description of these systems will be accompanied by guidelines describing factors to be considered by Federal librarians investigating automation of their libraries and descriptions of typical situations indicating when to automate or not to automate.

Role of Libraries in Information Systems

A proposed study which is closely related to the Automation study is one which will define the role of libraries in Government Information Systems. A literature search, financed by the ATLIS Program, is being conducted for the Committee by Dr. Anne Painter of Indiana University. This should be ready by August 1968. The balance of the study, for which we have received assurance of half the necessary funds, will examine the existing relationship between libraries and information centers, the decision-making process which led to the establishment of the information centers, the rationale for their existence and the patterns of their development including functions, technology, and use. Using the literature report and the status survey as a base, the Task Force on the Role of Libraries plans to develop a position paper which will state what relation should exist between libraries, information centers, and other units in an Information System.

Public Relations

One of the factors which promotes good library service within the Government, as elsewhere, is the creation of understanding and good will for the library and its program. The Committee has created a Task Force on Public Relations with responsibility for investigating the problems related to public relations within Government Agencies and devising guidelines and programs which will help Federal librarians in promoting use of their libraries and appreciation of its services. The Task Force has worked with the National Library Week program (2,000 copies of a poster suitable for Federal library promotion have been distributed.) It is engaged in developing guidelines for orientation programs for library clientele and is preparing a study of those basic aspects of public relations which may apply in Federal library situations.

• • • •

The funds provided by the CLR have been used primarily for the support of the Committee's secretariat during the past three years. Ten thousand dollars which were saved during the time the Executive Secretary was employed only part-time were used to procure necessary materials, to obtain a draft of the procurement study, to supplement the funds for the *Guide to Laws and Regulations,* and to support the two pilot studies on Library resources. These funds have been supplemented by administrative support from the Library of Congress at all levels which has been considerable, by more than $8,000 from the ATLIS Program and the Library of Congress, and by more than $300,000 in grants from the Office of Education. In addition, more than 100 librarians and other Federal officials are regularly devoting time and effort to furthering the work of the Committee. Indications are that this effort will become even more effective in the future.

The work of the Committee has created a new feeling of purpose, determination, and hope among Federal librarians that, in time, will develop a Federal library service which is dynamic and flexible and not only responsive but anticipatory of the Government's and the Nation's needs for information.

NOTES

[1] *The Federal Register,* 30:8557 (July 3, 1965).
[2] The word *agency* is used to cover not only separately organized units of the Federal Government, but also where appropriate, subordinate units thereof. The word *library* is used to cover not only a department library, but a library system, or libraries serving subordinate units.

V

SOCIAL MEASUREMENT & STATISTICS

Here we have excerpts from three readings, one "in esse" and two "in posse." *Toward A Social Report* is a very thought-provoking piece that tells us about some useful social statistics and indicators that we're not now collecting. The second reading comprises a valuable reference tool that describes the principal *existing* statistical sources available from the several agencies of the Government. And the last of this group goes into plans and methods for collecting much needed library statistics.

Statistical Services . . . describes the Census Bureau's publications briefly. Their publications and services are written up in more detail in several other places. I wanted to include more of them but space limitations . . . and all that jazz, prevent it. So I can only refer you to that Bureau's *Census Bureau Programs and Publications: Area and Subject Guide,* 1968, and *Guide to Census Bureau Data Files and Special Tabulations,* 1969. More recently, the Bureau's Data Access and Use Laboratory prepared a *1970 Census Users' Guide* in two parts, 1971. The first 70 pages of the first part should prove most interesting in that they describe the variety of data products and services not only available in book form but also on computer tape or microform.

Toward A Social Report

Prepared by the Staff of the Department of Health, Education, and Welfare

January 11, 1969

Dear Mr. President:

In March of 1966, you directed the Secretary of Health, Education and Welfare to search for ways to improve the Nation's ability to chart its social progress. In particular, you asked this Department "to develop the necessary social statistics and indicators to supplement those prepared by the Bureau of Labor Statistics and the Council of Economic Advisers. With these yardsticks, we can better measure the distance we have come and plan for the way ahead."

I have the honor to submit a report which reflects our efforts as of this time to assemble some relevant information that will lead to the development of such yardsticks. It deals with such aspects of the quality of American life as: health and illness; social mobility; the physical environment; income and poverty; public order and safety; learning, science, and art; and participation and alienation.

This document represents a preliminary step toward the evolution of a regular system of social reporting. We are offering it for the widest possible discussion, comment, and suggestion. We believe that it warrants the critical review not only of the Executive Branch and of the Congress, but also of the State and local officials, the academic community, and leaders of business and industry . . .

From the letter of transmittal submitted with this Report, written by Wilbur J. Cohen, then Secretary of Health, Education, and Welfare.

INTRODUCTION AND SUMMARY

The Nation has no comprehensive set of statistics reflecting social progress or retrogression. There is no Government procedure for periodic stock-taking of the social health of the Nation. The Government makes no Social Report.

We do have an Economic Report, required by statute, in which the President and his Council of Economic Advisors report to the Nation on its economic health. We also have a comprehensive set of economic indicators widely thought to be sensitive and reliable. Statistics on the National Income and its component parts, on employment and unemployment, on retail and wholesale prices, and on the balance of payments are collected annually, quarterly, monthly, sometimes even weekly. These economic indicators are watched by Government officials and private citizens alike as closely as a surgeon watches a fever chart for indications of a change in the patient's condition.

Although nations got along without economic indicators for centuries, it is hard to imagine doing without them now. It is hard to imagine governments and businesses operating without answers to questions which seem as ordinary as: What is happening to retail prices? Is National Income rising?

SOURCE: U.S. Department of Health, Education, and Welfare. *Toward a Social Report.* (Washington: 1969). pp. xi–xxii, and pp. 95–101.

Is unemployment higher in Chicago than in Detroit? Is our balance of payments improving?

Indeed, economic indicators have become so much a part of our thinking that we have tended to equate a rising National Income with national well-being. Many are surprised to find unrest and discontent growing at a time when National Income is rising so rapidly. It seems paradoxical that the economic indicators are generally registering continued progress—rising income, low unemployment—while the streets and the newspapers are full of evidence of growing discontent—burning and looting in the ghetto, strife on the campus, crime in the street, alienation and defiance among the young.

Why have income and disaffection increased at the same time? One reason is that the recent improvement in standards of living, along with new social legislation, have generated new expectations —expectations that have risen faster than reality could improve. The result has been disappointment and disaffection among a sizeable number of Americans.

It is not misery, but advance, that fosters hope and raises expectations. It has been wisely said that the conservatism of the destitute is as profound as that of the privileged. If the Negro American did not protest as much in earlier periods of history as today, it was not for lack of cause, but for lack of hope. If in earlier periods of history we had few programs to help the poor, it was not for lack of poverty, but because society did not care and was not under pressure to help the poor. If the college students of the fifties did not protest as often as those of today, it was not for lack of evils to condemn, but probably because hope and idealism were weaker then.

The correlation between improvement and disaffection is not new. Alexis de Tocqueville observed such a relationship in eighteenth century France: "The evil which was suffered patiently as inevitable, seems unendurable as soon as the idea of escaping from it crosses men's minds. All the abuses then removed call attention to those that remain, and they now appear more galling. The evil, it is true, has become less, but sensibility to it has become more acute."

Another part of the explanation of the paradox of prosperity and rising discontent is clearly that "money isn't everything." Prosperity itself brings its own problems. Congestion, noise, and pollution are byproducts of economic growth which make the world less livable. The large organizations which are necessary to harness modern technology make the individual feel small and impotent. The concentration on production and profit necessary to economic growth breeds tension, venality, and neglect of "the finer things."

Why a Social Report or Set of Social Indicators?

Curiosity about our social condition would by itself justify an attempt to assess the social health of the Nation. Many people want answers to questions like these: Are we getting healthier? Is pollution increasing? Do children learn more than they used to? Do people have more satisfying jobs than they used to? Is crime increasing? How many people are really alienated? Is the American dream of rags to riches a reality? We are interested in the answers to such questions partly because they would tell us a good deal about our individual and social well-being. Just as we need to measure our incomes, so we need "social indicators," or measures of other dimensions of our welfare, to get an idea how well off we really are.

A social report with a set of social indicators could not only satisfy our curiosity about how well we are doing, but it could also improve public policymaking in at least two ways. First, it could give social problems more visibility and thus make possible more informed judgments about national priorities. Second, by providing insight into how different measures of national well-being are changing, it might ultimately make possible a better evaluation of what public programs are accomplishing.

The existing situation in areas with which public policy must deal is often unclear, not only to the citizenry in general, but to officialdom as well. The normal processes of journalism and the observations of daily life do not allow a complete or balanced view of the condition of the society. Different problems have different degrees of visibility.

The visibility of a social problem can depend, for example, upon its "news value" or potential drama. The Nation's progress in the space race and the need for space research get a lot of publicity because of the adventure inherent in manned space exploration. Television and tabloid remind us almost daily of the problems of crime, drugs, riots, and sexual misadventure. The rate of infant mortality may be a good measure of the condition of a society, but this rate is rarely mentioned in the public press, or even percieved as a public problem. The experience of parents (or infants) does not insure that the problem of infant mortality is perceived as a social problem; only when we know that more than a dozen nations have lower rates of infant mortality than the United States can we begin to make a valid judgment about the condition of this aspect of American society.

Moreover, some groups in our society are well organized, but others are not. This means that the problems of some groups are articulated and advertised, whereas the problems of others are not. Public problems also differ in the extent to which they are immediately evident to the "naked eye." A natural disaster or overcrowding of the highways will be immediately obvious. But ineffectiveness of an educational system or the alienation of youth and minority groups is often evident only when it is too late.

Besides developing measures of the social conditions we care about we also need to see how these measures are changing in response to public programs. If we mount a major program to provide prenatal and maternity care for mothers, does infant mortality go down? If we channel new resources into special programs for educating poor children, does their performance in school eventually increase? If we mount a "war on poverty," what happens to the number of poor people? If we enact new regulations against the emission of pollutants, does pollution diminish?

These are not easy questions, since all major social problems are influenced by many things besides governmental action, and it is hard to disentangle the different effects of different causal factors. But at least in the long run evaluation of the effectiveness of public programs will be improved if we have social indicators to tell us how social conditions are changing.

The Contents of the Report

The present volume is not a social report. It is a step in the direction of a social report and the development of a comprehensive set of social indicators.

The report represents an attempt, on the part of social scientists, to look at several important areas and digest what is known about progress toward generally accepted goals. The areas treated in this way are health, social mobility, the condition of the physical environment, income and poverty,

public order and safety, and learning, science, and art.

There is also a chapter on participation in social institutions, but because of the lack of measures of improvement or retrogression in this area, it aspires to do no more than pose important questions.

Even the chapters included leave many—perhaps most—questions unanswered. We have measures of death and illness, but no measures of physical vigor or mental health. We have measures of the level and distribution of income, but no measures of the satisfaction that income brings. We have measures of air and water pollution, but no way to tell whether our environment is, on balance, becoming uglier or more beautiful. We have some clues about the test performance of children, but no information about their creativity or attitude toward intellectual endeavor. We have often spoken of the condition of Negro Americans, but have not had the data needed to report on Hispanic Americans, American Indians, or other ethnic minorities.

If the Nation is to be able to do better social reporting in the future, and do justice to all of the problems that have not been treated here, it will need a wide variety of information that is not available now. It will need not only statistics on additional aspects of the condition of the Nation as a whole, but also information on different groups of Americans. It will need more data on the aged, on youth, and on women, as well as on ethnic minorities. It will need information not only on objective conditions, but also on how different groups of Americans perceive the conditions in which they find themselves.

We shall now summarize each of the chapters in turn.

Health and Illness

There have been dramatic increases in health and life expectancy in the twentieth century, but they have been mainly the result of developments whose immediate effect has been on the younger age groups. The expectancy of life at birth in the United States has increased from 47.3 years at the turn of the century to 70.5 years in 1967, or by well over 20 years. The number of expected years of life remaining at age 5 has increased by about 12 years, and that at age 25 about 9 years, but that at age 65 not even 3 years. Modern medicine and standards of living have evidently been able to do a great deal for the young, and especially the very young, but not so much for the old.

This dramatic improvement had slowed down by the early fifties. Since then it has been difficult to say whether our health and life status have been improving or not. Some diseases are becoming less common and others are becoming more common, and life expectancy has changed rather little. We can get some idea whether or not there has been improvement on balance by calculating the "expectancy of *healthy* life" (i.e., life expectancy free of bed-disability and institutionalization). The expectancy of healthy life at birth seems to have improved a trifle since 1957, the first year for which the needed data are available, but certainly not as much as the improvements in medical knowledge and standards of living might have led us to hope.

The American people have almost certainly not exploited all of the potential for better health inherent in existing medical knowledge and standards of living. This is suggested by the fact that Negro Americans have on the average about seven years less expectancy of healthy life than whites, and the fact that at least 15 nations have longer life expectancy at birth than we do.

Why are we not as healthy as we could be? Though our style of life (lack of exercise, smoking, stress, etc.) is partly responsible, there is evidence which strongly suggests that social and economic deprivation and the uneven distribution of medical care are a large part of the problem.

Though the passage of Medicare legislation has assured many older Americans that they can afford the medical care they need, the steps to improve the access to medical care for the young have been much less extensive.

The Nation's system of financing medical care also provides an incentive for the relative underuse of preventive, as opposed to curative and ameliorative, care. Medical insurance may reimburse a patient for the hospital care he gets, but rarely for the checkup that might have kept him well. Our system of relief for the medically indigent, and the fee-for-service method of physician payment, similarly provide no inducements for adequate preventive care.

The emphasis on curative care means that hospitals are sometimes used when some less intensive form of care would do as well. This overuse of hospitals is one of the factors responsible for the extraordinary increases in the price of hospital care.

Between June 1967 and June 1968, hospital daily service charges increased by 12 percent, and in the previous 12 months they increased by almost 22 percent. Physicians' fees have not increased as much—they rose by $5\frac{1}{2}$ percent between June 1967 and June 1968—but they still rose more than the general price level. Medical care prices in the aggregate rose at an annual rate of 6.5 percent during 1965-67.

Social Mobility

The belief that no individual should be denied the opportunity to better his condition because of the circumstances of his birth continues to be one of the foundation stones in the structure of American values. But is the actual degree of opportunity and social mobility as great now as it has been?

It was possible to get a partial answer to this question from a survey which asked a sample of American men about their fathers' usual occupations as well as about their own job characteristics. Estimates based on these data suggest that opportunity to rise to an occupation with a higher relative status has not been declining in recent years, and might even have increased slightly. They also show that by far the largest part of the variation in occupational status was explained by factors other than the occupation of the father.

These encouraging findings, in the face of many factors that everyday observation suggest must limit opportunity, are probably due in part to the expansion of educational opportunities. There is some tendency for the sons of those of high education and status to obtain more education than others (an extra year of schooling for the father means on the average an extra 0.3 or 0.4 of a year of education for the son), and this additional education brings somewhat higher occupational status on the average. However, the variations in education that are not explained by the socioeconomic status of the father, and the effects that these variations have on occupational status, are much larger. Thus, on balance, increased education seems to have increased opportunity and upward mobility.

There is one dramatic exception to the finding that opportunity is generally available. The opportunity of Negroes appears to be restricted to a very great extent by current race discrimination and other factors specifically related to race. Though it is true that the average adult Negro comes from a family with a lower socioeconomic status than the average white, and has had fewer years of schooling, and that these and other "background" factors reduce his income, it does not appear to be possible to explain anything like all of the difference in income between blacks and whites in terms of such background factors. After a variety of background factors that impair the qualifications of the average Negro are taken into account, there remains a difference in income of over $1,400 that is difficult to explain without reference to current discrimination. So is the fact that a high status Negro is less likely to be able to pass his status on to his son than is a high status white. A number of other studies tend to add to the evidence that there is continuing discrimination in employment, as does the relationship between Federal employment and contracts (with their equal opportunity provisions) and the above-average proportion of Negroes in high status jobs.

The implication of all this is that the American commitment to opportunity is within sight of being honored in the case of whites, but that it is very far indeed from being honored for the Negro. In addition to the handicaps that arise out of history and past discrimination, the Negro also continues to obtain less reward for his qualifications than he would if he were white.

The Physical Environment

This chapter deals with the pollution of the natural environment, and with the manmade, physical environment provided by our housing and the structure of our cities.

Pollution seems to be many problems in many places—air pollution in some communities, water pollution in others, automobile junk yards and other solid wastes in still other places. These seemingly disparate problems can be tied together by one basic fact: The total weight of materials taken into the economy from nature must equal the total weight of materials ultimately discharged as wastes plus any materials recycled.

This means that, given the level and composition of the resources used by the economy, and the degree of recycling, any reduction in one form of waste discharge must be ultimately accompanied by an increase in the discharge of some other kind of waste. For example, some air pollution can be prevented by washing out the particles—but this can mean water pollution, or alternatively solid wastes.

Since the economy does not destroy the matter

it absorbs there will be a tendency for the pollution problem to increase with the growth of population and economic activity. In 1965 the transportation system in the United States produced 76 million tons of five major pollutants. If the transportation technology used does not greatly change, the problem of air pollution may be expected to rise with the growth in the number of automobiles, airplanes, and so on. Similarly, the industrial sector of the economy has been growing at about $4\frac{1}{2}$ percent per year. This suggests that, if this rate of growth were to continue, industrial production would have increased ten-fold by the year 2020, and that in the absence of new methods and policies, industrial wastes would have risen by a like proportion.

The chapter presents some measures of air and water pollution indicating that unsatisfactorily high levels of pollution exist in many places. There can be little doubt that pollution is a significant problem already, and that this is an area in which, at least in the absence of timely reporting and intelligent policy, the condition of society can all too easily deteriorate.

As we shift perspective from the natural environment to the housing that shelters us from it, we see a more encouraging trend. The physical quality of the housing in the country is improving steadily, in city center and suburb alike. In 1960, 84 percent of the dwelling units in the country were described as "structurally sound"; in 1966, this percentage had risen to 90 percent. In center cities the percentage had risen from 80 percent in 1960 to 93 percent in 1966. In 1950, 16 percent of the nation's housing was "overcrowded" in the sense that it contained 1.01 or more persons per room. But by 1960, only 12 percent of the nation's housing supply was overcrowded by this standard.

The principal reason for this improvement was the increased per capita income and demand for housing. About $11\frac{1}{2}$ million new housing units were started in the United States between 1960 and 1967, and the figures on the declining proportions of structurally unsound and overcrowded dwellings, even in central cities, suggest that this new construction increased the supply of housing available to people at all income levels.

Even though the housing stock is improving, racial segregation and other barriers keep many Americans from moving into the housing that is being built or vacated, and deny them a full share in the benefits of the improvement in the Nation's housing supply.

Income and Poverty

The Gross National Product in the United States is about $1,000 higher per person than that of Sweden, the second highest nation. In 1969 our GNP should exceed $900 billion. Personal income has quadrupled in this century, even after allowing for changes in population and the value of money.

Generally speaking, however, the distribution of income in the United States has remained practically unchanged over the last 20 years. Although the distribution of income has been relatively stable, the rise in income levels has meant that the number of persons below the poverty line has declined. The poor numbered 40 million in 1960 and 26 million in 1967.

A continuation of present trends, however, would by no means eliminate poverty. The principal cause of the decline has been an increase in earnings. But some of the poor are unable to work because they are too young, too old, disabled or otherwise prevented from doing so. They would not, therefore, be directly helped by increased levels of wages and earnings in the economy as a whole. Moreover, even the working poor will continue to account for a substantial number of persons by 1974: about 5 million by most recent estimates. This latter group is not now generally eligible for income supplementation.

The Nation's present system of income maintenance is badly in need of reform. It is inadequate to the needs of those who do receive aid and millions of persons are omitted altogether.

This chapter concludes with an analysis of existing programs and a discussion of new proposals which have been put forward in recent years as solutions to the welfare crisis.

Public Order and Safety

The concern about public order and safety in the United States is greater now than it has been in some time.

The compilations of the Federal Bureau of Investigation show an increase in major crimes of 13 percent in 1964, 6 percent in 1965, 11 percent in 1966, and 17 percent in 1967. And studies undertaken for the President's Crime Commission in 1965 indicate that several times as many crimes occur as are reported.

Crime is concentrated among the poor. Both its perpetrators and its victims are more likely to be residents of the poverty areas of central cities than of suburbs and rural areas. Many of those residents in the urban ghettoes are Negroes. Negroes have much higher arrest rates than whites, but it is less widely known that Negroes also have higher rates of victimization than whites of any income group.

Young people commit a disproportionate share of crimes. Part of the recent increase in crime rates can be attributed to the growing proportion of young people in the population. At the same time, the propensity of youth to commit crime appears to be increasing.

Fear of apprehension and punishment undoubtedly deters some crime. The crime rate in a neighborhood drops with much more intensive policing. But crime and disorder tend to center among young people in ghetto areas, where the prospects for legitimate and socially useful activity are poorest. It seems unlikely that harsher punishment, a strengthening of public prosecutors, or more police can, by themselves, prevent either individual crime or civil disorder. The objective opportunities for the poor, and their attitudes toward the police and the law, must also change before the problems can be solved.

Learning, Science, and Art

The state of the Nation depends to a great degree on how much our children learn, and on what our scientists and artists create. Learning, discovery, and creativity are not only valued in themselves, but are also resources that are important for the Nation's future.

In view of the importance of education, it might be supposed that there would be many assessments of what or how much American children learn. But this is not in fact the case. The standard sources of educational statistics give us hundreds of pages on the resources used for schooling, but almost no information at all on the extent to which these resources have achieved their purpose.

It is possible to get some insight into whether American children are learning more than children of the same age did earlier from a variety of achievement tests that are given throughout the country, mainly to judge individual students and classes. These tests suggest that there may have been a significant improvement in test score performance of children since the 1950's.

When the chapter turns to the learning and education of the poor and the disadvantaged, the results are less encouraging. Groups that suffer social and economic deprivation systematically learn less than those who have more comfortable backgrounds.

Even when they do as well on achievement tests, they are much less likely to go on to college. Of those high school seniors who are in the top one-fifth in terms of academic ability, 95 percent will ultimately go on to college if their parents are in the top socioeconomic quartile, but only half of the equally able students from the bottom socioeconomic quartile will attend college. Students from the top socioeconomic quartile are five times as likely to go to graduate school as comparably able students from the bottom socioeconomic quartile.

It is more difficult to assess the state of science and art than the learning of American youth. But two factors nonetheless emerge rather clearly. One is that American science is advancing at a most rapid rate, and appears to be doing very well in relation to other countries. The Nation's "technological balance of payments," for example, suggests that we have a considerable lead over other countries in technological know-how.

The other point that emerges with reasonable clarity is that, however vibrant the cultural life of the Nation may be, many of the live or performing arts are in financial difficulty. Since there is essentially no increase in productivity in live performances (it will always take four musicians for a quartet), and increasing productivity in the rest of the economy continually makes earnings in the society rise, the relative cost of live performances tends to go up steadily. This can be a significant public problem, at least in those cases where a large number of live performances is needed to insure that promising artists get the training and opportunity they need to realize their full potential.

Participation and Alienation: What We Need To Learn

Americans are concerned, not only about progress along the dimensions that have so far been described, but also about the special functions that our political and social institutions perform. It matters whether goals have been achieved in a democratic or a totalitarian way, and whether the group relationships in our society are harmonious and satisfying.

Unfortunately, the data on the performance of our political and social institutions are uniquely scanty. The chapter on "Participation and Alienation" cannot even hope to do much more than ask the right questions. But such questioning is also of use, for it can remind us of the range of considerations we should keep in mind when setting public policy, and encourage the collection of the needed data in the future.

Perhaps the most obvious function that we expect our institutions to perform is that of protecting our individual freedom. Individual liberty is not only important in itself, but also necessary to the viability of a democratic political system. Freedom can be abridged not only by government action, but also by the social and economic ostracism and discrimination that results from popular intolerance. There is accordingly a need for survey data that can discern any major changes in the degree of tolerance and in the willingness to state unpopular points of view, as well as information about the legal enforcement of constitutional guarantees.

Though liberty gives us the scope we need to achieve our individual purposes, it does not by itself satisfy the need for congenial social relationships and a sense of belonging. The chapter presents evidence which suggests (but does not prove) that at least many people not only enjoy, but also need, a clear sense of belonging, a feeling of attachment to some social group.

There is evidence for this conjecture in the relationship between family status, health, and death rates. In general, married people have lower age-adjusted death rates, lower rates of usage of facilities for the mentally ill, lower suicide rates, and probably also lower rates of alcoholism than those who have been widowed, divorced, or remained single. It is, of course, possible that those who are physically or mentally ill are less likely to find marriage partners, and that this explains part of the correlation. But the pattern of results, and especially the particularly high rates of those who are widowed, strongly suggest that this could not be the whole story.

There are also fragments of evidence which suggest that those who do not normally belong to voluntary organizations, cohesive neighborhoods, families, or other social groupings probably tend to have somewhat higher levels of "alienation" than other Americans.

Some surveys suggest that Negroes, and whites with high degrees of racial prejudice, are more likely to be alienated than other Americans. This, in turn, suggests that alienation has some importance for the cohesion of American society, and that the extent of group participation and the sense of community are important aspects of the condition of the Nation. If this is true, it follows that we need much more information about these aspects of the life of our society.

It is a basic precept of a democratic society that citizens should have equal rights in the political and organizational life of the society. Thus there is also a need for more and better information about the extent to which all Americans enjoy equality before the law, equal franchise, and fair access to public services and utilities. The growth of large scale, bureaucratic organizations, the difficulties many Americans (especially those with the least education and confidence) have in dealing with such organizations, and the resulting demands for democratic participation make the need for better information on this problem particularly urgent.

● ● ● ●

Though almost all Americans want progress along each of the dimensions of well being discussed in this Report, the Nation cannot make rapid progress along all of them at once. That would take more resources than we have. The Nation must decide which objectives should have the higher priorities, and choose the most efficient programs for attaining these objectives. Social reporting cannot make the hard choices the Nation must make any easier, but ultimately it can help to insure that they are not made in ignorance of the Nation's needs.

APPENDIX
How Can We Do Better Social Reporting in the Future?

Good decisions must be based on a careful evaluation of the facts. This truism is so often the basis for our most mundane behavior that we are seldom aware of its far-reaching significance. Most people do not decide whether to carry an umbrella without first checking the weather forecast or at least glancing out the window to see if it is raining. Yet, those policymakers and citizens who are concerned about the condition of American society often lack the information they need in order to decide what, if anything, should be done about the state of our society. Without the right kind of

facts, they are not able to discern emerging problems, or to make informed decisions about national priorities. Nor are they able to choose confidently between alternative solutions to these problems or decide how much money should be allocated to any given program.

Deficiencies of Existing Statistics

Only a small fraction of the existing statistics tell us anything about social conditions, and those that do often point in different directions. Sometimes they do not add up to any meaningful conclusion and thus are not very useful to either the policymaker or the concerned citizen. The Government normally does not publish statistics on whether or not children are learning more than they used to, or on whether social mobility is increasing or decreasing. It does publish statistics on life expectancy and the incidence of disability due to ill health, but some diseases are becoming more common and others less common, and no summary measure indicating whether we could expect more healthy life has been available.

This lack of data would not be surprising if it were simply a result of a lack of interest in statistics, or support for statistical collection, in the Government. But at the same time that some bemoan the lack of useful statistics, others are concerned about the supply of government statistics outrunning our capacity to make use of them. One Congressman recently argued that "we may be producing more statistics than we can digest," and argued that the Federal output of statistics may soon leave us "inundated in a sea of paper and ink." A detailed report by a Congressional Committee concluded that in 1967 more than 5,000 forms were approved by the Bureau of the Budget, which were estimated to take almost 110 million man-hours to complete. According to the same study, at the end of 1967 the Federal Government employed 18,902 Federal statistical workers, and spent $88 million on automatic data processing, computer equipment, and statistical studies under contract with private firms.[1] Comments and studies such as these do illustrate the fact that some are concerned about a plethora of statistics at the same time that the lack of particular types of statistical information stands in the way of better policy choices. This paradox suggests that the needed statistics cannot in practice be obtained simply through a general expansion of statistical efforts, but rather require new ideas about what statistics ought to be collected.

The problem does not appear to be unnecessary duplication of statistical efforts, or thoughtless decisions about what statistics should be collected. The Office of Statistical Standards of the Bureau of the Budget guards against any duplication in statistical collection, strives for comparability of different statistical series, and generally coordinates the Federal statistical effort. The Bureau of the Census and other agencies that collect statistics also seek the best advice, both inside and outside the Government, on what statistics ought to be collected. Thus the problem cannot be ascribed to poor management or foolish decisions—it evidently has deeper roots.

One of these roots is the fact that many of our statistics on social problems are merely a by-product of the informational requirements of routine management. This by-product process does not usually produce the information that we most need for policy or scholarly purposes, and it means that our supply of statistics has an accidental and imbalanced character.

Another source of the shortcomings of our statistical system is the *ad hoc* character of the decisions about what statistics should be collected. Numerous and gifted as those who advise us about what statistics we need may be, they cannot be expected to develop a system of data collection which maximizes the value and coverage of the statistics obtained with respect to the cost and number of the statistics gathered. A series of more or less independent decisions, however intelligent, may not provide the most coherent and useful system of statistics.

Social Indicators

A social indicator, as the term is used here, may be defined to be a statistic of direct normative interest which facilitates concise, comprehensive and balanced judgments about the condition of major aspects of a society. It is in all cases a direct measure of welfare and is subject to the interpretation that, if it changes in the "right" direction, while other things remain equal, things have gotten better, or people are "better off." Thus statistics on the number of doctors or policemen could not be social indicators, whereas figures on health or crime rates could be.

A large part of our existing social statistics are thus immediately excluded from the category of social indicators, since they are records of public expenditures on social programs or the quantity of inputs of one kind or another used for socio-economic purposes. It is not possible to say whether or not things have improved when Government expenditures on a social program, or the quantity of some particular input used, increase.

The phrase "social indicators" evidently emerged in imitation of the title of the publication called *Economic Indicators,* a concise compendium of economic statistics issued by the Council of Economic Advisers.

The National Income statistics are, in fact, one kind of social indicator; they indicate the amount of goods and services at our disposal. But they tell us little about the learning of our children, the quality of our culture, the pollution of the environment, or the toll of illness. Thus other social indicators are needed to supplement the National Income figures. However, the National Income statistics provide a useful model which can help guide the development of other social statistics.

One of the chief virtues of the National Income statistics is their extraordinary aggregativeness. Over any significant period of time, the output of some of the goods produced in a country increases while the output of other goods decreases. In a depression the output of glass jars for home preserves may increase; during a period of rapid growth the consumption of cheaper goods may decline as people switch to substitutes of higher quality. Changing technologies and fashions also insure that the tens of thousands of different types of goods produced in a modern economy do not show the same patterns of growth or decline. The achievement of the National Income and Product Accounts is that they summarize this incredible diversity of developments into a single, meaningful number indicating how much an economy has grown or declined over a period. They summarize this awesome variety of experience so well that we can usually spot even the minirecession, and allow the testing of meaningful hypotheses about the relationship between the National Income, or its major components, and other aggregative variables, such as consumption or investment. Changes in the Nation's health, or in the danger of crime, are in some sense narrower and simpler than changes in the whole economy, yet they have not heretofore been successfully aggregated.

The aggregation involved in the construction of the National Income and Product Accounts is so successful in part because relative prices are used to determine the relative weight or importance to be given to a unit of one kind of output as against a unit of a different type of output. If the number of automobiles produced has gone up by half a million since last year, while the output of potatoes has fallen by half a million bushels, we need to know the relative importance of these two developments before we can begin to make a judgment about the movement of the economy as a whole. It would obviously be arbitrary to determine the relative importance of these two developments by comparing the weight in pounds of an average automobile and a bushel of potatoes. Thus the relative prices of automobiles and potatoes are used to weigh the relative importance of two such developments in the National Income and Product Accounts.

Relative prices at any given moment of time provide weights that are presumably meaningful in welfare or normative terms. This is because a consumer who rationally seeks to maximize the satisfaction he gets from his expenditures, in terms of his own tastes or values, will allocate his expenditures among alternative goods in such a way that he gets the same amount of satisfaction from the last dollar spent on each type of good. If he obtained more benefit from the last dollar spent on apples than from the last dollar spent on oranges, he would obviously be better off if he spent more on apples and less on oranges.

The almost universal reliance on such aggregative measures of a society's income should not, however, obscure the dangers of failing to look behind the aggregates. Imagine these two cases: in one case, the National Income remains constant over a year, and all of the industries have the same level of output over the year; in the other case, the National Income also remains constant, but about half of the industries grow and the other half decline. Obviously, the first economy would be stagnant, whereas the second would be undergoing significant change, including presumably shifts of resources from some industries to others. We would not see the profound differences in these two hypothetical situations simply by looking at the aggregate figures for the National Income: we also have to disaggregate.

But disaggregation is not the enemy of aggregation. Indeed, a consciously constructed aggregate is usually easier to break down into its components than most other statistics. A well-constructed aggregative statistic, like the National Income, can (in principle at least) be compared to a pyramid. At the base are the individual firms, sites of production, and individual income recipients. Just above are the industries and communities, and above them are the major sectors and regions. When the same goods are processed by several firms, double counting is avoided by counting only the "value added." At the top there is the National Income. Such a pyramid can usually exist only when there has been the consistent definition and procedure that aggregation requires, and this systematic approach probably facilitates disaggregation as well as aggregation.

The relevant point that emerges from an examination of the National Income and Product Accounts is that aggregation can be extraordinarily useful, and is compatible with the use of the same data in disaggregated form. The trouble is that the "weights" needed for aggregative indexes of other social statistics are not available, except within particular and limited areas. It would be utopian even to strive for a Gross Social Product, or National Socioeconomic Welfare, figure which aggregated all relevant social and economic variables. There are no objective weights, equivalent to prices, that we can use to compare the importance of an improvement in health with an increase in social mobility. We could in principle have a sample survey of the population, and ask the respondents how important they thought an additional unit of health was in comparison with a marginal unit of social mobility. But the relevant units would be difficult even to define, and the respondents would have no experience in dealing with them, so the results would probably be unreliable. Thus the goal of a grand and cosmic measure of all forms or aspects of welfare must be dismissed as impractical, for the present at any rate.

Examples of Social Indicators

Within particular and limited areas, on the other hand, some modest degree of aggregation is now possible. And even over a limited area, such aggregation can be extremely useful. Some of the possibilities for useful aggregation over a limited span are illustrated in the chapters of this report.

One aggregative index is the expectancy of *healthy* life (strictly, life expectancy free of bed-disability and institutionalization). This index weights each disease or source of disability in proportion to its effect in reducing length of life or in keeping a person in bed or institutionalized. If there is either a reduction in bed-disability due to a reduction in disease, or an increase in life expectancy when bed-disability is unchanged, the index will increase, as it should. Admittedly, this aggregative index is, like the National Income statistics, imperfect in some respects.[2] Yet, its degree of aggregation makes it much easier to do systematic work at a general level on the relationship between health and life and various causal variables, such as medical inputs, income levels, and the like.

Another area in which limited aggregation is possible is that of crime. To determine how much the danger of being victimized by a criminal changes over time, we should weight each type of crime by the extent of harm suffered by the victim. The dollar values lost would provide good weights for larcenies and burglaries, but the loss from personal injury or death would have to be estimated or assumed.

Where changes in the extent of "criminality" (or conversely, "lawabidingness") in a population are at issue, different weights are needed. Though it presumably does not matter to the victim whether he is killed by manslaughter or murder, society puts a very different assessment on the two acts. Weights for an index of criminality can be obtained from surveys, which show that respondents of different classes and occupations tend to agree on the relative heinousness of different significant crimes. The results of the best known of these surveys are highly correlated (r = .97) with data on the average length of prison sentences for the same crimes.

Some aggregates do not require the cumulation of qualitatively quite different things. For example, in the Opportunity chapter the operative assumption is that social mobility along some one dimension tends to vary in proportion to social mobility along other dimensions. Thus the correlation coefficient indicating the association between the socioeconomic status of men working now, as measured by the social rank of their usual occupation, and the socioeconomic status of their fathers, measured in the same way, is an aggregative index of social mobility. Its aggregative character derives, not only from the geographic span of the sample, but also from the assumption that changes in occupational status are *representative* of the diverse and manifold changes entailed in any significant intergenerational change in socioeconomic status. The implicit aggregation entailed in using a representative variable is in principle inferior to the more explicit sorts of aggregation

discussed earlier, but it is usually easier in practice, and probably more congenial to those who are not familiar with aggregative theories or data constructs.

The Next Step: The Development of Policy Accounts

Although the potential usefulness of several social indicators has been illustrated in this report, this work represents only a beginning. Hopefully, there will be continued studies of social indicators and their method of construction. At the same time we also need to encourage the collection of new and more socially relevant data. If a balanced, organized, and concise set of measures of the condition of our society were available, we should have the information needed to identify emerging problems and to make knowledgeable decisions about national priorities.

The next step in any logical process of policy formation is to choose the most efficient program for dealing with the conditions that have been exposed. Then there must be a decision about how much should be spent on the program to deal with the difficulty. If these two decisions are to be made intelligently, the society needs information on the benefits and costs of alternative programs at alternative levels of funding.

It might seem at first glance that the benefits of an operating program could be obtained directly from the social indicators, which would measure any changes in the relevant social condition and therefore in the output of a program. In fact, it is much more difficult to obtain information on the output of even an existing program than to obtain a social indicator. The condition of an aspect of a nation depends, not only on a particular public program, but also on many other things. Health and life expectancy, for example, depend not only on public health programs, but also on private medical expenditures, the standard of living, the quality of nutrition, the exposure to contagious diseases, and the like. Thus to determine the output of a public program we normally have to solve something like what the econometrician would call the "specification problem"; we have to identify or distinguish those changes in the social indicator due to the changed levels of expenditure on the public program. This is often not a tractable task, but it could contribute much to truly rational decision making.

The fact that rational policy necessitates linking social indicators to program inputs means that social indicators alone do not provide all of the quantitative information needed for effective decision making. Ultimately, we must integrate our social indicators into policy accounts which would allow us to estimate the changes in a social indicator that could be expected to result from alternative levels of expenditure on relevant public programs.

Though an impressive set of social indicators could be developed at modest cost in the near-term future, a complete set of policy accounts is a utopian goal at present. This does not mean that work on a more integrative set of statistics should be postponed. These accounts will never be available unless we start thinking about the statistics we need for rational decision making now, even if this only entails marginal changes in the statistics we already have. The social statistics that we need will almost never be obtained as a by-product of accounting or administrative routine, or as a result of a series of *ad hoc* decisions, however intelligent each of these decisions might be. Only a systematic approach based on the informational requirements of public policy will do.

NOTES

[1] Subcommittee on Census and Statistics, Committee on Post Office and Civil Service, House of Representatives, *1967 Report of Statistical Activities of the Federal Government,* House Report 1071.

[2] It does not deal with the disability which does not force people to bed. Though it weighs the serious disease more heavily than the lesser disease, since the serious disease more often results in death or in longer bed-disability than the minor disease, it makes no allowance for the difference in pain and discomfort per day among various diseases. Finally, it ranks death and permanent bed disability equally, which may not be in accord with our values.

Statistical Services of the United States Government

Prepared by the Office of Statistical Standards,
Bureau of the Budget, Executive Office of the President.

This publication in spite of its publication date is still a valuable and concise reference tool, and a neat summary. My only criticism is that it lacks an index. Of the 3 parts described below only Part II is included in the pages that follow.

"Part I describes the statistical system of the Federal Government. In a section on "Organization" it describes the procedures followed to achieve coordination within a decentralized statistical system, and distinguishes between the various types of statistical agencies. Other sections describe the relations of Federal statistical programs to those of other governmental and nongovernmental organizations, the methods of collection and tabulation, and the presentation of data.

Part II presents brief descriptions of the principal economic and social statistical series collected by Government agencies. For each of about 50 subjects it tells what agencies are concerned and what kinds of data are collected and made available.

Part III contains a brief statement of the statistical responsibilities of each agency and a list of its principal statistical publications.

The booklet deals with economic and social statistics, with emphasis on what statistical information is made available to the public. Among statistical activities not dealt with here are statistical programs in the physical and natural sciences and the application of statistical methods and techniques in administrative processes. The collection and use of statistical data for operating purposes are not described in detail unless the data thus obtained are also available and used for informational purposes."
From the Introduction.

Note: the Budget Bureau is now called the Office of Management and Budget (as of July 1, 1970).

PRINCIPAL SOCIAL AND ECONOMIC STATISTICAL PROGRAMS

A. DEMOGRAPHIC STATISTICS

Population. The basic data on the size and characteristics of the population are those collected in the census of the population, which is taken every 10 years by the Bureau of the Census, in the Department of Commerce. The first population census was taken in 1790, and in 1810 the census was

SOURCE: Reprinted from U. S. Executive Office of the President, Bureau of the Budget. Office of Statistical Standards. *Statistical Services of the United States Government.* (Washington: Revised 1968). pp. vi-vii, 31-93

broadened to include other subjects. The 1960 Censuses of Population and Housing were taken as of April 1, 1960. The Census of Agriculture was taken in the fall of 1959.

The results of the decennial censuses are published in detail for geographic areas and in special reports and releases covering specific subjects. Demographic statistics are given on the number and characteristics of the population, including age, sex, race, marital status, family composition, place of birth, country of birth of parents, migration, education, and fertility. In addition, economic characteristics of the population are enumerated, including employment status, occupation and industry, and income. The data are presented, with varying degrees of detail, for the United States as a whole, four major regions, divisions, States, State economic areas, standard metropolitan statistical areas, counties, cities, and, in large cities, for tracts. In many of the tabulations, urban, rural-nonfarm and rural-farm parts are shown separately. In 1960, all the economic items and all except the most basic demographic items were collected for a 25-percent sample of households.

The Bureau of the Census also collects current data on the population in its current population survey—a monthly canvass of a scientifically selected sample of 52,500 households in 449 sample areas. The data are collected by Census Bureau enumerators who visit households and obtain information on population characteristics (such as marital status, school enrollment, household characteristics, internal migration, fertility, etc.), on individual and family incomes, and on the labor activity of each member of the household 14 years of age or older. The survey yields continuing monthly data on the labor force, as described below, and annual or less frequent data on other characteristics of the population. Results on demographic characteristics are published in the various series of *Current Population Reports* issued by the Bureau of the Census and labor force information is published by the BLS.

For intercensal periods the Bureau of the Census also publishes reports on the size, distribution, and composition of the population; estimates of the total population of States, by broad age groups, and estimates of the population of the largest standard metropolitan statistical areas (series P–25). These are nonsurvey-type estimates and are based on various reporting systems and administrative data which are used to measure directly and indirectly the components of population change, nationally, and for geographic areas. Population projections for the Nation as a whole are published at regular intervals, and State projections are published at somewhat less frequent intervals. Other Census Bureau reports include data on selected population characteristics (series P–20), estimates of the farm population issued jointly with the Economic Research Service (series Census–ERS P–27), and results of special censuses taken at the request and expense of local governments (series P–28). In addition to the Census–ERS estimate of the farm population for the United States, the Economic Research Service makes estimates of the farm population for the 9 major geographic divisions based on mailed questionnaire returns reporting on approximately 100,000 farms. This series also shows migration to and from farms.

Vital statistics. Major responsibility for compiling vital statistics rests in the National Center for Health Statistics. The country's official vital statistics are published by the Center's Division of Vital Statistics. The Division obtains its basic data either directly or indirectly from registration certificates (as of birth, death, marriage, etc.) which are filled out locally and film copies which are sent to the Division from vital statistics bureaus located in separate health departments in each of the 50 States, the District of Columbia, three separately reporting cities (Baltimore, New Orleans and New York City), Puerto Rico and the Virgin Islands. The certificates are used for legal and other purposes as well as to furnish vital statistics. Each data source is a separate jurisdiction, acting under its own laws and standards, and is subject only to advice, persuasion and leadership from the Federal Government.

To improve registration procedures and secure greater uniformity in vital statistics, a "death registration area" was established in 1880 for jurisdictions with satisfactory and sufficiently uniform practices. Not until 1933 did the area include every State. A birth registration area established in 1915 also gained complete State coverage in 1933. A marriage registration area established in January 1957 by 1968 included 44 of the 56 reporting jurisdictions; a divorce registration area established in January 1958 included 23 jurisdictions by 1968.

The program of the Division of Vital Statistics includes the following activities: (1) regular publication of certain monthly provisional statistics; (2) comprehensive annual statistics for the country as a whole, with geographic detail for States and lesser areas; (3) followback studies from samples of death and birth records for research and special factfinding; (4) special research studies, some in cooperation with other agencies within and outside the Public Health Service; (5) life tables; (6) special services to consumers of vital statistics on a reimbursable basis; (7) informational publications on vital registration; (8) promulgation of a model vital statistics act; (9) promulgation of standard vital certificates.

Immigration and naturalization. The Immigration and Naturalization Service compiles statistics on aliens and persons naturalized. The annual report of the Service presents data on admissions of both immigrants and nonimmigrants (tourists, students, visitors for business, foreign officials, temporary workers, etc.), including the country or region of birth and last permanent residence; the basis of admission under the immigration laws; and the age, sex, occupation, and marital status of immigrants. The alien population is also shown by nationality and State of residence. Data are presented on the characteristics (age, sex, occupation, year of entry into the United States) of persons naturalized as U.S. citizens, together with country of former allegiance. The Service also compiles statistics on arrival and departure of aliens and citizens by sea and air, by ports of entry or departure, by countries of embarkation or debarkation and by flag of carrier.

B. SOCIAL STATISTICS

Education. Administration of schools in the United States is a function of individual State and local governments rather than the Federal Government. Institutions of higher education are also independently administered in a decentralized manner. National education statistics are, therefore, largely a matter of compilation of results from independent systems— 50 State offices of education, 20,000 school districts, and 2,400 institutions of higher education. They are subject to the usual problems of assembling independently derived data, such as dealing with intrinsic differences among the units under study. Comparability of detail must therefore be watched very closely.

Many of the Federal education programs are centered in the Office of Education of the Department of Health, Education, and Welfare, whose National Center for Educational Statistics conducts a series of basic statistical surveys, as well as special studies. The data produced in OE, and much related educational data produced by other agencies, are summarized in their publication *Digest of Educational Statistics,* now an annual publication. Information on such subjects as schools, enrollments, teachers, graduates and degrees granted, and finances are presented for the elementary and secondary level and for institutions of higher education. Information on church related elementary and secondary schools is also being supplied after many years during which no data appeared for this type of school. Federal programs concerned with education and administered by the Office of Education and by other agencies are also summarized.

The National Center for Educational Statistics also produces the annual publication, *Projections of Educational Statistics.* This publication shows national 10-year projections of most of the main areas of educational statistics: enrollment, high school graduates, degrees, professional staff and expenditures. Projections of inter-

est to those studying education are also made by the Bureau of the Census, the Department of Labor, and the National Science Foundation.

In addition to the institutional data reported by the Office of Education and the data on the various Federal education programs, statistics on educational attainment of the population and on school enrollment are collected by the Bureau of the Census in its population surveys. The Department of Labor studies school dropouts and other problems relating to the development of skills in the labor force. The National Science Foundation reports on the development of scientific manpower. The Public Health Service reports on medical and dental training programs.

Reports on vocational education covering federally supported programs and data on public and school libraries are also issued by the Office of Education. Comparative studies with educational systems in other countries are made.

Health. The National Center for Health Statistics is a part of the Health Services and Mental Health Administration, Public Health Service, U.S. Department of Health, Education, and Welfare. The Center conducts three continuing sample surveys:

1. The Health Interview Survey, based on a sample of about 42,000 households each year, is conducted by carefully trained and supervised interviewers with the Bureau of the Census as collecting agent. Questions are asked about acute illnesses of all kinds, including accidental injuries; chronic conditions; disability; costs and uses of medical and dental care; hospitalization; other health-related topics; and personal, socioeconomic and demographic characteristics relevant to an understanding of the country's health

problems. Statistics from these household interviews are accumulated, analyzed, and published quarterly, annually or biennially, depending on the nature of the indexes and the degree of detail desired in the tables. Data collection began in July 1957 and the first report was issued in April 1958. As of mid-1968, 112 reports had been published including 87 detailed topical reports, 7 studies of population groups, 13 developmental and evaluative studies, and 5 reports giving program descriptions, survey designs, concepts and definitions.

2. The Health Examination Survey secures standardized data from direct examination, testing, and measurement of national samples of the country's population by sending mobile clinics manned by trained medical and auxiliary personnel to locations selected in the first stage of sampling. The desired information is then obtained by examining individuals selected in subsequent stages of sampling. Examination of a national sample of about 6,700 adults aged 18–79 years was completed with the first results published in 1964 and a total of 31 reports issued through mid-1968. The second cycle of the health examination survey included a national sample of about 7,000 children aged 6–11 years, ending in December 1965. A third cycle currently is examining a national sample of adolescents aged 12–17 years.

3. The Health Resources Surveys, the most recently established part of the National Health Survey program, is a group of surveys which is producing statistics on the health characteristics of the Nation's institutionalized population. This group includes the Institutional Population Survey, the Hospital Discharge Survey, and three companion surveys of ophthalmolo-gists, optometrists and dispensing opticians. The Institutional Population Survey's data are collected from establishments which provide some kinds of medical, nursing, personal, domiciliary or custodial care. These establishments are surveyed and information concerning all or a sample of their patients is obtained either from existing records or from questionnaires designed for this purpose. A master facility inventory of hospitals and all types of resident institutions has been prepared as the sampling frame for both the Institutional Population Survey and the Hospital Discharge Survey. The latter collects data on a sub-sample of discharges from a sample of short-stay hospitals in the Nation, excluding military and Veterans Administration hospitals and provides detailed medical data on diagnoses and surgical operations and procedures among hospitalized patients. The three companion surveys on ophthalmologists, optometrists and dispensing opticians will produce data on existing vision and eye-care manpower. In addition, a survey of the Nation's pharmacists is nearly completed. These four surveys will provide accurate and current information on the numbers, distribution and characteristics of manpower in these health occupations.

Various other programs of the Public Health Service yield statistics relating to health and medical services. Included are weekly reports on national morbidity and mortality from infectious diseases and on internationally reportable diseases occurring in various countries. Data are published periodically on the incidence and prevalence of specific diseases or disease categories, such as influenza, respiratory, neurotropic viral, hepatitis, malaria, venereal, and tuberculosis.

Other statistics deal with pesticide residues in the environment and in foods, state public health laboratory resources, laboratory diagnostic procedures, and other aspects of disease control.

From time to time, intensive community and state surveys are made to obtain data on the incidence and prevalence of general morbidity and medical care, and their relation to social, economic, and other factors in the observed populations. Other Public Health Service data refer to health personnel, resources, and activities; construction and operation of hospitals and other health care facilities; and the number and characteristics of patients in institutions providing health services.

Specialized reports are issued on various aspects of health, e.g., diabetes, cardiovascular disease, and smoking. In addition, data on accidental injuries and deaths are published throughout the year and an annual report to the President and the Congress is prepared.

Morbidity and mortality data and medical, dental, and hospital care statistics for direct beneficiaries of Federal programs are also available from the Veterans Administration, Social Security Administration, Railroad Retirement Board, and the Armed Forces (Army, Navy, and Air Force). The longest available series of data on illness and death is that for Army soldiers, which dates back to 1820.

Social insurance and related programs. Insurance against loss of income through old-age, disability, unemployment, or death of the breadwinner is provided in the United States under several different programs.

The most comprehensive system is the old-age, survivors, disability, and health insurance program (OASDHI) established by the Social Security Act of 1935, which is administered by the Social Security Administration in the Department of Health, Education, and Welfare. This program, which covers about 93 percent of all paid employment, now provides monthly benefits to retired workers (aged 62 and over), to disabled workers, and to specified dependents and survivors. In 1965 a health insurance program (Medicare) for those 65 and over was established.

The Railroad Retirement Act of 1935 brought railroad workers, many of whom had previously been covered by employers' pension plans, under a Federal system, which is administered by the Railroad Retirement Board. The retirement program now provides retirement and disability annuities for railroad employees, annuities for their spouses, and benefits for their survivors. The railroad retirement system and the general old-age, survivors, and disability insurance program are coordinated in several ways.

Most Federal Government employees are under the Federal civil service retirement system, established in 1920, which is administered by the Civil Service Commission and now provides retirement, disability, and survivor benefits. There are also a number of separate Federal retirement systems for special groups, such as regular military personnel, judges, and others.

Most State and local government employees are covered under special retirement systems, many of which also provide disability and survivor benefits. Nearly all State and local government employees are now eligible for OASDHI coverage, which is often in addition to their coverage under the special retirement system.

All States have workmen's compensation systems providing cash benefits and medical care in case of occupational injury and for illness of occupational origin. Four States have established temporary disability insurance programs with benefits, for limited periods, in case of nonoccupational illness.

Special compensation and pension programs for veterans, administered by the Veterans Administration, pay monthly benefits to disabled veterans and their dependents and survivors for service-connected disabilities and also, if the veteran or his family has less than a specified annual income, for non-service-connected disabilities.

The Social Security Administration publishes each month in the *Social Security Bulletin* data on the number of beneficiaries and total and average amount of insurance benefits, by type of benefit; status and operation of the OASDHI trust funds; and claims and reimbursements for hospital benefits and medical service benefits under Medicare. Quarterly series present data on reduced benefits for early retirement; cash benefits by State; detailed family beneficiary data; and covered employment and payroll figures. The annual statistical supplement to the *Social Security Bulletin* has trend and detailed data on benefits awarded and in current-payment status by beneficiary age, sex, race and family status; State benefit information; beneficiaries residing abroad; monthly amounts of cash benefits for selected types of beneficiaries; and on insured workers, and workers with taxable earnings by age, sex, and other special tabulations. Detailed statistics on applicants for disability benefits are published in the annual *Social Security Disability Applicant Statistics.*

The publication *Workers Under Social Security* replaces the *Handbook of Old-Age, Survivors, and Disability Insurance Statistics.* It provides comprehensive employment and earnings data and derivative program data for persons covered by OASDHI. The 1968 edition of *Workers Under Social Security* covers the period 1937–60 and for the year 1960. In addition, it has selected data on wage and salary workers reported for 1961 which includes annual and work history statistics. The next publication will have only annual sample data and the words "Annual Statistics" will appear on the cover. Issues containing both annual and work history statistics will be published at less frequent intervals and the next issue will have data for the period 1937–65.

In administering the OASDHI program, the Social Security Administration obtains quarterly reports from employers on the number of employees in a specified pay period in the last month of the quarter, the number of employees who worked at any time during the quarter, and taxable wages for the quarter. Information compiled from these reports has been published for the first calendar quarter of selected years since 1946 and annually since 1964 in *County Business Patterns.* Reporting unit data are classified by employment size and type of industry and are given for the entire U.S., by State, and by county or other equivalent political unit. Types of employment not included in the scope of *County Business Patterns* (although covered by OASDHI) are agriculture, domestic service, State and local government, and self-employed persons. Some State data on self-employed persons are available in the annual statistical supplement to the *Social Security Bulletin.* Other separate annual publications which provide information on certain types of covered employment are *Social Security Farm Statistics, Social Security Household Worker Statistics,* and *State and Local Government Employment Under OASDHI.*

For other social insurance programs, the *Social Security Bulletin* publishes monthly data on benefits and beneficiaries under the railroad, Federal civil service and veterans' benefit programs, and the State unemployment insurance programs. Annual benefit estimates only are available for the four State temporary disability and workmen's compensation programs. There are also monthly summary data on unemployment insurance operations, and contributions and taxes collected under the railroad, State unemployment insurance, and Federal civil service programs. Estimates of beneficiaries and benefit payments under State and local government retirement systems and the smaller Federal employee retirement systems are published in the annual statistical supplement.

Selected current statistics on the railroad retirement system, such as the number of beneficiaries in various categories with comparisons for the previous year, are published by the Railroad Retirement Board in its *Quarterly Review.* Additional data on this program are available in the annual report of the Railroad Retirement Board.

Detailed statistics on the veterans' programs are published in the annual report of the Veterans Administration. The data include the number of living veterans receiving compensation, pensions, disability allowances, and retirement pay; the number of deceased veterans whose dependents are receiving compensation or pension benefits; and the amounts paid under the various programs.

Total unemployment insurance claims for each State are published in a weekly bulletin, and data for 150 major local labor areas are included for one week in every month. Current operating data on the program are published monthly or quarterly by the Bureau of Employment Security in the monthly *Unemployment Insurance Review* and in *Unemployment Insurance Statistics.* Included are State figures on average number of insured unemployed and their characteristics, benefit payments, contributions activities, denials of benefits, appeals, summaries of monthly employment and quarterly wages covered by State unemployment insurance programs, and other details. The Bureau of Employment Security also compiles data, published monthly or quarterly in the Employment Service Statistics, on job applications, counseling, testing, job openings, referrals, placements, employer services, services to special applicant groups and other manpower activities carried on by State public employment service agencies.

Unemployment insurance for railroad workers was provided in the Railroad Retirement Act of 1935. This program is administered by the Railroad Retirement Board, which publishes current data on operation of the program in its *Quarterly Review* and annual data on operations since 1938 in its annual report.

Summary monthly and annual data on the operations of each of these unemployment insurance programs are published in the *Social Security Bulletin,* as noted above.

Social and rehabilitation services. *Public assistance.* The Social Security Act of 1935 provided for Federal financial participation in State programs for aid to the aged, the blind, and dependent children. The Social Security Act Amendments of 1950 provided for similar participation in programs of aid to the permanently and totally disabled. Under the Social Security Act Amendments of 1960, the Federal Government has also participated in State programs of medical assistance for the aged, providing medical care for older persons who have sufficient resources to meet their everyday needs but require help with medical expenses. The 1965 Amendments established a new program, medical assistance, which extended coverage to additional groups of people who need help in meeting their medical expenses. These programs are all administered by the States, but financed in part by grants of Federal funds to the States. To receive a Federal grant for payments and administrative expenses under any of these assistance programs, a State must have a plan approved as meeting the requirements of the Social Security Act. Each State establishes the conditions under which assistance is given to individuals in these groups and determines the amount of payments. The grants to the States for these programs are administered by the Assistance Payments Administration in the Social and Rehabilitation Service.

Statistics of the number of recipients and payments under these public assistance programs are published monthly or bimonthly, by State, in *Welfare in Review,* and summarized annually in the statistical supplement. The series are continuous since 1936 for old-age assistance, aid to the blind, and aid to dependent children; since 1950 for aid to the permanently and totally disabled; and since 1960 for medical assistance for the aged.

Aid to other needy persons is furnished principally through general assistance or relief programs of State or local governments, without Federal funds. Statistics on the number of recipients and the amount of payments under these programs are also presented in *Welfare in Review.*

Data on concurrent receipt of assistance and old-age, survivors, and disability health insurance cash benefits by aged public assistance recipients; on distribution of payments by amount; on reasons for opening and closing cases; and on source of funds for public assistance payments and administrative costs are also released by the Social and Rehabilitation Service, semi-annually or annually, in processed form. Data on utilization and cost of medical care under public assistance programs and on characteristics and financial resources of public assistance recipients are also released periodically.

Maternal and child welfare. Federal activities designed to promote the health and social welfare of children are administered by the Children's Bureau, established in 1912, now located in the Social and Rehabilitation Service, Department of Health, Education, and Welfare. Since 1935, the Children's Bureau has also administered grants provided in the Social Security Act to assist in extending and improving services to promote the health of mothers and children and in locating and serving children who are crippled or suffer from conditions that lead to crippling. In 1967 the Bureau was also assigned responsibility for services in the Aid to Families with Dependent Children program. Data on the number of mothers and children served under these programs by type of service, and on selected expenditures by type of expenditure and source of funds, are published in the annual statistical supplement to *Welfare in Review* and in the Children's Bureau's Statistical Series.

The Children's Bureau is also the major national collection agency for data on juvenile delinquency cases handled by juvenile courts in the United States and on related program statistics, such as data on training schools and other institutions serving delinquent children. (See below, Criminal and judicial statistics.)

Vocational rehabilitation. Under the Vocational Rehabilitation Act, as amended, the Rehabilitation Services Administration (RSA), an agency of the Social and Rehabilitation Service, U.S. Department of Health, Education, and Welfare, administers a program of grants to States and other sources for support of comprehensive vocational rehabilitation services for the physically and mentally handicapped. Other related programs operated under RSA authority include:

(1) special projects for the innovation and expansion of services in various program areas; (2) training programs to increase the supply of rehabilitation personnel; and (3) grants for constructing rehabilitation facilities and workshops and improving their services.

Under the Mental Retardation Facilities Construction Act, as amended, RSA administers special grant programs relating to mental retardation, including grants for constructing facilities, initiating community service programs, and improving services in State-operated mental retardation facilities.

Under Titles X and XIV of the Social Security Act, RSA administers social services programs for the recipients of Aid to the Blind and Aid to the Permanently and Totally Disabled.

Statistics are released periodically in the Rehabilitation Service Series and include information on State agency caseloads; characteristics of rehabilitated clients; Social Security Disability Insurance beneficiaries; turnover rates among State agency personnel in full-time positions; and special grant programs. Fiscal statistics and additional program data on grants to States are published annually in the Administrative Service Series.

Criminal and judicial statistics. There is no single source of comprehensive data on crime and the work of the courts in the United States as a whole. Under our constitutional system the police power (except for violations of Federal laws) is reserved to the States, and most national criminal and judicial statistics are based on voluntary reports from State or local governments. Several States have central agencies concerned with crime and correction, and issue reports which contain considerable data for those particular States. Nationwide statistics are of three types—those dealing with offenses and arrests, court statistics, and statistics on prisoners and parolees.

The Federal Bureau of Investigation in the Department of Justice has served since 1930, at the request of the International Association of Chiefs of Police, as a central clearinghouse for nationwide statistics on selected classes of serious offenses known to the police. In this capacity the Bureau publishes annually "Crime in the United States—Uniform Crime Reports— 19—," which includes statistics on seven classes of offenses known to police for the United States, the 50 States, and for each standard metropolitan statistical area. Summary data are also shown for offenses known, offenses cleared by arrest, and persons charged (held for prosecution) for these seven offenses; and data are presented on all arrests by offense, by age, sex, and race. These statistics are based on reports from nearly all city police departments and a large proportion of the rural law-enforcement agencies. Preliminary trends in summary form are also issued in quarterly releases.

In 1963, the FBI initiated a study of criminal careers. For Federal and certain other types of offenders data are available on sex, age, race, and number of previous arrests by type of offense. Recidivism is also shown by type of release and type of offense.

Operational statistics on crime are becoming available through the National Crime Information Center—a nationwide computerized law enforcement information system.

Annual reports on the business of the U.S. district courts, including data on civil cases by nature of suit, bankruptcy, and criminal cases by type of offense, number of defendants, and disposition of case, as well as data on probation, have been prepared since 1939 by the Administrative Office of the United States Courts. This report includes statistics on the U.S. Supreme Court and the U.S. Circuit Courts of Appeals. For persons appearing before the Federal courts as defendants and for those persons placed under the supervision of the Federal probation system separate annual reports are compiled. Juvenile court statistics have been collected and published annually since 1926 by the Children's Bureau in the Department of Health, Educa-

tion, and Welfare. Beginning with 1956, national estimates of the number of juvenile cases by type of court (urban, semi-urban and rural) and by sex have been made, based on a scientifically designed national sample of courts. In addition, the Bureau collects and publishes statistics on training schools for delinquent children. An annual series on State judicial criminal statistics, begun in 1932 by the Bureau of the Census, was discontinued in 1946, so that there are at present no nationwide data on State courts handling adult offenders.

The annual report on prisoners in State and Federal correctional institutions for adult offenders, begun by the Bureau of the Census in 1926, is now a part of the national prisoner statistics program of the Bureau of Prisons in the Department of Justice. This program also includes more detailed reports on admissions and releases as well as annual reports on executions. Data regarding Federal prisoners and parolees are presented in the annual publication of the Bureau of Prisons, *Statistical Report for 19—*. Prisoners in county and municipal penal institutions have not been enumerated on a national basis since 1933, except in connection with the decennial censuses of population.

C. MANPOWER, EMPLOYMENT, AND LABOR STATISTICS

Labor force. Current information on the labor force is collected by the Bureau of the Census, Department of Commerce, in its current population survey, acting as agent for the Bureau of Labor Statistics which analyzes and publishes the information. Monthly estimates are available from March 1940 to date. Current estimates of the labor force were formerly published in the monthly report on the labor

force (*Current Population Reports, series P–57*). Since July 1959 these estimates have been published monthly by the Bureau of Labor Statistics, Department of Labor, in *Employment and Earnings and Monthly Report on the Labor Force*.

The survey covers the week including the 12th of each month, and national estimates of the total labor force, of employment (including self-employment) in agricultural and non-agricultural industries, and of unemployment are issued early in the following month. These estimates are classified by sex, marital status, color, and age; the employed and unemployed are further classified by occupation, class of worker, and full- and part-time status. Persons at work are grouped within classes by the number of hours worked during the week, and the unemployed are sub-divided by duration and reasons for unemployment. Recent expansions of the program provide periodic tabulation and analysis of labor force statistics for the 20 largest metropolitan areas and 14 central cities and for the poverty and other urban neighborhoods of the 100 largest metropolitan areas.

Information on other characteristics of the labor force is published from time to time in special labor force reports which present information on such subjects as work experience during the course of the year, educational attainment, marital and family characteristics of workers, employment of students, etc. Seasonal adjustment of the labor force series is described in *Employment and Earnings and Monthly Report on the Labor Force* which provides seasonal adjustment factors for four age-sex components of agricultural employment, nonagricultural employment, and unemployment. The seasonally adjusted component figures are aggregated to produce seasonally adjusted totals for civilian labor force, total employment, unemployment, and the unemployment rate. Other selected series are also available on a seasonally adjusted basis.

The 1960 Census of Population provides labor force statistics, including statistics on occupation and industry, for every State, county, and urban place of 2,500 or more inhabitants.

Detailed cross-classifications of the data are prepared for the larger areas (States, cities of 100,000 or more, etc.), as well as for the United States and its urban and rural parts. Special reports in volume II provide detailed cross-classifications on such subjects as occupation by industry for the Nation as a whole.

Nonagricultural employment, hours, and earnings. Estimates of employment, hours, and earnings in nonagricultural establishments are prepared and issued monthly by the Bureau of Labor Statistics of the Department of Labor. The data are collected under a joint Federal-State program involving cooperation of the Bureau of Labor Statistics and the Bureau of Employment Security with State agencies, most of which are State employment security agencies affiliated with the Bureau of Employment Security.

Employment estimates are issued for "all employees" and for production workers in manufacturing and mining, construction workers in contract construction and nonsupervisory workers in most nonagricultural industries. Estimates of average hours paid for per week and of average weekly and hourly earnings are issued for production workers in manufacturing and mining; construction workers in contract construction; and nonsupervisory workers in wholesale and retail trade and finance, insurance and real estate. Reports and estimates refer to pay periods which include the 12th of each month. Comparable estimates for each State and more than 200 metropolitan areas are prepared and published by the cooperating State agencies, using data from the same reports on which the national estimates are based and conforming to the same procedural standards. National, State, and area estimates appear monthly in *Employment and Earnings and Monthly Report on the Labor Force,* published by the Bureau of Labor Statistics.

The estimates are based primarily on monthly reports to the Bureau of Labor Statistics, collected by the State agencies from a sample of 155,000 establishments, and are adjusted periodically to total (benchmark) figures as described below. The reports are supplemented by employment data for specific industries available from other Federal agencies—such as Interstate Commerce Commission data for railroad employment and Civil Service Commission data for employment by the Federal Government. The estimates are based on payroll records and hence do not include the self-employed, domestic service workers, or unpaid family workers. The joint program has been developed since 1947 and extends series prepared by the Bureau of Labor Statistics on a continuous basis since 1932, with some individual series available annually from 1919.

The benchmark totals to which the estimates are revised periodically are obtained primarily from information compiled by State employment security agencies, supplemented by data for small firms (not covered by unemployment compensation) from the old-age and survivors insurance program administered by the Social Security Administration, and by an annual sample survey of employment and payrolls of State and local governments conducted by the Governments Division of the Bureau of the Census. A variety of other sources are used to obtain benchmark information for other industries not covered or only partially covered by the social security programs.

The benchmark data compiled by State employment security agencies from reports submitted by approximately 2.5 million business establishments covered by State unemployment compensation programs include over 80 percent of total nonagricultural employment. The employers' reports also contain total wages paid and contributions (taxes) paid by employers for unemployment compensation purposes. These data are assembled quarterly by the Bureau of Employment Security to provide national and State totals by industry and published each quarter in the Bureau of Employment Security publication, *Employment and Wages of Workers Covered by State Unemployment Insurance Laws and Unemployment Compensation for Federal Employees.* In addition to serving as a source of benchmarks for national current employment estimates, the data are used similarly for State and local area estimates of nonagricultural employment and also as a major component in the national income estimates prepared by the Department of Commerce.

Current national employment estimates are published by the Bureau of Labor Statistics for all nonagricultural establishments and for the eight major industry divisions: manufacturing, mining, contract construction, transportation and public utilities, trade, finance, service, and government. All-employee estimates are also published for about 400 separate industry groups and subgroups, and estimates of production, construction, or nonsupervisory-worker employment are published for manufacturing and selected nonmanufacturing industries. For production workers in manufacturing and mining and nonsupervisory workers in some nonmanufacturing industries, weekly hours and average hourly and weekly earnings series are prepared for about 350 individual industry groups and subgroups. Average hours and average hourly and weekly earnings for all private nonagricultural establishments have been compiled monthly for periods since January 1964. The amount of industrial detail published for States and local areas varies from State to State, but in general is less than that available in the national estimates.

Studies of employment trends and appraisals of the long-range employment outlook in major industries, based on these and other data, are issued by the Bureau of Labor Statistics for use in planning programs of education, training, and recruitment and in vocational guidance. Information on occupations obtained in the decennial census of population, together with other information on specific occupations gathered from government and nongovernment sources, is combined with information on employment trends in the biennial Bureau of Labor Statistics publication, *Occupational Outlook Handbook,* and the periodical, *Occupational Outlook Quarterly,* which are prepared especially for vocational counselors. Similar information is used by the Bureau of Employment Security in the preparation of the *Job Guide for Young Workers* designed for use in counseling those with no more than a high school education.

Agricultural employment. Estimates of agricultural employment are issued monthly by the Statistical Reporting Service for 48 individual States. Regional and national totals, exclusive of Hawaii and Alaska, are also included in the monthly reports. These estimates are based on monthly reports collected from over 25,000 farmers. The data obtained in these reports are compared with data obtained in annual enumerative surveys and are checked against data collected in the periodic censuses of agriculture

and population. In addition to showing total farm employment, the published monthly estimates also provide separate estimates for family workers (including farm operators) and for hired workers, by States and combinations of States as listed above. Data on farm wage rates are published quarterly.

An annual report is also published on the hired farm working force showing the number of persons who worked for wages on farms at any time during the year, their characteristics, duration of employment at farm and nonfarm work, and their annual cash earnings. This report is based on information collected for the Economic Research Service by the Bureau of the Census, in the Current Population Survey.

Wages and related practices. Data on wages and related practices for general statistical use are collected by the Bureau of Labor Statistics in the Department of Labor and the Statistical Reporting Service in the Department of Agriculture. In addition, several other Federal agencies collect wage information in connection with administrative operations or responsibilities.

The Bureau of Labor Statistics has collected information since 1890 on hourly wage rates for selected occupations in a wide variety of manufacturing and nonmanufacturing industries. The present program provides for surveys of 50 manufacturing and 20 nonmanufacturing industries on a 2- to 5-year cycle basis. Earnings data presented in these studies pertain to occupational averages and distributions for a selected list of jobs. Information on overtime pay practices, shift differentials, holiday and vacation pay, and the occurrence and types of welfare and retirement plans, etc., is also obtained from the establishments visited. The program of wage studies also includes collection of annual data on union wage scales and standard hours in about 70 cities for 4 highly organized industries — construction (also collected quarterly for 7 major crafts), printing, local trucking, and local transit. These data are published in the form of national indexes as well as city wage scales.

In 1949 the Bureau of Labor Statistics began a program of area wage surveys which covers selected clerical, skilled maintenance, and unskilled worker occupations on a cross-industry basis. Eighty-five metropolitan areas, representative of all standard metropolitan statistical areas, are now surveyed annually. As in the industry studies, employer practices and supplementary pay benefits are also studied. Data are obtained mainly by field agents of the Bureau of Labor Statistics, with some collection by mail. The area wage surveys are supplemented by an annual survey of salaries of professional, administrative, and technical employees.

Occupational wage surveys in about 90 additional areas, both metropolitan and nonmetropolitan, are conducted for the purpose of setting rates to be paid by contractors under the Service Contracts Act of 1965. These surveys are of a more limited type, usually covering only a few service occupations.

Surveys are also undertaken to develop national statistics on the distribution of workers by straight-time earnings in a variety of industries and industry groups. These studies are nonoccupational and provide data by region and in some cases by product. The studies are conducted irregularly, usually in response to governmental

needs in connection with the determination of minimum wages under the Fair Labor Standards Act.

Beginning in 1959 the Bureau initiated a series of surveys of employer expenditures for selected supplementary remuneration practices ("fringe benefits"). These surveys also include information on the composition of payroll hours, showing ratios of paid leave (vacations, holidays, etc.) to total hours paid for. The current schedule involves covering all private nonagricultural employment biennially, with selected industry studies being made in the intervening years.

Since the war, increased emphasis has been placed by the Bureau of Labor Statistics on wage movements. A report on current wage developments is issued monthly, and detailed chronologies of wage developments over a period of years have been published for a substantial number of key companies or associations. Wage indexes have been prepared for a number of industries and occupational groups.

The Statistical Reporting Service of the Department of Agriculture, in connection with its crop reporting program, collects quarterly information from farmers on prevailing local wage rates for farm labor. Hourly, daily, weekly, and monthly averages are published by State and by geographic region, and indexes are computed and published. The Economic Research Service, USDA, publishes data on average earnings of hired farm workers collected annually as a supplement to the Census Bureau's Current Population Survey.

Some wage information for particular industries is collected by other Federal agencies in connection with regulatory activities. Such agencies include the Interstate Commerce Commission, the Civil Aeronautics Board, and the Federal Communications Commission (in cooperation with the Bureau of Labor Statistics). The Civil Service Commission publishes data on salaries of Federal employees by occupation and grade. The Commission also prescribes rules and designates a lead agency to conduct a wage survey in each area where there are substantial numbers of Federal "blue-collar" employees whose wages are set in accordance with prevailing locality rates. The results of these surveys are not published.

Local job market information. The Federal-State programs for unemployment insurance and public employment service are conducted by more than 2,000 local employment offices operated by State employment security agencies affiliated with the Bureau of Employment Security in the U.S. Department of Labor. The local offices are primary sources of information about local job market conditions and manpower resources, as well as about their unemployment insurance, job placement, and related operations. The Bureau of Employment Security, which assembles job market information from the State agencies and their local offices, serves as the Federal source of such information for areas throughout the country.

Area job market reports are prepared at bimonthly intervals by State employment security agencies for 150 major labor areas. These reports contain statistics and analyses of employment, anticipated labor requirements, and labor turnover, by industry; estimates of unemployment, including insured unemployment; and some information on labor demand and supply. "Area classifications" according to relative adequacy of local labor supply are assigned to the 150 major areas by the Bureau of Employment Security

on the basis of the information in the area labor reports. Smaller areas are classified if they have relatively substantial labor surpluses. In addition, areas with persistent unemployment are identified and recommended for consideration under the Public Works and Economic Development Act of 1965.

The area labor supply classifications of major and smaller areas, as well as a national summary of local labor market developments and outlook, are published monthly by the Bureau of Employment Security in its bulletin, *Area Trends in Employment and Unemployment.*

Occupational job market information is developed by the State employment security agencies under the guidance of the Bureau of Employment Security, primarily for use in employment counseling and job placement operations. One major source of such information consists of area skill surveys which analyze, by occupation, the manpower requirements and resources of individual labor areas. Local and State occupational guides prepared by the State employment security agencies present a picture of the job content and economic factors associated with individual occupations or groups of occupations. The Bureau of Employment Security also publishes selected occupational guidance materials in bulletins such as the *Job Guide for Young Workers, Career Guide for Demand Occupations,* and the *Health Careers Guidebook.*

The State employment security agencies also submit monthly reports to the Bureau of Employment Security during the active agricultural season, giving farm job market information for approximately 270 major agricultural areas. These reports show current employment and wages of seasonal hired farmworkers and information on current farm labor market conditions. Employment data for seasonal hired farmworkers are shown by origin of the labor supply (local, intrastate, interstate, offshore, and foreign). Once a year, the reports include information on the demand and supply situation for regular (year-round) hired farmworkers.

Scientific and technical manpower. The National Science Foundation has primary responsibility within the Government for statistics on scientific and technical manpower resources. It maintains the National Register for Scientific and Technical Personnel and in other ways acts as "focal agency" for the development, coordination, and analysis of statistical information relating to personnel in these occupations. Statistical activities in this connection are described in detail in section J, Resources for Research and Development, page 277.

The Bureau of Labor Statistics collects basic data on the employment of scientists and engineers in industry annually, by type of scientist and function. As part of its program of occupational outlook and manpower studies, the Department of Labor assembles and analyzes data on trends in supply, demand, employment characteristics, training requirements, and earnings of persons in scientific and technical occupations. The Public Health Service prepares estimates of the need for and supply of manpower for medical research.

Manpower development and training. The Manpower Administration of the Department of Labor is responsible for a number of programs which provide nationwide manpower training and services. These programs reflect many of the new directions in Federal manpower policy. With pro-

grams authorized by the Manpower Development and Training Act of 1962, as amended; the Economic Opportunity Act of 1964, as amended; and the Social Security Act amendments of 1967, the Manpower Administration is a focal point of the Federal Government's efforts to: provide for occupational training to meet skill shortages, meet the employment needs of the poor, take a more active and broader role in manpower policy, integrate the various manpower programs and related services which have been generated by the Congress, and continue the formal apprenticeship training program for which its Bureau of Apprenticeship Training has had continuing responsibility.

Statistical reporting for all manpower training programs is conducted by the Office of Manpower Management Data Systems of the Manpower Administration which gathers and disseminates statistical information on all manpower development and training programs administered under the aegis of the Department of Labor, as well as on some related programs administered by other Government agencies, such as the Office of Economic Opportunity and the Department of Health, Education, and Welfare. The information issued covers such matters as the extent of the training opportunities provided and their funding, occupational programs conducted, geographic dispersal of training programs and the socio-economic characteristics of participants in the various programs. This information is used for both administrative and public information purposes, including Congressional requests for information on manpower program operations both nationwide and within respective States. Pertinent program statistics are also developed for publication in the annual Manpower Report of the President and the annual report to the Congress prepared by the Department of Health, Education, and Welfare on the institutional training program conducted under the Manpower Development and Training Act.

Summary statistical information on program operations for the variety of manpower training and development functions encompassed within the Manpower Administration is regularly prepared for administrative use. This information provides cumulative and current statistics on the following specific programs administered within the Manpower Administration: the programs of classroom training in vocational institutions and the on-the-job training program authorized under the MDTA; the large Neighborhood Youth Corps training program authorized under the Economic Opportunity Act to provide work training and experience for disadvantaged youth both in- and out-of-school; three adult work training and experience programs for poverty-stricken and disadvantaged persons also enacted under the Economic Opportunity Act— Operation Mainstream, New Careers, and Special Impact; and the Work Incentive program enacted under recent amendments to the Social Security Act to provide work training and financial incentives for welfare recipients to enable them to achieve economic independence. Other manpower programs covered include two recently developed programs which draw upon the multiple resources now available under the combined Federal manpower effort and are aimed at deeper penetration of the hard-core and most disadvantaged of the unemployed. These are: Job Opportunities in the Business Sector (JOBS) which crystallizes a new thrust toward involvement of private industry in intensive train-

ing to prepare the hard-core unemployed to take their places in the steady labor force; and the Concentrated Employment Program operating in many urban areas to reach the hard-core unemployed by providing them with personalized manpower services and training opportunities to prepare them for full-time employment.

The Bureau of Apprenticeship and Training of the Department of Labor publishes statistics on apprenticeship and other types of industrial training. Data on numbers of apprentices enrolled in programs registered with Federal or State apprenticeship agencies are published semiannually, by trade and State. The Bureau publishes occasional reports on training programs and training needs based on sample surveys of particular industries. Finally, it conducts special studies designed to provide information on the extent to which apprenticeship and other planned training in industry are contributing to the Nation's skill requirements.

Productivity estimates. Current estimates of productivity in the private economy, by major sector, and in a number of nonagricultural industries are compiled by the Bureau of Labor Statistics in the Department of Labor. In addition, estimates of productivity in agriculture are compiled by the Economic Research Service in the Department of Agriculture.

Annual indexes have been compiled measuring the relationship between the production of goods and the input of labor in selected industries and industry groups since 1941, and in recent years the scope of the program has been broadened to include the private economy as a whole. Many of these series are extended back as far as 1909. Two types of indexes are prepared, based on different concepts:

1. Physical output per man-hour, in which output is measured in terms of physical units of goods produced per man-hour. This type of measure shows the changes in labor time required to produce a fixed composite of goods and services. It tends to reflect, primarily, the effects of technological change, utilization of plant capacity, and gains in worker and managerial efficiency. Physical output indexes are now compiled annually for approximately 30 manufacturing and non-manufacturing industries. The list of industries is currently being expanded.

2. Net output per man-hour, which relates the value added by processing (in constant dollars) to man-hours required. This measure reflects changes not only in technology and human skills, but also in materials utilization and shifts in relative importance between industries with different levels of value added per man-hour. Net output measures which are conceptually consistent with gross national product statistics are prepared for the total private economy, as well as for the following sectors: agriculture, non-agriculture, manufacturing, and non-manufacturing.

The most recent report for selected industries presented annual indexes for the years 1939 and 1947-66. Indexes of "Output per Man-Hour for the Private Economy," by major sectors are published annually and quarterly by the Bureau of Labor Statistics. The Bureau also publishes related annual and quarterly series on compensation per man-hour and unit labor costs for the private, nonfarm and manufacturing sectors, from 1947 on.

Projections of employment, output and productivity, utilizing the Office of Business Economics' input-output tables, are developed by the Bureau of Labor Statistics as part of the Inter-agency Economic Growth Project.

Projections 1970 presented projections of employment for about 80 industries.

The Bureau of Labor Statistics also prepares and publishes estimates of labor requirements for various types of construction projects, such as schools, hospitals, highways, public office buildings, and private and public housing. Data are available on labor requirements for both on- and off-site construction; also on materials and other nonlabor requirements.

Technological trends and impending developments in selected industries and some of their implications for productivity, production, and employment are intensively studied. Reports cover the impact of automation on labor requirements, occupational skills, transfer and retraining practices, collective bargaining, and adjustment of older workers. Recent publications include *Technological Trends in Major American Industries* and *Technology and Manpower in the Textile Industry of the 1970's.* (Earlier reports include *Technological Change and Productivity in the Bituminous Coal Industry, 1920–1960,* and *Impact of Technological Change and Automation in the Pulp and Paper Industry.*)

In addition, studies are made of the impact of major innovations that will affect broad sectors of the economy such as a study of the effects of numerical control in metalworking industries (*Outlook for Numerical Control of Machine Tools*) and several studies of the introduction of electronic computers in different industries (*Adjustments to the Introduction of Office Automation, Impact of Office Automation in the Insurance Industry,* and *Office Automation in the Internal Revenue Service*).

Case studies are also prepared dealing with manpower planning for worker adjustment to technological change in various industries or plants (*Manpower Planning for Technological Change: Case Studies of Telephone Operators*). (Earlier reports included case studies of adjustments to automation in a bakery, insurance company, electronics factory, petroleum refinery, an airline's reservation system, and an electric and gas utility.)

As part of the Department of Labor's study of the problem of the older worker, occasional studies are prepared dealing with such special aspects as redesigning jobs to accommodate the actual capacities of older workers (*Job Redesign for Older Workers: Ten Case Studies*).

The Economic Research Service of the Department of Agriculture prepares two types of productivity measures: (1) partial measures in which output is related to a single input such as labor or land, and (2) overall productivity in which output is related to total inputs committed to agriculture.

Annual estimates are made for the United States beginning with 1910 of farm production per man-hour in aggregate and separately for crops, livestock and livestock products, and for 12 major commodity groups within these 2 categories. Annual estimates are made of farm production per man-hour for 10 geographic regions beginning with 1939. Other partial productivity measures include crop production per acre, and persons supplied farm products by one farm-worker.

A measure of farm output per unit of total inputs committed to agriculture is estimated for the United States beginning with 1910. The index of farm output measures the year-to-year changes in the combined volume of crop and livestock production available for eventual human use. The index of total inputs is a weighted composite of labor, land, machinery, and service buildings, and various intermediate products such as fertilizer, lime, feed, seed, motor fuels, and other purchased inputs.

These index series of partial and total productivity are published in an annual report entitled *Changes in Farm Production and Efficiency*.

The Economic Research Service also makes annual estimates of production per unit of total input and per man-hour for 42 types of commercial farms in various type-of-farming areas. These series begin at different periods, some dating back to 1930. The data are published in an annual report entitled *Farm Costs and Returns, Commercial Farms by Type, Size, and Location*.

Labor turnover. The Bureau of Labor Statistics publishes monthly labor turnover rates in manufacturing industries for the United States as a whole, and for 21 major industry groups in manufacturing, 217 individual manufacturing industries, and 7 nonmanufacturing industries in mining and communications. The rates are based on reports submitted by about 40,000 cooperating establishments, covering a total of 12,300,000 employees.

Labor turnover measures the movement of wage and salary workers into and out of employment status with respect to individual firms. This movement is divided into accessions (additions to employment) and separations (terminations of employment). Monthly turnover rates are published for total accessions, showing new hires separately; and for total separations, showing quits (voluntary separations) and layoffs separately. Each type of action is cumulated for a calendar month and expressed as a rate per 100 employees on payrolls during the pay period including the 12th of the month. Separate rates for each of the component items are computed for each industry for which figures are published, and separate rates for men and women are published quarterly for the 21 major industry groups in manufacturing. Turnover information is not collected separately for production workers. Rates for manufacturing are seasonally adjusted.

In addition to the national program, the Bureau of Employment Security and the Bureau of Labor Statistics, both in the Department of Labor, have jointly made cooperative arrangements with the States and the District of Columbia for the compilation of labor turnover rates for manufacturing industries for States and for a considerable number of local areas. Under this system a manufacturing establishment submits a single report that can be used for compiling local area, State, and national labor turnover rates. The Bureau of Labor Statistics publishes State and area rates for manufacturing as a whole monthly in *Employment and Earnings and Monthly Report on the Labor Force*.

National labor turnover rates are available on a comparable basis from January 1930 for manufacturing as a whole, and from 1943 for two communications industries. Comparable rates for the amount of industrial detail now published are available from January 1958. Rates for individual industries prior to that date are not comparable with those now published because of a revision in the industrial classification structure. Most State and area rates begin with 1958 or later.

Industrial injuries. Statistics on the frequency and severity of disabling work injuries in about 670 manufacturing and nonmanufacturing industries are compiled annually by the Division of Industrial Safety in the Bureau of Labor Statistics, Department of Labor, according to the USA Standard Method of Recording and Measuring Work Injury Experience. The estimates are based on reports submitted by about 115,000 establishments employing nearly 14 million workers. In several States, cooperative arrangements for reporting work injuries have been worked out between the Bureau of Labor Statistics and the State agencies. The Bureau also makes periodic intensive surveys providing detailed information on injuries and accident causes in selected industries.

The Bureau of Mines in the Department of the Interior publishes statistics on causes, and the frequency and severity rates of disabling work injuries, the average number of men working, days active, man-days and man-hours of employment in minerals and minerals-related industries. These include coal mining, coke, petroleum and natural gas, peat, asphalt and related bitumens, metal and non-metal mining, slag (iron blast furnace), sand and gravel, and stone quarries. The Bureau collects coal mining data from mines employing 20 or more men on a monthly basis; all other data are collected on an annual basis. The monthly reports pertain to work injuries in anthracite and in bituminous coal mining which are presented in two reports: one on fatalities only; the other presenting data on all disabling work-connected injuries. Annual summaries of work injury data for all industries are presented in the *Minerals Yearbook* and in other annual publications.

Statistics are also published on work injury experience in safety competitions, sponsored in some instances by appropriate trade associations. Companies voluntarily enroll in the competition and submit their reports to the Bureau on a quarterly basis for summarization into the annual safety ratings. The safety competitions include the following: National Safety Competition (covering all minerals mining activities), Sand and Gravel Plants, National Lime Association, National Limestone Institute, and National Slag Association.

Significant data on work injuries are also available through systems of workmen's compensation (social insurance covering work injuries). In the United States workmen's compensation for almost all industries is a function of the State governments, and therefore most of the statistics are compiled by the States. This type of protection is provided by the Federal Government for Federal employees and certain other groups, notably longshore and harbor workers. The Federal workmen's compensation laws are administered by the Bureau of Employees' Compensation in the Department of Labor, which issues reports each year with statistics on fatal and nonfatal injuries reported under these laws and on money payments made to injured persons and survivors.

Data on the number of persons injured are collected as a part of the U.S. national health survey, initiated by the Public Health Service in 1957. The injury data collected in this survey are classified as motor vehicle, work, home, and other. The concept of work injuries used by the Public Health Service is broader than that of the Bureau of Labor Statistics or the Bureau of Mines, however, in that it covers not only disabling injuries but also nondisabling injuries if they are medically attended; and it covers any injury received while at work and not merely those "occurring in the course of and arising out of employment."

Furthermore, the concepts of disability are not the same.

Work stoppages and collective bargaining. The statistical series on work stoppages (strikes and lockouts) in the United States goes back as far as 1881. Reports have been published under the various titles of "Strikes and Lockouts," "Strikes," and "Work Stoppages." Data on the number of stoppages, number of workers involved, and the amount of resulting idleness, together with various classifications of the disputes by State, industry, causes, duration, etc., are available on an annual basis from 1927 to date. Statistics are released monthly on a preliminary basis showing the number of stoppages, number of workers involved, number of mandays idle, and the percent this represents of the estimated working time of all industries. Annual reports give detailed analyses by industry, location, major issues, etc. The Bureau tries to obtain complete coverage of all strikes and lockouts which involve six or more workers and last for one or more full shifts.

The Bureau of Labor Statistics maintains for Government and public use a current file of about 5,000 collective-bargaining agreements, including virtually all agreements (except railroad and airline) relating to 1,000 or more workers. The Bureau publishes a number of studies each year on such subjects as vacation benefits, union security provisions, and anti-discrimination provisions in major union contracts. Reports are also published on characteristics of health and insurance and pension plans, based on the plans filed under the Welfare and Pension Plans Disclosure Act and other sources.

A Directory of National and International Labor Unions in the United

States containing statistics on the size and composition of labor organizations, together with related matters, is published biennially by the Bureau of Labor Statistics. From time to time the Bureau also prepares analyses on union government based on provisions of union constitutions.

Foreign labor statistics. Special studies and statistical compilations dealing with labor conditions abroad are prepared by the Bureau of Labor Statistics. Such information is compiled from Foreign Service reports, national sources, international publications, and direct observation by staff, and is published in a variety of forms. Monographs on labor legislation and practices in individual countries are presented in the Bureau's *Labor Law and Practice* series. Brief summaries of labor in individual countries, in 3- to 5-page leaflet form, are regularly issued in a *Labor Digest* series. Listings of trade unions and their principal officers are also published for some countries. Individual reports in all country series are updated from time to time, depending upon the extent of change occurring in the countries.

Current reports and analyses of international labor activities and statistical data from selected countries are published monthly in *Labor Developments Abroad*. The *Foreign Labor Briefs* section of the *Monthly Labor Review* also provides brief accounts of foreign labor developments.

D. PRICE STATISTICS AND PRICE INDEXES

Wholesale prices. *Wholesale price indexes.* Monthly wholesale price indexes are compiled by the Bureau of Labor Statistics in the Department of Labor. An official monthly index has been prepared since 1902; the official series has been carried back to 1890, and the index has been extended, on an annual basis, back to 1720 by combining it with indexes from other sources. A comprehensive revision of the index was introduced in January 1952, based on approximately 5,000 price quotations for about 2,000 commodities.

The index is designed to measure price changes—that is, the general rate and direction of the composite of price movements in primary markets, and the specific rates and directions of price movements for individual commodities or groups of commodities. The price data used are those which apply at the primary market level—i.e., the first important commercial transaction for each commodity. Most of the quotations are for selling prices of representative manufacturers or producers, or prices quoted on organized exchanges. The weights represent the net selling values in the weight-base reference period. Sales of military goods, goods sold at retail by the producer, and interplant transfers are excluded from the weighting pattern. From 1947 through 1954 the weights were based primarily on data from the 1947 industrial censuses. Adjustments were made in January 1955 to aline the major group weight totals with the 1952–53 average values. In January 1958 a major revision of the weighting structure was introduced, based on data from the 1954 industrial censuses. Weights based upon the 1958 censuses were introduced early in 1961. Data for Alaska and Hawaii were included. Weights based upon the 1963 censuses were introduced in January 1967.

With release of data for January

1962, the indexes were shifted to a new base (1957–59=100). Data which had previously been available for each series on the 1947–49 base are available on the new base from the earliest date for which they were published on the former base.

In addition to the comprehensive index, indexes are released each month for 14 major groups, such as farm products and processed foods and feeds; 81 subgroups, such as grains and cotton products; 241 product classes; and most of the individual series. The Bureau of Labor Statistics indexes for 23 other special commodity groups are issued regularly, including an index of prices of construction materials; a series describing price changes by stage of fabrication; a series of separate indexes for durable and nondurable goods. These auxiliary indexes are recombinations of the data in the comprehensive wholesale price index. Monthly average prices are also published for some of the items in the index.

Industry - sector price indexes. Monthly industry-sector prices indexes for selected industries (4-digit SIC) and product classes are compiled by the Bureau of Labor Statistics in the Department of Labor. Annual average indexes have been prepared beginning with data for 1957. Monthly indexes are available beginning with January 1965.

An industry-sector price index is a composite index, derived from several price series combined to match the economic activity of a specified industry or sector. The indexes are industrial output indexes. They measure average changes in prices of commodities produced by a particular industry as defined by the Standard Industrial Classification of the Bureau of the Budget. Industry-sector indexes are relevant to studies of economic growth,

productivity, and other types of analysis where the emphasis is on industrial structure as distinct from market or commodity-use classifications.

Retail prices. The Consumer Price Index, compiled by the Bureau of Labor Statistics in the Department of Labor, is a measure of changes in prices for a fixed quantity of goods and services purchased by families of urban wage earners and salaried clerical workers. The index is a price barometer, not a measure of changes in the total amount of money spent by city families for living expenses. The index is based upon prices for food, apparel, housing, transportation, and miscellaneous goods and services (such as movies, beauty parlor services, medical, and dental care).

The index was initiated during World War I for use in wage negotiations, particularly in shipbuilding centers. Coverage was gradually extended to additional cities throughout the country, and the indexes were computed back to 1913. The national index is available on a monthly basis from January 1913 to date.

Beginning with the January 1962 index, the Consumer Price Index was converted to the standard reference base period 1957–59=100. No other aspects of the weight structure or the city and item samples were changed in connection with the rebasing. Historical tables of monthly and annual price changes on the 1957–59 base, for the United States and 23 large metropolitan areas, are available upon request to the Bureau of Labor Statistics.

The most recent comprehensive revision of the Consumer Price Index was introduced in January 1964 and linked to the existing index to maintain the continuity of the series. The revised index is based upon price data for about 400 items collected in 56 metropolitan areas and smaller urban places from a list of retail stores and service establishments selected as representative of the types of outlets in which wage earner and salaried clerical workers make their purchases. In addition, price data are collected from public utilities, other federal and local government agencies, and on such items as physicians' and dentists' fees, hospital rates, college tuition, and funeral services. The 400 items included in the current index were selected by the Bureau of Labor Statistics as representative of the thousands of commodities and services purchased by wage earner and clerical worker families, as actually reported in a survey of consumer expenditures covering the years 1960 and 1961.

Price data are collected at intervals ranging from every month to every third month. For some goods and services—such as foods, utilities, public transit, and a few other important items—prices are collected every month in each of the 56 cities. All other items are priced every month in the 5 largest metropolitan areas (except for rent which is priced every second month) and every third month in the remaining 51 areas and cities. Pricing of these goods and services in the 51 areas and cities is conducted on a rotating basis so that prices are collected in about one third of the cities, in each size category in any one month. Prices for nearly all of the items included in the index are collected through personal visit by specially trained agents of the Bureau of Labor Statistics. Prices for a few items (e.g., public utility rates, newspapers) are collected by mail; for several others, data are collected from secondary sources.

In addition to the national index, separate indexes are published for the 22 largest metropolitan areas (those having a population in 1960 of 1 million or more) and for Honolulu. These indexes are published monthly for the five largest areas and quarterly for the remaining 18. (Monthly food indexes are published for all 23 areas). Five major group indexes (e.g., food, housing, apparel) and 23 subgroup indexes (e.g., dairy products, housefurnishings, personal care) are published for the national and each of the 23 city indexes. Twenty-one special group indexes (e.g., all commodities, services, new and used cars) are also published for the national index. Estimated average prices for individual food items are published for each of the 23 large metropolitan areas and for the 56 cities combined. Average retail prices for various fuels and electricity are also published for each of these 23 areas and for the 56 cities combined.

At the present time average prices for other items are not available. Indexes for selected individual commodities and services (except foods and fuels) and for selected minor classes of related items are published quarterly. These indexes are based on prices reported in all cities in which prices are collected for the respective item. The revised index structure incorporates a replicated (double) sample of items as part of a sampling design aimed at estimating the index sampling error, but not every item is priced in every city.

Prices paid by farmers. The Statistical Reporting Service of the Department of Agriculture prepares an index, as of the 15th of each month, of prices paid by farmers for commodities and services used in family living and farm production, including interest on mortgages secured by farm real estate, taxes on farm real estate, and farm wage rates. The family living component is based upon prices paid by farmers for food and tobacco, clothing, household operations, household furnishings, building materials used in houses, and automobiles and automobile supplies. The farm production section is based upon prices paid by farmers for feed, livestock purchased, motor vehicles, motor supplies, farm machinery, farm equipment and supplies, building and fencing materials, fertilizer, and seed. Indexes of interest payable per acre on indebtedness secured by farm real estate, taxes payable per acre on farm real estate, and cash wages for hired labor are combined with the indexes of family living and farm production to form the comprehensive Index of Prices Paid by Farmers, Including Interest, Taxes, and Farm Wage Rates, legally defined as the "parity index."

The weights used for combining prices of individual items into group indexes represent the quantities of goods and services purchased by farmers during the year 1955. The index was revised using the new weights back to September 1952, and linked to the old index at that point.

The Index of Prices Paid by Farmers was first published in 1928. Annual indexes are available back to 1910 and quarterly indexes (March, June, September, December) to 1923, monthly indexes are available from 1937 to date. The index is used in calculating parity prices for farm products each month, pursuant to the Agricultural Adjustment Act of 1938, as amended.

The number of items included in the index has been increased from time to time as price series for items important in farmers' purchasing patterns have become available. The index of prices paid for items used in

family living includes about 250 price series for commodities and services, and the index for items used in farm production includes about the same number, with about 40 series being used in both indexes. Commodity prices are obtained by reports from both chain and independent stores.

Independent stores report by mail to field offices of the Statistical Reporting Service, quarterly for most surveys, and State average prices are calculated for each item. Feedstores report prices to field offices each month. Chainstores report each month, directly to the Washington office of the Statistical Reporting Service, and State average prices are also calculated from these reports. The chainstore reports are obtained mostly by mail, although prices are enumerated each month in a limited number of areas. For the quarterly months (March, June, September, December), independent store prices are combined with chainstore prices to obtain weighted national average prices, which are used in computing subgroup, group, and the overall parity indexes for these months. For the interquarterly months the changes shown by the chainstore prices are used, along with regular monthly data on prices paid for feed and livestock, to calculate monthly changes in the index.

Data on average costs of electricity and telephone services are obtained in an annual survey of farmers. Data on farm real estate taxes and interest charges are developed annually from special surveys. The wage rate index is based on information collected in a quarterly mail survey of farmers.

In addition to the monthly group indexes, 15 subgroup indexes, based on weighted average prices at independent and chainstores, are published quarterly. Quarterly average prices are also published currently for most items for the United States and, for some of the more important items, by States and for nine geographic areas.

Prices received by farmers. A monthly index of prices received by farmers is also published by the Statistical Reporting Service. This index is based on average prices received by farmers for products sold at local markets, or at the point to which farmers deliver their products. Mid-month prices of commodities sold by farmers were first collected in 1908 for crops, and in 1910 for livestock and livestock products. A comprehensive index was first published in 1921, with monthly series available from January 1910. Prices are collected either monthly or on a season-average basis for a large number of agricultural commodities. They are obtained from about 8,000 correspondents in the following broad classifications: (1) farm produce dealers at local shipping points; (2) country mill and elevator operators; (3) managers of local creameries and milk receiving stations; (4) cooperative marketing organizations; (5) country merchants; (6) country bankers; and (7) well-informed farmers. Average prices for most of the individual items are available by States, geographic regions, and for the United States.

The current index is based on prices of 55 individual commodities which account for approximately 93 percent of total cash receipts from sales of farm products. These prices are weighted by average annual quantities sold during the period 1954–57 to form group indexes for food grains; feed grains and hay; cotton; tobacco; oil-bearing crops; fruit; commercial vegetables; potatoes, sweetpotatoes, and dry edible beans; meat animals; dairy products; poultry and eggs; and wool. The group indexes are combined by weighting each group by the percentage of cash receipts which the group accounted for in 1953–57. The total index of prices received by farmers is compared with the index of prices paid, including interest, taxes, and wage rates, to determine the parity price position of agricultural commodities in general.

For a semitechnical description of the index of prices received by farmers and of the index of prices paid by farmers including interest, taxes, and farm wage rates see the April–July 1959 issue of *Agricultural Economics Research.*

Information on wholesale prices of agricultural commodities is discussed below, under "Marketing of agricultural products."

Implicit price deflators. In some cases prices indexes are not available directly but may be obtained indirectly as implicit deflators. For example, series on the gross national product and its components are published in both current and constant dollars in the *National Income and Product Accounts of the United States, 1929–1965,* a supplement to the *Survey of Current Business.* The major implicit deflators are also published in supplementary tables. The procedure used in obtaining the constant dollar estimates is generally to divide the components of the current dollar GNP by appropriate price indexes, utilizing as fine a product breakdown as possible. Implicit deflators as indexes of price changes in total GNP and its components can thus be obtained by dividing the constant dollar estimates into the corresponding current dollar figures.

Similarly, industry price deflators of the GNP originating in its component industries may be constructed by dividing the current dollar gross product estimates by corresponding physical volume measures (see GNP by Major Industries, *Survey of Current Business*, October 1962).

E. PRODUCTION STATISTICS

Censuses are conducted periodically which obtain data on the production of farms, manufacturing establishments, and mines. Data are also obtained on the basis of less complete coverage in each of these fields at more frequent intervals, in order to keep up to date the information obtained from the complete enumeration.

Manufacturing production. Current and benchmark statistics on manufacturing activity collected by the Bureau of the Census consist of four basic parts: (1) a quinquennial census of manufactures; (2) an annual survey of manufactures conducted for the four intervening years; (3) a monthly industrywide survey of manufacturing sales, orders, and inventories, and (4) monthly, quarterly and annual Current Industrial Reports dealing with production, shipments, and inventories of specific commodities.

The first census of manufactures was taken in 1810, covering activity in 1809, and censuses were taken at 10-year intervals thereafter (with the exception of 1830) through 1900, covering 1899. For the years 1904 through 1919 the censuses were taken at 5-year intervals, and from 1921 through 1939 at 2-year intervals. The census was suspended during World War II, but was taken for 1947.

Census legislation enacted in 1948, as amended in 1964, calls for complete censuses of manufactures, mineral industries, and business (wholesale, retail, and service trades) to be taken at 5-year intervals, covering activity during the years ending in 2 and 7. Censuses of manufactures were conducted covering 1954, 1958, 1963 and 1967. The next census is scheduled to cover activity in 1972.

Since 1939, censuses of manufactures have been conducted entirely by mail, based on lists obtained from Government administrative records supplemented by establishment lists for larger companies obtained in pre-census mail canvasses. Beginning with the 1967 census, data for companies with less than 10 employees were largely developed from administrative records of Internal Revenue Service and Social Security Administration rather than through direct collection of reports.

The 1967 census of manufactures obtained information on the quantity and value of products made and materials used, value added by manufacture, employment, payrolls, supplemental labor costs, capital expenditures, value of fixed assets, rental payments, fuels and electric energy consumed, and related data. Results of the census are published in a series of separate industry, area, and subject bulletins and in a series of bound volumes.

Volume I of the 1963 census shows summary statistics and reports by subject such as size of establishments, expenditures for plant and equipment, materials consumed, and concentration ratios. Volume II is a consolidation of reports for 80 groups of related industries and shows detailed information on individual industries and proucts. Volume III shows for each State and its important metropolitan areas and counties, general statistics, value added, and capital expenditures for each of the industries or industry groups of consequence in that State or in its smaller areas.

An essential part of the legislation changing the frequency of the manufactures census from a 2-year to a 5-year basis was the initiation of an annual survey of manufactures to carry forward key measures of manufacturing activity for intercensal years. In meeting the needs for census-type statistics in the interval between the full-scale censuses, the annual surveys provide up-to-date measures of the dollar value of shipments by product class, number of employees, payrolls, man-hours worked, value added by manufacture, cost of materials consumed, inven.ories, and new capital expenditures. The annual survey results are based on a sample of approximately 60,000 manufacturing establishments, including all larger plants and a representative sample of the smaller ones. Except for census years, this annual survey has been conducted continuously since 1949.

A basic monthly survey of manfacturers' sales, orders, and inventories is conducted by the Bureau of the Census covering a sample of manufacturing companies, including most of the larger firms; the data obtained constitute a key indicator of current activity in manufacturing. This survey is benchmarked to the annual survey of manufactures.

The Bureau of the Census collects and publishes monthly, quarterly, and annual data on production, shipments, orders, and inventories for approximately 5,000 important manufactured commodities in the Current Industrial Reports series. This series consists of about 100 separate reports representing virtually all major manufacturing areas such as textile mill products, apparel, pulp and paper, primary metals, and machinery.

The Office of Business Economics in the Department of Commerce conducts a quarterly survey of sales expectations and inventory anticipations by manufacturers.

Specialized information on industrial production is also assembled by other Federal agencies. The Department of Defense, for example, issues annual and more current reports on defense contracts. Data on alcoholic beverages and industrial alcohol are published by the Internal Revenue Service of the Treasury Department, and data on organic chemicals by the U.S. Tariff Commission.

The Business and Defense Services Administration conducts extensive studies and analyses in broad areas of the American economy and publishes the findings in various *Industry Reports* and *Outlook Studies*. Special attention has been given to the preparation of studies of export potential and the impact of imports on business and employment. Available data from other Federal agencies are used in carrying out these activities.

Mineral production. Censuses of mineral production were taken approximately every 10 years from 1840 through 1940, covering activity in the preceding year. The census legislation enacted in 1948 calls for censuses of mineral industries every fifth year. The first mineral industries census since that covering 1939 was taken for the year 1954 others cover the years 1958, 1963 and 1967; and the next will be taken to cover the year 1972.

Data collection procedures for censuses of mineral industries are the same as for censuses of manufactures described above, except that beginning with the 1967 census administrative records are used in lieu of direct reporting from companies with fewer than five employees instead of ten.

The 1967 census of mineral industries collected information on production of all minerals in terms of quantity and value; number of operating companies, number of mines, quarries, and oil wells; persons engaged; salaries and wages and supplemental labor costs; man-hours; contract work; supplies, minerals received for preparation, and fuel used; expenditures for development of mineral properties, buildings, machinery, and equipment; and value of fixed assets. For most of the mineral industries, data obtained in the censuses are classified by State, and selected statistics are presented by county.

Preliminary results of the censuses are published in separate reports giving summary data by State and industry and data on specific mineral industries. The final results are also published in separate reports as well as in two bound volumes, one presenting a general summary and industry statistics and the other giving State and county statistics.

The main source of current statistical information on minerals is the Bureau of Mines in the Department of the Interior, which collects annual and periodic statistics for all minerals. The data on annual production of minerals are collected under cooperative agreements between the Bureau of Mines and some 40 States and Puerto Rico.

The annual statistics are published in the *Minerals Yearbook,* which has been issued under varying titles each year since 1882. The Yearbook gives annual data on quantity and value of all minerals produced in the United States, as well as on mineral imports and exports, prices, employment and injuries in the mineral industries, consumption and inventory of important minerals, foreign mineral production, and trade. The Yearbook is issued in three volumes—minerals, metals, and fuels; area reports, domestic; and area reports international—each composed of separate chapters on individual minerals, metals, fuels, states, or countries. The chapters are available as separate reports, usually in advance of publication of the complete volume.

For a number of the more important minerals, metals, and fuels, the Bureau of Mines publishes weekly, monthly, and quarterly data on production, consumption, shipments, and inventories. These data are published in separate releases, and some also appear later in Yearbook volumes.

The Bureau publishes annually the Commodity Data Summaries, released initially in February 1963, which highlight (1) basic data on the domestic industry, production of minerals, metals, and fuels, stockpile information, import sources, tariff, depletion allowance, government incentive and procurement, world mine production and reserves; and (2) various economic factors.

A volume is published approximately every 5 years under the title *Mineral Facts and Problems,* the latest issue being for 1965. In addition to a review of technological trends, statistical data are given on size, organization, and geographic distribution of the industry; reserves; production, consumption, and foreign trade; prices, wage, and costs; employment and productivity; taxes and tariffs; and transportation.

Agricultural production. A complete census of agriculture has been taken every 10th year since 1840, and every 5th year beginning in 1925. The most recent census of agriculture, taken by the Bureau of the Census in 1964, collected information on acreage in farms, acreage of crops and other land uses, production and sales of agricultural products, tenure, race, age, and years on farm. In addition, information was obtained from all large farms and from a 20-percent sample of all other farms on farm labor, expenditures, facilities and equipment, value of land and buildings, mortgages, off-farm work, nonfarm income, and a few minor items. Another census of agriculture will be taken in 1969.

Current statistics on agricultural production are collected primarily by the Statistical Reporting Service in the Department of Agriculture. Continuous series of acreage and production of major crops and of livestock inventories extend back to 1866. In most cases the estimates are made on the basis of sample data reported in mailed questionnaires by farmers, processors, and others, adjusted to benchmark data available from the censuses of agriculture or other more frequent surveys. The Statistical Reporting Service is also using collection methods based on personal enumeration for major crop and livestock items in June and December and measurement surveys on sample plots for estimating yields of major crops during the growing year.

In March of each year the Statistical Reporting Service receives reports on the number of acres farmers intend to plant for 17 principal crops and a wide variety of minor crops. Data from these reports are used to estimate the total number of acres intended to be planted for each of the principal crops. In June, reports are obtained from farmers on acreage actually planted and preliminary estimates of production are prepared for about 20 major crops. Thereafter, the acreage estimates, along with monthly reports on the condition of crops, are used in making forecasts of production throughout the growing season. Monthly forecasts are also made of fruit production. (For some of the earlier crops, such as winter wheat, the monthly forecasts begin earlier than July.)

At the end of the growing season, the Statistical Reporting Service receives reports on the number of acres harvested, yield per acre, and production for most crops, including field crops, vegetables, fruits, and nuts. From these reports it prepares estimates of production for approximately 135 crops, on a national, regional, and State basis. The Statistical Reporting Service also makes estimates of livestock inventories as of January 1, of the spring and fall pig crops, and monthly estimates throughout the year of livestock slaughter and production of dairy and poultry products. Weekly reports are issued on weather-crop conditions, butter and cheese production, and chick placements for broiler production.

Yearly changes in the gross volume of crop production are measured in an index of volume of crop production which is computed from production data for the crop year. All production is included, regardless of its final disposition. This index is published monthly from August through December in *Crop Production*. Year-to-year changes in average level of yields of 28 crops are measured in an index of crop yields per acre harvested, subdivided into yield indexes of field and fruit crops. The series is published in the annual summary of *Crop Production*, issued each December.

The Economic Research Service in

cooperation with the Statistical Reporting Service estimates the total volume of farm output by combining crop and livestock production. These index series are published in an annual report entitled *Changes in Farm Production and Efficiency*.

Detailed data on the quantity and value of fishery products are published by the Bureau of Commercial Fisheries in the Department of the Interior.

Index of industrial production.

The Board of Governors of the Federal Reserve System compiles a monthly index of industrial production, with 1957–59 as 100. There are 207 monthly series, based on figures collected by Government agencies and by various trade organizations. The series are all in physical quantity terms representing output in the manufacturing, mining, and utility sectors of the economy.

The individual series are combined on the basis of the value added in 1957, converted to the 1957–59 base period. These series are combined following two systems of classification. One is on the basis of market groupings composed of (1) final products, which are further subdivided into consumer goods and equipment for business and government; and (2) materials, with about a dozen separately published components. The other system of classification is on the basis of industry groupings, such as primary metals, chemicals, and printing, which permit comparisons with similarly classified data on employment and the like. The industry grouping has as its principal categories durable manufactures, nondurable manufactures, mining, and utilities.

Durable manufactures account for 48 percent of the total index weight and include 11 of the SIC major groups covering primary metals, fabricated metal products, nonelectrical machinery, electrical machinery, transportation equipment, instruments, ordnance, stone, clay and glass, lumber, furniture, and miscellaneous manufactures. It also includes measures of the manufacturing activities of the Department of Defense.

Nondurable manufactures account for 38 percent of the total index weight and include 10 major groups covering food and beverages, tobacco, textiles, apparel, paper, printing, chemicals (including representation of the manufacturing establishments owned by the Atomic Energy Commission), petroleum, rubber and plastics, and leather.

Mining activities account for 8 percent of the index covering coal and metal mining, crude oil and natural gas extraction, oil and gas well drilling, and production of sand, clay, and other nonmetallic minerals. Utility output of electricity and gas includes both private and government-owned establishments, and accounts for 5 percent of the value in the 1957–59 base period.

In the market grouping of the individual series, consumer goods accounted for 32 percent of the total value during the base period, subdivided into automotive products, home goods, apparel, and consumer staples. The equipment series accounted for 15 percent of the total in 1957–59, divided between business equipment and an unpublished defense equipment category. The materials component accounts for 53 percent of the index base and consists of two major categories, durable goods materials and nondurable materials.

The industrial production index and its components are adjusted for the number of working days and for seasonal variation. These adjustments facilitate analysis of cyclical movements in analyzing economic change.

The index of industrial production for current months is published in detail in the monthly release, G. 12.3, Business Indexes and in partial detail in the *Federal Reserve Bulletin* as well as other current statistical publications such as the *Survey of Current Business*. Figures are available in convenient form in the biennial statistical supplement, *Business Statistics,* of the *Survey of Current Business*.

F. DISTRIBUTION STATISTICS

Wholesale, retail, and service trades. A wide range of statistics on wholesale and retail trade and the service trades is published every 5 years in the quinquennial census of business. Estimates of a number of key series, such as national estimates of wholesale and retail sales and inventories and accounts receivable and selected service trade receipts, are published by the Department of Commerce for intervening months and years and are kept up to date currently.

The Bureau of the Census also publishes a weekly series for retail sales by major kinds of retail business for the United States and monthly retail sales estimates for regions, divisions, and the larger States and standard metropolitan statistical areas. Department store sales figures are published monthly for standard metropolitan statistical areas, cities, and other local areas.

The quinquennial censuses, which provide a much wider variety of information than can be collected at reasonable cost at frequent intervals, serve several functions. In addition to providing broad national measures for such subjects as sales, payrolls, and employment for a great many kinds of retail, wholesale, and service establishments, the censuses obtain data for smaller geographic areas—States, standard metropolitan statistical areas, counties, and incorporated urban places. Statistics also are presented for central business districts of the larger cities, as well as for the more important retail centers in the standard metropolitan statistical areas in which these cities are located. Another important function of the census is to provide up-to-date listings of firms and establishments by size and location. These enable Census statisticians to design area probability samples of businesses which are used to estimate monthly retail and wholesale sales and related variables.

Censuses of business, including retail and wholesale trade and services, were first authorized by legislation passed in 1929, which directed that they be taken every 10 years as part of the decennial censuses. Complete censuses of business were taken in 1930 and 1940, covering activity in the preceding year, and in additional special censuses of business were taken covering the years 1933 and 1935. Legislation enacted in 1948, as amended in 1964, covering activity in the years ending in 2 and 7, directed that the censuses of manufactures and mineral industries, and other businesses be taken at 5-year intervals. Censuses of business were taken covering 1948, 1954, 1958. 1963, and 1967. The next census is scheduled to cover activity in 1972.

Before 1954, data for the censuses of business were collected by personal enumeration. Beginning with 1954 the censuses have been conducted by mail. Wholesale trade establishments without paid employees have been excluded from the scope of the censuses since 1954. Beginning then, also, data for retail trade and selected service establishments without paid employees were obtained from tax records of the Internal Revenue Service. In the 1967 censuses, Internal Revenue Service and Social Security Administration records were used in lieu of direct reporting from small retail, wholesale, and service trade establishments, the size varying with kind of business.

The business census volumes contain detailed information on sales, number of establishments, employment and payrolls, size of firm, and legal form of organization for each of a large number of different kinds of business. Volumes I, IV, and VI of the 1963 Census contain summary U.S. statistics for retail trade, wholesale trade, and service establishments, respectively. Area statistics for retail trade were contained in Volumes II and III, wholesale trade in V, and service establishments in VII. Volume I also contains sales by merchandise lines for retail employers; these data had been collected in 1948 but not in 1954 or 1958. Sales by commodity line have been published for wholesale trade in all censuses since 1948 and are published in Volume IV for 1963. Most of the data contained in the business census volumes have also been published as separate reports.

Area statistics include tabulations of business characteristics for each State, for 217 standard metropolitan statistical areas (in 1963), for all counties, and for incorporated cities and villages having a population of 2,500 (5,000 in wholesale trade publications) or more inhabitants. More detailed information was published for counties and cities with a significant business population. Since 1954, reports were published for the central business district of large metropolitan areas (116 in 1963), along with a U.S. summary; tabulations were also made in 1958 and 1963 for other major retail centers in the SMSA's in which these cities are located (972 such retail centers in 1963). These data are published in Volume III for 1963, as well as in a separate report for each standard metropolitan statistical area.

For wholesale trade, the Census collects some information which it does not gather for retail trade, sometimes because it is less relevant for retail trade, and sometimes because it is obtained by other means for retail trade—for example, receivables and bad debt losses and sales by class of customer.

The current business statistics program covers monthly estimates of retail and wholesale sales and inventories, retail accounts receivable, selected service trade receipts, and weekly estimates of retail sales. Estimates of the dollar volume of sales each month for the United States for all retail stores, and for such major types of business as grocery stores, department stores, apparel stores, furniture and homefurnishings stores, appliance dealers, lumber, building and hardware dealers, auto dealers, auto accessory stores, gasoline stations, are included in the *Monthly Retail Trade Report.* Estimates are shown on both an unadjusted basis and adjusted for trading days and seasonal variation. Limited geographic area data are included, as well as separate national statistics for firms having 11 or more outlets. Accounts receivable data, including separate estimates for charge accounts and installment accounts, are included.

The monthly retail trade estimates are based on a probability sample. All firms with 11 or more stores and all very large stores (as identified in previous censuses) are represented directly in the estimates each month. All remaining stores are represented by stores located in 233 Census sample areas. The large stores in these sample areas are canvassed each month. Smaller stores in a subsample of small land segments in the Census sample areas are personally enumerated, with a different set of about 2,000 land segments used for each of the 12 months of the year. New businesses, both large and small, located in these land segments are identified during the canvass of these segments and are included in the estimate.

This stratified probability sample has the advantage of permitting calculations of the probable range of error arising from the use of a sample rather than a complete enumeration. However, it should be recognized that there may be other types of errors (e.g., response errors, processing errors, etc.) in the estimates which affect their accuracy.

Statistics on department store sales are published monthly for approximately 200 standard metropolitan statistical areas, cities, and other local areas, based on a complete canvass of department stores in these areas. These statistics are included in the *Monthly Retail Trade Report* and are also published separately in the report *Monthly Department Store Sales in Selected Areas*.

Weekly estimates of retail trade are available starting in 1962. These are drawn from a small subsample of the monthly sample and are less reliable for this reason as well as for the reason that the weekly figures are based on estimates, rather than book records, to a greater extent than the monthly figures subsequently reported. Nevertheless, sales estimates for weeks and part weeks are used as a basis, in part, for advance monthly sales estimates, issued about 10 days after the end of the month.

Yearend inventory estimates are obtained from an annual retail trade survey, which utilizes a larger sample than the monthly retail survey. Monthly estimates of retail inventories are obtained by linking estimates of change to these annual benchmarks. Retail and wholesale inventory estimates are published in the release called *Business Sales and Inventories* and in the *Survey of Current Business*.

The Monthly Wholesale Trade Report furnishes national dollar volume estimates of sales and inventories of merchant wholesalers for a number of different kinds of business. Limited geographic division data are also shown. The estimates are based on a probability sample of firms, including a panel of 1,000 very large firms canvassed each month and 4 rotating panels each containing 4,000 smaller firms which report every fourth month. National estimates are issued both on an unadjusted basis and adjusted for seasonal variations and trading day differences.

The *Monthly Selected Service Receipts Report* provides national estimates of receipts of selected service trade establishments by major kind-of-business group. These estimates are based on a probability sample of firms, including a panel of about 2,000 large businesses canvassed each month and service trade establishments located in the sample of land segments enumerated for retail sales data (see above).

Marketing of agricultural products. Through its market news reports, the Consumer and Marketing Service in the Department of Agriculture publishes current information on the marketing of agricultural commodities, including cotton, wool, livestock, meats, dairy and poultry products, fruits and vegetables, grain, tobacco, and naval stores. These reports vary in frequency, kinds of data contained, and markets covered for different commodities and different seasons of the year. The kinds of information published in various market news reports include data on quality and prices of important farm products, arrivals in specific markets, commodity movements, supply and demand, and other market conditions. Daily reports are issued in bulletin form at important marketing centers and major shipping areas, and made available to press, radio and television. Often these reports are also mimeographed and mailed to those requesting them. Many of the reports which are issued daily or weekly by the field offices or the Washington headquarters of the Consumer and Marketing Service are summarized in monthly, quarterly, or annual reports.

Daily market news reports, with monthly and annual summaries, are also published for fishery products. These reports are issued by the Bureau of Commercial Fisheries in the Department of the Interior.

Monthly, quarterly, and annual data on the marketing and transportation of farm products are also compiled by the Economic Research Service in the Department of Agriculture. A quarterly report on *The Marketing and Transportation Situation* presents a summary, with statistical tables, of such data as price spreads between the farmer and the consumer, analysis of these spreads, marketing costs and profits, consumer expenditures for farm foods, and the share of the consumer's dollar received by the farmer for farm products. Data for the past year and comparisons with preceding years are presented in the annual volume of *Agricultural Statistics*.

G. TRANSPORTATION, PUBLIC UTILITY, AND COMMUNICATION STATISTICS

Transportation. Transportation data are collected and published primarily by regulatory agencies and agencies with administrative responsibilities for some aspects of transportation. The Bureau of the Census takes a census of transportation and conducts a continuing program of statistics relating to waterborne commerce.

The Department of Transportation was established in 1967. Through its Federal Aviation Administration, Federal Highway Administration, Federal Railroad Administration, and the U.S. Coast Guard, a wide variety of statistical activities are carried on which antedate the creation of the Department.

The Federal Aviation Administration publishes data on airports, air-

ways, air navigation facilities, and utilization of registered aircraft. The Federal Highway Administration publishes data on motor vehicle registrations, fuel consumption, characteristics, accidents and safety; and on traffic characteristics, mileage of public roads and streets, and highway costs and financing. The Federal Railroad Administration publishes data on railroad accidents, locomotives, signals, safety appliances, and hours of service. The U.S. Coast Guard publishes data on recreational boating accidents. The National Transportation Safety Board publishes data on civil aviation accidents.

The Interstate Commerce Commission publishes data on the traffic, operations, equipment, finances, and employment of interstate railroads; common and contract motor carriers (both property and passenger); coastwise, intercoastal, and inland waterways water carriers; oil pipeline companies; and freight forwarders. In addition, detailed statistics are published annually on the tonnage and revenue originated and terminated by rail, motor, and water carriers under Commission jurisdiction. These do not show point-to-point movements.

The Civil Aeronautics Board publishes data on the traffic, operations, and finances of commercial airlines.

The Bureau of the Census publishes vessel shipping statistics, including the number and registered tons of vessels entering and clearing U.S. ports and the value and shipping weight of import, export, and in-transit commodities. The statistics on number and registered tons of vessels are based on entrance and clearance forms prepared by local offices of the Bureau of Customs. Cargo statistics are compiled from import entries and export declarations filed by importers or exporters with collectors of customs at the time of import or export. These statistics are presented in commodity detail by port of loading and unloading, by dry cargo or tanker, and by flag of vessel (United States or foreign), and for dry cargo by type of service (liner or irregular). In 1962, statistical series were initiated showing value and shipping weight of airborne imports and exports.

The Corps of Engineers of the Army publishes data on cargo movements along the principal waterways and among the ports of the United States and on U.S.-flag transportation lines and their vessels operating in domestic trade.

The Maritime Administration publishes data on vessel utilization and performance, merchant fleets of the United States and other countries employed in Great Lakes and deep sea shipping, merchant ships built during recent periods, and collective bargaining in the U.S. maritime industry.

Census of Transportation. The first Census of Transportation was taken in 1963, the second in 1967, and subsequent ones are scheduled by law at five-year intervals. In order to avoid unnecessary duplication, the Census collects data only on aspects of transportation that are not reported by Federal regulatory or other agencies. For that reason, the program consists of a series of special surveys. These surveys include:

(1) A National Travel Survey: Data on national and regional travel by such characteristics as means of transportation, purpose of trip, duration, distance of trip, size of party, lodgings used, and origin and destination; also data on travel frequency of households and persons by socio-economic and travel characteristics.

(2) A Truck Inventory and Use Survey: Data on the number and characteristics of the Nation's trucks, such as major use, annual vehicle miles, gross vehicle weight, year model, body type and load length or capacity, vehicle size class, single unit or combination and axle arrangement, size of truck fleet, type of fuel, area of operation, and maintenance responsibility. Data are presented for each State, for Census divisions, and for the United States.

(3) A Commodity Transportation Survey: Data on the intercity shipments of commodities by manufacturers are presented in three series:

Commodity Series. Statistics on the flow of commodities in terms of the transportation commodity classification (TCC) showing tons and ton-miles of shipments by means of transport, length of haul, weight of shipment, origin and destination

Shipper Series. Manufacturing establishments are grouped into 25 shipper groups and 86 shipper classes or sub-groups. Data on tons and ton-miles are shown by means of transport, length of haul, origin, destination, commodity, and size of shipment for each group or class.

Area Series. Data on the flow of commodities from manufacturing plants located in each of 25 major industrial areas (called Production Areas") and major industrial States. Data on tons and ton-miles of commodities originated in each area are classified by weight of shipment, means of transport, length of haul, and destination area of shipment.

Public utilities. Statistics on various segments of the electric power and natural gas industries are collected and published by the Federal Power Commission. In general, these statistics cover utilities which are subject to regulation by the Federal Power Commission—i.e., privately-owned, state, and municipal utilities engaged in gas or electric service in interstate commerce—and in some cases all electric utilities whether privately or publicly owned and whether or not subject to regulation.

The Commission publishes various monthly and annual reports on the operations, equipment and construction, production, rates, and finances of the electric and gas utilities, as detailed fully in Part III of this booklet. In addition, the Commission issues periodic press releases showing related monthly and quarterly statistics. All reports submitted to the Federal Power Commission by electric utilities and interstate natural gas companies are available for public inspection.

Communications. Telephone, telegraph, and radio and television broadcasting industries are subject to regulation by the Federal Communications Commission. The Commission publishes an annual statistical report with detailed financial and operating data on the communications industry in the United States (telephone, wire telegraph, ocean cable, and radiotelegraph). It also publishes detailed annual reports for radio and television stations, and quarterly reports for telephone and telegraph carriers.

H. CONSTRUCTION AND HOUSING STATISTICS

Construction. Among the more important Federal statistics on construction are the monthly estimates of the value of new construction put in place. (Structural additions and alterations are considered to be new construction, but maintenance and repairs are not.) This is a measure of the extent to which new construction is currently contributing toward overall economic activity. These estimates are prepared by the Bureau of the Census of the U.S. Department of Commerce. The Census Bureau is now engaged in a long-range program of revising statistical concepts and methods. Since 1960 the Bureau has made a number of revisions affecting housing units, residential additions and alterations, private nonresidential buildings, public utilities, and State and local government construction. Further revisions of these and other categories of construction are planned.

For privately financed nonresidential building construction such as stores, warehouses, and factories, the Bureau of the Census bases its estimates largely on a monthly sample survey of project owners and contractors supplemented by construction contract award information supplied by the F. W. Dodge Company. These data are processed to reflect the value of work put in place each month. The estimates of public utility construction are derived from data reported by the Interstate Commerce Commission, the Federal Power Commission and other Federal regulatory agencies, and by private associations such as the American Gas Association, the Edison Electric Institute, and the American Telephone and Telegraph Co.

For publicly financed construction, data are obtained on projects undertaken by the Federal Government directly from the various Federal agencies. Estimates of State and local governmental construction activity are based on a quarterly sample survey of State and local governments. Construction expenditures data are collected and adjusted to provide estimates of the value of work put in place each month.

As an adjunct to the survey of housing starts, a survey of the sales of new private, nonfarm one-family homes was initiated in 1962 and is conducted by the Bureau of the Census under the sponsorship of the Department of Housing and Urban Development. The data cover number of homes built for sale, number sold and unsold, sales prices, types of financing, time interval from start and completion to sale, and physical characteristics of homes. Summary data are released monthly with more detailed statistics provided quarterly. Annual reports contain comprehensive financial information about sales transactions and extensive details about the physical characteristics of all new homes (those built for sale, those built for the exclusive use of the owner, etc.).

Monthly data on building construction authorized by local building permits, including residential and nonresidential building and additions and alterations, are prepared by the Bureau of the Census. The series give the number and permit valuation of new housing units and the permit valuation of various types of nonresidential buildings. Data are provided for major geographical areas and by States and selected standard metropolitan statistical areas. The number of new housing units covered by building permits is also published monthly for each of some 3,000 areas. Data are provided for each of the more than 12,000 places annually. In addition, statistics are compiled on contracts awarded for public housing units.

For Federal construction, information on the value of contracts awarded is published monthly for both residential and nonresidential construction. Contract award data are also presented for State and local highway construction. Contract award data for private construction are not compiled by the Federal Government but are reported by the F. W. Dodge Company.

Beginning with 1960, a continuing quarterly survey of residential alterations and repairs has been conducted by the Bureau of the Census. All residential units are covered, single family as well as multifamily, public and private. The survey covers expenditures for additions, alterations, maintenance, repairs, and replacements. The statistics provide separate figures for owner-occupants and nonresident owners. Distributions by major types of work as well as by selected household and property characteristics are also made available.

Housing. The first census of housing of the United States was taken in 1940. In the 1930 and earlier decennial censuses of population a few items on housing had been included, such as tenure, rent, and value of owned homes. In a law approved in 1949, a census of housing became an integral part of the regular decennial census program.

Although varying in some details, the information obtained in the censuses of 1940 and 1950 were substantially the same. Data were provided on type of structure, year built, tenure, color of occupants, number of rooms, persons per room, condition, rent or value, and facilities (such as water, toilet, bath, kitchen sink, refrigeration, and heating). In 1940, mortgage data were obtained only for owner-occupied homes. In 1950, mortgage data were collected, on a sample basis, for both owner- and renter-occupied homes.

Because of the social and economic significance of housing and the extent of change which was believed to have occurred after 1950, the Bureau of the Census was authorized to take a national housing inventory in 1956. Data were collected for the first time on the components of change in the housing inventory: i.e., the number of units added through new construction, conversion, and change from nonresidential to residential use; and those lost through demolition, merger, and change from residential to nonresidential use. The survey also obtained housing information on characteristics similar to that in the census of 1950. Data were obtained from a sample survey and are available for the United States, the four regions, and nine selected standard metropolitan statistical areas.

The 1960 Census of Housing contained a number of modifications in response to changing statistical needs in current housing programs. It included in 1960 a measure and description of the gross changes in the housing inventory, similar to the "components of change" program undertaken in the 1956 national housing inventory. A second change was the broadening of the coverage of private living accommodations to include units that were omitted from the 1950 Housing Census. Among the new items included in the 1960 census were: type of trailer, presence of basement in structure, number of bedrooms, number of bathrooms, elevator in structure, duration of vacancy, year occupancy started, hot water, heating fuel, source of water supply, method of sewage disposal, number of automobiles for personal use, and five equipment items—air conditioning, home food freezer, clothes washing machine, clothes dryer, and telephone. Most of the new items and some of those previously covered were collected on a sample basis. In addition, separate data were provided which presented cross-tabulations of housing and household characteristics of senior citizens.

Information on housing vacancies has been collected quarterly since early 1955 by the Bureau of the Census in connection with its current population survey. The housing vacancy rates are prepared for the United States, the four regions and inside-outside standard metropolitan statistical areas. The data are provided on type of vacancy and the condition of the unit—whether for rent, for sale, held off the market, or other status; whether for year-round or seasonal use; and whether in sound, deteriorating, or dilapidated condition. For the United States, and inside-outside standard metropolitan statistical areas, characteristics are provided for rental and sale vacancies—number of rooms, number of bedrooms, number of housing units in the structure, duration of vacancy, year structure built, and the sales price or monthly rent. Some of these characteristics are cross-tabulated by sales price or monthly rent.

Data on housing rents are collected by the Bureau of Labor Statistics for its Consumer Price Index. Data concerning housing covered by various insured or direct loan programs are available from the agencies administering those programs: Department of Housing and Urban Development and its constituent agencies, the Veterans Administration, and the Federal Home Loan Bank Board.

I. FINANCIAL REPORTS OF BUSINESS

Annual data on the finances of private business enterprises, based on Federal income tax returns, are published by the Internal Revenue Service of the Treasury Department in the *Statistics of Income* reports. Tabulations of selected items of financial data for sole proprietorships, partnerships, and corporations are published annually in the *U.S. Business Tax Returns* volume. Comprehensive annual financial data are published for corporations in a separate *Statistics of Income* volume which contains detailed income statement and balance sheet information and related tabulations. Special tabulations of data from tax returns are also a major source of important business statistics; recent studies have covered such items as corporate depreciable assets, depletion allowances, and corporate foreign income.

Current data on the financial position of manufacturing corporations have been provided since 1947 by a quarterly financial reports program conducted jointly by the Federal Trade Commission and the Securities and Exchange Commission. The Securities and Exchange Commission collects data from the manufacturing corporations registered with it, while the Federal Trade Commission collects data from a sample, stratified by size and industry, of the unregistered manufacturing corporations. The program provides quarterly income statement and balance sheet data, which are published in the *Quarterly Financial Report for Manufacturing Corporations*.

The Securities and Exchange Commission also publishes quarterly data on the current assets, current liabilities, and working capital position of all U.S. corporations except banks, insurance companies, savings and loan associations, and investment companies.

Information on actual and anticipated expenditures for plant and equipment is collected quarterly and annually by the Securities and Exchange Commission from registered corporations and by the Office of Business Economics in the Department of Commerce from a sample of unregistered companies in the manufacturing, mining, trade, service, construction, and finance industries. Similar information is collected by the Interstate Commerce Commission from interstate oil pipeline companies and from large interstate railroads, motor carriers, and water carriers. Estimates of plant and equipment expenditures for all industries and for major industrial groups are published jointly by the

Securities and Exchange Commission and Office of Business Economics in a quarterly report, *Plant and Equipment Expenditures of U.S. Business.*

Current financial data for industries subject to Federal regulation are collected by the Federal agency concerned.

J. RESOURCES FOR RESEARCH AND DEVELOPMENT

The National Science Foundation is the principal source of statistics on financial and manpower resources for research and development and higher education in the sciences. Largely through periodic surveys, basic data on resources and resource utilization are collected by or on behalf of the Foundation, which analyzes and publishes the results in series of annual or biennial reports. Although emphasis varies, the separate studies form an interlocking set of statistical analyses that together are intended to cover the national spectrum of resources for scientific activities.

Statistical distributions usually, but not always, are developed in three general patterns—by broad sector of the economy (government, industry, universities and colleges, and nonprofit institutions), by field of science or technical specialty, and by type of activity (basic research, applied research, and development). Studies may be broadly comprehensive or cover narrowly specific aspects. They often emphasize either the financial or the manpower resources, sometimes both.

Financial resources. Periodic reports in four principal economic sectors—Federal Government, industry, universities and colleges, and nonprofit institutions—are supplemented from time to time with others to complete the national coverage of R&D expenditures.

Government studies include the annual *Federal Funds for Research, Development, and Other Scientific Activities,* produced by the Foundation from information furnished by each Federal agency supporting R&D activities, R&D facilities, scientific information activities, or general-purpose data collection. A Foundation report on State government R&D expenditures for 1964 and 1965, in the 50 States, was based on data collected on behalf of the Foundation by the Bureau of the Census. The Foundation has also supported a Census survey of scientific activities of approximately 1,000 local government units. It is anticipated that the State and local government surveys will be repeated biennially hereafter in alternate years.

Industry studies include the annual report on *Research and Development in Industry,* prepared by the Foundation from data collected for it by the Bureau of the Census. This series provides continuity of data since 1953 on expenditures of major industry groups in a variety of relationships—source of funds, product field, cost components, geographic area, employment of scientists and engineers, etc.

Universities and colleges are surveyed biennially by the Foundation to obtain data on the financial and manpower characteristics of their scientific activities. The report series *Resources for Scientific Activities at Universities and Colleges* provides data on the sources of funds and the expenditures and personnel resources used for research, development, and instruction in the sciences and engineering. Separate data are shown for agricultural schools and experiment stations, medical schools, and university-administered Federally Funded Research and Development Centers.

Development of a data-collection system and statistical series reflecting impacts of Federal support on universities and colleges is a continuing project undertaken by the Foundation for the Federal Council on Science and Technology's Committee on Academic Science and Engineering (CASE). Initial reports, undertaken for Phase I of the project, detail the support given by eight principal Federal agencies to each university or college for research and development, R&D plant, other scientific activities, and non-science activities. A report of fiscal year 1963–67 activities is being prepared for release in fiscal year 1969. Phase II of the CASE project will provide more detailed information, including manpower data.

Nonprofit institutions, surveyed biennially by the Foundation for their R&D activities, are reported in the NSF series *Scientific Activities of Nonprofit Institutions*. The survey covers financial and manpower resources devoted to these activities in research institutes and operating foundations, science exhibitors (museums, zoological parks, botanical gardens, arboretums, etc.), professional and technical societies, private philanthropic foundations, other nonprofit organizations, and Federally Funded Research and Development Centers managed by nonprofit organizations.

Scientific manpower. The data on manpower resources published by the Foundation are of two general types: (1) professional characteristics, developed mainly from analyses of the National Register of Scientific and Technical Personnel, and (2) sources and utilization of personnel, mainly from periodic surveys. (See also page 251.)

The National Register, maintained since 1953 by the Foundation, collects data through questionnaires distributed every 2 years by professional scientific societies to members and other qualified scientists. Data are analyzed by the Foundation and published in occasional bulletins and a biennial report, *American Science Manpower*. Coverage includes physical, life, and some social scientists and comprises statistics on employment specialty and function, kind of employer, salary data, academic training, geographic location, foreign language and area knowledge, etc.

The National Register included 243,000 persons in 1966 and is expected to approach 280,000 in 1968.

A similar registration of engineers was started by the Foundation in 1964 through contract with the Engineers Joint Council, which also published the results. The 1964 registration consisted of 60,000 engineers; a 1967 registration of nearly 140,000 engineers is being processed in 1968.

Other Foundation studies analyze supply and utilization of scientists and engineers in particular situations. For example, a series on Federal Government employment of scientific and technical personnel (including salary data) is published biennially from data provided by the Civil Service Commission. Basic employment data on universities and colleges and on nonprofit institutions are collected in biennial surveys of their R&D activities.

Studies of private industry, State government, and local government employment of scientists and engineers are prepared by the Bureau of Labor Statistics with partial support by the Foundation.

Annual statistics on the immigration of scientists, engineers, and physicians and surgeons to the United States are published by the Foundation from data provided by the Immigration and Naturalization Service.

In addition, occasional studies are undertaken on particular segments, on national trends over a period of years, or on projections of requirements.

Special studies. The most broadly comprehensive study undertaken by the Foundation interrelates data on scientific activities of all sectors, summarizes trends in national patterns in research and development, both funds and manpower, and identifies the major intersectoral relationships that underlie R&D financing. The most recent report, *National Patterns of R&D Resources, Funds and Manpower in the United States, 1953–68,* was published in 1967.

Other special studies include analyses of resources for teaching science and engineering in universities and colleges, graduate education for science and engineering, special salary distributions, geographic distributions of funds from Federal sources, and scientific activities in foreign areas.

K. CONSUMER INCOME, EXPENDITURES, AND SAVING

Income. There are no estimates of "consumer income" in the strict sense. "Personal income," as defined in the national income accounts, includes income received by unincorporated businesses, nonprofit institutions (including trust and welfare funds), as well as by individuals or families. Personal income includes most receipts generally regarded as income, such as wages and salaries, dividends, interest, etc., but excludes capital gains and losses. Most of the income is in monetary form, but there are important exceptions—the rental value to owner-occupants of homes and the value of food produced and consumed on farms. Seasonally adjusted estimates of personal income by months are available since January 1946. Current estimates are carried in *Economic Indicators* and *Survey of Current Business.*

Estimates of personal income after taxes or "disposable personal income" are available annually since 1929 and quarterly since 1946. Advance estimates are published in *Economic Indicators* in the first month falling at the end of a quarter and revised estimates appear later in the *Survey.* Estimates of per capita disposable income in constant prices also appear in *Economic Indicators.*

Annual estimates of farm income, one of the two components of proprietors' income, are prepared by the Economic Research Service, U.S. Department of Agriculture. The series is available back to 1910, but is currently presented with related series in 5 year averages starting 1910 and annually from 1925 forward in the July issue of the *Farm Income Situation.* Annual estimates of the personal income of the farm population from farm and nonfarm sources are available back to 1934, and are presented on a disposable personal income per capita basis for comparison with the nonfarm population in the July issue of the *Farm Income Situation* of the U.S. Department of Agriculture.

Estimates of the size distribution of income for families and individuals are drawn from four sources: the Decennial Census of Population, an annual survey of the income of a sample of households (Series P–60, *Current Population Reports*), individual income tax returns, and periodic surveys of consumer income and expenditures conducted by the Bureau of Labor Statistics, U.S. Department of Labor and the U.S. Department of Agriculture. (See description under Expenditures, below.)

The 1960 Census of Population presents detailed cross-classifications of income distributions in 1959 by various family characteristics in 1960 and by areas (e.g., places, counties, metropolitan areas, states, and regions) as well as summary income distributions for the United States as a whole. Estimates of average income by county were published for the first time in the 1960 Census; aggregate income by county computed from this source is available in the 1967 *County and City Data Book*. Income estimates are based on a 25 percent sample of households enumerated in the 1960 Census of Population.

The periodic surveys of the Bureau of Labor Statistics and the U.S. Department of Agriculture provide information on the levels and distributions of income, before and after personal taxes, classified by family characteristics and by area. The most recent survey covered the years 1960 and 1961.

In the past, data obtained from these surveys were used by the National Income Division in the Office of Business Economics in a framework of data available from other sources to construct adjusted estimates of income distribution. The other sources include administrative records of the Internal Revenue Service and the Social Security Administration, estimates of earnings prepared by the Bureau of Labor Statistics, estimates of farm income prepared by the Economic Research Service, and the estimates of national income and expenditure prepared by the Office of Business Economics. Publication of this series was suspended following the 1963 estimates because the basic (benchmark) studies on which the annual series was founded had become obsolete. Publication will be resumed when improvements and updating of the techniques and sources are completed. Estimates for 1963 and prior years are available in *Income Distribution in the United States, by Size, 1944–50*, issued as a supplement to the *Survey of Current Business* in 1953 and in various issues of the *Survey*—the 1963 estimates are in the April 1964 issue.

Expenditures. The most detailed recent study of expenditures of urban consumers, the *Survey of Consumer Expenditures, 1960–61*, was made by the Bureau of Labor Statistics as part of the Consumer Price Index revision program. The survey obtained data on expenditures, with related information on income and savings, from a sample of about 9,500 families representing the total urban population of the United States. The study for 1961 was expanded, in cooperation with the U.S. Department of Agriculture, to include about 4,400 rural farm and rural non-farm families. This is the first nationwide survey of consumer expenditures, income, and saving since the 1941 *Study of Family Spending and Saving in Wartime*.

The results of the survey with varying amounts of detail, cross-classified by socio-economic characteristics of families, were summarized for four geographic regions and the United States for the total population and also separately for the urban and rural non-farm populations in BLS Report Series 237. This series also contains reports for 66 metropolitan areas and the smaller places in the 1960–61 sample. Similar U.S. and regional reports for rural farm areas in 1961 were published by the Agricultural Research

Service of the U.S. Department of Agriculture.

A somewhat larger survey of income and expenditures of farm operators' families was made in 1955 by the U.S. Department of Agriculture and the Bureau of the Census. Information on income and family living expenses was obtained from about 4,000 families. Results of the study were published in the U.S. Department of Agriculture Statistical Bulletin No. 224, *Farmers' Expenditures in 1955, by Regions,* and in Volume III of the 1954 Census of Agriculture.

Annual estimates of consumer expenditures by detailed category are published as part of the national income accounts each July in the *Survey of Current Business;* the issue of July 1967 covers the years 1963 through 1966. (Previous years, dating back to 1929, may be found in *The National Income and Product Accounts of the United States, 1929–1965,* issued as a supplement to the *Survey of Current Business.*)

Consumer expenditures for benchmark years are estimated primarily from data in the Censuses of Business and Manufactures, reports of the Department of Agriculture, Internal Revenue Service, and Interstate Commerce Commission. Current annual and quarterly estimates are carried forward by using the Census Bureau's Annual Survey of Manufactures and Monthly Report on Retail Trade, and other sources. These are later revised as benchmark data become available. Major groups of consumer expenditures are estimated in constant as well as current dollars.

Current quarterly estimates of major categories of consumer expenditures are published in *Economic Indicators* and the *Survey of Current Business.*

Information on the number of new and used cars consumers expect to purchase as well as their expected expenditures on houses and major household durables is obtained quarterly by the Bureau of the Census through its survey of Consumer Buying Expectations (CBE). The CBE also provides data on actual purchases of cars and other durables and on actual and expected changes in family income. The CBE is the successor to the Quarterly Survey of Consumer Buying Intentions which was conducted by the Census Bureau from January 1959 to January 1967.

Saving. Personal saving is estimated quarterly by the Office of Business Economics by subtracting personal outlays from disposable personal income. Quarterly estimates of individual saving are also made by the Securities and Exchange Commission on the basis of changes in personal assets, including currency and bank deposits, insurance equities, security holdings, real estate, and other types of assets. An annual reconciliation of these two estimates is published by the Securities and Exchange Commission and by the Office of Business Economics.

The consumer sector of the flow-of-funds accounts describes the financial flows absorbed by and emanating from consumers, including both income and credit transactions. It provides a third set of saving and investment figures for households.

L. GOVERNMENT TRANSACTIONS

Federal Government. Data on the financial operations of the Federal Government are compiled primarily by the Treasury Department and appear in its daily, monthly, and annual publications. Summary information on the public debt and cash transactions affecting the balance in the Treasurer's account is published in the *Daily Treasury Statement;* more detailed current information appears in the *Monthly Statement* and in the *Treasury Bulletin.* Extensive data on Government financial operations are published in the *Annual Report of the Secretary of the Treasury on the State of the Finances,* and in greater detail in the annual *Combined Statement.*

The annual *Budget of the United States,* issued by the Bureau of the Budget, presents both summary and detailed statistics on the Federal financial program, comparing estimates for the current and coming fiscal year with actual data for the previous year. Comparisons of major components of receipts and expenditures are shown for 10 or more years.

The Federal Budget is presented on a single, comprehensive basis and is the principal financial plan for conducting the affairs of the Federal government. The presentation encompasses two older budget concepts, the administrative budget and the consolidated cash statement. It includes all programs of the Federal government with outlays and deficit divided between an expenditure account and a loan account. A comparison of the new and old budget concepts is found in Special Analysis A of the *Budget of the United States* for fiscal year 1969.

Federal transactions as measured in the National Income and Product Accounts of the Department of Commerce are analyzed in Special Analysis B of the 1969 Budget. This data is widely used for the purposes of economic analysis and shows some tax receipts on an accrual basis and expenditures timed to correspond with the delivery of goods and performance of services.

As part of its government statistics program, the Bureau of the Census classifies Federal financial data on a basis comparable with that applied to State and local governments, and publishes annual unduplicated national totals of revenues by source and of expenditures by function for all levels of government.

A number of special analyses in the Federal Budget provide statistics of general interest. These cover transactions of public enterprises and trust funds; foreign currency availabilities and uses; investment, operating, and other expenditures; Federal credit programs; Federal activities in public works; research and development programs and selected scientific and technical activities of the Federal Government; Federal aid to State and local governments; principal Federal statistical programs; Civilian employment in the executive branch; Federal education and training; and Federal health programs.

A number of the Federal corporations or public enterprises, such as the Tennessee Valley Authority and the Commodity Credit Corporation, publish periodic financial statements.

State and local government finance. The Governments Division of the Bureau of the Census is the principal source of financial statistics of State and local governments. From 1850 through 1900 some information on these governments was obtained in connection with the decennial censuses of population. Beginning in 1902 special censuses were taken at decennial intervals covering all governmental units in the Nation—States, counties, cities, towns, townships, school districts, and special districts of various kinds. An act of Congress approved in September 1950 directed that a census of governments be taken in 1952 and at 5-year intervals thereafter. No funds were appropriated for a census of governments in 1952, but censuses were taken for 1957, 1962, and 1967 which obtained data on numbers and characteristics of governments; taxes and other governmental receipts, public expenditures, borrowing and indebtedness; government cash and security holdings; employment and payrolls; assessed values and the relationship of assessed value to sales price for various use classes of realty in each State. Preliminary reports for the 1967 Census of Governments have been issued, and the final reports have been or will be published in seven volumes: Volume I, Governmental Organization; Volume II, Taxable Property Values; Volume III, Compendium of Public Employment; Volume IV, Governmental Finances; Volume V, Local Government in Metropolitan Areas; Volume VI, Topical Studies; and Volume VII, State Reports. These reports show national, State, and county totals, and comparative statistics for the larger governmental units. Topical studies included in volume VI are: Popularly Elected Officials of State and Local Governments, Employee Retirement Systems of State and Local Governments, State Payments to Local Governments, State Reports on State and Local Government Finances, State Rankings for Selected Governmental Items, Graphic Summary of the 1967 Census of Governments, and Historical Statistics on Governmental Finances and Employment. The 52 State

reports in volume VII will present data on governmental structure and numbers, public employment, and State and local government finances for each State, the District of Columbia, and Puerto Rico.

Current statistics on State and local governments published by the Bureau of the Census include an annual report on State finances which dates back to 1915, and a similar report on finances of cities which was begun in 1898. Other annual reports supply National and State aggregates on governmental finances and on public employment, local finances data for major metropolitan areas, and a graphic summary of governmental finances and employment. These data are based on reports collected from all States and large local governmental units and a sample of the smaller local governments. A sample survey to provide quarterly data on State and local tax collections was initiated as part of the current statistics program in 1963. In 1965 a quarterly report on new construction expenditures of State and local governments was begun, also based on a sample survey.

In addition to these statistics covering all functions of State and local governments, data on particular functions or activities are published by various Federal agencies. Thus—to mention only two examples—the Office of Education in the Department of Health, Education, and Welfare publishes detailed information on finances of school systems; the Federal Highway Administration of the Department of Transportation publishes statistics on Federal, State, and local roads and highways.

M. FOREIGN TRADE AND TRAVEL STATISTICS

Foreign trade. Statistics on foreign trade are among the oldest compiled by the Federal Government. Annual data on merchandise exports and imports are available from 1790, and monthly data from 1866.

The official foreign trade statistics are compiled by the Bureau of the Census, from documents filed by importers and exporters with Customs directors at the time of import or export. The basic data include the value of merchandise imports and exports, classified by commodity, country of origin (for imports) or destination (for exports), and customs district through which the goods move, together with quantity figures for most commodity classes. Exports are classified into approximately 3,600 commodity classifications provided in the 1965 edition of Schedule B, Statistical Classification of Domestic and Foreign Commodities Exported From the United States, which was based on the Standard International Trade Classification, Revised, established by the United Nations. Imports, which are compiled initially in accordance with about 10,000 classifications in the Tariff Schedules of the United States Annotated, are also reported in terms of approximately 2,300 classifications listed in Schedule A, Statistical Classification of Commodities Imported Into the United States, also based on the SITC. Data for certain other summary groupings are also compiled.

The basic data are published by the Bureau of the Census in monthly and annual reports, with cumulative data included in many of the monthly reports. Printed machine tabulation sheets, with more detail than is published, are also made available for reference at selected cities in advance of, or in lieu of, publication.

In many of the current Census publications, data are presented showing imports and exports by vessel and by air as well as by all methods of transportation combined. In addition, sep-arate tabulations on waterborne trade are also prepared.

The import and export data compiled by the Bureau of the Census are used by other agencies, such as the Department of Agriculture and the Bureau of Mines in the Department of the Interior, in preparing specialized summaries of foreign trade. They are also used by the Bureau of International Commerce in the Department of Commerce in its analyses of foreign commerce and in its compilation of quantum and unit value indexes of foreign trade, and by the Office of Business Economics, Department of Commerce, in preparing estimates of the balance of international payments.

Travel statistics. No single agency in the U.S. Government is responsible for collection and analysis of all travel statistics. Data on various aspects of the subject are available from several agencies.

A monthly measure of the general pattern of international passenger travel is published by the Immigration and Naturalization Service, Department of Justice, with data on arrivals and departures by mode of travel and other classifications, including country of embarkation and debarkation.

A more precise measure of travel by foreign visitors to the United States is offered by the tabulations of the Immigration and Naturalization Service covering admissions of nonimmigrant aliens by class (tourists, students, business, etc.). These, supplemented by data on border traffic, form the basis for official submittals to the United Nations, to the Organization for Economic Cooperation and Development, and to the International Union of Official Travel Organizations of statistics on visitors to the United States. The United States Travel Service publishes data monthly and annually on travel of foreigners in the United States, including transits and students as well as business and pleasure visitors—the classes to which its promotional efforts are particularly directed.

Estimates of travel and travel expenditures reflecting balance of payments definitions are prepared by the Office of Business Economics, Department of Commerce. These estimates are based on passenger data from the Immigration and Naturalization Service, information obtained from a continuing sample survey of international travelers, and other sources. Expenditure data appear as components of the quarterly figures on international balance of payments, and additional travel market data are presented in special articles in the *Survey of Current Business*.

The Passport Office in the Department of State publishes data on passports issued and renewed, including the number of passport holders intending to visit specific countries. Forecasts of citizen departures to Europe, based on passport applications, are also made.

In the field of domestic travel, there is no continuing source of data. In 1957 the Bureau of the Census made a travel survey, obtaining information from a probability sample of households from which national estimates were derived for the total volume of civilian travel, classified by means of transport, purpose and length of trip, origin and destination areas, and other factors. Since 1963, the travel survey has been an integral part of the quinquennial census of transportation.

N. MONEY, CREDIT, AND THE SECURITIES MARKETS

Detailed statistics are available from the Federal Government on money, the central banking system, the privately owned commercial and mutual savings banks, the securities markets, savings and loan institutions, and other aspects of the financial system.

Responsibility for statistics in this field reflects the division of administrative responsibilities among several agencies. Not only does the catalog of available series range over a number of agencies, but any one statistical table may be a synthesis of data drawn from several sources.

Since the discussion below is in terms of subjects rather than agencies, a brief mention of the contributions of the several agencies will serve as a useful background. The major contributing agencies include Treasury, with statistics on the currency, the national banks, the Federal debt, and international finance; the Federal Reserve Board with data on central banking, the Federal Reserve System including the member commercial banks, and banking and monetary developments generally; the Federal Deposit Insurance Corporation covering all insured banks and related commercial banking data; the Federal Home Loan Bank Board with data on the Federal home loan banks, the savings and loan industry, and the mortgage market generally; the Securities and Exchange Commission covering the organized securities exchanges and the private securities market; and several other agencies with various contributions, including Census, Department of Housing and Urban Development, Veterans Administration, and the Department of Agriculture.

Statistics on the money supply illustrate the composite nature of money and banking statistics noted above.

The Federal Reserve issues weekly and monthly data on the money supply, defined as an aggregate of currency outside the Treasury and the Federal Reserve Banks and the vaults of all commercial banks and of privately held demand deposits, as well as related series on time deposits and U.S. Government demand deposits. Money supply and time deposits are available on a seasonally adjusted basis. These may be found in the monthly *Federal Reserve Bulletin*. Data in greater detail on deposits are found in banking reports, and on currency in circulation by type and denomination in the *Treasury Bulletin*.

The key statistics on central bank operation and related matters include the weekly and end-of-month reports of the 12 Federal Reserve banks, available individually and as a consolidated statement, and a special tabulation available at similar intervals, but on a weekly average basis as well, called *Member Bank Reserves, Federal Reserve Bank Credit, and Related Items*. The latter tabulation shows in detail the factors "supplying reserve funds" (Federal Reserve bank credit outstanding, gold stock, and Treasury currency outstanding) and the factors "absorbing reserve funds" (currency in circulation, member bank required reserves, etc.).

Data concerned specifically with operations of commercial and mutual banks reflect the division of responsibility for supervision of the several segments of the banking system among three Federal agencies: the Comptroller of the Currency in the Treasury Department, the Federal Reserve System, and the Federal Deposit Insurance Corporation, with particular responsibilities, respectively, for the national, the State member, and the nonmember insured banks.

Perhaps the most basic source of banking statistics is the so-called "call report"—a detailed report of assets and liabilities currently tabulated semi-annually by each agency for the banks under its supervision, and brought together in comprehensive tabulations. With the aid of similar reports covering the small number of noninsured banks, the Federal Deposit Insurance Corporation compiles "all-bank" statistics. Data on the earnings, expenses, and profits of all insured commercial, and mutual savings banks are also published annually.

Of particular interest are the data on commercial and mutual savings bank loans and investments. These may be found in the call report tabulations. Also, with less detail, they are available monthly in the *Federal Reserve Bulletin* series and semimonthly in a mimeographed release. Major credit items for all commercial banks are also available monthly on a seasonally adjusted basis. An additional series based on reports from a group of "weekly reporting large commercial banks" provides weekly asset and liability data for virtually all large banks in the country. Information on business loans by industry is available from a considerable part of this weekly sample, including data on term loans by industry as of the last Wednesday of each month. Detailed loan studies are made from time to time by Federal Reserve.

Other balance sheet data are available in corresponding series, including reserves and deposits. A table of special interest for current analyses shows weekly averages of daily figures for member banks, total reserves, required reserves, excess reserves, borrowings at Federal Reserve banks, and free reserves.

In addition, seasonally adjusted

monthly average data are available for total, required, and nonborrowed reserves and for member bank deposits subject to reserve requirements—time and savings, private demand, and U.S. Government demand.

A variety of other types of data on commercial and savings banking are made available by the supervisory agencies, each with emphasis on its own special sphere of interest, although the comprehensive data are in general available, particularly in Federal Reserve publications. These include data on number and classification of banks, and changes in the banking structure. Monthly series on bank debits are issued by Federal Reserve for New York City and 232 other Standard Metropolitan Statistical Areas, with corresponding series for annual rates of deposit turnover. Important series are issued in advance releases, as well as in the *Federal Reserve Bulletin*.

Data on consumer credit, both installment and noninstallment, are assembled by the Federal Reserve from several sources. Monthly series show consumer credit classified by type, and installment credit classified by type of holder. For installment credit, monthly data are available not only for credit outstanding but for credit extended and repaid. These series are based on data from commercial banks, sales finance companies, retail stores advancing credit, and various other types of lending agencies.

A variety of series on short-term interest rates and the money market are available. Federal Reserve collects from commercial banks data on rates on short-term business loans, and publishes a quarterly series showing average rates by size of loan for 35 financial centers, with regional grouping. Also

shown is the percentage distribution of the dollar amount of loans reported at each rate or in each rate range. In addition to collecting data on interest rates, the Federal Reserve has, since late 1964, conducted quarterly surveys to obtain information from large commercial banks concerning changes in their nonprice lending policies and practices and their appraisal of current and anticipated demand for business loans. Beginning with data for 1967 the results of these surveys are being published annually in the *Federal Reserve Bulletin*. Other Federal Reserve series include money market rates based on dealer reports. Treasury data show yields on short-, intermediate-, and long-term government securities. The Federal Reserve issues monthly data on commercial and finance company paper and bankers acceptances outstanding.

There is also a variety of data on aspects of the market for mortgage funds. Estimates of nonfarm mortgage debt outstanding are made by the Federal Reserve and the Federal Home Loan Bank Board. Monthly series on nonfarm foreclosures are also issued by the Board. Activity of savings and loan associations, including deposits and loans made and loans outstanding, and the operations of the Federal Home Loan Banks are available monthly from the Federal Home Loan Bank Board.

A monthly series on interest rates and terms of nonfarm conventional first mortgages is compiled by the Federal Home Loan Bank Board with the cooperation of the Federal Deposit Insurance Corporation. This series covers mortgages made on new and existing single family homes by savings and loan associations, commercial and mutual savings banks, and life insurance and mortgage companies.

Data are provided for the United States as a whole and for 18 major standard metropolitan statistical areas. Federal agencies active in the mortgage market—The Federal Housing Administration and other constituent agencies of the Department of Housing and Urban Development, as well as the Veterans Administration—issue useful administrative and other data on loans, interest rates, and characteristics of properties and borrowers.

Considerable information is available on agricultural credit. The Department of Agriculture assembles and publishes semiannually in the *Agricultural Finance Review* data by States on the agricultural loans of commercial and savings banks, insurance companies, the Farmers Home Administration, the Rural Electrification Administration, the Commodity Credit Corporation, and agencies supervised by the Farm Credit Administration; State estimates of the farm mortgage debt held by nonreporting lenders annually; data on farm mortgage loans made or recorded annually; and data on farm mortgage interest rates and annual interest charges on the farm mortgage debt. This publication includes data on farm insurance and farm taxes. The USDA also publishes "Farm Real Estate Market Developments" which reports trends in farmland values and in the means by which farm transfers are financed.

In its annual *Balance Sheet of Agriculture,* the Department of Agriculture reviews changes in the agricultural credit situation and in farm assets, debts, equities, and income. Data on farm mortgage debt are obtained each 5 years by the Bureau of the Census as part of the census of agriculture program. In 1966, sample surveys of the characteristics of farm loans and borrowers were undertaken by several agencies. Lending by commercial banks was surveyed by the Federal Reserve System, that by the production credit agencies was examined by the Farm Credit Administration, while the Department of Agriculture studied lending by the Federal land banks, insurance companies, and the Farmers Home Administration. Results have been or are to be published by the respective agencies. Data on the operation of the Farm Credit Administration, the Farmers Home Administration, the Rural Electrification Administration, and the Commodity Credit Corporation are available from the annual reports and other publications of these agencies.

The primary source of Federal statistics on the securities markets, including the issuance of corporate securities and trading on major securities exchanges, is the Securities and Exchange Commission. Important series of this agency include summary monthly data on new security issues, both public and private and both registered and nonregistered; special reports on the cost of flotation of corporate securities; monthly data on the volume and value of trading on securities exchanges with additional weekly releases on round- and odd-lot trading on the two New York exchanges; monthly summaries of securities transactions and holdings of officers, directors, and principal stockholders; and weekly price indexes on common stocks listed on the New York Stock Exchange. The Federal Reserve System issues monthly data on stock market credit, including the borrowings of stock exchange members and their loans to customers.

Information on Government securities comes primarily from the Treasury Department. This includes detailed current data on Government securities, including characteristics, amounts outstanding, distribution of ownership, prices and yields, and monthly average yields for taxable Treasury bonds.

O. NATIONAL ECONOMIC ACCOUNTS

National income and product. Estimates of gross national product, national income, personal income, and related series are prepared by the National Income Division in the Office of Business Economics, Department of Commerce. These basic measures of the national economy are published regularly in the *Survey of Current Business,* and annual summaries and additional detail are presented in the July issue.

In 1965 the Office of Business Economics published a comprehensive revision of the national income and product accounts. This revision incorporated the benchmark data obtained in the 1958 economic censuses as well as other additions to the statistical source data on which the national income and product estimates are based. It also included certain changes in the definitions of the income and product totals and some of their components. The revised figures on an annual basis since 1929 and on a quarterly basis since 1946 are shown in *The National Income and Product Accounts of the United States, 1929–1965,* issued as a supplement to the *Survey of Current Business.*

Descriptions of the conceptual framework and of the sources and methods of estimation of statistics on national income and product are contained in three publications. The main reference continues to be *National Income: 1954* edition, issued as a supplement to the *Survey.* The conceptual and statistical changes introduced in the 1965 revision are discussed in the August 1965 *Survey.* Changes associated with the previous benchmark revision are covered in the 1959 publication *U.S. Income and Output,* issued as a supplement to the *Survey.*

Gross national product (GNP) is defined as the market value of goods and services produced by the labor and property of the Nation's residents. It is the broadest measure we have of the overall functioning of the economy. It is designed to answer such questions as whether the dollar value of total output of goods and services is rising or falling, and how the composition and distribution of this output are changing. Estimates are also prepared to measure the trend of gross national product after allowance has been made for price changes, that is, GNP in constant dollars.

Annual estimates from 1929 and quarterly estimates from 1946 have been prepared of gross national product and each of its chief components: personal consumption expenditures, gross private domestic investment, net exports, and Government purchases of goods and services. Estimates of GNP and its major components in constant dollars have been published for each year beginning 1929 and each quarter beginning 1947.

The gross national product estimates have also been prepared by sector—business, households and institutions, rest of world, and general government—and by type of product—goods, services and structures. These estimates are available annually since 1929 and quarterly since 1947 in current and constant dollars. Further breakdowns of the gross national product which are available are estimates by major industries, presented annually since 1947 in current and constant dollars; gross auto product, which shows output originating from the production and sale of passenger cars, available annually and quarterly, in current and constant dollars, beginning with 1947; and gross corporate product, presented annually and quarterly in current dollars since 1946 and in constant dollars for nonfinancial corporation since 1948.

National income is the sum of labor and property earnings from the current production of goods and services by the Nation's economy. As such, it measures national output at factor cost as reflected in the payments made to the factors—labor, capital, and land—which directly produce this output. It differs from the gross market value of output in that it excludes the portions of the market price which are added on to cover depreciation and certain business taxes.

Annual estimates from 1929 and quarterly estimates from 1946 have been prepared of national income and its chief components: wages and salaries, proprietors' income, corporate profits, rental income, and net interest. The annual estimates of total national income in the aggregate and by factor shares, presented in the July issue of the *Survey of Current Business,* are also classified by about 70 industry groups.

Personal income is composed of the income currently received by individuals, unincorporated enterprises, nonprofit institutions, and private welfare funds, in the form of wage and salary receipts, other labor income, proprietors' and rental income, interest and dividends, and transfers of income from business and from the Government (such as military pensions, old-

age benefits, and relief payments). Disposable income measures personal incomes after deduction for income taxes and related payments. Seasonally adjusted monthly totals of personal income at annual rates are available for the period beginning January 1946. Estimates of disposable income are available annually since 1929 and quarterly since 1946.

A comprehensive summary of the annual estimates of personal income by States for the years 1929–55, with a review of the concepts and estimating methods for this series, was presented in *Personal Income by States Since 1929,* published in 1956 as a supplement to the *Survey of Current Business.* Comparable data with supporting detail are published each year in the April (preliminary estimates) and August (final estimates) issues of the *Survey.* The August 1967 *Survey* presents data back to 1948 that revise the data shown in the 1956 supplement. Quarterly estimates of personal income by States were first published in the December 1966 *Survey.* The quarterly series begin in 1964 and are now published each year in the January, April, August and October issues of the *Survey.* Annual estimates of personal income in 97 SMSA's for 5 selected years from 1929 to 1962 were published in the May 1967 *Survey.* In the August 1968 *Survey* estimates for 1966 will be presented and the coverage extended to include all SMSA's.

Interindustry sales and purchase (input-output) accounts. These accounts represent a deconsolidation of the income and product account along industry lines. Estimates of the flows of goods and services among the various industries, as well as to final markets, are provided. The accounts are designed to show the relationships among the various industries and final markets of the economy and to permit tracing the impact of final expenditures on the product and income originating in each of the industries.

Interindustry sales and purchase accounts are prepared by the Office of Business Economics for the quinquennial census years. Intercensal year updating is also programed.

The basic description of the concepts and methods and the estimates for 1958, the first year covered in this series, were included in the *Survey of Current Business* for November 1964 and September 1965. Additional articles have appeared in the *Survey* for May 1965, October 1965, and April 1966. An updated table for 1961 has been completed.

The input-output table for 1963 will present interindustry sales and purchases for more than 350 industries compared with the 86 industries shown in the 1958 and 1961 tables.

Balance of international payments; Government foreign transactions. Comprehensive data on the U.S. "balance of payments" are published by the Office of Business Economics in the Department of Commerce. Its reports summarize the economic transactions between residents of the United States and those of other countries, including "unilateral transfers" such as gifts, reparations, contributions, etc., whether in cash or in kind. Annual summaries are available for each year since 1919 and quarterly statements since 1946. Details by major geographic areas have been published for annual data since 1940 and for quarterly data since 1948.

The balance-of-payments statistics are published quarterly and annually in the *Survey of Current Business*. In addition, annual data are published for selected major transactions with individual countries (such as travel, investments, and Government aid) and for the debtor-creditor position of the United States. More comprehensive and detailed statistics are presented in occasional special bulletins covering extended periods. The latest, issued early in 1963, provides estimates of the balance of payments for the years 1919–1961, and gives detailed data for major types of foreign transactions over extended periods.

Periodically the Office of Business Economics conducts comprehensive mandatory surveys of U.S. direct private foreign investments and of foreign direct private investments in the United States. The reports, *U.S. Business Investments in Foreign Countries,* issued in 1960, and *Foreign Business Investments in the United States,* issued in 1962, give the complete results of the most recent surveys of these investments. Another survey of U.S. direct investments abroad has been taken for the year 1966, results of which will be published in 1969. These surveys provide broad ranges of data on the value and operations of these enterprises and on their role in economic development. Data from these surveys provide the benchmarks for the quarterly statistics on investment flows and income in the balance-of-payments accounts and also for annual estimates of sources and uses of funds of the direct foreign investment firms.

Detailed statements of the volume and nature of U.S. Government foreign aid are also provided by the Office of Business Economics in the annual report *Foreign Grants and Credits by the U.S. Government,* which shows a consolidated record of all such Government expenditures abroad, by agency, program, and geographic area. The report contains breakdowns of aid provided under all past and present programs, as well as grants and credits tables showing the national recipients of such aid. For the most part the records begin with the fiscal year 1941, although additional information on earlier years is available.

Flow-of-funds accounts. The Board of Governors of the Federal Reserve System publishes a set of tables intended to show somewhat more explicitly than the national income and product accounts the processes through which saving finances investment in the economy. The Board's table are termed flow-of-funds accounts, since they are focused on payments and receipts—the transfer of funds among transactors—rather than income and production. The flow-of-funds accounts are an extension of the national income and product accounts in which the national totals of saving and investment in the latter system are allocated to the several major sectors of the economy—governments, business, households, etc.—and expanded in detail to show the financial investment of each sector as well as its investment in physical assets. Flow of funds is thus a deconsolidation of the national saving and investment account, within which all borrowing and lending within the economy are consolidated and cancel out. The process of deconsolidation generates, in addition to sector data on saving and investment, summary national totals of funds raised in credit markets, flows through financial intermediaries to credit markets, and the reflection of borrowing in financial investment by the public. The investment may take the form of cash, institutional deposits, or securities purchased directly. For individual sectors the tables also include major current-account payments and receipts such as income, taxes, consumption, etc.

The flow-of-funds accounts are currently published quarterly, with the first data for each quarter appearing on a preliminary basis about one month after the end of the quarter. These preliminary figures are in separate publications for seasonally adjusted and unadjusted data that are available on request.

The seasonally adjusted data are then published later with more complete information in the *Federal Reserve Bulletin*. Annual revisions are published once a year in the *Bulletin,* together with tables of asset and liability structure for the economy and for each major sector. The revisions reflect national income and product revisions appearing in July issues of the *Survey of Current Business* and annual benchmark data on financial accounts that become available over the course of the year. The schedule of *Bulletin* appearances is shown on page A–3 of all copies of the *Bulletin*. Supplementary tables become available periodically that include unadjusted as well as adjusted data and cover much sector and transaction detail not shown in the *Bulletin*.

The structure of the accounts is described in *Flow of Funds Accounts, 1945–47,* published 1968 by the Board of Governors of the Federal Reserve System and available on request. Seasonal adjustments are discussed in the November 1962 *Bulletin,* p. 1393 ff.

Planning For A Nationwide System of Library Statistics

David C. Palmer, ALA Project Director and General Editor

"In 1966, a National Conference on Library Statistics was cosponsored by ALA and USOE. At this conference, the major topics of discussion were needs for the uses of library statistics and proposed methods of establishing an efficient nationwide data-collection system. It was this conference that stimulated the Library Administration Division of the American Library Association to submit its proposal for the current project to the U. S. Office of Education.

In its present form, the publication contains the considered opinions and recommendations of a relatively small group of expert librarians. However, it also represents the distillation of several decades of work by a much larger number of librarians, and their contribution to this ultimate product is gratefully acknowledged . . ."

From the Foreword *by Joel Williams, Former Chief, Library Surveys Branch, National Center for Educational Statistics (retired, August 1970).*

SUMMARY OF MAJOR RECOMMENDATIONS

1. Planning for standardized, meaningful, and even minimal library statistics must continue—indefinitely. Other research efforts, especially in the areas of management systems, data bank development, user data, and impact of library services are needed and should be coordinated with these guidelines.

2. Efforts to standardize terminology must be continued and intensified. Definitions found in *Library Statistics: A Handbook of Concepts, Definitions, and Terminology* should be reviewed, refined, and expanded. While this is primarily the obligation of the profession at large, the terminology should be promulgated by the U.S. Government and revised as needed. Continued recognition by the United States of America Standards Institute, and its cooperation, will contribute to the widest acceptance of this standardized terminology.

3. The National Center for Educational Statistics (NCES) should be assisted by an advisory committee which represents fairly the numerous governmental, professional, and commercial interests in library statistics. This advisory input into planning and operating a national library statistics system should be augmented and supplemented by the National Commission on Libraries and Information Science and by State advisory committees. The Statistics Coordinating Committee of the American Library Association should continue its strong advisory and promotional roles.

4. A program of shared responsibility between NCES and the States in nationwide (as well as State) library statistical coverage is essential and should be highly defined, coordinated, and regularized. NCES will have to take a close look at the library functions at the State level to determine which agencies are responsible for which functions.

5. Federal financial assistance to the States to enable them to carry out their responsibilities in the foregoing system is mandatory. This assistance should be designed to both stimulate State investment in this area and to be used as a tool for regularization and compliance.

SOURCE: Reprinted from U. S. Department of Health, Education, and Welfare. Office of Education. National Center for Educational Statistics. *Planning For A Nationwide System Of Library Statistics.* David C. Palmer, ALA Project Director and General Editor. OE-15070. (Washington: 1970 i.e. 1971), pp. 1-21, 31-36, 49-56, and p. 117.

6. Determination of library universes should take place at the State level according to definitions supplied by NCES.

7. Training programs, with appropriate instructors, manuals, meetings, etc., are essential to the national statistics program, both at the State and local levels, for general understanding, accuracy of returns, and compliance.

8. States should be encouraged to collect data beyond Federal and national needs and should distribute these data widely. They should serve as true information centers on libraries and library conditions in the respective States.

9. Continued national planning should incorporate appropriate steps toward the formation of a national data bank system for library statistics. Such a system should allow for retrieval of specialized library data at cost.

THE PROJECT

Almost a century has passed since the first American Library Association Conference in 1876 took special note of the problems of library statistics. One of the most comprehensive reports on libraries ever compiled was published that year. Entitled *Public Libraries in the United States,* it was produced by the Bureau of Education (now the U.S. Office of Education), itself only 9 years old at the time. As John Lorenz points out in his paper in appendix A: "If we knew as much about libraries today as was compiled and published in 1876, we would be in a much better position to plan for future library development." But the fact is that we have not yet achieved even the most elemental body of recurring statistical data about our public libraries, much less those for school, college, university, and special libraries. In addition, we know relatively little about the needs and uses for such data.

The present effort to formulate planning for a nation-wide library data system is the latest in the profession's long and valiant struggle to standardize, codify, and regularize reporting techniques for the Nation's libraries of all types. Standardized terminology and definitions, common methods of counting, regularized coverage and periodicity, and assigned levels of responsibility for State and national reporting are reasonable goals. But they require basic agreement throughout the profession, leadership at authoritative levels, and most importantly, a review mechanism to enable response to the forces of change.

When we recall the developments over the last hundred years of librarianship, it is small wonder that many of the efforts attempted have been abortive, or short lived at best, for the following reasons:

1. Libraries have proliferated and have taken on different characteristics.

2. The relationships of libraries to each other and to emerging systems and networks have undergone a

rapid evolution which promises to accelerate even further.

3. Library materials have branched far beyond the conventional printed word, and this diversity is matched with unprecedented output.

4. Funding patterns for library service are now much more complex, and the responsibilities of local, State, and Federal governments in their support is shifting.

5. Even our concept of just what a librarian is, and what he does, is far from that held a generation ago. The move toward recognized paraprofessionals and library technicians will affect this even more.

These developments have a direct bearing upon the units to be counted and the way they are counted. When the remarkable technological advances in statistical techniques, automated counting, and data processing, storage, and retrieval are added to these factors, it becomes apparent that any immutable plan for national library statistics is impossible and undesirable. What *is* essential is national *planning* as a continuous process, sensitive to and adaptive to new tools, new concepts and attitudes, and new uses of library data.

Defining what is meant by a "nationwide system of library statistics" has been difficult. Each of the special groups and individual consultants who have been involved in this project sees such a "system" from a particular vantage point and with a certain vested interest based upon the type of library, library service, or information need with which he is associated. To be sure, each has realized the "system" must be broad enough to encompass all the others' interests. A general feeling of unanimity has been present, but when the tough decisions such as exact perimeters of scope, frequency, and detail of data collection have to be made, vested interests come to the fore. It must be remembered, however, that this has been so for the past hundred years. It is not new; hopefully, it is not insurmountable.

A utopian system would satisfy all of the needs identified by all these various points of view. It would provide easy access to a complete bank of library data from which both desirable samples and complete universes could be drawn at will. The age of the computer, and man's increasing ability to reach the stars he grasps for, give us hope and promise which pervade our approach to complex problems, especially statistical ones. But it also engenders frustration when we come face to face with fiscal and political realities. Who is going to be responsible for the input? Where is the money coming from? What are the priorities? For how many audiences are we designing this statistical system?

This report attacks these questions from various points of view and with specific needs in mind. It is hoped that the report will provide a broad rationale upon which a nationwide system of library statistics can be designed, and that the specific recommendations will guide its structure and development. The recommendations certainly do not profess to encompass all of the concerns which can be raised by users of library data. A nationwide system must, at this stage, be a direction toward which the concerned parties agree to move together, rather than a specific final destination they wish to reach. Moreover, it must contain a proposed program of implementation. These guidelines, therefore, will become a data system as they are translated into action.

The American Library Association's statistics planning project, which resulted in this report, is a direct outgrowth of two recent efforts: (1) the Statistics Coordinating Project, which produced the volume *Library Statistics: A Handbook of Concepts, Definitions, and Terminology* (hereafter referred to as the *Handbook*) in 1966, and (2) the National Conference on Library Statistics, the proceedings of which were published in 1967. Events leading up to these efforts are summarized in the overview paper by G. Flint Purdy in appendix A and in appendix C.

Further historical background can be found in the overview paper by John Lorenz in appendix A. Essentially, the project for nationwide system planning is the result of continued efforts by the Statistics Coordinating Committee, which is organized within the Library Administration Division of ALA. Under its aegis, the project proposal was designed and funds were secured from the National Center for Educational Statistics of the U.S. Office of Education.

The design of the project is simple, if somewhat eclectic.

Nationally know authorities were asked to produce general position or overview papers which could guide a group of specialists representing the major types of libraries and library concerns. The overview papers and the papers of the specialists, presented in appendixes A and B, deserve a few words of explanation and background. First, the overview papers (appendix A):

1. **Professional:** This paper establishes a backdrop of concern for library statistics as felt by the profession at large. Against such a setting, the specific needs for data of the various types of libraries can be highlighted. Its broad approach includes an historical perspective, as well as the present-day considerations which should shape a nationwide system. G. Flint Purdy, Director of Libraries, Wayne State University, was engaged to produce this segment of the report but died prior to completion of editorial work. A note of appreciation is appended to his paper, presenting his unique qualifications for this task.

2. **Federal:** The statistical needs of the Federal Government and its role in the compilation and dissemination of library data were felt to require special attention. This paper reviews the authority under which the Federal Government has concerned itself with library statistics and the specific agencies which should be involved in any nationwide data system. John Lorenz, Deputy Librarian of Congress and former head of the Library Services Branch of the U.S. Office of Education, views this area from his long experience in Washington with matters relating to library data needs.

3. **Legislative:** Increasing governmental support of library programs at the local, State, and Federal levels carries with it special needs for data. Not only is this a concern for accountability, but detailed information is also essential in order to draft library-related legislation and to justify appropriations. Paul Howard, former Executive Secretary of the Federal Library Committee, has been intimately involved with library legislation for more than 25 years. His paper on statistical support of legislation reviews the kinds of data needed and why they are vital to the legislative process. A nationwide system for the collection and dissemination of library statistics would have to meet these needs if library programs are to compete favorably for the tax dollar.

4. **State:** S. Gilbert Prentiss, former State Librarian of New York, was engaged as a specialist for State libraries. As his work progressed, however, it became evident that the roles of the State library as collector and as producer of library statistics should be separated. The potential for State agencies as partners with the Federal Government and national associations in implementing a nationwide data system is so central to its

design that this portion of his work has been placed with the overview papers and was used as a general guide for the specialists.

5. **Library Networks and Systems:** The statistical problems of library systems are particularly evident in the papers on public libraries and school libraries. They are enormously perplexing and must be resolved if one is to measure in any meaningful way the impact of library systems upon library development. When the dimension of multiple-type library arrangements is added, special attention must be given to this whole area. Concurrent with the work of the statistics planning project were the efforts of Ruth Boaz in the National Center for Educational Statistics to formulate a survey of public libraries which would reflect these concerns. The article, "The Dilemma of Statistics for Public Libraries," which appeared in the *ALA Bulletin* of December 1969, presents the problems encountered in this survey. The implications of networks and systems for library statistics have been summarized in a paper written as an introduction to a survey proposal made by the Office of Education. Although this paper was not written as a part of the statistics planning project, it has been included here as an overview paper because it presents an innovative approach to data collection for comprehensive library planning. Miss Boaz worked on the 1963-66 evaluation of the New York State public library systems and in the statistical unit of the Division of Library Development of the New York State Library prior to joining the U.S. Office of Education in April of 1968.

6. **Research:** While several of the papers touch upon the data needs for research into library matters, this paper is intended to focus specifically upon these needs from the outset. The information collected determines in large measure the extent, depth and quality of the research possible. Gaps in data, as well as inconsistency in terminology and definitions, have severely limited our research capability. This is particularly evident when one attempts to determine trends within the profession, and to measure progress in any documented way. Computer and other techniques will undoubtedly enable us to learn more from the data available, but a nationwide system will have to concern itself with data which are not now available, but which are essential to the conduct of penetrating inquiry and analysis. Kenneth Beasley, Dean of the Graduate School, University of Texas, El Paso, has for many years looked at library problems and research needs through the eyes of a political scientist and public administration expert. His overview paper on research builds upon his studies for the Pennsylvania State Library and subsequent research into library matters.

Specific Statistical Concerns (appendix B): While the

Statistics Coordinating Committee was anxious that the statistics planning project not go over the same ground covered by the *Handbook,* there was, understandably, the intent that the specific fields covered would match and build upon those in the 1966 volume. Special consultants, therefore, were engaged in the areas of college and university, public, State, school, and special libraries and in the field of library education. Because of the emergence of Federal libraries as an organized group, and the increasing importance of the role of this group in the development of a nationwide library data system, the area of Federal libraries was added to this list.

Fiscal, temporal, and other practical limitations precluded detailed coverage of a number of distinct types of libraries, as it did in the *Handbook,* for example: law libraries, libraries connected with religious organizations, patient and inmate libraries in hospitals and institutions, and association and labor union libraries designed for member use. The *Handbook* stated in regard to these special types of libraries:

> Although these libraries do not qualify for inclusion in the basic types of libraries . . . they must be considered in the evaluation of total library resources in the United States. Also, when one is evaluating library use and library resources on a national basis, it is readily apparent that libraries of this type will have an impact on the statistics.[1]

Exclusion from specific coverage of special classes of libraries caused concern following the publication of the *Handbook,* and perhaps a word of explanation here would help place this matter in perspective. First, the categories included were, to a great extent, predicated by those represented on the ALA Statistics Coordinating Committee, either by virtue of their membership as distinct statistics committees within the American Library Association or by their representation on the Coordinating Committee through liaison membership arrangements. Second, the included categories constitute those in which a considerable body of statistical experience has accumulated. Third, in some cases the included categories are broad enough to encompass specialized areas. For example, law libraries not only can be considered to be a subgroup within special libraries but they also have a relationship to State, Federal, and college and university libraries.

While these considerations may seem expedient, it should be recognized that a nationwide system will have to include specialized library interests and constituen-

---

[1] American Library Association, *Library Statistics: A Handbook of Concepts, Definitions, and Terminology,* p. 7.

cies. Omission of specific focus upon special types of libraries in this project should be considered a limitation, perhaps, but not an oversight. Several of the chapters refer to the problems of overlap which multitype library systems, which may be involved in basic and special categories of libraries, raise. Particular attention will have to be given those libraries which are quasi-public, quasi-academic, and those whose functions and allegiances cut across the traditional stratification now used by the profession. The overview paper on library networks directs attention to these complexities, and a nationwide, comprehensive library data system will have to concern itself increasingly with the emerging cross-cut presaged in today's use of library and information networks and systems.

The papers covering specific statistical concerns may be considered addenda to the chapters in the *Handbook*. An effort was made to obtain consultants other than those who authored the *Handbook* chapters, and this was possible in every case except that of school libraries. Each of these consultants was provided with a set of the overview papers and was asked to direct attention to the following:

1. Gaps in the *Handbook*.

2. The universe for his category of statistics, along with possible sampling techniques.

3. Priorities.

4. Periodicity.

5. Financing.

6. The allocation of responsibilities for statistics collection and dissemination by Federal, State, and professional agencies.

Public Libraries: Rose Vainstein, Professor of Library Science at the University of Michigan, produced the paper on public library statistics. Long associated with library statistics at the Library Services Branch of the U.S. Office of Education, Vainstein addresses herself to the emerging statistical problems of library systems, providing detailed inquiry into questions raised by Ruth Boaz in the overview "Library Systems and Networks."

School Libraries: Richard L. Darling, then Director, Department of Educational Media and Technology, Montgomery County, Md., Public Schools, was one of the consultants to the Library Statistics Coordinating Project of 1963-64. His paper on school library statistics is an extension and refinement of his contribution on

this subject in the *Handbook*. Darling is also known for his former work with national statistics at the U.S. Office of Education. He is now dean of the School of Library Service, Columbia University.

College and University Libraries: Academic libraries are covered by Jay K. Lucker, Associate Librarian, Princeton University and George M. Bailey, Professor and Chief Librarian, York College, City University of New York. This joint effort brings together the concerns of the whole academic library spectrum from the large university to the 2-year college.

Library Education and Manpower: Consideration of the statistics of library schools as essential to those of library manpower in general is provided in the paper by Frank L. Schick, Director, School of Library and Information Science, University of Wisconsin at Milwaukee. Schick is known for his extensive work with library statistics at the Federal and international levels and is currently chairman of the Statistics Coordinating Committee of ALA. His paper "Status of Library Statistics Publications, 1970" is included in appendix C of this report by permission of the R. R. Bowker Company.

State Libraries: S. Gilbert Prentiss' coverage of State library statistics, as explained previously, is divided into two parts. The first, "State Libraries as Collectors of Statistics," appears as an overview paper. The paper included under Specific Statistical Concerns deals with State libraries as producers of statistics, an area which presents many complexities and which has had only the most rudimentary coverage in statistical compilations.

Special Libraries: Logan Cowgill, of the Office of Water Resources Research of the U.S. Department of the Interior, contributed the paper on special libraries. As chairman of the Statistics Committee of the Special Libraries Association, Cowgill is a liaison member of ALA's Statistics Coordinating Committee. The American Library Association is particularly grateful for his efforts on behalf of this project. Thanks are also extended to the Special Libraries Association for facilitating Cowgill's work and for its cooperative efforts to include the concerns of special libraries, which constitute such a large segment of the profession.

Federal Libraries: Paul Howard, then Executive Secretary of the Federal Library Committee and since retired, was prevailed upon to write a paper on the subject of Federal library statistics in addition to his paper on the legislative process. Federal libraries comprise many types and are scattered throughout this country and over the world. They have long been neglected in any overall statistical compilation and planning.

The diversity of interests, the varing levels of detail required, and the overall intent of the statistics planning project not to restrict or overstructure the efforts of the 12 consultants, made it impossible for all papers to present parallel deductions and suggestions. The conclusions and recommendations presented in chapter 3 were prepared by the editor as an analysis and distillation of the implications of all the papers and project discussions.

The Statistics Coordinating Committee (Library Organization and Management Section, Library Administration Division, American Library Association) served as an advisory board to the entire project, and insofar as possible, each of the individual statistics committees was asked to review the papers of concern to it with the specialist, to act as a sounding board, and to submit comments and recommendations to the Coordinating Committee, whose chairman (1963-69) served as project director and general editor.

Assisting the project director was a small steering committee which was invaluable in working out the many logistical problems of the study, as well as those in which seeming conflicts and contradictions emerged. Ruth Frame, Executive Secretary of the Library Administration Division, ALA, handled all scheduling, fiscal matters, and general correspondence and contributed substantively to decisions made along the way. Alphonse

Trezza, now director of the Illinois State Library, continued to contribute the kind of insight and support to this project which was so productive during the Coordinating Project of 1963-64. Joel Williams, who directed that project, served as Federal monitor to the present effort, and from his vantage point as Chief of the Library Surveys Branch of the National Center for Educational Statistics, provided insight into the needs and exigencies of the U.S. Office of Education. Further continuity and assistance was generously provided by Frank L. Schick who has been identified previously in connection with the paper "Library Education and Manpower."

The editor is also very grateful to Nettie Taylor, Director, Library Extension Division, Maryland State Department of Education, and past president of the American Association of State Libraries, for her critical review and expenditure of time and effort on behalf of the project, and to Ray Fry of the Division of Library Programs, U.S. Office of Education, and his staff, for their willingness to act as a sounding board.

The guidelines presented in this report are designed to serve as directions toward development of a nationwide system of library statistics, focused on the collection, evaluation, and dissemination of pertinent, meaningful, complete, and accurate library statistics.

CONCLUSIONS AND RECOMMENDATIONS

This chapter, written after the papers presented in the appendixes were prepared, had the advantage of a number of meetings and joint deliberations not afforded the authors of these papers. It presents, hopefully, a wider agreement on certain central issues, but it does not presume to answer each and every question raised in the overview and statistical papers. Reference should be made to appendix B, "Specific Statistical Concerns," for detail as to statistical problems and proposed solutions by type of library and for library education and manpower.

A number of concurrent developments outside the framework of the Statistics Coordinating Committee of the American Library Association have influenced this chapter—many of them associated with the U.S. Office of Education and its National Center for Educational Statistics (NCES). The following trends undoubtedly will have an impact upon future library statistics programs:

1. The present austerity in which the Federal Government's programs operate restricts considerably the ability of NCES to make major commitments toward the

assumption of new responsibilities regarding any nationwide library statistical program. Emphasis, therefore, must be placed on shared responsibility among governmental and nongovernmental agencies. At the same time, there is an indication that modest grants made specifically for improvement of State statistical programs along the line of title X of the National Defense Education Act might be feasible. In conjunction with nationwide planning, this seed money could do much to improve the situation.

2. The library and information science community can anticipate a number of research efforts and surveys which will bear directly on statistics programs, such as inquiries which will relate to new administrative techniques (program planning and budgeting, management systems, etc.) and to the measurement of impact of social programs (user satisfaction, relevance to pressing issues of urban life, poverty, equalized opportunity, etc.). In this respect, a hope of the National Center for Educational Statistics to augment its own staff with contracts for supplementary work should be mentioned.

3. There will be increased emphasis on factors of accountability. Governmental units which are the major

gatherers and disseminators of library statistics will place priority on those data items which are considered to be the best measures of the results of their investments and which help to satisy the informational needs of their legislative bodies and executive decisionmakers. It can be assumed that USOE's primary inhouse efforts will be directed to providing the information needed by the Federal Government for its own program control and evaluation.

4. The library community will be asked to reevaluate some time-honored concepts such as the value of institutional listings vs. comparison by stratified norms and medians, and the use of sampling techniques vs. total data collections. It will be challenged to catch up statistically with its own evolution and technology as well as with the nationwide data systems of other fields. This development is a part of the new emphasis on accountability and evaluation.

The following problems are illustrative of those arising from the forces of change acting on today's libraries and media centers:

1. Centralized cataloging vs. local cataloging operations.

2. Multipurpose libraries vs. separate units designed to serve certain portions of the user's total informational needs.

3. Population "served" vs. population eligible for service.

4. Service measurements vs. workload data.

5. Size of collection vs. use, recency, and relevance of the collection (with implications for central storage of little-used materials, facsimile transmission, and other retrieval devices).

6. Reduction of duplication vs. necessary duplication for more immediate satisfaction, and the use of expendable materials.

7. Traditional hierarchy of professional librarianship vs. selective skills training, work allocation, and skills sharing,

8. Autonomy and status vs. systems and networks development.

These problems have significant bearing upon statistics and upon the kinds of data needed. The presence of so many unresolved questions and the general foment for

change within the information and communication sciences make it difficult to keep pace with the needs of the profession and preclude a tidy, finite, and static plan.

The recommendations presented here are admittedly transitional and evolutionary. They are more concerned with planning as a process than with a plan, or blueprint, as an objective. They are guidelines for implementation and it is hoped they will inventory a number of areas beyond the scope of this study which need concerted attention, research, and resolution.

Standardization of Terminology

The *Handbook,* or more particularly, its "Glossary: Terms Used in Statistical Surveys," represents a point of departure for what must be a continuous effort to standardize and refine terminology. Such a body of definitions is essential to national aggregates and to any program of shared responsibility. In the 5 years since it was published, a number of needed refinements have come to light, as well as some significant additions. The statistics committees of ALA's Library Administration Division have continued this work and some major segments are now ready for adoption. A set of definitions has been completed for physical facilities of libraries, has been adopted as a formal supplement to the *Handbook,* and is expected to be published at an early date. Considerable progress has also been made in formulating a standard vocabulary for technical services. Elsewhere in ALA, work is progressing on a revision of the *ALA Glossary of Library Terms,* last published in 1943. The publication in 1969 of the *USA Standard for Library Statistics* should also be noted.

The standardization of terminology is particularly appropriate to all library and related associations and every effort should be made by ALA to seek the assistance and involvement of other major national library associations. Although committee activity undertaken primarily at semiannual conferences is limited and slow, reasonable debate and concensus is built into this process. While coordination and authoritative publication of terminology of library statistics are properly the responsibilities of the National Center for Educational Statistics, the actual defining of terminology should take place in the library and information science community. ALA, through its Statistics Coordinating Committee should:

1. Outline areas in which standard terminology has not been developed and set priorities for their coverage.

2. Develop an orderly program by which suggested

revisions to existing definitions can be reviewed and acted upon.

3. Commence planning a project which will lead to the publication by NCES of a document which would revise and expand the glossary that appears in the *Handbook* and in the *USA Standard for Library Statistics*. The Coordinating Committee should bear the following in mind as it designs and implements such a project:

a. Coordination insofar as possible with present efforts to issue a new ALA glossary of library terms.

b. Continued representation of NCES on the Statistics Coordinating Committee. If NCES is to utilize, further develop, and promulgate the standardized terminology, it must be significantly involved.

c. The desirability of special funding for the project. The mechanics which produced the *Handbook,* i.e., a funded project staff, advisory assistance, and a series of regional conferences at which the broadest possible spectrum of reaction and suggestion was obtained, were basic to its success and general acceptance.

4. Strengthen ties with other professional associations, particularly with appropriate subdivisions of the Special Libraries Association, the Association of Research Libraries, the Canadian Library Association, and others working on standard glossaries and related activities regarding library automation and computerization.

5. Seek advice and guidance from specialists in other disciplines whose work involves them in library statistics (e.g., statisticians, public administrators, political scientists, sociologists, etc.). A relatively small expenditure might enable the committee to hold special meetings with such persons at crucial moments of planning, policysetting, and decision-making.

6. Seek to involve in its membership persons actively engaged in library statistics and research, recruiting on the basis of skill and involvement rather than prominence in the profession and in the ALA structure.

7. Hold for its own membership workshops in "data-banking," program planning and budgeting, and other techniques which affect statistical terminology and procedures.

Against this background of wide professional participation in developing and recommending statistical terms for library data gathering, the National Center for Educational Statistics should adopt and promulgate the terminology along with such additions and qualifications as it might have to adopt, through a U.S. Government manual for library statistics. It should be guided in this matter by its liaison membership on the Coordinating Committee and by its own advisory committee on library statistics described later in this chapter.

A Nationwide System of Library Statistics

An official statistical language for libraries, however, is only a small portion of what should constitute a nationwide system of library statistics. Basic to the recommendations of this chapter is the necessity to decentralize, to articulate, and to coordinate the responsibilities for statistics gathering and dissemination. The proposed system depends upon a much more active role of the States and upon the input of research, interaction of advisory groups, inservice training, and relatively small amounts of money at strategic points along the way. The role of the States can be seen from the diagrammatic presentation in chart I and is interwoven throughout the steps to be outlined next. Research should be encouraged by all possible means and should involve the widest spectrum of professional participation. Reference is made to Beasley's overview paper in this context.

Chart I lists the major ingredients which should be part of a statistics system. Some of these are already incorporated in present programs and work effectively; others are additions to present practice.

NCES Advisory Committee: An important factor of the system is the formation of an advisory group on library statistics within the U.S. Office of Education.[1] Such a group should be broadly representative of users of library statistics, library and information science associations, research and computer experts, publishers, and other related groups.

National Commission on Libraries and Information Science: The activities of an NCES advisory group should be distinguished from those of the newly created National Commission on Libraries and Information Science. While the Commission will be concerned that adequate data on library conditions are available, it has a much broader charge. It will, therefore, be subject to many pressures involving national planning for library

---

[1] Also recommended in *National Conference on Library Statistics,* p. 93.

resources, services, and information transmission techniques which will meet the needs of the future. Its membership will reflect broad concerns of the profession and will be unable to give the detailed attention to statistical matters *per se* which will be required for the implementation of the system proposed in this report, much less to the ultimate formation of a data bank system. The Commission will, however, constitute a useful and much needed higher authority for financial support and determination of priorities. Naturally, the Commission would be directly concerned with that legislation necessary to implement the statistics program of the States as proposed and with efforts to secure its passage and implementation.

Coordination With Other Agencies: Several other influences should be brought to bear upon major policy and priority determination before NCES initiates forms for specific surveys. Expanded communication with the USOE Bureau of Library Programs and Educational Technology and with the USOE regional library program officers would be essential. In addition, other statistics-producing agencies (such as the Bureau of the Census) should be kept in mind for optimum correlation of data, derived statistics, etc.; and the Federal Library Committee could also make a contribution at this stage.

Forms Development: Development of standardized forms for the collection of national library data is the responsibility of the National Center for Educational Statistics and a major concern of its advisory committee. This activity should encompass the development of forms for both the State and local levels as well where national data are concerned. NCES could play a very important role as adviser to governmental and private agencies in the design of statistical forms which are consistent and effective. In addition, NCES should commission work on the development of forms from research centers (e.g., academic institutions and/or government-sponsored institutes) as appropriate and as required by the specialized nature of the particular form.

Review; Pretesting: Forms should be reviewed by the appropriate State agencies and the professional associations and should be pretested on a carefully constructed sample of the agencies to be surveyed. Sufficient lead-time must be provided for questions which necessitate the keeping of new records at the local level. The State agencies can be useful in assisting in the construction of pretest samples which are representative of the variety of local conditions the questionnaires must serve.

Forms Clearance, Further Coordination: NCES should coordinate its data collection activities with those required by other Federal agencies which administer programs affecting libraries. For example, data collected by the Bureau of Libraries and Educational Technology of the USOE in the course of administering various grant programs should be tapped by NCES and utilized. Local agencies should not have to answer the same questions for each of several agencies of the Federal Government if the data can be pooled and shared. Coordination and communication between NCES and the Bureau of Libraries and Educational Technology should be strenghtened. If this requires some formal intrastructure, then one should be established.

A central data bank serving all parts of the USOE would seem highly productive, but care would have to be taken to see that all pertinent information were indeed "deposited" in the bank. Such a system would presuppose standardization of terminology and procedure in all USOE data-gathering activities. Whether or not a data bank is established, a forms clearance program beyond that exercised by the Office of Management and Budget (formerly the Bureau of the Budget), which must pass on all governmental forms, is essential. The data bank aspect is discussed in detail later in this chapter.

NCES is obviously not responsible for all information released by the Federal Government on the Nation's libraries. Evaluations of grant programs, research reports, and other major pieces of information are the responsibility of the offices which execute these programs and may include statistical information. Much of this information tends to be of an inventory type (the number of libraries which have, or have not, certain characteristics; do, or do not, provide certain services, etc.). This type of information is highly useful and needed, but it is not necessarily statistical nor subject to derived data and interpretation. Much more inventory-type information should be issued by the USOE but would generally be beyond the scope of NCES, at least in its present form and until a well-developed data bank system is operative. The effort represented by this report should not be confused with a total national information system on libraries which would be capable of infinite expansion.

Printing and Distribution: The national Center for Educational Statistics should have survey questionnaires printed in sufficient supply for distribution to each State according to the demands of its self-determined universe(s). Franking privileges should be extended for the mailing by the States of all questionnaires designed by the Federal Government for national statistical surveys.

Library Universes: Library universes should be defined by NCES but can only be determined with any accuracy and economy at the State level. The American Library Association and other professional associations should study the question of library universes and establish a minimum standard for statistically significant units, and make recommendations for meaningful samples when the sampling technique can be used judiciously. Further study is also required in adopting appropriate statistical terminology for library systems, especially those which include more than one type of library. Although NCES can provide basic building-block-unit survey forms, it is the responsibility of the States to produce aggregate systems reports.

Education; Training: NCES has an obligation to assist the States in the data-collecting activities which it delegates to them. Workshops should be regularly scheduled on a regional or interstate basis, at which the questionnaires, their distribution within the States, and editing requirements would be discussed. The State personnel directly responsible for these activities should attend the meetings. The resultant forum for comment and criticism about the forms and procedures would be as useful to NCES as to the participants, since reaction and feedback can be used to refine the program and correct errors and misjudgements. One of the serious problems of library statistics has been the lack of opportunity to involve middle management directly responsible for their collection. In addition to involving such personnel at training sessions, it would be desirable to encourage participation of appropriate representatives of ALA and other professional associations in order that the consumers and major advisers would have more immediate contact with the pragmatic issues involved.

Procedures Manual; Instructions for Survey Forms: Essential to the workshops and to the statistical activities of the States on behalf of the Federal Government, would be the development of Federal manuals of instructions and procedures. These manuals should embody the standardized terminology adopted and promulgated by NCES and should delineate desired procedures and editing instructions in detail as well as provide general understanding of the objectives of the various surveys. The manuals should be reviewed by the NCES advisory committee on library statistics and revised as appropriate. Considerable care should be exercised to continue the same procedures from year to year and to revise them only after thoughtful deliberation and expert advice. The more familiar the State and local agencies become with the forms, the terminology, and the procedures, the better will be the product, and irritation and confusion can be minimized. Also, if changes in the manual or the instructions are adopted, considerable leadtime should be allowed (at least a year) for the State and local agencies to become thoroughly aware of them and institute necessary adjustments. Inservice training and workshop activities would probably have to be intensified to facilitate understanding and compliance.

Additional State Statistical Needs: In addition to the Federal statistics activities for national library data, there should be the careful construction by the States of additional questions and statistical instruments needed individually by them to satisy legal requirements under State law, to meet the more detailed data requirements they would have in their day-to-day contacts with local agencies, and to evaluate specific programs. The Federal Government has a role here in assisting the States to adopt certain uniform procedures and forms in order to improve comparability among the States. But we are speaking of areas of data which are for the most part beyond the Federal purview and would not normally be published centrally as part of the national library statistics. The States must take the responsibility of refining their own data-gathering programs, and ALA's American Association of State Libraries should direct attention to coordination of these activities and such uniform survey instruments as are feasible.

State Advisory Groups: In each State, an advisory committee on library statistics should be appointed to assist in these matters. Care should be taken to see that the various State agencies concerned in this area are represented. For example, library statistics have a bearing upon accreditation programs, State and community planning, urban affairs, and research activities, to mention only a few. Also the statistics program must take into account the many ways in which library activities are organized at the State level, e.g., separate State library commissions, public library extension agencies organized within State departments of education, school library development agencies within or outside the State library structure, separate departments of higher education, separate State historical agencies, etc. If intertype library systems and networks are to continue to develop, and if the number of separate Federal programs affecting libraries continues, then all the State agencies concerned should participate in the development of meaningful library statistics programs.

State Library Agencies; State Agencies Concerned with Libraries: In referring to State agencies which would act as the NCES links in the national library statistics system, it must be understood that we are not necessarily speaking only of the "State library agencies." The various forms of State organization mentioned before imply that for particular surveys (college libraries, for example), the appropriate State agency would have to be contacted, whether it be in the State department of education, the department of higher education, or the State library. While it would be convenient, and in many cases desirable, for the Federal Government to assign responsibility for all library surveys to a central State agency (such as the State library), such an action would be unrealistic and unworkable. It must work through existing State organizational patterns. In order to activate the appropriate State agency for comprehensive statistics collection, NCES must, therefore, develop relations with a number of relevant agencies in each State. On the other hand, to effectively coordinate such a program, each State agency will need to tap local groups for advice—library associations, library schools, research centers, etc. The States have an obligation to analyze the users of library statistics and, insofar as possible, include all of them in their library data program planning.

Distribution; Training: We are assuming much more sophisticated questionnaires and the use of standardized terminology which will be new to the local agencies. We are assuming, also, surveys by the States of library agencies with which they have had little or no contact heretofore. The State, then, has the obligation to assist the local libraries to understand and comply with its statistical requirements. Considerable effort will have to go into the development of effective workshop techniques and manuals. On the State and Federal levels, timing will be a sensitive factor. Leadtime in which to commence new recordkeeping procedures at the local level and in which to become thoroughly acquainted with the procedures, objectives, and vocabulary is essential. With respect to the core questions which are being asked on behalf of the Federal Government, the States should be able to call upon "instructors" from NCES to assist with workshops. The cooperation and participation of State professional associations through their appropriate committees could also be of help in focusing attention on such meetings.

State Editing: At the heart of this recommended system is the decentralization of the program and the shared responsibility for editing the questionnaire returns. The Federal manual of procedures should contain editing guides for the States. The State agencies are close enough to the local units to spot obvious misunderstandings of the respondents and to clear them up through direct contact. They are also in a position to maintain an overview of local activities which impinge upon each other and must be correlated for a statistically sound picture of library system activities. Vainstein's chapter on public library statistics discusses some of these problems. Suffice it to say that meaningful statistics regarding networks and systems, especially those composed of different types of libraries, will make the editing process at the State level of crucial importance.

Coordination at the State Level: It is important that one central State agency be assigned the responsibility for this editorial process. It is recommended that the State library, or the State library extension agency, act as the central editing unit for core library data being forwarded to the Federal Government. It may have to work with other State agencies to obtain expertise in interpreting certain portions of the data. In any event, the advisory group(s) mentioned above should review and react to editorial policy. Obviously, leverage must be applied at this point, and some form of Federal financial assistance with regulatory guidance and control would seem the most effective. Should a central State educational statistics center evolve outside the State library or State library extension agency, then State library personnel should be assigned to the center to work with the coordination and editing of library data, and the State library should be a fully participating member of the center's planning and review activities.

Publication and Dissemination of Data: It is recommended that two parallel data publication and dissemination activities be defined, regularized, and implemented as soon as possible. NCES, upon receipt of the core data from the States should edit it again for its own purposes and publish it as promptly as the Federal governmental structure permits. Meanwhile, at the State level, the data which have been collected for State purposes should be published as soon as possible, using uniform table shells developed by NCES. This plan assumes that the primary responsibility (pro tem) for institutional data will rest with the States, and that the Federal Government will be primarily responsible for national aggregates.

State publication should allow for enough copies to satisfy individual requests from local agencies in other States through reciprocal distribution of all statistical publications of library data. State libraries have an obligation to provide information on libraries and library programs within their own States.[2] The State publications should receive wide distribution beyond the State borders: to other State library agencies, national associations, the Library of Congress, the National Center for Educational Statistics, the Bureau of Libraries and Educational Technology, and other Federal agencies.

National Library Statistics Depository: To provide a central resource for all those engaged in library statistics research, it is recommended that a library statistics depository be established and consist of all library statistics publications and survey instruments published

---

[2] For example, an academic librarian in New Jersey wishing access to the statistics of one or several comparable institutions in California could contact the institutions directly but should have other avenues of access to the desired information as well—the State library being one of them.

CHART I

A NATIONWIDE SYSTEM OF LIBRARY STATISTICS

NCES professional
staff

NCES Consultants;
research institutes

NCES Advisory
Committee

RESEARCH; DETERMINATION
OF NCES QUESTIONNAIRE
CONTENT

National Commission on Libraries
and Information Science

Bureau of Libraries and Educational Technology; other
related Federal agencies

ALA and other professional
association advice

Approval by NCES
Advisory Committee

FORMS DEVELOPMENT; USE
OF STANDARDIZED TERMINOLOGY

Coordination with other
Federal agencies

State agency cooperation
in determining pretest
samples

PRETESTING
OF
QUESTIONNAIRES

Professional association
consultation and
recommendations

USOE interagency
review

FORMS CLEARANCE
AND
PRINTING

Office of Management and
Budget (formerly Bureau of
the Budget)

State agency determination
of survey
universe(s)

DISTRIBUTION
TO
STATES

Professional association
recommendations on survey
universe(s)

Trainees directly involved in
library statistics

NCES-hired
instructors

INSERVICE TRAINING;
REGIONAL WORKSHOPS

ALA, other professional
participation

Procedures manuals,
definitions, etc.

Federal requirements
to be met

State agency research
activities

STATE DETERMINATION
OF ADDITIONAL
STATISTICS NEEDS

State Statistics Advisory
Committee

State professional
associations

Federal financial
assistance

STATE DISTRIBUTION OF
FEDERAL QUESTIONNAIRES
AND STATE SUPPLEMENTS

Additions, supplements to
questionnaire for State and
local needs

Local
librarians

State agency instructors

Procedures manuals,
definitions, etc.

INSERVICE TRAINING;
LOCAL WORKSHOPS

Federal representatives as
required

State professional association(s)
participation

CHART I—(Continued)

A NATIONWIDE SYSTEM OF LIBRARY STATISTICS—Continued

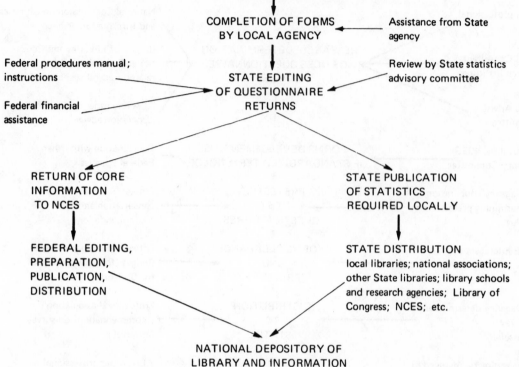

in the United States. Such information should be made available on request to researchers in the field. The depository could be established at the Library of Congress, the National Center for Educational Statistics, the American Library Association, or any other appropriate agency.

Chart I: The above diagram presents a visual overview, albeit a somewhat oversimplified presentation of a nationwide statistics program as it would involve NCES and the State agencies in a shared-responsibility operation.

The process outlined in the preceding diagram should, at some time, contain another important element—the utilization of a national data bank system. An argument is made for data banking later on, but before we describe such an *ultima Thule,* present limitations must be faced up to, along with possible methods for alleviating them.

Interim Limitations and Considerations

The last decade has seen the gradual diminution of the library statistical publications of USOE. (Even in the most productive period of the former Library Services Branch, the library statistical publications were neither entirely synchronized nor complete.) A number of factors contributed to this program reduction:

1. Several reorganizations have taken place within USOE and are continuing to take place. Of particular interest was the creation of the National Center for Educational Statistics in 1965, at which time library statistics were separated from library programs, occasioning the reassignment of personnel, budget adjustments, etc.

2. An unprecedented spate of education programs was thrust upon the Office of Education by legislative action. Data gathering and distribution were forced to take a lower priority than the solution to pressing problems of implementing these programs and establishing necessary administrative and regulatory machinery. The magnitude of the programs directed toward education *per se* also tended to overshadow those of supportive services such as library service, and to preempt its already unsteady hold on the priorities scale.

3. The rapid growth of computer technology has forced the conversion of traditional statistical survey techniques—a conversion which is slow and laborious. Communication among computer and library experts has far to go and is impeded by a language barrier.

4. Confusion has always existed within the profession as to what information it considered essential and what terminology should constitute a standard. Although the *Handbook* provided the nascent NCES some guidance, it has been difficult for the Federal Government to respond to conflicting professional demands. One need only ask "what is a library system" or "what is meant by population served" to recognize the impasse which faced the national library statistics program.

5. The present austerity in which USOE must operate (the small staff allotted to library surveys at present and the reduced funds for all their attendant needs such as travel, publication, etc.) makes it impossible to assume that NCES is in a position to satisfy the profession's demands for continuing all the traditional surveys at a frequency known in the past in addition to initiating new survey techniques which will incorporate improvements sought by the Statistics Coordinating Committee and other interested professional groups. This reason overshadows almost any other for adopting the shared responsibility described in the preceding pages.

At this point in time and at this point in its development, NCES will, of necessity, have to direct its attentions foremost to the needs of the Federal Government rather than to those of private associations and individual users. This is regrettable, and one can only hope that a compromise between Federal and extra-Federal needs can be achieved which will ease this interim period. The Boaz overview paper, "Library Networks and Systems," is an indication of the direction of such a compromise.

The National Center for Educational Statistics, however, has no monopoly on problems which have circumscribed library statistical publications. The diversity of data needs within the library community has made it difficult to establish even a limited core of library information which can be aggregated nationally.

Chart II represents recurring categories of library data which are identified by the contributors to this project as needed regularly and which constitute a bare minimum. With the exception of information on physical facilities, and detailed personnel data (such as fringe benefits, etc.), these statistics are desired on an annual basis. Even so, there is considerable variation in expressed need, as can be seen in the following tally:

1. All seven categories want:

   a. Salaries.
   b. Staff data (number of positions).
   c. Population or clientele served.
   d. Expenditure by type or program.

2. All categories, except library education, want:

   a. Book stock.
   b. Periodicals.
   c. Microform.
   d. Nonbook materials.
   e. Interlibrary loan data.

3. All categories except library education and special libraries want:

   a. Number of outlets.
   b. Circulation.

4. Only public, school, and State libraries, and library education want income by source.

5. Only public and State libraries want reference statistics.

6. Only public, school, and college and university libraries want data on hours open.

While the number of data in which there is expressed unanimity of need is disappointingly small, there is an indication that a body of "core" questions which would apply across the board for all types of libraries could be developed for meaningful national aggregates. These core questions would constitute a central body of data gathered regularly and in standardized form by NCES, hopefully with the assistance of the States. To them would be added other questions (depending upon the type of library surveyed) which would make up less frequent (perhaps biennial) national surveys published by the Federal Government. During this interim—pending the growth of NCES, progress toward a data bank system, and other factors—the bulk of annual, detailed data should be gathered at the State level and made accessible as described before.

Such guidelines as may be gathered from chart II would need further review by the professional associations once this line of attack was fully understood. It is possible that more common ground can be found and the

CHART II

NATIONAL LIBRARY STATISTICS
BASIC ANNUAL DATA REQUIREMENTS

Basic data required	Public	School	College and university	Library education	State	Special	Federal
Income by source	X	X		X	X		
Expenditure by type of program	X	X	X	X	X	X	X
Salaries	X	X	X	X	X	X	X
Fringe benefits[1]	X	X	X	X	X	X	X
Staff	X	X		X	X	X	X
Book stock	X	X	X		X	X	X
Periodicals	X	X	X		X	X	X
Microform	X	X	X		X	X	X
Nonbook materials	X	X	X		X	X	X
Reference	X				X		
Circulation	X	X	X		X		X
Interlibrary loans	X	X	X		X	X	X
Physical facilities[1]	X	X	X	X	X	X	X
Hours open	X	X	X				
Number of outlets		X	X		X		X
Population or clientele served		X	X	X	X	X	X

[1] To be reported approximately every 5 years.

assurance that publication would be regularized might influence the present desire for annual publication of some of the data items.

But it would seem clear that more concentrated expertise is needed to determine the nature of the core questions which might be adopted by NCES. The advisory committee recommended for NCES, the National Commission on Libraries and Information Science, further advice from the Statistics Coordinating Committee, and other national organizations (once the urgency of determining the scope of core data is known), plus the professional input of NCES itself, should be able to perfect and delineate essential data categories to be included in "core surveys" cutting across types of libraries. The fact that the library community, acting solely through its various association and committee structures, has so far proved itself inadequate to such determination cannot be escaped. To summarize, NCES should put primary emphasis on perfecting a multipurpose survey instrument (LIBGIS, as it is called in the Boaz paper) for the collection of core data on the local and system activities of public, school, college and university, State, and special libraries (and possibly Federal libraries) intended to produce annually:

1. National aggregates for each type of library, by State.

2. Information on libraries and library development functions at the local, State, and Federal levels. By library development functions is meant those activities and services which extend beyond the traditional service areas as defined by source of local support and which are developed on behalf of a network of library and information services.

NCES should also develop more detailed surveys by type of library. The frequency with which each type can be covered, however, will depend in large measure upon the rapidity with which the shared-responsibility system involving the States can be established and made fully operational.

Given the difficulties under which NCES must operate, this approach would seem rational and pragmatic. The library profession will want to review carefully the data which are to be included in core surveys, and NCES should make sure that adequate opportunity to do so is afforded. But while the profession can, and should, influence this coverage, it cannot expect to enlarge it to cover all the many aspects it might wish to have covered annually. Budget and staff limitations at the Federal level preclude this, as do the philosophic issues which require better definition and further stabilization (e.g., the questions of library systems and population served). Of great importance will be the concerted deliberations and assistance which the advisory committee to NCES can afford.

How long this admittedly restricted, interim program would continue depends upon three factors:

1. The rapidity with which the State agencies can assume their full statistical responsibilities in a nationwide system of library statistics (as illustrated in chart I).

2. The extent to which professional groups can develop supplementary data surveys which are sufficiently coordinated with the national effort to produce meaningful extensions of it.

3. The gradual development of a data bank system which would provide regular dissemination of essential core data, as well as access (at cost) to particular levels of detail, as needed.

State Statistical Capability: If the States are to assume responsibilities, many of which will be new, then some incentive program is needed to secure their cooperation. It is therefore recommended that participation in a standard, minimal program be recommended to State library agencies and, upon consent of a majority, be made a mandatory factor in Federal library aid programs. The statistics program can be financed entirely by Federal funds, or on some matching basis. The latter would have the advantage of encouraging State governments to recognize the need for strenghtening State library agencies generally with realistic support of their own library and information needs.

There are a number of ways this incentive program could be designed. It would be out of scope for this report to attempt to design new legislation, though this would be one approach. Regulatory interpretation of existing statutes, such as the Library Services and Construction Act, the State Technical Services Act (administered by the U.S. Department of Commerce), the Elementary and Secondary Education Act, the Higher Education Act, and others, or amendments to them, would be another.

Whatever the legal mechanics, this federally supported and coordinated program should require the following factors at the State level:

1. Submission of an approvable State plan under which the statistics activities will be developed and carried out.

2. Identification of legal authority in State statutes for gathering, interpreting, publishing, and disseminating library statistics for all types of libraries.

3. Identification of the agency or agencies within State government which will carry out these responsibilities, and the means by which efforts in this area will be coordinated.

4. Identification of a State library statistics advisory committee which will represent all types of libraries and major information interests within the State.

5. Compliance with NCES requirements concerning terminology and procedures as developed in official U.S. Government instructions and manuals.

6. Agreement to act as the Federal Government's agent in surveying libraries within the State with regard to core information needed nationally.

7. Identification of the means by which the State will encourage and train local libraries to participate in the statistics system.

8. Identification by each State of the various library universes as defined by the Federal Government and the use of such national, standard coding system as might be developed for both individual library units and for library systems.

9. Submission of data on the library functions at the State level as required by the Federal Government for national use. (See Prentiss's paper on State libraries as producers of statistics in appendix B.)

10. Provision of statistically skilled personnel to coordinate, interpret, and edit State statistics on libraries, to develop forms, and to assist local libraries in filling them out, etc.

11. Allowance for coordinated, cooperative, multi-State programs where population and library density would make this more feasible. (Advice from the regional library program officers of USOE could be valuable in these considerations.)

12. Compliance with standardized format requirements of electronic data processing (e.g., punched cards, machine readable tape, etc.) as data bank development proceeds.

At the Federal level, NCES would have to assume the responsibilities outlined for it in a nationwide library statistics system. Realistic budgetary support of NCES will be essential. In addition, of course, the Federal Government must provide grant funds to the States to enable them to comply with the 12 factors just cited. NCES, in cooperation with the American Association of State Libraries of ALA, should cost out the elements of State responsibility involved in the system, namely:

1. State determination of library universes.

2. State forms development, distribution.

3. State advisory committee expenses.

4. Development and publication of State statistical manual.

5. Local inservice training workshops.

6. Research activities directly concerned with refining the program.

7. Staffing (including competent statistical person-'nel).

8. Editing of data.

9. Publication and distribution of individual library data by the States.

10. Other elements.

A very rough estimate of this cost for all 50 States and the outlying areas would be approximately $3 million annually—a very small national investment considering the large sums which have gone into library development programs in this Nation.

In addition, and especially in view of any attempt to establish a national library data bank system, NCES (or the Bureau of Libraries and Educational Technology, whichever is appropriate) should be enabled to conduct specialized library surveys and to provide detailed data on particular aspects of library activity (beyond the normal statistical program) *at cost* to the user. Defraying cost in this way would enable research centers, publishers, governmental and private agencies, and individuals to tap into the data mass as accumulated and produced by the system without placing undue burden upon NCES. (A precedent for this activity can be found in the special studies of the U.S. Bureau of the Census.)

Supplemental Professional Activity: Statistical publication by the profession itself has been significant in the past and should not be discounted for the future. In the main, and with such notable exceptions as college and university library statistics published prior to 1960 and certain recurring selected salary surveys, these contributions have been sporadic and uncoordinated. Professional associations, libraries, and other private agencies are ill equipped to sustain major portions of the national statistical coverage on libraries. As nonprofit organizations, they have not had sufficient funds to do the work; they must respond to their particular memberships or governances rather than to the dictates of an overall plan; and compliance of agencies surveyed is on a courtesy basis and therefore cannot be assured.

This is not to say that such agencies, and especially research units of academic institutions, do not respond ably when commissioned to do a particular survey or to analyze, edit, and publish data already gathered. NCES should exercise great freedom in commissioning such work and in supplementing its own publication capacity with the skills and services of outside agencies. Indeed, it is hoped that these arrangements will be expanded and intensified. Not only do they disperse the workload and make possible the keeping of certain deadlines, they also promote healthy exchange, communication, understanding, and trust between the Federal Government and the profession.

What portion of national library statistics commitments can be borne by the profession itself?

Adequate personnel statistics to meet the needs of professional planning (such as individual salaries, fringe benefits, certification, and tenure data) may be impossible to acquire through general statistical programs of the Federal and State Governments. The national library associations must take the initiative and responsibility for the availability of annual personnel data to enable librarians and the general library community as a whole to recognize needs and to take informed action.

The American Library Association is currently considering ways and means of conducting annual salary surveys. This is considered to be a step toward the establishment of annual library salary goals. The ALA also expects to develop employment standards including fringe benefit guidelines. These two programs will require the investment of funds and man-hours by association members and staff.

The Special Libraries Association and the Association of Research Libraries each has periodically collected and distributed personnel statistics regarding their own individual or institutional members. The ALA should work closely with the other library associations in the development and support of a program of adequate personnel statistics for the profession. These professional associations must also work with the national and State agencies to acquire all possible data through, and from, ongoing statistical programs of the governments.

It must also be clearly understood that all libraries must cooperate fully in providing requested personnel data to governmental and professional statistical programs. Failure to cooperate completely with such programs will mean the profession cannot assess the status of the profession with accuracy.

This report emphasizes the wisdom and necessity for the use of sampling techniques in statistical reporting. Sampling techniques should be used whenever possible by the profession in fulfilling its commitment of providing personnel data.

It is suggested that, at the Federal level, the annual personnel studies of the associations be supplemented by occasional, intensive surveys by NCES which correlate and interpret data of the various types of libraries. Sampling techniques, again, would be essential.

In addition to bearing the responsibility for adequate personnel data, the profession may also need to sponsor other "special studies" which cannot be included in periodic library statistics studies. These might include statistical reports on holdings by subject and by form, space requirements, and user needs.

Again, for the interim, responsibility will have to be borne by many specialized agencies for much of their own statistical needs. For example, The American Association of Law Libraries, Music Librarians Association, Medical Libraries Association, and the numerous chapters of the Special Libraries Association represent crosscuts of the profession which the present system is unprepared for. In time, the proposed data bank system could provide much needed information for the various interest groups, and should be designed to do so. But NCES is obviously unable to render this kind of service now (except as specifically commissioned) and will be unable to do so for some time to come.

Professional organizations should be encouraged to supplement the nationwide system outlined in this chapter in every way they can. They should not be asked, however, to bear responsibility for basic minimal, annual statistical coverage of the Nation's library activity.

A National Data Bank System: In the long range, the statistical needs of all users of library data can best be satisfied by an electronic data bank system. Many factors lead us to such a conclusion:

First, each user, whether stratified by type of library unit or by type of need (administrative, research, political, etc.), wants more, not less, detail for his area of concern than is now or has been hitherto available and can cite compelling reasons why such level of detail is needed. The increasing complexity of information control and of organizational and fiscal factors surrounding the knowledge explosion is among the more obvious. Also, as society attempts to mobilize its forces to deal with such massive problems as urban change, social and economic equalization, and evolution and revolution in any number of directions; the variety and number of users of library related data expand. Detailed data are increasingly of interest in the areas of sociology, political science, education, commerce, industry, and others beyond librarianship *per se*.

In spite of this multiplication of detail to be collected and the uses to which it can be put, or indeed perhaps because of it, those concerned with library statistics have all too often tried to control data by establishing some delimiting framework—by sorting out the absolutely necessary from the postponable. What data are needed, how often, who is to be responsible, etc. are questions which are repeated throughout the literature and are faced in almost every paper in this report. One of the oldest and simplest ways of controlling massive detail is to reduce it. But this method runs contrary to the major forces at work in an era of exploding population, information, economy, and technology. Our need for detailed data grows in proportion to its mass. Fortunately, this growth tends to be equaled by the technical ability to cope with it.

Attempts to delineate the areas and the frequency of library statistics which are to be produced have been frustrating. Who is to decide what is essential, what is postponable? Even if librarians can achieve a consensus, what of those who produce and allocate the funds for libraries? Electronic data processing and the data bank concept are the only techniques which will accommodate the mass of detail and the multiplicity of uses which now exist and can be expected to expand.

As pointed out by Boaz, Vainstein, Prentiss, Howard, and others, new fiscal and service relationships among libraries of the same type and of different types are gradually breaking down the distinctions which have been preserved in traditional library statistics. For example, the National Center for Educational Statistics is coming to the realization that the categories which shaped their publications on public library statistics (i.e., population served—25,000-99,999; 100,000 and over, etc.) are now totally meaningless and unworkable. Because of emerging system and network relationships, the same library may serve different sized populations according to different functions.

In order to assess the gamut of resources and services available to a given population, from a variety of library units and at varying levels of sophistication and intensity, we must combine bits of library data in ways hitherto untried. Not only is this need apparent as library systems and information networks proliferate and become more complex, but it can be observed within the single library unit which may simultaneously serve a number of purposes—the institutional library, for example, which serves the public and academic needs of inmates as well as the special, technical library needs of its staff; or the combinations of public, school, and special library services found in the same agency in the military; or the unpredictable mixtures found in State libraries. Considerably more flexibility is needed to sort out these data and to arrange them in a way that is statistically significant for the use made of them.

The computerized data bank affords the degree of flexibility of data manipulation which is increasingly called for as libraries and library systems evolve.

The need for research and for correlation of research findings and the scarcity of data which have been standardized to a degree which make them acceptable to multiple research applications are covered in the Beasley research overview paper. These concerns lead him to conclude that a data bank is central to any program of general research in library service. The ability of the electronic data bank system to cope with a mass of detail, yet provide maximum flexibility of access to any category, obviously characterizes the kind of tool needed to satisfy the research needs which have been identified.

One need not belabor the point to conclude that the data bank approach affords the ultimate, long-range solution which a nationwide, comprehensive library statistics program should provide. NCES has for some time set its sights upon computerization of its activities and is moving in this direction.

But the development of a data bank system will require more than a large memory capacity machine, the sums needed for hardware and software, and the personnel to convert data to machine readable form. It is absolutely dependent upon standardization of terminology, inquiry into what should occupy the computer cells, systematic collecting and editing of data, and the cooperative relationships illustrated in the foregoing diagram and explanatory test. The data bank will involve the interlocking, coordinated efforts of the many advisory groups which have been cited and the designing of an electronic information system by highly skilled professionals. Beasley's suggestion that a consortium of agencies—Federal, State, and private—working together as a data bank system, each bearing part of the responsibility, the workload, and the financing, should be explored carefully and would constitute a highly useful research project in itself. In the meantime, the steps taken now should be guided with the ultimate data bank solution in mind.

FEDERAL OVERVIEW

by John G. Lorenz

The collection of national statistics of many types and varieties is one of the most important responsibilities of the Federal Government.

Some of the principal types of statistics as specifically identified in the *U.S. Government Organization Manual* are: agricultural, business, carriers, census, construction, cost of living, cotton, educational, employment, fisheries, foreign, government services, health, housing, industrial, labor, manpower, manufactures, mineral, monetary, population, price, research, social security, State and local governments, tax, trade, transportation, and wage.

Some of the principal agencies of the Federal Government with a primary responsibility for statistics are:

Bureau of Accounts and Statistics, Civil Aeronautics Board

Bureau of Labor Statistics, Department of Labor

Division of Research and Statistics, Federal Reserve System

National Center for Educational Statistics, Office of Education, Department of Health, Education, and Welfare

National Center for Health Statistics, Public Health Service, Department of Health, Education, and Welfare

Office of Research and Statistics, Social Security Administration, Department of Health, Education, and Welfare

Statistics Division, Internal Revenue Service, Department of the Treasury

Agricultural Statistics Division, Department of Agriculture

Research and Statistics Division, Selective Service System

Reports and Statistics Service, Veterans Administration

The Bureau of the Census, of course, has as its primary mission providing basic statistics about the people and the economy of the Nation in order to assist the Congress, Federal, State, and local governments, business and industry, and the public generally in planning, carrying out, and evaluating public and private programs. It collects, tabulates, and publishes a wide variety of statistical data and provides statistical information to Government and private users. This Federal agency first began collecting library statistics in 1850 when it reported on public school, Sunday school, college, and church library statistics in 31 States, the District of Columbia, and four territories including Minnesota, New Mexico, Oregon, and Utah. This Census report also included a tabulation for 31 States and the District of Columbia on State libraries, social libraries, students' libraries, libraries of academies and professional schools, and scientific and historical societies. The latest general Census, the 1960 decennial, does not illustrate any progress in national library statistics from this source but rather retrogression since no detailed library statistics are included. Librarians are only included as one of the occupations to be analyzed as part of the "experienced civilian labor force."

In the broader field of education, the Office of Education was established in 1867 to collect such statistics and facts as shall show the condition and progress of education, to diffuse such information as shall aid the people of the United States in the establishment and maintenance of efficient school systems, and otherwise to promote the cause of education. The Office included libraries in its field of responsibility and in 1876 published one of the most comprehensive reports on libraries ever compiled, *Public Libraries in the United States*. Library statistics in this publication included college libraries, information on printed catalogs, public library statistics on appropriations, benefactions, loss and wear of books, and circulation by various classes of material. This remains an amazing compilation of information. If we knew as much about

libraries today as was compiled and published in 1876 we would be in a much better position to plan for future library development.

The library services unit was established in the Office in 1937 as a result of language inserted in an appropriation bill. That language read in part: "For expenses necessary for the Office of Education, including surveys, studies, investigations and reports regarding libraries...." This provision has been repeated in every appropriation bill for the U.S. Office of Education from that year to this, clearly indicating that the Office has this specific and definite responsibility and part of the salaries and expenses appropriation of the Office each year is expected to be used for this purpose.

The new library services unit in USOE took its statistics collecting responsibilities seriously and, following its formal establishment in 1938 under Ralph Dunbar, the first unit chief, began nationwide statistical surveys on public, college and university, and school libraries. These were done at intervals of 5-7 years along with shorter annual surveys of public libraries serving over 100,000 population. During this period, in response to the need for annual statistics of college and university libraries, the American Library Association took the responsibility for collecting and publishing such data as complete and accurate as a professional association with volunteer membership labor could manage.

The passage of the Library Services Act in 1956 enabled the Office of Education to strengthen the staff of the Library Services Branch, not only to administer the act but to enable it to do a better job of research and consultant services including statistical studies and reports. With this expansion, the Library Services Branch was able to assume the responsibility from the American Library Association for the annual collection of college and university library statistics on a comprehensive and official basis. In addition, the collection of statistics of State library administrative agencies was undertaken as a measurement of the impact of the Library Services Act.

The Federal responsibility for educational statistics was considerably sharpened and made more specific by the passage of the National Defense Education Act of 1958 with title X providing for the "Improvement of Statistical Services of State Educational Agencies" with the following specifications:

(a) For the purpose of assisting the States to improve and strengthen the adequacy and reliability of educational statistics provided by State and local reports and records and the methods and techinques for collecting and processing educational data and disseminating information about the condition and progress of education in the States, there are authorized to be appropriated for the fiscal year ending June 30, 1959, and each of the nine succeeding fiscal years, for grants to States under this section, such sums as the Congress may determine.

(b) Grants under this section by the Commissioner shall be equal to one-half of the cost of State educational agency programs to carry out the purposes of this section, including (1) improving the collection, analysis, and reporting of statistical data supplied by local educational units, (2) the development of accounting and reporting manuals to serve as guides for local educational units, (3) the conduct of conferences and training for personnel of local educational units and of periodic reviews and evaluation of the program for records and reports, (4) improving methods for obtaining, from other State agencies within the State, educational data not collected by the State educational agency, or (5) expediting the processing and reporting of statistical data through installation and operation of mechanical equipment. The total of the payments to any State under this section for any fiscal year may not exceed $50,000.

This law has improved the collection of school library statistics in some States but the term "educational statistics" has not been generally applied. As a result statistics of other types of libraries or library services have not been similarly strengthened at the State level.

In the Library Services Branch, the creation of a new position of research library specialist in 1963 made possible the collection of some special library statistics for the first time. Data on library education programs and library manpower were brought together by a new library education specialist position.

Plans for cooperation with the States in collecting public library and college and university library statistics had begun to be worked out so that the advantages of conformity of State and Federal library statistical standards could be achieved as well as the advantages of decentralization of collection and centralization of analysis. Plans were also made for conducting future public and school library surveys using sampling techniques.

These plans were interrupted in July 1965 by a reorganization of the USOE which created a National Center for Educational Statistics to which were trans-

ferred the staff of the Library Services Branch that had carried out the library statistical program. The responsibility for the program was also removed from the Branch. The primary objective of the Center, however, was placed on educational statistics related to the evaluation of new educational grant programs. The Center did make a few grants to outside agencies to complete the collection and analysis of college and university library statistics and a survey of special libraries serving the Federal Government.

Some efforts have been made to have the U.S. Bureau of Census collect more library statistical data in special or decennial censuses but the many demands on the Census for specialized data rather preclude great expectations that such collection can ever be in the detail needed by Federal, State, local and institutional library administrators and their governing bodies.

Federal library agencies would, of course, be responsible for statistics of their own agencies. The Library of Congress has detailed statistics of its own programs. Now that it is administering the National Program for Acquisitions and Cataloging under title II-C of the Higher Education Act, it also has been collecting statistics from participating research libraries on the impact of that program.

The National Library of Medicine has also conducted a survey of medical libraries in the United States, and the National Agricultural Library has a similar interest in agricultural libraries in the United States.

The Federal Library Committee, created in 1965 as the result of the cooperation of the Library of Congress and the Bureau of the Budget, with a grant from the Council on Library Resources, has promoted the development and improvement of Federal library statistical information. The Committee was influential in establishing a cooperative arrangement with the USOE National Center for Educational Statistics under which the Committee prepared survey forms with the assistance of the Office of Education which were in turn circularized to Federal libraries for response. The Center then contracted with the University of Wisconsin at Milwaukee for the editing and processing of the returns which were published in 1968 as the *Survey of Special Libraries Serving the Federal Government.*

The Federal Government needs national library statistics to determine at any particular point in time what the condition and progress of the various types of libraries and library services are, how these facts relate to national needs, what Federal library programs and Federal library support are necessary. Such statistics are also needed to evaluate those programs already being administered and funded and to provide information to State, local agencies, institutions, governing boards, professional associations, and other groups and individuals concerned with libraries so that sound judgments can be made on which to base all library development and improvement programs.

Firm and competent planning is needed at the national level so that library statistics collected, analyzed and disseminated will be as reliable, valid and consistent as possible in order that national totals can be projected and reliable judgements made based upon them. Standardization of statistical terms and definitions are essential to achieve uniformity of reporting and analysis which will result in comparable data. At the suggestion of the Library Services Branch in the U.S. Office of Education, the ALA Statistics Coordinating Committee prepared in 1960 a proposal for a National Survey of Library Statistics which would provide a systematic approach for coordinating and unifying the national needs for library statistics. The proposal resulted in a grant from the Council on Library Resources with supplementary assistance by the National Science Foundation and the National Library of Medicine for the development of a handbook and the formulation of a comprehensive program for the systematic collection of statistics for all types of libraries. The essential role of the Federal Government and specifically the U.S. Office of Education in this basic enterprise is evidenced by the fact that the Director of the project was drawn from the staff of the statistics unit of the U.S. Office of Education and several staff members of the Library Services Branch served in key roles in the work of the project.

Since the potential need for library statistics is great and resources to produce the needed statistics will usually be less than that required, a wisely and carefully constructed national program of essential library statistics must be developed specifying types of libraries and programs to be covered, periodicity, degree of detail and analysis, potential for sampling techniques, and the sharing of responsibility and costs between Federal, State, and local levels. An interesting proposal based on sampling was made at the National Conference on Library Statistics in 1966. The Library Services Branch and the National Center might establish a team of experts—two to three outstanding librarians, an expert in research management, statistics and computers, an urban social scientist. This group would plan and implement a small, but strategic national network of statistical research teams placed permanently in selected libraries across the country, to collect national information. Perhaps a hundred libraries would be involved, representing a scientifically selected group in the various categories of libraries.

These local teams might vary in size and be persons trained in graduate library schools and exposed to pre- and inservice programs in other disciplines. The teams could be distributed on the basis of market areas, types of collection, etc. The libraries could be typical of X number of libraries of which they are a prototype. The teams would be financed by Federal funds, but be an integral part of local library staffs. Their job would be to compile and analyze and collect local library statistics called for in a plan developed by the national team of experts.

There is no doubt that the collection of library statistics by the Office of Education has already played an important role in the wider use of standard library statistical terms and definitions at State, local, and institutional levels. This has been partially accomplished by thorough review of Federal statistical forms while still in draft form with responsible professional library groups and leaders before review and approval by the Bureau of the Budget. Through conferences, meetings, articles, and other forms of communication, OE library officials have had considerable success in having State library agencies and local and institutional libraries adopt standard library statistical terms and definitions. With continuing and hopefully growing involvement in the collection and analyses of library statistics there is every reason to believe that this trend toward the widest possible use of standard terms and definitions will continue.

The responsibility for developing a national library statistical program rests clearly with the U.S. Office of Education. If a National Commission on Libraries and Information Science is created, the review and full support of this body in the implementation of such a national program would be most helpful.[1] The National Conference on Library Statistics made a similar recommendation in June 1966, several months before the National Advisory Commission on Libraries was created by President Johnson in September 1966. The Conference further recommended that a National Commission have a subgroup on library statistics.

In pursuing their studies and deliberations, the National Advisory Commission on Libraries was appalled at the lack of adequate library statistics. Their report includes the following references and recommendations regarding

[1] Editor's note: This paper was written prior to the establishment of a National Commission on Libraries and Information Science in July 1970.

library statistics: "...The National Center for Educational Statistics must be in a position to collect on a continuing basis the pertinent and adequate library data...urgently required and not now available...for an appraisal of present programs and formulating plans for the future."[2]

The National Center has recently established a unit and designated a staff with the responsibility for library statistics. It is to be hoped that this will form the nucleus of a developing program of national library statistics so badly needed for national library development.

---

[2] National Advisory Commission on Libraries, *Library Services for the Nation's Needs*, p. 43.

LEGISLATIVE OVERVIEW

by Paul Howard

Legislation in the United States occurs at three levels—local, State, and national. At each level the legislative process is basically the same. A problem is encountered, a program is envisioned, supporting groups are organized, supporting data and information are developed, legislative sponsors are indoctrinated, staff work is initiated, an ordinance or bill is drafted, it is introduced, is referred to a Legislative Committee, additional staff work is done, hearings are held, a report is made, a ruling is established for consideration by the Legislative Body, the legislation is debated, a vote is taken, the bill is forwarded to the other Legislative Branch or to the Executive. With the signature of the Executive, the ordinance or bill becomes law. The program so authorized is now in its most critical phase. To become effective, legislation usually requires the appropriation of funds. The budgeting process is fully as complicated, and is often surrounded by more secrecy than the legislative process. Legislative authorization is not always compulsory and may be negated through failure in budgeting or in appropriating. The budgeting and appropriating processes are often much more difficult than authorizing legislative processes.

On the national level, the budgeting and appropriating process contains the following basic steps (a very simplified version). At the agency request, each of its components develops an estimate and justification for its proposed expenditures. (This is usually 16 to 18 months before the beginning of the appropriate fiscal year.) These estimates are consolidated and reviewed at the bureau level, then consolidated and reviewed at the agency level. Agency budgets are transmitted to the Office of Management and Budget (formerly the Bureau of the Budget), usually in September, nine or ten months before the beginning of the fiscal year. The Office of Management and Budget reviews agency requests in the light of overall program requirements. Hearings are held by Budget Examiners in order to allow agencies to defend their requests. The Office of Manage-ment and Budget consolidates and revises the appropriation requests and recommends a budget to the President.

The consolidated budget is transmitted to the Congress together with the budget message. This occurs in January, approximately one year after the start of the budget process. The budget then goes through the legislative process just described.

For the purpose of this overview, the steps mentioned will be considered to comprise the legislative process. Actions entirely within the purview of the Executive will not be considered as legislative. Although there may be variations of this procedure and in some cases, especially at the local level, a telescoping of some steps may occur and others may be especially emphasized or added. In many cases the steps are taken in different sequence. Supporting groups may be organized long before a problem is discovered. In fact, they may discover or create the problem, or at least call attention to its existence.

Library legislative programs have long been handicapped by lack of adequate statistical data. These deficiencies arise from lack of a coordinated program, lack of continuity, lack of relevance, and from lack of competence in statistical techniques.

As the legislative process and the framers of legislation grow more sophisticated, the demand for supporting data and information becomes more exacting. Sale techniques become, if not less emotional, at least less flamboyant. The presentation of facts and supporting data becomes more and more necessary at each step of the legislative process.

Such information is of six kinds:

1. General description of a situation and analysis of problems involved.

2. Illustrative examples.

3. Information concerning extent of need.

4. Quantitative measures of the effect of previous actions in the same or similar situations.

5. The nature of legislative solutions proposed.

6. Estimates of the effect of proposed legislation.

Four of these kinds of information (numbers 1, 3, 4, and 6) *require* the use of statistics, while in the case of the other two, statistics can be of definite value.

In the early days of ALA's national legislative program, statistical data were even less developed than now. For this reason, the first version of the Library Services and Construction Act was the Library Demonstration Act, and the proposed program among other things, was designed to produce the data necessary to support permanent legislation. In 1946 the author's article "Whither ALA"[1] attempted to define the responsibilities of the library associations and of the Government in national library program development. Responsibility for statistical research was logically assigned (in the author's opinion) to the Government. This was based on the theory that the Government could, and would, develop a more consistent, long-range, and comprehensive program of statistical research than the various professional associations could.

At first, it appeared that this assumption was valid. The Library Services Branch of the Office of Education continued its efforts to develop a comprehensive statistical program covering all types of libraries. Passage of the Library Services Act in 1956 was enough of a stimulus that the continuing programs of the Branch were also enhanced and the statistical program appeared to be well established and developing in the manner planned and requested by the associations. However, in 1965, a reorganization of the Office of Education transferred all statistical work to the National Center for Educational Statistics. This was followed by a series of reorganizations which, with other factors, including a change in policy on collection methods, significantly hampered library statistics activity for about 3 years; but since that time, the establishment of a Library Surveys Branch in the National Center, which concentrates exclusively on the collection of library data, is reversing this trend.

The Report of the National Advisory Commission on Libraries stresses the need for a strong statistical program and emphasizes the difficulties it encountered because of the lack of statistical and other data upon which findings and programs can be based.[2] One of its principal recommendations is the establishment of an institute for the purpose of remedying this type of defect.[3]

Although there has been much justified criticism of the nature and quality of library statistics, it is noteworthy that the greatest surge of library legislation occurred from 1956 to 1965 when the statistical program of the Office of Education reached its peak. It may be argued that the same pressures which produced the legislation also produced the statistical program.

It took 10 years to pass the first Federal aid to libraries program amounting to $5,000,000. In the next 10 years this was increased to approximately $630,000,000. Among the many factors which influenced this build-up, effective use of available statistics was among the more important. This chicken and egg argument can be extended indefinitely without resolution. The pertinent point is that legislation and statistics go together.

---

[1] Paul Howard, "Whither ALA," *ALA Bulletin* 40 (October 1, 1946): 304-308.
[2] National Advisory Commission on Libraries, *Library Services for the Nation's Needs,* pp. 9, 43.
[3] Ibid., p. 39.

RESEARCH OVERVIEW

by Kenneth E. Beasley

For many years, as we now view the scene, the status of library development could be described best by that famous hymn, "There is a Balm in Gilead." Librarians and many members of the public hoped for a little heaven on earth, but it always seemed elusive and yet close enough to be viewed and on occasions even enjoyed vicariously. Then, all of a sudden, reality began to change at a pace that surprised all, frightened many, and was accepted by a few almost nonchalantly. The change was caused by many social forces originating in the general social discontent after World War II, forces which were spurred by the realization that concentrated research could produce answers to almost any apparently insoluble problem.

Social movements tend to generate part of their own

momentum but eventually the intensity diminishes. The present one, though, is different because after two decades there is considerable evidence that the peak has not been reached. Since libraries are an integral part of the social system, it must be assumed that they too have not reached their final form and in the next few years will depart even further from the pre-1945 norm.[1] This change, even though it is partially predictable in intensity and duration, can be quite discontinuous in the absence of decisive direction by informed persons.[2] This direction will not be easy to formulate because the alternatives from a social point of view almost approach infinity. Even in the limited area of library services, the number of proven programs exceed the most optimistic estimates of available manpower. The demand will exist, the knowledge to support numerous courses of action will be available, but the wherewithal to act will be limited. How to maximize social benefit in this setting of frustration and conflict is the task assigned to us!

Much of the success of the direction will depend on the quality and quantity of research. In its broadest sense, and as used in this paper, research means gathering data about unknown phenomena, organizing them, drawing conclusions that explain or describe, and in the case of social science research to articulate alternatives and trends. Although there are few administrators in any of the major social programs who question the need for research, the intensity of the feeling varies markedly. In some professions like mental health and education, research finds are widely accepted, supported, and implemented whereas in others like the library field acceptance is still spotty. Similarly, the type (quality) of research covers a broad range that includes at one extreme simple data gathering to prove a predetermined point and at the opposite end complex analyses of problems that may or may not have relevance in current decisionmaking. The distinction between pure and applied or sponsored and independent research is discussed often but in practice is blurred as university personnel engage in consultation and sponsored projects and the consulting companies reserve part of their intellectural resources for basic studies. Inhouse organizational research can be described similarly. Indeed, one can argue easily that research has reached a state of development

where researchers constitute a cult that is messianic and strongly defensive to outside criticisms, and yet it is quite productive.

It is in this general research setting that one must comment about and evaluate library research. Although obviously an integral part of the whole and indistinguishable in many respects from its counterpart in other social programs, research efforts in library administration and services have two unique features which describe them more accurately and provide a better basis for understanding their function in library development.

The present state of organized research is controlled in a large measure by its recency, dating back only 10 or 15 years. As will be noted later, efforts were made in the 1930's; but they were never pursued and not until the early 1950's do they reappear. Some of the lag in knowledge caused by this late entry can be offset by the experience gained from some of the unproductive methodological experiments of other research, but the lag will still be noticeable for several years to come. For example, the body of data that comes from gradual accretion in "trial and error" research is almost wholly-lacking in the library field. We are still devoting priceless time to such mundane subjects as *how* to measure a collection, *how* to evaluate reference questions, and whether circulation is a meaningful statistic. Not until publication of *Library Statistics: A Handbook* . . . in 1966 was there a systematic national definition of many basic terms used in public library service, but there still has been minimal adoption. Because schools and institutions of higher learning are essentially a closed system, the lag in their research is not as noticeable and is not as much an impediment for future development; for these, the impact of the new methodologies of systems analysis and behavioral sciences have more than offset previous deficiencies.

Librarians as a group are still not research oriented despite the fact that their national professional organization has sponsored research projects for many years and the fact that their daily work places them in constant association with the research products of other fields.[3] Several factors explain this attitude. Until recently, libraries were small and unchanging and as a result could be researched in their entirety in a short time. Also, budgets were minimal and were used almost entirely for direct operations of well-established programs. Philoso-

---

[1] The rate of change will not necessarily be the same for all types of libraries. Blasingame has commented aptly that in certain respects the intensity of the public library movement has diminished while the intensity of the special library movement is still very marked. Academic libraries are probably somewhere in between.

[2] It is recognized that this line of reasoning resembles closely the traditional arguments of the conservative who strives to maintain the status quo by the controlled direction of the future. Some reflection, however, on the emphasis on research as a tool of change will reveal that there is a significant difference.

---

[3] Many of the research projects sponsored by the ALA in the past have really been a combination of promotion and research, with the two not being distinguished properly in all cases. This observation can be made now as we look back. At the time the research was carried out, the distinction was probably not so identifiable.

phically, public libraries were in effect elitist, even though they were called "free" or "public," and as such they minimized the necessity for one of the current major areas of research; impact of services on various social subgroups.

No doubt a further significant contributing factor is that only a few graduate library schools are research oriented, and even at these institutions there are too few faculty trained to do or teach research. For many older librarians, a serious problem is the fact that research is disconcerting and anxiety-laden since in technique it is amoral and tends to challenge traditional concepts and operations. For them to accept research, there must be positive assurances that their identity and social reference points will not be changed, or if changed, that their contributions and talents will still be meaningful. Parenthetically, it can be noted that the professional organizations could do much to relieve this uneasiness, but so far they have not given this task a high priority.

Finally, note must be made that many administrative decisions in the larger local areas and at the State and Federal level are still not required to be based on the careful analysis of data. What little research is done, therefore, tends to be undermined at this stage. In one sense, this "undermining" has not been too costly because, as I have stated on other occasions, library service started its recent expansion from such a low base that almost any new program was probably right and a major error would require premeditation. This situation no longer prevails in most States. Now, the cost of delay (including the social costs of lack of service) while planning and organizing more systematically is less than the cost of errors associated with the present decision-making process.

The current status of library research has been stated well by numerous members of the profession, one of the latest being the series of short articles in the May 1967 issue of the *Wilson Library Bulletin.* The editor very aptly described the array of opinions as "A Kaleidoscopic View of Library Research." The comments range from Philip Enis' critical phrases of "fragmentary, noncumulative, generally weak and relentlessly oriented to practice" to the moderate position of Robert L. Gitler who argues that research has been going on but too little attention has been given to its application. Both of these positions, which are reflective of other observations in the library literature, are correct. Their differences stem from the fact that (a) they are talking about different types of research, (b) the type of research is not related to the function it is to serve, and (c) the research of a former period is evaluated according to the more advanced techniques of a later period. A review of the types of library research at this point will

be useful to explain these differences and to provide a backdrop for later comments about a future research program.

Dating from the 1930's, a major part of the data on library operations has come from demonstration projects and surveys.[4] Demonstration projects, not as common in recent years, were designed to determine if a certain kind of service was feasible and desirable. By their nature, they were field studies of action programs and were concerned with active ongoing decisionmaking, political and administrative interaction, and philosophical justifications. In some respects, they were the forerunner of the case study that became so popular in the social sciences in the early 1950's. They never quite gained this stature, partly because there was insufficient general research support in the social sciences and partly because many projects were never reported in the literature. Those that were reported were often addressed to a broad or popular audience and hence tended to be general statements with failures and deficiencies not being recognized or revealed. Despite their limited usefulness as articulated research findings, the reports of demonstration projects are the source of a wealth of data which have not been fully exploited by doctoral students and other researchers for the insights they might shed on library service during a transition period of nearly two decades and the possible hypotheses that might be compared with current assumptions about the "whys" of library service in a supposedly new era.

If there is anything truly unique about library research it is the extensive use (bordering on dedication) of surveys. Their widespread acceptance and general pattern has been stated well by Charles A. Bunge in "Statewide Library Surveys and Plans: Development of the Concept and Some Recent Patterns"[5] and need not be recounted here. Like demonstration projects, surveys have been action oriented but with one difference in that they supposedly preceded all decisions on programs except the belief that some kind of change was probably in order. In reality, the decisions had been made and the purpose of most surveys has been to prove their correctness and to show that services were adequate.

From one point of view, this simplistic approach has been salutary because it made most surveys focus

---

[4] Demonstration projects began in the 1930's and continued through the 1940's and were supported quite commonly by funds under the 1956 Library Services Act. By the early 1960's, however, they received less support from the profession, largely because projects were being duplicated and hence not really demonstrations.

[5] Charles A. Bunge, "Statewide Library Surveys and Plans: Development of the Concept and Some Recent Patterns," *Library Quarterly* 36(January 1966): 25-37.

sharply enough that the better ones have provided some comparative data. Had the profession been able to agree on definitions several years ago, and had the surveyors been more alert to their responsibilities to the profession as well as to the communities for whom the surveys were being made, the collective results of many surveys would comprise by now a valuable array of descriptive data which could be used for both more advanced theoretical and applied research.

This criticism is not meant to downgrade the survey or to argue that all should follow an identical format. *The Public Library Inquiry* (1949-1952) and the later survey of library services in the Pacific Northwest are examples of almost unexcelled survey work which have as their objective the identification of the major patterns of library service, and later statewide surveys (e.g. West Virginia and Ohio) were built on the experiences of prior efforts.[6] Surveys, furthermore, need to be continued because they serve a useful function in direct program decisionmaking, are a device to disseminate knowledge to the public, and can be a symbol around which an action program can be organized easily. Efforts spent on surveys, however, should produce general research data along with the information needed by the community or State, and to this end must be systematized with perhaps the following features:

1. Surveys which are designed to answer the questions whether there is adequate library service, are standards being met, what kinds of new services or organization would be desirable, etc., should follow a fairly standard format. Books like *Library Surveys* by Maurice Tauber and Irlene Roemer (eds.) satisfy part of this requirement; but to this kind of presentation there should be added some of the features of a manual—and there should be general professional agreement.

2. This format should be designed by personnel associated with research at library schools and disseminated by the profession's national organization. This is the kind of function the profession should do for itself in the interest of assisting the public.

3. In the case of community surveys, or where direct

citizen participation is important, the format should be detailed so that nonprofessional researchers can do all or most of the data gathering.

4. In surveys made by outsiders, the detailed format should be followed with the additional requirements of a description of the methodology, reasons for departure from the format if such seems desirable, and evidence that the surveyor is acquainted with the results of other surveys.

These requirements are not as rigid as they may seem at first. No one is prevented from doing surveys, but communities would know what an acceptable minimum is. If a survey were done in less than a professional manner, subsequent communities in which a person intended to work would be entitled to know this. *The profession, with the direct assistance of the library schools, must assume this or a similar responsibility.* The alternatives are much less pleasing.[7]

In the 1960's, there was a surge forward in the use of the newer social science research methodologies—statistics quantitative measurements, systems analysis, behavioral techniques, computers, etc. From these efforts, at first by social and physical scientists and engineers, and now including a few librarians with research training, there have been several excellent reports. At the top of any listing, for example, would be Fusler and Simon's study of the use of the University of Chicago Library.[8] The projected reports of the manpower study by Mary Lee Bundy and Paul Wasserman should also be of top caliber considering the carefully constructed methodology and use of leading researchers in several disciplines.[9]

Although very few examples of this type of research can be cited in the public and school library areas (with the latter being unusually weak), a good base is developing rapidly to support major studies on academic libraries involving empirical testing and leading to statements of a comprehensive theory of the function of the research library. Articles have already been published on the application of systems analysis, quantitative measurements of use, computers, and the latest concepts of budgeting. Although still in embryonic form, measure-

[6] Robert D. Leigh, *The Public Library in the United States* (New York: Columbia University Press, 1950); Pacific Northwest Library Association, *Libraries and Librarians of the Pacific Northwest* (Seattle: University of Washington Press, 1960); Ralph Blasingame, *Survey of Ohio Libraries and State Library Services* (Columbus: State Library of Ohio, 1968). See also Grace Stevenson, *Arizona Library Survey* (Phoenix: Bureau of Educational Research and Services, 1968).

[7] This recommendation is made with a full awareness that some present unsatisfactory procedures will be frozen into the standard format. New procedures are certainly difficult to get adopted, some might argue, without the hurdle of the sanctity of a standard system. Still, the alternatives are less pleasing.

[8] Herman Fusler and Julian Simon, *Patterns in the Use of Books in Large Research Libraries* (Chicago: University of Chicago Library, 1961).

[9] For a short summary statement, see Paul Wasserman and Mary Lee Bundy, "Maryland's Manpower Project: A Progress Report," *Library Journal* 93 (April 1, 1968): 1409-14.

ments of quality and quantity have already been translated in several State university systems into formulae as guides for systematic development.[10]

The best literature and research by far deals with special libraries. Here one finds numerous illustrations of efforts to apply certain methodologies and concepts in all the sciences, including engineering, behavioral sciences, and business; modified cost-benefit ratios, cost-time-motion/efficiency, multilevel file structure to determine user interest, mathematical formula for evaluating machine retrieval systems, formula to determine when interlibrary loans become too costly, marginal utility theory, simulation of search process, etc. Information retrieval problems is the object of many of the inquiries. Despite their advancement over similar studies about other types of library service, these are still relatively simple and general and tend to be discontinuous.

The reasons for this uneven development in research among the areas of library services can be identified and need to be noted here as a background for later recommendations. The leading reason is that there are still too few library trained researchers. Members of the nonlibrary disciplines can make a contribution for a short time and can perform a very useful service as critics; *but the real insights are most likely to come from persons steeped in the specialty and, second, possessing the detachment characteristic of the true researcher.* Until this kind of person can assume the major part of library research, it will continue to be below the optimum level.

Another factor is the small amount of reliable descriptive data on which to construct advanced studies. Spottiness, furthermore, stems from the lack of reporting of the better research in the leading journals, and particularly the failure to report methodology. An outsider should always be restrained in commenting on editorial policies in journals outside his discipline, but it seems to me that the present library journals are oriented too much to a broad library audience. Perhaps what is needed is a new journal similar to *Administrative Science Quarterly* which reports the best of the research and theoretical statements, jargon and all if such is necessary to express something precisely.[11] Right now, its active reading audience would be small compared to the total membership of the American Library Associa-

tion, but its use would be an indispensable feature of graduate training. Hopefully, as the younger graduates accepted administrative positions, they would continue to follow the publication and provide the atmosphere in their organization for inhouse testing of basic findings. Currently, the procedure for disseminating research data is awkward and haphazard and places a premium on lengthy articles in order to assure publication in a symposium or book of readings.

Finally, library research will always have the same handicap faced by all social science researchers in that library service is determined by many variables which can change rapidly within short periods of time. Consequently, experimenting and testing never produce as precise results as one would like, and their application to other situations may be very limited.

An overall program for the collection of statistics on library services must be interrelated with general library research as it exists now and as it has developed in the immediate past. As I have stated elsewhere in writing, an essential requirement for collecting any statistics is that they measure or describe specific and identifiable characteristics.[12] It is the identification and description of these characteristics to which general library research is addressed, and in so doing a variety of research techniques and methodologies must be employed. Ideally, they would be identified first, and perhaps even general theories formulated, before statistics were gathered. Practically, this procedure is not feasible because the statistics provide part of the raw data for identifying characteristics, and the demand for decisions will not permit us to wait this long. Moving ahead in both areas is mandatory even though there will be serious problems of circular reasoning to overcome by mixing the two types of research. It is with these ideas in mind that the following comments are presented as recommendations for an integrated or comprehensive research program.

The profession should prepare a plan of priority research, particularly as a guideline for younger researchers. Although a plan of this type has overtones of predetermining what is important, it need not go so far as to be the equivalent of *control.* Unfortunately, research dollars are limited as to both location and time, but library problems respect neither. Judicious use of scarce resources, therefore, is paramount; and judiciousness inevitably implies value judgments. Indeed, library research is heavily *controlled now,* but it is vague and is exercised by various persons and organizations for

[10] For example, Verner W. Clapp and Robert J. Jordan, "Quantitative Criteria for Adequacy of Academic Library Collections," *College and Research Libraries,* September 1965, pp. 371-80.

[11] The ideal would be reorientation of an existing journal. However, editorial policies of professional journals are not the easiest thing to change, witness the great growth in new journals recently.

[12] Kenneth E. Beasley, *A Statistical Reporting System for Local Public Libraries.*

different reasons—witness the common phrase used by researchers, "I must sell this project to____." One way to start setting priorities would be a series of working meetings[13] at which leading practitioners and acknowledged library researchers could assess the current scene and suggest some orderly ways of development. This discussion would also force a look at the interrelationships of different types of library service and perhaps some expression of a general theory of library development. Equally important, a program of recommended research is a way to communicate to administrators the types of survey and demonstration projects that would be useful to support general research.

A top priority should be projects which address themselves to the interrelationships of public, academic, special, and school libraries just noted. Various efforts have been made along these lines, usually involving only two of the types, but no significant work has treated all of them as a unit.[14] Indeed, one of the most urgent needs of the profession is a modern comprehensive theory of the function of libraries. Parenthetically one might note what many librarians have discovered: New techniques of cooperation and organization create as many new demands as they meet. It can be argued that as these demands grow, essentially "closed" facilities (e.g. academic libraries) will be opened up, general facilities (public libraries) will specialize more, and the public will view all of them generically as "libraries" with less interest in their origin. In this setting, studies of the users of a library would only have limited value for short term operating decisions rather than as a revelation of a basic social phenomenon.[15]

If accepted, a plan of priority research would decrease the number of similar projects, particularly surveys, and would force librarians to evaluate the geographic transferability of research findings, something that the profession has avoided doing up to now. The presumption would certainly be that quality research in one jurisdiction would be valid in another one unless the latter demonstrated clearly significant uniqueness; it would have to assume the burden of proof if it argued

there was a difference. So-called research designed for its immediate catalytic effect in getting an action program started would be identified clearly for what it is!

Inhouse (staff) research must be developed and directed by persons trained in both librarianship and research. Staff research is oriented toward data gathering for administrative decisionmaking, but the data are indispensable for comparative studies. National determination of the proper data or statistics to be collected is feasible in the short run, but in the final analysis it will be (and must be) the librarian-researcher who sets the pattern. Accuracy in reporting depends on them, they know what nuances should be noted to explain apparent deviations from the norm, they interpret research findings to the administrator, and they will be the ones who will test the validity of whatever data are gathered.

Staff research is probably the weakest element in the organizational structure of libraries, and compared to such social programs as education, mental health, penology, it is far below par. There will always be some difficulty in providing the desired amount because so many libraries are small and cannot afford full time positions for research. This is but reality, which must be met by devising alternative ways and insisting that larger library units sponsor a high level of inhouse research in their organization.[16]

There must be a resolution of the current confusion about the collection and reporting of statistics. In at least the past 7 years there has been much discussion, some effort, but little improvement. I have commented formally on the subject as it pertains to public libraries on several occasions, the latest one being a statement of "A Theoretical Framework for Public Library Measurements."[17] Based on this experience and the writings of others the following summary judgments. can be suggested:

1. The major difficulty in untangling the statistics mess is the confusion by many librarians of descriptive statistics, standards, and qualitative evaluations. Statistics merely describe what has been determined previously as that which ought to be described. They are neutral, expressing neither good nor bad. Qualitative evaluations are expres-

---

[13] Many of the meetings in the past with this general orientation have not been at the level of sophistication envisioned in this recommendation.

[14] Although there is no theoretical statement on which to base their actions, several States have already proceeded on the assumption that a unity exists. The efforts of Rhode Island, New York, and Pennsylvania should be noted in particular.

[15] Paradoxically, this observation does not mean that fewer user studies are necessary. Although many of them have been made in recent years, the methodologies, sophistication, and purpose have differed so much that we still do not have a good picture of the user. Perhaps if the focus of such studies were sharper by relating them to the short run decisionmaking process, we could get better results.

[16] "Staff research" is a subject that needs much more attention in the literature. No major implementation of this recommendation can be made without retraining present staff personnel. Although I do not claim to have seen all programs for inservice training conducted by State libraries and library schools, I have never seen one that treated this subject.

[17] Kenneth E. Beasley, "A Theoretical Framework for Public Library Measurement," in *Research Methods in Librarianship: Measurement and Evaluation,* ed. Herbert Goldhor, Ch. 1.

sions of value assigned to certain statistical results. The values may be derived in part from the statistics but may also stem from other observations. Standards are only statements of what should be, based in part on what is! The latter may come from descriptive statistics in whole or in part.

Because descriptive statistics are so poor in all areas of library administration, evaluations and standards are often no more than guesses which can be challenged by all extremists and proved wrong by their own statistics. As a first step in untangling, there should be an agreement on those aspects of library service which are subject to quantitative measurement and which describe some meaningful aspect of service. For example, the number of people who enter a library says something about service whereas the number of cardholders does not. The total number of books (and other material) indicates the probability of a certain item being present.[18] Similarly, the number of professional employees is more significant than the total employees.[19] Some things cannot be measured quantitatively, such as the impact of Book A on Mr. X, but with behavioral research techniques we can make some generalizations about all of the Mr. X's and these generalizations will be useful for decisionmaking. Because libraries deal in large numbers (books, people, etc.) a large number of descriptive characteristics can be quantified.

2. Qualitative measures of a library are no more difficult to set than for many other private and public services. The major requirements are (a) systematic determination of characteristics as just noted, (b) willingness to be critical of the status quo, and (c) clear definition of functions. The last item has posed the most difficulty with public librarians because they have not fully admitted that the functions of different sizes of

libraries vary, and that it is only proper to compare libraries falling in the same category. School libraries also tend wrongly to be considered monolithic. Academic libraries, in contrast, are viewed differently with a frank recognition that libraries at a junior college, 4-year college, and graduate institution have very unique characteristics. What needs to be done is to compare the functions of some of the subtypes or categories of each of the three basic kinds of libraries. For example, are high school, junior college, and undergraduate libraries of 4-year colleges similar in "x" number of characteristics? Is the purpose of elementary and junior high libraries and public children's collections the same or so supplementary that they are a part of a whole? Once functions have been defined, the applicability of descriptive statistics, quality evaluations, and standard to all or part of them can be determined.

Qualitative measures originate in two ways: One set of them is *internal* to the library and is determined essentially by librarians from both empirical data and their collective judgments. In this category are such factors as age of material, types of periodicals, training of personnel, classification of material, accessibility, etc. The second set, which overlaps the first, is *external* to the library (and the profession) and represents that body of knowledge describing the needs of the individual and society. These needs are articulated as a result of research employing all of the techniques of social science research. The librarians can do part of this research to determine these needs, but not all because of the requirement of specialized training. In most instances, they must take already articulated conclusions, translate them into the library setting, and then apply them to an operating program.

Examples of these factors would be needs established by research in bibliotherapy, social trends in employment as described by the economist and sociologist, business information as stated by business administrators, educational needs as stated by educators, general reading matters as expressed by the public in their actual reading habits, etc. In summary, qualitative measures must be set by the library profession in active consultation with other groups. A large part of the misunderstanding of present quality measurements stems from the fact that they tend to be confined to the *internal* set, which is the one most familiar to librarians, and do not reflect enough of the *external* set.

---

[18] This relationship will be challenged by some members of the profession who know about certain libraries with reported large collections which are reputed to be quite poor. I, too, can recall visiting such facilities. However, I think these cases are the exception and should not control our efforts to determine statistical relationships in the "upper 90 percent" of libraries. On the other hand, if these libraries are not exceptions, then there are some fundamental problems in library development which have not as yet been explored fully.

[19] The number of professional employees must obviously be related to other factors before it can be evaluated. The professional employees, for example, could be doing clerical work. Where this occurs, it should show up as overstaffed with professional personnel. Other data on employees will still be necessary, but their use will be for short term administrative decisionmaking.

Implied in this reasoning is that standards should also be set by librarians working actively with outside forces.[20] Academic libraries come the closest to fulfilling this requirement since in most institutions of higher learning book selection is a responsibility of each discipline.

3. The present confusion on statistics also results from not understanding that there are two levels or types of statistics which overlap in some instances but still have clear identities. One kind includes those statistics which are the basis for a qualitative measurement and setting of standards. They are the result of rather basic research and may be complex and technical. An illustration would be the data needed for a formula to measure *access* to a library.

A lower order of statistics is concerned with operations. These data are significant to the administrator for certain types of information and control, and of the two the latter usually takes precedence. Illustrations would be expenditures by type, income by source, number of books, (inventory), number of cardholders, population of the taxing jurisdiction, salary scale, number of employees, etc. This kind of information is commonly reported to the public, Federal, and State executive and legislative policymakers. No matter what steps are taken to develop qualitative measures and standards, data of this order will continue to serve a useful purpose. For one thing, they make possible comparisons with other social programs, in terms of investment or allocation and use of resources. They are also useful base data in certain situations to determine what quality of library service is possible from a given amount of resources—quality does not necessarily mean efficiency. The important thing to recognize is that, contrary to the general practice, this lower order of data has very limited value for comparing library programs and quality.

A general research program or nationwide program for statistics must incorporate both levels and sponsor both with the same enthusiasms. This proposal may sound like a plan to use two languages to explain the same thing, and to a

certain extent it is true. There is no harm in this approach—in fact it leads to more precise descriptions—if the profession uses each language correctly and in the proper place.

4. Central to any program of statistics or general research is a data bank. "Bank" is used in the broad sense to mean a depository for not only statistical data but other research findings as well. Enough banks have been established in other academic and business areas to demonstrate that they are feasible technically and within financial capabilities. They not only provide data more rapidly for operating decisions, but they are a major force for improving research by building on past studies. *A data bank, however, should not be created to report formally the kind of current library statistics.* Knowing details about every library in the United States is not meaningful, although it would be interesting. This does not mean a bank should not be established now for "imperfect" data as long as it is understood that certain corrective steps in the system are essential.

The two major issues are who should be responsible for the development and operation and whether the profession is motivated enough to resolve some of the problems noted in this paper in order to maximize the value received from the investment. The second matter cannot be answered here—although much more can be done than many *leaders* are willing to try—but some comments on the former can be offered.

Who should operate it? There are arguments in favor of one organization assuming responsibility for the bank and functioning also as the agent to collect and publish general library statistics. Such an arrangement has the earmark of administrative simplicity and would undoubtedly facilitate some development of uniformity in reporting. These advantages, however, are not likely to be controlling in any final decision, largely because they are hypothetical and consensus on the one agency to do the work is unlikely in the near future.

There are other compelling reasons against centralization. Research and library services are not as yet a part of a unitary system. Although more uniformity is desirable, and indeed necessary, there are still significant differences. Statistical data, for example, should be collected at a source where it can be processed rapidly for fairly immediate use and with a minimum of diversions from other demands. Other research data may be

---

[20]Many librarians will claim that this active participation already exists. What they are really referring to in most cases is a form of general conversation or consultation. A librarian in a large system can specialize enough that he or she can develop an identity (and liaison) with special groups, but these are the exception. It can be argued that some of the present standards are stated so generally because the librarians have tried to be too "self contained!"

collected at points where specialized research personnel are available to edit and code them. Also, because statistics are used for different purposes, it is not necessarily more efficient for one agency to try to collect for every possible use, and in some cases the form will have to be mandated because of demands by policymakers (*e.g.* Congress). Private groups could not (and should not) do the latter. Some individual collecting, therefore, will still be necessary.

A more practical solution might be formation of a consortium of agencies desiring to develop data banks, with each one assuming responsibility for a specialty but with a sufficiently strong interlocking directorate to assure coordination. The American Library Association would certainly be a logical place to house the secretariat for it and to assume the general responsibilities of administration and development. At this time, it seems that likely members would be universities with strong library research programs, corporate entities having a strong interest in technical library services, and such public agencies as might be appropriate. There would certainly be no reason, in the case of the last group, why a State library might not be the most feasible repository of certain kinds of data.

BIBLIOGRAPHY

American Library Association. *Library Statistics: A Handbook of Concepts, Definitions, and Terminology.* Prepared by the staff of the Statistics Coordinating Project, Joel Williams, Director. Chicago: American Library Association, 1966.

American Library Association. *National Conference on Library Statistics.* Proceedings of a conference held June 6-8, 1966. Chicago: American Library Association, 1967.

American Library Association. *National Inventory of Library Needs.* Chicago: American Library Association, 1965.

American Library Association. *North American Library Education Directory and Statistics 1966-68,* edited by Frank L. Schick. Chicago: American Library Association, 1968.

Beasley, Kenneth E. *A Statistical Reporting System for Local Public Libraries.* Pennsylvania State Library Monograph No. 3. Harrisburg: Pennsylvania State Library, 1964.

Council of National Library Associations. *USA Standard for Library Statistics.* New York: USA Standards Institute, 1969.

Goldhor, Herbert, ed. *Research Methods in Librarianship: Measurement and Evaluation.* University of Illinois Graduate School of Library Science Monograph No. 8. Champaign-Urbana: University of Illinois Graduate School, 1968.

National Advisory Commission on Libraries. *Library Services for the Nation's Needs; toward fulfillment of a national policy.* Report of the National Advisory Commission on Libraries. Mimeographed. Washington, D.C.: The Commission, 1968. The report is also published as chapter 12 of *Libraries at Large; tradition, innovation, and the national interest,* edited by Douglas M. Knight and E. Shepley Nourse. New York: R. R. Bowker, 1969. The report is also reprinted in the January 1969 *ALA Bulletin.*

Nelson Associates. *Public Library Systems in the United States; a Survey of Multijurisdictional Systems.* Chicago: American Library Association, 1969.

Social Science Research Council. *Public Library Inquiry.* New York: Columbia University Press, 1949-52.

Tauber, Maurice and Irlene R. Stephens, eds. *Library Surveys.* New York: Columbia University Press, 1967.

Thompson, Elizabeth H. *A.L.A. Glossary of Library Terms.* Chicago: American Library Association, 1943.

U.S. Office of Education. *Public Libraries in the United States; their history, condition, and management.* Special report, Department of the Interior, Bureau of Education. Washington, D.C.: U.S. Government Printing Office, 1876.

VI

INFORMATION HANDLING SYSTEMS

Libraries across the nation are currently feeling the effects of the information explosion. The production of books, journals, analytical reports, and miscellany threatens to overwhelm even the most sophisticated information handling centers. Conventional library methods are presenting problems to users and librarians alike. On the following pages you'll find some efforts at solving those problems. For more detail on this subject see: *Development Trends in Federal Library and Information Center Automation.* Final Report. June 1969. 429p. Prepared by Information Dynamics Corporation, Bethesda, Md. for the Bureau of Research, Office of Education, Department of Health, Education, and Welfare. Available as ERIC (Educational Resources Information Center) Report No. 030773, from ERIC, Leasco Information Products, Inc., P. O. Drawer 0, Bethesda, Md. 20014.

Information Retrieval Systems

Prepared by the Office of Records Management, National Archives and Records Service

"The methods and equipment used in most offices for storing and retrieving information have changed insignificantly in the past 50 years, and many of these systems are still adequate today. However, the situation is rapidly changing and has already become a serious problem in some offices, The information explosion that began with World War II and the increased complexity in Government operations make it necessary for many managers to consider improved methods and equipment. Fortunately, because of pioneering efforts in the scientific and engineering communities and developments in records miniaturization, computer technology, and electronic communications, today's manager has new answers to his information retrieval problems. This handbook contains descriptions of representative nonconventional systems in use today, with a view toward providing managers, management analysts, supervisors, and others with ideas as to how they might improve the dissemination, storage, and retrieval of information in their offices.

Although this handbook is issued as one of a series of Records management Handbooks produced by the National Archives and Records Service, General Services Administration (GSA), the United States Air Force shared in its development. It was produced under a contract jointly funded and administered by the Air Force and GSA."
From the Foreward.

NAME OF SYSTEM:

DDC Information Storage, Dissemination, and Retrieval

ORIGINATOR:

Defense Documentation Center (DDC)

Defense Supply Agency

Cameron Station, Alexandria, Virginia 22314

OBJECTIVE. To maintain and operate a centralized national documentation dissemination and retrieval service for the scientific and engineering disciplines, in order to improve the utilization of research reports and the effectiveness of Government research and development activities.

BACKGROUND. The Defense Department (DOD) must spend several billion dollars a year on research, development, testing, and evaluation of new operational and support systems. As a by-product of these thousands of individual programs, an avalanche of technical reports are produced. Collectively, there is a treasure of scientific and technical information among these many documents. A major problem in the design of any information collecting, processing, and disseminating system is the need to channel the required information to the interested persons as efficiently and effectively as possible.

SOURCE: Reprinted from U. S. General Services Administration. National Archives and Records Service. Office of Records Management. *Information Retrieval Systems.* A Records Management Handbook. (Washington: 1970). p. 75-77, 80-81, 96-100, 107-118.

To better understand user characteristics, the DOD undertook a comprehensive study of the problem by interviewing many users of the information. The sampling encompassed about 1,350 of the more than 100,000 scientists, engineers, and technical people involved in Department of Defense research and development work. The investigation revealed that, as for type of information interest, almost half desired engineering information while about 40 percent had scientifically-oriented interests. In regard to the depth of the information need, 60 percent wished specific facts, perhaps from one document, while about a third of those interviewed desired enough material to make detailed analyses.

In terms of information system utilization, about 95 percent of the users relied upon their organizational technical libraries, with most agreeing that abstracts of information media would have been useful in completing past projects. About one third of the users utilized the DDC, while the remainder, at the time of the interview, were unaware of its services.

THE NEW METHOD.   The Defense Documentation Center collects, processes, announces, and distributes scientific, engineering, and technical information to personnel of the Department of Defense and related agencies and activities. Documents processed and distributed by this system fall into the subject categories listed in the COSATI (Committee on Scientific and Technical Information) Subject Category List, which covers 22 scientific and engineering fields.

The full collection of research and development documents dates from 1947 and totals about one million accessions. The descriptive data for accessions acquired since 1953 is stored on magnetic tape and is computer-retrievable. All documents are microfilmed as they are processed into the system. Those documents received before 1965 are stored on 35-mm. roll microfilm while the later acquisitions are reproduced in microfiche. The microfiche is used to reproduce hard copies for pre-stocking and to meet user needs. Incoming documents are arranged by a six digit AD number in consecutive order within three separate blocks of numbers, which are based on classification needs.

Document analysis processing includes descriptive cataloging, subject categorization, subject indexing, and abstracting, which is accomplished by means of remote input terminals. The objective of this treatment is to bring the technical report literature under bibliographic control and to simultaneously produce input data for processing into the computer record.

Documents are categorized under as many as 13 characteristics that are machine-stored for subsequent retrieval. Characteristics include corporate author entry, personal author, and the source report number.

The Technical Abstract Bulletin (TAB), together with its companion TAB indexes, are published semimonthly and announce new accessions to a limited group of users. Should these subscribers desire a copy of the document they may choose between hard copy or microfiche format. (By special arrangement, DDC will furnish magnetic tape containing cataloging data covering current accessions.)

REMARKS.   The objective of this system is to provide the right information to the user at the right time and in an economically acceptable format. It is the largest and the most used system of its kind anywhere in the world. A first step in meeting these responsibilities is to understand users' needs and then to establish procedures that will fulfill their requirements.

DDC is continuing to take actions within the processing framework to reduce the time for document information to reach users. For example, during the past year the time span between initial receipt of documents by the DDC and the receipt of abstracts and indexes by subscribers has been greatly reduced. This improvement resulted from the installation of new electronic photocomposition equipment at the Government Printing Office (GPO) and from the cooperative efforts of the GPO and the DDC to fully utilize the equipment's productive capabilities.

DDC INFORMATION STORAGE, DISSEMINATION, AND RETRIEVAL

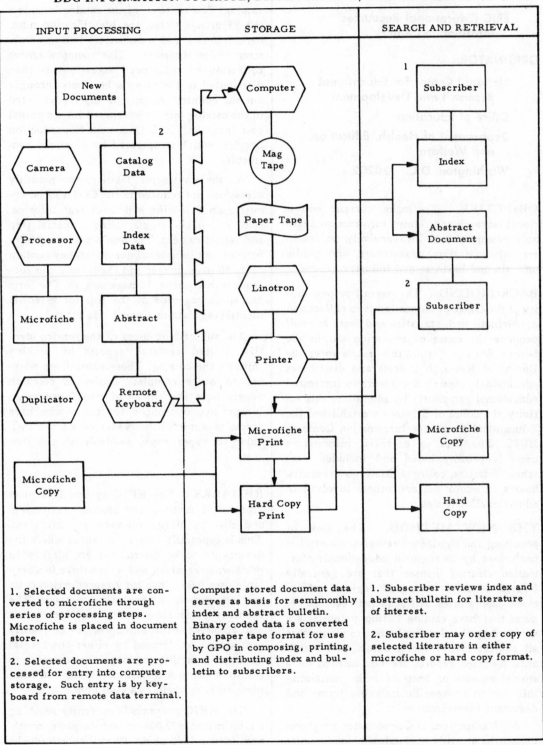

INPUT PROCESSING	STORAGE	SEARCH AND RETRIEVAL

1. Selected documents are converted to microfiche through series of processing steps. Microfiche is placed in document store.

2. Selected documents are processed for entry into computer storage. Such entry is by keyboard from remote data terminal.

Computer stored document data serves as basis for semimonthly index and abstract bulletin. Binary coded data is converted into paper tape format for use by GPO in composing, printing, and distributing index and bulletin to subscribers.

1. Subscriber reviews index and abstract bulletin for literature of interest.

2. Subscriber may order copy of selected literature in either microfiche or hard copy format.

NAME OF SYSTEM:

   ERIC (Educational Resources
   Information Center)

ORIGINATOR:

   National Center for Educational
   Research and Development

   Office of Education

   Department of Health, Education,
   and Welfare

   Washington, D.C.   20202

OBJECTIVE.   To make current educational research and related information available promptly and inexpensively to teachers, administrators, researchers, and public officials, and business and industry groups.

BACKGROUND.   The overall responsibility of the Office of Education is to collect and disseminate such statistics and facts as shall promote the cause of education within the United States. Within this framework, the Bureau of Research collects and distributes educational research documents to interested educational personnel. To administer this activity, the Office of Education established the Educational Resources Information Center— ERIC. The field of potential information users is broadly based and includes local school districts, colleges, State governments, boards of education, and others involved in educational activities.

THE NEW METHOD.   The task of acquiring the significant research material is performed by 20 regional educational information clearing houses that are generally located at universities and regional educational laboratories. All acquired research reports that have catalog listing potential are screened by the clearing houses to insure that all subject matter meets established standards. Selected reports are documented on a special resume or abstract form containing information on specific indexing terms and document identifications.

   At Washington, D.C., computer programs permit the monthly field submissions in paper tape format to be quickly machine processed. The resultant product is a computer printout that serves as the basis for the monthly catalog. The contents of the catalog include a list of article titles, the identification numbers, indexes, and a numerical listing of abstract identifications. This comprehensive collection of referenced accessions is then distributed to the many subscribers throughout the country. A copy of any report listed in the catalog may be purchased for a nominal cost from the ERIC Document Reproduction Service, which is operated by a private contractor.

   At the contractor facility, the monthly accessions are reduced to the COSATI (Committee on Scientific and Technical Information) microfiche format using a special step and repeat camera. The first 4 x 6 inch microfiche of any individual document may contain up to 60 page images and the second and subsequent microfiche, 72 page images. The form has space reserved at the top for essential identifying data in normal size print.

   The subscribing users of the service identify desired research reports by looking through the catalog. Those subscribers wishing to order complete copies of research papers have the choice of two formats: an inexpensive microfiche for those who have access to a microfiche reader or a 6 x 8 inch enlarged paper copy, available at a higher cost.

REMARKS.   The ERIC system is a most economical method for storing, retrieving, and disseminating full-page reproductions. This is especially true in instances where the documents to be distributed are already in print when received and where there is a very large user base, since copy reproduction costs are less expensive than other methods. The economy of storage at the user location is also apparent. Further, copies can be readily reproduced on demand by either the central or the user facility, making it unnecessary to maintain any stock. Last, packaging and shipment costs are held to a minimum.

   The ERIC program is currently reaching an estimated 477,000 educators each month, and during 1969 about 10 million microfiche were sold by the ERIC Document Reproduction Service.

ERIC (EDUCATIONAL RESOURCES INFORMATION CENTER)

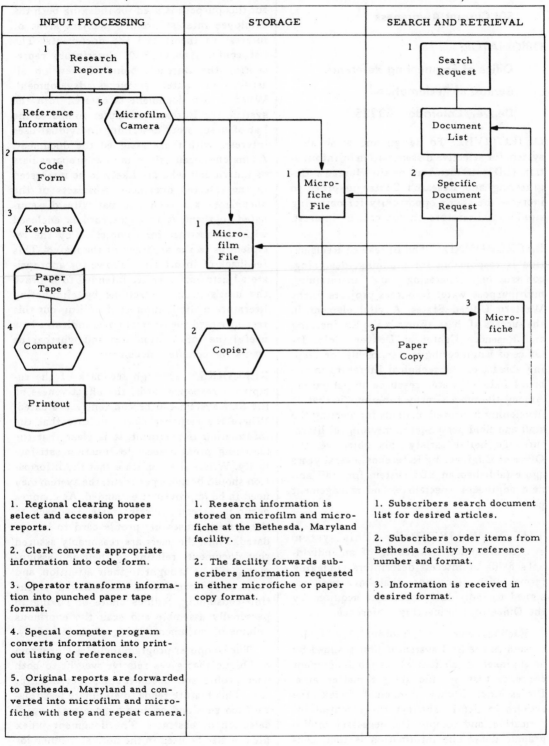

INPUT PROCESSING	STORAGE	SEARCH AND RETRIEVAL

1. Regional clearing houses select and accession proper reports.

2. Clerk converts appropriate information into code form.

3. Operator transforms information into punched paper tape format.

4. Special computer program converts information into printout listing of references.

5. Original reports are forwarded to Bethesda, Maryland and converted into microfilm and microfiche with step and repeat camera.

1. Research information is stored on microfilm and microfiche at the Bethesda, Maryland facility.

2. The facility forwards subscribers information requested in either microfiche or paper copy format.

1. Subscribers search document list for desired articles.

2. Subscribers order items from Bethesda facility by reference number and format.

3. Information is received in desired format.

NAME OF SYSTEM:

SDI Current Awareness

ORIGINATOR:

Office of Engineering Reference
Bureau of Reclamation
Denver, Colorado   80225

OBJECTIVE.   To design and establish a system for selective dissemination of information (SDI) to members of the Bureau's Engineering and Research Center in order to increase the staff's opportunity for obtaining significant literature on subjects of interest.

BACKGROUND.   The Bureau of Reclamation is responsible for planning, designing, constructing, operating, and maintaining multipurpose water resources projects in the Western United States. A vital element in the success of these efforts is the Engineering and Research Center at Denver, Colo. Its Office of Engineering is responsible for keeping abreast of the technical literature in the broad field of water resource investigation. Among the office's many functions is that of developing improved methods for alerting the staff and field personnel to meaningful literature. To better satisfy this objective, the Office of Engineering Reference several years ago established an SDI system for staff and field engineers, specialists, and management personnel.

THE NEW METHOD.   This system evolves around the matching of an individual's fields of interest descriptors (indexing terms) with descriptors that have been assigned to individual documents acquired by the Office of Engineering Reference.

Each document selected for possible inclusion in the SDI system is first scanned by an engineer or scientist whose job assignment concerns that specific subject matter area. Professional library personnel index the articles in depth, abstract the essential information, and compile the necessary bibliographic data. The information is then converted to magnetic tape format for entry into the computer's SDI matching program.

A thesaurus wordlist specially developed for this purpose is used for indexing both the employee interest profiles (subject areas of interest to them) and the documents. The list contains about 3,300 descriptors representing the Bureau's point of view on all aspects of water resources development. When a new document is entered into the system, the Bureau's computer compares the list of descriptors describing individual user interests with those assigned the document. As matches occur, the computer prepares lists of individuals who are likely to be interested in the selected document. Abstracts of the documents are then automatically disseminated to them. A response card is enclosed with the abstract for completion by the recipient as to the accuracy of the match. This feedback of information allows for appropriate adjustments that are intended to improve the user's profile selections by eliminating literature of little interest. In filling out this response card the recipient also indicates how useful the information was and whether he wants the complete document.

REMARKS.   Through feedback of the recipient's response cards, the effectiveness of the SDI system can be constantly evaluated. Where the response cards indicate that the information is pertinent, it is clear that the matching profiles seem to function satisfactorily. Where they indicate that the information should be more pertinent, the system may need to be improved or expanded. As changes occur in a recipient's interests, feedback to the system causes his profile card to be updated. Thus, the users are reasonably assured that documents relating to their job assignments will be brought to their attention, and they, at the same time, are relieved of the time-consuming, tedious chore of having to personally assemble and scan the enormous volume of documents being produced today.

The computer program includes a program technique that gives relative weight to both user profile and document abstract descriptors. This feature tends to eliminate less relevant matches and assures a more meaningful selection of abstracts. The document index file can also be used in the normal manner for conducting retrospective searches upon request of the users.

SDI CURRENT AWARENESS

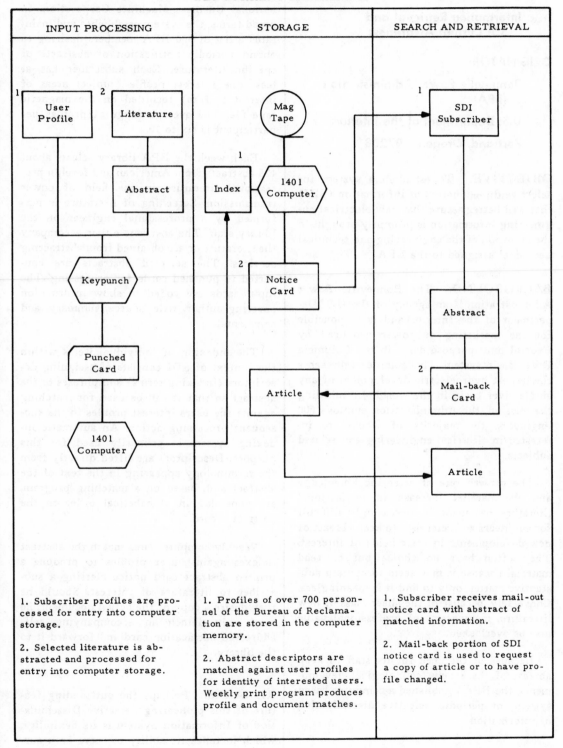

INPUT PROCESSING	STORAGE	SEARCH AND RETRIEVAL
1. Subscriber profiles are processed for entry into computer storage. 2. Selected literature is abstracted and processed for entry into computer storage.	1. Profiles of over 700 personnel of the Bureau of Reclamation are stored in the computer memory. 2. Abstract descriptors are matched against user profiles for identity of interested users. Weekly print program produces profile and document matches.	1. Subscriber receives mail-out notice card with abstract of matched information. 2. Mail-back portion of SDI notice card is used to request a copy of article or to have profile changed.

NAME OF SYSTEM:

**Information Retrieval and
SDI Current Awareness**

ORIGINATOR:

**Bonneville Power Administration
(BPA)**

U.S. Department of the Interior

Portland, Oregon   97208

OBJECTIVE.   To establish a system for selective dissemination of information (SDI) that will better assure that new electrical engineering information is promptly brought to the attention of the engineering and technical personnel assigned to the BPA.

BACKGROUND.   The Bonneville Power Administration is an agency of the U.S. Department of the Interior and is responsible for the marketing of power produced by Federal multipurpose dams in the Columbia River Basin system. This complex represents the largest hydroelectric development of any single river basin in the world. In fulfilling the mission, the Administration employs 600 engineers, the majority of whom are interested in electrical engineering and related subjects.

The growth rate of scientific knowledge and the parallel increase in professional literature has made it increasingly difficult for engineers and scientists to keep abreast of new developments in their fields of interest. They often have no choice but to read material because it may seem to contain substantive matter, only to find it is meaningless. Conversely, because of the sheer mass of new literature, many items of professional value may be overlooked.

Because of the need for its staff to keep abreast of these new technological developments, the BPA established a computer-based system for periodic, selective dissemination of information.

THE NEW METHOD.   This SDI system is based on a BPA modification of a System 1401 computer program developed by the International Business Machines Corporation. In broad terms, the system establishes and maintains a list of 400 BPA members desiring to obtain periodic notification of abstracts of specific literature. Each subscriber has at least one interest profile (subject areas of interest to him) recorded on the magnetic tape file. The average range of profiles per participant is six to 10.

Each week the BPA library selects about 125 abstracts from American and foreign professional literature in the field of power transmission. Screening of literature is performed by a professional engineer on the library staff. The abstracts either accompany the literature or are obtained from abstracting services. The selected abstracts are converted to punched cards for processing. The input cards are coded to show information covering author, title, source, summary, and comments.

The indexing of individual items within the context of SDI consists of assigning descriptors (indexing terms) and phrases to the abstract so that it can be used for matching against the users interest profiles in the subsequent processing action. An automatic indexing system is primarily used for this purpose. Descriptors are lifted directly from the terminology appearing in the text of the abstract and, based on a matching program, are appended in alphabetical order to the abstract record.

Weekly computer runs match the abstract indexes against user profiles to produce a printed abstract card notice alerting a subscriber to literature of interest. Should he then desire a copy of the actual document, he need only detach an accompanying self-addressed notification card and forward it to the library.

REMARKS.   Perhaps the outstanding feature of this pioneering Selective Dissemination of Information System is its flexibility, which includes its ability to serve both current awareness and retrospective search functions.

For retrospective search, the abstracts are retained on a cumulative magnetic tape file and processed against special inquiries as needed. When the file approaches unreasonable limits, a special program purges the abstracts appearing to have the least retention value. About 1,400 output notices are printed per week for the current awareness processing.

Engineers enrolled in the Bonneville SDI system have expressed satisfaction with its ability to disseminate a higher proportion of meaningful information. Evaluation cards completed by subscribers reveal that 57 percent have a direct interest in information received. Of particular interest, only 4.5 percent of those having a direct interest had seen the subject matter before being alerted by the SDI system.

INFORMATION RETRIEVAL AND SDI CURRENT AWARENESS

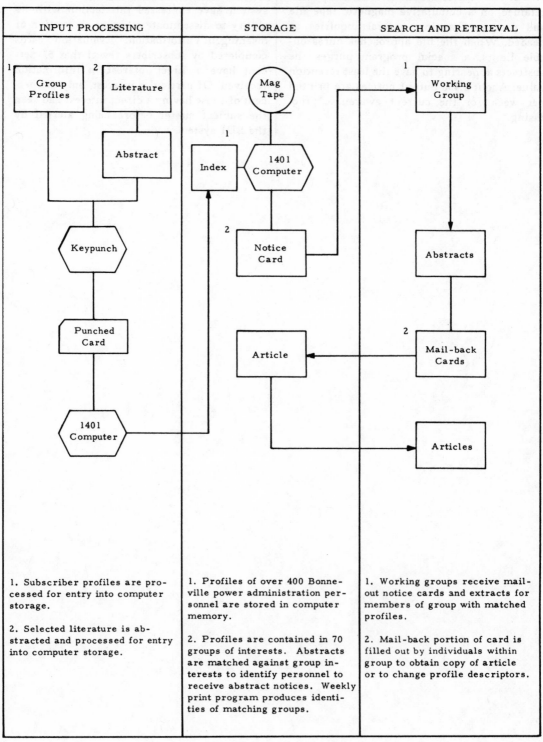

INPUT PROCESSING	STORAGE	SEARCH AND RETRIEVAL
1. Subscriber profiles are processed for entry into computer storage. 2. Selected literature is abstracted and processed for entry into computer storage.	1. Profiles of over 400 Bonneville power administration personnel are stored in computer memory. 2. Profiles are contained in 70 groups of interests. Abstracts are matched against group interests to identify personnel to receive abstract notices. Weekly print program produces identities of matching groups.	1. Working groups receive mailout notice cards and extracts for members of group with matched profiles. 2. Mail-back portion of card is filled out by individuals within group to obtain copy of article or to change profile descriptors.

NAME OF SYSTEM:

Congressional Information Network

ORIGINATOR:

Legislative Reference Service

Library of Congress

Washington, D.C.   20540

OBJECTIVE. To develop and operate a document storage and dissemination system capable of providing the members of Congress with current information as to the status of legislation, committee hearings, the budget, and other significant matters.

BACKGROUND. The United States Congress, as it enters the decade of the 1970's, is faced with legislative demands of extraordinary complexity. Each congressional member must function effectively in his several distinctive roles of office. These activities include that of legislator, rendering decisions of national and often world-wide importance; of prime representative of his State or district; and of helper to constituents having specific problems or complaints. The ability of the Congressmen and their committees to effectively discharge their duties is often hindered by the great number of routine tasks to be performed, the great variety of information to be acquired, and the diverse issues to be evaluated.

The stresses upon the members and their staffs have been augmented by the effects of the information explosion. The profusion of books, articles, analytical reports, and miscellany threatens to overwhelm the present information handling centers. Traditional procedures for acquiring, indexing, abstracting, storing, processing, retrieving, and disseminating urgent information do not effectively meet present demands. Thus, the Congressman must evaluate new methods, techniques, and tools to assist him in the performance of his legislative and administrative tasks. Steady advances in information handling technology over the past 20 years now demonstrate the proven potential of technology to better support the Congress in a number of application areas.

The following example is but a beginning in a series of automated information processing programs aimed at enhancing the chamber, committee, and individual member performance.

THE NEW METHOD. The Library of Congress, Legislative Reference Service (LRS), is now providing more responsive support to Congressional members and committees in the information sciences. The first application of the system for the Congress was the "Digest of Public General Bills," which summarizes the essential features of all public bills and resolutions. Essential identifying information on each piece of legislation includes the name of sponsor(s), the date introduced, the bill number, and the committee to which assigned, plus synoptic and indexing information. This information is placed in the disk storage unit of an IBM 360, Model 40 computer through use of a remote ATS (administrative terminal system) text processing system. Six IBM Model 2741 remote terminal selectric typewriters are used for insertion, recall, and editing of the "Bill Digest" information. The Digest is produced cumulatively every two months, with supplements produced every two weeks. Each of these publications is printed by photo-offset methods by the Government Printing Office (GPO).

Each month a "Legislative Status Report" encompassing digests and status information on 200 to 300 major bills is produced, using the same ATS remote terminal and storage system. The 11 by 15 inch computer output continuous paper form is reduced to an 8½ by 11 inch master copy through use of a Xerox 2400 Mark IV duplicator. The necessary copies for distribution to the Congress and other interested agencies and individuals are produced by a Multilith duplicator. The ability of the computer to add data elements without regard to sequence and to rapidly change obsolete material have proven to be particularly useful in this application.

The Congressional Information Network is also used for producing and disseminating the periodic "Congressional Committee Calendars." Additionally, bibliographic reports in the form of a weekly list of about 10 significant citations is disseminated on a selective basis to individuals whose areas of subject matter interest match the indexing terms covering the contents of the selected citations. About 190 personnel in the Legislative Branch are currently using this service.

Currently there are 29 active remote ATS terminals involved in the overall system. Of these, 23 are located in LRS and two are located with congressional committees.

REMARKS. As the complexity and diversity of the tasks confronting the Congress increase, the importance of utilizing every pos-sible means of acquiring and analyzing selected priority information before making decisions will become increasingly critical. The role of electronic technology will assume broader proportions as the legislator strives to fulfill his responsibilities and is willing to rely upon support from such systems.

The above-cited examples are only the start of a greater utilization of the benefits of computer and associated technologies. For example, during 1971, Data Central—a powerful, full-text, on-line retrieval system—will be used for retrieval of bill digests and legislative status information. The bill digest data base is already available in the computer as a by-product of the current "Bill Digest" production.

CONGRESSIONAL INFORMATION NETWORK

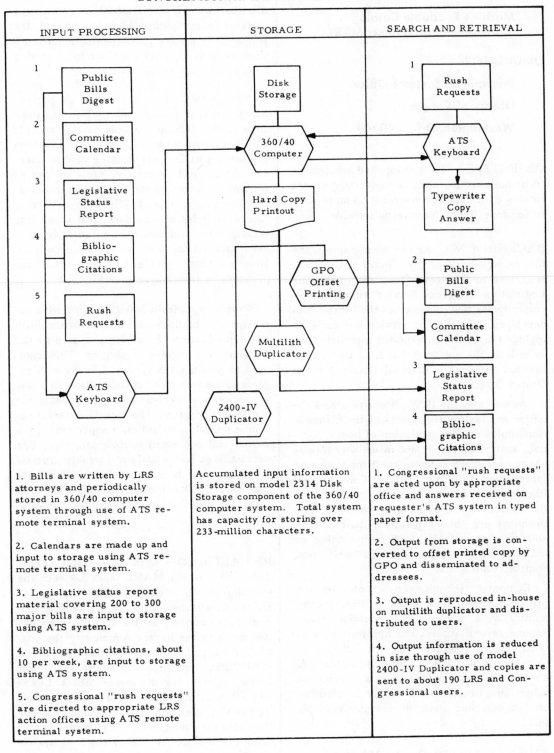

INPUT PROCESSING	STORAGE	SEARCH AND RETRIEVAL

1. Bills are written by LRS attorneys and periodically stored in 360/40 computer system through use of ATS remote terminal system.

2. Calendars are made up and input to storage using ATS remote terminal system.

3. Legislative status report material covering 200 to 300 major bills are input to storage using ATS system.

4. Bibliographic citations, about 10 per week, are input to storage using ATS system.

5. Congressional "rush requests" are directed to appropriate LRS action offices using ATS remote terminal system.

Accumulated input information is stored on model 2314 Disk Storage component of the 360/40 computer system. Total system has capacity for storing over 233-million characters.

1. Congressional "rush requests" are acted upon by appropriate office and answers received on requester's ATS system in typed paper format.

2. Output from storage is converted to offset printed copy by GPO and disseminated to addressees.

3. Output is reproduced in-house on multilith duplicator and distributed to users.

4. Output information is reduced in size through use of model 2400-IV Duplicator and copies are sent to about 190 LRS and Congressional users.

NAME OF SYSTEM:

   **Machine Readable Catalog
   Dissemination (Project MARC)**

ORIGINATOR:

   Information Systems Office

   Library of Congress

   Washington, D.C.   20540

OBJECTIVE.   To develop and implement techniques and methods for converting source catalog card data into machine-readable form to improve library service nationwide.

BACKGROUND.   As the name implies, the first responsibility of the Library of Congress is service to Congress. One department, the Legislative Reference Service, functions exclusively for that purpose. As the Library has developed, its range of service has come to include the entire Government establishment, as well as the public at large, so that it has become, in effect, a national library for the United States.

As we enter the 1970's, libraries across the nation are feeling the effects of the information explosion. The profusion of books, journals, analytical reports, and miscellany threatens to overwhelm even the most sophisticated information handling centers. Conventional library methods are presenting problems to the librarians and users alike. Among these problems are the preparation, maintenance, and searching of the 3 x 5 inch catalog or index cards, and preparation of shelf lists, control records, etc.

Computer technology now possesses the proven potential to support the library community in a number of application areas. Among several studies and applications currently being conducted by the Library of Congress is the MARC (*MA*chine-*R*eadable *C*ataloging) system that is now serving 90 subscribing libraries with weekly distribution of bibliographic data in machine-readable form.

THE NEW METHOD.   The MARC System converts records for selected current catalog card entries into machine-readable form and distributes the information on magnetic tape reels to participating libraries around the Nation. The library participants, in turn, use these records as input for their local catalog card processing requirements.

The MARC tape distributed to participants contains separate files of information such as the machine-readable catalog record; an abbreviated author-title record, to include the Library of Congress catalog card number; and subject and descriptive cross-references for tracing records generated by the machine-readable catalog record. The machine catalog record includes all the data with which the cataloger and reference librarian have long been familiar, as well as certain new data elements that provide for augmented approaches to the catalog.

Processing within MARC begins with the receipt of a bibliographic record in the form of a reproduction of the card prepared by the Library of Congress catalogers. This card, used to produce the typeset Library of Congress catalog card, is reproduced on an input worksheet and becomes the source data for the MARC System. The worksheet information is edited, punched on a paper tape typewriter, and converted to magnetic tape. The data undergo both a daily and weekly processing cycle prior to output as a MARC master tape record. The master tape is then duplicated for distribution to participating libraries weekly.

REMARKS.   One immediate result of the distribution of the MARC tapes has been the stimulation of interest in the concept of library data transmission. It has become evident, for example, that the MARC system has suggested to the library community the possibility that individual libraries can use a MARC-like system to contribute their own cataloging data for the use of others. Libraries will not only receive data from a centralized source like the Library of Congress, but they also may send data. This feature would bring much closer to reality the long anticipated concept of a network of libraries that can create and utilize a common data base.

A library participant, in evaluating the early results of the MARC Pilot Project, estimated that the system will minimize the searching, editing, keypunching, and verifying for about 24,000 volumes during the year. The MARC magnetic tape record represents a valuable potential for reducing operating costs and improving service since it can be used in a wide variety of ways, such as the automatic preparation of index cards, purchase orders, shelf lists, book spine labels, and charge-out cards; automatic searching of index records by computer; and on-line searching using remote terminals.

This example of dissemination of catalog data in digital form between the Library of Congress and the growing number of participating libraries throughout the Nation is only the forerunner of many additional library applications to be developed over the next few years. Since many of these concepts have application in the office world, their progress should be watched closely.

MACHINE READABLE CATALOG DISSEMINATION (PROJECT MARC)

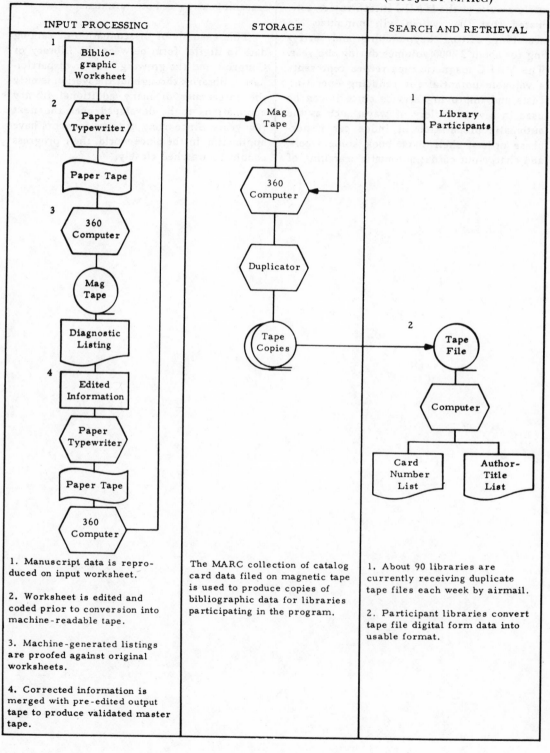

INPUT PROCESSING	STORAGE	SEARCH AND RETRIEVAL

INPUT PROCESSING

1 — Bibliographic Worksheet

2 — Paper Typewriter → Paper Tape

3 — 360 Computer → Mag Tape → Diagnostic Listing

4 — Edited Information → Paper Typewriter → Paper Tape → 360 Computer

STORAGE

Mag Tape → 360 Computer → Duplicator → Tape Copies

SEARCH AND RETRIEVAL

1 — Library Participants

2 — Tape File → Computer → Card Number List / Author-Title List

1. Manuscript data is reproduced on input worksheet.

2. Worksheet is edited and coded prior to conversion into machine-readable tape.

3. Machine-generated listings are proofed against original worksheets.

4. Corrected information is merged with pre-edited output tape to produce validated master tape.

The MARC collection of catalog card data filed on magnetic tape is used to produce copies of bibliographic data for libraries participating in the program.

1. About 90 libraries are currently receiving duplicate tape files each week by airmail.

2. Participant libraries convert tape file digital form data into usable format.

NAME OF SYSTEM:

> Aerospace Information
> Dissemination

ORIGINATOR:

> Office of Technology Utilization
>
> Scientific & Technological
> Information Division
>
> National Aeronautics and
> Space Administration
>
> Washington, D.C.   20546

OBJECTIVE.   To assure that scientists and engineers working on NASA's advanced aeronautical and space projects, as well as other interested institutions and individuals, are kept informed of significant developments in their areas of interest and to provide a rapid economical means for obtaining needed information.

BACKGROUND.   The NASA Office of Technology Utilization is responsible for the collection, processing, and communicating of scientific and technical information resulting from space program experience. Much emphasis has been directed toward placing this vast collection of knowledge in the hands of those who would explore its nonaerospace applications. Thus the information program managers have broadened the base of interest to a marked degree. The current Master Authority Address List reveals that an audience of over 2,700 public and private institutions are interested in NASA's collection of documents and publications.

THE NEW METHOD.   The NASA information collection comprises more than one-half million documents and publications. This collection encompasses acquisitions from Government, industry, research institutes, and the academic community. In addition, NASA regularly receives technical literature and specialized reports covering various projects, laboratory findings, and new patent information.

Hundreds of additions to the document file are received daily at the NASA Scientific and Technical Information Facility at College Park, Md. Each document accepted as a potentially valuable addition is first given an accession number for control purposes. Those documents with a potential of broad interest are selected for conversion to microfiche format. Indexers then examine each selected document for pertinent bibliographic data and select the terms under which the document will be listed in the index. Abstractors review each newly-received document and develop appropriate abstracts, or may rewrite the abstract that accompanied the document if it does not conform with NASA standards.

The microfiche is roughly 4 x 6 inches and conforms with the COSATI (Committee on Scientific and Technical Information) microfiche standards. The distribution copy consists of a diazo sheet of negative film carrying images of as many as 60 pages. The bibliographic citation of the document appears in normal size print across the top.

The most widely used reference guides to the NASA scientific and technical information system's growing file of knowledge are two complementary bibliographical and abstract bulletins, *Scientific and Technical Aerospace Reports* (STAR) and *International Aerospace Abstracts* (IAA). STAR abstracts cover worldwide report literature on space and aeronautics, while those in the IAA provide similar coverage of scientific and trade journals, books, and papers presented at meetings. Expert processing and modern methods of printing keep the coverage of both journals remarkably current. Indexes are organized to show subjects pertinent to a variety of disciplines.

Users of the STAR and IAA document reference services may identify a desired document by citing its accession number. In addition to the accession number, the bulletin also includes such bibliographic information as the corporate source, the title of the report, and an abstract of the report. Requesters may order a microfiche copy of the document or an enlarged paper copy. In most instances, the microfiche copies cost substantially less than the paper reproductions.

REMARKS. Without the benefits of microfilm as a storage and dissemination medium, it would almost be impossible to effectively serve the scientific and technical community. In addition to the problems of making, assembling, and warehousing paper copies, the packaging and shipping would represent a formidable effort. Fortunately, the steady improvement in microfilm technology has made it possible for information handling activities to keep abreast of the increased creation of paper documents. In 1969 NASA distributed almost 10 million microfiche under its information dissemination program. This in itself was a gain of almost one million microfiche over the previous year's total.

AEROSPACE INFORMATION DISSEMINATION

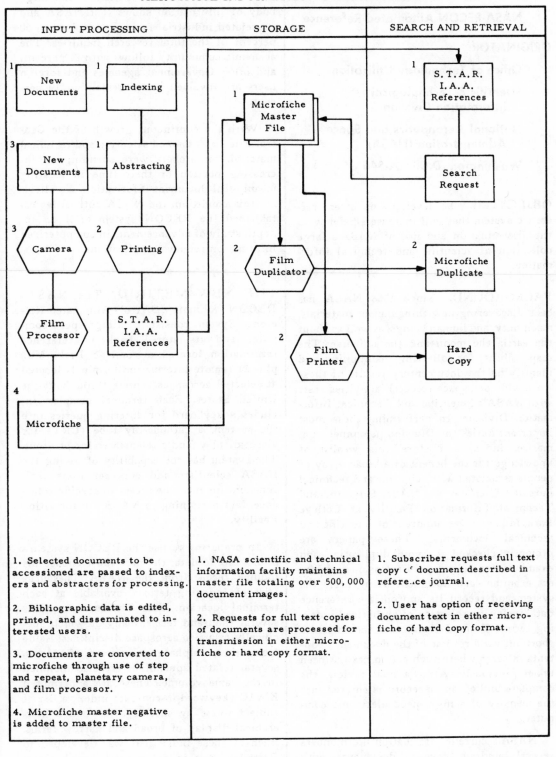

INPUT PROCESSING	STORAGE	SEARCH AND RETRIEVAL

1. Selected documents to be accessioned are passed to indexers and abstracters for processing.

2. Bibliographic data is edited, printed, and disseminated to interested users.

3. Documents are converted to microfiche through use of step and repeat, planetary camera, and film processor.

4. Microfiche master negative is added to master file.

1. NASA scientific and technical information facility maintains master file totaling over 500,000 document images.

2. Requests for full text copies of documents are processed for transmission in either microfiche or hard copy format.

1. Subscriber requests full text copy of document described in reference journal.

2. User has option of receiving document text in either microfiche of hard copy format.

NAME OF SYSTEM:

NASA-RECON Automated Reference

ORIGINATOR:

Office of Technology Utilization

Scientific & Technological Information Division

National Aeronautics and Space Administration (NASA)

Washington, D.C.   20546

OBJECTIVE.   To develop a document reference system that will increase efficiency in the dissemination and use of NASA's large collection of scientific and technical information.

BACKGROUND.   Since 1958 NASA has been discovering new things about materials, machinery, and human beings, as well as about the earth, the moon and the universe. The responsibility for collecting, maintaining, and identifying the documentary results of these worldwide aerospace research activities rests with NASA's Scientific and Technical Information Division. In performing these most important duties the Division personnel summarize, index, and store this wealth of knowledge for the benefit of a broad array of people associated with scientific and technical pursuits. Each day the NASA Scientific and Technical Information Facility at College Park, Md., receives hundreds of scientific and technical documents.   These papers are promptly checked to avoid duplication and examined for relevance. Professional indexers examine each document as it enters the system and record its appropriate reference data, including selection of authorized indexing terms. Trained abstractors then write a short but valid resume of the document's contents in cases where such action has not been taken previously. After a final review, the complete bibliographic record is entered into the memory of a high-speed electronic computer.

NASA's current information file numbers several hundred thousand documents, with most of the material maintained in microform.

An analysis of the various users of this large body of information shows that NASA and its related industrial firms are involved in 60 percent of the total research inquiries. The academic community follows with 21 percent, and other Government agencies and foreign users are involved in the remaining 19 percent.

With the continuous growth of the Central File's accessioned scientific and technical material, researchers were spending an increasing portion of their time in locating meaningful document information. To alleviate this condition, the NASA authorities established the RECON system after an indepth study of advancements in computerized information retrieval applications.

THE NEW METHOD.   The NASA-RECON (*RE*mote *CON*trol) Automated Reference System consists of a high-speed computer and its stored bank of reference information located at College Park, Md., plus 21 remote information terminals located at selected aerospace centers throughout the United States. Each terminal complex includes a keyboard for entering queries into the system, a cathode-ray tube (CRT) for visual display, and a teleprinter for printout. The system has the capability of giving the NASA scientists and engineer users real-time, on-line machine access to specific reference data pertaining to NASA's Information Facility.

In preparing to use the RECON system's bibliographic data, the user must choose his inquiry terms from the NASA Thesaurus (list of indexing terms), available at each terminal location. This Thesaurus contains several thousand terms, many of which specifically relate to aerospace disciplines. Aside from these alphabetically-arranged terms, several related appendixes are also included in the same volume. These are a permuted KWIC (keyword-in-context) index; a list of subject terms by subcategories, and a heirarchical display of broad and narrow terms. Each of these index lists was developed to assist the user in determining which terms to use when conducting his search.

The user starts the search by entering his identification code on the console keyboard and then typing out his search question. Within seconds the bibliographic replies are displayed on the CRT. Depending upon the user's input query, the answer might cover accession numbers and titles, or display a catalog listing of information on a particular scientific discipline. If the list is long, he can instruct the computer to printout the selected citations on a printer located next to the CRT.

As an example of the system's flexibility, suppose a user needed detailed information on an ultrahigh-frequency radio transmitter used on a Lincoln Experimental Satellite. The search could be conducted under three indexing terms: Lincoln Experimental Satellites, ultrahigh frequency, and radio transmitters, terms that can be recognized by the computer. In response to how many documents were indexed under these terms, the CRT display showed ten under the first, 93 under the second, and 110 under the third. The computer could then be asked to display the titles, authors' names and other information on each of the three sets of terms. However, this action would be impractical due to the number of reports. To save time, the computer could be asked to cite the number of documents indexed under all three terms. The computer's reply would quickly reveal on the CRT display that only one document was indexed under the three terms specified. By pushing another button the CRT would show that the item was a 26-page report, dated July 19, 1968, and prepared by Dr. R. E. Jones. With this information, the user would be able to obtain an abstract of the paper or a microfiche copy of the complete report.

REMARKS. This real-time, on-line, time-sharing automated information system with remote access terminals possesses a wide range of coordinate reference capabilities. With proper search preparation on the part of the user, it can be used to correlate and manipulate reference data in a variety of ways to achieve search satisfaction. Its great speed and search flexibility reduce the search time of hundreds of scientists and technicians to a minimum and thus afford them a higher percentage of time for more creative pursuits.

Costs for development, acquisition, and operation of such a sophisticated system are high in relation to other automated retrieval systems. In time, such costs will become lower and thus more competitive as improvements in hardware and programing occur.

NASA/RECON AUTOMATED REFERENCE

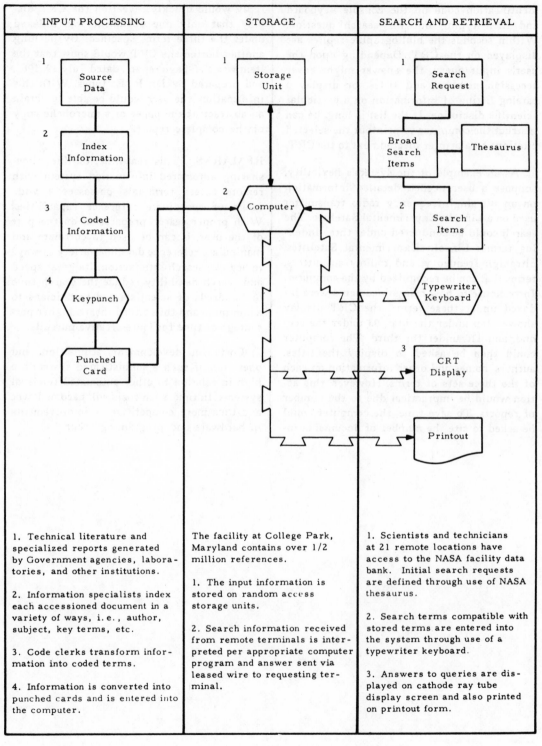

INPUT PROCESSING	STORAGE	SEARCH AND RETRIEVAL
1. Technical literature and specialized reports generated by Government agencies, laboratories, and other institutions. 2. Information specialists index each accessioned document in a variety of ways, i.e., author, subject, key terms, etc. 3. Code clerks transform information into coded terms. 4. Information is converted into punched cards and is entered into the computer.	The facility at College Park, Maryland contains over 1/2 million references. 1. The input information is stored on random access storage units. 2. Search information received from remote terminals is interpreted per appropriate computer program and answer sent via leased wire to requesting terminal.	1. Scientists and technicians at 21 remote locations have access to the NASA facility data bank. Initial search requests are defined through use of NASA thesaurus. 2. Search terms compatible with stored terms are entered into the system through use of a typewriter keyboard. 3. Answers to queries are displayed on cathode ray tube display screen and also printed on printout form.

VII

COPYRIGHTS, PATENTS, AND TRADEMARKS

I feel that basic information on patents, copyrights, and trademarks: definitions, procedure for obtaining, protection, and searching procedures—all should be readily available to the librarian. For more details than provided here, write the respective offices.

General Information On Copyright

Prepared by Copyright Office, Library Of Congress.

This Circular attempts to (and does) answer some of the questions that are frequently asked about copyright, such as: What is a copyright? Who can claim copyright? What can be copyrighted? and the like. Basic info for all librarians.

WHAT IS A COPYRIGHT

A copyright is a form of protection given by the law of the United States (Title 17, U. S. Code) to the authors of literary, dramatic, musical, artistic, and other intellectual works. The owner of a copyright is granted by law certain exclusive rights in his work such as:

* the right to print, reprint and copy the work.
* the right to sell or distribute copies of the work.
* the right to transform or revise the work by means of dramatization, translation, musical arrangement, or the like.
* the right to perform and record the work.

The rights granted by the copyright law are not unlimited in scope. For example, in the case of musical compositions, the performance right is limited to public performances for profit. Recording rights in musical works are limited by the so-called "compulsory license" provision, which permits recordings upon payment of certain royalties after the initial recording has been authorized by the copyright owner.

WHO CAN CLAIM COPYRIGHT

Only the author or those deriving their rights through him can rightfully claim copyright. Mere ownership of a manuscript, painting, or other copy does not necessarily give the owner the right to copyright. In the case of works made for hire, it is the employer, and not the employee, who is regarded as the author.

There is no provision for securing a blanket copyright to cover all the works of a particular author. Each work must be copyrighted separately if protection is desired.

Minors may claim copyright. However, state law may regulate or control the conduct of business dealings involving copyrights owned by minors; for information on this subject, it would be well to consult an attorney.

WHAT CAN BE COPYRIGHTED

The copyright law (Title 17, U.S. Code) lists 13 broad classes of works in which copyright may be claimed, with the provision that these are not to limit the subject matter of copyright. Within the classes are the following kinds of works:

Books (Class A). Published works of fiction and nonfiction, poems, compilations, composite works, directories, catalogs, annual publications, information in tabular form, and similar text matter, with or without illustrations, that appear as a book, pamphlet, leaflet, card, single page, or the like.

Periodicals (Class B). Publications, such as newspapers, magazines, reviews, newsletters, bulletins, and serial publications, that appear under a single title at intervals of less than a year. Also contributions to periodicals, such as stories, cartoons, or columns published in magazines or newspapers.

Lectures or similar productions prepared for oral delivery (Class C). Unpublished works such as lectures, sermons, addresses, monologs, recording scripts, and certain forms of television and radio scripts.

SOURCE: U. S. Library of Congress. Copyright Office. *General Information on Copyright.* Circular 1. (Washington: 1971). pp. 1-11.

Dramatic and dramatico-musical compositions (Class D). Published or unpublished dramatic works such as the acting versions of plays for the stage, for filming, radio, television, and the like, as well as pantomimes, ballets, operas, operettas, etc.

Musical compositions (Class E). Published or unpublished musical compositions (other than dramatico-musical compositions) in the form of visible notation, with or without words. Also new versions of musical compositions, such as adaptations, arrangements, and editing when it represents original authorship. The words of a song, unaccompanied by music, are not registrable in Class E.

Maps (Class F). Published cartographic representations of area, such as terrestrial maps and atlases, marine charts, celestial maps, and such three-dimensional works as globes and relief models.

Works of art; or models or designs for works of art (Class G). Published or unpublished works of artistic craftmanship, insofar as their form but not their mechanical or utilitarian aspects are concerned, such as artistic jewelry, enamels, glassware, and tapestries, as well as works belonging to the fine arts, such as paintings, drawings, and sculpture.

Reproductions of works of art (Class H). Published reproductions of existing works of art in the same or a different medium, such as a lithograph, photoengraving, etching, or drawing of a painting, sculpture, or other works of art.

Drawings or sculptural works of a scientific or technical character (Class I). Published or unpublished diagrams or models illustrating scientific or technical works, such as an architect's or an engineer's blueprint, plan, or design, a mechanical drawing, an astronomical chart, or an anatomical model.

Photographs (Class J). Published or unpublished photographic prints and filmstrips, slide films, and individual slides. Photoengravings and other photomechanical reproductions of photographs are registered in Class K.

Prints, pictorial illustrations, and commercial prints or labels (Class K). Published prints or pictorial illustrations, greeting cards, picture postcards, and similar prints, produced by means of lithography, photoengraving, or other methods of reproduction. A print or label, not a trademark, published in connection with the sale or advertisement of articles of merchandise also is registered in this class.

Motion-picture photoplays (Class L). Published or unpublished motion pictures that are dramatic in character, such as feature films, filmed or recorded television plays, short subjects and animated cartoons, musical plays, and similar productions having a plot.

Motion pictures other than photoplays (Class M). Published or unpublished non-dramatic motion pictures, such as newsreels, travelogs, training or promotional films, nature studies, and filmed or recorded television programs having no plot.

WHAT CANNOT BE COPYRIGHTED

Even though a work does not fit conveniently into one of the 13 classes, this does not necessarily mean that it is uncopyrightable. However, there are several categories of material which are generally not eligible for statutory copyright protection. These include among others:

- Titles, names, short phrases and slogans; familiar symbols or designs; mere variations of typographic ornamentation, lettering, or coloring; mere listings of ingredients or contents.
- Ideas, plans, methods, systems, or devices, as distinguished from a description or illustration.
- Sound recordings, and the performances recorded on them.
- Works that are designed for recording information and do not in themselves convey information, such as time cards, graph paper, account books, diaries, bank checks, score cards, address books, report forms, and the like.
- Works consisting entirely of information that is common property and containing no original authorship. For example: standard calendars, height and weight charts, tape measures and rulers, schedules of sporting events, and lists or tables taken from public documents or other common sources.

UNPUBLISHED WORKS

An unpublished work is generally one for which copies have not been sold, placed on sale, or made available to the public. Unpublished works are eligible for one or the other of two types of protection:

Common Law Literary Property. This type of protection against unauthorized use of an unpublished work is a matter of state law, and arises automatically when the work is created. It requires no action in the Copyright Office. It may last as long as the work is unpublished, but it ends when the work is published or copyright is secured.

Statutory Copyright. This is the protection afforded by the federal law upon compliance with certain requirements. Only the following types of works can be registered for statutory copyright before they have been published: musical compositions, dramas, works of art, drawings and sculptural works of a scientific or technical character, photographs, motion pictures, and works prepared for oral delivery. There is no requirement that any of these works be registered for statutory copyright in unpublished form, but there may be advantages in doing so. If they are registered in their unpublished form, the law requires that another registration be made after publication with the copyright notice affixed to the copies (see page 354).

The following types of material cannot be registered for statutory protection in unpublished form: books (including short stories, poems and narrative outlines), prints, maps, reproductions of works of art, periodicals, and commercial prints and labels. These works secure statutory copyright by the act of publication with notice of copyright.

COPYRIGHT PROCEDURE FOR AN UNPUBLISHED WORK

Statutory copyright for unpublished works is secured by registering a claim in the Copyright Office. For this purpose it is necessary to forward the following material:

Application Form. The appropriate form may be ordered from the Copyright Office from the list printed on page 355. Forms are supplied without charge.

Copy. In the case of manuscripts of music, dramas, lectures, etc., one complete copy should accompany the application. It will be retained by the Copyright Office. For photographs, deposit one photographic print. Special requirements concerning motion pictures, and certain graphic and artistic works, are stated on the application forms.

Fee. The registration fee for unpublished works is $6.

See pages 355 and 356 for mailing instructions.

PUBLISHED WORKS

Published works are works that have been made available to the public in some way, usually by the sale or public distribution of copies. The copyright law defines the "date of publication" as "the earliest date when copies of the first authorized edition were placed on sale, sold, or publicly distributed by the proprietor of the copyright or under his authority, . . ."

No specific number of copies or method of distribution is required for a general publication. However, it is sometimes difficult to determine the dividing line between a general publication and a limited distribution (such as sending copies to agents, publishers, or some other limited group for a specific purpose). If you are in doubt about publication in a particular case, it may be advisable to consult an attorney.

The rights in a work will be permanently lost unless all published copies bear a notice of copyright in the form and position described on page 354. When a work has been published without notice of copyright it falls into the public domain and becomes public property. After that happens it serves no purpose to add the notice to copies of the work, and doing so may be illegal.

In the case of works that cannot be registered in advance of publication, it is the act of publication with notice of copyright, rather than registration in the Copyright Office, that secures statutory copyright. While the Copyright Office registers claims to copyright, it does not grant copyright protection.

COPYRIGHT PROCEDURE FOR PUBLISHED WORKS

Three steps should be taken to secure and maintain statutory copyright in a published work:

- *Produce copies with copyright notice.* Produce the work in copies by printing or other means of reproduction. It is essential that all copies bear a copyright notice in the required form and position (see page 354).
- *Publish the work.*
- *Register your claim in the Copyright Office.* Promptly after publication, you should forward the following material:

Application Form. The appropriate form may be requested from the Copyright Office from the list printed on page 355.

Copies. Send two copies of the best edition of the work as published.

Fee. The registration fee for published works is $6.

See pages 355 and 356 for mailing instructions.

NOTE: The law requires that, after a work is published with the prescribed notice, two copies "shall be promptly deposited," accompanied by a claim of copyright and a fee.

THE COPYRIGHT NOTICE

Form of the Notice. As a general rule, the copyright notice should consist of three elements:

- *The word "Copyright," the abbreviation "Copr.," or the symbol ©.* Use of the symbol © may have advantages in securing copyright in countries that are members of the Universal Copyright Convention.
- *The name of the copyright owner (or owners).*
- *The year date of publicaiton.* This is ordinarily the year in which copies are first placed on sale, sold, or publicly distributed by the copyright owner or under his authority. However, if the work has previously been registered for copyright in unpublished form, the notice should contain the year date of registration for the unpublished version. Or, if there is new copyrightable matter in the published version, it is advisable to include both the year date of the unpublished registration and the year date of publication.

These three elements should appear together on the copies. Example:

© John Doe 1971

Optional Form of Notice. A special form of the notice is permissible for works registrable in Classes F through K (maps; works of art, models or designs for works or art; reproductions of works of art; drawings or sculptural works of a scientific or technical character; photographs; prints and pictorial illustrations; and prints or labels used for articles of merchandise). This special notice may consist of the symbol ©, accompanied by the initials, monogram, mark, or symbol of the copyright owner, if the owner's name appears upon some accessible portion of the copies. A detachable tag bearing a copyright notice is not acceptable as a substitute for a notice permanently affixed to the copies.

Position of the Notice. For a book or other publication printed in book form, the copyright notice should appear upon the title page or the page immediately following. The "page immediately following" is normally the reverse side of the page bearing the title. For a periodical, the notice should appear upon the title page, upon the first page of text, or under the title heading. For a musical composition, the notice may appear either upon the title page or upon the first page of music.

Notice for Unpublished Works. The law does not specify a notice for unpublished works. Nevertheless, to avoid the danger of inadvertent publication without notice, it may be advisable for an author to affix notices to any copies that leave his control.

HOW LONG DOES COPYRIGHT PROTECTION LAST

The first term of statutory copyright runs for 28 years. The term begins on the date the work is published with the notice of copyright, or, in the case of unpublished works registered in the Copyright Office, on the date of registration. A copyright may be renewed for a second term of 28 years if an acceptable renewal application and fee are received in the Copyright Office during the last year of the original term of copyright, which is measured from the exact date on which the original copyright began. Several recent Acts of Congress have extended second-term copyrights that would have expired on or after September 19, 1962; however, these extensions have no effect on the time limits for renewal registration. For further information about renewal copyright and these extensions, write to the Copyright Office.

INTERNATIONAL COPYRIGHT PROTECTION

If a work is by an author who is neither a citizen nor a domiciliary of the United States and the work is first published outside the United States, special conditions determine whether or not the work can be protected by U.S. copyright. Specific questions on this subject, and questions about securing protection for U.S. works in foreign countries, should be addressed to the Register of Copyrights, Library of Congress, Washington, D.C. 20540.

For general information regarding international copyright matters, request Circular 38 from our Office. We also furnish on request the current lists showing the copyright relations of various countries.

For information about the requirements and protection provided by other countries, it may be advisable to consult an expert familiar with foreign copyright laws. The U.S. Copyright Office is not permitted to recommend agents or attorneys or to give legal advice or information on foreign laws.

TRANSFER OR ASSIGNMENT OF STATUTORY COPYRIGHT

A copyright may be transferred or assigned by an instrument in writing, signed by the owner of the copyright. The law provides for the recordation in the Copyright Office of transfers of copyright. The original signed instrument should be submitted for the purpose of recording. It will be returned following recordation. For effective protection, an assignment executed in the United States should be recorded within 3 months from the date of execution. Assignments executed abroad should be recorded within 6 months. For information about assignments and related documents, request Circular 10.

APPLICATION FORMS

The following forms are provided by the Copyright Office, and may be obtained free of charge upon request:

*Class A   Form A: Published book manufactured in the United States of America.

Form A–B Foreign: Book or periodical manufactured outside the United States of America (except works subject to the ad interim provisions of the Copyright Law of the United States of America; see Form A–B Ad Interim).

*Class A
or B   Form A–B Ad Interim: Book or periodical in the English language manufactured and first published outside the United States of America and subject to the ad interim provisions of the Copyright Law of the United States of America.

Form B: Periodical manufactured in the United States of America.

*Class B   Form BB: Contribution to a periodical manufactured in the United States of America.

Class C   Form C: Lecture or similar production prepared for oral delivery.

Class D   Form D: Dramatic or dramatico-musical composition.

Class E   Form E: Musical composition by an author who is a citizen or domiciliary of the United States of America or which is first published in the United States of America.

Form E Foreign: Musical composition by an author who is not a citizen or domiciliary of the United States of America and which is not first published in the United States of America.

*Class F   Form F: Map.

Class G   Form G: Work of art; model or design for work of art.

*Class H   Form H: Reproduction of a work of art.

Class I   Form I: Drawing or plastic work of a scientific or technical character.

Class J   Form J: Photograph.

Form K: Print or pictorial illustration.

*Class K   Form KK: Print or label used for article of merchandise.

Class L
or M   Form L–M: Motion picture.

Form R: Renewal copyright.

Form U: Notice of use of musical composition on mechanical instruments.

*NOT TO BE USED FOR UNPUBLISHED MATERIAL (SEE PAGES 352 AND 353).

MAILING INSTRUCTIONS

Address. All communications should be addressed to the Register of Copyrights, Library of Congress, Washington, D.C. 20540.

Fees. Do not send cash. Fees sent to the Copyright Office should be in the form of a money order, check, or bank draft, payable to the *Register of Copyrights.*

Mailing. Processing of the material will be more prompt if the application, copies, and fee are all mailed at the same time and in the same package.

AVAILABLE INFORMATION

This circular attempts to answer some of the questions that are frequently asked about copyright. For a list of other material published by the Copyright Office, write for "Publications of the Copyright Office." Any requests for Copyright Office publications or special questions relating to copyright problems not dealt with in this circular should be addressed to the Register of Copyrights, Library of Congress, Washington, D.C. 20540.

The Copyright Office cannot give legal advice. If you need information or guidance on matters such as disputes over the ownership of a copyright, getting a work published, obtaining royalty payments, or prosecuting possible infringers, it may be necessary to consult an attorney.

A pamphlet edition of "The Copyright Law of the United States of America" (Bulletin 14), with the Regulations of the Copyright Office, is available for 45 cents from the Superintendent of Documents, U.S. Government Printing Office, Washington, D.C. 10402.

General Information Concerning Patents

Prepared by the Patent Office

"The purpose of this booklet is to give the reader some general information about patents and the operations of the Patent Office . . . It attempts to answer many of the questions commonly asked of the Patent Office but is not intended to be a comprehensive textbook on patent law or a guide for the patent lawyer. Consequently, many details are omitted and complications have been avoided as much as possible. It is hoped that this pamphlet will be useful to inventors and prospective applicants for patents, to students, and to others who may be interested in patents by giving them a brief general introduction to the subject." From the Preface.

FUNCTIONS OF THE PATENT OFFICE

The Patent Office is an agency of the U.S. Department of Commerce, the Department of the Federal Government primarily concerned with assisting and encouraging the development of the business and industry of the United States.

The role of the Patent Office in carrying out this mission is to provide patent protection for inventions and the registration of trademarks to serve the interests of inventors and businesses with respect to their inventions and corporate and product identifications, to advise and assist other bureaus and offices of the Department of Commerce and other agencies of the Government in matters involving patents and inventions and the transfer of technology, and, through the preservation, classification, and dissemination of patent information, to aid and encourage innovation and the scientific and technical advancement of the Nation.

In discharging its duties, the Patent Office examines applications and grants patents on inventions when applicants are entitled to them; it publishes and disseminates patent information, records assignments of patents, maintains search files of U.S. and foreign patents and a Patent Search Center for public use, and supplies copies of patents and official records to the public. Similar functions are performed relating to trademarks.

Additional information may be obtained from the Patent Office publications *Patent Laws* and *Rules of Practice in Patent Cases* listed on page 361. The Patent Office does not publish any textbooks on patent law, but a number of such works for the specialist and for the general reader have been published by private concerns.

WHAT IS A PATENT?

A patent for an invention is a grant by the Government to an inventor of certain rights.

A patent is granted by the Government acting through the Patent Office.

The subject matter of the patent is an invention.

The person entitled to receive the patent grant is the inventor (or his heirs or assigns).

The duration of the patent grant is 17 years.

The right conferred by the patent grant extends throughout the United States and its territories and possessions.

The right conferred by the patent grant is, in the language of the statute and of the grant itself, "the right to exclude others from making, using, or selling" the invention. What is granted is not the right to make, use, or sell, but the right to exclude others from making, using, or selling the invention.

Most of the statements in the preceding paragraphs will be explained in greater detail in later sections.

Some persons occasionally confuse patents,

SOURCE: Reprinted from U.S. Department of Commerce. Patent Office. *General Information Concerning Patents.* (Washington: reprinted 1970). pp. 1–9.

copyrights, and trademarks. Although there may be some resemblance in the rights of these three kinds of intangible property, they are completely different and serve different purposes.

Copyrights

Copyright protects the writings of an author against copying. Literary, dramatic, musical and artistic works are included within the protection of the copyright law, which in some instances also confers performing and recording rights. The copyright goes to the form of expression rather than to the subject matter of the writing. A description of a machine could be copyrighted as a writing, but this would only prevent others from copying the description—it would not prevent others from writing a description of their own or from making and using the machine. Copyrights are registered in the Copyright Office in the Library of Congress and the Patent Office has nothing whatever to do with copyrights. Information concerning copyrights may be obtained by addressing: Register of Copyrights, Library of Congress, Washington, D.C. 20540.

Trademarks

A trademark relates to the name or symbol used in trade with goods to indicate the source or origin of the goods. Trademark rights will prevent others from using the same name on the same goods, but do not prevent others from making the same goods without using the trademark. Trademarks which are used in interstate or foreign commerce may be registered in the Patent Office. The procedure relating to the registration of trademarks and some general information concerning trademarks is given in a pamphlet called *General Information Concerning Trademarks,* which may be obtained from the Patent Office on request.

PATENT LAWS

The Constitution of the United States gives Congress the power to enact laws relating to patents, in Article 1, section 8, which reads "Congress shall have power . . . to promote the progress of science and useful arts, by securing for limited times to authors and inventors the exclusive right to their respective writings and discoveries." Under this power Congress has from time to time enacted various laws relating to patents. The first patent law was enacted in 1790. The law now in effect is a general revision which was enacted July 19, 1952, and which came into effect January 1, 1953. This law is reprinted in a pamphlet entitled *Patent Laws,* which is sold by the Superintendent of Documents, U.S. Government Printing Office, Washington, D.C. 20402.

The patent law specifies the subject matter for which a patent may be obtained and the conditions for patentability. The law establishes the Patent Office for administering the law relating to the granting of patents, and contains various other provisions relating to patents.

WHAT CAN BE PATENTED

The patent law specifies the general field of subject matter that can be patented, and the conditions under which a patent may be obtained.

In the language of the statute, any person who "invents or discovers any new and useful process, machine, manufacture, or composition of matter, or any new and useful improvements thereof, may obtain a patent," subject to the conditions and requirements of the law. By the word "process" is meant a process or method, and new processes, primarily industrial or technical processes, may be patented. The term "machine" used in the statute needs no explanation. The term "manufacture" refers to articles which are made, and includes all manufactured articles. The term "composition of matter" relates to chemical compositions and may include mixtures of ingredients as well as new chemical compounds. These classes of subject matter taken together include practically everything which is made by man and the processes for making them.

The Atomic Energy Act of 1954 excludes the patenting of inventions useful solely in the utilization of special nuclear material or atomic energy for atomic weapons.

The statute specifies that the subject matter must be "useful." The term "useful" in this connection refers to the condition that the subject matter has a useful purpose and also includes operativeness, that is, a machine which will not operate to perform the intended purpose would not be called useful. Alleged inventions of perpetual motion machines are refused patents.

Interpretations of the statute by the courts have defined the limits of the field of subject matter which can be patented, thus it has been held that methods of doing business and printed matter cannot be patented. In the case of mixtures of ingredients, such as medicines, a patent cannot be granted unless there is more to the mixture than the effect of its components. (So-called patent medicines are ordinarily not patented; the phrase "patent medicine" in this connection does not have the meaning that the medicine is patented.) It is often said that a patent cannot be obtained upon a mere idea or suggestion. The patent is granted upon the new machine, manufacture, etc., as has been said, and not upon the idea or suggestion of the new machine. As will be stated later, a complete description of the actual machine or other subject matter sought to be patented is required.

NOVELTY AND OTHER CONDITIONS FOR OBTAINING A PATENT

In order for an invention to be patentable it must be new as defined in the statute. The statute provides that an invention cannot be patented if—

"(a) The invention was known or used by others in this country, or patented or described in a printed publication in this or a foreign country, before the invention thereof by the applicant for patent, or

"(b) The invention was patented or described in a printed publication in this or a foreign country or in public use or on sale in this country more than one year prior to the date of the application for patent in the United States . . . .

If the invention has been described in a printed publication anywhere in the world, or if it has been in public use or on sale in this country before the date that the applicant made his invention, a patent cannot be obtained. If the invention has been described in a printed publication anywhere, or has been in public use or on sale in this country more than one year before the date on which an application for patent is filed in this country, a valid patent cannot be obtained. In this connection it is immaterial when the invention was made, or whether the printed publication or public use was by the inventor himself or by someone else. If the inventor describes the invention in a printed publication or uses the invention publicly, or places it on sale, he must apply for a patent before one year has gone by, otherwise any right to a patent will be lost.

Even if the subject matter sought to be patented is not exactly shown by the prior art, and involves one or more differences over the most nearly similar thing already known, a patent may still be refused if the differences would be obvious. The subject matter sought to be patented must be sufficiently different from what has been used or described before so that it may be said to amount to invention over the prior art. Small advances that would be obvious to a person having ordinary skill in the art are not considered inventions capable of being patented. For example, the substitution of one material for another, or changes in size, are ordinarily not patentable.

THE UNITED STATES PATENT OFFICE

Congress has established the United States Patent Office to perform the function of issuing patents on behalf of the Government. The Patent Office as a distinct bureau may be said to date from the year 1802 when a separate official in the Department of State who became known as "Superintendent of Patents" was placed in charge of patents. The revision of the patent laws enacted in 1836 reorganized the Patent Office and designated the official in charge as Commissioner of Patents. The Patent Office remained in the Department of State until 1849 when it was transferred to the Department of the Interior, and in 1925 it was transferred to the Department of Commerce, in which Department it is today.

The chief functions of the Patent Office are to administer the patent laws as they relate to the granting of letters patent for inventions, and to perform other duties relating to patents. It examines applications for patents to ascertain if the applicants are entitled to patents under the law, and grants the patents when they are so entitled; it publishes issued patents and various publications concerning patents and patent laws, records assignments of patents, maintains a search room for the use of the public to examine issued patents and records, supplies copies of records and other papers, and the like. Analogous and similar functions are performed with respect to the registration of trademarks. The Patent Office has no jurisdiction over questions of infringement and the enforcement of patents, nor over matters relating to the promotion or utilization of patents or inventions.

The head of the Office is the Commissioner of Patents and his staff includes several assistant commissioners of patents and other officials. As head of the office, the Commissioner superintends or performs all duties respecting the granting and issuing of patents and the registration of trademarks; exercises general supervision over the entire work of the Patent Office; prescribes the rules, subject to the approval of the Secretary of Commerce, for the conduct of proceedings in the Patent Office and for recognition of attorneys and agents; decides various questions brought before him by petition as prescribed by the rules, and performs other duties necessary and required for the administration of the Patent Office and the performance of its functions.

The examination of applications for patents is the largest and most important function of the Patent Office. The work is divided among a number of examining groups, each group having jurisdiction over certain assigned fields of invention. Each group is headed by a group director and staffed by a number of examiners. The examiners perform the work of examining applications for patents and determine whether patents can be granted. An appeal can be taken to the Board of Appeals from their decisions refusing patents and a review by the Commissioner of Patents may be had on other matters by petition. The examiners also determine when an interference exists between pending applications, or a pending application and a patent, institute interference proceedings in such cases and hear and decide certain preliminary questions raised by contestants.

In addition to the examining groups, the Patent Office has a number of sections, divisions, or branches which perform various other services, such as receiving and distributing mail, receiving new applications, handling sales of printed copies of patents, making copies of records, inspecting drawings, recording assignments, and so on.

At the present time the Patent Office has about 2,700 employees, of whom about half are examiners and others with technical and legal training. Patent applications are received at the rate of over 90,000 per year. The Patent Office receives over two and a half million pieces of mail each year.

PUBLICATIONS OF THE PATENT OFFICE

Patents. – The specification and accompanying drawings of all patents are published on the day they are granted, and printed copies are sold to the public by the Patent Office. About 3,500,000 patents have been issued.

Printed copies of any patent identified by its patent number, may be purchased from the Patent Office at a cost of 50 cents each, postage free, except design patents which are 20 cents each.

Future patents classified in subclasses containing subject matter of interest may be obtained, as they issue, by prepayment of a deposit and a service charge. For the cost of such subscription service, a separate inquiry should be sent to the Patent Office.

Official Gazette of the United States Patent Office. – The *Official Gazette* of the United States Patent Office is the official journal relating to patents and trademarks. It has been published weekly since January 1872 (replacing the old Patent Office Reports), and is now issued each Tuesday, simultaneously with the weekly issue of the patents. It contains an abstract and a selected figure of the drawings of each patent granted on that day; decisions in patent and trademark cases rendered by the courts and the Patent Office; notices of patent and trademark suits; indexes of patents and patentees; list of patents available for license or sale; and much general information such as orders, notices, changes in rules, changes in classification, etc. The *Official Gazette* is sold on subscription and by single copies by the Superintendent of Documents, U.S. Government Printing Office, Washington, D.C. 20402.

Since July 1952, the illustrations and claims or abstracts fo the patents have been arranged in the *Official Gazette* according to the Patent Office classification of subject matter, permitting ready reference to patents in any particular field. Street addresses of patentees have been published since May 24, 1960, and a geographical index of residences of inventors has been included since May 18, 1965. Since January 2, 1968, abstracts, when available, have been published instead of claims. Copies of the *Official Gazette* may be found in public libraries of larger cities.

Index of Patents. – This annual index to the *Official Gazette* is currently issued in two volumes, one an index of patentees and the other an index by subject matter of the patents. Sold by Superintendent of Documents.

Index of Trademarks. – An annual index of registrants of trademarks. Sold by Superintendent of Documents.

Decisions of the Commissioner of Patents. – Issued annually, reprinting the decisions which have been published weekly in the *Official Gazette*. Sold by Superintendent of Documents.

Manual of Classification. – A looseleaf book containing a list of all the classes and subclasses of inventions in the Patent Office classification system, a subject matter index, and other information relating to classification. Substitute pages are issued from time to time. Annual subscription includes the basic manual and substitute pages. Sold by Superintendent of Documents.

Classification Definitions. – Contain the changes in classification of patents as well as definitions of new and revised classes and subclasses. Sold by Patent Office.

Weekly Class Sheets. – Lists showing classification of each patent in the weekly issue of the *Official Gazette.* Sold on annual subscription by Patent Office.

Patent Laws. – A compilation of patent laws in force. Sold by Superintendent of Documents.

Rules of Practice in Patent Cases. – Rules governing the procedures in the Patent Office which have been adopted by the Commissioner of Patents under the authority of the patent statutes and approved by the Secretary of Commerce, with supplementary materials including forms and relevant sections of the patent law. Sold by Superintendent of Documents.

Trademark Rules of Practice of the Patent Office With Forms and Statutes. – Rules governing the procedures in the Patent Office in Trademark matters and a compilation of trademark laws in force. Sold by Superintendent of Documents.

General Information Concerning Trademarks. – Serves the same purpose with regard to trademarks as does this pamphlet concerning patents. Single copies are distributed by the Patent Office on request. Multiple copies may be purchased from Superintendent of Documents.

Patents and Inventions–An Information Aid for Inventors. – The purpose of this pamphlet is to provide information which may help inventors decide whether to apply for patents and aid them in obtaining patent protection and promoting their inventions. Sold by Superintendent of Documents.

Directory of Registered Patent Attorneys and Agents Arranged by States and Countries. – A geographical listing of patent attorneys and agents registered to practice before the U.S. Patent Office. Sold by Superintendent of Documents.

Manual of Patent Examining Procedure. – A loose-leaf manual which serves primarily as a detailed reference work on patent examining practice and procedure for the Patent Office's Examining Corps. Subscription service includes basic manual, quarterly revisions, and change notices. Sold by Superintendent of Documents.

Guide for Patent Draftsmen. – Patent Office requirements for patent drawings. Illustrated. Sold by Superintendent of Documents.

The Story of the United States Patent Office. – A chronological account of the development of the U.S. Patent Office and patent system and of inventions which had unusual impact on the American economy and society. Sold by Superintendent of Documents.

Patents: Spur to American Progress. – Outlines the functioning of the patent system in layman's language, illustrating how the system nurtures discovery upon which the partnership of inventor, industry, and the public builds American prosperity. A publication in the U.S. Department of Commerce's series, "Know Your Economic ABC's." Sold by Superintendent of Documents.

GENERAL INFORMATION AND CORRESPONDENCE

All business with the Patent Office should be transacted in writing. The personal attendance of applicants at the Office is unnecessary. Mail should be addressed to "Commissioner of Patents, Washington, D.C. 20231." The physical location of the Office is Crystal Plaza, 2021 Jefferson Davis Highway, Arlington, Va.

Applicants and attorneys are required to conduct their business with the Office with decorum and courtesy. Papers presented in violation of this requirement will be returned.

A separate letter (but not necessarily in a separate envelope) should be written in relation to each distinct subject of inquiry such as assignments for recording, payment of issue fees, orders for printed copies of patents, orders for photographic copies of records, and requests for other services. None of these should be included with letters responding to Office actions in applications.

When a letter concerns a patent, it should state the name of the patentee, the invention, and the patent number and date.

In making inquiry concerning the status of his application, the inventor should be sure to give its serial number and filing date.

The zip code should be included as part of the address in all correspondence.

An order for a copy of an assignment must give the book and page or reel and frame of the record, as well as the name of the inventor; otherwise, an additional charge is made for the time consumed in making a search for the assignment.

Applications for patents are not open to the public, and no information concerning them is released except on written authority of the applicant, his assignee, or his attorney, or when necessary to the conduct of the business of the Office. Patents and related records, including records of any decisions, the records of assignments of patent applications, books, and other records and papers in the Office are open to the public. They may be inspected in the Patent Office Search Center or copies may be ordered.

The Office cannot respond to inquiries concerning the novelty and patentability of an invention in advance of the filing of an application; give advice as to possible infringement of a patent; advise of the propriety of filing an application; respond to inquiries as to whether or to whom any alleged invention has been patented; act as an expounder of the patent law or as counselor for individuals, except in deciding questions arising before it in regularly filed cases. Information of a general nature may be furnished either directly or by supplying or calling attention to an appropriate publication.

THE PATENT OFFICE SEARCH CENTER

In addition to copies of United States patents, the Patent Office Search Center at Crystal Plaza, 2021 Jefferson Davis Highway, Arlington, Va., has available for public use over 120,000 volumes of scientific and technical books in various languages, about 90,000 bound volumes of periodicals devoted to science and technology, the official journals of foreign patent offices, and over 8 million foreign patents in bound volumes. (In many cases there are two sets of foreign patents, one set arranged in numerical order and another set arranged according to the subject classification system of the country of origin of the patents.)

A Search Room is provided where the public may search and examine United States patents granted since 1836. Patents are arranged according to the Patent Office classification system of over 300 subject classes and 64,000 subclasses. By searching in these classified patents, it is possible to determine, before actually filing an application, whether an invention has been anticipated by a United States patent, and it is also possible to obtain the information contained in patents relating to any field of endeavor.

A Record Room also is maintained where the public may inspect the records and files of issued patents and other open records. The Record Room contains a set of United States patents arranged in numerical order and a complete set of the *Official Gazette.*

Applicants and their attorneys or agents may examine their own cases in the Record Room, and public records may be examined wherever they may be maintained in the Patent Office Search Center. Applicants, their attorneys or agents, and the general public are not entitled to use the records and files in the examiners' rooms.

The Search Room is open from 8 a.m. to 8 p.m. Monday through Friday except on legal holidays.

Since a patent is not always granted when an application is filed, many inventors attempt to make their own investigation before applying for a patent. This may be done in the Search Room of the Patent Office, and to a limited extent in some public libraries. Patent attorneys or agents may be employed to make a so-called preliminary search through the prior United States patents to discover if the particular device or one similar to it has been shown in some prior patent. This search is not always as complete as that made by the Patent Office during the examination of an application, but only serves, as its name indicates, a preliminary purpose. For this reason, the Patent Office examiner may, and often does, reject claims in an application on the basis of prior patents or publications not found in the preliminary search.

Those who cannot come to the Search Room may order from the Patent Office copies of lists of original patents or of crossreferenced patents contained in the subclasses comprising the field of search, and inspect printed copies of the patents in a library which has a numerically arranged set of patents. These libraries and their locations are: Albany, N.Y., University of State of New York; Atlanta, Ga., Georgia Tech Library; Boston, Mass., Public Library; Buffalo, N.Y., Buffalo and Erie County Public Library; Chicago, Ill., Public Library; Columbus, Ohio, Ohio State University Library; Detroit, Mich., Public Library; Kansas City, Mo., Linda Hall Library; Los Angeles, Calif., Public Library; Madison, Wis., State Historical Society of Wisconsin; Milwaukee, Wis., Public Library; Newark, N.J., Public Library; New York, N.Y., Public Library; Philadelphia, Pa., Franklin Institute; Pittsburgh, Pa., Carnegie Library; Providence, R.I., Public Library; St. Louis, Mo., Public Library; Stillwater, Okla., Oklahoma Agricultural and Mechanical College; Sunnyvale, Calif., Public Library;[1] Toledo, Ohio, Public Library.

The Patent Office has also prepared on microfilm lists of the numbers of the patents issued in each of its subclasses, and many libraries have purchased copies of these lists. In libraries which have the lists and a copy of the Manual of Classification, and also a set of patent copies or the *Official Gazette,* it will be unnecessary for the searcher to communicate with the Patent Office before commencing his search, as he can learn from the Manual of Classification the subclasses which his search should include, then identify the numbers of the patents in these subclasses from the microfilm lists, and examine the patent copies so identified, or the disclosures of these patents in the *Official Gazette* volumes.

While the classification printed on any patent is correct at the time the patent is issued, it should be noted that the constantly expanding arts often require reclassification. As a result, the classification indicated on the patent may be incorrect at a later date.

NOTE

[1] Arranged by subject matter, collection dates from Jan. 2, 1962.

General Information Concerning Trademarks

Prepared by the Patent Office

Some people tend to confuse patents, copyrights, and trademarks. Although there may be some resemblance in the rights of these three kinds of intangible property, they are completely different and serve different purposes, as this general guide on trademarks shows for one of the three.

TRADEMARK STATUTES AND RULES

This pamphlet is intended to serve only as a general guide in regard to trademark matters in the Patent Office.

Applications for registration of trademarks must conform to the requirements of the Trademark Act of 1946, as amended, and the Trademark Rules of Practice. This Act, Public Law 489, Seventyninth Congress, Chapter 540, 60 Stat. 427, popularly known as the Lanham Act, and forming Chapter 22, Title 15 of the U.S. Code, became effective July 5, 1947, superseding the Trademark Acts of 1905 and 1920. A copy of the *Trademark Rules of Practice With Forms and Statutes* can be obtained from the Superintendent of Documents, Washington, D.C., 20402, for 45¢.

DEFINITION AND FUNCTIONS OF TRADEMARKS

Definition of Trademarks

A "trademark," as defined in section 45 of the 1946 Act, "includes any word, name, symbol, or device, or any combination thereof adopted and used by a manufacturer or merchant to identify his goods and distinguish them from those manufactured or sold by others."

Function of Trademarks

The primary function of a trademark is to indicate origin. However, trademarks also serve to guarantee the quality of the goods bearing the mark and, through advertising, serve to create and maintain a demand for the product. Rights in a trademark are acquired only by use and the use must ordinarily continue if the rights so acquired are to be preserved. Registration of a trademark in the Patent Office does not in itself create or establish any exclusive rights, but is recognition by the Government of the right of the owner to use the mark in commerce to distinguish his goods from those of others.

Mark Must Be Used in Commerce

In order to be eligible for registration, a mark must be in use in commerce which may lawfully be regulated by Congress, for example, interstate commerce, at the time the application is filed. "Use in commerce" is defined in section 45 as follows:

> For the purposes of this Act a mark shall be deemed to be used in commerce (a) on goods when it is placed in any manner on the goods or their containers or the displays associated therewith or on the tags or labels affixed thereto and the goods are sold or transported in commerce and (b) on services when it is used or displayed in the sale or advertising of services and the services are rendered in commerce, or the services are rendered in more than one State or in this and a foreign country and the person rendering the services is engaged in commerce in connection therewith.

Trade and Commercial Names

Trademarks differ from trade and commercial names which are used by manufacturers, industri-

SOURCE: Reprinted from U.S. Department of Commerce. Patent Office. *General Information Concerning Trademarks.* (Washington: Reprinted 1970). pp. 1–3, 10–11, 17–18.

alists, merchants, agriculturists, and others to identify their businesses, vocations or occupations, or the names or titles lawfully adopted by persons, firms, associations, companies, unions and other organizations. The latter are not subject to registration unless actually used as trademarks.

REGISTRATION OF TRADEMARKS

Marks Not Subject to Registration

A trademark cannot be registered if it—

(a) Consists of or comprises immoral, deceptive, or scandalous matter or matter which may disparage or falsely suggest a connection with persons, living or dead, institutions, beliefs, or national symbols, or bring them into contempt or disrepute.

(b) Consists of or comprises the flag or coat of arms or other insignia of the United States, or of any State or municipality, or of any foreign nation, or any simulation thereof.

(c) Consists of or comprises a name, portrait, or signature identifying a particular living individual except by his written consent, or the name, signature, or portrait of a deceased President of the United States during the life of his widow, if any, except by the written consent of the widow.

(d) Consists of or comprises a mark which so resembles a mark registered in the Patent Office or a mark or trade name previously used in the United States by another and not abandoned, as to be likely when applied to the goods of another person, to cause confusion, or to cause mistake, or to deceive.

Principal and Supplemental Register Marks

The Trademark Act of 1946 provides for the establishment of two registers, designated as the Principal Register and the Supplemental Register. Coined, arbitrary, fanciful, or suggestive marks, generally referred to as "technical marks," may, if otherwise qualified, be registered on the Principal Register. Marks not qualified for registration on the latter register but which, nevertheless, are capable of distinguishing applicant's goods and have been in lawful use in commerce for at least one year, may be registered on the Supplemental Register.

Registrable Marks—Principal Register

A trademark, if otherwise eligible, may be registered on the Principal Register unless it consists of a mark which, (1) when applied to the goods of the applicant is merely descriptive or deceptively misdescriptive of them, or (2) when applied to the goods of the applicant is primarily geographically descriptive or deceptively misdescriptive of them, except as indications of regional origin, or (3) is primarily merely a surname.

Such marks, however, may be registered on the Principal Register, provided they have become distinctive as applied to the applicant's goods in commerce. The Commissioner may accept as prima facie evidence that the mark has become distinctive as applied to applicant's goods in commerce, proof of substantially exclusive and continuous use thereof as a mark by the applicant in commerce for the 5 years next preceding the date of filing of the application for registration.

Registrable Marks—Supplemental Register

All marks capable of distinguishing applicant's goods and not registrable on the Principal Register, which have been in lawful use in commerce for the year preceding the filing of the application for registration, may be registered on the Supplemental Register. For the purpose of registration on the Supplemental Register a mark may consist of any trademark, symbol, label, package, configuration of goods, name, word, slogan, phrase, surname, geographical name, numeral, or device, or any combination of any of the foregoing.

SERVICE, CERTIFICATION, AND COLLECTIVE MARKS

The Trademark Act of 1946 also provides for the registration of service marks, certification marks, and collective marks.

Service Marks

The term "service mark" means a mark used in the sale or advertising of services to identify the services of one person and distinguish them from the services of others. Titles, character nemes and other distinctive features of radio or television programs may be registered as service marks notwithstanding that they, or the programs, may advertise the goods of the sponsor.

Certification Marks

The term "certification mark" means a mark used upon or in connection with the products or services of one or more persons other than the owner of the mark to certify regional or other origin, material, mode of manufacture, quality, accuracy or other characteristics of such goods or services or that the work or labor on the goods or services was performed by members of a union or other organization.

Collective Marks

The term "collective mark" means a trademark or service mark used by the members of a cooperative, an association, or other collective group or organization. Marks used to indicate membership in a union, an association, or other organization may be registered as Collective Membership Marks.

REGISTERED MARKS

Constructive Notice and Evidence of Ownership

Registration of a mark on the Principal Register of the 1946 Act, or under the Acts of 1881 or 1905, is constructive notice of the registrant's claim of ownership thereof, and prima facie evidence of the validity of the registration, registrant's ownership of the mark, and of registrant's exclusive right to use the mark in commerce in connection with the goods or services specified in the certificate, subject to any conditions and limitations stated therein. Such registrations give the right to sue in the United States courts and to prevent importation of goods bearing an infringing mark.

Registration on the Supplemental Register of the 1946 Act or under the Act of 1920 does not constitute constructive notice or prima facie evidence and does not give the right to prevent importation

of goods bearing an infringing mark, but does give the right to sue in the United States courts.

Notice of Registration

A registrant should give notice that his mark is registered by displaying with the mark as used the words "Registered in U.S. Patent Office," or "Reg. U.S. Pat. Off.," or the letter R enclosed within a circle, thus ®. Use of such notice before the actual issuance of a certificate of registration for the mark is improper and may be the basis for refusal of registration.

RECORDS AND PUBLICATIONS OF THE PATENT OFFICE

Digest of Registered Marks

A digest of registered marks is maintained in the Search Room of Trademark Operations and is open open to the public. This digest comprises a set of the registered word marks arranged alphabetically and a set of registrations comprising symbols, birds, animals, etc., arranged according to the classification of the goods or services with which they are used. It is advisable to search this digest before adopting a trademark so as to avoid possible conflict with previously registered marks. The Office has a card index of articles of commerce indicating their classification in the various classes of goods which have been established under the law.

Printed Copies of Registrations

Printed copies of registrations will be furnished by the Patent Office upon payment of the fee therefor. These copies may be merely copies of the registration as issued or status copy showing all effective actions taken on the registrations, including renewal affidavits, publication under section 12 (c), cancellation, etc.

Registration Files

After a mark has been registered or published for opposition, the file of the application and all proceedings relating thereto are available for public inspection and copies of the papers may be furnished upon paying the fee therefor.

Pending Applications

A digest of pending applications with a reproduction of the mark, the name and address of the applicant, the goods or services with which the mark is used, the dates of first use, and the serial number of the application is maintained for public inspection. Access to the file of a particular pending trademark application will be permitted prior to publication upon the showing in writing of good cause for such access. Decisions of the Trade Trademark Trial and Appeal Board in applications and proceedings relating thereto are published or available for inspection or publication.

Assignment Records

The assignment records of the Patent Office are open to public inspection and copies of any recorded assignment may be obtained upon payment of the fee therefor. An order for a copy of an assignment should give the liber (book) and page or the reel and frame of the record.

Official Gazette

The Official Gazette of the Patent Office is published weekly and contains in addition to material relating to patents, information relating to trademarks, including marks published for opposition, marks registered, amended, cancelled and renewed, and marks published under section 12 (c) of the 1946 Act.

Single copies and subscriptions of the Official Gazette are sold by the Superintendent of Documents, U.S. Government Printing Office, Washington, D.C., 20402. The trademark material is reprinted separately as the trademark section and may be purchased or subscribed to separately.

Annual Trademark Index.

An annual index of registrants of trademarks is published and sold by the Superintendent of Documents.

VIII

AMENDING THE LIBRARY SERVICES & CONSTRUCTION ACT

Enactment by the 84th Congress of the Rural Library Services Act of 1956 (Public Law 84-597) provided the first Nation-wide Federal support for public library services. In 1960 the law was extended for 5 years (Public Law 86-679), and amendments to the original law enacted in 1964 (Public Law 88-269) extended eligibility to urban areas and authorized use of Federal funds for construction of public library facilities.

Two years later, the law was again extended (Public Law 89-511). This enactment also made State library administrative agencies responsible for planning future library development, especially through interlibrary cooperation, and for providing specialized library services in each State. In 1967 certain technical amendments were enacted (Public Law 90-154).

The Library Services and Construction Act expired on June 30, 1971. Prior to that date, hearings were held to extend it for another five years. In the pages that follow you'll find some interesting and informative excerpts from those hearings and then the Public Law that resulted from these hearings. Reading these pages will give you some idea of the legislative process in action and of the time and intelligent effort put in by some of your legislators and colleagues in seeing to it that this law is extended.

Library Services and Construction Amendments of 1970 Hearing Before the Select Subcommittee on Education

"The record of the Library Services and Construction Act has been one of steady success since its inception. From Fiscal 1957 to Fiscal 1969, the Federal Government has committed $200 million to extending public library services to areas without adequate services. Some 45 millions books and other library materials has been purchased for this purpose from Federal funds matched by funds from local and State sources.

An estimated 85 million people have benefited in one way or another from library programs which have frequently used "outreach" services to bring the advantages of libraries to ghetto residents, migrant workers, and residents of isolated areas." These are the accomplishments in general. The excerpts that follow tell of specific accomplishments and needs in several areas of the United States. And some tell why LSCA needs to be extended, and explain the several parts of the proposed act. These several statements, some presented orally to the committee, some inserted into the record, were made by some of the top librarians in the United States. They include Jersey City Library Director William J. Roehrenbeck, New Jersey State Librarian Roger H. McDonough, Idaho State Librarian Helen Miller, Philadelphia Library Director Carlton Rochell, Trustee Margaret S. Warden, Great Falls, Montana, Public Library, Trustee Alexander Peter Allain, St. Mary Parish Library, Franklin, Louisiana, John A. Humphry, Assistant Commissioner for Libraries, New York State Education Department, and L. Quincy Mumford, Librarian of Congress.

Mr. BRADEMAS. The Select Subcommittee on Education will come to order for the purpose of consideration of the Library Services and Construction Amendments of 1970.

National concern for the development of good library services was demonstrated by the 84th Congress which passed the Rural Library Services Act of 1956. The act authorized an annual appropriation of $7.5 million for 5 years to assist the States and territories in extending and developing libraries in areas of under 10,000 population.

In 1960, Congress extended the act for an additional 5 years.

In 1964, the programs changed and expanded with amendments to the basic law which extended participation to libraries in urban areas and made available for the first time Federal funds for the construction of public library facilities.

The Library Services and Construction Act has had a record of steady success. Through the funds appropriated under this act, an estimated 85 million people have benefited from library services.

The program has grown by 45 million books; 650 bookmobiles have taken library services to people outside the reach of existing library facilities, and some 1,500 library construction projects have been undertaken to serve an estimated 50 million people.

SOURCE: U.S. Congress. House of Representatives. Committee on Education and Labor. Select Subcommittee on Education. *Library Services and Construction Amendments of 1970.* Hearing, Ninety First Congress, second session, H.R. 16365 and S. 3318 . . . September 10, 1970. (Washington: 1970). pp. 47–49, 58–65, 73–75, 81–84, 86–90, 93–97, 101–108, 113–115.

Today, we are very pleased to hear testimony from individuals concerned with libraries at the local, State and Federal level.

The Chair is pleased at this time to recognize his distinguished colleague on the subcommittee and of the full committee, the gentleman from New Jersey, Mr. Daniels, for the purpose of presenting our first witness.

Mr. Daniels.

Mr. DANIELS. Thank you, Mr. Chairman.

I appreciate the fact that you called upon me to present the first witness this morning.

I would like to say, at the outset, I regret very much that I shall be unable to stay and listen to the testimony of the witness I am about to introduce because of the fact that, as chairman of the Subcommittee on Insurance and Health Benefits of the House Post Office and Civil Service, I have called an executive session of my subcommittee at 10 a.m. Consequently, I must be there because we have important legislation under consideration which I would like the subcommittee to consider and report favorably so that some action may be taken on this legislation in this session of Congress.

Mr. McDonough is from the Garden State of New Jersey, a man well known to this committee, who has testified innumerable times, whose testimony has been most important in framing the library legislation. His interest in this field dates back a number of years. In fact, he testified on the Library Services Act of 1956 which, as you recall, was a landmark piece of legislation.

I would like to present to the subcommittee Mr. Roger H. McDonough, director of the State library of New Jersey, and director of the division of State library of arts and history of the New Jersey Department of Education.

I might also point out that he was also past president of the American Library Association.

Undoubtedly he will refer to his background in his testimony.

I would also like to request, Mr. Chairman, that I may move at this particular time to insert in the record a statement by William J. Roehrenbeck, director of the Jersey City Library. I believe the statement will be very interesting to you and members of the subcommittee because it sets forth a particularly innovative program introduced in Jersey City, my hometown, which program is referred to as Outreach.

(The statement referred to follows:)

LIBRARY OUTREACH PROGRAM, 1970

A REPORT BY WILLIAM J. ROEHRENBECK, DIRECTOR, JERSEY CITY (N.J.) PUBLIC LIBRARY

During the summer of 1970, the Jersey City Public Library received Federal funds granted by the New Jersey State Library under the provisions of the Library Services and Construction Act to initiate a special "Outreach" program focused on the Bergen-Lafayette section of the city—a predominantly black, low income, densely populated area. The basic purpose of the program is to reach out beyond the walls of the Library to non-users with books, records, programs, and information which can be of practical value to them, to demonstrate that the Library can provide enjoyment and recreation, and to dissipate any negative attitudes toward the Library as a middle-class institution intended only for the better-educated or more affluent.

Two methods are being used: sidewalk service in the target area provided by a small Volkswagen bus, the "Mini-Mobile"; and a corps of community aides working out in the neighborhoods from the two storefront branches in the area.

The most colorful feature of the Outreach program is the red-and-white "Mini-Mobile", whose function is to carry library materials out of the building into the streets of the target area and to provide sidewalk service for people who are not normally library users—who are either unaware of the Library's existence or who feel it has no relevance for them.

The Mini-Mobile carries a collection of paperbacks for all ages: picture and easy books for younger children, a wide range of recreational and informative reading for older boys and girls and teen-agers, and practical, easy-to-read books for adults on consumer education, vocational guidance, self-improvement, child care, health and hygiene, sports, home decoration, drug addiction, etc. There is special emphasis on black history and achievement. All titles have been heavily duplicated, and several supplemental orders have been placed for easy books, and for such items as *Soul on Ice, Manchild in the Promised Land, Down These Mean Streets, and Autobiography of Malcolm X*, which are in constant demand. Phonograph records, pamphlets on subjects of current interest, and magazines are also carried on the Mini-Mobile.

Materials are not cataloged, but are simply stamped with Library ownership and given a book pocket and charge card. No library cards are required, and people may borrow all materials on their names. Fines are not charged.

The Mini-Mobile went into service on July 1, 1970. During its first six weeks of operation, the Mini-Mobile provided approximately 90 hours of service at 60 stops, and loaned a total of 4,029 items. Four hundred and eighty-five adults and 2,183 children were contacted. This, despite the fact that two full days were lost because of rain, and that operations were seriously hampered on several other days by showers and/or intense heat.

Cold figures present an inadequate picture of the Mini-Mobile operation, since much time is spent by staff in just talking with people, telling them about the Library and its services, listening to them, hearing about their problems and "gripes," and discovering their interests, attitudes, and hopes.

The approach of the Library staff has been warm, friendly, and service directed. When the Mini-Mobile parks at a stop, a small table and chairs are set out on the sidewalk. Portable book racks are set up with a variety of books of interest to the people in the area, and the staff goes to work, in a "soft-sell" manner, speaking to people as they pass by, telling them about the Library and its services, asking about their interests, answering questions, filling requests for subjects and titles, giving impromptu story hours for children, etc. Flyers about the Library are distributed, as are applications for library cards. Public reaction is encouraging and ranges from overwhelming enthusiasm from children to open-mouthed amazement from adults who had no idea that the Library had books they might like or phonograph records they could borrow. The lack of red tape and complete informality of the service has proven beneficial in attracting patrons.

The following are representative comments made by patrons:
This is wonderful.
When are you coming back?
Hey, man, look at all the books!
You mean I can take it without a card? You trust me?
Are these books for sale?
I thought it was just for kids.
Hey, records too!
The Library had a good idea.
It's free?

Return visits to stops are always greeted with great enthusiasm. When the children hear the distinctive Mini-Mobile horn they come running from all directions, books in hand.

As part of its service, the Mini-Mobile staff has presented film programs at a housing project, and many impromptu, on-the-spot story hours and record programs at various locations.

The Library has also been carried outside the walls into the community by "Project Outreach", a corps of work-study students from Jersey City State College who have been working out of the two branches in the target area under the direction of a Program Coordinator. Their primary objectives are to make the initial contact with potential users of the library, to inform them about its materials and services, focusing on its relevance in their lives, and to break down barriers which may exist in their minds about the use of a public institution. These community aides are all thoroughly familiar with the target area and have been able to establish excellent rapport with both adults and children. They interpret the Library to residents and provide helpful feedback on community reactions, opinions, and needs.

The community aides have made face-to-face contact with individuals on the streets, in the parks, at housing projects, and with established groups such as churches, schools, the housing authority, municipal community relations councils, family guidance centers, etc., with whom they have cooperated in arranging and presenting programs, supplying books, records, and films, and offering story hours and cultural programs of all kinds in and outside the Library.

They are working in the two branches in a variety of book-oriented activities for neighborhood children, including story hours, film programs, creative writing, dramatics, black history, poetry reading, etc. Adult activities have included programs on consumer education and family guidance, and a seminar for minority businessmen.

Elderly residents of the target area's two housing projects have been visited with large print books, magazines, and records. The aides found that while many of the old people enjoyed books and magazines, some were unable to read. For these, the visit itself and the genuine, friendly interest displayed by the young aides, did much to brighten an otherwise dreary day. Phonograph records which were brought and played, especially gospel songs and spirituals, were much enjoyed and repeatedly requested.

Portable libraries of fifteen or twenty paperbacks, stressing black history and experience, have been deposited in some 18 neighborhood barberships and laundromats as a result of contacts made by aides. The books are set up in small racks or "shoe boxes", with signs inviting customers to read while they wait, and suggesting that they visit the neighborhood branch for other good books. These deposits have been very successful.

Several field trips have been arranged by the Program Coordinator for adults and children, including visits to the Schomburg Library and the Studio Museum in Harlem, the United Nations, the Bronx Zoo, and a special performance of "Cinderella" at Jersey City State College.

It is too early to evaluate results, but it is evident that many people in Jersey City have already acquired a new image of the Library—not as a remote, stodgy, forbidding city institution—but as a group of friendly, enthusiastic people with exciting, interesting books, records, films, and activities to share with them and their children.

STATEMENT OF ROGER H. McDONOUGH, STATE LIBRARIAN, NEW JERSEY

My name is Roger H. McDonough. I am the State Librarian of New Jersey, and Director of the Division of the State Library, Archives and History of New Jersey Department of Education. My responsibilities include administration of the Library Services and Construction Act in the State of New Jersey.

I am also a past president of the American Library Association. I am speaking in support of the bill to extend the Library Services and Construction Act.

I have had the honor and the privilege of testifying in support of Federal assistance to libraries a number of times, beginning with that landmark piece of legislation, the Library Services Act of 1956. It has been highly gratifying to see successive Congresses respond to the needs of the people through extension and expansion of this legislation, and I am sure that the reason this program has been so popular with the Congress is because so many good things have happened through the stimulus provided by the presence of these relatively modest Federal monies.

My personal knowledge of these programs as they have been conducted nationwide convinces me that the LSCA monies have made the difference between poor library service and good library service for millions of Americans. I have had the good fortune to be able to inspect at firsthand the manifold uses to which these Federal monies have been put in various States. I have seen citizens, young and old, in rural areas of the deep South, for example, receiving bookmobile library service for the first time. In sharp contrast, I have visited and observed with keen interest vital outreach programs in Bedford-Stuyvesant, Brooklyn, and in our own Jersey City and Camden. Taking the libraries to the people appears to work just as well in our inner cities as it does in the country. Good buildings are still essential, however, and the new, attractive and inviting buildings that have been erected with the encouragement of Title II funds across the country have replaced crowded, antiquated structures, many of which had outlived their usefulness a generation and more ago.

The 1966 addition of Titles IV–A and IV–B expanded services to the blind and handicapped and to the patients and residents of State institutions, thus bringing a new service dimension to a segment of our population who previously had received only token library service.

As I have observed it, a considerable portion of the Federal money has been used to provide new and different kinds of services. It has allowed the States to experiment and demonstrate structures or patterns of service, particularly under Titles I and III, for which no other funds would have been available. The Federal monies have helped to demonstrate the vital educational and informational function of libraries in our democratic society. I hardly need remind you that the public library is one of the few major social, educational institutions in the country in which an individual may, in the privacy of his own need or interest, pursue his vocational or business improvement or his cultural goals.

Because of long years of financial neglect, however, libraries are still forced to fight vigorously for their fair share of the tax dollar. Not only are they forced to compete with other public agencies but they are also fighting against inflationary trends in the cost of library materials and operating expenses, as well as the increase in the number and kinds of informational materials required. It is with good reason that this proliferation of educational materials is aptly characterized as an "information explosion." For example, in 1956 when I testified before the Senate Education Subcommittee, some 12,000 books were published annually. Last year, over 29,000 titles were published. During this same period, the number of periodical titles increased by 150 percent.

In 1956, local tax support for libraries in New Jersey amounted to $7.4 million, as compared to the $23 million provided in 1969 (an increase of 300 percent). In 1956, the State of New Jersey provided no money for public library support. This year, the State legislature appropriated $6,000,000. Progress is being made at all levels but it must be remembered in citing these figures that inflation and increased populations have seriously offset these apparent gains.

While the States and municipal governments have made valiant efforts to provide better support for their public libraries, they have simply not been able to do everything that is required. The mayors of the two largest cities in New Jersey, for example, have informed their public library boards that the cities have reached the limit of their ability to finance the library programs and any additional support must come from outside. Some support, in the form of State and Federal aid, is now going to these city libraries, and it is clear that these funds are essential if the high levels of service that these libraries have provided for many years is to be preserved.

Let me highlight for you some of the ways the LSCA has benefited the people of New Jersey. Through the use of Federal money, we were able to demonstrate the desirability of establishing key strong-point libraries in strategic locations across the State in order that they might provide reference, consultative and coordinative services to all of the libraries and citizens in the region. Federal funds were also used to recompense major research libraries for providing citizen access throughout the State to these magnificent collections. The research libraries included the Rutgers and Princeton University libraries and the Newark Public Library. The demonstration was so successful that in a short time State legislation was enacted incorporating the three-level system approach, and providing the area and research libraries with State funds to build upon the results of Federal seed money. Continuing the development of system programs, Federal funds are being used to help strengthen weaker libraries so that they will be in a better position to offer area-wide services. It is worth mentioning, I think, that under our coordinated program, local autonomy has been preserved and our 350 municipal libraries run their own affairs using the area reference libraries and the research libraries as needed through a voluntary cooperative arrangement.

Another major program under Title I of the present Act is the special stimulation of services to the disadvantaged citizens of New Jersey in both rural and urban areas. Under this program, the funds are granted to a given project for a maximum of three years to encourage the local library to perfect the new service and to seek out local support for the activity. A wide variety of projects have been initiated in New Jersey. These range from a multi-purpose program in Monmouth County which contains urban, suburban and rural areas and which provides, for example, quiet study areas in urban locations, outlets in housing projects, and film, book and story hour services to migrant workers. Other projects include the support of a library unit in an adult basic education center, and a highly successful and imaginative program in the inner-city area of Jersey City featuring a mini-bookmobile operation which sets up shop itinerantly at various streetcorners, plus a new branch outlet in a converted storefront. Similar experimental programs are being developed in many parts of the country.

One of the most significant projects supported under Title III (Interlibrary Cooperation) is New Jersey's Micro-Automated Catalog Project. This is a unique idea developed by a member of my staff, Mr. Kenneth Richards, Head of our Bureau of Archives and History. The full catalog of the State Library has been placed on microfilm and deposited in area libraries, together with a rapid access Reader-Printer. The area libraries now know what titles are owned by the State Library or what materials are available on a given subject and can produce a patron request by simply pushing the print-out button. This year we intend to expand this particular program and tie it into a TWX network in order to provide faster service to the library users. In another area, Title IV-B, the availability of funds to assist in the provision of library services to the blind and handicapped came at a most fortunate time in New Jersey. We were just establishing a regional library for this purpose in New Jersey and LSCA funds were of great benefit to us in building a strong foundation program.

The need for library services in State institutions is so immense that the money provided thus far under Title IV-A allows us only to begin to scratch the surface.

The most disappointing factor in Federal support to public libraries has been the recent reduction in funds under Title II, Construction. Before Title II Construction was authorized in 1964, New Jersey was building an average of two public library buildings per year. During the first four years of Title II, an average of approximately 15 libraries per year was constructed in New Jersey. The Federal funds have definitely stimulated building activity as evidenced by the fact that over the years $4½ million of Federal funds has resulted in more than $28½ million worth of public library construction. Last year New Jersey received only $200,000 under Title II. Consequently, because of this low funding, we had to reject a dozen worthy construction applications. Few of these construction projects will now move forward without the stimulation of LSCA.

The combination of programs now under Titles I & IV of the LSCA would have the potential of allowing the States to respond to their particular needs. Because of ongoing commitments to programs currently supported by the specific titles, the promise of flexibility would be an illusion, however, unless considerable increases in funds are provided.

It is clear to me that the continuation of the incentive of Federal money for libraries is essential. In the past, these funds have stimulated four to five times as much State and local effort. The same result can be expected in the future.

Having presented my views, documented with data relating to my own State of New Jersey, I would like to call to your attention the official position of the members of the American Association of State Libraries (ASL) representing the fifty States, regarding the extension of the LSCA.

The ASL recommends a five-year extension of LSCA beyond its current expiration date of June 30, 1971. In the extension of this Act, specific attention must be directed to the following points:

    1. High priority to library services to the disadvantaged;

    2. Fiscal support for strong and vital metropolitan public library service;

    3. Increase in the relative importance of inter-type library cooperation;

    4. Consideration of some consolidation of separate titles for administrative convenience and flexibility;

    5. Strengthening of State library agencies, particularly in capacity for planning, research and evaluation.

I would like to mention an additional point in regard to the Ayres bill (HR 16365) before closing. This has to do with the provision under Section 201, p. 15, providing for a one percent set aside of appropriations for program evaluation.

We have been concerned with the need to evaluate the effectiveness of the various programs under LSCA and indeed there is need to evaluate the total LSCA program. A number of factors are likely to affect the success of any evaluation program. Among these are: 1) placement of the responsibility for evaluation; 2) reporting requirements; and 3) scope and complexity of the programs.

It is our feeling that in considering where responsibility lies for evaluating a grant program such as LSCA, a distinction should be made between the operational programs at the State and local levels and the program considered as a whole. The operational programs may be evaluated objectively within the granting agency but not necessarily by the individuals responsible for administering the grants. However, the overall program shall be reviewed and evaluated outside the granting agency. For this purpose the National Commission on Libraries and Information Science which this Congress has recently established will be ideal and is legally empowered to act.

The nature and cost of evaluating a program is affected more by its scope and complexity than by its size. It will probably cost more to evaluate work in 10,000 units spending a total of one million dollars than to evaluate work in 1,000 units spending a total of 10 million dollars. For this reason we would recommend that the cost of evaluating the programs be justified through the regular appropriation process rather than be established as an automatic percentage over which Congress will have no control. In any case, the minimal funds appropriated to the States for programs should not be further reduced by the proposed percentage cut. Instead, an additional amount should be appropriated for evaluation.

In closing, I again urge that the Library Services and Construction Act, which has done so much to extend, improve and help equalize public library service throughout the country, be extended at least for another five years to enable the States to do effective, long-range planning.

Thank you for the privilege of testifying before you today.

STATEMENT OF MISS HELEN MILLER, STATE LIBRARIAN OF THE STATE OF IDAHO

Miss MILLER. Thank you, Mr. Chairman.

I am Helen Miller. I am State librarian of Idaho, a member of the

American Library Association for 25 years, and the current chairman of the Association's Committee on National Library Week.

I was born on a farm in rural Missouri, and raised in a town of 500 with no library, so I feel especially close to those persons who even today don't have library service, or who have service which is inadequate for their needs.

I wish to speak in support of the 5-year extension of the Library Services and Construction Act. The present act expires June 30, 1971, and I feel that it is vital to the information needs of the entire Nation that act be renewed at this time.

As I have been State librarian in Idaho for 8½ years, and directly in charge of administering the LSCA program there, I would like to tell of the use which we have made of the funds, and the information needs which we still have not met.

SERVICES

When the original LSA began in 1956, the Idaho State Library had the lowest income of any State library in the Nation—$16,000—and could not match for Federal funds. Now, in 1970, we have a State appropriation of $130,000—about a 700 percent increase.

In addition, the 1970 annual session of the Idaho Legislature finally answered our recurring pleas for a State grant-in-aid program to help local public libraries, and appropriated $100,000 for this purpose.

This may sound like Idaho has done so well that there is no need for further help—but the truth is that we started at such a low level that we still have a long way to go to catch up with other States.

In 1956, the local tax income for our public libraries was only $334,000. Now, our 100 public libraries together receive just a bit more than $1 million annually.

Idaho's total State population is less than that of a major city like Washington, D.C.; yet our area is greater than that of all New England. Nine of our counties have less than 3,000 population—and only eight have more than 25,000.

Federal funds have been the impetus for most library improvements in Idaho in the past 13 years. We see the six major public libraries of Idaho as library leaders, each in a geographical area. These city libraries serve as a foster parent to smaller libraries in the multicounty area. The city taxpayers shoulder a greater burden—and we use LSCA funds to help strengthen these six library centers. This is a concept like that proposed priority in the new LSCA—to strengthen metropolitan public libraries which serve as national or regional resource centers.

In 1963, Idaho had only seven public librarians with professional training—and no trained public librarian in the 500 miles from Boise north to the Canadian border. Thanks to LSCA funds, which have helped with scholarships, and with grants to enable the large libraries to pay enough to attract a librarian, we now have a total of 17½ professionals in our public libraries.

This month we are expecting to add four new graduates as regional assistants. This increase of 300 percent in professional staff will surely improve the quality of library service in Idaho.

DISADVANTAGED

I wish to endorse the concept of some priority for the disadvantaged in urban and rural areas, as proposed for LSCA.

Idaho's disadvantaged are the Indian, the migrant, the small farmer, the lumberman who has seasonal work. We have very few blacks, no Puerto Ricans, a few Chinese and Japanese, and a large Basque colony.

As all of our library service has been at a near-beginning level, service to the disadvantaged has not varied much from the service to the advantaged. Bookmobiles go to the major Indian reservations. The younger Indians use the library, but the adults largely shun it.

There is a similar situation with the migrants, who are now becoming permanent residents in increasing numbers. Library service is limited by the ability to read, and the materials which are available. We find that the migrant may speak a Tex-Mex mixture, but finds Spanish books as difficult as English. The vocabulary in the home is very limited, and the students are not able to compete with Anglo children at the same age level.

Indian parents may not talk much, may use a dialect which is not a written language. The children are taught English in school, and there is a deplorable lack of reading material of interest to a reservation child.

In a small effort to gain Indian material, we are sponsoring a project for the taping of Nez Perce Indian tales—in the original Nez Perce, followed by an English translation, and then an English typescript is made.

A followup should be printing and illustrating these stories, so that the Indian children can read stories which belonged to their elders. We aren't sure when or how this can be done. But we do hope that we can proceed with the taping before the few older Indians are dead.

The Indians of the Bannock-Shoshone, at Fort Hall, have received national publicity for the high suicide rate among the young men, and the sense of desperation and futility which this reflects. The Pocatello Public Library gives bookmobile service to the reservation residents—but something more is needed. Perhaps young Indians who have a sense of commitment to the reservation and its people would be willing to undertake an "outreach" library program—and take books to the lodges, plan programs for the small children, manage discussion groups for the teenagers, show films, tape stories. Working with the Indians is very slow, and the white man is not very welcome.

In the past, we have made our LSCA grants to existing public libraries, to improve their services, or to extend services to unserved areas with the object of establishing new libraries with a local tax base. The Indians and the migrants, however, do not contribute a property tax. Thus, if we are to give library service to these groups, I now believe that we must do it directly with Federal and State moneys, and not depend on a grant to the local public library.

I do hope that the new LSCA will authorize sufficient appropriations to allow us to continue to help the established libraries—who certainly need help—and also to begin to provide direct service to these special groups.

INTERLIBRARY COOPERATION

Interlibrary Cooperation, funded with title III of LSCA, means a lot in a sparsely settled State like Idaho. No library has adequate funds, adequate materials, or staff. Therefore, cooperation is a necessity.

As one of our first projects under title III, we established a teletype network. It now operates among the three largest academic libraries, the six regional center public libraries, and the State library. All other libraries have access to the network through a telephone credit card.

Idaho is accustomed to looking to its neighbors, Washington, and

Oregon, for most examples of progress—but in our Litty (Libraries of Idaho Teletype) we have been the innovator in the Northwest. Approximately 1,700 messages are sent each month, requesting books or reference materials.

Another pioneer teletype service which the Idaho State Library administers is a medical TWX tie-in, providing a link between Idaho and the Health Sciences Library at the University of Washington, Seattle. An average of 100 medical requests are forwarded each month, and a photocopy of the needed material is mailed directly to the patron.

Other Idaho title III projects which are significant include the microfilming of old Idaho newspapers so that these early records can be preserved and available for library users. A union list of magazines and other serials in our 20 major libraries is just coming off the press. We have helped fund a new program sponsored by the Western Interstate Commission on Higher Education (known in the West as WICHE) to provide continuing education for library personnel in the 12 Western States.

I endorse the proposal to give title III 100-percent Federal funding. These projects of cooperation are for the benefit of libraries of all types, and their users. Staff time in the many participating libraries more than matches the Federal share.

CONSTRUCTION

I wish to include a plea for the continuation of a separate LSCA title for construction, rather than consolidating these building projects with service activities as proposed in H.R. 16365.

Idaho's construction projects have surely been the smallest in the Nation—four have been for less than $2,000—but have been very important to the communities where they are located. They have included building a 16 by 20 concrete block library in Idaho City—population 188 and the county seat of an old gold mining county, and buying a Boise-Cascade prefab unit for a library in the Teton Valley—where there was no contractor and the building season was too short for contractors to come in and build on the site.

The total cost of our 29 building projects has been $787,324 in local funds and $891,601 in Federal. The major libraries are still the ones which need the buildings the most. As a conservative estimate, $15 million are needed now just to replace the old Carnegie buildings and enable the major libraries to cope with their 1970 population instead of the 1910 population for which the buildings were designed.

In view of the fact that we have so far to go, in terms of our construction needs, I urge that title II be given continued emphasis as a separate title, and that increasing funds be authorized to carry on this essential program. The meager amounts appropriated in the past 2 years have very effectively impeded progress in extending adequate library service to all our people.

In fiscal 1970, only $7,807,000 was appropriated, which provided funds for 65 building projects throughout the country. However, 271 projects requiring $51,525,945 in Federal matching grants had originally been planned. The States represented on this subcommittee, alone, could have used $20,019,840 in Federal dollars. For your information, I have attached to my statement a summary of public library construction needs in fiscal 1970.

SPECIALIZED SERVICES

Idaho's service to residents of State institutions has been another service where we had to begin at the bottom. We only have seven fully State-supported institutions—there are some advantages in having a low population. But it means that there often aren't enough residents to make full-time library staff feasible.

We have, with LSCA money, helped all the institutions to purchase books, employ staff, begin programs. Above all, we have tried to get the institutions' administrative staff to realize that the library can help in the treatment program. We are making headway slowly. The prison library, for example, now has a carpet on the floor and tables and chairs.

But we still have no professional librarians in the institutions, and the bookstock is far from adequate.

Our service to the blind and handicapped is being purchased on contract from the Utah State Library in Salt Lake City. Now we are considering setting up this program in Idaho. It may cost more, but we believe that we can give a better service to our residents by having the materials and staff in Idaho.

SUMMARY

Finally, Mr. Chairman, I do urge passage of the proposed LSCA, and that it be done by this Congress, this year.

In addition to opposing the outright consolidation in H.R. 16365 of all the programs currently authorized by the existing law, I also oppose the provision in that bill of a $200,000 basic allotment. That would be $85,000 less than we are currently eligible to receive. With increasing needs, this lower figure is totally unrealistic.

Furthermore, since any remainder is to be apportioned on the basis of population, a low $200,000 allotment would be detrimental to the smaller States, such as my own State of Idaho.

Thank you, Mr. Chairman, for the privilege of appearing before the Select Subcommittee on Education, on behalf of libraries.

APPENDIX

THE LSCA RECORD

From fiscal year 1957 to fiscal year 1969, Title I committed $200 million in Federal resources to extending public library services to areas without adequate services. Forty-five million books and other library materials have been supplied to libraries through Title I funds, plus the required State and local matching funds; an estimated 85 million people have benefitted from the new or improved services provided by the program. "Outreach" projects supported by Title I are bringing imaginative library services to places and people never reached by traditional libraries: to disadvantaged urban ghetto residents; to migrant workers; to residents of isolated areas. Sometimes, reaching these people has meant the creation of promising new kinds of flexible library services: the storefront library, new uses of the bookmobile, and so on. With a boost from Title I, public libraries are growing more responsive to community needs. Especially among poor and minority populations inadequately served by public libraries, there is a growing awareness that libraries must reach out to people where they are, and that their materials and services must meet community needs.

Since 1965, Title II has provided approximately $140 million for new library construction, matched with $343 million in State and local funds. These funds have provided assistance for about 1,565 new, enlarged and remodeled library facilities within reach of over 50 million people, some for the first time.

Title III of the LSCA provides for the creation and operation of library networks, for sharing resources among all kinds of libraries within localities, regions, States, and among States. Through Title III, libraries of all kinds (such as school, public, and academic libraries and information centers) are coordinating and sharing their resources to offer better services to the special clientele of each. After an initial planning year and 2 full years of operation, the program has aided in the creation of 45 interlibrary networks and centers serving 904 libraries. Thirty-five Title III-supported telecommunications systems now connect 800 libraries; and 14 technical processing centers, available to 300 libraries, have been established. During Title III's first 3 years, $4,563,000 has been obligated to States for the program.

One project funded under the program in FY 1969 brought together Arizona, Colorado, Idaho, Montana, Nevada, New Mexico, Utah and Wyoming in the development of a Regional Information Network Group (RING). Another example of last year's activities was a project continuing and expanding the services of North Dakota's Northwest Library Federation with headquarters in Minot. An LSCA Title II construction project, it bolsters the resources of small libraries in an 11-county area, through inservice training, consultant services, and centralized processing and cataloging. Other kinds of Title III undertakings included conferences and workshops on interlibrary cooperative activities and developing and/or updating computer-produced union catalogs of books, periodicals, etc.

Title IV of LSCA contains two different programs. Part A authorizes the provision of library materials and services to patients, inmates, and residents of State-operated or substantially State-supported institutions; Part B encourages the provision of special materials and services to the physically handicapped (including the blind) who, because of their handicaps, cannot use ordinary library materials. The programs have separate authorizations and separate State plans.

By the end of FY 1969, $4,189,000 in funds obligated under Title IV–A had brought library services to an estimated 300,000 people, in 500 State institutions. Of these, 400 were correctional institutions, 65 were State hospitals, and 20 were residential schools. Some States spread their allocations among all eligible institutions, for improving existing library collections and training library staff for specialized service. Other States chose to concentrate funds on fewer institutions, organizing new libraries and expanding services.

Beyond the expansion of library services and training of library staff, the program has produced three kinds of long-lasting accomplishments. During FY 1968, several States carried out surveys to assess the state of library services to their State institutions, finding most deplorable at best, nonexistent at worst. The required State advisory councils for Title IV–A have often proven invaluable, in interpreting the library needs of State institutions and in demonstrating to these States the need for State support for institutional library services. Finally, 20 States have added Title IV–A consultants to their State library agency staffs. In sum, then, perhaps the program's most important contribution has been to focus State attention on the desperate needs of libraries in State residential institutions.

An example of the program's impact is the Kings Park State Hospital in New York. Kings Park State Hospital received a title IV–A grant of $20,000 for each of 2 years, 1968 and 1969, to investigate the effects of intensive library service upon culturally deprived and emotionally disturbed patients.

As a result of the project, the hospital has added to the library staff, increased the library budget, and is planning a new library in a future rehabilitation building. The library is now a firstline department in the hospital and the librarian a vital member of the rehabilitation team.

In Wisconsin, 15 of the 19 institutions which have participated in LSCA title IV–A activity now have librarians on their staffs. Eleven are full time, four are part time. Three more institutions have hired librarians on a consultant basis to direct work done by other staff members. The full-time librarian of one institution initiated a library project in a small neighboring institution on a volunteer basis, and volunteers have contributed valuable services. The State reports with 3 years of funding, book and periodical collections have been greatly improved, and experimentation in audiovisual techniques has progressed rapidly. Additional library space has been acquired in several cases.

Title IV–B is aiding States and localities to begin to serve an estimated 2 million physically handicapped, many of them blind or partially blind, who cannot use ordinary library materials and who would benefit from special materials, equipment, and services. It is estimated that 70,000 handicapped people have already been reached by IV–B programs. States have used a total of $2,610,000 in title IV–B funds in a variety of ways: adding staff to regional libraries for the handicapped, building public awareness of the special library needs of the handicapped, identifying potential users and informing them of available materials and services, and expanding library resources in general for the handicapped. These resources include braille materials, books and periodicals in large print, records, tapes, "talking book" machines, and other specialized equipment such as book holders, page turners, prism glasses, etc.

Since one main obstacle to providing special library services to the handicapped is their "invisibility" in their communities, several States have invested program funds in locating the handicapped and registering them for services. In Louisiana, for example, the State library hired part-time consultants in a "case finding project." Operating out of seven urban public libraries, they enlisted members of professions, agencies and organizations serving the handicapped in a drive to identify and contact potential recipients of Title IV–B services.

In summary, the Library Services and Construction Act has led to a number of significant accomplishments. It has provided library services for the first time to many people never before reached by a library, such as the poor, the isolated, the institutionalized, the handicapped. It has focused State and local attention on the library needs of people and institutions inadequately served. The LSCA has encouraged the commitment of State and local resources to improving and extending the provision of libraries to serve all citizens.

STATEMENT OF KEITH DOMS, DIRECTOR, FREE LIBRARY OF PHILADELPHIA

Mr. Doms. Mr. Chairman and Mr. Hansen, while I would like to respond to your suggestion as much as possible, I am here in a unique position.

My name is Keith Doms. I am vice president and president-elect of the American Library Association, and director of the Free Library of Philadelphia. I am the immediate past chairman of the ALA Coordinating Committee on Library Service to the Disadvantaged. Currently, I am a member of the Pennsylvania advisory council on titles III, IV–A, and IV–B under the Library Services and Construction Act.

Today I am representing the American Library Association, a nonprofit educational organization of approximately 30,000 members devoted to the purpose of developing public, school, college, and other types of libraries throughout the Nation.

The American Library Association strongly supports legislation to extend and amend the Library Services and Construction Act. A 5-year extension of the LSCA, which expires June 30, 1971, is essential if the United States hopes to provide adequate library facilities, resources, and services for its citizens in the decade of the seventies.

Under the stimulation of Federal funds—matched by State and community funds in a ratio of 3 to 1—85 million people across this country have benefited from new or improved library services since the original passage of this act in 1956. On the national level, because of LSCA, 1,500 public library buildings were constructed from 1965 to 1969 to serve 50 million people. The $135 million of Federal funds used for this construction were matched by $326 million in State and local funds.

To dramatize the benefits of this act on the State level: in my own State of Pennsylvania, for example, 56 projects under title II were realized between 1964 and 1970. With new buildings, or replacement of inadequate quarters, or improved facilities, close to 1,800,000 Pennsylvanians benefited from construction money in those 6 years. Of the $20 million in total construction costs for new and renovated libraries in Pennsylvania, approximately $8 million were Federal dollars ($12 million constituted State and local matching money).

How has this Federal aid helped in large metropolitan areas? In Philadelphia we established a reader development program to provide up-to-date pertinent materials for adults who are semiliterate and who have only a grade school reading ability but need information on consumers' goods, nutrition, and a wide variety of other important matters. In fiscal 1969, 75,500 pieces of material on these subjects were circulated through 126 agencies cooperating with the library and working directly with these disadvantaged adults.

Eight new branch libraries were built with the use of LSCA funds in eight areas of the city of Philadelphia where the people previously had no library.

A regional film center, located in Philadelphia and administered by the Free Library, funded by LSCA and serving all of eastern Pennsylvania, circulated educational films for 37,000 showings attended by 1,874,800 persons in fiscal 1969–70.

A new package-program of specialized library service coordinated with the Model Cities program is now getting underway in Philadelphia. This includes mobile units, a library service and abstracting unit as part of a community information center and data bank, and the use of community personnel in the operation of the services.

Such projects in Philadelphia are only examples of similar programs in other urban areas of the Nation—all made possible by the stimulation of LSCA funds.

Neither these accomplishments nor the promise held out for the millions of still unreached should be wasted away by failure to extend this legislation. It has been an invaluable concept and support for the people of all ages and education and cultural levels and in aiding librarians to serve them.

Urban and rural communities from coast to coast have benefited. The funds have been well used. But the needs still existing are very real, very vital. And the deficits and gaps still existing between present conditions and adequate conditions call for continuing work.

More books are needed—to keep up with the population and information explosions. Americans were borrowing 3 million books daily from their public libraries in 1968. To meet the increasing needs of the 1970's, public library collections must be increased substantially. For 1970, the estimated deficit is 357 million volumes, or slightly below 50 percent of recognized requirements (3.5 volumes per capita). While students use public libraries significantly, we are also talking here about millions of citizens engaged in purely self-educating endeavors. This is encouraging and timely in an age when the traditional patterns of formalized education are merging more and more with the public availability of information and opinion through multiple means.

There is already a shortage of personnel in our metropolitan libraries, and because of the lack of funds for staffing these systems, further deficiencies can be expected. Of 1,102 authorized staff positions in the public library system of Philadelphia, for example, 189 were unfilled as of August this year because of metropolitan fiscal problems, now all too typical across the Nation.

More regional library centers must be established. Of the 67 counties in Pennsylvania, the people in 31 of them had no county or regional library service as recently as 1968.

More films are needed. In Philadelphia, the regional film center (already mentioned as serving the eastern half of the State) needs 7,500 prints to keep up with the demand. It now has less than 1,500. And there are some 11½ million people in Pennsylvania. The western half of the State is served from Pittsburgh—with an equivalent gap between resources and demand.

Additional materials are needed for the physically handicapped. National estimates are that there will be 2,250,000 of these persons by fiscal 1971. They need talking books, braille books, page turners, and other special materials for reading. With the fiscal 1971 budget recommendation only 70,000 of these people can be served. The situation in Pennsylvania is no better.

For the record, I should like to submit a statement detailing the equally dire lack of library service to persons in State-supported institutions in Pennsylvania.

For all of these reasons, we urge the extension of the Library Services and Construction Act for another 5-year term, with increased funding each year.

A key element in continuing the progress made under LSCA grants thus far is the continued encouragement of interlibrary cooperation— at the local, State, regional, and interstate level. Such cooperation and mutual planning guarantee more efficient and more equitable improvement for all patrons in need of library services and resources. It is recommended, therefore, that title III be continued in its present form, with 100 percent Federal funding. The legislation should also serve to support the priority which the American Association of State Libraries places on strengthening State libraries and strengthening metropolitan libraries serving as resource centers, under title I.

At the annual conference of the American Library Association in Detroit this past July, it was voted that the association establish an office for library service to the disadvantaged and unserved. This new office will help implement ALA's long-standing goal of reaching out to the entire community. In view of this action, the strongest recommendation I would like to leave with this committee is the need for high priority attention to be given to library service to the disadvantaged.

An important breakthrough has now been made in this area. In Philadelphia we see it in the construction and rehabilitation of library buildings in inner city neighborhoods. We see it in the growing outreach of our reader development program. We see it in our unfolding projects in cooperation with the model cities program. We see it in the acquisition of all kinds of special and relevant materials, including materials in Spanish.

We are now reaching persons never before served.

The American people have benefited significantly from what Congress has provided in previous LSCA legislation.

This work must not only go forward: it must be given increased support and attention.

I thank the committee for the privilege of testifying here today on these matters of such importance to the welfare of the people of the United States.

(The attachments referred to follow:)

LIBRARY SERVICE INSTITUTIONS—PENNSYLVANIA

There are over 90 State-supported institutions in Pennsylvania. In 1968, not five of those institutions had a library program worthy of the name. The descriptions below explain the situation:

1. A prison reported 14,000 volumes. About 10,000 were fiction. Of that number, over 8,000 were women's novels with pre-1950 publication dates (some as far back as 1890) and as many as 10 copies of some titles. The small amount of non-fiction was largely sets of fiction (Dickens, Kipling, etc.). A *Television Today* dated 1936 is representative of the actual non-fiction books.

2. A mental hospital has a small building which is a combination canteen and library. The collection of materials is not bad, but it is only available to residents able to walk over, probably less than 5 percent.

3. A home for the elderly has a book collection of about 10,000 volumes. 90 percent of the books are either sets (Dickens, Kipling, etc.) in the small print of the early 1900s or books copyrighted before 1890 (memorial gifts for servicemen of the Civil War).

4. A youth institution has a library, an empty room with 14 books, their ESEA Title II books from the previous year. These are not loaned out so they will not be lost.

5. A hospital for crippled children (65 percent in bed throughout their stay) has book stacks 7 feet tall, and so close together that a wheelchair cannot be maneuvered conveniently.

6. A rehabilitation center with a large percentage of the population having some type of physical disability has 8 foot stacks, 2 areas that are too close to walk between to get at the shelves and practically no materials in the areas of the program of the institution.

Most institutions had no materials at all, or a motley collection of gifts stacked wherever there are shelves, or materials only available to a small segment of the population.

The picture has changed somewhat today. There are perhaps 10 institutions out of the total of 90 which have adequate library programs which will get better. There are another 20 in process of improvement. But, there is still a great deal to be done.

Title IV of LSCA has the responsibility for the development of library service to Pennsylvania residents who are outside the normal service responsibility of the libraries specifically mentioned in LSCA Titles I–III. The residents of State-supported institutions and non-institutionalized blind and physically handicapped are the specific residents mentioned in the Act.

At present, due to the small amount of funds available, no direct grants are being made from the program. The present funds are being used to support State-wide service in the following areas:

1. Consultant aid in the development of libraries and library programs.

2. Development of certain central collection services.

3. In-service education of untrained and partially trained personnel with responsibility for library management.

4. Coordination of agencies, organizations and groups concerned with these aspects of library service.

5. Liaison with agencies, organizations, groups and libraries concerned with the provision of library services to these patrons.

These areas and others which are presently involved in various aspects of work of the Special Library Service Division staff are being met to a greater or lesser extent. As the library service to these patrons improves, this constantly changing library program will alter its approach to reflect current needs and development.

STATEMENT OF CARLTON ROCHELL, DIRECTOR, PUBLIC LIBRARY OF ATLANTA

Mr. ROCHELL. Mr. Chairman and Mr. Perkins, my name is Carlton Rochell. I am director of the Atlanta Public Library. Since 1960, I have directed libraries in Mississippi, Alabama, Tennessee, and Georgia. Prior to that I was a student at Florida State University. I was born in rural middle Tennessee. You might say that I know the South.

I am indeed pleased to be here today and to have the opportunity to speak in support of a 5-year extension and expansion of the Library Services and Construction Act.

These are trying years, we would all concede. They are so demanding that they do more than try men's souls. They test the fullest of our mental capacity, our intellectual ability. We in the educational world are especially sensitive to the crucial nature of change.

I was struck by a quotation I read recently from Governor Berkeley of Virginia in 1670. He was opposed to free schools, and he said—

I thank God there are no free schools. I hope we shall not have them these hundred years; for learning has brought disobedience and heresy and sects into the world.

Governor Berkeley doubtless gaged correctly, by his own standards, the effects of education. Freedom to develop and exchange ideas will always bring change.

Having studied mathematics and economics as an undergraduate, I am continually struck by the simple fact that the public library is the most economical and most effective educational tool yet devised by man. In these times of throwing around dollar figures in the billions, it is truly amazing to consider that for a mere $6 a year every person in this country can have total access to an information system capable of opening all doors. Without a doubt, there is a potential in libraries that is just now being tapped. I speak specifically of programs for the educationally, socially, and culturally disadvantaged of this country. It is a simple, irrefutable fact that funds made available through the Library Services and Construction Act have caused a national awareness of the potential for constructive social change through books and libraries.

It is also a fact that, without a continuing and increasing commitment of funds at the local, State, and national level, this long overdue awakening will be all for nought. When the Library Services Act was first passed in 1956, we talked in terms of the expensive nature of launching bookmobiles into the rural areas of this Nation. In the 1970's the cost of mounting effective programs that will be used in the ghettos of our cities is 10 times that same amount. Extending library service into deprived neighborhoods to reach the nonreader, to serve most meaningful those now unserved, calls for sizable sums.

There are two programs made possible in the State of Georgia through Library Services and Construction Act funds which I would briefly like to mention. First, the program for the blind and physically handicapped—a program established in 1967 to provide direct mail service of Braille talking books tapes, and large-type books. During the 2 years 1967–69, circulation of these materials has increased 50 percent (100,334 to 148,400). During the same time, the number of readers participating has jumped 150 percent (from 2,546 to 5,510). Significantly, the number of volumes per reader has shrunk from 37 to 20. The service is growing faster than the availability of materials.

The director of the program has complained that the staff has not grown with these impressive statistics. He went on to say that without Federal grants to support the project, objectives of the State plan would have been, and would continue to be, hopelessly utopian.

Under a still fledgling title IV–A program, we now have book collections in every prison and prison branch in Georgia. Because of limited funds and the nature of the service, much of this work has been carried on through use of paperbacks, newspapers, magazines, and prints. The program has enjoyed phenomenal popularity and success. The following statement by the director of the program on goals for 1970 indicates how far we have yet to travel in this area: "We hope in 1970 to increase the ratio of books to men from 1:1 to 2:1. As you know, the school media standards now call for a ratio of 25 books per student in our public schools." If we are serious about rehabilitating those in our penal institutions, we must provide them with quality library service to give them the educational, recreational and vocational resources they need to return to society.

The framework for improved programs is there. It is working. It is needed. Without continuing commitments through the Library Services and Construction Act, these efforts will all have been in vain.

I would like to spend the remainder of my time discussing some concrete results of the Library Services and Construction Act which exist in my own professional background. As director of the Knoxville, Tenn., and Anniston, Ala. public libraries, it was my good fortune to be a part of two very similar plans to abolish separate city and county libraries, establish joint libraries, and replace two 60-year-old central buildings with modern facilities. Federal and State money under titles I and II of the Library Services and Construction Act enabled us to make these improvements. It is a matter of record that neither of these accomplishments would have reached reality if we had not had the promise of construction funds and additional book funds. Of some $3 million expended for construction, less than one-fourth came from LSCA and Appalachian Redevelopment funds, yet that was enough to make the partnership click.

Shortly after my arrival in Atlanta, I was instrumental in establishing a committee under the local council on governments to study the problems of library service to the Metropolitan Atlanta area. As chairman of this committee for the past year and a half, it is quite evident to me at this point that the only way we will ever get library service across county lines on a nonfee basis in Metropolitan Atlanta is through a source of funds filtering down from the State and/or Federal level.

Atlanta, as you know, is a national city. It is indeed the melting pot for the entire Southeast. It is also, along with a number of our other great cities, facing almost insurmountable financial problems. The city library is an island in a sea of suburbia, maintaining the only in-depth collection of public library materials for an area of almost 1½ million people. Over one-third of the use of central library collections is by nonresidents or, in more specific terms, by people who do not help support the collections. At the present level of funding, the State library is so over-extended in the maintenance of a regional library system in the State that, without new money coming into the city, we see no way of alleviating this situation. Somehow, in some way, we need direct money into the city at a level sufficient to develop and nurture the collections and open the door to all residents. Therefore, I particularly urge adoption of the proposed amendment to make funds available under title I of LSCA for the strengthening of metropolitan public libraries which serve as national or regional resource centers.

In other areas, the Atlanta Public Library is fast assuming the role of catalyst in the social revolution which is taking place in our region. Informal, flexible, adaptable, and with a definition that leans more heavily on the term "communications" than that of "reservoir," the Atlanta Public Library has made significant strides in assisting various agencies in solving the educational and social ills in our city. Some of these projects are made possible through LSCA funds; others, through other grants, largely Federal.

Among those I will briefly mention are:

(1) Project Enlarge: In this program, a portable darkroom was constructed out of scrap lumber in the basement of the public library and was then moved from neighborhood to neighborhood where teenagers were encouraged to learn to become expert photographers while interacting with pre-school children in a story-hour situation. The results of this project have been amazing. The cumulative body of materials is now on national tour in 15 of the major cities in the United States. The attached brochure, with quotes from the Honorable Julian Bond and the Honorable Sam Massell, will give you some idea of the respect which this program gained in the community.

I might mention one item. This program is now associated with the newly established Postal Street Academy in Atlanta and the 17-year-old, part-time director of that project is Donald Carmichael, one of the first participants in the program.

(2) Mobile service: When I arrived in Atlanta on January 2, 1968, the library was in the process of surplusing a 1954 bookmobile. It was retrieved, painted brick yellow and orange, stocked with magazines, paperbacks, children's books, and black history materials, and became the initial prong of a multifaceted inner city program. This program has now grown to three such bookmobiles and an additional mobile unit called the Free Reeler which is equipped with rear projection equipment, seating for 25 people, a stereo-player, and shelves for small book collections. The success of this program has been phenomenal. The investment has been modest. I might point out that the entire program was made possible through our LSCA grants.

In regard to the proposed LSCA amendments of 1970. I favor a broad public library service program under title I, emphasizing special programs to meet the needs of the disadvantaged, with increased funds for this purpose and for metropolitan public libraries which serve as national or regional resource centers.

However, I firmly oppose the bill which would consolidate construction projects with service programs—H.R. 16365. Public library construction should be retained as a separate program under title II. Unless rather rigid safeguards were incorporated into an act consolidating construction with service libraries there would be pressured, to construct buildings at every crossroad in every rural county commissioner's district across the South. Consequently, funds sorely needed for books, services, and interlibrary cooperation would be drained off for buildings.

To summarize: The evidence from my experience indicates that continuation of LSCA is essential to provide flexible library programs adapted to current needs of modern society. The effect of increased motivation, of stimulation of imaginative planning and programing in local and regional libraries, is of far greater value than the money involved. I am attaching some examples of the effects of this stimulation which support this concept and ask that they be inserted in the record as a part of my testimony.

In conclusion, I wish again to urge a 5-year extension and expansion of the Library Services and Construction Act, and further, to thank the members of this committee for the privilege of speaking before you today.

(The attachments accompanying statement follow:)

EXAMPLES OF THE CATALYTIC EFFECT OF LSCA ON THE ATLANTA PUBLIC LIBRARY

These projects are not necessarily significant in themselves but they point out that, because of an initial program started with an obsolete 1954 bookmobile and developed through Library Services and Construction Act funds, the Atlanta Public Library is becoming the agency foremost in the minds of the many cultural, educational, and social agencies that need catalytic help in the form of information and resources. This, to me, is the city library at its best. This also explains why increasing Federal funds for building library collections and services should be channeled into the national cities of this country, so that the metropolitan library can indeed come into its own.

Late last year, the Library began operation of a new program called Institute for Urban Communications. With private donations and a grant through the Georgia Commission on the Arts, using National Endowment for the Humanities funds, a notable start has been made toward documenting (through sound and visuals) the process of growing up in today's city. There is a high probability that this program will be picked up by either educational or commercial television, and we are hopeful that it will even be syndicated. Again, this is the library as communicator.

Just about a year ago, the Atlanta Public Library received the first Model Cities grant for public libraries in this country. Through this grant, storefront libraries in two communities were opened and two more are in the process of opening. Deposits were placed in Federal housing projects, film programs established through Economic Opportunity Atlanta centers and other places where people of the area congregate. Just this week, as the City attempted to cool an explosive situation in the Summer Hill community of Atlanta, the Library was called on for special projects such as film programs, field trips, etc. It was significant that the Library was the only agency of government located directly in the heart of the most explosive area of Summer Hill.

In still other programs, we are presently working with the Atlanta Housing Authority to set aside space in all major public housing facilities for libraries to be placed there and operated under a cooperative program with the tenants' association in each. We are also working closely with Economic Opportunity Atlanta and the recently established Postal Street Academy. We are in the final stages of negotiating contracts with the Postal Street Academy to operate libraries in connection with their educational programs. We were struck by the similarity of approach used by this innovative and successful program with that of the Library. In still another area, the Library mounted over the past year one of the most extensive film programs ever attempted through a city library and its branches. To date in 1970, some 110,000 persons have viewed films and enjoyed corresponding programs through the Library.

Over the past several weeks, I have met with representatives of the Academy

Theatre, which recently received a major grant through the Ford Foundation for experimental theatre projects, and with the Youth Experimental Opera Workshop, working under grants from the National Endowment for the Humanities and the city schools. In these programs, young people will stage productions through branch libraries and intermingle with younger children to gain an appreciation for the spoken and written word.

STATEMENT OF MRS. MARGARET S. WARDEN, TRUSTEE, GREAT FALLS PUBLIC LIBRARY, GREAT FALLS, MONT.

Mrs. WARDEN. It is a great pleasure to be here. I am Mrs. Margaret S. Warden, chairman of the board of trustees of the Great Falls Public Library, in Great Falls, Mont. Library trustees in Montana, as in other States, are charged with the control of free public libraries to give the people of the State the fullest opportunity to enrich and inform themselves through reading. I have been a trustee for 13 years, and regard my position as one of considerable responsibility.

I am appearing today under the auspices of the American Library Association, to endorse the proposed legislation to amend and extend the Library Services and Construction Act.

When I think of libraries, a kaleidoscope of memories sweeps over me. From the age of 5, I was a confirmed library user. It was exciting to me then to race 17 blocks to the public library to get a book for a special occasion; to skate with Hans Brinker; to race with Amundson toward the North Pole; to hide in the dark shadows with Poe; to share the love lyrics of Robert Browning. I was fortunate to be a child in a community which had a public library to give me those joys.

Certainly not everyone has had the opportunity to grow up with libraries, but since the Library Services Act programs began in 1957, a wealth of opportunities has been made available for the first time to many people. I want to tell you that the Library Services and Construction Act has meant the difference between life and death to the libraries of Montana.

As a direct result of the stimulation of LSCA, almost 150,000 people have received public library service for the first time. This one fact alone would justify the cost in Montana, but there is more. Library service which has been poor to mediocre for many of those receiving it has had a new infusion of life. The increased resources have made it more vital, more stimulating, and more worthwhile than would have been possible without the help of LSCA.

Our State is the fourth largest in the Union, encompassing 147,148 square miles, but it has only 682,000 people. Some three-tenths of 1 percent of the Nation's people live in this State, which makes up 4 percent of the total land area of the United States. I would like to support Miss Miller's statement that the $200,000 basic allotment in H.R. 16365 discriminates against those of us who live in States that have small populations and large areas. We need service points and services, but we can't compete on a per capita basis. I think we could compete on what we are providing for our people with the basic allotment we have in the existing law but not with the reduced basic allotment and greater per capita distribution proposed in H.R. 16365.

Prior to 1956 and the passage of the Library Services Act, we had scattered municipal library service and a number of county libraries, but there were many people who had no library at all. Almost 200,000 lived in counties where there were no libraries, or in rural areas not served by city libraries.

Our State library agency was a small agency trying to provide books to people throughout the State and to help local public libraries become better, subject to the limits imposed by a $21,000 annual appropriation in 1956–57 from the State legislature (now increased to $161,600 for 1970–71).

The Library Services Act and its successor, Library Services and Construction Act, have stimulated the development of public library service in Montana, the growth of the State library in strength, and fostered a spirit of genuine cooperation between libraries to make resources available to more people.

With the incentive of Federal matching funds which increased from $40,000 in 1957 to $315,354 in 1969, the State and local governments were encouraged to increase their library support by nearly $1 million—almost quadrupling their effort.

Where prior to this legislation we had no instance of library service crossing county lines, Montana now has five multicounty federations of libraries, one encompassing seven large counties and the others growing toward this number. (See map No. 1.) The residents of 18 counties in these federations have access to all of the public libraries, broadening the range of material available to them almost beyond measure.

We have accomplished this only because funds under title I of the Library Services and Construction Act were available to assist these counties in the formation of federations. Bookmobiles have been purchased, books and other library materials have enriched limited local collections, staff members have been trained, and service has expanded.

Each month, bookmobiles in these 18 counties visit 229 communities to bring library service to people who are quite remote from any library building. In one instance, in the town of Capitol, residents would have to drive more than 80 miles to the nearest library if it were not for the bookmobile. That is a round trip of 160 miles, 57 miles on paved roads and 30 miles on gravel road.

The State library has compiled some remarkable statistics showing the increase in State appropriation for State library services and in local appropriation for public library support, stimulated by accomplishments under LSA and LSCA, since the Library Services Act was first passed. I would like your permission to have these entered in the record of this hearing, and have them attached to this statement. (See enclosure I.)

In 1956, Montana had 32 counties which had countywide library service, and 24 which had only scattered municipal libraries. In 1970, because of the federation program under title I of the Library Services and Construction Act, Montana has 44 counties with countywide library service. We are closing the gap with the help of this program. (See map No. 2.)

Title IV of the Library Services and Construction Act has made possible the beginning of a system of service to residents and inmates of Montana's State institutions. To those people who have been shut up in correctional institutions, or confined to custodial institutions, the availability of quality library service for the first time has done much for therapy and rehabilitation.

I want to give you two remarkable statistics reported by the State library. Our walk-in State prison library serving an inmate population of less than 300, reports an impressive circulation of more than 28,000 books in the year ending June 30, 1970. Our State mental hospital library, offering patients a place to get books and to come to read magazines and newspapers, reports 1,200 people coming to the library every month.

Also, under title IV of the Library Services and Construction Act, the State library has been able to offer, to blind and physically handicapped residents of the State, access to library materials and library service which far exceeds that available earlier. Almost 900 individuals are regularly receiving service from the State library in this program, nearly double the number served through a more distant regional library 3 years ago.

But Montana's story cannot be told only in terms of growth in library programs or in library support.

The construction program, title II of the LSCA, has meant tremendous stimulation in the fact of its assistance to 14 communities scattered across the State, in erection of new buildings or remodeling of older buildings for better public library service. These facilities are in areas participating in multicounty federations; from new headquarters libraries for our two largest cities to small grants to help smalltown branches of county libraries, these buildings are significant evidence of citizen interest in and pride in good library service. (See map No. 3.)

Title II funds have been particularly helpful to Montana: with our population spread over so wide an area, we require more buildings—more service points—than would a more compact State, or a city with our total population. A more compact State or large city has closer access. I can't stress too much the fact that we need more service points.

I feel that to cut the basic grant for all programs down to $200,000 and to allot the remainder on a per capita basis would really hinder us in providing these service points.

Title III of the Library Services and Construction Act, which assists in programs of interlibrary cooperation, has given Montanans a network that provides access to far more resources than any one city could possibly provide. A statewide telephone system permits public libraries direct access to the State library, and the State library direct access to academic and special library collections throughout the State. Plans are being made for expanding a telecommunications system to major resource centers beyond Montana's boundaries.

Sharing of library resources is of perhaps more importance to us in Montana and to people in other less populous States because we have no large public library and our largest university libraries fall far short of having the collections which are available in the university libraries of the more populous States. This communications network, however, means that an individual living in an isolated rural community may have available as close as his telephone and as quickly as the mails can bring it, the resources not only of any library in the State, but of the major research libraries throughout the region and the Nation.

Montana—and the other States and territories—has benefited significantly in 15 years of these programs. It is important to every one of us that they be continued so that better library service can be offered to more people to help them in their educational, informational, and recreational pursuits. These programs have been a tremendous stimulus to us in Montana and their continuation will help us in meeting our goals.

I earnestly recommend passage of the Library Services and Construction Amendments of 1970 and I would like the three titles.

I thank you for the opportunity of appearing before you today to make this statement on this essential legislation and the programs which have benefited us in Montana.

(The attachments referred to follow:)

GROWTH AND SUPPORT OF STATE AND PUBLIC LIBRARY SERVICE IN MONTANA—1956-69

Year	State appropriation for State library operation	Local appropriation for public library service	LSCA funding for Montana (excluding construction)	Population served by public libraries
1956	21,507	676,323	0	464,116
1957	21,507	601,757	40,000	465,012
1958	31,173	674,029	59,282	465,363
1959	31,173	746,130	63,486	473,022
1960	39,272	817,952	72,427	529,929
1961	39,272	891,113	72,427	579,385
1962	46,335	945,419	73,006	579,385
1963	46,335	945,420	73,006	576,350
1964	52,994	960,669	72,932	568,821
1965	52,994	1,039,872	175,179	576,649
1966	75,000	1,164,185	173,214	587,654
1967	75,000	1,194,188	192,099	586,852
1968	100,000	1,375,056	312,451	587,386
1969	100,000	1,440,822	315,354	595,589
1970	157,500	(1)	305,875	(1)
1971	161,600	(1)	(1)	(1)

1 Figures not available at report date.

Source: Montana State Library, and annual reports from public libraries submitted to the State Library during the perioo. Reports for the year ending June 30, 1970, are not complete as of the date of this table (Aug. 20, 1970).

EXAMPLES

In Great Falls, we had two libraries. One was operated by the city and the other by the County of Cascade. Now we have consolidated these resources. The same is true in Kalispell, where the Flathead County Library and the Kalispell Library are now combined. This provides more and better services, using funds more widely.

The State Training School for Boys in Miles City, now has books in the cottages and films in the recreation department. When the service by bookmobile started in 1968, the boys wanted to know how to restore old cars and other "do-it-yourself" information.

On an Indian reservation, the copies of "Stay Away, Joe" are worn out because the boys like to read about one of their own.

In the Helena Girls' Training School, they have learned to read stories to "Head Start" youngsters so that they, too, can share these adventures with the brothers and sisters at home.

The love of poetry was revived in the Center for the Aged in Lewiston when Mrs. Alma Jacobs, Great Falls Librarian, recited the poems the elderly people had learned in their youth. Some even recited bits or partial lines. Now student library assistants of St. Leo's Parochial school come weekly to read aloud and talk to the senior citizens.

The Library Laws of Montana are up to date for the first time since 1915 because so many people are involved in libraries and aware of their needs.

Earlier in my testimony, I mentioned Capitol. This tiny town is on the State line near South Dakota. Leaving Broadus, the bookmobile travels on paved road for 57 miles to Alzada. From here only a graveled road goes to Capitol, another 30 miles away. The Sage Brush bookmobile does a booming business for there is no library in the entire county.

In my home at Great Falls, without $239,000 from Title II, the bond issue for a new library would have failed as it had in two previous tries. This made the difference in construction of the $1,200,000 building.

Choteau, in a county that had token library service until a bookmobile and contractual service with my library provided good library service, had a chance to buy a new building for practically nothing if some Title II money could match the local funds. They collected $20,000 in a fund drive and with matching monies were able to buy and remodel this fine building that will be the hub of community activity.

In the beginning of library service in Montana in a mountain town of Yaak, even a saloon, "The Dirty Shame, Jr.," served as a library for a day when it provided the only source of electricity for the bookmobile and closed down as a bar. People brought pot-luck, had films and music, and left loaded with books.

From my own knowledge, for I've traveled into every city and town in Montana having a newspaper, I have seen what the Library Services and Construction Act has done for our people. I have seen the hope in their faces. I have seen their change of attitude. Earlier they accepted the fact that only limited library service was possible because of our huge geographical area, scattered population and low taxable valuation. Through effective demonstrations, it is now recognized that good library service in each community can be a reality.

STATEMENT OF ALEXANDER PETER ALLAIN, TRUSTEE, ST. MARY PARISH (COUNTY) LIBRARY, FRANKLIN, LA.

Mr. ALLAIN. I am Alex Allain, a Louisiana attorney, a library trustee, president of the St. Mary Parish Public Library Board, a member of the American Library Trustee Association, and a former member of its board of directors. From 1967 to 1969, I served as chairman of the Louisiana Library Development Committee, a standing committee of the Louisiana Library Association charged with planning programs for the development of all libraries and of library services throughout the State of Louisiana.

I am here today to speak in support of the proposed 5-year extension of the Library Services and Construction Act which expires June 30, 1971. Speaking from my experience as chairman of a State library development committee, I would say that at least a 5-year extension period is essential to provide adequate time in which to formulate long-range plans to serve the library and information needs of the country. I also support the new priority programs to meet the needs of disadvantaged persons, in both urban and rural areas, for library services; for strengthening the capacity of State library administrative agencies for meeting the needs of all the people of the States; and for strengthening metropolitan public libraries which serve as national or regional resource centers.

I am speaking on behalf of the American Library Association and on behalf of thousands of board members responsible for the operations of State and local public libraries.

Basically, trustees have developed the philosophy that all libraries, that is, public, school, academic, special, and institutional libraries form the basis, the core, and the very heart of our educational process. Without these libraries, the educational process, formal and informal, as it is conceived today, would be greatly endangered. The quality of American education depends upon the quality of these libraries. Furthermore, the future of the United States, politically, socially, culturally, and economically depends primarily on the state of education. Education is an implicit requisite in the development of the ability to think, reason, and understand. Libraries are the most economic, the finest, and most practical device invented by man for education.

The question involved in Federal support in the form of the Library Services and Construction Act as seen by the trustees of the Nation is not whether libraries and education will survive, but rather whether these institutions will be of the caliber necessary to prepare the Nation for continued growth. This is the basic reason that I urge the extension of the act as generally proposed and full appropriation of the amounts authorized.

Hopefully, priority will be placed on special programs to meet the needs of disadvantaged persons in both rural and urban areas. This is of particular importance in this complex age, when basic reading ability and access to current information is vital to job security. Equality of man presupposes the right to equal treatment, but is meaningless unless man has access to equal knowledge. Yet this access is too often determined by circumstances over which he has no control. This priority, if it is authorized in the proposed legislation, would be an acknowledgment of these needs and hopefully the beginning of an attempt to fill them. We assume that these programs would include an attempt to solve the functional illiteracy which plagues both the disadvantaged and the advantaged, and makes dependent beings of otherwise intelligent men. I am pleased to say that our American Library Trustee Association this year adopted a resolution in support of the Nation's "Right to Read" program. With your permission, I would like to insert it in the record at this point.

(The document referred to follows:)

RESOLUTION ADOPTED BY THE BOARD OF DIRECTORS OF THE AMERICAN LIBRARY TRUSTEE ASSOCIATION AT THE ASSOCIATION'S MIDWINTER CONFERENCE, JANUARY 24, 1970

Whereas, education is one of the essential requirements for the maintenance of a free government by informed, thoughtful citizens; and

Whereas, education is impossible without the facility to read the printed word and comprehend its meaning: and

Whereas, modern, well-stocked, well-staffed libraries, accessible to all the population, are necessary in order to provide our citizens with a wide range of materials that will promote the enjoyment of reading, as well as meet their educational needs; and

Whereas, it has been reliably shown that too large a proportion of Americans do not read with facility and understanding: Now, therefore, be it

Resolved, That we, the members of the American Library Trustee Association, lend our full support and cooperation to the President's stated goal of assuring that every American will have the opportunity to learn to read with ease and enjoyment, and have access to a full range of reading materials to meet his need; and be it further

Resolved, That we do hereby endorse President Nixon's "Right to Read" program and urge that full funding of existing legislation in order adequately to support libraries, and additional necessary funds to assure the success of the "Right to Read" program, be provided by the Congress.

In connection with the title III program, interlibrary cooperation, I would like to point out that the various kinds and types of libraries of the Nation are independent from each other in terms of their governing bodies but they are interrelated in their information function. The weakness of one casts additional demands upon others. For example, a weakness in school libraries at the elementary, secondary or even college level, forces students to use the public libraries excessively, thus straining resources. For this reason, I urge that special attention continue to be focused on strengthening cooperative programs among the various types of libraries as a separate program, as currently authorized under title III (interlibrary cooperation) rather than consolidating these activities with the other LSCA programs as proposed by H.R. 16365.

However, to stimulate greater cooperative effort, I recommend 100 percent Federal funding of these projects, eliminating the 50 percent matching now required, for two reasons: First, to avoid the time-consuming procedures and redtape involved in trying to arrive at equitable cost-sharing formulas and in mixing the funds of the various types of libraries involved. Second, and even more important, to overcome the financial barriers to cooperative participation by poor libraries in economically depressed areas, unable to raise the required matching funds.

As you know, only a very limited amount of money has been appropriated to carry on title III programs. In my own State of Louisiana, we are making progress but much more needs to be accomplished in terms of providing adequate library service to all our citizens.

The services of a librarian-management consultant on planning and establishing a processing center at the State library was funded under this title, as was the operation of a TWX communications system connecting 12 academic, eight public and three special libraries with the State library's reference department. A statewide survey of library resources was begun in this year, a project considered basic and essential to the implementation of the State plan for seven (tentative) regional library systems connecting all types of libraries. Title III funds were earmarked for preparing for a demonstration of one regional (multiparish) library system including all types of libraries. In cooperation with the office of the Secretary of State, a cards-with-documents program was initiated which made funds available to the recorder of State documents for the purchase of Library of Congress cards which will be distributed to selected academic, public, and special libraries.

Finally, I urge that Federal money spent for education as well as libraries, which are a part of the educational process should not be viewed as an expense, but rather as an investment in the future of America.

A dramatic example of the benefits derived from the Federal investment in LSCA programs can be cited in Louisiana's title IV–A program which, among other things, provides library service to correctional institutions. Following the establishment of this specialized State library service, officials in both the State department of corrections and the individual institutions recognized immediately the value of the library in the rehabilitation process and entered into a joint financing agreement with the State library. Since State funds are not presently available, the officials and the inmates themselves have approved the use of the inmates' welfare fund for the projects. The books and other library materials for each project are carefully selected to meet the needs of the residents and to correlate with the education, rehabilitation, and recreation programs of the institutions. The current issue of the Louisiana Library Association Bulletin carries a brief account of this highly successful program, which I would like to submit for the record. We have now six projects going. We have 28 projects left to complete in Louisiana of this nature. We certainly hope that money will be forthcoming for these.

In conclusion, I urge passage of amendments to the Library Services and Construction Act which will: (1) extend the Library Services and Construction Act for at least 5 years; (2) include a provision for strengthening metropolitan public libraries and indeed any library, whether it is a metropolitan library or not, which serve as national or regional resource centers; (3) recognize as a new priority, programs designed to meet the needs of disadvantaged persons, in both urban and rural areas for library services; and (4) provide funds for strengthening the capacity of State library administrative agencies for meeting the needs of all the people of the State.

I also urge that Congress fully fund all appropriations authorized.

Thank you for the privilege of appearing before you today.

(The attachments accompanying the statement follow:)

[Louisiana Library Association Bulletin, Winter 1970]

INSIDE LOUISIANA'S CORRECTIONAL INSTITUTION LIBRARIES

INTRODUCTION

(By Vivian Cazayoux, Associate State Librarian and Formerly Library Consultant for Institutional Service)

With the addition of Title IV–A to the Library Services and Construction Act in 1967, the Louisiana State Library was able to begin to fulfill its responsibility to provide library service to the health, welfare and correctional institutions maintained by the State of Louisiana. Enacted as a legal function in 1946, and long recognized as a moral obligation, this service was not implemented previously because of a shortage of personnel and funds.

Today, two and one-half years since the passage of the title, library service has been inaugurated at all three of the adult correctional institutions in Louisiana: State Penitentiary, Angola—April, 1968; Correctional and Industrial School, DeQuincy—February, 1969; and Women's Penitentiary, St. Gabriel—July, 1969.

Officials in both the State Department of Corrections and the individual institutions recognized immediately the value of the library in the rehabilitation process and entered into a joint financing agreement with the State Library. Since state funds are not presently available, the officials and the inmates themselves have approved the use of the Inmates' Welfare Fund for the projects.

Following the plan found to be successful in the parish demonstration libraries, the State Library is administering these libraries as pilot programs for two years. At the end of that time the Department of Corrections will assume the responsibility for full financing and administration, with the State Library giving advice and assistance on a continuing basis.

The books and other library materials for each project are carefully selected to meet the needs of the residents and to correlate with the education, rehabilitation and recreation programs of the institutions. The wide range of reading interests as well as reading levels are given special attention. There is a good selection of paperbacks and current magazines on a wide variety of subjects. The paperbacks, available on a "Borrow one, Return one" basis, are especially popular.

The initial success of the program can be attributed in large measure to the enthusiasm and real dedication of the librarians. They have shown an interest and concern for the welfare of these men and women, who somehow have gone wrong, and a desire to help the inmates use the library to improve their lives.

Though the libraries are similar, each has been adapted to the institution and the inmates served. Each librarian has been asked to describe some of the unique features of his program.

LCIS LIBRARY

(By Robert Ivy, Librarian, Louisiana Correctional and Industrial School)

The response and enthusiasm to the library and its service since it opened its doors to some 470 trainees has been gratifying. In the words of one trainee "When you enter, it's like being in a free world. There's an atmosphere of tranquility."

After browsing for a while, another young man noted, "The advantages are great! You can get just about all the education you want!"

Two Great Books discussion groups with approximately 12 trainees in each section have been active for 7 months. Each group meets twice monthly for 2 hours. The purpose of the program is to provide the trainees with a life-long program of liberal self-education through reading and discussion. The program is designed to teach members to think constructively and express themselves.

The library also sponsors monthly film discussion sessions in which some 20 to 25 trainees participate. A trainee "leader" chairs discussions following the viewing of a film or films selected by a committee made up of trainees.

Trainees state that they have become more observant and aware since participating in the film and book discussion groups. They feel that these two new educational and rehabilitative methods have given them the opportunity to express themselves freely and the opportunity to "disagree agreeably."

Other activities include a library orientation program on an individual basis for new trainees, recommended reading lists, tours and a reading program in which State Library reading certificates are awarded. Fifteen trainees were presented reading certificates in an impressive presentation ceremony held in the library during National Book Week.

Three trainees assist in operating the library, each having a specific job assignment such as maintaining the circulation desk, shelving books, checking in periodicals and newspapers and assisting in interlibrary loan service. There is also opportunity to work together in carrying out some duties.

The carpeted and airconditioned library is furnished with shelving, tables, desks, office and work room counters made in the carpentry shops at LCIS. The trainees, in contributing their own special talents in the planning of the library, felt that they were a part of it long before its doors were officially opened.

The library program is actively stimulating interest and concern on the part of both staff members and trainees. One of the trainees summed up the two-year demonstration program this way: "A library is like the value of a dollar. You have to learn the value of a dollar before you can make it work for you. Well, the same thing applies to the library. After you learn what it has to offer, you can begin to gain from it."

READING AT ANGOLA

(By Jim Johnson, Librarian, Louisiana State Penitentiary)

After more than one and one-half years of service, the library at the Louisiana State Penitentiary can now begin to answer the question of whether the service was necessary. Based upon the circulation statistics for the period April 1968 to October 1969, the service was indeed long overdue. A total of 45,969 books were circulated during this period.

Prison records throughout the country reveal a number of case histories when men have educated themselves in prison. Self-education is possible at Angola, too, because of the amount of time available for reading. After working hours, the men are free to pursue whatever leisure time activity they enjoy, within the scope of the institution's rules. Reading occupies a good portion of this time for many inmates. After the evening meal, it is either television or books. Thus it can be seen that enough time is available to begin a reading habit, which hopefully will continue in post-institutional life.

At the Louisiana State Penitentiary, fiction accounts for approximately 35 percent of all books circulated. Since Angola is a "closed" society, the popular authors maintain their popularity long after it has waned on the outside. Particular books are in demand long after they have ceased to be popular "on the streets" (inmates terminology meaning the free world), because the prison market cannot be saturated by paperbacks and movies.

Popular areas of fiction are ones with lots of action: mysteries, science fiction, western and historical fiction by authors such as Zane Grey, Jack Schaffer, Isaac Asimov, Andre Norton, Ian Fleming, Earl Stanley Gardner and Frank Yerby.

In addition to being male-oriented, these works are very easy to read, permitting the less-than-adequately prepared reader to enjoy them. Prisons are notorious for having a large percentage of their populations illiterate or nearly so, and Angola is no exception.

Adventure and excitement are very important in nonfiction reading at Angola. History, especially when it concerns World War II, is exceedingly popular. Because of the numerous motion pictures and television shows about World War II, the men bring a large amount of knowledge to their reading. Inmates are interested in adventurous wartime activities about frogmen, pilots and paratroopers. This type of reading allows the reader a release from the everyday tensions of prison life.

American history has not been as popular as general world history, all through the Civil War and the expansion of the westward territories have captured the fascination of many.

Many library patrons are armchair travelers and can tell you all about Piccadilly or the Kremlin without ever having been farther than their public library. This is also true of Angola patrons. Latin America is a popular area of reading. Interest in the TIME-LIFE series is high.

Since the penitentiary's population is entirely male, it is understandable that books about sports are favored by many and include both how-to-books and books about particular teams, heroes and general sports.

Sports serve as an excellent leisure time activity, allowing men to enjoy themselves while keeping physically fit. Angola has a wider-ranging recreational schedule, and the library's books on sports complement this program.

Art is another means of recreational expression at Angola where many artists use the library's art collection.

Games, such as chess and bridge, are also popular, and clubs have been organized to play these games. Again the library's collection aids the players in their strategy.

Sociologically speaking, a prison can be called an artificial society with its inhabitants coming from various subcultures. Many of the men are aware of certain social shortcomings, and for this reason the social sciences are read rather extensively.

Negro history holds a commanding lead in circulation within the social sciences. The prison community at Angola is approximately 60 per cent Negro, and the Negro inmate, just as his brother on the outside, is feeling the same pains of a social awakening; therefore, there is constant demand for books which relate to the Negro.

The inmate is practically cut off from society, and he must have something to make him realize that the end of the world is not at hand. The suffering of the inmates is slight compared to that which some of history's famous, and sometimes tragic, figures have endured. By reading biographies of some of these men, the inmate can gain the knowledge that he has not sunk to the nadir of existence, that there is still something to be realized from life.

Poetry seems to hold a wide fascination among the inmate population. Anthologies containing the works of many poets, rather than those of one particular bard, are especially appealing. The greatest use is made in volumes on love poetry, possibly indicating the insecurity of the men. Some of these poems find their way into the letters which the men write home to their loved ones.

Popularized accounts of the pure sciences, particularly those of Isaac Asimov, have been popular. Biology and its allied sciences have been read more than any others, with mathematics following a close second.

The applied sciences are well represented in the library by books on automobile mechanics, carpentry, welding and electronics. All of these subjects are taught at the vocational school at Angola.

Alcoholism and narcotic addiction are two illnesses which frequently send men to prison. In an effort to better understand their problems, the alcoholics and the addicts have formed organizations to discuss ways of combating their problems. They read extensively and view films in an effort to better understand what it is all about.

Psychology is a field which interests many inmates. They are constantly trying to understand what makes them tick and have discovered that the library is the place to begin exploration.

The writings of Billy Graham and Norman Vincent Peale comprise the bulk of religious reading. Stories from the Bible and popularizations of the life of Christ and of His disciples are also valuable. The more philosophic theological tracts are not read as much.

The requests are as varied as the backgrounds of the men, making selection of materials a challenging experience.

A NEW LIBRARY AT THE WOMEN'S PENITENTIARY

(By Lois le Blanc, Librarian, Women's Penitentiary at St. Gabriel)

A bright yellow bookmobile filled with new books is a popular place at the Women's Penitentiary at St. Gabriel. During library hours, many women can be seen on their way to the used bookmobile which was renovated and installed to house the library because of limited physical facilities at the prison. The unit is secured on concrete supports. The motor and driving controls were removed, and storage cabinets, a card catalog, magazine display shelves and a dictionary shelf were built. Colorful curtains of gold and yellow, a carpet of gold and red, and new paneling make the library cheerful and comfortable. An air-conditioning and heating unit was installed in the rear window.

A metal canopy attached to the "immobile bookmobile" covers the area between the library and the building housing the prison's ceramics shop, garment factory, classrooms and dining hall. A sidewalk was recently built here. A folding table and bright canvas chairs provide reading and browsing space. Here the women read the latest newspapers from Baton Rouge, New Orleans and Shreveport, and pore over magazines. The buildings at the prison are light green so the sunshiny yellow library and the colorful canopy and chairs provide a bright spot on the prison landscape.

The majority of the women at St. Gabriel are Negroes, and most of them are under 35 years of age. The average educational level is eighth grade. These women have a wide range of interests and come to the library for facts and information on a variety of subjects.

One group meets to discuss and study ontology (the science of being), and the library fills requests for information for them. There is usually a special Christmas program staged by the women. Several came to the library to get material to plan this event. Ideas for inexpensive Christmas gifts were supplied from the library's collection to readers interested in making small gifts and items to sell.

Many readers want books on religion and the Bible. One woman reads all she can find about Che Guevara. Another is interested in Louisiana history and especially in the folklore of the state.

One woman looked through the library copy of *Good Reading* and launched her own planned reading program. Her selections include Kierkegaard, Nietzsche, Martin Buber, Shakespeare, Francis Bacon and many others.

Witchcraft is a popular subject with many readers. They have enjoyed Petry's *Tituba of Salem Village* and Tallant's *Voodoo in New Orleans* and are always requesting more on this subject.

Many of the women studying for high school diplomas read to supplement their textbooks. Vocational information is available on a variety of occupations. Books on beauty culture are most in demand. Materials on drugs and alcoholism are provided to support rehabilitative programs. Many books on crafts, needlework and art are in the collection. The books on ceramics are popular with the women who work in the prison's ceramics shop.

The most generally asked for items are books by and about Negroes. The library provides personal experiences of Negroes, Negro history, commentaries on current social changes and ideas about the future of the Negro. Martin Luther King, Jr., Langston Hughes, and Lerone Bennett are popular authors at St. Gabriel.

Other subjects in demand are philosophy, psychology, jazz, poetry and written experiences of other prison inmates, especially Bill Sands' *The Seventh Step* and *My Shadow Ran Fast*.

Special requests for books and information from the State Library have included the following: yoga, ontology, Hinduism, famous opera houses, Chinese paperfolding, how to stop smoking, and hotel and restaurant management.

The library is open Monday through Thursday from 4 p.m. until dark when the women must return to the dormitories. Saturday hours are 2 to 5 p.m. Mrs. Frances Peltier, library assistant, is in the library for most of these hours. She is very enthusiastic about library work and has a good knowledge of books, although she has no formal library education. She is sincerely interested in people and her relationship with the women at St. Gabriel is a major factor in the success of the library there. Mrs. Peltier has become a good friend to many of the women and many times when one is leaving the prison, she will come by to tell Mrs. Peltier good bye. At these times one hears comments about how much the library has meant to an inmate. One person said that reading library books had made her time at St. Gabriel seem shorter and more pleasant. Several have said they would keep up the reading they started in prison by becoming library patrons in places where they will be living. One girl, who had been paroled the day before, came to tell Mrs. Peltier good bye and said she had told the parole board and Colonel Sowers, head of the Department of Corrections, that the library at St. Gabriel has been "the best thing that ever happened to me."

The library has received the full support and cooperation of the prison staff. Matrons and other personnel often stop in to borrow books. Loss of books and damage to them has been very slight. Overdue books are usually easily recovered by posting notices in the dining hall. One reader has become the library "scout"; she tracks down borrowers of overdue books.

Plans for the future include the development of a record collection and the organization of a regular film forum.

That the readers are appreciative of this new library is apparent from this quote by an inmate in the prison newspaper: "A small library just opening up might not seem like much to the rest of Louisiana, but it is something that we have never had here, and because of this, we appreciate it much more than most people would a great new building filled with all imaginable books."

STATEMENT OF JOHN A. HUMPHRY, ASSISTANT COMMISSIONER FOR LIBRARIES, NEW YORK STATE EDUCATION DEPARTMENT

My name is John A. Humphry, Assistant Commissioner for Libraries, New York State Education Department. I am writing on behalf of the Association of Research Libraries, the principal organization of university and research libraries in this country, to express support for a five year extension of the Library Services and Construction Act, the major federal legislation in support of public library service. May I ask that this statement become a part of the official record.

While the membership of the Association of Research Libraries is made up primarily of academic libraries, there are also some major public libraries and one state (New York) library among its members. The Library Services and Construction Act has been of substantial assistance in improving public library service throughout the United States. During the early years of federal support of libraries through this and other library legislation, emphasis was placed on developing quality programs of service that would better meet the book and information needs of various publics. In later years, however, much greater emphasis has been placed on effective cooperation among all types of libraries with impetus given by Title III of this Act under consideration. Users may need the services and resources of school, public, college, university, state and even special libraries to satisfy their ever-increasing demands. Thus major support of one aspect of library effort results in an overall improvement in service. Title III, Library Cooperation, of the Library Services and Construction Act is so significant in present-day library development that I should like to recommend that it be retained as an identifiable program within the Act and that realistic funding be authorized for it. It is essential to continue to encourage cooperative coordinated library programs.

We in the New York State Library are particularly interested in interlibrary cooperation, and I should like to describe one of the exemplary programs. It is known as the New York State Interlibrary Loan program, commonly referred to as NYSILL. As many of you know, interlibrary loan has been a fact of library life for nearly 100 years. Libraries have a long record of being willing to share resources, especially those of a research nature, for the serious user. In New York State, the interlibrary loan program has been coordinated by the New York State Library. By 1969, the total volume of interlibrary loan requests throughout the State was estimated at approximately 675,000 requests, of which approximately 80% were filled. Thus, one can readily see the activity generated by students, members of the general public, scholars, business, industry, government and others who need books and information.

In 1964. a new configuration and dimension was added to this program, whereby the New York State Library became the center and focal point for a sophisticated exchange of books of particular value in research. Since the New York State Library is especially strong, with a collection in excess of one million volumes, an additional 3 million pamphlets, maps, films, recordings and other media, it supplies more than half of all the requests that come to it from individual libraries via the public library systems and the reference and research library resources systems. Not content to rest on these laurels, the State Library has entered into contract with 12 additional libraries to improve the New York State record in meeting requests for materials. Three area libraries are searched if the requests cannot be met at the State Library. These 3 libraries are the Brooklyn Public Libary, the Rochester Public Library and the Buffalo and Erie County Public Library. After clearance with these 3 strong general collections, contracts exist with 9 subject research libraries, such as those at Cornell University, New York University, the Libraries of the New York Academy of Medicine. American Museum of Natural History. Engineering Societies, the Union Theological Seminary, and the Research Libraries of The New York Public Library which comprise the second echelon of the referral process. More than 100,000 requests now clear through the network on an annual basis and more than half are met by the New York State Library. An additional 30% are met by the contracting libraries. This type of activity lends itself naturally for funding under Title III of the Library Services and Construction Act. It represents large public libraries, small and medium sized public libraries, college, university, research and special libraries working together to serve the serious research needs of many segments of our population.

This successful operation will lead us into further cooperative projects. One of these is a research library collection improvement fund to support these strong contracting libraries and further improve their collections. In addition, this effort can guide us in developing joint acquisitions programs among research libraries. Most of the requests for materials on interlibrary loan originate in public libraries or the public library systems.

More than 90% of such requests sent to the New York State Library are received via teletype or some other method of rapid communication. At the present time, plans are being developed to computerize our system so that the all-important factor of speed can be improved and that searching the various contracting libraries can be done more rapidly. That is, the computer can help us determine the most effective sequence of search based on load per library and strength of collection. New York State has been a leader in applying the system concept to its library programs and, therefore, has a network of libraries in existence which serve to expedite and enhance the concept of interlibrary cooperation.

The Association of Research Libraries urges the Committee to continue to support the Library Services and Construction Act and to grant funds for Title III that will encourage coordinated rather than competitive programs of library service.

THE LIBRARIAN OF CONGRESS,
Washington, D.C., September 8, 1970.

DEAR MR. BRADEMAS: It is my understanding that your Subcommittee has under consideration bills to amend and extend the Library Services and Construction Act.

This legislation has had an impact on the majority of this country's citizens. As a result of funds provided under Title-II of the Library Services and Construction Act, communities in every State have been able to replace outmoded libraries—many of them originally funded by Andrew Carnegie—with up-to-date, attractive, and functional structures. Title-I has enabled these libraries to provide the library services so necessary in our confused, complicated society. Not only have bookmobiles become a regular part of the scene in rural communities, but bookmobiles have been able to bring library services to those individuals living in crowded urban areas. Because of the impetus given by this legislation, store-front libraries, properly staffed and stocked, are bringing books and other library materials to the disadvantaged, who for the first time have an understanding of what a public library is and what horizons it can open.

I do not believe that we would have advanced as far as we have in providing free library services if it had not been for the passage of the Library Services and Construction Act. State legislatures and city councils have increased the budgets for libraries because of the matching provision of this Act. Certainly this was the intent of Congress in approving this legislation. Because of the increase in funds, public libraries have been able to reach citizens in the community and to educate them as to the services they can offer and the advantages of making use of free library service. Innovative library programs tailored to the needs of the community have resulted to the advantage of the entire populace.

Under funds provided by Title-III of the Act, a more effective use of total library resources has resulted. Because of the increasing amount of literature available as well as the eclectic needs of the community, no library, be it special, public, or academic, can claim to have all of the resources its clientele needs. The establishment of cooperative networks of libraries has not only improved services, but has provided for a more effective and economical use of the financial resources available to libraries. In addition, these networks have contributed to the ultimate goal of a national information network.

As you know, the Library of Congress administers the national books-for-the-blind and physically handicapped program. Originally, this program was designed for blind readers only, but in 1965 it was extended to include all the handicapped who could not read a conventional book. This influx of new blind and physically handicapped readers has exceeded our original expectations. In fact, the number of readers has doubled during this period.

The Library of Congress provides the talking books and books in braille to 47 regional libraries who in turn service the handicapped readers in their areas. Sixteen new regional libraries have been established as a result of the stimulation provided by funding under Title-IV-B of the Library Services and Construction Act. Without these additional regional libraries, service of books to this specialized population would have been seriously hampered during these years of expansion to include the physically handicapped.

No librarian would say that State institutional library service is adequate but funds provided under Title-IV-A of the Act have at least provided additional incentive to librarians to improve these services. Much remains to be done and I would hope that money appropriated under this Act would continue to be used for institutional library service.

I know that the bills before you provide for consolidation in varying degrees of the Titles in this Act. I would hope that your Subcommittee, in reporting a bill, would provide the safeguard that an amount not less than the amount expended by the States from such sources for State institutional library services and library services to the physically handicapped during fiscal year 1971 be expended.

I urge that Congress approve this most important legislation.

Sincerely yours,

L. QUINCY MUMFORD, *Librarian of Congress.*

O

Public Law 91-600,

91st Congress

In 1970, prior to the passage of this law spelled out below, House Report 91-1659 said the following, among other things:

"Useful and economical as the library services supported and expanded under this Act have been, much still remains to be done. Public library income this year is expected to be $450 million short of the level of $5 per capita recommended by the American Library Association. Enactment and full funding of H.R. 19363 can assure no more than half the construction of public library facilities known to be needed. For lack of funds, less than half the institutions either operated or substantially supported by States which are eligible for assistance under this Act actually receive it. Only half the physically handicapped persons who need library service are eligible for indirect aid under this statute can be assisted at the current level of funding."

Let us hope that the much that "still remains to be done" will be accomplished, now that this Act has been passed. You should know the particulars that follow. Read it! It's yours!

AN ACT

To amend the Library Services and Construction Act, and for other purposes.

Be it enacted by the Senate and House of Representatives of the United States of America in Congress assembled, That this Act may be cited as the "Library Services and Construction Amendments of 1970."

Purpose: Amendment to the Library Services and Construction Act

Sec. 2. (a) It is the purpose of this Act to improve the administration, implementation, and purposes of the programs authorized by the Library Services and Construction Act, by lessening the administrative burden upon the States through a reduction in the number of State plans which must be submitted and approved annually under such Act and to afford the States greater discretion in the allocation of funds under such

Act to meet specific State needs and, by providing for special programs to meet the needs of disadvantaged persons, in both urban and rural areas, for library services and for strengthening the capacity of State library administrative agencies for meeting the needs of all the people of the States.

(b) The Library Services and Construction Act (20 U.S.C. 351 et seq.), is amended by striking out all that follows the first section and inserting in lieu thereof the following:

"Declaration of Policy

"Sec. 2. (a) It is the purpose of this Act to assist the States in the extension and improvement of public library services in areas of the States which are without such services or in which such services are inadequate, and with public library construction, and in the improvement of such other State library services as library services for physically handicapped, institutionalized, and disadvantaged persons, in strengthening State

SOURCE: U.S. Laws, Statutes, etc. *Library Services and Construction Amendments of 1970.* Public Law 91-600. 91st Congress, S. 3318. Approved December 30, 1970. (Washington: 1970), pp. 1–12.

library administrative agencies, and in promoting interlibrary cooperation among all types of libraries.

"(b) Nothing in this Act shall be construed to interfere with State and local initiative and responsibility in the conduct of library services. The administration of libraries, the selection of personnel and library books and materials, and, insofar as consistent with the purposes of this Act, the determination of the best uses of the funds provided under this Act shall be reserved to the States and their local subdivisions.

"Definitions

"Sec. 3. The following definitions shall apply to this Act:

"(1) 'Commissioner' means the Commissioner of Education.

"(2) 'Construction' includes construction of new buildings and acquisition, expansion, remodeling, and alteration of existing buildings, and initial equipment of any such buildings, or any combination of such activities (including architects' fees and the cost of acquisition of land). For the purposes of this paragraph, the term 'equipment' includes machinery, utilities, and built-in equipment and any necessary enclosures or structures to house them; and such term includes all other items necessary for the functioning of a particular facility as a facility for the provision of library services.

"(3) 'Library service' means the performance of all activities of a library relating to the collection and organization of library materials and to making the materials and information of a library available to a clientele.

"(4) 'Library services for the physically handicapped' means the providing of library services, through public or other nonprofit libraries, agencies, or organizations, to physically handicapped persons (including the blind and other visually handicapped) certified by competent authority as unable to read or to use conventional printed materials as a result of physical limitations.

"(5) 'Public library' means a library that serves free of charge all residents of a community, district, or region, and receives its financial support in whole or in part from public funds.

"(6) 'Public library services' means library services furnished by a public library free of charge.

"(7) 'State' means a State, the District of Columbia, the Commonwealth of Puerto Rico, Guam, American Samoa, the Virgin Islands, or the Trust Territory of the Pacific Islands.

"(8) 'State Advisory Council on Libraries' means an advisory council for the purposes of clause (3) of section 6(a) of this Act which shall—

"(A) be broadly representative of the public, school, academic, special, and institutional libraries, and libraries serving the handicapped, in the State and of persons using such libraries, including disadvantaged persons within the State;

"(B) advise the State library administrative agency on the development of, and policy matters arising in the administration of the State plan; and

"(C) assist the State library administrative agency in the evaluation of activities assisted under this Act:

"(9) 'State institutional library services' means the providing of books and other library materials, and of library services, to (A) inmates, patients, or residents of penal institutions, reformatories, residential training schools, orphanages, or general or special institutions or hospitals operated or substantially supported by the State, or (B) students in residential schools for the physically handicapped (including mentally retarded, hard of hearing, deaf, speech impaired, visually handicapped, seriously emotionally disturbed, crippled, or other health impaired persons who by reason thereof require special education) operated or substantially supported by the State.

"(10) 'State library administrative agency' means the official agency of a State charged by law of that State with the extension and development of public library services throughout the State, which has adequate authority under law of the State to administer State plans in accordance with the provisions of this Act.

"(11) 'Basic State plan' means the document which gives assurances that the officially designed State library administrative agency has the fiscal and legal authority and capability to administer all aspects of this Act: provides assurances for establishing the State's policies, priorities, criteria, and procedures necessary to the implementation of all programs under provisions of this Act; and submits copies for approval as required by regulations promulgated by the Commissioner.

"(12) 'Long-range program' means the comprehensive five-year program which identifies a State's library needs and sets forth the activities to be taken toward meeting the identified needs supported with the assistance of Federal funds made available under this Act. Such long-range programs shall be developed by the State library administrative agency and shall specify the State's policies, criteria, priorities, and procedures consistent with the Act as required by the regulations promulgated by the Commissioner and shall be updated as library progress requires.

"(13) 'Annual program' means the projects which are developed and submitted to describe the specific activities to be carried out annually toward achieving fulfillment of the long-range program. These annual programs shall be submitted in such detail as required by regulations promulgated by the Commissioner.

"AUTHORIZATIONS OF APPROPRIATIONS

"Sec. 4. (a) For the purpose of carrying out the provisions of this Act the following sums are authorized to be appropriated:

"(1) For the purpose of making grants to States for library services as provided in title I, there are authorized to be appropriated $112,000,000 for the fiscal year ending June 30, 1972, $117,600,000 for the fiscal year ending June 30, 1973, $123,500,000 for the fiscal year ending June 30, 1974, $129,675,000 for the fiscal year ending June 30, 1975, and $137,-150,000 for the fiscal year ending June 30, 1976.

"(2) For the purpose of making grants to States for public library construction, as provided in title II, there are authorized to be appropriated $80,000,000 for the fiscal year ending June 30, 1972, $84,-000,000 for the fiscal year ending June 30, 1973, $88,000,000 for the fiscal year ending June 30, 1975, and $97,000,000 for the fiscal year ending June 30, 1976.

"(3) For the purpose of making grants to States to enable them to carry out inter-library cooperation programs authorized by title III, there are hereby authorized to be appropriated $15,000,000 for the fiscal year ending June 30, 1972, $15,750,000

for the fiscal year ending June 30, 1973, $16,500,000 for the fiscal year ending June 30, 1974, $17,300,000 for the fiscal year ending June 30, 1975, and $18,200,-000 for the fiscal year ending June 30, 1976.

"(b) Notwithstanding any other provision of law, unless enacted in express limitation of the provisions of this subsection, any sums appropriated pursuant to subsection (a) shall (1), in the case of sums appropriated pursuant to paragraphs (1) and (3) thereof, be available for obligation and expenditure for the period of time specified in the Act making such appropriation, and (2), in the case of sums appropriated pursuant to paragraph (2) thereof, subject to regulations of the Commissioner promulgated in carrying out the provisions of section 5(b), be available for obligation and expenditure for the year specified in the Appropriation Act and for the next succeeding year.

"ALLOTMENTS TO STATES

"Sec. 5. (1)(1) From the sums appropriated pursuant to paragraph (1), (2), or (3) of section 4(a) for any fiscal year, the Commissioner shall allot the minimum allotment, as determined under paragraph (3) of this subsection, to each State. Any sums remaining after minimum allotments have been made shall be allotted in the manner set forth in paragraph (2) of this subsection.

"(2) From the remainder of any sums appropriated pursuant to paragraph (1), (2), or (3) of section 4(a) for any fiscal year, the Commissioner shall allot each State such part of such remainder as the population of the State bears to the population of all the States.

"(3) For the purposes of this subsection, the 'minimum allotment' shall be—

"(A) with respect to appropriations for the purposes of title I, $200,000 for each State, except that it shall be $40,000 in the case of Guam, American Samoa, the Virgin Islands, and the Trust Territory of the Pacific Islands;

"(B) with respect to appropriations for the purposes of title II, $100,000 for each State, except that it shall be $20,000 in the case of Guam, American Samoa, the

Virgin Islands, and the Trust Territory of the Pacific Islands: and

"(C) with respect to appropriations for the purposes of title III, $40,000 for each State, except that it shall be $10,000 in the case of Guam, American Samoa, the Virgin Islands, and the Trust Territory of the Pacific Islands.

If the sums appropriated pursuant to paragraph (1), (2), or (3) of section 4(a) for any fiscal year are insufficient to fully satisfy the aggregate of the minimum allotments for that purpose, each of such minimum allotments shall be reduced ratably.

"(4) The population of each State and of all the States shall be determined by the Commissioner on the basis of the most recent satisfactory data available to him.

"(5) There is hereby authorized for the purpose of evaluation (directly or by grants or contracts) of programs authorized by this Act, such sums as Congress may deem necessary for any fiscal year.

"(6) The amount of any State's allotment under subsection (a) for any fiscal year from any appropriation made pursuant to paragraph (1), (2), or (3) of section 4(a) which the Commissioner deems will not be required for the period and the purpose for which such allotment is available for carrying out the State's annual program shall be available for reallotment from time to time on such dates during such year as the Commissioner shall fix. Such amount shall be available for reallotment to other States in proportion to the original allotments for such year to such States under subsection (a) but with such proportionate amount for any of such other State being reduced to the extent that it exceeds the amount which the Commissioner estimates the State needs and will be able to use for such period of time for which the original allotments were made and the total of such reductions shall be similarly reallotted among the States not suffering such a reduction. Any amount reallotted to a State under this subsection for any fiscal year shall be deemed to be a part of its allotment for such year pursuant to subsection (a).

"STATE PLANS AND PROGRAMS

"Sec. 6. (a) Any State desiring to receive its allotment for any purpose under this Act for any fiscal year shall (1) have in effect for such fiscal year a basic State plan as defined in section 3(11) and meeting the requirements set forth in subsection (b), (2) submit an annual program as defined in section 3(13) for the purposes for which allotments are desired, meeting the appropriate requirements set forth in titles I, II, and III, and shall submit (no later than July 1, 1972) a long-range program as defined in section 3(12) for carrying out the purposes of this Act as specified in subsection (d), and (3) establish a State Advisory Council on Libraries which meets the requirements of section 3(8).

"(b) A basic State plan under this Act shall—

"(1) provide for the administration, or supervision of the administration, of the programs authorized by this Act by the State library administrative agency;

"(2) provide that any funds paid to the State in accordance with a long-range program and an annual program shall be expended solely for the purposes for which funds have been authorized and appropriated and that such fiscal control and fund accounting procedures have been adopted as may be necessary to assure proper disbursement of, and account for, Federal funds paid to the State (including any such funds paid by the State to any other agency) under this Act;

"(3) provide satisfactory assurance that the State agency administering the plan (A) will make such reports, in such form and containing such information, as the Commissioner may reasonably require to carry out his functions under this Act and to determine the extent to which funds provided under this Act have been effective in carrying out its purposes, including reports of evaluations made under the State plans, and (B) will keep such records and afford such access thereto as the Commissioner may find necessary to assure the correctness and verification of such reports; and

"(4) set forth the criteria to be used in determining the adequacy of public library services in geographical areas and for groups of persons in the State, including criteria designed to assure that priority will be given to programs or projects which serve urban and rural areas with high concentrations of low-income families.

"(c) (1) The Commissioner shall not approve any basic State plan pursuant to this Act for any fiscal year unless—

"(A) the plan fulfills the conditions specified in section 3(11) and subsection (b) of this section and the appropriate titles of this Act;

"(B) he has made specific findings as to the compliance of such plan with requirements of this Act and he is satisfied that adequate procedures are subscribed to therein insure that any assurances and provisions of such plan will be carried out.

"(2) The State plan shall be made public as finally approved.

"(3) The Commissioner shall not finally disapprove any basic State plan submitted pursuant to subsection (a) (1), or any modification thereof, without first affording the State reasonable notice and opportunity for hearing.

"(d) The long-range program of any State for carrying out the purposes of this Act shall be developed in consultation with the Commissioner and shall—

"(1) set forth a program under which the funds received by the State under the programs authorized by this Act will be used to carry out a long-range program of library services and construction covering a period of not less than three nor more than five years;

"(2) be annually reviewed and revised in accordance with changing needs for assistance under this Act and the results of the evaluation and surveys of the State library administrative agency;

"(3) set forth policies and procedures (A) for the periodic evaluation of the effectiveness of programs and projects supported under this Act, and (B) for appropriate dissemination of the results of such evaluations and other information pertaining to such programs or projects; and

"(4) set forth effective policies and procedures for the coordination of programs and projects supported under this Act with library programs and projects operated by institutions of higher education or local elementary or secondary schools and with other public or private library services programs.

Such program shall be developed with advice of the State advisory council and in consultation with the Commissioner and shall be made public as it is finally adopted.

"(e) Whenever the Commissioner, after reasonable notice and opportunity for hearing to the State agency administering a program submitted under this Act finds—

"(1) that the program has been so changed that it no longer complies with the provisions of this Act, or

"(2) that in the administration of the program there is a failure to comply substantially with any such provisions or with any assurance or other provision contained in the basic State plan,

then, until he is satisfied that there is no longer any such failure to comply, after appropriate notice to such State agency, he shall make no further payments to the State under this Act or shall limit payments to programs or projects under, or parts of, the programs not affected by the failure, or shall require that payments by such State agency under this Act shall be limited to local or other public library agencies not affected by the failure.

"(f) (1) If any State is dissatisfied with the Commissioner's final action with respect to the approval of a plan submitted under this Act or with his final action under subsection (e) such State may, within sixty days after notice of such action, file with the United States court of appeals for the circuit in which such State is located a petition for review of that action. A copy of the petition shall be forthwith transmitted by the clerk of the court to the Commissioner. The Commissioner thereupon shall file in the court the record of the proceedings on which he based his action as provided in section 2112 of title 28, United States Code.

"(2) The findings of fact by the Commissioner, if supported by substantial evidence, shall be conclusive; but the court, for good cause shown, may remand the case to the Commissioner to take further evidence, and the Commissioner may thereupon take new or modified findings of fact and may modify his previous action, and shall certify to the court the record of further proceedings.

"(3) The court shall have jurisdiction to affirm the action of the Commissioner or to set it aside, in whole or in part. The judgment of the court shall be subject to review by the Supreme Court of the United States upon certiorari or certification as provided in section 1254 of title 28, United States Code.

"Payments to States

"Sec. 7. (a) From the allotments available therefor under section 5 from appropriations pursuant to paragraph (1), (2), or (3) of sections 4(a), the Commissioner shall pay to each State which has a basic State plan approved under section 6(a) (1), an annual program and a long-range program as defined in sections 3 (12) and (13) an amount equal to the Federal share of the total sums expended by the State and its political subdivisions in carrying out such plan, except that no payments shall be made from appropriations pursuant to such paragraph (1) for the purposes of title I to any State (other than the Trust Territory of the Pacific Islands) for any fiscal year unless the Commissioner determines that—

"(1) there will be available for expenditure under the programs from State and local sources during the fiscal year for which the allotment is made—
"(A) sums sufficient to enable the State to receive for the purpose of carrying out the programs payments in an amount not less than the minimum allotment for that State for the purpose, and
"(B) not less than the total amount actually expended, in the areas covered by the programs for such year, for the purposes of such programs from such sources in the second preceding fiscal year; and
"(2) there will be available for expenditure for the purposes of the programs from State sources during the fiscal year for which the allotment is made not less than the total amount actually expended for such purposes from such sources in the second preceding fiscal year.

"(b) (1) For the purpose of this section, the 'Federal share' for any State shall be, except as is provided otherwise in title III, 100 per centum less the State percentage, and the State percentage shall be that percentage which bears the same ratio to 50 per centum as the per capita income of such State bears to the per capita income of all the States (excluding Puerto Rico, Guam,

American Samoa, the Virgin Islands, and the Trust Territory of the Pacific Islands), except that (A) the Federal share shall in no case be more than 66 per centum, or less than 33 per centum, and (B) the Federal share for Puetro Rico, Guam, American Samoa, and the Virgin Islands shall be 66 per centum, and (C) the Federal share for the Trust Territory of the Pacific Islands shall be 100 per centum.

"(2) The 'Federal share' for each State shall be promulgated by the Commissioner within sixty days after the beginning of the fiscal year ending June 30, 1971, and of every second fiscal year thereafter, on the basis of the average per capita incomes of each of the States and of all the States (excluding Puerto Rico, Guam, American Samoa, the Virgin Islands, and the Trust Territory of the Pacific Islands), for the three most recent consecutive years for which satisfactory data are available to him from the Department of Commerce. Such promulgation shall be conclusive for each of the two fiscal years beginning after the promulgation.

"TITLE I–LIBRARY SERVICES

"Grants for States for Library Services

"Sec. 101. The Commissioner shall carry out a program of making grants from sums appropriated pursuant to section 4(a) (1) to States which have had approved basic State plans under section 6 and have submitted annual programs under section 103 for the extension of public library services to areas without such services and the improvement of such services in areas in which such services are inadequate, for making library services more accessible to persons who, by reason of distance, residence, or physical handicap, or other disadvantage, are unable to receive the benefits of public library services regularly made available to the public, for adapting public library services to meet particular needs of persons within the States, and for improving and strengthening library administrative agencies.

"Uses of Federal Funds

"Sec. 102. (a) Funds appropriated pursuant to paragraph (1) of section 4(a) shall be available for grants to States from allotments under section 5(a) for the purpose of paying the Federal share of the cost of carrying out State plans submitted and approved under section 6 and section 103. Except as is provided in subsection (b), grants to States under this title may be used solely—

"(1) for planning for, and taking other steps leading to the development of, programs and projects designed to extend and improve library services, as provided in clause (2); and

"(2) for (A) extending public library services to geographical areas and groups of persons without such services and improving such services in such areas and for such groups as may have inadequate public library services; and (B) establishing, expanding, and operating programs and projects to provide (i) State institutional library services, (ii) library services to the physically handicapped and (iii) library services for the disadvantaged in urban and rural areas; and (C) strengthening metropolitan public libraries which serve as national or regional resource centers.

"(b) Subject to such limitations and criteria as the Commissioner shall establish by regulation, grants to States under this title may be used (1) to pay the cost of administering the State plans submitted and approved under this Act (including obtaining the services of consultants), statewide planning for and evaluation of library services, dissemination of information concerning library services, and the activities of such advisory groups and panels as may be necessary to assist the State library administrative agency in carrying out its functions under this title, and (2) for strengthening the capacity of State library administrative agencies for meeting the needs of the people of the States.

"State Annual Program for Library Services

"Sec. 103. Any State desiring to receive a grant from its allotment for the purposes of this title for any fiscal year shall, in addition to having submitted, and having had approved, a basic State plan under section 6, submit for that fiscal year an annual program for library services. Such program shall be submitted at such time, in such

form, and contain such information as the Commissioner may require by regulation, and shall—

"(1) set forth a program for the year submitted under which funds paid to the State from appropriations pursuant to paragraph (1) of section 4(a) for that year will be used, consistent with its long-range program, solely for the purposes set forth in section 102;

"(2) set forth the criteria used in allocating such funds among such purposes, which criteria shall insure that the State will expend from Federal, State, and local sources an amount not less than the amount expended by the State from such sources for State institutional library services, and library services to the physically handicapped during the fiscal year ending June 30, 1971;

"(3) include such information, policies, and procedures as will assure that the activities to be carried out during that year are consistent with the long-range program; and

"(4) include an extension of the long-range program, taking into consideration the results of evaluations.

"TITLE II–PUBLIC LIBRARY CONSTRUCTION

"Grants to States for Public Library Construction

Sec. 201. The Commissioner shall carry out a program of making grants to States which have had approved a basic State plan under section 6 and have submitted a long-range program and submit annually appropriately updated programs under section 203 for the construction of public libraries.

"Uses of Federal Funds

"Sec. 202. Funds appropriated pursuant to paragraph (2) of section 4(a) shall be available for grants to States from allotments under section 5(a) for the purpose of paying the Federal share of the cost of construction projects carried under State plans. Such grants shall be used solely for the construction of public libraries under approved State plans.

"State Annual Program for the Construction of Public Libraries

"Sec. 203. Any State desiring to receive a grant from its allotment for the purpose of this title for any fiscal year shall, in addition to having submitted, and having had approved, a basic State plan under section 6, submit such projects as the State may approve and are consistent with its long-range program.

"Such projects shall be submitted at such time and contain such information as the Commissioner may require by regulation and shall—

"(1) for the year submitted under which funds are paid to the State from appropriations pursuant to paragraph (2) of section 4(a) for that year, be used, consistent with the State's long-range program, for the construction of public libraries in areas of the State which are without the library facilities necessary to provide adequate library services;

"(2) follow the criteria, policies, and procedures for the approval of applications for the construction of public library facilities under the long-range program;

"(3) follow policies and procedures which will insure that every local or other public agency whose application for funds under the plan with respect to a project for construction of public library facilities is denied will be given an opportunity for a hearing before the State library administrative agency;

"(4) include an extension of the long-range program taking into consideration the results of evaluations.

"TITLE III—INTERLIBRARY COOPERATION

"Grants to States for Interlibrary Cooperation Programs

"Sec. 301. The Commissioner shall carry out a program of making grants to States which have an approved basic State plan under section 6 and have submitted a long-range program and an annual program under section 303 for interlibrary cooperation programs.

"Uses of Federal Funds

"Sec. 302. (a) Funds appropriated pursuant to paragraph (3) of section 4(a) shall be available for grants to States from allotments under paragraphs (1) and (3) of section 5(a) for the purpose of carrying out the Federal share of the cost of carrying out State plans submitted and approved under section 303. Such grants shall be used (1) for planning for, and taking other steps leading to the development of, cooperative library networks; and (2) for establishing, expanding, and operating local, regional, and interstate cooperative networks of libraries, which provide for the systematic and effective coordination of the resources of school, public, academic, and special libraries and information centers for improved supplementary services for the special clientele served by each type of library or center.

"(b) For the purposes of this title, the Federal share shall be 100 per centum of the cost of carrying out the State plan.

"State Annual Program for Interlibrary Cooperation

"Sec. 303. Any State desiring to receive a grant from its allotment for the purposes of this title for any fiscal year shall, in addition to having submitted, and having had approved, a basic State plan under section 6, submit for that fiscal year an annual program for interlibrary cooperation. Such program shall be submitted at such time, in such form, and contain such information as the Commissioner may require by regulation and shall—

"(1) set forth a program for the year submitted under which funds paid to the State from appropriations pursuant to paragraph (3) of section 4(a) will be used consistent with its long-range program for the purposes set forth in section 302.

"(2) include an extension of the long-range program taking into consideration the results of evaluations."

(c) (1) The amendment made by subsection (b) shall be effective after June 30, 1971.

(2) In the case of funds appropriated to carry out programs under the Library Services and Construction Act for the fiscal year ending June 30,

1971, each State is authorized, in accordance with regulations of the Commissioner of Education, to use a portion of its allotment for the development of such plans as may be required by such Act, as amended by subsection (b).

Amendments to the Adult Education Act

Sec. 3. (a) Effective on and after July 1, 1969, section 305(a) of the Adult Education Act is amended—

(1) by striking out in the first sentence "any fiscal year" and inserting in lieu thereof "the fiscal year ending June 30, 1972, and for any succeeding fiscal year"; and

(2) by inserting at the end thereof the following new sentence: "From the sums available for purposes of section 304(b) for the fiscal year ending June 30, 1970, and the succeeding fiscal year, the Commissioner shall make allotments in accordance with section 305(a) of the Adult Education Act of 1966 as in effect on June 30, 1969."

(b) Section 312(b) of the Adult Education Act is amended by inserting at the end thereof the following new sentence: "For the fiscal year ending June 30, 1970, and the succeeding fiscal year, nothing in this subsection shall be construed to prohibit the use of any amounts appropriated pursuant to this Act to pay such costs, subject to such limitations as the Commissioner may prescribe."

Approved December 30, 1970.

LEGISLATIVE HISTORY:
  HOUSE REPORT No. 91-1659 accompanying H.R. 19363 (Comm. on Education and Labor).
  SENATE REPORT No. 91-1162 (Comm. on Labor and Public Welfare).
  CONGRESSIONAL RECORD, Vol. 116 (1970):
    Sept. 18, 21, considered and passed Senate.
    Dec. 7, considered and passed House, amended.
    Dec. 15, Senate concurred in House amendment.

IX

CAREERS IN FEDERAL LIBRARIES

This Reader wouldn't be complete unless it had something on library work in the Federal government. And, so we have a few pages from a brochure on the subject. It's too bad that the pictures from that brochure couldn't have been included. They show some good looking Federal librarians and some very attractive Federal library buildings. The *Roster of Federal Libraries,* a directory that you might want to look at, came out in 1970. It tells us that there are "more than 1900 individual libraries serving the many departments, committees, agencies, courts, and other formal organizational entities in the Federal government. They include six types: Presidential, national, general, academic, school, and special or technical." This *Roster* was compiled by Mildred Benton et al. and published by the George Washington University Medical Center, Department of Medical and Public Affairs, Biological Sciences Communication Project, 2001 S. Street, N. W., Washington, D. C. 20009.

Professional Careers for Librarians

Prepared by the U.S. Civil Service Commission

Towards the end of this reading, under the heading: Step 2—Finding the Right Job, *it says in part: ". . . it is advisable to supplement IAB referrals with personal contacts . . . finding the right job is often up to you." So don't just fill out the forms and sit back and wait for a job to come to you. Make contacts! Know the field! Read the* Library Vacancy Roster *every month. You can get this last by writing to Federal Library Committee, Library of Congress, Washington, D. C. 20540. And, good luck!*

WHY BE A FEDERAL LIBRARIAN?

What does a Federal library offer that other libraries don't? According to the librarians who work in them, advantages like . . .

Service

What other organization serves so many publics? The Federal Government with the District of Columbia government, brings public library services to residents of Washington, D. C. and to servicemen and their families the world over. It operates hospital libraries, serving patients and supporting vital medical research. And, its technical and specialized libraries in all Federal agencies provide policy-makers with the latest findings and proposals in their area of interest, with balanced and accurate information on controversial subjects. Your work in a Government library will reflect the special kind of service your agency gives its public. In a hospital library, for instance, you may recommend books for use in psychiatric group therapy sessions. Acquisitions in some military library systems include developing paperback collections for a combat zone. In a scientific library, the first step in cataloging may be creation of new vocabulary to bring subject headings in step with expanding technology.

Variety

As one Federal librarian put it, "A typical day provides enough variety to make the work interesting. And in addition I find that I have many atypical days." Your days will be divided between face-to-face assistance and behind the scenes assignments, between long term projects and rush requests. And, don't be surprised if you're asked to develop a library orientation course for students from low-income families hired by your library for summer jobs. Or if someone assigned to developing a new agency insignia drops in for some information on heraldry.

Scope

Whatever your special talents, a Federal library will expect you to use and develop them. Do you like the freedom of running a one-man show? The smallest Federal libraries have only one or two staff members. Do you see yourself as the executive type? Chief librarians in larger Federal libraries and library systems coordinate the work of 20 or more people and may administer operations of several field offices. Do you want to make a creative contribution to agency management? Federal libraries must develop improved techniques for handling their ever growing volume of materials. A streamlined cataloging system or plan for automated information retrieval may set a pattern adopted by libraries throughout the world.

Mobility and career opportunity

Do you want to move up or move around? The breadth of Government activity lets you move

SOURCE: Reprinted from U. S. Civil Service Commission. *Professional Careers For Librarians.* Announcement 442. (Washington: 1970), p. 3-18.

among libraries in many subjects or carve out a career in just one. Within a single library, you may advance by becoming an expert in a specialized field or by taking on administrative responsibility. It is also possible to move among the many different Federal libraries without competitive examination. As for location, there are many possibilities since Federal libraries are scattered throughout the United States as well as overseas.

Other Benefits

The benefits of Federal employment are well known, and include such things as paid vacations, liberal sick leave, health benefits, and retirement; not to mention job security for capable employees. Opportunities to continue professional development and education are usually available, and many agencies will pay or help pay for relevant courses.

WHAT ARE THE MAJOR FEDERAL LIBRARIES?

Almost three-fourths of all librarians in the Federal Service are found in five library systems— Army, Navy, Air Force, Veterans Administration, and the Department of Interior—and in the Library of Congress. In addition, all Cabinet departments have sizable library staffs, and practically every Government agency has at least a few librarians to handle its reference collection. To give you an idea of the kinds of opportunities available, the following pages describe a representative selection of some dynamic Federal libraries.

The National Library of Medicine, Bethesda, Maryland, is the world's largest research library in a single scientific and professional field. To meet the demands of doctors, medical researchers and students for the most up-to-date information available on biomedical topics, the Library maintains a permanent collection of nearly 1,500,000 pieces in more than 40 languages. Materials are collected exhaustively in some 40 biomedical areas and, to a lesser degree, in a number of related areas such as chemistry, physics, zoology, botany, psychology, and instrumentation. The Library acquires new material at the rate of approximately 100,000 items a year. To get this information to the people who ask for it—35 or 40 may request bibliographies in an average day—NLM makes use of

new technology. A computerized information retrieval system with stations in a number of large medical libraries contains over a million citations from the world's leading biomedical journals and has been in operation since 1964. Each month, articles from about 2,300 publications are added to this system, and additions total about 200,000 articles a year. Through its National Medical Audiovisual Center in Atlanta, Georgia, NLM operates a national program for the development, production, evaluation and distribution of films and videotapes on biomedical subjects. In addition to a staff of artists, photographers and technicians who produce the films, the Audiovisual Center employs five librarians and about 25 information specialists who administer a collection of 250,000 audiovisual materials.

The National Library of Medicine employs approximately 60 librarians and 30 technical information specialists with subject-matter specializations in scientific fields. Some of these jobs may require knowledge of at least one foreign language. For additional information on opportunities with NLM, write:

Personnel Officer
National Library of Medicine
8600 Rockville Pike
Bethesda, Md. 20014

The National Agricultural Library is a unified and comprehensive source of information on subjects connected with agriculture, serving not only Department of Agriculture employees but also colleges and universities, research institutions, agricultural associations, industry and other Government agencies. Its collection, which now exceeds a million and a quarter volumes, includes material on all phases of botany, chemistry, animal industry, veterinary medicine, biology, agricultural engineering, rural sociology, forestry, entomology, law, food and nutrition, soils and fertilizers, water resources, marketing, transportation and other economic aspects of agricultural products, as well as agriculture in general. Information on materials received by the Library is publicized through the "Bibliography of Agriculture," the "Pesticides Documentation Bulletin," and other special bibliograhies. Through organization and participation in an international network of agricultural knowledge, which will eventually involve all Land Grant colleges and universities, the Library intends to bring a more comprehensive pool of information to researchers, scholars and students. The Library pioneered in the use of photocopies of Library materials and in development of a photocopying machine that uses a continuous-roll process, enabling the Library to provide photoprints quickly and economically. Library services are being restructured to pave the way for total automation, with computers and electronic data processing equipment now being adapted for acquisitions, cataloging and indexing. Future applications are planned in information retrieval and preparation of bibliographies.

The national Agricultural Library is located in a new 14-story building providing space for two million volumes, on the grounds of the Agricultural Research Center in Beltsville, Maryland. In addition, the Library system includes a Law Branch, Bee Culture Library, and a number of libraries serving Department of Agriculture research laboratories at field installations. The Library employs librarians with specializations in scientific fields, foreign languages, and computer technology. For additional information on opportunities with the National Agricultural Library, write:

Program Coordination Services
National Agricultural Library
Beltsville, Md. 20705

The Department of the Interior Library is an active, research oriented library, offering comprehensive reference service in all areas of conservation. The Department is involved in environmental quality, water pollution, reclamation and conservation of lands and water, marine resources, electric power, mineral production, National Parks, American Indians, territories, fish, wildlife, outdoor recreation, oceanographic research, and geological surveys of the earth (as well as the moon). In order to service all these programs, the Library has an extensive collection of 750,000 monographs, 4,500 periodicals, 8,000 serials, and 300 indexing and abstracting services. Its research staff compiles bibliographies of these materials on a regular basis and upon requests from Government and private researchers.

The library is developing a national library system for natural resources. As the headquarters for the National Library for Natural Resources, the Interior Library will utilize new computer technology to coordinate and optimize usage of valuable collections scattered in field libraries throughout the United States. There are some 32 full fledged field libraries at present and approximately 50 others in various stages of development. This expanding system holds many opportunities for librarians interested in implementing their ideas and making full use of their talents. The Department of the Interior Library offers librarians in the physical, biological, and social sciences a chance to increase their knowledge while playing an active role in expanding library services. For further information about opportunities available at the Department of the Interior Library, contact:

Director of Library Services
U. S. Department of the Interior
Department Library
18th and C Streets NW.
Washington, D. C. 20240

The Veterans Administration maintains libraries in all 165 VA hospitals across the country. The smallest of these, with about 2,000 volumes in its collection, employs a single librarian who carries out the entire library program. At larger hospitals, up to a dozen librarians and assistants may work under the direction of a Chief Librarian with collections up to 20,000 volumes. Service common to all VA libraries, regardless of size, include across-the-desk service to ambulatory patients, book cart service to the bedfast, and reference and bibliographic service to physicians and other hospital staff members. There are special reading aids such as large-print books, automatic page turners and ceiling projectors for the handicapped. All together, VA patients' libraries contain over 1,200,000 volumes of general interest and circulate about 800,000 of them each year. In addition, more than 800,000 books and periodicals as well as biomedical information and data in other formats provide a network of learning resources centers in all VA hospital libraries. The services of these libraries support VA research, education, and clinical programs. Small wonder, then, that VA medical libraries answer 90,000 reference questions and circulate 400,000 publications in a year. The Veterans Administration employs over 300 librarians with varying subject-matter backgrounds. For more information about opportunities with the VA, write:

Director, Library Service (11A3)
Veterans Administration
Washington, D. C. 20420

The Departments of the Army, Navy, and Air Force maintain worldwide library operations supporting all types of Department of Defense activities. Army, Navy, and Air Force librarians may work in academic libraries, such as those as the Military, Naval, and Air Force Academies, or they may work in technical libraries serving physicians, scientists, engineers, and other specialists. Many work in general libraries, providing public and school library service to military personnel, dependents, and civilians at military bases and hospitals. Since the base library staff is responsible for all aspects of library operation, some assignments require a background in administration, planning and budgeting of library services. And, in some overseas, isolated or small stateside locations, where libraries have only one or two librarians, the job demands flexibility and ability to work alone. Quite a few jobs with base libraries and some in dependent school libraries are overseas (mostly at GS-9) in the Pacific, Alaska, Europe, and the Canal Zone. For these jobs, you must agree to stay from one to three years depending on location. Once overseas, you may be reassigned or promoted to libraries in other countries; and, when you return to the States, you can receive placement assistance in the locality of your choice.

Department of the Army's is one of the world's largest library programs. There are more than 400 post libraries, 200 school and technical libraries, as well as academic libraries at the Command and General Staff College in Kansas, the U. S. Army War College in Pennsylvania, and, of course, the U. S. Military Academy at West Point. Their combined holdings total over ten million books and other materials. The career program for the more than 600 librarians in this system is Army-wide, offering excellent opportunities for training and advancement. For information on openings with Army libraries within the United States, contact the Civilian Personnel Officer at the installation where you want to work, or write:

Functional Chief, Librarian Career Program
The Adjutant General's Office
Department of the Army
ATTN: AGMG–L
Washington, D. C. 20315

For information and a brochure on overseas opportunities, write:

Department of the Army
DCSPER Office of Civilian Personnel
EMDSS
Interchange and Recruitment Branch
Old Post Office Building
12th St. and Pennsylvania Avenue NW.
Washington, D. C. 20315

Additional information on opportunities with

the dependent school system is available through U. S. Employment Services offices.

Department of the Navy librarians, almost 400 in all, man about 150 libraries ranging from those at the Naval Academy and Naval War College to one and two person libraries at naval stations and hospitals. For most station library positions, the Navy prefers persons with military or public library experience. Librarians with such technical libraries as those at the Naval Ordnance Laboratory or Naval Electronics Laboratory need appropriate technical backgrounds. For more information on employment opportunities, contact the naval installation where you want to work or, for overseas positions, write to:

Overseas and Return Placement Staff
Office of Civilian Manpower Management
Navy Department
Washington, D. C. 20390

Department of the Air Force employs nearly 400 librarians in base libraries and in specialized and academic libraries serving such activities as the School of Aerospace Medicine in Texas, Cambridge Research Laboratories in Massachusetts, the Air Force Academy, and the Air Force Institute of Technology in Ohio. The total Air Force library system includes over 600 facilities having more than six million books and other materials. For specific information on Air Force librarian positions, contact the installation where you want to work. For overseas employment information, visit your nearest U. S. Air Force Civilian Personnel Office. They will furnish you with addresses and telephone numbers of your nearest Air Force overseas recruiting representative.

The Department of Housing and Urban Development boasts a newly formed consolidated library supporting the work of this new agency. Now with branches in seven major cities in addition to Washington, D. C., and with plans to add three more, the HUD library hopes to become the definitive national resource in housing and city planning. Already over a third of the library's work is with people outside the agency—experts on city planning, housing, economics, mortgage finance, transportation, race relations, and a host of other topics related to today's metropolitan development. They come from universities, local action groups, public interest associations, and consulting firms. Users request over 22,000 bibliographies a year on subjects ranging from new communities to open housing law. The HUD library contains one of the most comprehensive law collections of any Federal Executive agency outside the Justice Department. The Library's total collection, mostly in periodicals and reports, numbers about 400,000 pieces and brings together 1,500 periodicals in the housing and urban development field. From this material HUD librarians compile "Housing and Planning References" indexing significant books, documents, and articles to aid researchers in keeping up with the latest thinking in the field. Future plans call for automation of this activity along with all other information retrieval.

The Department of Housing and Urban Development employs 19 librarians in Washington, D. C. and a smaller number at each regional office. For more information on these positions, which generally require a background in social sciences, sometimes with knowledge of architecture and technology, write:

Director
Library
Department of HUD
451 7th Street SW.
Washington, D. C. 20410

The Department of Transportation is another new agency formed to combat problems of growing national concern. Still being consolidated, its centralized library in Washington, D. C. employs 24 librarians and technical information specialists. In addition, the Department's Federal Aviation Administration employs librarians in nine regional offices ranging from Anchorage to Atlanta. Reflecting the rapid expansion of activities in the transportation field, libraries of three major organizations within the Department—the Federal Aviation Administration, the Bureau of Public Roads, and the Coast Guard—already answer over 2,000 reference and research questions a month from Government employees, consulting firms, contractors, and the public. And the subjects of these inquiries are no longer limited to the best mixture for concrete. Although most emphasis in the last few years has been on urban mass transit and highway safety, inquiries come in on airplane specifications, aviation medicine, environmental factors in roadside planning, right-of-way law, motor vehicle exhaust, navigational safety, parking—anything that has to do with getting people from here to there. Library staff members prepare continuing bibliographies on "highways" and "Urban Transportation Research and Planning" and support departmental research activities in such related subjects as electronics and engineering, soil mechanics for road construction, and

radar and radio traffic control. To meet the burgeoning demand for information on transportation subjects, the Department includes among its future plans for the library automation of all reference services.

Because of the technical nature of many of its services, the Department of Transportation prefers to hire librarians with some scientific background although there may be occasional openings for those with other specializations. For further information on opportunities with DOT, write:

Librarian, TAD-49
Department of Transportation
400 7th Street SW.
Washington, D. C. 20410

The Library of Congress is the Nation's largest and most comprehensive library. No other library in the country employs almost 1,000 librarians and a total staff of 4,500 people with over 150 different types of positions. Located in Washington, D. C., across from the U. S. Capitol Building and beside the Supreme Court Building, the Library also maintains 14 offices in foreign countries, which together with other offices in the library under the National Program for Acquisitions and Cataloging are engaged in gathering and cataloging materials for its own collections as well as for other libraries throughout the nation. Through acquisition and exchange the Library received over 8 million pieces last year, including more than 3 million additions to its permanent collections in many written languages and from all countries of the world. These collections presently number over 58 million pieces, and supply information through its diversified reference and research staff to Congress, Government agencies, academic communities, and individuals throughout the country. Last year, the Library answered over one million inquiries, ranging from the simplest from John Q. Public to the most complex from the Congress or from the President of the United States. In cooperation with the National Library of Medicine and National Agricultural Library, which share responsibility for making available materials from around the world, the Library of Congress is developing a uniform system of computerized information retrieval. At present, the Library has or is developing automated cataloging and reporting systems in almost every major subject area—science and technology, maps and geography, and folk music to name a few.

Librarians at the Library of Congress enjoy similar pay and benefits as do librarians under the

Federal civil service system. However, they are covered by a separate merit system. For information on qualifications required and how you can apply for Library of Congress jobs, write:

Personnel Office
Library of Congress
Washington, D. C. 20540

HOW CAN YOU BECOME A FEDERAL LIBRARIAN?

Getting a Federal librarian job is generally a two step process. First, you must establish your qualifications for librarian jobs in general. Once you have done this, you should contact Federal agencies to find out about openings and locate the particular job that's right for you.

Step 1—Qualifying

Jobs in almost all Federal libraries except the Library of Congress and the D. C. Public Library require civil service eligibility. You can obtain this eligibility by meeting the requirements on page 420. The usual entrance level is Grade GS-9, for which a master's degree in library science is the typical means of qualifying. However, eligibility under this announcement is the *basic* requirement for librarian jobs. Some agencies also require study in a particular field, such as physical science or law, ability to translate foreign language materials, or additional experience beyond that shown for a given grade. You will be considered for such positions only if you meet the specific requirements of the job.

If you meet the qualifications requirements, on page 420, submit your application to:

Interagency Board of U. S. Civil Service
   Examiners—WAS
1900 E Street NW.
Washington, D. C. 20415

The Washington, D. C., board will maintain the list of eligibles for positions throughout the U. S. and overseas.

Your application should consist of:

Form 5001 ABC.
SF 171. In filling this out, please be sure to indicate the lowest grade or salary you will accept and to give a positive indication of where you are willing to work. If you have knowledge of a foreign language, please indi-

cate the degree of your ability using the guidelines below:

Excellent—Can read specialized material in a subject-matter field with which you are familiar with infrequent use of a dictionary.

Good—Can read newspapers or popular magazines without use of a dictionary or specialized material using a dictionary.

Fair—Can read newspapers and popular magazines using dictionaries and grammars.

SF 15, with the documentary proof required, it you are claiming 10-point veteran preference (disability, widow, wife, or mother preference).

You will be evaluated for the minimum grade or salary which you indicate you will accept and for any higher grades for which you qualify. Your notice of rating will indicate whether you are eligible or ineligible and, if eligible, for which grade levels. Then, as vacancies occur at these grades, your qualifications will be evaluated in relation to the agency's specific requirements, and you will be ranked relative to other candidates for the job in question. Your eligibility for consideration will remain in effect for one year from the date of your notice of rating. For continued eligibility, you must submit updated information on your experience at intervals of not less than 11 nor more than 12 months.

Step 2—Finding the Right Job

Looking for work in a Federal library is much like finding a job anywhere. The Interagency Board is similar to an employment agency in that it can refer your name to libraries requesting people with your background to fill vacancies and may even call your attention to other libraries which have continuing needs for librarians with your qualifications. However, the IAB cannot know until a specific request is received which agencies are expecting to hire librarians in the near future or whether the agency you may prefer has any openings for someone with your background. The Federal Library Committee compiles a monthly listing of vacancies which agencies are anxious to fill. This list, which may be obtained from the Committee at the Library of Congress, will give you an idea of which agencies are looking for librarians, but may not include every prospective employer. If you want specific information on your chances for employment or want to acquaint yourself with Federal library operations, it is advisable to supplement IAB referrals with personal contacts. If you are interested in any agencies not discussed in this announcement, you can address your inquiry to the agency's library. Or, if you live near a Federal office, you may prefer to visit its library and see for yourself the kind of work that goes on. The librarians will be glad to discuss their jobs and answer any questions you might have. Remember, in Government as in industry, finding the right job is often up to you.

Librarian Positions at GS–13/15

If you are interested in positions at grades GS–13 through 15, file two copies of SF 171, Form 5001 ABC, and SF 15 if needed with Desk 408, U. S. Civil Service Commission, 1900 E Street NW., Washington, D. C. 20415. Jobs at these grades are filled through Announcement 408 for Senior Level Positions, which is available at Federal Job Information Centers and most large Post Offices.

Students

If you expect to complete within the next 9 months all educational requirements for a given grade level, you may be rated eligible for that grade and may be given a provisional appointment. However, you may not enter on duty until you furnish proof that you have completed the required education.

A few libraries have work-study programs for students working toward a master's degree in library science. Contact the agencies in which you are interested to find out whether they have such a plan.

Travel Expenses and Other Allowances

For overseas assignments, the agency will provide free transportation for you and your household goods provided you complete the required tour of duty. You will receive on-base quarters or a housing allowance, as well as commissary privileges. If you can't take your family to a particular post, you may be entitled to a separate maintenance allowance for them.

For some positions within the United States, the agency may pay your travel costs and the cost of transporting your household goods and personal belongings to your first post of duty. The agency will tell you after you are selected if this is the case.

Equal Employment Opportunity

All qualified applicants will receive consideration for employment without regard to race, creed, color, sex, or national origin.

General Information

For information about citizenship, age, kinds of appointments, physical abilities, veteran preference, and similar information, see Civil Service Commission Pamphlet 4, "Working for the U.S.A.," which can be obtained most places where applications are available.

Previous Eligibilities

Lists of eligibles established under all current librarian announcements will be superseded by lists established under this announcement. If you acquired eligibility before April 1, 1969, this eligibility will be terminated. If your current eligibility was acquired on or after that date, you will be rerated under the terms of this announcement, and a new notice of rating will be sent to you.

REQUIREMENTS FOR BASIC ELIGIBILITY

To be rated for grade	You must have . . . Experience	OR	Education
GS–7* $7,639 a year	Five years of relevant experience including at least 1 year comparable in difficulty and responsibility to the GS–5 level in the Federal service. (To qualify on this basis, you must pass a written test in library science and must demonstrate conclusively that your experience and/or education has provided a knowledge and understanding of the theories, principles, and techniques of professional librarianship. If you qualify on the basis of experience alone, you must have had two years of experience at the GS–5 level. VA does not hire persons who qualify under the written test provision.)		Completion of 1 full academic year of graduate study in library science at an accredited college or university; or

Completion of all requirements for a "fifth-year" bachelor's degree in library science in addition to a previously earned degree in another field of study from an accredited college or university. (To qualify for most jobs on this basis, you must also have 1 year of professional experience.); or

A bachelor's degree from an accredited college or university which included or was supplemented by 24 semester hours, or equivalent, in library science, plus 1 year of work experience which included duties in one or more functional areas of librarianship comparable to the GS–5 level in the Federal service. (For Veterans Administration jobs.) |
| GS–9 $9,320 a year | Meet the requirements for GS–7 and have had 1 year of professional or advanced experience in librarianship or in an appropriate subject-matter or language field which was comparable in difficulty and responsibility to the GS–7 level in the Federal service. | | Completion of all requirements for a master's degree or 2 full academic years of graduate study in library science at an accredited college or university; or

Meet the requirements for GS–7 and have completed all requirements for a master's degree or 2 full academic years of graduate study in an appropriate subject-matter or language field at an accredited college or university. |
| GS–11 $11,233 a year | Meet the requirements for GS–9 and have one year of professional or advanced experience in librarianship or in appropriate subject-matter or language field which was comparable in difficulty and responsibility to the GS–9 level in the Federal service. | | Completion of all requirements for a master's degree or 3 full academic years of graduate study in library science at an accredited college or university; or

Meet the requirements for GS–7 and have completed all requirements for a doctoral degree or 3 full academic years of graduate study in an appropriate subject-matter or language field at an accredited college or university. |
| GS–12 $13,289 a year | Meet the requirements for GS–11 and have had 1 year of professional or advanced experience in librarianship or an appropriate subject-matter or language field which was comparable in difficulty and responsibility to the GS–11 level in the Federal service. | | |

*This is the lowest grade held by professional librarians. A very few trainee jobs may be filled at GS–5 from the GS–7 list. Please indicate if you would accept the lower salary.

NOTE.–At each grade equivalent combinations of professional experience and education of the types described above are acceptable on the basis of one full academic year (30 semester hours or equivalent) of education for one year of experience.